Latin Authors

AMMIANUS MARCELLINUS. J. C. Rolfe.

CELSUS. W. G. Spencer.

CICERO, IN CATILINAM, PRO FLACCO, PRO MURENA, PRO SULLA. B. L. Ullman.

CICERO, DE NATURA DEORUM. H. Rackham.

CICERO, DE ORATORE, ORATOR, BRUTUS. Charles Stuttaford and W. E. Sutton.

CICERO, PRO SEXTIO, IN VATINIUM, PRO CAELIO, PRO PROVINCIIS CONSULARIBUS, PRO BALBO. J. H. Freese.

ENNIUS, LUCILIUS and other specimens of Old Latin. E. H. Warmington.

PLINY, NATURAL HISTORY. W. H. S. Jones.

PRUDENTIUS. J. H. Baxter.

ST. JEROME'S LETTERS. F. A. Wright.

SIDONIUS, LETTERS & POEMS. E. V. Arnold and W. B. Anderson.

SILIUS ITALICUS. J. D. Duff.

VALERIUS FLACCUS. J. H. Mozley.

DESCRIPTIVE PROSPECTUS ON APPLICATION

| London | - | - | WILLIAM HEINEMANN |
| New York | - | - | - G. PUTNAM'S SONS |

THEOPHRASTUS: CHARACTERS. J. M. Edmonds; HERODES, etc. A. D. Knox.

THEOPHRASTUS: ENQUIRY INTO PLANTS. Sir Arthur Hort, Bart. 2 Vols.

THUCYDIDES. C. F. Smith. 4 Vols. (Vols. I., II. and III. 2nd Imp. revised.)

TRYPHIODORUS. Cf. OPPIAN.

XENOPHON: CYROPAEDIA. Walter Miller. 2 Vols. (2nd Imp.)

XENOPHON: HELLENICA, ANABASIS, APOLOGY, AND SYMPOSIUM. C. L. Brownson and O. J. Todd. 3 Vols. (2nd Imp.)

XENOPHON: MEMORABILIA AND OECONOMICUS. E. C. Marchant.

XENOPHON: SCRIPTA MINORA. E. C. Marchant.

IN PREPARATION

Greek Authors

ARISTOTLE, ATHENIAN CONSTITUTION. H. Rackham.

ARISTOTLE, ECONOMICS. W. G. Armstrong.

ARISTOTLE, METAPHYSICS. H. Tredennick.

ARISTOTLE, ON THE MOTION AND PROGRESSION OF ANIMALS. E. S. Forster.

ARISTOTLE, ORGANON. H. P. Cooke.

DEMOSTHENES, MEIDIAS, ANDROTION, ARISTO-CRATES, TIMOCRATES. J. H. Vince.

DEMOSTHENES, PRIVATE ORATIONS. G. M. Calhoun.

DIODORUS SICULUS. C. H. Oldfather.

GREEK MATHEMATICAL WORKS. J. Thomas.

MYTHOGRAPHI GRAECI.

SEXTUS EMPIRICUS. Rev. R. G. Bury.

THE LOEB CLASSICAL LIBRARY

EDITED BY

T. E. PAGE, LITT.D.

E. CAPPS, PH.D., LL.D.   W. H. D. ROUSE, LITT.D.

THE GEOGRAPHY OF STRABO

VIII

THE GEOGRAPHY
OF STRABO

WITH AN ENGLISH TRANSLATION BY
HORACE LEONARD JONES, Ph.D., LL.D.

CORNELL UNIVERSITY

IN EIGHT VOLUMES

VIII

LONDON : WILLIAM HEINEMANN LTD
NEW YORK : G. P. PUTNAM'S SONS
MCMXXXII

Printed in Great Britain

ΣΤΡΑΒΩΝΟΣ ΓΕΩΓΡΑΦΙΚΩΝ

ΙΖ΄

Ι

1. Ἐπεὶ δὲ τὴν Ἀραβίαν ἐφοδεύοντες καὶ τοὺς
κόλπους συμπεριελάβομεν τοὺς σφίγγοντας αὐτὴν
καὶ ποιοῦντας χερρόνησον, τὸν Περσικὸν καὶ τὸν
Ἀράβιον, τούτῳ δέ τινα συμπεριωδεύθη καὶ τῆς
Αἰγύπτου καὶ τῆς Αἰθιοπίας, τὰ τῶν Τρωγλοδυ-
τῶν καὶ τῶν ἑξῆς μέχρι τῶν ἐσχάτων τῆς κινναμωμοφόρου, τὰ λειπόμενα καὶ συνεχῆ τοῖς ἔθνεσι
τούτοις, ταῦτα δ᾽ ἐστὶ τὰ περὶ τὸν Νεῖλον,
ἐκθετέον· μετὰ δὲ ταῦτα τὴν Λιβύην ἔπιμεν,
ἥπερ ἐστὶ λοιπὴ τῆς συμπάσης γεωγραφίας.
κἀνταῦθα δ᾽ Ἐρατοσθένους ἀποφάσεις προεκθε-
τέον.

2. Φησὶ δὴ τοῦ Ἀραβίου κόλπου πρὸς τὴν
ἑσπέραν ἐννακοσίους ἢ χιλίους [1] σταδίους διέχειν
τὸν Νεῖλον, παραπλήσιον ὄντα κατὰ τὸ σχῆμα [2]
τῷ γράμματι τῷ Ν [3] κειμένῳ ἀνάπαλιν· ῥυεὶς
γάρ, φησίν, ἀπὸ Μερόης ἐπὶ τὰς ἄρκτους ὡς
δισχιλίους καὶ ἑπτακοσίους σταδίους, πάλιν
ἀναστρέφει πρὸς [4] μεσημβρίαν καὶ τὴν χειμερινὴν

C 786

---

[1] ἐννακοσίους ἢ χιλίους, Groskurd, for ἐννακισχιλίους (F has
α in margin) ; ἐννακοσίους, Corais ; χιλίους, Kramer.
[2] σχῆμα, C. Müller, for στόμα.   Meineke ejects κατὰ τὸ
στόμα.
[3] τῷ νυ EFDr, though D has N above νυ.

2

THE

GEOGRAPHY OF STRABO

BOOK XVII

CONTENTS

THE GEOGRAPHY OF STRABO

BOOK XVII

I

1. SINCE, in my description of Arabia, I have also included the gulfs which pinch it and make it a peninsula, I mean the Persian and Arabian Gulfs, and at the same time have gone the rounds of certain parts both of Aegypt and of Aethiopia, I mean the countries of the Troglodytes and the peoples situated in order thereafter as far as the Cinnamon-bearing country, I must now set forth the remaining parts that are continuous with these tribes, that is, the parts in the neighbourhood of the Nile; and after this I shall traverse Libya, which is the last remaining subject of my whole geography. And here too I must first set forth the declarations of Eratosthenes.

2. Now according to him the Nile is nine hundred or a thousand stadia distant towards the west from the Arabian Gulf, and is similar in shape to the letter N written reversed; [1] for after flowing, he says, from Meroê towards the north about two thousand seven hundred stadia, it turns back towards the south and the winter sunset about three thousand

---

[1] *i.e.* И. This is true, roughly speaking, of the course of the Nile from Meroê to Syenê (see critical note).

---

[4] D*h* insert τήν after πρός.

δύσιν ὡς τρισχιλίους καὶ ἑπτακοσίους σταδίους,
καὶ σχεδὸν ἀντάρας τοῖς κατὰ Μερόην τόποις καὶ
εἰς τὴν Λιβύην πολὺ προπεσὼν[1] καὶ τὴν ἑτέραν
ἐπιστροφὴν ποιησάμενος πρὸς τὰς ἄρκτους φέρεται
πεντακισχιλίους μὲν καὶ τριακοσίους σταδίους
ἐπὶ τὸν μέγαν καταράκτην, μικρὸν παρεπι-
στρέφων πρὸς τὴν ἕω, χιλίους δὲ καὶ διακοσίους
τοὺς ἐπὶ τὸν ἐλάττω τὸν κατὰ Συήνην, πεντακισχιλίους δὲ ἄλλους καὶ τριακοσίους ἐπὶ τὴν
θάλατταν. ἐμβάλλουσι δ' εἰς αὐτὸν δύο ποταμοί,
φερόμενοι μὲν ἔκ τινων λιμνῶν ἀπὸ τῆς ἕω, περι-
λαμβάνοντες δὲ νῆσον εὐμεγέθη τὴν Μερόην· ὧν
ὁ μὲν Ἀσταβόρας καλεῖται κατὰ τὸ πρὸς ἕω
πλευρὸν ῥέων, ἅτερος δ' Ἀστάπους· οἱ δ' Ἀστα-
σόβαν καλοῦσι, τὸν δ' Ἀστάπουν ἄλλον εἶναι,
ῥέοντα ἔκ τινων λιμνῶν ἀπὸ μεσημβρίας, καὶ
σχεδὸν τὸ κατ' εὐθεῖαν σῶμα τοῦ Νείλου τοῦτον
ποιεῖν· τὴν δὲ πλήρωσιν αὐτοῦ τοὺς θερινοὺς
ὄμβρους παρασκευάζειν. ὑπὲρ δὲ τὰς συμβο-
λὰς τοῦ Ἀσταβόρα καὶ τοῦ Νείλου σταδίοις
ἑπτακοσίοις Μερόην εἶναι πόλιν ὁμώνυμον τῇ
νήσῳ· ἄλλην δ' εἶναι νῆσον ὑπὲρ τῆς Μερόης, ἣν
ἔχουσιν οἱ Αἰγυπτίων φυγάδες οἱ ἀποστάντες
ἐπὶ[2] Ψαμμιτίχου,[3] καλοῦνται δὲ Σεμβρῖται, ὡς
ἂν ἐπήλυδες· βασιλεύονται δὲ ὑπὸ γυναικός,
ὑπακούουσι[4] δὲ τῶν ἐν Μερόῃ. τὰ δὲ κατωτέρω
ἑκατέρωθεν Μερόης, παρὰ μὲν τὸν Νεῖλον πρὸς

[1] προπεσών D, προσπεσών other MSS.
[2] ἐπί, Corais emends to ἀπό, citing Herodotus 2. 30 ; and
so Meineke, but both ἐπὶ Ψαμμητίχου and ἀπὸ Ψαμμητίχου are
found in that passage.
[3] Ψαμμητίχου CDF*hiuz*.
[4] ὑπακούουσι, Corais emends to ἐπαρχούσης (cp. 16. 4. 8).

4

seven hundred stadia, and after almost reaching the
same parallel as that of the region of Meroê and
projecting far into Libya and making the second
turn, flows towards the north five thousand three
hundred stadia to the great cataract, turning aside
slightly towards the east, and then one thousand
two hundred stadia to the smaller cataract at Syenê,
and then five thousand three hundred more to the
sea. Two rivers empty into it, which flow from
some lakes on the east and enclose Meroê, a rather
large island. One of these rivers, which flows on
the eastern side of the island, is called Astaboras [1]
and the other is called Astapus,[2] though some call it
Astasobas and say that another river, which flows
from some lakes from the south,[3] is the Astapus and
that this river forms almost all the straight part of
the body of the Nile, and that it is filled by the
summer rains. Above the confluence of the Astaboras and the Nile, he says, at a distance of seven
hundred stadia, lies Meroê, a city bearing the same
name as the island; and there is another island above
Meroê which is held by the Aegyptian fugitives
who revolted in the time of Psammitichus, and are
called "Sembritae," meaning "foreigners." [4] They
are ruled by a queen, but they are subject to the
kings of Meroê.[5] The lower parts of the country
on either side of Meroê, along the Nile towards the

---

[1] Now Atbara or Takazze.

[2] Now Bahr el-Abiad.   [3] Now Bahr el-Asrek.

[4] See 16. 4. 8. According to Herodotus (2. 30), the original
number of these fugitives was 240,000 (see Rawlinson's note,
Vol. II, p. 37).

[5] This statement is inconsistent with that in 16. 4. 8,
which, however, appears to have been taken from Artemidorus.

τὴν Ἐρυθρὰν Μεγάβαροι καὶ Βλέμμυες, Αἰθιόπων
ὑπακούοντες, Αἰγυπτίοις δ᾽ ὅμοροι· παρὰ θάλατταν δὲ Τρωγλοδύται· διεστᾶσι δὲ εἰς δέκα ἢ
δώδεκα ἡμερῶν ὁδὸν οἱ κατὰ τὴν Μερόην Τρωγλοδύται τοῦ Νείλου. ἐξ ἀριστερῶν δὲ τῆς ῥύσεως
τοῦ Νείλου Νοῦβαι κατοικοῦσιν ἐν τῇ Λιβύῃ,
μέγα ἔθνος, ἀπὸ τῆς Μερόης ἀρξάμενοι μέχρι τῶν
ἀγκώνων, οὐχ ὑποταττόμενοι τοῖς Αἰθίοψιν, ἀλλ᾽
ἰδίᾳ κατὰ πλείους βασιλείας διειλημμένοι. τῆς δ᾽
Αἰγύπτου τὸ παρὰ τὴν θάλατταν ἐστιν ἀπὸ τοῦ
Πηλουσιακοῦ στόματος πρὸς τὸ Κανωβικὸν στάδιοι
χίλιοι¹ τριακόσιοι. Ἐρατοσθένης μὲν οὖν οὕτως.

3. Δεῖ δὲ ἐπὶ πλέον εἰπεῖν, καὶ πρῶτον τὰ περὶ
τὴν Αἴγυπτον, ὅπως ἀπὸ τῶν γνωριμωτέρων ἐπὶ
τὰ ἑξῆς προΐωμεν· κοινὰ μὲν γάρ τινα καὶ ταύτῃ
τῇ χώρᾳ καὶ τῇ συνεχεῖ καὶ ὑπὲρ αὐτὴν τῇ τῶν
Αἰθιόπων ὁ Νεῖλος παρασκευάζει, ποτίζων τε
αὐτὰς κατὰ τὰς ἀναβάσεις καὶ τοῦτ᾽ οἰκήσιμον
αὐτῶν τὸ μέρος ἀπολείπων μόνον τὸ καλυπτό-
μενον ἐν ταῖς πλημμυρίσι, τὸ δ᾽ ὑπερδέξιον καὶ
μετεωρότερον τοῦ ῥεύματος πᾶν ἀοίκητον διεξιὼν
ἑκατέρωθεν καὶ ἔρημον διὰ τὴν αὐτὴν ἀνυδρίαν.
C 787 ἀλλὰ τὴν μὲν Αἰθιοπίαν οὔτε πᾶσαν διέξεισιν ὁ
Νεῖλος οὔτε μόνος οὔτ᾽ ἐπ᾽ εὐθείας οὔτ᾽ οἰκουμένην
καλῶς· τὴν δὲ Αἴγυπτον καὶ μόνος καὶ πᾶσαν καὶ
ἐπ᾽ εὐθείας ἀπὸ τοῦ μικροῦ καταράκτου ὑπὲρ
Συήνης καὶ Ἐλεφαντίνης ἀρξάμενος, οἵπερ εἰσὶν
ὅροι τῆς Αἰγύπτου καὶ τῆς Αἰθιοπίας, ἕως τῶν ἐπὶ

---

¹ χίλιοι (as in 15. 1. 33 ; cp. 1. 4. 5), the editors, for τρισχίλιοι (E reads γσ´).

Red Sea, are inhabited by Megabari and Blemmyes, who are subject to the Aethiopians and border on the Aegyptians, and, along the sea, by Troglodytes (the Troglodytes opposite Meroê are a ten or twelve days' journey distant from the Nile), but the parts on the left side of the course of the Nile, in Libya, are inhabited by Nubae, a large tribe, who, beginning at Meroê, extend as far as the bends of the river, and are not subject to the Aethiopians but are divided into several separate kingdoms. The extent of Aegypt along the sea from the Pelusiac to the Canobic mouth is one thousand three hundred stadia. This, then, is what Eratosthenes says.

3. But it is necessary to speak at greater length, and first of the parts about Aegypt, in order to proceed from those that are better known to those that come in order thereafter; for the Nile effects certain common results in this country and in that which is continuous with it and lies above it, I mean the country of the Aethiopians, in that it waters them at the time of its rise and also leaves only those parts of them habitable which have been covered during the overflows, and in that it merely passes through all the higher parts that are at a greater altitude than its current, leaving them uninhabited and desert on both sides because of the same lack of water. However, the Nile does not pass through the whole of Aethiopia, nor alone, nor in a straight line, nor through country that is well inhabited, but it alone passes through Aegypt, through the whole of it and in a straight line, beginning from the little cataract above Syenê and Elephantinê, which are the boundaries of Aegypt and Aethiopia, to its outlets on the sea-coast. And

7

θάλατταν ἐκβολῶν.¹ καὶ μὴν οἵ γε Αἰθίοπες τὸ
πλέον νομαδικῶς ζῶσι καὶ ἀπόρως διά τε τὴν λυπ-
ρότητα τῆς χώρας καὶ τὴν τῶν ἀέρων ἀσυμμετρίαν
καὶ τὸν ἀφ' ἡμῶν ἐκτοπισμόν, τοῖς δ' Αἰγυπτίοις
ἅπαντα τἀναντία συμβέβηκε· καὶ γὰρ πολιτικῶς
καὶ ἡμέρως ἐξ ἀρχῆς ζῶσι καὶ ἐν γνωρίμοις
ἵδρυνται τόποις, ὥστε καὶ αἱ διατάξεις αὐτῶν
μνημονεύονται. καὶ ἐπαινοῦνταί γε, δοκοῦντες
ἀξίως χρήσασθαι τῇ τῆς χώρας εὐδαιμονίᾳ, μερί-
σαντές τε εὖ καὶ ἐπιμεληθέντες· βασιλέα γὰρ
ἀποδείξαντες τριχῇ τὸ πλῆθος διεῖλον, καὶ τοὺς
μὲν στρατιώτας ἐκάλεσαν, τοὺς δὲ γεωργούς, τοὺς
δὲ ἱερέας· καὶ τοὺς μὲν τῶν ἱερῶν ἐπιμελητάς,
τοὺς δ' ἄλλους τῶν περὶ τὸν ἄνθρωπον· καὶ τοὺς
μὲν τὰ ² ἐν τῷ πολέμῳ, τοὺς δ' ὅσα ἐν εἰρήνῃ, γῆν
τε καὶ τέχνας ἐργαζομένους,³ ἀφ' ὧνπερ καὶ αἱ
πρόσοδοι συνήγοντο τῷ βασιλεῖ. οἱ δ' ἱερεῖς καὶ
φιλοσοφίαν ἤσκουν καὶ ἀστρονομίαν· ὁμιληταί τε
τῶν βασιλέων ἦσαν. ἡ δὲ χώρα τὴν μὲν πρώτην
διαίρεσιν εἰς νομοὺς ἔσχε, δέκα μὲν ἡ Θηβαΐς,
δέκα δ' ἡ ἐν τῷ Δέλτα, ἑκκαίδεκα δ' ἡ μεταξύ
(ὡς δέ τινες, τοσοῦτοι ἦσαν οἱ σύμπαντες νομοί,
ὅσαι αἱ ἐν τῷ λαβυρίνθῳ αὐλαί·⁴ αὗται δ' ἐλάττους τῶν τριάκοντα⁵)· πάλιν δ' οἱ νομοὶ τομὰς
ἄλλας ἔσχον, εἰς γὰρ τοπαρχίας οἱ πλεῖστοι

---

¹ τοῦ Νείλου, after ἐκβολῶν, Groskurd and later editors
eject.
² τά, added from the Epitome.
³ ἐργαζομένους, Kramer, for ἐργαζομένων.
⁴ αὐλαί F, αὐταί other MSS.
⁵ τριάκοντα, Meineke, following conj. of Groskurd, emends
to τριάκοντα ἕξ.

indeed the Aethiopians lead for the most part a nomadic and resourceless life, on account of the barrenness of the country and of the unseasonableness of its climate and of its remoteness from us, whereas with the Aegyptians the contrary is the case in all these respects; for from the outset they have led a civic and cultivated life and have been settled in well-known regions, so that their organisations are a matter of comment. And they are commended in that they are thought to have used worthily the good fortune of their country, having divided it well and having taken good care of it; for when they had appointed a king they divided the people into three classes, and they called one class soldiers, another farmers, and another priests; and the last class had the care of things sacred and the other two of things relating to man; and some had charge of the affairs of war, and others of all the affairs of peace, both tilling soil and following trades, from which sources the revenues were gathered for the king. The priests devoted themselves both to philosophy and to astronomy; and they were companions of the king. The country was first divided into Nomes,[1] the Thebaïs containing ten, the country in the Delta ten, and the country between them sixteen (according to some, the number of the Nomes all told was the same as that of the halls in the Labyrinth, but the number of these is less than thirty[2]); and again the Nomes were divided into other sections, for most of them were divided into

---

[1] The Greek word (Νομοί) here means Districts or Provinces. Pliny (5. 9) refers to them as *praefecturae oppidorum*.

[2] Meineke and others unnecessarily emend the text to read "thirty-six" (see critical note).

διήρηντο, καὶ αὗται δ' εἰς ἄλλας τομάς· ἐλάχισται
δ' αἱ ἄρουραι μερίδες. ἐδέησε δὲ τῆς ἐπ' ἀκριβὲς
καὶ κατὰ λεπτὸν διαιρέσεως διὰ τὰς συνεχεῖς τῶν
ὅρων συγχύσεις, ἃς ὁ Νεῖλος ἀπεργάζεται κατὰ
τὰς αὐξήσεις, ἀφαιρῶν καὶ προστιθεὶς καὶ ἐναλ-
λάττων τὰ σχήματα καὶ τἆλλα σημεῖα ἀποκρύπ-
των, οἷς διακρίνεται τό τε ἀλλότριον καὶ τὸ
ἴδιον· ἀνάγκη δὴ ἀναμετρεῖσθαι πάλιν καὶ πάλιν.
ἐντεῦθεν δὲ καὶ τὴν γεωμετρίαν συστῆναί φασιν,
ὡς τὴν λογιστικὴν καὶ ἀριθμητικὴν παρὰ Φοινίκων
διὰ τὰς ἐμπορίας. τριχῆ δὲ διήρητο, ὥσπερ τὸ
σύμπαν, καὶ τὸ ἐν ἑκάστῳ τῷ νομῷ πλῆθος, εἰς
τρία ἴσα μερισθείσης τῆς χώρας. ἡ δὲ περὶ τὸν
ποταμὸν πραγματεία διαφέρει τοσοῦτον, ὅσον τῇ
ἐπιμελείᾳ νικᾶν τὴν φύσιν. φύσει γὰρ πλείονα
φέρει καρπὸν καὶ ποτισθεῖσα μᾶλλον, φύσει καὶ
C 788 ἡ μείζων ἀνάβασις τοῦ ποταμοῦ πλείω ποτίζει
γῆν, ἀλλ' ἡ ἐπιμέλεια πολλάκις καὶ τῆς φύσεως
ἐξίσχυσεν ἐπιλιπούσης, ὥστε καὶ κατὰ τὰς ἐλάττους ἀναβάσεις τοσαύτην ποτισθῆναι γῆν, ὅσην
ἐν ταῖς μείζοσι, διά τε τῶν διωρύγων καὶ τῶν
παραχωμάτων· ἐπὶ γοῦν τῶν πρὸ Πετρωνίου
χρόνων ἡ μεγίστη μὲν ἦν φορὰ καὶ ἀνάβασις,
ἡνίκα ἐπὶ τεσσαρεσκαίδεκα πήχεις ἀνέβαινεν ὁ
Νεῖλος, ἡνίκα δ' ἐπ' ὀκτώ, συνέβαινε λιμός· ἐπ'
ἐκείνου δὲ ἄρξαντος τῆς χώρας καὶ δώδεκα μόνον

---

[1] By "arourae" Strabo refers to the Aegyptian land-measure,
which was 100 Aegyptian cubits square (Herodotus 2. 168),
i.e. about seven-elevenths of our acre. Each soldier was

toparchies, and these also into other sections; and the smallest portions were the arourae.[1] There was need of this accurate and minute division on account of the continuous confusion of the boundaries caused by the Nile at the time of its increases, since the Nile takes away and adds soil, and changes conformations of lands, and in general hides from view the signs by which one's own land is distinguished from that of another. Of necessity, therefore, the lands must be re-measured again and again. And here it was, they say, that the science of geometry[2] originated, just as accounting and arithmetic originated with the Phoenicians, because of their commerce.[3] Like the people as a whole, the people in each Nome were also divided into three parts, since the land had been divided into three equal parts. The activity of the people in connection with the river goes so far as to conquer nature through diligence. For by nature the land produces more fruit than do other lands, and still more when watered; and by nature a greater rise of the river waters more land; but diligence has often-times, even when nature has failed, availed to bring about the watering of as much land even at the time of the smaller rises of the river as at the greater rises, that is, through the means of canals and embankments. At any rate, in the times before Petronius[4] the crop was the largest and the rise the highest when the Nile would rise to fourteen cubits, and when it would rise to only eight a famine would ensue; but in the time of his reign over the

granted the free use of twelve arourae of land without tax-ation (Herodotus 2. 168).

   [2] Literally, "land-measuring."   [3] See 16. 2. 24.

   [4] C. Petronius (see 17. 1. 54).

πληρώσαντος πήχεις τοῦ Νείλου μέτρου,[1] μεγίστη
ἦν ἡ φορά, καὶ ὀκτώ ποτε μόνον πληρώσαντος,
λιμοῦ οὐδεὶς ᾔσθετο. τοιαύτη μὲν ἡ διάταξις, τὰ
δ᾽ ἑξῆς λέγωμεν νυνί.

4. Ἀπὸ γὰρ τῶν Αἰθιοπικῶν τερμόνων ῥεῖ ἐπ᾽
εὐθείας ὁ Νεῖλος πρὸς ἄρκτους, ἕως τοῦ καλου-
μένου χωρίου Δέλτα· εἶτ᾽ ἐπὶ κορυφὴν σχιζόμενος
ὁ Νεῖλος, ὥς φησιν ὁ Πλάτων, ὡς ἂν τριγώνου
κορυφὴν ἀποτελεῖ τὸν τόπον τοῦτον, πλευρὰς δὲ
τοῦ τριγώνου τὰ σχιζόμενα ἐφ᾽ ἑκάτερα ῥεῖθρα
καθήκοντα μέχρι τῆς θαλάττης, τὸ μὲν ἐν δεξιᾷ
τῆς κατὰ Πηλούσιον, τὸ δ᾽ ἐν ἀριστερᾷ τῆς κατὰ
Κάνωβον καὶ τὸ πλησίον Ἡράκλειον προσα-
γορευόμενον, βάσιν δὲ τὴν παραλίαν τὴν μεταξὺ
τοῦ Πηλουσίου καὶ τοῦ Ἡρακλείου. γέγονε δὴ[2]
νῆσος ἔκ τε τῆς θαλάττης καὶ τῶν ῥευμάτων
ἀμφοῖν τοῦ ποταμοῦ, καὶ καλεῖται Δέλτα διὰ
τὴν ὁμοιότητα τοῦ σχήματος· τὸ δ᾽ ἐπὶ τῇ κορυφῇ
χωρίον ὁμωνύμως κέκληται διὰ τὸ ἀρχὴν εἶναι τοῦ
λεχθέντος σχήματος, καὶ ἡ κώμη δὲ ἡ ἐπ᾽ αὐτῷ
καλεῖται Δέλτα. δύο μὲν οὖν ταῦτα τοῦ Νείλου
στόματα, ὧν τὸ μὲν Πηλουσιακὸν καλεῖται, τὸ δὲ
Κανωβικὸν καὶ Ἡρακλειωτικόν, μεταξὺ δὲ τούτων
ἄλλαι πέντε εἰσὶν ἐκβολαὶ αἵ γε ἀξιόλογοι, λεπτό-
τεραι δὲ πλείους· ἀπὸ γὰρ τῶν πρώτων μερῶν
ἀπορρῶγες πολλαὶ καθ᾽ ὅλην μερισθεῖσαι τὴν
νῆσον πολλὰ καὶ ῥεῖθρα καὶ νήσους ἐποίησαν,
ὥσθ᾽ ὅλην γενέσθαι πλωτὴν διωρύγων ἐπὶ διώρυξι
τμηθεισῶν, αἳ κατὰ ῥᾳστώνην πλέονται τοσαύτην,

---

[1] Νείλου μέτρον r; Νειλομετρίου, Corais; πηχέων . . . μέτρον
conj. Villebrun.
[2] δή, Groskurd, for δ᾽ ἡ.

country, and when the Nilometer registered only twelve cubits, the crop was the largest, and once, when it registered only eight cubits, no one felt hunger. Such is the organisation of Aegypt; but let me now describe the things that come next in order.

4. The Nile flows from the Aethiopian boundaries towards the north in a straight line to the district called "Delta," and then, being "split at the head," as Plato says,[1] the Nile makes this place as it were the vertex of a triangle, the sides of the triangle being formed by the streams that split in either direction and extend to the sea—the one on the right to the sea at Pelusium and the other on the left to the sea at Canobus and the neighbouring Heracleium, as it is called,—and the base by the coast-line between Pelusium and the Heracleium. An island, therefore, has been formed by the sea and the two streams of the river; and it is called Delta on account of the similarity of its shape; and the district at the vertex has been given the same name because it is the beginning of the above-mentioned figure; and the village there is also called Delta. Now these are two mouths of the Nile, of which one is called Pelusiac and the other Canobic or Heracleiotic; but between these there are five other outlets, those at least that are worth mentioning, and several that are smaller; for, beginning with the first parts of the Delta, many branches of the river have been split off throughout the whole island and have formed many streams and islands, so that the whole Delta has become navigable —canals on canals having been cut, which are

---

[1] *Timaeus* 21 E.

ὥστε καὶ ὀστράκινα ἐνίοις εἶναι πορθμεῖα. τὴν
μὲν οὖν περίμετρον ὅσον τρισχιλίων σταδίων
ἐστὶν ἡ σύμπασα νῆσος· καλοῦσι[1] δ᾽ αὐτὴν καὶ
τὴν κάτω χώραν σὺν ταῖς ἀπαντικρὺ ποταμίαις
τοῦ Δέλτα· ἐν δὲ ταῖς ἀναβάσεσι τοῦ Νείλου
καλύπτεται πᾶσα καὶ πελαγίζει πλὴν τῶν οἰκή-
σεων· αὗται δ᾽ ἐπὶ λόφων αὐτοφυῶν ἢ χωμάτων
C 789 ἵδρυνται, πόλεις τε ἀξιόλογοι καὶ κῶμαι, νησίζου-
σαι κατὰ τὴν πόρρωθεν ὄψιν. πλείους δ᾽ ἢ[2]
τετταράκοντα ἡμέρας τοῦ θέρους διαμεῖναν τὸ
ὕδωρ ἔπειθ᾽ ὑπόβασιν λαμβάνει κατ᾽ ὀλίγον,
καθάπερ καὶ τὴν αὔξησιν ἔσχεν· ἐν ἑξήκοντα δὲ
ἡμέραις τελέως γυμνοῦται καὶ ἀναψύχεται τὸ
πεδίον· ὅσῳ δὲ θᾶττον ἡ ἀνάψυξις, τοσῷδε θᾶττον
ὁ ἄροτος καὶ ὁ σπόρος· θᾶττον δέ, παρ᾽ οἷς τὰ
μείζω θάλπη. τὸν αὐτὸν τρόπον καὶ τὰ ἐπάνω
τοῦ Δέλτα ποτίζεται, πλὴν ὅτι ἐπ᾽ εὐθείας ὅσον
τετρακισχιλίοις σταδίοις δι᾽ ἑνὸς ῥείθρου τοῦ
ποταμοῦ φερομένου, πλὴν εἴ πού[3] τις ἐντρέχει
νῆσος, ὧν ἀξιολογωτάτη ἡ τὸν Ἡρακλειωτικὸν
νομὸν περιέχουσα, ἢ εἴ πού τις ἐκτροπὴ διώρυγι
ἐπὶ πλέον εἰς λίμνην μεγάλην καὶ χώραν, ἣν
ποτίζειν δύναται, καθάπερ ἐπὶ τῆς τὸν Ἀρσινοΐτην[4]
νομὸν ποτιζούσης[5] καὶ τὴν Μοίριδος λίμνην καὶ
τῶν εἰς τὴν Μαρεῶτιν[6] ἀναχεομένων. συλλήβδην
δ᾽ εἰπεῖν, ἡ ποταμία μόνον ἐστὶν Αἴγυπτος ἡ
ἑκατέρωθεν ἐσχάτη τοῦ Νείλου, σπάνιον εἴ που

---

[1] καλοῦσι, Brequigny, for κολποῦσι; κατοικοῦσι, Corais.
[2] δ᾽ ἢ hmox, ἤ E, δέ other MSS.
[3] εἴ που EF; εἰ μή που other MSS.
[4] Ἀρσινοΐτην D; Ἀρσινοήτην other MSS.
[5] ποτιζούσης Letronne, for ποιούσης.

navigated with such ease that some people even use earthenware ferry-boats.[1]   Now the island as a whole is as much as three thousand stadia in perimeter; and they also call it, together with the opposite river-lands of the Delta, Lower Egypt;[2] but at the rising of the Nile the whole country is under water and becomes a lake, except the settlements; and these are situated on natural hills or on artificial mounds, and contain cities of considerable size and villages, which, when viewed from afar, resemble islands.   The water stays more than forty days in summer and then goes down gradually just as it rose; and in sixty days the plain is completely bared and begins to dry out; and the sooner the drying takes place, the sooner the ploughing and the sowing; and the drying takes place sooner in those parts where the heat is greater.   The parts above the Delta are also watered in the same way, except that the river flows in a straight course about four thousand stadia through only one channel, except where some island intervenes, of which the most noteworthy is that which comprises the Heracleiotic Nome, or except where the river is diverted to a greater extent than usual by a canal into a large lake or a territory which it can water, as, for instance, in the case of the canal which waters the Arsinoïte Nome and Lake Moeris[3] and of those which spread over Lake Mareotis.[4]   In short, Aegypt consists of only the river-land, I mean the last stretch of river-

[1] Cp. Juvenal 15. 126.
[2] Cp. 1. 2. 23 and 16. 2. 35.
[3] See Herodotus 2. 149 and Breasted's *A History of Egypt*, pp. 191–94.
[4] Now Lake Mariout.

---

[6] Μαρεῶτιν E, Μαραιῶτιν other MSS.

τριακοσίων σταδίων ἐπέχουσα συνεχῶς πλάτος
τὸ οἰκήσιμον, ἀρξαμένη ἀπὸ τῶν ὅρων[1] τῆς
Αἰθιοπίας, μέχρι τῆς κορυφῆς τοῦ Δέλτα. ἔοικεν
οὖν κειρία[2] ψυχομένη[3] ἐπὶ μῆκος, ὑπεξαιρου-
μένων τῶν ἐπὶ πλέον ἐκτροπῶν. ποιεῖ δὲ τὸ
σχῆμα τοῦτο τῆς ποταμίας, ἧς λέγω, καὶ τῆς
χώρας τὰ ὄρη τὰ ἑκατέρωθεν ἀπὸ τῶν περὶ
Συήνην τόπων καταγόμενα μέχρι τοῦ Αἰγυπτίου
πελάγους· ἐφ' ὅσον γὰρ ταῦτα παρατείνει καὶ
διέστηκεν ἀπ' ἀλλήλων, ἐπὶ τοσοῦτον καὶ ὁ
ποταμὸς συνάγεταί τε καὶ διαχεῖται καὶ διασχη-
ματίζει τὴν χώραν διαφόρως τὴν οἰκήσιμον. ἡ δὲ
ὑπὲρ τῶν ὁρῶν ἐπὶ συχνὸν ἀοίκητός ἐστιν.

5. Οἱ μὲν οὖν ἀρχαῖοι στοχασμῷ τὸ πλέον, οἱ
δ' ὕστερον αὐτόπται γενηθέντες ᾔσθοντο ὑπὸ
ὄμβρων θερινῶν πληρούμενον τὸν Νεῖλον, τῆς
Αἰθιοπίας τῆς ἄνω κλυζομένης, καὶ μάλιστα ἐν τοῖς
ἐσχάτοις ὄρεσι, παυσαμένων δὲ τῶν ὄμβρων
παυομένην κατ' ὀλίγον τὴν πλημμυρίδα. τοῦτο
δ' ὑπῆρξε μάλιστα δῆλον τοῖς πλέουσι τὸν
Ἀράβιον κόλπον μέχρι τῆς κινναμωμοφόρου καὶ
τοῖς ἐκπεμπομένοις ἐπὶ τὴν τῶν ἐλεφάντων θήραν,
καὶ εἴ τινες ἄλλαι χρεῖαι παρώξυνον ἐκεῖσε ἄνδρας προχειρίζεσθαι τοὺς τῆς Αἰγύπτου βασιλέας
τοὺς Πτολεμαϊκούς. οὗτοι γὰρ ἐφρόντισαν τῶν
τοιούτων, διαφερόντως δ' ὁ Φιλάδελφος ἐπικλη-

---

[1] ὅρων, Corais, for ὁρῶν.
[2] κηρία CEFs (C adding υ above η), κει̣ι̣ξ D*himowxz* (D
adding the ει above η), κυ̣ρι̣ξ Ald.
[3] ψυχομένη, Corais (who conj. τεταμένη, however), for
ψυχομένη; ἀναπτυσσομένη or ἀνεπτυγμένη conj. Kramer.

---

[1] But the text seems corrupt (see critical note). Strabo
may have written, "Accordingly, it resembles length-wise an

land on either side of the Nile, which, beginning at the boundaries of Aethiopia and extending to the vertex of the Delta, scarcely anywhere occupies a continuous habitable space as broad as three hundred stadia. Accordingly, when it is dried, it resembles lengthwise a girdle-band,[1] the greater diversions of the river being excepted. This shape of the river-land of which I am speaking, as also of the country, is caused by the mountains on either side, which extend from the region of Syenê down to the Aegyptian Sea; for in proportion as these mountains lie near together or at a distance from one another, in that proportion the river is contracted or widened, and gives to the lands that are habitable their different shapes. But the country beyond the mountains is for a great distance uninhabited.[2]

5. Now the ancients depended mostly on conjecture, but the men of later times, having become eye-witnesses, perceived that the Nile was filled by summer rains, when Upper Aethiopia was flooded, and particularly in the region of its farthermost mountains, and that when the rains ceased the inundation gradually ceased. This fact was particularly clear to those who navigated the Arabian Gulf as far as the Cinnamon-bearing country, and to those who were sent out to hunt elephants[3] or upon any other business which may have prompted the Ptolemaic kings of Aegypt to despatch men thither. For these kings were concerned with things of this kind; and especially the Ptolemy surnamed Philadelphus, since he was of an

unwound girdle-band," or else, "Accordingly, it resembles a hand outstretched to full length," meaning both arm and hand, and thus referring to the Delta as well as to the stretch of river-land from Aethiopia to the vertex.
[2] See 1. 2. 25. [3] See 16. 4. 7.

17

θείς, φιλιστορῶν καὶ διὰ τὴν ἀσθένειαν τοῦ
σώματος διαγωγὰς ἀεί τινας καὶ τέρψεις ζητῶν
καινοτέρας. οἱ πάλαι δὲ βασιλεῖς οὐ πάνυ
C 790 ἐφρόντισαν τῶν τοιούτων, καίπερ οἰκεῖοι σοφίας
γεγονότες καὶ αὐτοὶ καὶ οἱ ἱερεῖς, μεθ' ὧν ἦν
αὐτοῖς ὁ πλείων βίος· ὥστε καὶ θαυμάζειν ἄξιον
καὶ διὰ τοῦτο καὶ διότι Σέσωστρις τὴν Αἰθιοπίαν
ἐπῆλθεν ἅπασαν μέχρι τῆς κινναμωμοφόρου, καὶ
ὑπομνήματα τῆς στρατείας αὐτοῦ καὶ νῦν ἔτι
δείκνυται, στῆλαι καὶ ἐπιγραφαί. Καμβύσης τε
τὴν Αἴγυπτον κατασχὼν προῆλθε καὶ μέχρι τῆς
Μερόης μετὰ τῶν Αἰγυπτίων· καὶ δὴ καὶ τοὔνομα
τῇ τε νήσῳ καὶ τῇ πόλει τοῦτο παρ' ἐκείνου
τεθῆναί φασιν, ἐκεῖ τῆς ἀδελφῆς ἀποθανούσης
αὐτῷ Μερόης (οἱ δὲ γυναῖκά φασι)· τὴν ἐπωνυμίαν
οὖν ἐχαρίσατο αὐτῇ τιμῶν τὴν ἄνθρωπον. θαυ-
μαστὸν οὖν, πῶς ἐκ τῶν τοιούτων ἀφορμῶν οὐ
τελέως ἐναργὴς ἦν ἡ περὶ τῶν ὄμβρων ἱστορία
τοῖς τότε, καὶ ταῦτα τῶν ἱερέων φιλοπραγμονέσ-
τερον ἀναφερόντων εἰς τὰ ἱερὰ γράμματα καὶ
ἀποτιθεμένων, ὅσα μάθησιν περιττὴν ἐπιφαίνει.[1]
εἰ γὰρ ἄρα, τοῦτ' ἐχρῆν ζητεῖν, ὅπερ καὶ νῦν ἔτι
ζητεῖται, τί δή ποτε θέρους, χειμῶνος δὲ οὔ, καὶ
ἐν τοῖς νοτιωτάτοις, ἐν δὲ τῇ Θηβαΐδι καὶ τῇ περὶ
Συήνην οὐ συμπίπτουσιν ὄμβροι· τὸ δ' ὅτι ἐξ
ὄμβρων αἱ ἀναβάσεις μὴ ζητεῖν, μηδὲ τοιούτων
δεῖσθαι μαρτύρων, οἵους Ποσειδώνιος εἴρηκε.
φησὶ γὰρ Καλλισθένη λέγειν τὴν ἐκ τῶν ὄμβρων

---

[1] ὑποφαίνει *moz*, ἐπιτείνει E, marg. F, D first hand but
changed to ἐπιφαίνει.

---

[1] Diodorus Siculus (1. 33) says his mother.
[2] So 15. 1. 19.

inquiring disposition, and on account of the infirmity
of his body was always searching for novel pastimes
and enjoyments. But the kings of old were not at
all concerned with such things, although they proved
themselves congenial to learning, both they and the
priests, with whom they spent the greater part of
their lives; and therefore we may well be surprised,
not only on this account, but also by the fact that
Sesostris traversed the whole of Aethiopia as far as
the Cinnamon-bearing country, and that memorials
of his expedition, pillars and inscriptions, are to be
seen even to this day. Further, when Cambyses
took possession of Aegypt, he advanced with the
Aegyptians even as far as Meroê; and indeed this
name was given by him to both the island and the
city, it is said, because his sister Meroê—some say his
wife—[1] died there. The name, at any rate, he
bestowed upon the place in honour of the woman.
It is surprising, therefore, that the men of that time,
having such knowledge to begin with, did not possess
a perfectly clear knowledge of the rains, especially
since the priests rather meticulously record in their
sacred books, and thus store away, all facts that reveal any curious information; for they should have
investigated, if they made any investigations at all,
the question, which even to this day is still being
investigated, I mean why in the world rains fall in
summer but not in winter, and in the southernmost
parts but not in Thebaïs and the country round Syenê;[2]
but the fact that the rising of the river results from
rains should not have been investigated, nor yet
should this matter have needed such witnesses as
Poseidonius mentions; for instance, he says that
it was Callisthenes who states that the summer rains

19

αἰτίαν τῶν θερινῶν, παρὰ Ἀριστοτέλους λαβόντα,
ἐκεῖνον δὲ παρὰ Θρασυάλκου τοῦ Θασίου (τῶν
ἀρχαίων δὲ φυσικῶν εἷς οὗτος), ἐκεῖνον δὲ παρ'
ἄλλου,[1] τὸν δὲ παρ' Ὁμήρου διπετέα φάσκοντος
τὸν Νεῖλον·

   ἂν δ' εἰς Αἰγύπτοιο διπετέος ποταμοῖο.

   Ἀλλ' ἐῶ ταῦτα, πολλῶν εἰρηκότων, ὧν ἀρκέσει
δύο μηνῦσαι τοὺς ποιήσαντας καθ' ἡμᾶς τὸ περὶ τοῦ
Νείλου βιβλίον, Εὔδωρόν τε καὶ Ἀρίστωνα τὸν
ἐκ τῶν περιπάτων· πλὴν γὰρ τῆς τάξεως τά γε
ἄλλα καὶ τῇ φράσει καὶ τῇ ἐπιχειρήσει ταῦτά[2]
ἐστι κείμενα παρ' ἀμφοτέροις. ἐγὼ γοῦν ἀπορού-
μενος ἀντιγράφων εἰς τὴν ἀντιβολὴν ἐκ θατέρου
θάτερον ἀντέβαλον· πότερος δ' ἦν ὁ τἀλλότρια
ὑποβαλλόμενος, ἐν Ἄμμωνος εὕροι τις ἄν. Εὔδωρος
δ' ᾐτιᾶτο τὸν Ἀρίστωνα· ἡ μέντοι φράσις Ἀρισ-
τώνειος μᾶλλόν ἐστιν.

   Οἱ μὲν οὖν ἀρχαῖοι τὸ οἰκούμενον αὐτὸ καὶ
ποτιζόμενον ὑπὸ τοῦ Νείλου μόνον Αἴγυπτον
ἐκάλουν, ἀπὸ τῶν περὶ Συήνην τόπων ἀρξάμενοι
μέχρι τῆς θαλάττης· οἱ δ' ὕστερον μέχρι νῦν
προσέλαβον ἐκ μὲν τῶν πρὸς ἔω μερῶν τὰ[3]
μεταξὺ τοῦ Ἀραβίου κόλπου καὶ τοῦ Νείλου
C 791 σχεδόν τι πάντα (οἱ δ' Αἰθίοπες οὐ πάνυ χρῶνται
τῇ Ἐρυθρᾷ θαλάττῃ), ἐκ δὲ τῶν ἑσπερίων τὰ

---

[1] For ἄλλου C. Müller conj. παρὰ Θαλοῦ (citing 1. 1. 11).
[2] ταῦτά, Corais, for ταῦτα.
[3] τά, before μεταξύ, Corais inserts.

---

[1] Literally "antigraphs"; *i.e.*, apparently, "copies" of
parallel passages from the two works.

are the cause of the risings, though Callisthenes took the assertion from Aristotle, and Aristotle from Thrasyalces the Thasian (one of the early physicists), and Thrasyalces from someone else, and he from Homer, who calls the Nile "heaven-fed" : "And back again to the land of Aegyptus, heaven-fed river."

But I dismiss this subject, since it has been discussed by many writers, of whom it will suffice to report only the two who in my time have written the book about the Nile, I mean Eudorus and Ariston the Peripatetic philosopher ; for except in the matter of arrangement everything found in the two writers is the same as regards both style and treatment. I, at any rate, being in want of copies [1] with which to make a comparison, compared the one work with the other ;[2] but which of the two men it was who appropriated to himself the other's work might be discovered at Ammon's temple! Eudorus accused Ariston ; the style, however, is more like that of Ariston.

Now the early writers gave the name Aegypt to only the part of the country that was inhabited and watered by the Nile, beginning at the region of Syenê and extending to the sea ; but the later writers down to the present time have added on the eastern side approximately all the parts between the Arabian Gulf and the Nile (the Aethiopians do not use the Red Sea at all [3]), and on the western side the parts

[2] In the Alexandrian library, apparently.

[3] The other translators interpret πάνυ as meaning "much," or "to such an extent," or the like. But Strabo is speaking of Aethiopians in the strict sense of the term ; for "the country between the Nile and Arabian Gulf is Arabia" (17.1. 21), and even Aegyptian Heliupolis (17. 1. 30) and Thebes (17. 1. 46) are in "Arabia."

μέχρι τῶν Αὐάσεων καὶ ἐν τῇ παραλίᾳ τὰ ἀπὸ
τοῦ Κανωβικοῦ στόματος μέχρι Καταβαθμοῦ καὶ
τῆς Κυρηναίων ἐπικρατείας. οἵ τε γὰρ ἀπὸ τοῦ
Πτολεμαίου βασιλεῖς ἴσχυσαν τοσοῦτον, ὥστε[1]
καὶ τὴν Κυρηναίαν αὐτὴν κατέσχον καὶ διενεί-
μαντο πρὸς τὴν Αἴγυπτον καὶ τὴν Κύπρον.
Ῥωμαῖοί τε οἱ διαδεξάμενοι τὴν ἐκείνων ἐπαρχίαν
κρίναντες τὴν Αἴγυπτον ἐν τοῖς αὐτοῖς ὅροις
διεφύλαξαν. Αὐάσεις δ' οἱ Αἰγύπτιοι καλοῦσι
τὰς οἰκουμένας χώρας περιεχομένας κύκλῳ μεγάλαις ἐρημίαις, ὡς ἂν νήσους πελαγίας. πολὺ δὲ
τοῦτ' ἔστι κατὰ τὴν Λιβύην, τρεῖς δ' εἰσὶν αἱ
πρόσχωροι τῇ Αἰγύπτῳ καὶ ὑπ'[2] αὐτῇ τεταγμέναι.
τὰ μὲν οὖν καθ' ὅλου καὶ ἀνωτάτω περὶ τῆς
Αἰγύπτου ταῦτα λέγομεν, τὰ καθ' ἔκαστα δὲ καὶ[3]
τὰς ἀρετὰς αὐτῆς νῦν διέξιμεν.

6. Ἐπεὶ δὲ τὸ πλεῖστον τοῦ ἔργου τούτου καὶ
τὸ κυριώτατον ἡ Ἀλεξάνδρειά ἐστι καὶ τὰ περὶ
αὐτήν, ἐντεῦθεν ἀρκτέον. ἔστι τοίνυν ἡ ἀπὸ
Πηλουσίου παραλία πρὸς τὴν ἑσπέραν πλέουσι
μέχρι μὲν τοῦ Κανωβικοῦ στόματος χιλίων που
καὶ τριακοσίων σταδίων, ὃ δὴ καὶ βάσιν τοῦ
Δέλτα ἔφαμεν· ἐντεῦθεν δ' ἐπὶ Φάρον τὴν νῆσον
ἄλλοι στάδιοι πεντήκοντα πρὸς τοῖς ἑκατόν. ἡ
δὲ Φάρος νησίον ἐστὶ παράμηκες, προσεχέστατον
τῇ ἠπείρῳ, λιμένα πρὸς αὐτὴν ποιοῦν ἀμφίστομον.

---

[1] ὥστε, Letronne and Groskurd, for οἵ γε.
[2] ὑπ' m for ἐπ'; so Corais and Meineke.
[3] The text of F from καί to Πτολεμαῖος (17. 1. 11) is lost.

---

[1] Ptolemy I (Soter), reigned 323–285 B.C.

extending as far as the oases, and on the sea-coast the parts extending from the Canobic mouth to Catabathmus and the domain of the Cyrenaeans. For the kings after Ptolemy [1] became so powerful that they took possession of Cyrenaea itself and even united Cypros with Aegypt. The Romans, who succeeded the Ptolemies, separated their three dominions and have kept Aegypt within its former limits.[2] The Aegyptians call "oases "[3] the inhabited districts which are surrounded by large deserts, like islands in the open sea. There is many an oasis in Libya, and three of them lie close to Aegypt and are classed as subject to it. This, then, is my general, or summary, account of Aegypt, and I shall now discuss the separate parts and the excellent attributes of the country.

6. Since Alexandria [4] and its neighbourhood constitute the largest and most important part of this subject, I shall begin with them. The sea-coast, then, from Pelusium, as one sails towards the west, as far as the Canobic mouth, is about one thousand three hundred stadia—the "base" of the Delta, as I have called it ; [5] and thence to the island Pharos, one hundred and fifty stadia more. Pharos is an oblong isle, is very close to the mainland, and forms with it a harbour with two mouths ; for

[2] The Romans made Cyrenaea an "allied state" (*civitas foederata*) in 96 B.C., a Roman province in 88 B.C., and later (see 17. 3. 25) united it with Crete. Cypros was annexed to the province of Cilicia in 47 B.C., presented by Antony to Cleopatra in 32 B.C., made an imperial province in 27 B.C., and a senatorial province in 22 B.C.

[3] The Greek spelling is "auases."

[4] See Map of Alexandria at end of volume.

[5] 17. 1. 4.

ἠιὼν γάρ ἐστι κολπώδης, ἄκρας εἰς τὸ πέλαγος
προβεβλημένη δύο· τούτων δὲ μεταξὺ ἡ νῆσος
ἵδρυται κλείουσα τὸν κόλπον, παραβέβληται γὰρ
αὐτῷ κατὰ μῆκος. τῶν δ' ἄκρων τῆς Φάρου τὸ
μὲν ἑῷον μᾶλλόν ἐστι προσεχὲς τῇ ἠπείρῳ καὶ
τῇ κατ' αὐτὴν ἄκρᾳ (καλεῖται δ' ἄκρα Λοχιάς),
καὶ ποιεῖ τὸν λιμένα ἀρτίστομον·[1] πρὸς δὲ τῇ
στενότητι τοῦ μεταξὺ πόρου καὶ πέτραι εἰσίν, αἱ
μὲν ὕφαλοι, αἱ δὲ καὶ ἐξέχουσαι, τραχύνουσαι
πᾶσαν ὥραν τὸ προσπῖπτον ἐκ τοῦ πελάγους
κλυδώνιον. ἔστι δὲ καὶ αὐτὸ τὸ τῆς νησῖδος
ἄκρον πέτρα περίκλυστος, ἔχουσα πύργον
θαυμαστῶς κατεσκευασμένον λευκοῦ λίθου πο-
λυόροφον, ὁμώνυμον τῇ νήσῳ. τοῦτον δ' ἀνέθηκε
Σώστρατος Κνίδιος, φίλος τῶν βασιλέων, τῆς
τῶν πλωϊζομένων σωτηρίας χάριν, ὥς φησιν ἡ
ἐπιγραφή·[2] ἀλιμένου γὰρ οὔσης καὶ ταπεινῆς
τῆς ἑκατέρωθεν παραλίας, ἐχούσης δὲ καὶ χοιρά-
δας καὶ βράχη τινά, ἔδει σημείου τινὸς ὑψηλοῦ

---

[1] ἀμφίστομον w, Corais.

[2] After ἐπιγραφή C, in the margin, adds: Ἐπίγραμμα.
Σώστρατος Κνίδιος Δεξιφάνους θεοῖς σωτῆρσιν ὑπὲρ τῶν πλωϊζο-
μένων· The same words are found in Dhirw, and also, with
Ἐπίγραμμα omitted, in moxz.

---

[1] This tower, one of the "Wonders of the World," cost
800 talents (Pliny 6. 18). According to Eusebius (*Chron. ad
Olymp.* 124. 1), it was built in the time of Ptolemy Philadelphus, but, according to Suidas, at the beginning of the
reign of Pyrrhus (299 B.C.), *i.e.* in the time of Ptolemy Soter.
According to Josephus (*Bell. Jud.* 4. 10. 5, or L.C.L. edition,
Vol. III, pp. 181 and 251), it was visible from the sea at
300 stadia ; according to Epiphanes (Steph. Byz., s.v. Φάρος),
it was 306 fathoms high ; and the *Schol.* Lucian *ad Icaro-
menippum*, § 12, says that it was visible 300 miles away ! See

'the shore of the mainland forms a bay, since it thrusts two promontories into the open sea, and between these is situated the island, which closes the bay, for it lies lengthwise parallel to the shore. Of the extremities of Pharos, the eastern one lies closer to the mainland and to the promontory opposite it (the promontory called Lochias), and thus makes the harbour narrow at the mouth; and in addition to the narrowness of the intervening passage there are also rocks, some under the water, and others projecting out of it, which at all hours roughen the waves that strike them from the open sea. And likewise the extremity of the isle is a rock, which is washed all round by the sea and has upon it a tower that is admirably constructed of white marble with many stories and bears the same name as the island.[1] This was an offering made by Sostratus of Cnidus, a friend of the kings, for the safety of mariners, as the inscription says:[2] for since the coast was harbourless and low on either side, and also had reefs and shallows, those who were sailing from the open sea thither needed some lofty and

A. M. de Zogheb, *Études sur L'Ancienne Alexandrie*, Paris, 1910; and Thiersch's restoration of the tower in Rostovtzeff's *A History of the Ancient World*, Vol. I, p. 369.

[2] Some of the MSS. (see critical note) record the inscription, which is preserved in Lucian, *How to Write History*, § 62 (but is obviously a gloss in Strabo): "Sostratus of Cnidus, son of Dexiphanes, on behalf of mariners, to the Divine Saviours." "The Divine Saviours" might refer to Ptolemy Soter and Berenicê (see the Corais-Letronne edition, which cites Spannheim, *De Praestantia et Usu Numismat.* I, p. 415, and Visconti, *Iconographie Grecque* II, 18, p. 564), but it was the Dioscuri (Castor and Pollux) who were known by "all" as "guardians of the sea" and "the saviours of sailors" (1. 3. 2 and 5. 3. 5).

καὶ λαμπροῦ τοῖς ἀπὸ τοῦ πελάγους προσπλέου-¹
C 792 σιν, ὥστ᾽ εὐστοχεῖν τῆς εἰσβολῆς τοῦ λιμένος.
καὶ τὸ ἑσπέριον δὲ στόμα οὐκ εὐείσβολόν ἐστιν,
οὐ μὴν τοσαύτης γε δεῖται προνοίας. ποιεῖ δὲ
καὶ τοῦτο ἄλλον λιμένα τὸν τοῦ Εὐνόστου καλού-
μενον· πρόκειται δ᾽ οὗτος τοῦ ὀρυκτοῦ καὶ κλεισ-
τοῦ λιμένος· ὁ μὲν γὰρ ἐκ τοῦ λεχθέντος πύργου
τῆς Φάρου τὸν εἴσπλουν ἔχων ὁ μέγας ἐστὶ
λιμήν· οὗτοι δὲ συνεχεῖς ἐν βάθει ἐκείνῳ, τῷ
ἑπτασταδίῳ καλουμένῳ χώματι διειργόμενοι ἀπ᾽
αὐτοῦ, παράκεινται. τὸ δὲ χῶμά ἐστιν ἀπὸ τῆς
ἠπείρου γέφυρα ἐπὶ τὴν νῆσον κατὰ τὸ ἑσπέριον
αὐτῆς μέρος ἐκτεταμένη, δύο διάπλους ἀπολείπουσα μόνον εἰς τὸν Εὐνόστου λιμένα, καὶ αὐτοὺς
γεγεφυρωμένους· ἦν δ᾽ οὐ γέφυρα μόνον ἐπὶ τὴν
νῆσον τὸ ἔργον τοῦτο, ἀλλὰ καὶ ὑδραγώγιον, ὅτε
γε ᾠκεῖτο· νῦν δ᾽ ἠρήμωσεν αὐτὴν ὁ θεὸς Καῖσαρ
ἐν τῷ πρὸς Ἀλεξανδρέας πολέμῳ, τεταγμένην
μετὰ τῶν βασιλέων· ὀλίγοι δ᾽ οἰκοῦσι πρὸς τῷ
πύργῳ ναυτικοὶ ἄνδρες. ὁ γοῦν μέγας λιμὴν πρὸς
τῷ κεκλεῖσθαι καλῶς τῷ τε χώματι καὶ τῇ φύσει,
ἀγχιβαθής τέ ἐστιν, ὥστε τὴν μεγίστην ναῦν ἐπὶ
κλίμακος ὁρμεῖν, καὶ εἰς πλείους σχίζεται λιμένας.
οἱ μὲν οὖν πρότεροι τῶν Αἰγυπτίων βασιλεῖς,

---

¹ i.e. "Harbour of the happy return." This harbour might
have been so named after Eunostus, king of Soli in Cypros
and son-in-law of Ptolemy Soter (C. Wachsmuth, *Göttinger
Festrede*, 1876, 4), the idea being inspired, perhaps, by the
fact that Eunostus was so good a harbour as compared with
the eastern.

² This harbour (called "Cibotus," i.e. "Chest" or "Box"),
which was fortified, was connected with Lake Mareotis by
a canal. Its shape and size are to-day problematical, for it

conspicuous sign to enable them to direct their course aright to the entrance of the harbour. And the western mouth is also not easy to enter, although it does not require so much caution as the other. And it likewise forms a second harbour, that of Eunostus,[1] as it is called, which lies in front of the closed harbour which was dug by the hand of man.[2] For the harbour which affords the entrance on the side of the above-mentioned tower of Pharos is the Great Harbour, whereas these two lie continuous with that harbour in their innermost recess, being separated from it only by the embankment called the Heptastadium.[3] The embankment forms a bridge extending from the mainland to the western portion of the island, and leaves open only two passages into the harbour of Eunostus, which are bridged over. However, this work formed not only a bridge to the island but also an aqueduct, at least when Pharos was inhabited. But in these present times it has been laid waste by the deified Caesar[4] in his war against the Alexandrians, since it had sided with the kings. A few seamen, however, live near the tower. As for the Great Harbour, in addition to its being beautifully enclosed both by the embankment and by nature, it is not only so deep close to the shore that the largest ship can be moored at the steps, but also is cut up into several harbours. Now the earlier kings of the

has been filled up and its site lies within that of the present Heptastadium.

[3] So called from its being "Seven Stadia" in length. It has been so much enlarged by alluvial deposits and debris from the old city that it is now, generally speaking, a mile wide, and forms a large part of the site of the city of to-day.

[4] Julius Caesar.

ἀγαπῶντες οἷς εἶχον καὶ οὐ πάνυ ἐπεισάκτων
δεόμενοι, διαβεβλημένοι πρὸς ἅπαντας τοὺς πλέον-
τας, καὶ μάλιστα τοὺς Ἕλληνας (πορθηταὶ γὰρ
ἦσαν καὶ ἐπιθυμηταὶ τῆς ἀλλοτρίας κατὰ σπάνιν
γῆς), ἐπέστησαν φυλακὴν τῷ τόπῳ τούτῳ, κελεύ-
σαντες ἀπείργειν τοὺς προσιόντας· κατοικίαν δ'
αὐτοῖς ἔδοσαν τὴν προσαγορευομένην Ῥακῶτιν,
ἣ νῦν μὲν τῆς Ἀλεξανδρέων πόλεώς ἐστι μέρος τὸ
ὑπερκείμενον τῶν νεωρίων, τότε δὲ κώμη ὑπῆρχε·
τὰ δὲ κύκλῳ τῆς κώμης βουκόλοις παρέδοσαν,
δυναμένοις καὶ αὐτοῖς κωλύειν τοὺς ἔξωθεν
ἐπιόντας. ἐπελθὼν δὲ Ἀλέξανδρος, ἰδὼν τὴν
εὐκαιρίαν, ἔγνω τειχίζειν ἐπὶ τῷ λιμένι τὴν πόλιν·
τῆς δ' ὕστερον ἐπηκολουθηκυίας εὐδαιμονίας τῇ
πόλει μνημονεύουσί τι σημεῖον κατὰ τὴν ὑπο-
γραφὴν τοῦ κτίσματος συμβάν· τῶν γὰρ ἀρχιτεκ-
τόνων γῇ [1] λευκῇ διασημαινομένων τὴν τοῦ
περιβόλου γραμμήν, ἐπιλιπούσης τῆς γῆς καὶ
τοῦ βασιλέως ἐπιόντος, οἱ διοικηταὶ τῶν ἀλφίτων
μέρος τῶν παρεσκευασμένων τοῖς ἐργάταις
παρέσχον, δι' ὧν καὶ αἱ ὁδοὶ κατετμήθησαν εἰς
πλείους·[2] τοῦτ' οὖν οἰωνίσθαι λέγονται [3] πρὸς
ἀγαθοῦ γεγονός.[4]

7. Ἡ δ' εὐκαιρία πολύτροπος· ἀμφίκλυστόν
τε γάρ ἐστι τὸ χωρίον δυσὶ πελάγεσι, τῷ μὲν [5]

[1] γῇ, Groskurd, for τῇ.
[2] εἰς πλείους, Tozer suspects as being a gloss.
[3] λέγεται moz.   [4] γεγονότος Dhi.
[5] τῷ μὲν . . . τῷ δέ E, τὸ μὲν . . . τὸ δέ other MSS.

---

[1] Literally, "white earth."
[2] According to Plutarch (*Alexander* 26), birds of all kinds
settled on the place like clouds and ate up all the barley-

28

Aegyptians, being content with what they had and not wanting foreign imports at all, and being prejudiced against all who sailed the seas, and particularly against the Greeks (for owing to scarcity of land of their own the Greeks were ravagers and coveters of that of others), set a guard over this region and ordered it to keep away any who should approach; and they gave them as a place of abode Rhacotis, as it is called, which is now that part of the city of the Alexandrians which lies above the ship-houses, but was at that time a village; and they gave over the parts round about the village to herdsmen, who likewise were able to prevent the approach of outsiders. But when Alexander visited the place and saw the advantages of the site, he resolved to fortify the city on the harbour. Writers record, as a sign of the good fortune that has since attended the city, an incident which occurred at the time of tracing the lines of the foundation: When the architects were marking the lines of the enclosure with chalk,[1] the supply of chalk gave out; and when the king arrived, his stewards furnished a part of the barley-meal which had been prepared for the workmen, and by means of this the streets also, to a larger number than before, were laid out. This occurrence, then, they are said to have interpreted as a good omen.[2]

7. The advantages of the city's site are various; for, first, the place is washed by two seas, on the

meal with which the area had been marked out, so that Alexander was greatly disturbed at the omen; but the seers assured him that the omen was good. The barley-meal betokened an abundance of food (Ammianus Marcellinus 22. 16. 7).

STRABO

C 793 ἀπὸ τῶν ἄρκτων τῷ Αἰγυπτίῳ λεγομένῳ, τῷ
δ' ἀπὸ μεσημβρίας τῷ τῆς λίμνης τῆς Μαρείας,
ἢ καὶ Μαρεῶτις¹ λέγεται· πληροῖ δὲ ταύτην
πολλαῖς διώρυξιν ὁ Νεῖλος, ἄνωθέν τε καὶ ἐκ
πλαγίων, δι' ὧν τὰ εἰσκομιζόμενα πολλῷ πλείω
τῶν ἀπὸ θαλάττης ἐστίν, ὥσθ' ὁ λιμὴν ὁ λιμναῖος
ὑπῆρχε πλουσιώτερος τοῦ θαλαττίου· ταύτῃ δὲ
καὶ τὰ ἐκκομιζόμενα ἐξ Ἀλεξανδρείας πλείω τῶν
εἰσκομιζομένων ἐστί· γνοίη δ' ἄν τις ἔν τε τῇ
Ἀλεξανδρείᾳ καὶ τῇ Δικαιαρχίᾳ γενόμενος, ὁρῶν
τὰς ὁλκάδας ἔν τε τῷ κατάπλῳ καὶ ἐν ταῖς
ἀναγωγαῖς, ὅσον βαρύτεραί τε καὶ κουφότεραι
δεῦρο κἀκεῖσε πλέοιεν. πρὸς δὲ τῷ πλούτῳ τῶν
καταγομένων ἑκατέρωσε εἴς τε τὸν κατὰ θάλατταν
λιμένα καὶ εἰς τὸν λιμναῖον, καὶ τὸ εὐάερον ἄξιον
σημειώσεώς ἐστιν· ὃ καὶ αὐτὸ συμβαίνει διὰ τὸ
ἀμφίκλυστον καὶ τὸ εὔκαιρον τῆς ἀναβάσεως τοῦ
Νείλου. αἱ μὲν γὰρ ἄλλαι πόλεις αἱ ἐπὶ λιμνῶν
ἱδρυμέναι βαρεῖς καὶ πνιγώδεις ἔχουσι τοὺς ἀέρας
ἐν τοῖς καύμασι τοῦ θέρους· ἐπὶ γὰρ τοῖς χείλεσιν
αἱ λίμναι τελματοῦνται διὰ τὴν ἐκ τῶν ἡλίων
ἀναθυμίασιν· βορβορώδους οὖν ἀναφερομένης
τοσαύτης ἰκμάδος, νοσώδης ὁ ἀὴρ ἕλκεται καὶ
λοιμικῶν κατάρχει παθῶν· ἐν Ἀλεξανδρείᾳ δὲ
τοῦ θέρους ἀρχομένου πληρούμενος ὁ Νεῖλος
πληροῖ καὶ τὴν λίμνην καὶ οὐδὲν ἐᾷ τελματῶδες
τὸ τὴν ἀναφορὰν ποιῆσον² μοχθηράν· τότε δὲ
καὶ οἱ ἐτησίαι πνέουσιν ἐκ τῶν βορείων καὶ τοῦ
τοσούτου πελάγους, ὥστε κάλλιστα τοῦ θέρους
Ἀλεξανδρεῖς διάγουσιν.

¹ Μαρείας . . . Μαρεῶτις E, Μαρίας . . . Μαραιῶτις other
MSS.   ² ποιῆσον moz, ποιῆσαν other MSS.

30

north by the Aegyptian Sea, as it is called, and on
the south by Lake Mareia, also called Mareotis. This
is filled by many canals from the Nile, both from
above and on the sides, and through these canals
the imports are much larger than those from the sea,
so that the harbour on the lake was in fact richer
than that on the sea; and here the exports from
Alexandria also are larger than the imports; and
anyone might judge, if he were at either Alexandria
or Dicaearchia[1] and saw the merchant vessels both
at their arrival and at their departure, how much
heavier or lighter they sailed thither or therefrom.
And in addition to the great value of the things
brought down from both directions, both into the
harbour on the sea and into that on the lake, the
salubrity of the air is also worthy of remark. And
this likewise results from the fact that the land
is washed by water on both sides and because of the
timeliness of the Nile's risings; for the other cities
that are situated on lakes have heavy and stifling
air in the heats of summer, because the lakes then
become marshy along their edges because of the
evaporation caused by the sun's rays, and, accordingly, when so much filth-laden moisture rises, the
air inhaled is noisome and starts pestilential diseases,
whereas at Alexandria, at the beginning of summer,
the Nile, being full, fills the lake also, and leaves
no marshy matter to corrupt the rising vapours.
At that time, also, the Etesian winds blow from
the north and from a vast sea,[2] so that the Alexandrians pass their time most pleasantly in summer.

[1] Now Puteoli.
[2] The Aegyptian monsoons, here called the "Etesian"
(*i.e.* "Annual") winds, blow from the north-west all
summer.

31

8. Ἔστι δὲ χλαμυδοειδὲς τὸ σχῆμα τοῦ ἐδάφους
τῆς πόλεως· οὗ τὰ μὲν ἐπὶ μῆκος πλευρά ἐστι τὰ
ἀμφίκλυστα, ὅσον τριάκοντα σταδίων ἔχοντα διάμετρον, τὰ δὲ ἐπὶ πλάτος οἱ ἰσθμοί, ἑπτὰ ἢ ὀκτὼ
σταδίων ἑκάτερος, σφιγγόμενος τῇ μὲν ὑπὸ θαλάττης, τῇ δ' ὑπὸ τῆς λίμνης. ἅπασα μὲν ὁδοῖς
κατατέτμηται ἱππηλάτοις καὶ ἁρματηλάτοις, δυσὶ
δὲ πλατυτάταις, ἐπὶ πλέον ἢ πλέθρον ἀναπεπτα-
μέναις, αἳ δὴ δίχα καὶ πρὸς ὀρθὰς τέμνουσιν
ἀλλήλας. ἔχει δ' ἡ πόλις τεμένη τε κοινὰ κάλλιστα καὶ τὰ βασίλεια, τέταρτον ἢ καὶ τρίτον
τοῦ παντὸς περιβόλου μέρος· τῶν γὰρ βασιλέων
ἕκαστος ὥσπερ τοῖς κοινοῖς ἀναθήμασι προσεφι-
λοκάλει τινὰ κόσμον, οὕτω καὶ οἴκησιν ἰδίᾳ

---

[1] According to Plutarch (5. 11), the shape was like that of
a *Macedonian* chlamys, or military cloak ; and the plan was
designed by "Diochares" (probably an error for "Deinocrates"). Likewise, "the inhabited world is chlamys-
shaped" (see Vol. I, p. 435 and footnote 3). See Tarbell,
Classical Philology, I, p. 283, for a discussion of this passage
as bearing on the shape of the chlamys.

[2] Strabo is thinking apparently of a line drawn from the
centre of the skirt of the chlamys, which was circular, to
the centre of the collar.

[3] According to Philo (*In Flaccum* 973 A) the city was
divided into five sections, which were designated as Alpha,
Beta, Gamma, Delta, and Epsilon. Beta apparently com-
prised the palaces, including the Museum, the Sema and
many other buildings ; Delta, the Jewish quarter (Josephus,
Bell. Jud. 2. 8) ; but the sites of the three others are doubtful.
On the dimensions of the city, cp. Josephus, *Bell. Jud.*
2. 16. 4 (30 × 10 stadia) ; Philo, *In Flaccum* 757 (10 stadia in
breadth) ; Stephanus Byzantinus, *s.v.* Ἀλεξάνδρεια (34 × 8,

8. The shape of the area of the city is like a chlamys;[1] the long sides of it are those that are washed by the two waters, having a diameter[2] of about thirty stadia, and the short sides are the isthmuses, each being seven or eight stadia wide and pinched in on one side by the sea and on the other by the lake.[3] The city as a whole is intersected by streets practicable for horse-riding and chariot-driving, and by two that are very broad, extending to more than a plethrum in breadth, which cut one another into two sections and at right angles.[4] And the city contains most beautiful public precincts and also the royal palaces, which constitute one-fourth or even one-third of the whole circuit of the city; for just as each of the kings, from love of splendour, was wont to add some adornment to the public monuments, so also he would invest himself at his own expense with a residence, in addition to those

and 110 in circuit); Pliny 5. 10 (15 miles in circuit); and Diodorus Siculus 17. 59 (40 in breadth), who obviously means by " breadth " what others call " length," and seems to include suburban districts on east and west.

[4] The main longitudinal street ran straight through from the "Canobic Gate," or "Gate of the Sun," on the east to the "Gate of the Moon" on the west. Its site has been identified in part with that of the present Rosetta Street (see A. M. de Zogher, *Études sur L'Ancienne Alexandrie,* p. 11); but Dr. Botti (cited by Zogher) takes a different view. "The most important of the latitudinal streets was that of the Sema, which had on its right the tomb of Alexander the Great, and, on its left, very probably the Museum. Then it crossed the Canobic avenue, passed the Adrianum and Caesareum on the right, the temple of Isis-Plousia and the Emporium on the left, and ends on the quay of the great maritime port and the place of embarkation, near the two obelisks" (Neroutsos-Bey, quoted by Zogher, p. 15). See Map at end of volume.

περιεβάλλετο πρὸς ταῖς ὑπαρχούσαις, ὥστε νῦν
τὸ τοῦ ποιητοῦ,

　　　　ἐξ ἑτέρων ἕτερ᾿ ἐστίν·

ἅπαντα μέντοι συναφῆ καὶ ἀλλήλοις καὶ τῷ
λιμένι, καὶ ὅσα ἔξω αὐτοῦ. τῶν δὲ βασιλείων
μέρος ἐστὶ καὶ τὸ Μουσεῖον, ἔχον περίπατον καὶ
C 794 ἐξέδραν καὶ οἶκον μέγαν, ἐν ᾧ τὸ συσσίτιον τῶν
μετεχόντων τοῦ Μουσείου φιλολόγων ἀνδρῶν.
ἔστι δὲ τῇ συνόδῳ ταύτῃ καὶ χρήματα κοινὰ καὶ
ἱερεὺς ὁ ἐπὶ[1] τῷ Μουσείῳ, τεταγμένος τότε μὲν
ὑπὸ τῶν βασιλέων, νῦν δ᾿ ὑπὸ Καίσαρος. μέρος
δὲ τῶν βασιλείων ἐστὶ καὶ τὸ καλούμενον Σῆμα,[2]
ὃ περίβολος ἦν, ἐν ᾧ αἱ τῶν βασιλέων ταφαὶ καὶ
ἡ Ἀλεξάνδρου· ἔφθη γὰρ τὸ σῶμα ἀφελόμενος
Περδίκκαν ὁ τοῦ Λάγου Πτολεμαῖος, κατακομί-
ζοντα ἐκ τῆς Βαβυλῶνος καὶ ἐκτρεπόμενον ταύτῃ
κατὰ πλεονεξίαν καὶ ἐξιδιασμὸν τῆς Αἰγύπτου·

---

[1] ὑπό Dhi.
[2] Σῆμα, Tzschucke, for Σῶμα; so later editors.

---

[1] Odyssey, 17. 266 (concerning the palace of Odysseus).
[2] i.e. on the promontory called Lochias (see § 9 following).
[3] Cp. the structure described by Vitruvius, De Architectura
(5. 11 2): "Spacious exedras within three porticoes with
seats, where philosophers, rhetoricians and all others who
take delight in studies can engage in disputation." Suidas
(s.v. ἐξέδρα) seems to make the Exedra a building distinct
from the Museum: "They live near the Museum and the
Exedra."
[4] i.e. "Tomb" However, the MSS. (see critical note)
read Soma, i.e. "Body." And so does the Greek version
of the Pseudo-Callisthenes (C. Müller, Didot Edition, Scrip-
tores Rerum Alexandri Magni III. 3. 4): "And Ptolemy
made a tomb in the holy place called 'Body of Alexander,'
and there he laid the body, or remains, of Alexander"; but

already built, so that now, to quote the words of
the poet,[1] "there is building upon building." All,
however, are connected with one another and the
harbour, even those that lie outside[2] the harbour.
The Museum is also a part of the royal palaces; it
has a public walk, an Exedra with seats, and a large
house,[3] in which is the common mess-hall of the
men of learning who share the Museum. This group
of men not only hold property in common, but also
have a priest in charge of the Museum, who formerly
was appointed by the kings, but is now appointed
by Caesar. The Sema also,[4] as it is called, is a part
of the royal palaces. This was the enclosure which
contained the burial-places of the kings and that of
Alexander; for Ptolemy,[5] the son of Lagus, fore-
stalled Perdiccas by taking the body away from him
when he was bringing it down from Babylon and
was turning aside towards Aegypt, moved by greed
and a desire to make that country his own.[6] Further-

the Syrian version (*Alexander the Great*, trans. by E. A. W.
Budge, p. 142) reads: "and they call that place 'The tomb
of Alexander' unto this day." But more important is the
statement of Zenobius (*Proverbia* III, 94): "Ptolemy (Philopator) built in the middle of the city a *mnema* (μνῆμα οἰκο-
δομήσας), which is now called the *Sema*, and he laid there all
his forefathers together with his mother, and also Alexander
the Macedonian."

[5] Ptolemy Soter.

[6] The accounts vary. According to Diodorus Siculus
(18. 26–28), Arrhidaeus spent two years making elaborate
preparations for the removal of Alexander's body; and
Ptolemy I went as far as Syria to meet him, and thence took
the body to Aegypt for burial. Pausanias (1. 6. 3, 1. 7. 1)
says that Ptolemy I buried it at Memphis and Ptolemy II
transferred it to Alexandria. The Pseudo-Callisthenes (*l.c.*)
says that the Macedonians were at first determined to take
the body back to Macedonia, but later, upon consulting the

καὶ δὴ καὶ ἀπώλετο διαφθαρεὶς ὑπὸ τῶν στρατιωτῶν, ἐπελθόντος τοῦ Πτολεμαίου καὶ κατακλεί-
σαντος αὐτὸν ἐν νήσῳ ἐρήμῃ· ἐκεῖνος μὲν οὖν
ἀπέθανεν ἐμπεριπαρεὶς [1] ταῖς σαρίσσαις, ἐπελθόντων ἐπ᾽ αὐτὸν [2] τῶν στρατιωτῶν, σὺν αὐτῷ
δὲ καὶ οἱ βασιλεῖς, Ἀριδαῖός τε καὶ τὰ παιδία
τὰ Ἀλεξάνδρου, καὶ ἡ γυνὴ Ῥωξάνη ἀπῆραν εἰς
Μακεδονίαν· τὸ δὲ σῶμα τοῦ Ἀλεξάνδρου κομίσας
ὁ Πτολεμαῖος ἐκήδευσεν ἐν τῇ Ἀλεξανδρείᾳ, ὅπου
νῦν ἔτι κεῖται· οὐ μὴν ἐν τῇ αὐτῇ πυέλῳ· ὑαλίνη
γὰρ αὕτη, ἐκεῖνος δ᾽ ἐν χρυσῇ κατέθηκεν· ἐσύλησε
δ᾽ αὐτὴν [3] ὁ Κόκκης καὶ Παρείσακτος ἐπικληθεὶς
Πτολεμαῖος, ἐκ τῆς Συρίας ἐπελθὼν καὶ ἐκπεσὼν
εὐθύς, ὥστ᾽ ἀνόνητα αὐτῷ τὰ σῦλα γενέσθαι.

9. Ἔστι δ᾽ ἐν τῷ μεγάλῳ λιμένι κατὰ μὲν τὸν
εἴσπλουν ἐν δεξιᾷ ἡ νῆσος καὶ ὁ πύργος ὁ Φάρος,
κατὰ δὲ τὴν ἑτέραν χεῖρα αἵ τε χοιράδες καὶ ἡ

---

[1] περιπαρείς Corais.   [2] ἐπ᾽ αὐτῷ στρατιωτῶν Dhi.
[3] αὐτήν Emoz, αὐτόν other MSS.

---

oracle of the Babylonian Zeus, all agreed that "Philip
Ptolemy" (surely an error for "Philip Arrhidaeus," the
immediate successor of Alexander, or for "Ptolemy I")
should take it from Babylon to Aegypt and bury it at
Memphis; and that he took the body to Memphis, but, by
order of the chief priest of the temple there, immediately
took it to Alexandria. There, according to Diodorus Siculus
(*l.c.*), Ptolemy devised a sacred precinct (τέμενος), which in
size and construction was worthy of Alexander's glory.
When Augustus was in Alexandria, he saw the body, having
had the coffin and body brought forth from its shrine,
penetrali (Suetonius, *Augustus* 18); and "he not only saw the
body, but touched it, whereupon, it is said, a piece of nose
broke off" (Dio Cassius 51. 16).

[1] Perdiccas first attacked Ptolemy on the Pelusiac branch
of the Nile "not far from a fortress called 'Camel's Wall,'"

more, Perdiccas lost his life, having been slain by
his soldiers at the time when Ptolemy attacked him
and hemmed him up in a desert island.[1] So Perdiccas was killed, having been transfixed by his
soldiers' sarissae[2] when they attacked him; but the
kings who were with him, both Aridaeus[3] and the
children of Alexander, and also Rhoxanê, Alexander's
wife, departed for Macedonia; and the body of
Alexander was carried off by Ptolemy and given
sepulture in Alexandria, where it still now lies—not,
however, in the same sarcophagus as before, for the
present one is made of glass,[4] whereas the one
wherein Ptolemy laid it was made of gold. The
latter was plundered by the Ptolemy nicknamed
"Cocces"[5] and "Pareisactus,"[6] who came over
from Syria but was immediately[7] expelled, so that
his plunder proved unprofitable to him.

9. In the Great Harbour at the entrance, on the
right hand, are the island and the tower Pharos,
and on the other hand are the reefs and also the

---

where he was unsuccessful; and then later near Memphis,
where his soldiers mutinied (Diodorus Siculus 18. 33 ff.).

[2] Long Macedonian pikes.

[3] Also spelled Arrhidaeus.

[4] Or, possibly, "alabaster." Cp. the *so-called* "Sarcophagus
of Alexander" found at Sidon and now at the Ottoman
Museum in Constantinople.

[5] *i.e.* "scarlet."

[6] Literally, "Pareisactus" means "one who has been
brought in (*i.e.* upon the throne) privily," *i.e.* "usurper."
But scholars take the word to mean "Illegitimate" (*i.e.*
"Pretender") in this passage and identify this Ptolemy
with Ptolemy XI (so Tozer, *Selections*, p. 350).

[7] This must mean "immediately" after his violation of
the tomb, for Ptolemy XI mounted the throne in 80 B.C.
and, so far as is known, he was never expelled till 58 B.C.

Λοχιὰς ἄκρα, ἔχουσα βασίλειον. εἰσπλεύσαντι
δ' ἐν ἀριστερᾷ ἐστι συνεχῆ τοῖς ἐν τῇ Λοχιάδι
τὰ ἐνδοτέρω βασίλεια, πολλὰς καὶ ποικίλας
ἔχοντα διαίτας καὶ ἄλση· τούτοις δ' ὑπόκειται
ὅ τε ὀρυκτὸς λιμὴν καὶ κρυπτός,¹ ἴδιος τῶν
βασιλέων, καὶ ἡ Ἀντίρροδος, νησίον προκείμενον
τοῦ ὀρυκτοῦ λιμένος, βασίλειον ἅμα καὶ λιμένιον
ἔχον· ἐκάλεσαν δ' οὕτως, ὡς ἂν τῇ Ῥόδῳ ἐνά-
μιλλον. ὑπέρκειται δὲ τούτου τὸ θέατρον· εἶτα
τὸ Ποσείδιον, ἀγκών τις ἀπὸ τοῦ Ἐμπορίου καλου-
μένου προπεπτωκώς, ἔχων ἱερὸν Ποσειδῶνος· ᾧ
προσθεὶς χῶμα Ἀντώνιος ἔτι μᾶλλον προνεῦον
εἰς μέσον τὸν λιμένα ἐπὶ τῷ ἄκρῳ κατεσκεύασε
δίαιταν βασιλικήν, ἣν Τιμώνιον προσηγόρευσε.
τοῦτο δ' ἔπραξε τὸ τελευταῖον, ἡνίκα προλειφθεὶς
ὑπὸ τῶν φίλων ἀπῆρεν εἰς Ἀλεξάνδρειαν μετὰ
τὴν ἐν Ἀκτίῳ κακοπραγίαν, Τιμώνειον² αὑτῷ
κρίνας τὸν λοιπὸν βίον, ὃν διάξειν ἔμελλεν ἔρημος
τῶν τοσούτων φίλων. εἶτα τὸ Καισάριον καὶ τὸ
Ἐμπόριον καὶ αἱ³ ἀποστάσεις· καὶ μετὰ ταῦτα
τὰ νεώρια μέχρι τοῦ ἑπτασταδίου. ταῦτα μὲν
τὰ περὶ τὸν μέγαν λιμένα.

10. Ἑξῆς δ' Εὐνόστου λιμὴν μετὰ τὸ ἑπτα-
C 795 στάδιον· καὶ ὑπὲρ τούτου ὁ ὀρυκτός, ὃν καὶ
Κιβωτὸν καλοῦσιν, ἔχων καὶ αὐτὸς νεώρια. ἐνδο-
τέρω δὲ τούτου διῶρυξ πλωτὴ μέχρι τῆς λίμνης

---

¹ κρυπτός, the reading of all MSS., Jones restores, for
κλειστός. Corais and the later editors.
² Τιμώνειον E, Τιμώνιον other MSS.
³ αἱ, Corais inserts ; καὶ ἀποστάσεις E.

---

¹ Cp. § 6 above.   ² 31 B.C.

promontory Lochias, with a royal palace upon it; and on sailing into the harbour one comes, on the left, to the inner royal palaces, which are continuous with those on Lochias and have groves and numerous lodges painted in various colours. Below these lies the harbour that was dug by the hand of man and is hidden from view,[1] the private property of the kings, as also Antirrhodos, an isle lying off the artificial harbour, which has both a royal palace and a small harbour. They so called it as being a rival of Rhodes. Above the artificial harbour lies the theatre; then the Poseidium—an elbow, as it were, projecting from the Emporium, as it is called, and containing a temple of Poseidon. To this elbow of land Antony added a mole projecting still farther, into the middle of a harbour, and on the extremity of it built a royal lodge which he called Timonium. This was his last act, when, forsaken by his friends, he sailed away to Alexandria after his misfortune at Actium,[2] having chosen to live the life of a Timon[3] the rest of his days, which he intended to spend in solitude from all those friends.[4] Then one comes to the Caesarium and the Emporium and the ware-houses; and after these to the ship-houses, which extend as far as the Heptastadium. So much for the Great Harbour and its surroundings.

10. Next, after the Heptastadium, one comes to the Harbour of Eunostus, and, above this, to the artificial harbour, which is also called Cibotus; it too has ship-houses. Farther in there is a navigable

[3] Timon the Athenian was nicknamed the "Misanthrope." Antony, like Timon, felt that he himself also had been wronged and treated with ingratitude, and therefore hated all men (Plutarch, *Antony* 69).

[4] He slew himself in 30 B.C.

τεταμένη τῆς Μαρεώτιδος.¹ ἔξω μὲν οὖν τῆς
διώρυγος μικρὸν ἔτι λείπεται τῆς πόλεως· εἶθ' ἡ
Νεκρόπολις² τὸ προάστειον, ἐν ᾧ κῆποί τε
πολλοὶ καὶ ταφαὶ καὶ καταγωγαὶ πρὸς τὰς
ταριχείας τῶν νεκρῶν ἐπιτήδειαι. ἐντὸς δὲ τῆς
διώρυγος τό τε Σαράπιον καὶ ἄλλα τεμένη ἀρχαῖα
ἐκλελειμμένα πως διὰ τὴν τῶν νέων³ κατασκευὴν
τῶν ἐν Νικοπόλει· καὶ γὰρ ἀμφιθέατρον καὶ
στάδιον καὶ οἱ πεντετηρικοὶ ἀγῶνες ἐκεῖ συντε-
λοῦνται· τὰ δὲ παλαιὰ ὠλιγώρηται. συλλήβδην
δ' εἰπεῖν ἡ πόλις μεστή ἐστιν ἀναθημάτων καὶ
ἱερῶν· κάλλιστον δὲ τὸ γυμνάσιον, μείζους ἢ
σταδιαίας ἔχον τὰς στοάς. ἐν μέσῳ δὲ τό τε⁴
δικαστήριον καὶ τὰ ἄλση. ἔστι δὲ καὶ Πάνειον,
ὕψος τι χειροποίητον στροβιλοειδὲς ἐμφερὲς ὄχθῳ
πετρώδει διὰ κοχλίου τὴν ἀνάβασιν ἔχον· ἀπὸ δὲ
τῆς κορυφῆς ἔστιν ἀπιδεῖν ὅλην τὴν πόλιν ὑπο-
κειμένην αὐτῷ πανταχόθεν. ἀπὸ δὲ τῆς Νεκροπόλεως ἡ ἐπὶ τὸ μῆκος πλατεῖα διατείνει παρὰ τὸ
γυμνάσιον μέχρι τῆς πύλης τῆς Κανωβικῆς· εἶθ'
Ἱππόδρομος καλούμενός ἐστι καὶ αἱ παρακείμεναι⁵
ἄλλαι μέχρι τῆς διώρυγος τῆς Κανωβικῆς διὰ

¹ Μαρεώτ.δος E, Μαραιώτιδος other MSS.
² Emoz read καὶ after Νεκρόπολις.
³ νέων, Groskurd, for νεκρῶν s, νεῶν other MSS.
⁴ στοάς. ἐν μέσῳ δὲ τό τε, Corais, for στοὰς ἐν μέσῳ. τὸ δέ.
⁵ D (?) and the editors before Kramer add αἱ before ἄλλαι.
Kramer conj. that κατοικίαι, or some word of similar meaning,
has fallen out after ἄλλαι. Meineke conj. καλιαί ("wooden
dwellings"), Vogel ἅλαι ("salt-works"), for ἄλλαι.

---

¹ Cp. the Nicopolis near Actium, and its sacred precinct,
and its quinquennial games (7. 7. 6 and footnote 1).
² Of the *city*, not the *gymnasium*.

canal, which extends to Lake Mareotis. Now outside the canal there is still left only a small part of the
city; and then one comes to the suburb Necropolis,
in which are many gardens and graves and halting-
places fitted up for the embalming of corpses, and,
inside the canal, both to the Sarapium and to other
sacred precincts of ancient times, which are now
almost abandoned on account of the construction of
the new buildings at Nicopolis; for instance, there
are an amphitheatre and a stadium at Nicopolis, and
the quinquennial games are celebrated there;[1] but
the ancient buildings have fallen into neglect. In
short, the city is full of public and sacred structures;
but the most beautiful is the Gymnasium, which has
porticoes more than a stadium in length. And in
the middle[2] are both the court of justice and the
groves. Here, too, is the Paneium,[3] a "height," as
it were, which was made by the hand of man; it has
the shape of a fir-cone, resembles a rocky hill, and is
ascended by a spiral road; and from the summit one
can see the whole of the city lying below it on all
sides. The broad street that runs lengthwise[4]
extends from Necropolis past the Gymnasium to the
Canobic Gate; and then one comes to the Hippodrome, as it is called, and to the other (streets?)[5]
that lie parallel, extending as far as the Canobic

[3] Sanctuary of Pan.
[4] See § 8 above.
[5] Both the text and the interpretation are doubtful. ὁδοί
("streets") is not found in the MSS.; but, although it is the
natural word to supply, just as ὁδός *must* be supplied above
with πλατεῖα ("broad"), it hardly suits the context, as
Kramer, who conjectures κατοικίαι ("settlements"), insists.
Vogel (see critical note) simply emends ἄλλαι ("other") to
ἅλαι ("salt-works").

δὲ τοῦ Ἱπποδρόμου διελθόντι ἡ Νικόπολίς ἐστιν,
ἔχουσα κατοικίαν ἐπὶ θαλάττῃ πόλεως οὐκ ἐλάττω·
τριάκοντα δέ εἰσιν ἀπὸ τῆς Ἀλεξανδρείας στάδιοι.
τοῦτον δὲ ἐτίμησεν ὁ Σεβαστὸς Καῖσαρ τὸν
τόπον, ὅτι ἐνταῦθα ἐνίκα τῇ μάχῃ τοὺς ἐπεξιόντας
ἐπ᾽ αὐτὸν μετὰ Ἀντωνίου· καὶ λαβὼν ἐξ ἐφόδου
τὴν πόλιν ἠνάγκασε τὸν μὲν Ἀντώνιον ἑαυτὸν
διαχειρίσασθαι, τὴν δὲ Κλεοπάτραν ζῶσαν ἐλθεῖν
εἰς τὴν ἐξουσίαν· μικρὸν δ᾽ ὕστερον κἀκείνη ἑαυτὴν
ἐν τῇ φρουρᾷ διεχειρίσατο λάθρα δήγματι ἀσπίδος
ἢ φαρμάκῳ ἐπιχρίστῳ (λέγεται γὰρ ἀμφοτέρως),
καὶ συνέβη καταλυθῆναι τὴν τῶν Λαγιδῶν ἀρχήν,
πολλὰ συμμείνασαν ἔτη.

11. Πτολεμαῖος γὰρ ὁ Λάγου διεδέξατο Ἀλέξανδρον, ἐκεῖνον δὲ ὁ Φιλάδελφος, τοῦτον δὲ ὁ
Εὐεργέτης, εἶθ᾽ ὁ Φιλοπάτωρ ὁ τῆς Ἀγαθοκλείας,
εἶθ᾽ ὁ Ἐπιφανής, εἶθ᾽ ὁ Φιλομήτωρ, παῖς παρὰ
πατρὸς ἀεὶ διαδεχόμενος· τοῦτο δ᾽ ἀδελφὸς διεδέξατο ὁ δεύτερος Εὐεργέτης, ὃν καὶ Φύσκωνα
προσαγορεύουσι, τοῦτον δ᾽ ὁ Λάθουρος ἐπικληθεὶς
C 796 Πτολεμαῖος, τοῦτον δ᾽ ὁ Αὐλητὴς ὁ καθ᾽ ἡμᾶς,
ὅσπερ ἦν τῆς Κλεοπάτρας πατήρ. ἅπαντες μὲν
οὖν οἱ μετὰ τὸν τρίτον Πτολεμαῖον ὑπὸ τρυφῆς
διεφθαρμένοι χεῖρον ἐπολιτεύσαντο, χείριστα δ᾽
ὁ τέταρτος καὶ ἕβδομος καὶ ὁ ὕστατος, ὁ Αὐλητής·
ὃς χωρὶς τῆς ἄλλης ἀσελγείας χοραυλεῖν¹ ἤσκησε,

---

¹ χοραυλεῖν E, χοραύλην other MSS.

¹ Josephus (*Bell. Jud.* 4. 11. 5) says "twenty."
² Cp. Plutarch, *Antony* 86.

42

canal. Having passed through the Hippodrome, one comes to Nicopolis, which has a settlement on the sea no smaller than a city. It is thirty [1] stadia distant from Alexandria. Augustus Caesar honoured this place because it was here that he conquered in battle those who came out against him with Antony; and when he had taken the city at the first onset, he forced Antony to put himself to death and Cleopatra to come into his power alive; but a little later she too put herself to death secretly, while in prison, by the bite of an asp or (for two accounts are given) by applying a poisonous ointment; [2] and the result was that the empire of the sons of Lagus, which had endured for many years, was dissolved.

11. For Ptolemy the son of Lagus succeeded Alexander; and he in turn was succeeded by Philadelphus, and he by Euergetes, and then he by Philopator the son of Agathocleia, and then he by Epiphanes, and then he by Philometor, a son always succeeding a father; but Philometor was succeeded by a brother, the second Euergetes, who is also called Physcon, and he by the Ptolemy nicknamed Lathurus, [3] and he by Auletes of our own time, who was the father of Cleopatra. Now all the kings after the third Ptolemy, being corrupted by luxurious living, have administered the affairs of government badly, but worst of all the fourth, seventh, and the last, Auletes, who, apart from his general licentiousness, practised the accompaniment of choruses with

[3] *i.e.* Ptolemy VII.   Strabo here skips Ptolemy IX (Alexander I) and Ptolemy X (Alexander II), who apparently had no place in the official list of legitimate kings (cp. Letronne edition, note *ad loc.*).

καὶ ἐπ' αὐτῷ γε[1] ἐσεμνύνετο[2] τοσοῦτον, ὥστ' οὐκ
ὤκνει συντελεῖν ἀγῶνας ἐν τοῖς βασιλείοις, εἰς
οὓς παρῄει διαμιλλησόμενος τοῖς ἀνταγωνισταῖς.
τοῦτον μὲν οὖν οἱ Ἀλεξανδρεῖς ἐξέβαλον, τριῶν
δ' αὐτῷ θυγατέρων οὐσῶν, ὧν μία γνησία ἡ
πρεσβυτάτη, ταύτην ἀνέδειξαν βασίλισσαν· οἱ
υἱοὶ δ' αὐτοῦ δύο νήπιοι τῆς τότε χρείας ἐξέπιπτον
τελέως. τῇ δὲ κατασταθείσῃ μετεπέμψαντο ἄνδρα
ἐκ τῆς Συρίας Κυβιοσάκτην[3] τινά, προσποιησά-
μενον τοῦ γένους εἶναι τῶν Συριακῶν βασιλέων·
τοῦτον μὲν οὖν ὀλίγων ἡμερῶν ἀπεστραγγάλισεν
ἡ βασίλισσα, οὐ φέρουσα τὸ βάναυσον καὶ τὸ
ἀνελεύθερον. ἧκε δ' ἀντ' ἐκείνου προσποιησά-
μενος καὶ αὐτὸς εἶναι Μιθριδάτου υἱὸς τοῦ
Εὐπάτορος Ἀρχέλαος, ὃς ἦν μὲν Ἀρχελάου υἱὸς
τοῦ πρὸς Σύλλαν διαπολεμήσαντος καὶ μετὰ
ταῦτα τιμηθέντος ὑπὸ Ῥωμαίων, πάππος δὲ τοῦ
βασιλεύσαντος Καππαδόκων ὑστάτου καθ' ἡμᾶς,
ἱερεὺς δὲ τῶν ἐν Πόντῳ Κομάνων. Γαβινίῳ δὲ
τότε συνδιέτριψεν ὡς συστρατεύσων ἐπὶ Παρ-
θυαίους, λαθὼν δὲ τοῦτον κομίζεται διά τινων
εἰς τὴν βασίλισσαν καὶ ἀναδείκνυται βασιλεύς.
ἐν τούτῳ τὸν Αὐλητὴν ἀφικόμενον εἰς Ῥώμην
δεξάμενος Πομπήιος Μάγνος συνίστησι τῇ συγ-

---

¹ γε, Corais, for δέ.   ² Cx have ἐπί before τοσοῦτον.
³ Κυβισάκτην C.

---

¹ Hence "Auletes" ("Flute-player").
² According to Dio Cassius (39. 13), this was Berenicè
(IV). She reigned with her mother Cleopatra Tryphaena for
one year (58–57 B.C.) and then alone for one year.
³ Later, Ptolemy XII and XIII.
⁴ A nickname, "Salt-fish Dealer." Dio Cassius (39. 57)
says, "a certain Seleucus."

the flute,[1] and upon this he prided himself so much
that he would not hesitate to celebrate contests
in the royal palace, and at these contests would
come forward to vie with the opposing contestants.
He, however, was banished by the Alexandrians;
and since he had three daughters, of whom one,
the eldest, was legitimate, they proclaimed her
queen;[2] but his two sons,[3] who were infants, were
completely excluded from service at the time.
When she had been established on the throne, they
sent after a husband for her from Syria, a certain
Cybiosactes,[4] who had pretended that he belonged
to the family of the Syrian kings. Now the queen
had this man strangled to death within a few days,
being unable to bear his coarseness and vulgarity;
but in his place came a man who likewise had
pretended that he was a son of Mithridates Eupator
—I mean Archelaüs, who was son of the Archelaüs
who carried on war against Sulla and afterwards was
honoured by the Romans, and was grandfather of
the man who was last to reign as king over the
Cappadocians in our time,[5] and was priest of Comana
in Pontus.[6] At that time he had been tarrying
with Gabinius,[7] in the hope of joining with him
on an expedition against the Parthians, but without
the knowledge of Gabinius he was brought by
certain agents to the queen and proclaimed king.[8]
In the meantime Pompey the Great, having received
Auletes, who had arrived at Rome, recommended

[5] 12. 1. 2.
[6] On this Archelaüs, see 12. 3. 34.
[7] Proconsul of Syria, 57 B.C.
[8] He reigned only six months, being slain in battle by
Gabinius (12. 3. 34).

κλήτῳ καὶ διαπράττεται κάθοδον μὲν τούτῳ, τῶν
δὲ πρέσβεων τῶν πλείστων, ἑκατὸν ὄντων, ὄλεθρον
τῶν καταπρεσβευσάντων αὐτοῦ· τούτων δ᾽ ἦν καὶ
Δίων ὁ Ἀκαδημαϊκός, ἀρχιπρεσβευτὴς γεγονώς.
καταχθεὶς οὖν ὑπὸ Γαβινίου Πτολεμαῖος τόν τε
Ἀρχέλαον ἀναιρεῖ καὶ τὴν θυγατέρα, χρόνον δ᾽
οὐ πολὺν τῇ βασιλείᾳ προσθεὶς τελευτᾷ νόσῳ,
καταλιπὼν δύο μὲν υἱεῖς, δύο δὲ θυγατέρας, πρεσ-
βυτάτην δὲ Κλεοπάτραν. οἱ μὲν οὖν Ἀλεξανδρεῖς
ἀπέδειξαν βασιλέας τόν τε πρεσβύτερον τῶν
παίδων καὶ τὴν Κλεοπάτραν, οἱ δὲ συνόντες τῷ
παιδὶ κατασταστιάσαντες ἐξέβαλον τὴν Κλεοπάτραν, καὶ ἀπῆρε μετὰ τῆς ἀδελφῆς εἰς τὴν
Συρίαν. ἐν τούτῳ Πομπήιος Μάγνος ἧκε φεύγων
ἐκ Παλαιφαρσάλου πρὸς τὸ Πηλούσιον καὶ τὸ
Κάσιον[1] ὄρος. τοῦτον μὲν οὖν δολοφονοῦσιν οἱ
μετὰ τοῦ βασιλέως, ἐπελθὼν δὲ Καῖσαρ τόν τε
μειρακίσκον διαφθείρει καὶ καθίστησι τῆς Αἰγύπτου βασίλισσαν τὴν Κλεοπάτραν, μεταπεμ-
ψάμενος ἐκ τῆς φυγῆς· συμβασιλεύειν δ᾽ ἀπέδειξε
τὸν λοιπὸν ἀδελφὸν αὐτῇ, νέον παντελῶς ὄντα.
C 797 μετὰ δὲ τὴν Καίσαρος τελευτὴν καὶ τὰ ἐν Φιλίπ-
ποις διαβὰς Ἀντώνιος εἰς τὴν Ἀσίαν ἐξετίμησεν
ἐπὶ πλέον τὴν Κλεοπάτραν, ὥστε καὶ γυναῖκα
ἔκρινε καὶ ἐτεκνοποιήσατο ἐξ αὐτῆς, τόν τε
Ἀκτιακὸν πόλεμον συνήρατο ἐκείνῃ καὶ συνέφυγε·
καὶ μετὰ ταῦτα ἐπακολουθήσας ὁ Σεβαστὸς
Καῖσαρ ἀμφοτέρους κατέλυσε καὶ τὴν Αἴγυπτον
ἔπαυσε παροινουμένην.

---

[1] Κάσιον Dhx, κάσσιον other MSS.

---

[1] So Dio Cassius (39. 13).

him to the Senate and effected, not only his
restoration, but also the death of most of the
ambassadors, one hundred in number, who had
undertaken the embassy against him,[1] and among
these was Dion the academic philosopher, who had
been made chief ambassador. Accordingly, on
being restored by Gabinius, Ptolemy slew both
Archelaüs and his own daughter. But before he had
added much time to his reign, he died of disease,
leaving behind two sons and also two daughters,
the eldest daughter being Cleopatra.[2] Now the
Alexandrians proclaimed as sovereigns both the
elder of the boys and Cleopatra; but the associates
of the boy caused an uprising and banished Cleopatra,
and she set sail with her sister to Syria. In the
meantime Pompey the Great had come in flight
from Palaepharsalus to Pelusium and Mt. Casius.
Now Pompey was treacherously slain by the king's
party, but when Caesar arrived he put the lad
to death, and, having summoned Cleopatra from
exile, established her as queen of Aegypt; and
he appointed her remaining brother to reign as king
with her, although he was exceedingly young.
After the death of Caesar and the battle of Philippi,[3]
Antony crossed over to Asia and held Cleopatra
in such extraordinary honour that he chose her
as wife and had children by her; and he under-
took the battle at Actium with her and fled with
her; and after this Augustus Caesar pursued them,
destroyed both, and put an end to Aegypt's being
ruled with drunken violence.

[2] The famous Cleopatra.   [3] 42 B.C.

12. Ἐπαρχία δὲ νῦν ἐστι, φόρους μὲν τελοῦσα
ἀξιολόγους, ὑπὸ σωφρόνων δὲ ἀνδρῶν διοικουμένη
τῶν πεμπομένων ἐπάρχων ἀεί. ὁ μὲν οὖν
πεμφθεὶς τὴν τοῦ βασιλέως ἔχει τάξιν· ὑπ᾽ αὐτῷ
δ᾽ ἐστὶν ὁ δικαιοδότης, ὁ τῶν πολλῶν κρίσεων
κύριος· ἄλλος δ᾽ ἐστὶν ὁ προσαγορευόμενος
ἰδιόλογος,[1] ὃς τῶν ἀδεσπότων καὶ τῶν εἰς
Καίσαρα πίπτειν ὀφειλόντων ἐξεταστής ἐστι·
παρέπονται δὲ τούτοις ἀπελεύθεροι Καίσαρος καὶ
οἰκονόμοι, μείζω καὶ ἐλάττω πεπιστευμένοι πράγ-
ματα. ἔστι δὲ καὶ στρατιωτικοῦ τρία τάγματα,
ὧν τὸ ἓν κατὰ τὴν πόλιν ἵδρυται, τἆλλα δ᾽ ἐν
τῇ χώρᾳ· χωρὶς δὲ τούτων ἐννέα μέν εἰσι σπεῖραι
Ῥωμαίων, τρεῖς μὲν ἐν τῇ πόλει, τρεῖς δ᾽ ἐπὶ
τῶν ὅρων τῆς Αἰθιοπίας ἐν Συήνῃ, φρουρὰ τοῖς
τόποις, τρεῖς δὲ κατὰ τὴν ἄλλην χώραν. εἰσὶ
δὲ καὶ ἱππαρχίαι τρεῖς ὁμοίως διατεταγμέναι
κατὰ τοὺς ἐπικαιρίους τόπους. τῶν δ᾽ ἐπιχωρίων
ἀρχόντων κατὰ πόλιν μὲν ὅ τε ἐξηγητής ἐστι,
πορφύραν ἀμπεχόμενος καὶ ἔχων πατρίους τιμὰς
καὶ ἐπιμέλειαν τῶν τῇ πόλει χρησίμων, καὶ ὁ
ὑπομνηματογράφος καὶ ὁ ἀρχιδικαστής, τέταρτος
δὲ ὁ νυκτερινὸς στρατηγός. ἦσαν μὲν οὖν καὶ
ἐπὶ τῶν βασιλέων αὗται αἱ ἀρχαί, κακῶς δὲ
πολιτευομένων τῶν βασιλέων ἠφανίζετο καὶ ἡ
τῆς πόλεως εὐκαιρία διὰ τὴν ἀνομίαν. ὁ γοῦν
Πολύβιος γεγονὼς ἐν τῇ πόλει βδελύττεται τὴν

---

[1] ἰδιόλογος, Corais, for κύριος λόγος s, ἴδιος λόγος other
MSS.

---

[1] e.g. Strabo's friend Aelius Gallus (2. 5. 12).
[2] Juri dicendo praefectus.

12. Egypt is now a Province; and it not only pays considerable tribute, but also is governed by prudent men[1]—the praefects who are sent there from time to time. Now he who is sent has the rank of the king; and subordinate to him is the administrator of justice,[2] who has supreme authority over most of the law-suits; and another is the official called Idiologus,[3] who inquires into all properties that are without owners and that ought to fall to Caesar; and these are attended by freedmen of Caesar, as also by stewards, who are entrusted with affairs of more or less importance. There are also three legions of soldiers, one of which is stationed in the city and the others in the country; and apart from these there are nine Roman cohorts, three in the city, three on the borders of Aethiopia in Syenê, as a guard for that region, and three in the rest of the country. And there are also three bodies of cavalry, which likewise are assigned to the various critical points. Of the native officials in the city, one is the Interpreter,[4] who is clad in purple, has hereditary prerogatives, and has charge of the interests of the city; and another the Recorder;[5] and another the Chief Judge;[6] and the fourth the Night Commander.[7] Now these officers existed also in the time of the kings, but, since the kings were carrying on a bad government, the prosperity of the city was also vanishing on account of the prevailing lawlessness. At any rate, Polybius, who had visited the city, is disgusted with the state of

---

[3] A kind of "Special Agent," or "Procurator," of Caesar.
[4] Interpres.
[5] Scriba publicus.
[6] Judicum praefectus.
[7] Praetor nocturnus.

τότε κατάστασιν, καί φησι τρία γένη τὴν πόλιν
οἰκεῖν, τό τε Αἰγύπτιον καὶ [1] ἐπιχώριον φῦλον,
ὀξὺ καὶ ἀπολιτικόν,[2] καὶ τὸ μισθοφορικόν, βαρὺ
καὶ [3] πολὺ καὶ ἀνάγωγον· ἐξ ἔθους γὰρ παλαιοῦ
ξένους ἔτρεφον τοὺς τὰ ὅπλα ἔχοντας, ἄρχειν
μᾶλλον ἢ ἄρχεσθαι δεδιδαγμένους διὰ τὴν τῶν
βασιλέων οὐδένειαν· τρίτον δ' ἦν γένος τὸ τῶν
Ἀλεξανδρέων, οὐδ' αὐτὸ εὐκρινῶς πολιτικὸν διὰ
τὰς αὐτὰς αἰτίας, κρεῖττον δ' ἐκείνων ὅμως· καὶ
γὰρ εἰ μιγάδες, Ἕλληνες ὅμως ἀνέκαθεν ἦσαν
καὶ ἐμέμνηντο τοῦ κοινοῦ τῶν Ἑλλήνων ἔθους.
ἠφανισμένου δὲ καὶ τούτου τοῦ πλήθους, μάλιστα
C 798 ὑπὸ τοῦ Εὐεργέτου τοῦ Φύσκωνος, καθ' ὃν ἧκεν
εἰς τὴν Ἀλεξάνδρειαν ὁ Πολύβιος (καταστασιαζό-
μενος γὰρ ὁ Φύσκων πλεονάκις [4] τοῖς στρατιώταις
ἐφίει τὰ πλήθη καὶ διέφθειρε), τοιούτων δή,
φησίν, ὄντων τῶν ἐν τῇ πόλει, λοιπὸν ἦν τῷ ὄντι
τὸ τοῦ ποιητοῦ·

Αἴγυπτόνδ' ἰέναι δολιχὴν ὁδὸν ἀργαλέην τε.

13. Τοιαῦτα δ' ἦν, εἰ μὴ [5] χείρω, καὶ τὰ τῶν
ὑστέρων βασιλέων.[6] Ῥωμαῖοι δ' εἰς δύναμιν, ὡς
εἰπεῖν, ἐπηνώρθωσαν τὰ πολλά, τὴν μὲν πόλιν
διατάξαντες ὡς εἶπον, κατὰ δὲ τὴν χώραν

---

[1] Except F, the MSS. read τό before ἐπιχώριον.
[2] Before πολιτικόν (MSS.) Tyrwhitt conj. οὐ; Kramer conj.
ἀπολιτικόν; C. Müller ὀχλητικόν.
[3] The words βαρὺ καί are found only in C.
[4] πολλάκις moz.　　　　[5] F has καί after μή.
[6] Except Fx, the MSS. have καί before Ῥωμαῖοι.

things then existing; and he says that three classes
inhabited the city: first, the Aegyptian or native
stock of people, who were quick-tempered and not [1]
inclined to civic life; and, secondly, the mercenary
class, who were severe and numerous and intractable
(for by an ancient custom they would maintain
foreign men-at-arms, who had been trained to rule
rather than to be ruled, on account of the worth-
lessness of the kings); and, third, the tribe of the
Alexandrians, who also were not distinctly inclined
to civil life, and for the same reasons, but still they
were better than those others,[2] for even though
they were a mixed people, still they were Greeks
by origin and mindful of the customs common to
the Greeks. But after this mass of people had also
been blotted out, chiefly by Euergetes Physcon, in
whose time Polybius went to Alexandria (for, being
opposed by factions, Physcon more often sent the
masses against the soldiers and thus caused their
destruction)—such being the state of affairs in the
city, Polybius says, in very truth there remained for
one, in the words of the poet, merely

" to go to Aegypt, a long and painful journey." [3]

13. Such, then, if not worse, was the state of
affairs under the later kings also; but the Romans
have, to the best of their ability, I might say, set
most things right, having organised the city as
I have said,[4] and having appointed throughout the

---

[1] The MSS. omit the negative ("not"), without which one
would naturally interpret ὀξύ as meaning "acute" rather
than "quick-tempered."

[2] *i.e.* the first class.

[3] *Odyssey* 4. 483. [4] § 12 above.

STRABO

ἐπιστρατήγους τινὰς καὶ νομάρχας καὶ ἐθνάρχας
καλουμένους ἀποδείξαντες, πραγμάτων οὐ μεγάλων ἐπιστατεῖν ἠξιωμένους. τῆς δ' εὐκαιρίας
τῆς κατὰ τὴν πόλιν τὸ μέγιστόν ἐστιν, ὅτι τῆς
Αἰγύπτου πάσης μόνος ἐστὶν οὗτος ὁ τόπος πρὸς
ἄμφω πεφυκὼς εὖ, τά τε ἐκ θαλάττης διὰ τὸ
εὐλίμενον, καὶ τὰ ἐκ τῆς χώρας, ὅτι πάντα
εὐμαρῶς ὁ ποταμὸς πορθμεύει συνάγει τε εἰς
τοιοῦτον χωρίον, ὅπερ μέγιστον ἐμπόριον τῆς
οἰκουμένης ἐστί.

Τῆς μὲν οὖν πόλεως ταύτας ἄν τις λέγοι τὰς
ἀρετάς· τῆς Αἰγύπτου δὲ τὰς προσόδους[1] ἔν
τινι λόγῳ Κικέρων φράζει, φήσας κατ' ἐνιαυτὸν
τῷ τῆς Κλεοπάτρας πατρὶ τῷ Αὐλητῇ προσ-
φέρεσθαι φόρον ταλάντων μυρίων δισχιλίων
πεντακοσίων. ὅπου οὖν ὁ κάκιστα καὶ ῥαθυμό-
τατα τὴν βασιλείαν διοικῶν τοσαῦτα προσω-
δεύετο, τί χρὴ νομίσαι τὰ νῦν, διὰ τοσαύτης
ἐπιμελείας οἰκονομούμενα καὶ τῶν Ἰνδικῶν
ἐμπορίων καὶ τῶν Τρωγλοδυτικῶν ἐπηυξημένων
ἐπὶ τοσοῦτον; πρότερον μέν γε οὐδ' εἴκοσι πλοῖα
ἐθάρρει τὸν Ἀράβιον κόλπον διαπερᾶν, ὥστε ἔξω
τῶν στενῶν ὑπερκύπτειν, νῦν δὲ καὶ στόλοι
μεγάλοι στέλλονται μέχρι τῆς Ἰνδικῆς καὶ τῶν
ἄκρων τῶν Αἰθιοπικῶν, ἐξ ὧν ὁ πολυτιμότατος

[1] Except E, the MSS. have ἅς after προσόδους.

[1] Strabo seems not to have known that the office of
Epistrategus was in existence as far back as 181 B.C. (Victor
Martin, *Les Epistratiges*, pp. 11, 173, Geneva, 1911). But in
the time of the Ptolemies only the Thebaïs had an Epistra-
tegus (*l.c.* p. 22), and, as the title indicates, he was a
Military Governor. The *several* Epistrategi appointed by the

country officials called Epistrategi [1] and Nomarchs [2] and Ethnarchs,[3] who were thought worthy to super-intend affairs of no great importance. Among the happy advantages of the city, the greatest is the fact that this is the only place in all Aegypt which is by nature well situated with reference to both things—both to commerce by sea, on account of the good harbours, and to commerce by land, because the river easily conveys and brings together everything into a place so situated—the greatest emporium in the inhabited world.

Now one might call these the excellent attributes of the city; and as for the revenues of Aegypt, Cicero tells about them in a certain speech,[4] saying that a tribute of twelve thousand five hundred talents [5] was paid annually to Auletes, the father of Cleopatra. If, then, the man who administered the kingdom in the worst and most careless way obtained so large a revenue, what should one think of the present revenues, which are managed with so much diligence, and when the commerce with the Indians and the Troglodytes has been increased to so great an extent? In earlier times, at least, not so many as twenty vessels would dare to traverse the Arabian Gulf far enough to get a peep outside the straits, but at the present time even large fleets are despatched as far as India and the extremities of Aethiopia, from which the most valuable cargoes

Romans, however, were given only administrative power, being wholly deprived of military power (*l.c.* p. 57).

[2] " Rulers of Nomes " (on the " Nomes," see 17. 1. 3).

[3] Rulers of Tribes.   [4] No longer extant.

[5] Cp. Diodorus Siculus (17. 52), who says six thousand talents.

κομίζεται φόρτος εἰς τὴν Αἴγυπτον, κἀντεῦθεν
πάλιν εἰς τοὺς ἄλλους ἐκπέμπεται τόπους· ὥστε
τὰ τέλη διπλάσια συνάγεται, τὰ μὲν εἰσαγωγικά,
τὰ δὲ ἐξαγωγικά· τῶν δὲ βαρυτίμων βαρέα καὶ
τὰ τέλη. καὶ γὰρ δὴ καὶ μονοπωλίας ἔχει· μόνη
γὰρ ἡ Ἀλεξάνδρεια τῶν τοιούτων ὡς ἐπὶ τὸ
πολὺ καὶ ὑποδοχεῖόν ἐστι καὶ χορηγεῖ τοῖς
ἐκτός. ἔτι δὲ μᾶλλόν κατιδεῖν ἔστι τὴν εὐφυΐαν
ταύτην περιοδεύοντι τὴν χώραν, καὶ πρῶτον τὴν
παραλίαν ἀρξαμένην ἀπὸ τοῦ Καταβαθμοῦ·
μέχρι δεῦρο γάρ ἐστιν ἡ Αἴγυπτος, ἡ δ' ἐξῆς
ἐστι Κυρηναία καὶ οἱ περιοικοῦντες βάρβαροι
Μαρμαρίδαι.

14. Ἀπὸ μὲν οὖν Καταβαθμοῦ εἰς Παραιτόνιον[1]
εὐθυπλοοῦντι σταδίων ἐστὶν ἐννακοσίων ὁ δρόμος.
πόλις δ' ἐστὶ καὶ λιμὴν μέγας τετταράκοντά που
C 799 σταδίων· καλοῦσι δ' οἱ μὲν Παραιτόνιον τὴν
πόλιν, οἱ δ' Ἀμμωνίαν. μεταξὺ δὲ ἥ τε Αἰγυπτίων
κώμη καὶ ἡ Αἰνησίσφυρα[2] ἄκρα, καὶ Τυνδάρειοι
σκόπελοι, νησίδια τέτταρα ἔχοντα λιμένα· εἶθ'
ἐξῆς ἄκρα Δρέπανον καὶ νῆσος Αἰνησίππεια[3]
ἔχουσα λιμένα καὶ κώμη Ἆπις, ἀφ' ἧς εἰς μὲν
Παραιτόνιον στάδιοι ἑκατόν, εἰς δὲ Ἄμμωνος
ὁδὸς ἡμερῶν πέντε. ἀπὸ δὲ τοῦ Παραιτονίου εἰς
Ἀλεξάνδρειαν[4] χίλιοί που καὶ τριακόσιοι στάδιοι. μεταξὺ δὲ πρῶτον μὲν ἄκρα λευκόγειος,
Λευκὴ ἀκτὴ καλουμένη, ἔπειτα Φοινικοῦς λιμὴν

---

[1] Παραιτόμιον E, Παρατόνιον F, Παραιτώνιον moxz.
[2] Αἰνησίσφυρα, Xylander and later editors, following
Ptolemaeus (4. 5), for νησίφιρα F, νησισφύρα other MSS.
[3] ἐνισσίπεια DEFhi, ἐνισίσπεια Cxz, ἐνισίσπια r, ἐνισίπεια m,
ἐνίσπεια o, Αἰνησίππη Ptolemaeus.

are brought to Aegypt, and thence sent forth again to the other regions; so that double duties are collected, on both imports and exports; and on goods that cost heavily the duty is also heavy. And in fact the country has monopolies also; for Alexandria alone is not only the receptacle of goods of this kind, for the most part, but also the source of supply to the outside world. And, further, one can perceive more clearly these natural advantages if one travels round the country, visiting first of all the part of the coast which begins at Catabathmus—for Aegypt extends as far as that place, though the country next thereafter belongs to the Cyrenaeans and to the neighbouring barbarians, the Marmaridae.

14. Now the run from Catabathmus to Paraetonium, if one sails in a straight course, is nine hundred stadia. It is a city and large harbour of about forty stadia.[1] Some call the city Paraetonium, but others Ammonia. In the interval, one comes to the village of the Aegyptians, to the promontory Aenesisphyra, and to the Tyndareian Rocks, which latter are four small islands with a harbour; then next to Drepanum, a promontory, and to Aenesippeia, an island with a harbour, and to Apis, a village, from which the distance to Paraetonium is one hundred stadia, and to the temple of Ammon, a five days' journey. The distance from Paraetonium to Alexandria is approximately one thousand three hundred stadia; and in the interval one comes first to a promontory of white earth, Leucê Actê, as it is called, and then to Phoenicus, a harbour, and to

[1] *i.e.* in circuit.

---

[4] εἰς 'Αλεξάνδρειαν, inserted by Mannert and the editors.

καὶ Πνιγεὺς κώμη· εἶτα νῆσος Πηδωνία¹ λιμένα
ἔχουσα, εἶτ᾽ Ἀντίφραι μικρὸν ἀπωτέρω τῆς
θαλάττης. ἅπασα μὲν ἡ χώρα αὕτη οὐκ εὔοινος,
πλείω δεχομένου τοῦ κεράμου θάλατταν ἢ οἶνον,
ὃν δὴ καλοῦσι Λιβυκόν, ᾧ δὴ καὶ τῷ ζύθῳ² τὸ
πολὺ φῦλον χρῆται τῶν Ἀλεξανδρέων· σκώπτονται
δὲ μάλιστα αἱ Ἀντίφραι· εἶθ᾽ ὁ Δέρρις³ λιμήν,
καλούμενος οὕτως διὰ τὴν πλησίον πέτραν
μέλαιναν δέρρει ἐοικυῖαν· ὀνομάζουσι δὲ καὶ
Ζεφύριον τὸν πλησίον τόπον, εἶτ᾽ ἄλλος λιμὴν
Λεύκασπις καὶ ἄλλοι πλείους· εἶτα Κυνὸς σῆμα·
εἶτα Ταπόσειρις,⁴ οὐκ ἐπὶ θαλάττῃ, πανήγυριν
δεχομένη μεγάλην. (καὶ ἄλλη δ᾽ ἐστὶ Ταπόσειρις
ἐπέκεινα τῆς πόλεως ἱκανῶς.) αὐτῆς δὲ πλησίον
πετρῶδες ἐπὶ τῇ θαλάττῃ χωρίον, καὶ αὐτὸ
δεχόμενον πολλοὺς τοὺς ἀκμάζοντας⁵ ἅπασαν
ὥραν ἔτους· εἶθ᾽ ἡ Πλινθίνη⁶ καὶ Νικίου κώμη
καὶ Χερρόνησος φρούριον, πλησίον ἤδη τῆς
Ἀλεξανδρείας καὶ τῆς Νεκροπόλεως ἐν ἑβδομήκοντα σταδίοις. ἡ δὲ Μαρεία⁷ λίμνη παρατεί-
νουσα μέχρι καὶ δεῦρο πλάτος μὲν ἔχει πλειόνων

¹ Σιδονία Cmoz.
² ζύθῳ, Xylander, for ζύγῳ.
³ Δέρρις EF, Δέρις other MSS.
⁴ Ταφόσειρις Ehi, Ταπόσειρις with φ above π, D.
⁵ ἀκμάζοντας, the later editors, following conj. of Tyrwhitt,
emend to κωμάζοντας.
⁶ Πλινθηνή DEh, Πλιθήνη CFx.
⁷ Μαρεία E, Μαρίνα F, Μαρία other MSS.

¹ i.e. apparently, as distinguished from the two other
classes of people at Alexandria (see § 12 above), and not
"most of the people at Alexandria," as others interpret it.
² i.e. because of the bad wine.   ³ i.e. a "hide."
⁴ i.e. like that mentioned in § 16 below.

Pnigeus, a village, and then to Pedonia, an island
with a harbour, and then to Antiphrae, which is at
only a little distance from the sea. The whole of
this country is without good wine, since the wine-jars
receive more sea-water than wine; and this they
call "Libyan" wine, which, as also beer, is used by
most of the tribe of Alexandrians;[1] but Antiphrae
is ridiculed most.[2] Then one comes to the harbour
Derrhis, so called because of the black rock near by,
which resembles a "derrhis";[3] and the neighbouring
place is also called Zephyrium.[4] Then to another
harbour, Leucaspis[5] and several others; and then
to Cynos-Sema;[6] and then to Taposeiris, not on the
sea, which holds a great public festival. (There is
also another Taposeiris on the other side of the city
and quite far from it.) And near it[7] there is a rocky
place on the sea where likewise crowds of people in
the prime of life[8] assemble during every season of
the year. And then[9] one comes to Plinthinê and
to the village of Nicias, and to Cherronesus, a
stronghold, where we are now near Alexandria and
Necropolis, a distance of seventy stadia. Lake
Mareia,[10] which extends even as far as this,[11] has a

---

[5] "White-shield."

[6] "Bitch's Monument" (cp. Vol. III, p. 377).

[7] The translator understands "it" to refer to the *first*
Taposeiris, and parenthesises the preceding statement
accordingly, though "it" might refer to the *second* (cp. §§ 16
and 17 below), in which case the parenthesis should end
with "season of the year."

[8] The later editors, except Müller-Dübner, very plausibly
emend the text to read, "crowds of 'revellers'" (see
critical note, and cp. §§ 16 and 17 below).

[9] *i.e.* continuing from the first Taposeiris.

[10] Also called "Mareotis" (§ 7 above).

[11] *i.e.* Cherronesus.

ἢ πεντήκοντα καὶ ἑκατὸν σταδίων, μῆκος δ' ἐλαττόνων ἢ τριακοσίων. ἔχει δ' ὀκτὼ νήσους καὶ τὰ
κύκλῳ πάντ' οἰκούμενα καλῶς· εὐοινία τέ ἐστι
περὶ τοὺς τόπους, ὥστε καὶ διαχεῖσθαι πρὸς
παλαίωσιν τὸν Μαρεώτην [1] οἶνον.

15. Φύεται δ' ἐν τοῖς Αἰγυπτιακοῖς ἕλεσι καὶ
ταῖς λίμναις ἥ τε βύβλος καὶ ὁ Αἰγύπτιος κύαμος,
ἐξ οὗ τὸ κιβώριον, σχεδόν τι ἰσοΰψεις ῥάβδοι
ὅσον δεκάποδες. ἀλλ' ἡ μὲν βύβλος ψιλὴ ῥάβδος
ἐστὶν ἐπ' ἄκρῳ χαίτην ἔχουσα, ὁ δὲ κύαμος κατὰ
πολλὰ μέρη φύλλα καὶ ἄνθη ἐκφέρει καὶ καρπὸν
ὅμοιον τῷ παρ' ἡμῖν κυάμῳ, μεγέθει μόνον καὶ
γεύσει διαλλάττοντα. οἱ οὖν κυαμῶνες ἡδεῖαν
ὄψιν παρέχουσι καὶ τέρψιν τοῖς ἐνευωχεῖσθαι
βουλομένοις· εὐωχοῦνται δ' ἐν σκάφαις θαλαμη-
γοῖς, ἐνδύοντες εἰς τὸ πύκνωμα τῶν κυάμων καὶ
C 800 σκιαζόμενοι τοῖς φύλλοις· ἔστι γὰρ σφόδρα
μεγάλα, ὥστε καὶ ἀντὶ ποτηρίων καὶ τρυβλίων
χρῆσθαι· ἔχει γάρ τινα καὶ κοιλότητα ἐπιτηδείαν
πρὸς τοῦτο· καὶ δὴ καὶ ἡ Ἀλεξάνδρεια μεστὴ
τούτων ἐστὶ κατὰ τὰ ἐργαστήρια, ὡς σκεύεσι
χρωμένων· καὶ οἱ ἀγροὶ μίαν τινὰ τῶν προσόδων
καὶ ταύτην ἔχουσι τὴν ἀπὸ τῶν φύλλων. ὁ μὲν
δὴ κύαμος τοιοῦτος· ἡ δὲ βύβλος ἐνταῦθα μὲν οὐ
πολλὴ φύεται (οὐ γὰρ ἀσκεῖται), ἐν δὲ τοῖς
κάτω μέρεσι τοῦ Δέλτα πολλή, ἡ μὲν χείρων,

---

[1] Μαραιώτην CDE*h*, Μαρεῶτιν F*moxz*.

---

[1] *i e.* drawn off from the lees, not merely once or twice, for
early consumption, but time and again, with a view to ageing it into old wine of superior quality. The special name

breadth of more than one hundred and fifty stadia and a length of less than three hundred. It contains eight islands; and all the shores round it are well inhabited; and the vintages in this region are so good that the Mareotic wine is racked off with a view to ageing it.[1]

15. The byblus[2] grows in the Aegyptian marshes and lakes, as also the Aegyptian cyamus,[3] from which comes the ciborium;[4] and it has stalks approximately equal in height, about ten feet. But though the byblus is a bare stock with a tuft on top, the cyamus produces leaves and flowers in many parts, and also a fruit like our cyamus, differing only in size and taste. Accordingly, the bean-fields afford a pleasing sight, and also enjoyment to those who wish to hold feasts therein. They hold feasts in cabin-boats, in which they enter the thick of the cyami and the shade of the leaves; for the leaves are so very large that they are used both for drinking-cups and for bowls, for these even have a kind of concavity suited to this purpose; and in fact Alexandria is full of these in the work-shops, where they are used as vessels; and the farms have also this as one source of their revenues—I mean the revenue from the leaves. Such, then, is the cyamus. As for the byblus, it does not grow in large quantities here (for it is not cultivated), but it grows in large quantities in the lower parts of the Delta, one kind

---

"Mareotic" indicates both the quality and the wide use of this wine.

[2] The Aegyptian papyrus.

[3] *i.e.* "bean."

[4] *i.e.* the "seed-vessel," of which drinking-cups were made (cp. Horace, *Carmina* 2. 7. 22).

ἡ δὲ βελτίων, ἡ ἱερατική· κἀνταῦθα δέ τινες τῶν
τὰς προσόδους ἐπεκτείνειν βουλομένων μετήνεγκαν
τὴν Ἰουδαϊκὴν ἐντρέχειαν,[1] ἣν ἐκεῖνοι παρεῦρον
ἐπὶ τοῦ φοίνικος (καὶ μάλιστα τοῦ καρυωτοῦ) καὶ
τοῦ βαλσάμου· οὐ γὰρ ἐῶσι πολλαχοῦ φύεσθαι,
τῇ δὲ σπάνει τιμὴν ἐπιτιθέντες τὴν πρόσοδον
οὕτως[2] αὔξουσι, τὴν δὲ κοινὴν χρείαν διαλυ-
μαίνονται.

16. Ἐν δεξιᾷ δὲ τῆς Κανωβικῆς πύλης ἐξιόντι
ἡ διῶρύξ ἐστιν ἡ ἐπὶ Κάνωβον συνάπτουσα τῇ
λίμνῃ· ταύτῃ δὲ καὶ ἐπὶ Σχεδίαν ὁ πλοῦς ἐπὶ τὸν
μέγαν ποταμὸν καὶ ἐπὶ τὸν Κάνωβον, πρῶτον δὲ
ἐπὶ τὴν Ἐλευσῖνα· ἔστι δ᾽ αὕτη κατοικία πλησίον
τῆς τε Ἀλεξανδρείας καὶ τῆς Νικοπόλεως ἐπ᾽
αὐτῇ τῇ Κανωβικῇ διώρυγι κειμένη, διαίτας
ἔχουσα καὶ ἀπόψεις τοῖς καπυρίζειν βουλομένοις
καὶ ἀνδράσι καὶ γυναιξίν, ἀρχή τις Κανωβισμοῦ
καὶ τῆς ἐκεῖ λαμυρίας. ἀπὸ δὲ τῆς Ἐλευσῖνος
προελθοῦσι μικρὸν ἐν δεξιᾷ ἐστιν ἡ διῶρυξ ἀνά-

---

[1] For ἐντρέχειαν, Cobet conj. κακεντρέχειαν, citing 7. 3. 7.
[2] ὄντως CDFhnsx ; αὐτοῖς, Corais.

---

[1] *i.e.* the kind "devoted to sacred purposes." The superior
quality consisted of the middle and broadest (about 9½ inches)
strips of the plant ; but though originally called Hieratica,
it was later called Augusta in honour of Augustus (see
Encyclopœdia Britannica, s. v. "Papyrus.")

[2] Dr. F. Zucker (*Philologus* 70, N.F. 24, 1911, pp. 79–105)
shows that the Romans established a government monopoly
of Aegyptian papyrus ; but his conclusion that under the
Ptolemies there was no such monopoly and that Strabo's
words, "some of those who wished to enhance the revenues,
etc.," mean that "a number of large proprietors misused their
power, and through limiting the cultivation to their own

being inferior, and the other superior, that is, the Hieratica.[1] And here, too, certain of those who wished to enhance the revenues adopted the shrewd practice of the Judaeans, which the latter had invented in the case of the palm tree (particularly the caryotic palm) and the balsam tree ; for they do not allow the byblus to grow in many places, and because of the scarcity they set a higher price on it and thus increase the revenues, though they injure the common use of the plant.[2]

16. On the right of the Canobic Gate, as one goes out, one comes to the canal which is connected with the lake and leads to Canobus ;[3] and it is by this canal that one sails, not only to Schedia, that is, to the great river, but also to Canobus, though first to Eleusis. Eleusis is a settlement near both Alexandria and Nicopolis, is situated on the Canobic canal itself, and has lodging-places and commanding views for those who wish to engage in revelry, both men and women, and is a beginning, as it were, of the " Canobic " life [4] and the shamelessness there current. On proceeding a slight distance from Eleusis, and on the right, one

---

advantage and to the injury of the public produced a rise in the price of papyrus," is vigorously opposed by Professor J. P. Mahaffy (*Hermathena*, 16, 1911, pp. 237–41), who rightly understands Strabo to refer to "certain chancellors of the exchequer (διοικηταί) who had to meet a sudden demand by raising money as best they could." However, in a later article (*Philologus* 74, N. F. 28, pp. 184–85) Zucker retracts his former interpretation of the passage, accepting Mahaffy's. See also Wilcken, *Papyruskunde, Grundzüge* I, 1, pp. 255–56.

[3] *i.e.* " connected " indirectly, by a short tributary south-west of the city.

[4] *i.e.* the luxurious life at Canobus, which was proverbial.

STRABO

γουσα ἐπὶ τὴν Σχεδίαν. διέχει δὲ τετράσχοινον
τῆς Ἀλεξανδρείας ἡ Σχεδία, κατοικία πόλεως,
ἐν ᾗ τὸ ναύσταθμον τῶν θαλαμηγῶν πλοίων, ἐφ'
οἷς οἱ ἡγεμόνες εἰς τὴν ἄνω χώραν ἀναπλέουσιν·
ἐνταῦθα δὲ καὶ τὸ τελώνιον τῶν ἄνωθεν καταγομένων καὶ ἀναγομένων· οὗ χάριν καὶ σχεδία
ἔζευκται ἐπὶ τῷ ποταμῷ, ἀφ' ἧς καὶ τοὔνομα τῷ
τόπῳ. μετὰ δὲ τὴν διώρυγα τὴν ἐπὶ Σχεδίαν
ἄγουσαν ὁ ἐξῆς ἐπὶ τὸν Κάνωβον πλοῦς ἐστι
παράλληλος τῇ παραλίᾳ τῇ ἀπὸ Φάρου μέχρι
τοῦ Κανωβικοῦ στόματος· στενὴ γάρ τις ταινία
μεταξὺ διήκει τοῦ τε πελάγους καὶ τῆς διώρυγος,
ἐν ᾗ ἐστιν ἥ τε μικρὰ Ταπόσειρις μετὰ τὴν Νικό-
πολιν καὶ τὸ Ζεφύριον, ἄκρα ναΐσκον ἔχουσα
Ἀρσινόης Ἀφροδίτης· τὸ δὲ παλαιὸν καὶ Θῶνίν
τινα πόλιν ἐνταῦθά φασιν, ἐπώνυμον τοῦ
βασιλέως τοῦ δεξαμένου Μενέλαόν τε καὶ Ἑλένην
ξενίᾳ. περὶ οὖν τῶν τῆς Ἑλένης φαρμάκων
C 801 φησὶν οὕτως ὁ ποιητής·

ἐσθλά, τά οἱ Πολύδαμνα πόρεν Θῶνος παρά-
κοιτις.

17. Κάνωβος δ' ἐστὶ πόλις ἐν εἴκοσι καὶ ἑκατὸν
σταδίοις ἀπὸ Ἀλεξανδρείας πεζῇ ἰοῦσιν, ἐπώνυμος
Κανώβου τοῦ Μενελάου κυβερνήτου, ἀποθανόντος
αὐτόθι, ἔχουσα τὸ τοῦ Σαράπιδος ἱερὸν πολλῇ
ἁγιστείᾳ τιμώμενον καὶ θεραπείας ἐκφέρον, ὥστε
καὶ τοὺς ἐλλογιμωτάτους ἄνδρας πιστεύειν καὶ

---

[1] See § 24 below.
[2] *i.e.* "raft" or "pontoon bridge."
[3] Thonis was situated at the Canobic mouth of the Nile, and in early times was the emporium of Aegypt (Diodorus

comes to the canal which leads up to Schedia. Schedia is four schoeni [1] distant from Alexandria; it is a settlement of the city, and contains the station of the cabin-boats on which the praefects sail to Upper Aegypt. And at Schedia is also the station for paying duty on the goods brought down from above it and brought up from below it; and for this purpose, also, a schedia [2] has been laid across the river, from which the place has its name. After the canal which leads to Schedia, one's next voyage, to Canobus, is parallel to that part of the coast-line which extends from Pharos to the Canobic mouth; for a narrow ribbon-like strip of land extends between the sea and the canal, and on this, after Nicopolis, lies the Little Taposeiris, as also the Zephyrium, a promontory which contains a shrine of Aphroditê Arsinoê. In ancient times, it is said, there was also a city called Thonis here,[3] which was named after the king who received Menelaüs and Helen with hospitality. At any rate, the poet speaks of Helen's drugs as follows: "goodly drugs which Polydamna, the wife of Thon, had given her." [4]

17. Canobus is a city situated at a distance of one hundred and twenty stadia from Alexandria, if one goes on foot, and was named after Canobus, the pilot of Menelaüs, who died there. It contains the temple of Sarapis, which is honoured with great reverence and effects such cures that even the most reputable men believe in it and sleep in it—them-

Siculus 1. 19); and King Thon was the warden of the Canobic mouth in the time of the Trojan war (Herodotus 1. 113).

[4] *Odyssey* 4. 228.

ἐγκοιμᾶσθαι αὐτοὺς ὑπὲρ ἑαυτῶν ἢ ἑτέρους·
συγγράφουσι δέ τινες καὶ τὰς θεραπείας, ἄλλοι
δὲ ἀρετὰς τῶν ἐνταῦθα λογίων.¹ ἀντὶ πάντων
δ᾽ ἐστίν ὁ τῶν πανηγυριστῶν ὄχλος τῶν ἐκ τῆς
Ἀλεξανδρείας κατιόντων τῇ διώρυγι· πᾶσα γὰρ
ἡμέρα καὶ πᾶσα νὺξ πληθύει τῶν μὲν ² ἐν τοῖς
πλοιαρίοις καταυλουμένων καὶ κατορχουμένων
ἀνέδην ³ μετὰ τῆς ἐσχάτης ἀκολασίας, καὶ ἀνδρῶν
καὶ γυναικῶν, τῶν δ᾽ ἐν αὐτῷ τῷ Κανώβῳ καταγωγὰς ἐχόντων, ἐπικειμένας τῇ διώρυγι εὐφυεῖς
πρὸς τὴν τοιαύτην ἄνεσιν καὶ εὐωχίαν.

18. Μετὰ δὲ τὸν Κάνωβόν ἐστι τὸ Ἡράκλειον ⁴
Ἡρακλέους ἔχον ἱερόν· εἶτα τὸ Κανωβικὸν στόμα
καὶ ἡ ἀρχὴ τοῦ Δέλτα. τὰ δ᾽ ἐν δεξιᾷ τῆς
Κανωβικῆς διώρυγος ὁ Μενελαΐτης ἐστὶ νομός
ἀπὸ τοῦ ἀδελφοῦ τοῦ πρώτου Πτολεμαίου καλούμενος, οὐ μὰ Δία ἀπὸ ⁵ τοῦ ἥρωος, ὡς ἔνιοί φασιν,
ὧν καὶ Ἀρτεμίδωρος. μετὰ δὲ τὸ Κανωβικὸν
στόμα ἐστὶ τὸ Βολβίτινον, εἶτα τὸ Σεβεννυτικόν,
καὶ τὸ Φατνιτικόν, τρίτον ὑπάρχον τῷ μεγέθει
παρὰ τὰ πρῶτα δύο, οἷς ὥρισται τὸ Δέλτα· καὶ
γὰρ οὐ ⁶ πόρρω τῆς κορυφῆς σχίζεται εἰς τὸ ἐντὸς
τοῦ Δέλτα. τῷ δὲ Φατνιτικῷ συνάπτει τὸ
Μενδήσιον, εἶτα τὸ Τανιτικὸν καὶ τελευταῖον τὸ
Πηλουσιακόν. ἔστι δὲ καὶ ἄλλα τούτων μεταξύ,
ὡς ἂν ψευδοστόματα, ἀσημότερα· ἔχει μὲν οὖν

---

¹ ἀρεταλογίων CDFh, ἀρετολογίων x, τερατολογίων i.
² μέν, Corais inserts.
³ ἀνέδην h, and second hand in D ; ἀναίδην other MSS.
⁴ τό, after Ἡράκλειον Ex omit.
⁵ ἀπό EF, ὑπό other MSS.
⁶ οὐ F, οὐδέ other MSS.

selves on their own behalf or others for them.[1]
Some writers go on to record the cures, and others
the virtues, of the oracles there. But to balance
all this is the crowd of revellers who go down from
Alexandria by the canal to the public festivals; for
every day and every night is crowded with people
on the boats who play the flute and dance without
restraint and with extreme licentiousness, both men
and women, and also with the people of Canobus
itself, who have resorts situated close to the canal
and adapted to relaxation and merry-making of this
kind.

18. After Canobus one comes to the Heracleium,
which contains a temple of Heracles; and then to
the Canobic mouth and the beginning of the Delta.
The parts on the right of the Canobic canal are the
Menelaïte Nome, so called from the brother of the
first Ptolemy [2]—not, by heaven, from the hero, as
some writers say, among whom is also Artemidorus.
After the Canobic mouth one comes to the Bolbitine
mouth, and then to the Sebennytic, and to the
Phatnitic, which is third in size as compared with
the first two,[3] which form the boundaries of the
Delta; for not far from the vertex of the Delta the
Phatnitic splits, sending a branch into the interior
of the Delta. Lying close to the Phatnitic mouth
is the Mendesian; and then one comes to the
Tanitic, and, last of all, to the Pelusiac. There
are also others in among these, pseudo-mouths as
it were, which are rather insignificant. Their mouths

---

[1] Even Moses advocated this practice (16. 2. 35).
[2] On this Menelaüs see Diodorus Siculus (20. 21–53) and
Plutarch (*Demetrius* 15–17).
[3] The Canobic and Pelusiac.

65

εἰσαγωγὰς τὰ στόματα, ἀλλ' οὐκ εὐφυεῖς οὐδὲ
μεγάλοις πλοίοις, ἀλλ' ὑπηρετικοῖς διὰ τὸ
βραχέα εἶναι καὶ ἑλώδη. μάλιστα μέντοι τῷ
Κανωβικῷ στόματι ἐχρῶντο ὡς ἐμπορίῳ, τῶν
κατ' Ἀλεξάνδρειαν λιμένων ἀποκεκλειμένων,[1] ὡς
προείπομεν. Μετὰ δὲ τὸ Βολβίτινον στόμα ἐπὶ
πλέον ἔκκειται ταπεινὴ καὶ ἀμμώδης ἄκρα·
καλεῖται δὲ Ἄγνου κέρας· εἶθ' ἡ Περσέως σκοπὴ
καὶ τὸ Μιλησίων τεῖχος· πλεύσαντες γὰρ ἐπὶ
Ψαμμιτίχου τριάκοντα ναυσὶ Μιλήσιοι (κατὰ
Κυαξάρη δ' οὗτος ἦν τὸν Μῆδον) κατέσχον εἰς τὸ
στόμα τὸ Βολβίτινον, εἶτ' ἐκβάντες ἐτείχισαν τὸ
λεχθὲν κτίσμα· χρόνῳ δ' ἀναπλεύσαντες εἰς τὸν
Σαϊτικὸν νομὸν καταναυμαχήσαντες Ἰνάρων πόλιν
C 802 ἔκτισαν Ναύκρατιν οὐ πολὺ τῆς Σχεδίας ὕπερθεν.
μετὰ δὲ τὸ τῶν Μιλησίων τεῖχος ἐπὶ τὸ Σεβεννυ-
τικὸν προϊόντι[2] στόμα λίμναι εἰσίν, ὧν ἡ ἑτέρα
Βουτικὴ καλεῖται ἀπὸ Βούτου πόλεως, καὶ ἡ
Σεβεννυτικὴ δὲ πόλις καὶ ἡ Σάϊς, μητρόπολις τῆς
κάτω χώρας, ἐν ᾗ τιμῶσι τὴν Ἀθηνᾶν· ἐν δὲ τῷ
ἱερῷ αὐτῆς ἡ θήκη κεῖται τοῦ Ψαμμιτίχου.
περὶ δὲ τὴν Βούτον καὶ Ἑρμοῦ πόλις ἐν νήσῳ
κειμένη· ἐν δὲ τῇ Βούτῳ Λητοῦς ἐστι μαντεῖον.
19. Ἐν δὲ τῇ μεσογείῳ τῇ ὑπὲρ τοῦ Σεβεννυ-
τικοῦ καὶ Φατνιτικοῦ στόματος Ξόις ἐστὶ καὶ
νῆσος καὶ πόλις ἐν τῷ Σεβεννυτικῷ νομῷ. ἔστι

---

[1] ἀποκεκλειμένων D, ἀποκεκλιμένων other MSS.
[2] προϊόντι E, προσιόντι other MSS.

---

[1] i.e. to foreign imports (§ 6 above).
[2] Meaning "Willow-Horn," apparently.

indeed afford entrance to boats, but are adapted, not to large boats, but to tenders only, because the mouths are shallow and marshy. It is chiefly, however, the Canobic mouth that they used as an emporium, since the harbours at Alexandria were kept closed,[1] as I have said before. After the Bolbitine mouth one comes to a low and sandy promontory which projects rather far into the sea; it is called Agnu-Ceras.[2] And then to the Watch-tower of Perseus [3] and the Wall of the Milesians; for in the time of Psammitichus (who lived in the time of Cyaxares the Mede) the Milesians, with thirty ships, put in at the Bolbitine mouth, and then, disembarking, fortified with a wall the above-mentioned settlement; but in time they sailed up into the Saïtic Nome, defeated the city Inaros in a naval fight, and founded Naucratis, not far above Schedia. After the Wall of the Milesians, as one proceeds towards the Sebennytic mouth, one comes to two lakes, one of which, Buticê, has its name from the city Butus, and also to the Sebennytic city, and to Saïs, the metropolis of the lower country, in which Athena is worshipped; and in her temple lies the tomb of Psammitichus. In the neighbourhood of Butus is also an Hermupolis,[4] which is situated on an island; and in Butus there is an oracle of Leto.[5]

19. In the interior above the Sebennytic and Phatnitic mouths lies Xoïs, both an island and a city, in the Sebennytic Nome. Here, also, are an

---

[3] Herodotus (2. 15) appears to place the watch-tower at the Canobic mouth.

[4] "City of Hermes."

[5] On Leto's shrine and oracle in Butus, see Herodotus 2. 155.

δὲ καὶ Ἑρμοῦ πόλις καὶ Λύκου πόλις καὶ Μένδης,
ὅπου τὸν Πᾶνα τιμῶσι καὶ τῶν ζώων τράγον·
ὡς δὲ Πίνδαρός φησιν, οἱ τράγοι ἐνταῦθα γυναιξὶ
μίγνυνται·

Μένδητα παρὰ κρημνὸν θαλάσσης,
ἔσχατον Νείλου κέρας, αἰγιβάται
ὅθι τράγοι γυναιξὶ μίσγονται.[1]

πλησίον δὲ Μένδητος καὶ Διὸς πόλις καὶ αἱ περὶ
αὐτὴν λίμναι καὶ Λεοντόπολις· εἶτ' ἀπωτέρω ἡ
Βούσιρις πόλις ἐν τῷ Βουσιρίτῃ νομῷ καὶ Κυνὸς
πόλις. φησὶ δ' Ἐρατοσθένης κοινὸν μὲν εἶναι
τοῖς βαρβάροις πᾶσιν ἔθος τὴν ξενηλασίαν, τοὺς
δ' Αἰγυπτίους ἐλέγχεσθαι διὰ τῶν περὶ τὸν
Βούσιριν μεμυθευμένων ἐν τῷ Βουσιρίτῃ νομῷ,
διαβάλλειν τὴν ἀξενίαν βουλομένων τοῦ τόπου
τούτου τῶν ὕστερον, οὐ βασιλέως, μὰ Δία, οὐδὲ
τυράννου γενομένου τινὸς Βουσίριδος· προσεπι-
φημισθῆναι δὲ καὶ τὸ

Αἴγυπτόνδ' ἰέναι δολιχὴν ὁδὸν ἀργαλέην τε,

προσλαμβάνοντος πρὸς τοῦτο πάμπολυ καὶ τοῦ
ἀλιμένου καὶ τοῦ μηδὲ τὸν ὄντα λιμένα ἀνεῖσθαι
τὸν πρὸς τῇ Φάρῳ, φρουρεῖσθαι δ' ὑπὸ βουκόλων
ληστῶν ἐπιτιθεμένων τοῖς προσορμιζομένοις·
Καρχηδονίους δὲ καταποντοῦν, εἴ τις τῶν ξένων
εἰς Σαρδὼ παραπλεύσειεν ἢ ἐπὶ Στήλας· διὰ δὲ

---

[1] The words Μένδητα . . . μίσγονται are not found in EF.
Kramer and later editors reject them.

---

[1] "City of Lycus."   [2] Frag. 201 (215), Schroeder.
[3] So Herodotus (2. 46), who also says that "In the
Aegyptian language both the he-goat and Pan are called
'Mendes.'"

Hermupolis and a Lycupolis,[1] and Mendes, at which place they worship Pan and, among animals, a he-goat; and, as Pindar [2] says, the he-goats have inter-course with women there: [3] "Mendes, along the crag of the sea, farthermost horn of the Nile, where the goat-mounting he-goats have intercourse with women." Near Mendes lie also a Diospolis [4] and the lakes in its neighbourhood and Leontopolis; [5] and then, at a greater distance, the city Busiris in the Busirite Nome, and Cynospolis.[6] According to Eratosthenes, the expulsion of foreigners is a custom common to all barbarians, and yet the Aegyptians are condemned for this fault because of the myths which have been circulated about Busiris in connection with the Busirite Nome,[7] since the later writers wish falsely to malign the inhospi-tality of this place, although, by heavens, no king or tyrant named Busiris ever existed; and, he says, the poet's words are also constantly cited—"to go to Aegypt, long and painful journey"—the want of harbours contributing very much to this opinion, as also the fact that even the harbour which Aegypt did have, the one at Pharos, gave no access, but was guarded by shepherds who were pirates and who attacked those who tried to bring ships to anchor there; and the Carthaginians likewise, he adds, used to drown in the sea any foreigners who sailed past their country to Sardo [8] or to the Pillars, and

---

[4] "City of Zeus."   [5] "Lion City."
[6] "Dog's City."
[7] The mythical king Busiris sacrificed all foreigners who entered Aegypt, but at last was slain by Heracles (Apollo-dorus 2. 5. 11).
[8] Sardinia.

69

ταῦτ᾽ ἀπιστεῖσθαι τὰ πολλὰ τῶν ἑσπερίων· καὶ
τοὺς Πέρσας δὲ κακῶς ἡγεῖσθαι τοῖς πρέσβεσι
τὰς ὁδοὺς κύκλῳ καὶ διὰ δυσκόλων.

20. Συνάπτει δὲ καὶ ὁ Ἀθριβίτης νομὸς καὶ
Ἄθριβις πόλις καὶ ἔτι ὁ Προσωπίτης νομός, ἐν
ᾧ Ἀφροδίτης πόλις. ὑπὲρ δὲ τὸ Μενδήσιον
στόμα καὶ τὸ Τανιτικὸν λίμνη μεγάλη καὶ ὁ
Μενδήσιός ἐστι νομὸς καὶ ὁ Λεοντοπολίτης καὶ
πόλις Ἀφροδίτης καὶ ὁ Φαρβητίτης νομός· εἶτα
τὸ Τανιτικὸν στόμα, ὅ τινες Σαϊτικὸν λέγουσι,
καὶ ὁ Τανίτης νομὸς καὶ πόλις ἐν αὐτῷ μεγάλη
Τάνις.

21. Μεταξὺ δὲ τοῦ Τανιτικοῦ καὶ τοῦ Πηλουσιακοῦ λίμναι καὶ ἕλη μεγάλα καὶ συνεχῆ κώμας
πολλὰς ἔχοντα· καὶ αὐτὸ δὲ τὸ Πηλούσιον κύκλῳ
C 803 περικείμενα ἔχει ἕλη, ἅ τινες Βάραθρα καλοῦσι,
καὶ τέλματα· ᾤκισται δ᾽ ἀπὸ θαλάττης ἐν
πλείοσιν ἢ εἴκοσι σταδίοις, τὸν δὲ κύκλον ἔχει
τοῦ τείχους σταδίων εἴκοσιν· ὠνόμασται δ᾽ ἀπὸ
τοῦ πηλοῦ καὶ τῶν τελμάτων. ταύτῃ δὲ καὶ
δυσείσβολός ἐστιν ἡ Αἴγυπτος ἐκ τῶν ἑωθινῶν
τόπων τῶν κατὰ Φοινίκην καὶ τὴν Ἰουδαίαν, καὶ
ἐκ τῆς Ἀραβίας δὲ τῆς Ναβαταίων, ἥπερ ἐστὶ
προσεχής· διὰ τούτων ἐπὶ τὴν Αἴγυπτον ἡ ὁδός.
ἡ δὲ μεταξὺ τοῦ Νείλου καὶ τοῦ Ἀραβίου κόλπου
Ἀραβία μέν ἐστι, καὶ ἐπί γε τῶν ἄκρων αὐτῆς
ἵδρυται τὸ Πηλούσιον, ἀλλ᾽ ἔρημος ἅπασά ἐστι
καὶ ἄβατος στρατοπέδῳ. ὁ δὲ μεταξὺ ἰσθμὸς
Πηλουσίου καὶ τοῦ μυχοῦ τοῦ καθ᾽ Ἡρώων πόλιν
χιλίων[1] μέν ἐστι σταδίων, ὡς δὲ Ποσειδώνιός

---

[1] χιλίων (as in 1. 2. 29 and Herodotus 2. 158, 4 11),
Epitome and editors, for ἐννακοσίωι.

it is for this reason that most of the stories told about the west are disbelieved; and also the Persians, he says, would treacherously guide the ambassadors over roundabout roads and through difficult regions.

20. Bordering on this Nome is the Athribite Nome and the city Athribis, and also the Prosopite Nome, in which is a City of Aphroditê. Above the Mendesian and Tanitic mouths lie a large lake and the Mendesian and Leontopolite Nomes and a City of Aphroditê and the Pharbetite Nome; and then one comes to the Tanitic mouth, which some call Saïtic, and to the Tanite Nome, and to Tanis, a large city therein.

21. Between the Tanitic and Pelusiac mouths lie lakes, and large and continuous marshes which contain many villages. Pelusium itself also has marshes lying all round it, which by some are called Barathra,[1] and muddy ponds; its settlement lies at a distance of more than twenty stadia from the sea, the wall has a circuit of twenty stadia, and it has its name from the *pelos*[2] and the muddy ponds. Here, too, Aegypt is difficult to enter, I mean from the eastern regions about Phoenicia and Judaea, and from the Arabia of the Nabataeans, which is next to Aegypt; these are the regions which the road to Aegypt traverses. The country between the Nile and the Arabian Gulf is Arabia, and at its extremity is situated Pelusium; but the whole of it is desert, and impassable for an army. The isthmus between Pelusium and the recess of the gulf at Heroönpolis[3] is one thousand stadia, but, according to Poseidonius, less than one thousand

---

[1] "Pits."   [2] *i.e.* "mud."
[3] "City of Heroes."

φησιν, ἐλαττόνων ἢ χιλίων καὶ πεντακοσίων·
πρὸς δὲ τῷ ἄνυδρος εἶναι καὶ ἀμμώδης ἑρπετῶν
πλῆθος ἔχει τῶν ἀμμοδυτῶν.

22. Ἀπὸ δὲ Σχεδίας ἀναπλέουσιν ἐπὶ Μέμφιν
ἐν δεξιᾷ μέν εἰσι πάμπολλαι κῶμαι μέχρι τῆς
Μαρείας [1] λίμνης, ὧν ἐστι καὶ ἡ Χαβρίου κώμη
καλουμένη· ἐπὶ δὲ τῷ ποταμῷ Ἑρμοῦ πόλις ἐστίν·
εἶτα Γυναικῶν πόλις καὶ νομὸς Γυναικοπολίτης·
ἐφεξῆς δὲ Μώμεμφις καὶ Μωμεμφίτης νομός·
μεταξὺ δὲ διώρυγες πλείους εἰς τὴν Μαρεῶτιν.
οἱ δὲ Μωμεμφῖται τὴν Ἀφροδίτην τιμῶσι, καὶ
τρέφεται θήλεια βοῦς ἱερά, καθάπερ ἐν Μέμφει
ὁ Ἄπις, ἐν Ἡλίου δὲ πόλει ὁ Μνεῦις· οὗτοι μὲν
οὖν θεοὶ νομίζονται, οἱ δὲ παρὰ τοῖς ἄλλοις (παρὰ
πολλοῖς γὰρ δὴ ἔν τε τῷ Δέλτα καὶ ἔξω αὐτοῦ
τοῖς μὲν ἄρρην, τοῖς δὲ θήλεια τρέφεται), οὗτοι δὲ
θεοὶ μὲν οὐ νομίζονται, ἱεροὶ δέ.

23. Ὑπὲρ δὲ Μωμέμφεώς εἰσι δύο νιτρίαι
πλεῖστον νίτρον ἔχουσαι καὶ νομὸς Νιτριώ-
της. τιμᾶται δ᾽ ἐνταῦθα ὁ Σάραπις καὶ παρὰ
μόνοις τούτοις θύεται ἐν Αἰγύπτῳ πρόβατον·
πλησίον δὲ καὶ ἐνταῦθα πόλις Μενέλαος, ἐν
ἀριστερᾷ δὲ ἐν τῷ Δέλτα ἐπὶ μὲν τῷ ποταμῷ
Ναύκρατις, ἀπὸ δὲ τοῦ ποταμοῦ δίσχοινον διέχουσα ἡ Σάϊς· καὶ μικρὸν ταύτης ὕπερθε τὸ τοῦ
Ὀσίριδος ἄσυλον, ἐν ᾧ κεῖσθαι τὸν Ὄσιρίν
φασιν. ἀμφισβητοῦσι δὲ τούτου πολλοί, καὶ
μάλιστα οἱ τὰς Φιλὰς οἰκοῦντες τὰς ὑπὲρ Συήνης

---

[1] Μαρείας E, Σαμαρείας Dh, Σαμαρίας CF, Μαρίας moswxz.

---

[1] "City of Women."
[2] "City of the Sun."

five hundred; and in addition to its being waterless and sandy, it contains a multitude of reptiles, the sand-burrowers.

22. From Schedia, as one sails towards Memphis, there are, on the right, a very large number of villages, extending as far as Lake Mareia, among which is the Village of Chabrias, as it is called; and, on the river, one comes to an Hermupolis, and then to Gynaeconpolis [1] and the Gynaeconpolite Nome, and, next in order, to Momemphis and the Momemphite Nome; but in the interval there are several canals which empty into Lake Mareotis. The Momemphitae honour Aphroditê; and a sacred cow is kept there, as is Apis in Memphis and Mneuïs in Heliupolis. [2] Now these animals are regarded as gods, but those in the other places (for in many places, indeed, both in the Delta and outside of it, either a bull or cow is kept)—those others, I say, are not regarded as gods, though they are held sacred.

23. Above Momemphis are two nitre-beds, which contain very large quantities of nitre, [3] and the Nitriote Nome. Here Sarapis is held in honour; and they are the only people in Aegypt who sacrifice a sheep. Near by, and in this Nome, is a city Menelaüs; and on the left, in the Delta, lies Naucratis, which is on the river, whereas Saïs lies at a distance of two schoeni from the river. A little above Saïs is the asylum of Osiris, in which the body of Osiris is said to lie; but many lay claim to this, and particularly the inhabitants of the Philae which

[3] The ancients meant by "nitre" native sodium carbonate, not potassium nitrate (saltpetre), the present meaning. Pliny (31. 6) mentions the various kinds and their uses.

καὶ τῆς Ἐλεφαντίνης. μυθεύουσι γὰρ δή, διότι ἡ Ἶσις κατὰ πολλοὺς τόπους κατὰ γῆς θείη σοροὺς τοῦ Ὀσίριδος (μία δὲ τούτων ἦν ἔχουσα τὸν Ὄσιριν, ἀφανὴς πᾶσι), τοῦτο δὲ πράξειε λαθεῖν βουλομένη τὸν Τυφῶνα, μὴ ἐπελθὼν ἐκρίψειε τὸ σῶμα τῆς θήκης.

24. Ἀπὸ μὲν δὴ τῆς Ἀλεξανδρείας ἐπὶ τὴν τοῦ Δέλτα κορυφὴν αὕτη ἡ περιήγησις, φησὶ δ' ὁ Ἀρτεμίδωρος σχοίνων ὀκτὼ καὶ εἴκοσι τὸν ἀνά-
C 804 πλουν, τοῦτο δ' εἶναι σταδίους ὀκτακοσίους τετταράκοντα, λογιζόμενος τριακονταστάδιον τὴν σχοῖνον· ἡμῖν μέντοι πλέουσιν ἄλλοτ' ἄλλῳ μέτρῳ χρώμενοι τῶν σχοίνων ἀπεδίδοσαν τὰ διαστήματα, ὥστε καὶ τετταράκοντα σταδίους καὶ ἔτι μείζους κατὰ τόπους ὁμολογεῖσθαι παρ' αὐτῶν. καὶ διότι παρὰ τοῖς Αἰγυπτίοις ἄστατόν ἐστι τὸ τῆς σχοίνου μέτρον, αὐτὸς ὁ Ἀρτεμί-δωρος ἐν τοῖς ἑξῆς δηλοῖ. ἀπὸ μὲν γὰρ Μέμφεως μέχρι Θηβαΐδος τὴν σχοῖνον ἑκάστην φησὶν εἶναι σταδίων ἑκατὸν εἴκοσιν, ἀπὸ δὲ τῆς Θηβαΐδος μέχρι Συήνης ἑξήκοντα, ἀπὸ δὲ Πηλουσίου πρὸς τὴν αὐτὴν ἀναπλέουσι κορυφὴν σχοίνους μὲν πέντε καὶ εἴκοσί φησι, σταδίους δὲ ἑπτακοσίους πεντήκοντα, τῷ αὐτῷ μέτρῳ χρησάμενος. πρώτην δ' ἐκ τοῦ Πηλουσίου προελθοῦσιν εἶναι διώρυγα τὴν πληροῦσαν τὰς κατὰ τὰ ἕλη καλουμένας λίμνας, αἳ δύο μέν εἰσιν, ἐν ἀριστερᾷ δὲ κεῖνται τοῦ μεγάλου ποταμοῦ ὑπὲρ τὸ Πηλούσιον ἐν τῇ Ἀραβίᾳ· καὶ ἄλλας δὲ λέγει λίμνας καὶ διώρυγας

---

¹ So Diodorus Siculus (1. 22. 3).

is situated above Syenê and Elephantinê;[1] for they tell the mythical story, namely, that Isis[2] placed coffins of Osiris beneath the earth in several places (but only one of them, and that unknown to all, contained the body of Osiris), and that she did this because she wished to hide the body from Typhon,[3] fearing that he might find it and cast it out of its tomb.

24. Now this is the full description of the country from Alexandria to the vertex of the Delta; and, according to Artemidorus, the voyage up the river is twenty-eight schoeni, that is, eight hundred and forty stadia, reckoning the schoenus at thirty stadia. When I made the voyage, however, they used different measures at different times when they gave the distances, so that even forty stadia, or still more, was the accepted measure of the schoenus, according to the place. That the measure of the schoenus among the Aegyptians is unstable is made clear by Artemidorus himself in his next statement; for from Memphis to Thebaïs each schoenus, he says, is one hundred and twenty stadia, and from Thebaïs to Syenê sixty, and, as one sails up from Pelusium to the same vertex of the Delta, the distance, he says, is twenty-five schoeni, that is, seven hundred and fifty stadia, using the same measure. The first canal, as one proceeds from Pelusium, he says, is the one which fills the Marsh-lakes, as they are called, which are two in number and lie on the left of the great river above Pelusium in Arabia; and he also speaks of

[2] This goddess was both sister and wife of Osiris.
[3] Typhon came to be identified with the Aegyptian god "Set" (brother of Osiris and Isis), who murdered Osiris.

ἐν τοῖς αὐτοῖς μέρεσιν ἔξω τοῦ Δέλτα. ἔστι δὲ
καὶ νομὸς Σεθρωίτης παρὰ τὴν ἑτέραν λίμνην· ἕνα
δὲ τῶν δέκα τῶν ἐν τῷ Δέλτα διαριθμεῖται καὶ
τοῦτον· εἰς δὲ τὰς αὐτὰς [1] λίμνας συμβάλλουσι
καὶ ἄλλαι δύο διώρυγες.

25. Ἄλλη δ' ἐστὶν ἐκδιδοῦσα εἰς τὴν Ἐρυθρὰν
καὶ τὸν Ἀράβιον κόλπον κατὰ [2] πόλιν Ἀρσινόην,
ἣν ἔνιοι Κλεοπατρίδα καλοῦσι. διαρρεῖ δὲ καὶ
διὰ τῶν πικρῶν καλουμένων λιμνῶν, αἳ πρότερον
μὲν ἦσαν πικραί, τμηθείσης δὲ τῆς διώρυγος τῆς
λεχθείσης μετεβάλοντο [3] τῇ κράσει τοῦ ποταμοῦ,
καὶ νῦν εἰσιν εὔοψοι, μεσταὶ δὲ καὶ τῶν λιμναίων
ὀρνέων. ἐτμήθη δὲ [4] ἡ διῶρυξ κατ' ἀρχὰς μὲν
ὑπὸ Σεσώστριος πρὸ τῶν Τρωικῶν· οἱ δὲ ὑπὸ
τοῦ Ψαμμιτίχου παιδός, ἀρξαμένου μόνον, εἶτ'
ἐκλιπόντος τὸν βίον· ὕστερον δὲ ὑπὸ Δαρείου τοῦ
πρώτου, διαδεξαμένου τὸ ἑξῆς ἔργον. καὶ οὗτος
δὲ δόξῃ ψευδεῖ πεισθεὶς ἀφῆκε τὸ ἔργον περὶ
συντέλειαν ἤδη· ἐπείσθη γὰρ μετεωροτέραν εἶναι
τὴν Ἐρυθρὰν θάλατταν τῆς Αἰγύπτου καί, εἰ
διακοπείη πᾶς ὁ μεταξὺ ἰσθμός, ἐπικλυσθήσεσθαι
τῇ θαλάττῃ τὴν Αἴγυπτον· οἱ μέντοι Πτολεμαϊκοὶ
βασιλεῖς διακόψαντες κλειστὸν ἐποίησαν τὸν
εὔριπον, ὥστε, ὅτε βούλοιντο, ἐκπλεῖν ἀκωλύτως
εἰς τὴν ἔξω θάλατταν καὶ εἰσπλεῖν πάλιν. εἴρηται

---

[1] τὰς αὐτάς Groskurd, for ταύτας τάς Ex, τοσαύτας other
MSS. So Kramer and later editors.
[2] κατά, Brequigny, for καί; so the editors.
[3] μετεβαλοντο, x and the editors, for μετεβάλοντο.
[4] D*h*i insert καί before ἡ.

---

[1] The others are named in §§ 18–20 above. Pliny (5. 9)
names still more.

other lakes and canals in the same regions outside the Delta. There is also the Sethroïte Nome by the second lake, although he counts this Nome too as one of the ten[1] in the Delta; and two other canals meet in the same lakes.

25. There is another canal which empties into the Red Sea and the Arabian Gulf near the city Arsinoê, a city which some call Cleopatris. It flows also through the Bitter Lakes, as they are called, which were indeed bitter in earlier times, but when the above-mentioned canal was cut they underwent a change because of the mixing with the river, and now are well supplied with fish and full also of aquatic birds. The canal was first cut by Sesostris before the Trojan War—though some say by the son of Psammitichus,[2] who only began the work and then died—and later by Dareius the First,[3] who succeeded to the next work done upon it. But he, too, having been persuaded by a false notion, abandoned the work when it was already near completion; for he was persuaded that the Red Sea was higher than Aegypt, and that if the intervening isthmus were cut all the way through, Aegypt would be inundated by the sea. The Ptolemaïc kings,[4] however, cut through it and made the strait a closed passage,[5] so that when they wished they could sail out without hindrance into the outer sea and sail in again. But I have

[2] *i.e.* by Necos (Diodorus Siculus 1. 33. 9), or Necho, who lost 120,000 men in the effort (Herodotus 2. 158).

[3] So Diodorus Siculus (1. 33. 9).

[4] "Ptolemy II" (Diodorus Siculus 1. 33. 11).

[5] "At the most advantageous place he built a cleverly contrived barrier" (Diodorus Siculus 1. 33. 11).

δὲ καὶ περὶ τῆς τῶν ὑδάτων ἐπιφανείας καὶ ἐν τοῖς πρώτοις ὑπομνήμασι.

26. Πλησίον δὲ τῆς Ἀρσινόης καὶ ἡ τῶν Ἡρώων ἐστὶ πόλις καὶ ἡ Κλεοπατρὶς ἐν τῷ μυχῷ τοῦ C 805 Ἀραβίου κόλπου τῷ πρὸς Αἴγυπτον καὶ λιμένες καὶ κατοικίαι διώρυγές τε¹ πλείους καὶ λίμναι πλησιάζουσαι τούτοις· ἐνταῦθα δ᾽ ἐστὶ καὶ ὁ Φαγρωριοπολίτης νομὸς καὶ πόλις Φαγρωριόπολις. ἡ δὲ ἀρχὴ τῆς διώρυγος τῆς ἐκδιδούσης εἰς τὴν Ἐρυθρὰν ἀπὸ κώμης ἄρχεται Φακούσσης, ᾗ συνεχής ἐστι καὶ ἡ Φίλωνος κώμη· πλάτος δ᾽ ἔχει πηχῶν ἑκατὸν ἡ διῶρυξ, βάθος δ᾽ ὅσον ἀρκεῖν μυριοφόρῳ νηί· οὗτοι δ᾽ οἱ τόποι πλησιάζουσι τῇ κορυφῇ τοῦ Δέλτα.

27. Αὐτοῦ δὲ καὶ ἡ Βούβαστος πόλις καὶ ὁ Βουβαστίτης νομός· καὶ ὑπὲρ αὐτὸν ὁ Ἡλιοπολίτης νομός. ἐνταῦθα δ᾽ ἐστὶν ἡ τοῦ Ἡλίου πόλις ἐπὶ χώματος ἀξιολόγου κειμένη, τὸ ἱερὸν ἔχουσα τοῦ Ἡλίου καὶ τὸν βοῦν τὸν Μνεῦιν ἐν σηκῷ τινι τρεφόμενον, ὃς παρ᾽ αὐτοῖς νενόμισται θεός, ὥσπερ καὶ ἐν Μέμφει ὁ Ἄπις. πρόκεινται δὲ τοῦ χώματος λίμναι, τὴν ἀνάχυσιν ἐκ τῆς πλησίον διώρυγος ἔχουσαι. νυνὶ μὲν οὖν ἐστι πανέρημος ἡ πόλις, τὸ ἱερὸν ἔχουσα τῷ Αἰγυπτίῳ τρόπῳ κατεσκευασμένον ἀρχαῖον, ἔχον πολλὰ τεκμήρια τῆς Καμβύσου μανίας καὶ ἱεροσυλίας, ὃς τὰ μὲν πυρί, τὰ δὲ σιδήρῳ διελωβᾶτο τῶν ἱερῶν, ἀκρωτηριάζων καὶ περικαίων, καθάπερ καὶ τοὺς ὀβελίσκους· ὧν δύο καὶ εἰς Ῥώμην ἐκομίσθησαν οἱ μὴ κεκακωμένοι τελέως, ἄλλοι δ᾽ εἰσὶ κἀκεῖ καὶ ἐν Θήβαις, τῇ νῦν Διοσπόλει, οἱ μὲν ἑστῶτες ἀκμὴν πυρίβρωτοι, οἱ δὲ καὶ κείμενοι.

¹ τε, Corais, for δέ; so the later editors.

already discussed the levels of the bodies of water in my first commentaries.[1]

26. Near Arsinoê one comes also to Heroönpolis and Cleopatris, in the recess of the Arabian Gulf towards Aegypt, and to harbours and settlements, and near there, to several canals and lakes. Here, too, is the Phagroriopolite Nome and the city Phagroriopolis. The canal which empties into the Red Sea begins at Phacussa, to which the Village of Philo is contiguous; the canal has a breadth of one hundred cubits and a depth sufficient for very large merchant-vessels; and these places are near the vertex of the Delta.

27. Here are both the city Bubastus and the Bubastite Nome; and above it is the Heliopolite Nome. In this Nome is Heliupolis, which is situated upon a noteworthy mound; it contains the temple of Helios, and the ox Mneuïs, which is kept in a kind of sanctuary and is regarded among the inhabitants as god, as is Apis in Memphis. In front of the mound are lakes, which receive the overflow from the neighbouring canal. The city is now entirely deserted; it contains the ancient temple constructed in the Aegyptian manner, which affords many evidences of the madness and sacrilege of Cambyses, who partly by fire and partly by iron sought to outrage the temples, mutilating them and burning them on every side, just as he did with the obelisks. Two of these, which were not completely spoiled, were brought to Rome, but others are either still there or at Thebes, the present Diospolis— some still standing, thoroughly eaten by the fire, and others lying on the ground.

[1] 1. 1. 20 and 1. 3. 8 ff.

28. Τῆς δὲ κατασκευῆς τῶν ἱερῶν ἡ διάθεσις τοιαύτη· κατὰ τὴν εἰσβολὴν τὴν εἰς τὸ τέμενος λιθόστρωτόν ἐστιν ἔδαφος, πλάτος μὲν ὅσον πλεθριαῖον ἢ καὶ ἔλαττον, μῆκος δὲ καὶ τριπλάσιον καὶ τετραπλάσιον, ἔστιν ὅπου καὶ μεῖζον· καλεῖται δὲ τοῦτο δρόμος, καθάπερ Καλλίμαχος εἴρηκεν·

ὁ δρόμος ἱερὸς οὗτος Ἀνούβιδος.

διὰ δὲ τοῦ μήκους παντὸς ἑξῆς ἐφ' ἑκάτερα τοῦ πλάτους σφίγγες ἵδρυνται λίθιναι, πήχει εἴκοσιν ἢ μικρῷ πλείους ἀπ' ἀλλήλων διέχουσαι, ὥσθ' ἕνα μὲν ἐκ δεξιῶν εἶναι στίχον τῶν σφιγγῶν, ἕνα δ' ἐξ εὐωνύμων· μετὰ δὲ τὰς σφίγγας πρόπυλον μέγα, εἶτ' ἄλλο προελθόντι πρόπυλον, εἶτ' ἄλλο· οὐκ ἔστι δὲ διωρισμένος ἀριθμὸς οὔτε τῶν προπύλων οὔτε τῶν σφιγγῶν, ἄλλα δ' ἐν ἄλλοις ἱεροῖς, ὥσπερ καὶ τὰ μήκη καὶ τὰ πλάτη τῶν δρόμων. μετὰ δὲ τὰ προπύλαια ὁ νεὼς πρόναον ἔχων μέγα καὶ ἀξιόλογον, τὸν δὲ σηκὸν σύμμετρον, ξόανον δ' οὐδέν, ἢ οὐκ ἀνθρωπόμορφον, ἀλλὰ τῶν ἀλόγων ζῴων τινός· τοῦ δὲ προνάου παρ' ἑκάτερον πρόκειται τὰ λεγόμενα[1] πτερά· ἔστι δὲ ταῦτα ἰσουψῆ τῷ νεῷ τείχη δύο, κατ' C 806 ἀρχὰς μὲν ἀφεστῶτα ἀπ' ἀλλήλων μικρὸν[2] πλέον ἢ τὸ πλάτος ἐστὶ τῆς κρηπῖδος τοῦ νεώ, ἔπειτ' εἰς τὸ πρόσθεν προϊόντι κατ' ἐπινευούσας[3] γραμ-

---

[1] Instead of λεγόμενα C reads μεγάλα.   [2] μικρῷ Dz.
[3] ἐπινευούσας, Corais and Groskurd emend to ἀπονευούσας.

---

[1] Strabo means the Aegyptian temples in general.
[2] A sketch of the plan may be found in Tozer's *Selections*, p. 356 ; but cp. the sketch of the pronaos in the Corais-Latronne edition.

28. The plan of the construction of the temples [1] is as follows: [2] at the entrance into the sacred precinct there is a floor paved with stones, with a breadth of about a plethrum, or less, and a length either three or four times as great, or in some cases more; and this is called the dromus, [3] as Callimachus states: "This is the dromus, sacred to Anubis." [4] Throughout its whole length are stone sphinxes placed in order on each of its two sides, at a distance from one another of twenty cubits or a little more, so that one row of the sphinxes is on the right and one row on the left. And after the sphinxes one comes to a large propylum, [5] and then, as one proceeds, another, and then another; but there is no prescribed number either of propyla or of sphinxes, and they are different in different temples, as are also the lengths and the breadths of the dromi. After the propylaea one comes to the naos, [6] which has a large and noteworthy pronaos, [7] and to a sanctuary of commensurate size, though it has no statue, or rather no statue of human form, but only of some irrational animal. On either side of the pronaos project the wings, as they are called. These are two walls equal in height to the naos, which are at first distant from one another a little more than the breadth of the foundation of the naos, and then, as one proceeds onward, follow

[3] Literally, "course" or "run."
[4] The Aegyptian Anpu, worshipped as "Lord of the Grave."
[5] Literally, "Front Gate"; but, like the Propylaea on the Acropolis at Athens, the propylum was a considerable building forming a gateway to the temple.
[6] *i.e.* the temple proper.
[7] *i.e.* front hall-room.

μὰς μέχρι πηχῶν πεντήκοντα ἢ ἑξήκοντα· ἀναγ-
λυφὰς δ' ἔχουσιν οἱ τοῖχοι οὗτοι μεγάλων εἰδώλων,
ὁμοίων τοῖς Τυρρηνικοῖς καὶ τοῖς ἀρχαίοις σφόδρα
τῶν παρὰ τοῖς Ἕλλησι δημιουργημάτων. ἔστι
δέ τις καὶ πολύστυλος οἶκος, καθάπερ ἐν Μέμφει,
βαρβαρικὴν ἔχων τὴν κατασκευήν· πλὴν γὰρ τοῦ
μεγάλων εἶναι καὶ πολλῶν καὶ πολυστίχων τῶν
στύλων¹ οὐδὲν ἔχει χαρίεν οὐδὲ γραφικόν, ἀλλὰ
ματαιοπονίαν ἐμφαίνει μᾶλλον.

29. Ἐν δὲ τῇ Ἡλίου πόλει καὶ οἴκους εἴδομεν
μεγάλους, ἐν οἷς διέτριβον οἱ ἱερεῖς· μάλιστα γὰρ
δὴ ταύτην κατοικίαν ἱερέων γεγονέναι φασὶ τὸ
παλαιόν, φιλοσόφων ἀνδρῶν καὶ ἀστρονομικῶν·
ἐκλέλοιπε δὲ καὶ τοῦτο νυνὶ τὸ σύστημα καὶ ἡ
ἄσκησις. ἐκεῖ μὲν οὖν οὐδεὶς ἡμῖν ἐδείκνυτο τῆς
τοιαύτης ἀσκήσεως προεστώς, ἀλλ' οἱ ἱεροποιοὶ
μόνον καὶ ἐξηγηταὶ τοῖς ξένοις τῶν περὶ τὰ ἱερά.
παρηκολούθει δέ τις ἐξ Ἀλεξανδρείας ἀναπλέοντι
εἰς τὴν Αἴγυπτον Αἰλίῳ Γάλλῳ τῷ ἡγεμόνι
Χαιρήμων τοὔνομα, προσποιούμενος τοιαύτην τινὰ
ἐπιστήμην, γελώμενος δὲ τὸ πλέον ὡς ἀλαζὼν
καὶ ἰδιώτης. ἐκεῖ δ' οὖν ἐδείκνυντο οἵ τε τῶν
ἱερέων οἶκοι καὶ Πλάτωνος καὶ Εὐδόξου διατριβαί·
συνανέβη γὰρ δὴ τῷ Πλάτωνι ὁ Εὔδοξος δεῦρο
καὶ συνδιέτριψαν τοῖς ἱερεῦσιν ἐνταῦθα ἐκεῖνοι
τρισκαίδεκα ἔτη, ὡς εἴρηταί τισι· περιττοὺς γὰρ
ὄντας κατὰ τὴν ἐπιστήμην τῶν οὐρανίων, μυστι-

¹ moz change all these genitives to accusatives; so Corais.

¹ i.e. in the Etruscan tombs.
² Hardly Chaeremon the Alexandrian philosopher and
historian, as some think. Aelius Gallus made the voyage

converging lines as far as fifty or sixty cubits ; and these walls have figures of large images cut in low relief, like the Tyrrhenian[1] images and the very old works of art among the Greeks. There is also a kind of hall with numerous columns (as at Memphis, for example), which is constructed in the barbaric manner ; for, except for the fact that the columns are large and numerous and form many rows, the hall has nothing pleasing or picturesque, but is rather a display of vain toil.

29. In Heliupolis I also saw large houses in which the priests lived ; for it is said that this place in particular was in ancient times a settlement of priests who studied philosophy and astronomy ; but both this organisation and its pursuits have now disappeared. At Heliupolis, in fact, no one was pointed out to me as presiding over such pursuits, but only those who performed the sacrifices and explained to strangers what pertained to the sacred rites. When Aelius Gallus the praefect sailed up into Aegypt, he was accompanied by a certain man from Alexandria, Chaeremon[2] by name, who pretended to some knowledge of this kind, but was generally ridiculed as a boaster and ignoramus. However, at Heliupolis the houses of the priests and schools of Plato and Eudoxus were pointed out to us ; for Eudoxus went up to that place with Plato, and they both passed thirteen years[3] with the priests, as is stated by some writers ; for since these priests excelled in their knowledge of the heavenly bodies,

about 25 B.C., but that Chaeremon was a tutor of Nero after A.D. 49.

[3] The Epitome reads "three years," and Diogenes Laertius (8. 87) "sixteen months."

κοὺς δὲ καὶ δυσμεταδότους, τῷ χρόνῳ καὶ ταῖς
θεραπείαις ἐξελιπάρησαν, ὥστε τινὰ τῶν θεωρη-
μάτων ἱστορῆσαι· τὰ πολλὰ δὲ ἀπεκρύψαντο οἱ
βάρβαροι. οὗτοι δὲ τὰ ἐπιτρέχοντα τῆς ἡμέρας
καὶ τῆς νυκτὸς μόρια ταῖς τριακοσίαις ἑξήκοντα
πέντε ἡμέραις εἰς τὴν ἐκπλήρωσιν τοῦ ἐνιαυσίου
χρόνου παρέδοσαν. ἀλλ᾽ ἠγνοεῖτο τέως ὁ ἐνιαυ-
τὸς παρὰ τοῖς Ἕλλησιν, ὡς καὶ ἄλλα πλείω,
ἕως οἱ νεώτεροι ἀστρολόγοι παρέλαβον παρὰ
τῶν μεθερμηνευσάντων εἰς τὸ Ἑλληνικὸν τὰ τῶν
ἱερέων ὑπομνήματα· καὶ ἔτι νῦν παραλαμβάν-
ουσι τὰ ἀπ᾽ ἐκείνων, ὁμοίως καὶ τὰ τῶν Χαλδαίων.

30. Ἐντεῦθεν δὴ[1] ὁ Νεῖλός ἐστιν ὁ ὑπὲρ τοῦ
Δέλτα· τούτου δὴ τὰ μὲν δεξιὰ καλοῦσι Λιβύην
ἀναπλέοντι, ὥσπερ καὶ τὰ περὶ τὴν Ἀλεξάνδρειαν καὶ τὴν Μαρεῶτιν, τὰ δ᾽ ἐν ἀριστερᾷ
Ἀραβίαν. ἡ μὲν οὖν Ἡλίου πόλις ἐν τῇ Ἀραβίᾳ
ἐστίν, ἐν δὲ τῇ Λιβύῃ Κερκέσουρα πόλις κατὰ
C 807 τὰς Εὐδόξου κειμένη σκοπάς· δείκνυται γὰρ
σκοπή τις πρὸ τῆς Ἡλίου πόλεως, καθάπερ καὶ
πρὸ τῆς Κνίδου, πρὸς ἣν ἐσημειοῦτο ἐκεῖνος τῶν
οὐρανίων τινὰς κινήσεις· ὁ δὲ νομὸς Λητοπολίτης
οὗτος. ἀναπλεύσαντι δ᾽ ἐστὶ Βαβυλών, φρούριον
ἐρυμνόν, ἀποστάντων ἐνταῦθα Βαβυλωνίων τινῶν,

---

[1] Instead of δή, Dh read δέ.

---

[1] As stated in § 46 (below), they divided the year into
twelve months of thirty days each, and at the end of the

albeit secretive and slow to impart it, Plato and
Eudoxus prevailed upon them in time and by
courting their favour to let them learn some of
the principles of their doctrines; but the barbarians
concealed most things. However, these men did
teach them the fractions of the day and the night
which, running over and above the three hundred
and sixty-five days, fill out the time of the true
year.[1] But at that time the true year was unknown
among the Greeks, as also many other things, until
the later astrologers learned them from the men
who had translated into Greek the records of the
priests; and even to this day they learn their
teachings, and likewise those of the Chaldaeans.

30. From Heliupolis, then, one comes to the Nile
above the Delta. Of this, the parts on the right, as
one sails up, are called Libya, as also the parts
round Alexandria and Lake Mareotis, whereas
those on the left are called Arabia. Now Heliupolis is in Arabia, but the city Cercesura, which
lies near the observatories of Eudoxus, is in Libya;
for a kind of watch-tower is to be seen in front of
Heliupolis, as also in front of Cnidus, with reference
to which Eudoxus would note down his observations
of certain movements of the heavenly bodies. Here
the Nome is the Letopolite. And, having sailed
farther up the river, one comes to Babylon, a stronghold, where some Babylonians had withdrawn in
revolt and then successfully negotiated for permission

---

twelve months added five days (so Herodotus 2. 4), and then
at the end of every fourth year added another day. Diodorus
Siculus (1. 50), however, puts it thus : "They add five and
one-fourth days to the twelve months and in this way complete
the annual period."

85

εἶτα διαπραξαμένων ἐνταῦθα κατοικίαν παρὰ τῶν
βασιλέων· νυνὶ δ᾽ ἐστὶ στρατόπεδον ἑνὸς τῶν
τριῶν ταγμάτων τῶν φρουρούντων τὴν Αἴγυπτον.
ῥάχις δ᾽ ἐστὶν ἀπὸ τοῦ στρατοπέδου καὶ μέχρι
Νείλου καθήκουσα, δι᾽ ἧς ἀπὸ τοῦ ποταμοῦ
τροχοὶ καὶ κοχλίαι τὸ ὕδωρ ἀνάγουσιν, ἀνδρῶν
ἑκατὸν πεντήκοντα ἐργαζομένων δεσμίων· ἀφ-
ορῶνται δ᾽ ἐνθένδε τηλαυγῶς αἱ πυραμίδες ἐν τῇ
περαίᾳ ἐν Μέμφει καί εἰσι πλησίον.

31. Ἐγγὺς δὲ καὶ ἡ Μέμφις αὐτή, τὸ βασίλειον
τῶν Αἰγυπτίων· ἔστι γὰρ ἀπὸ τοῦ Δέλτα τρίσχοι-
νον εἰς αὐτήν. ἔχει δὲ ἱερά, τό τε τοῦ Ἄπιδος,
ὅς ἐστιν ὁ αὐτὸς καὶ Ὄσιρις, ὅπου ὁ βοῦς ὁ
Ἄπις ἐν σηκῷ τινι τρέφεται, θεός, ὡς ἔφην,
νομιζόμενος, διάλευκος τὸ μέτωπον καὶ ἄλλα τινὰ
μικρὰ τοῦ σώματος, τἆλλα δὲ μέλας· οἷς ση-
μείοις ἀεὶ κρίνουσι τὸν ἐπιτήδειον εἰς τὴν δια-
δοχήν, ἀπογενομένου τοῦ τὴν τιμὴν ἔχοντος.
ἔστι δ᾽ αὐλὴ προκειμένη τοῦ σηκοῦ, ἐν ᾗ καὶ
ἄλλος σηκὸς τῆς μητρὸς τοῦ βοός· εἰς ταύτην
δὲ τὴν αὐλὴν ἐξαφιᾶσι τὸν Ἄπιν καθ᾽ ὥραν τινά,
καὶ μάλιστα πρὸς ἐπίδειξιν τοῖς ξένοις· ὁρῶσι
μὲν γὰρ καὶ διὰ θυρίδος ἐν τῷ σηκῷ, βούλονται
δὲ καὶ ἔξω· ἀποσκιρτήσαντα δ᾽ ἐν αὐτῇ μικρὰ
ἀναλαμβάνουσι πάλιν εἰς τὴν οἰκείαν στάσιν.

---

[1] Strabo's statement is too concise to be clear. He refers
to certain Babylonian captives who, being unable to endure
the hard work imposed upon them *in Aegypt*, revolted from
the king, seized the stronghold along the river, and gained
the concession in question after a successful war (Diodorus
Siculus, 1. 56. 3).

[2] *i.e.* to Babylon.

[3] The pyramids of Gizeh, described by Herodotus (2. 124 ff.)
and Pliny (36. 16).

from the kings to build a settlement;[1] but now it is
an encampment of one of the three legions that
guard Aegypt. There is a ridge extending from
the encampment even as far as the Nile, on which
the water is conducted up from the river [2] by wheels
and screws; and one hundred and fifty prisoners are
employed in the work; and from here one can
clearly see the pyramids[3] on the far side of the
river at Memphis, and they are near to it.[4]

31. Memphis itself, the royal residence of the
Aegyptians, is also near Babylon; for the distance
to it from the Delta is only three schoeni.[5] It
contains temples, one of which is that of Apis, who
is the same as Osiris; it is here that the bull Apis is
kept in a kind of sanctuary, being regarded, as I
have said, as god; his forehead and certain other
small parts of his body are marked with white, but
the other parts are black;[6] and it is by these marks
that they always choose the bull suitable for the
succession, when the one that holds the honour has
died. In front of the sanctuary is situated a court,
in which there is another sanctuary belonging to the
bull's mother. Into this court they set Apis loose at
a certain hour, particularly that he may be shown to
foreigners; for although people can see him through
the window in the sanctuary, they wish to see him
outside also; but when he has finished a short bout
of skipping in the court they take him back again to
his familiar stall.

---

[4] According to Pliny (36. 16) the pyramids were seven and
one-half miles (*i.e.* sixty stadia) from Memphis.

[5] On the "schoenus," see 17. 1. 24.

[6] "He is black, and has on his forehead a triangular white
spot and on his back the likeness of an eagle" (Herodotus
3. 28). Pliny (8. 71) says, "a crescent-like white spot on
the right side."

Τό τε δὴ τοῦ Ἄπιδός ἐστιν ἱερόν, παρακείμενον
τῷ Ἡφαιστείῳ, καὶ αὐτὸ τὸ Ἡφαίστειον πολυ-
τελῶς κατεσκευασμένον ναοῦ τε μεγέθει καὶ τοῖς
ἄλλοις. πρόκειται δ' ἐν τῷ δρόμῳ καὶ μονόλιθος
κολοσσός· ἔθος δ' ἐστὶν ἐν τῷ δρόμῳ τούτῳ
ταύρων ἀγῶνας συντελεῖσθαι πρὸς ἀλλήλους, οὓς
ἐπίτηδες τρέφουσί τινες, ὥσπερ οἱ ἱπποτρόφοι·
συμβάλλουσι γὰρ εἰς μάχην ἀφέντες, ὁ δὲ κρείτ-
των νομισθεὶς ἄθλου τυγχάνει. ἔστι δ' ἐν Μέμφει
καὶ Ἀφροδίτης ἱερόν, θεᾶς Ἑλληνίδος νομιζομένης·
τινὲς δὲ Σελήνης¹ ἱερὸν εἶναί φασιν.

32. Ἔστι δὲ καὶ Σαράπιον ἐν ἀμμώδει τόπῳ
σφόδρα, ὥσθ' ὑπ' ἀνέμων θῖνας ἄμμων σωρεύεσ-
θαι, ὑφ' ὧν αἱ σφίγγες αἱ μὲν καὶ μέχρι κεφαλῆς
ἑωρῶντο ὑφ' ἡμῶν κατακεχωσμέναι, αἱ δ' ἡμιφα-
νεῖς· ἐξ ὧν εἰκάζειν παρῆν τὸν κίνδυνον, εἰ τῷ
βαδίζοντι πρὸς τὸ ἱερὸν λαῖλαψ ἐπιπέσοι. πόλις
δ' ἐστὶ μεγάλη τε καὶ εὔανδρος,² δευτέρα μετὰ
Ἀλεξάνδρειαν, μιγάδων ἀνδρῶν, καθάπερ καὶ τῶν
ἐκεῖ συνῳκισμένων. πρόκεινται δὲ καὶ λίμναι
τῆς πόλεως καὶ τῶν βασιλείων, ἃ νῦν μὲν κατέ-
C 808 σπασται καί ἐστιν ἔρημα, ἵδρυται δ' ἐφ' ὕψους
καθήκοντα μέχρι τοῦ κάτω τῆς πόλεως ἐδάφους·
συνάπτει δ' ἄλσος αὐτῷ καὶ λίμνη.

33. Τετταράκοντα δ' ἀπὸ τῆς πόλεως σταδίους

¹ For Σελήνης, Nolt conj. Ἑλένης, citing Herod. 2. 112.
² εὔδενδρος E.

---

¹ Diodorus Siculus refers to "images made of one stone,
both of himself (Sesostris) and of his wife, thirty cubits high,
and of his sons, twenty cubits, in the temple of Hephaestus
at Memphis."

There is here, then, not only the temple of Apis, which lies near the Hephaesteium, but also the Hephaesteium itself, which is a costly structure both in the size of its naos and in all other respects. In front, in the dromus, stands also a colossus made of one stone ;[1] and it is the custom to hold bull-fights in this dromus, and certain men breed these bulls for the purpose, like horse-breeders ; for the bulls are set loose and join in combat, and the one that is regarded as victor gets a prize. And at Memphis there is also a temple of Aphroditê, who is considered to be a Greek goddess,[2] though some say that it is a temple of Selenê.[3]

32. There is also a Sarapium at Memphis, in a place so very sandy that dunes of sand are heaped up by the winds ; and by these some of the sphinxes which I saw were buried even to the head and others were only half-visible ; from which one might guess the danger if a sand-storm should fall upon a man travelling on foot towards the temple. The city is both large and populous, ranks second after Alexandria, and consists of mixed races of people, like those who have settled together at Alexandria. There are lakes situated in front of the city and the palaces, which latter, though now in ruins and deserted, are situated on a height and extend down to the ground of the city below ; and adjoining the city are a grove and a lake.

33. On proceeding forty stadia from the city, one

[2] Herodotus (2. 112) refers to the temple of the " Foreign Aphroditê" at Memphis and identifies her with Helen ; but see Rawlinson (Vol. II, p. 157, footnote 9), who very plausibly identifies her with Astarte, the Phoenician and Syrian Aphroditê.
[3] Goddess of the Moon.

προελθόντι ὀρεινή τις ὀφρύς ἐστιν, ἐφ᾽ ᾗ πολλαὶ
μέν εἰσι πυραμίδες, τάφοι τῶν βασιλέων, τρεῖς
δ᾽ ἀξιόλογοι· τὰς δὲ δύο τούτων καὶ ἐν τοῖς ἑπτὰ
θεάμασι καταριθμοῦνται· εἰσὶ γὰρ σταδιαῖαι τὸ
ὕψος, τετράγωνοι τῷ σχήματι, τῆς πλευρᾶς
ἑκάστης μικρῷ μεῖζον τὸ ὕψος ἔχουσαι· μικρῷ
δὲ καὶ ἡ ἑτέρα τῆς ἑτέρας ἐστὶ μείζων· ἔχει δ᾽
ἐν ὕψει μέσως πως [1] τῶν πλευρῶν λίθον ἐξαιρέ-
σιμον· ἀρθέντος δὲ σύριγξ ἐστὶ σκολιὰ μέχρι τῆς

---

[1] Letronne conj. μιᾶς after πως; Groskurd, Meineke and
others so read.

---

[1] Cheops.   [2] Khafra.
[3] *i.e.* "high up, approximately midway" (*horizontally*)
"between the sides" (the *two* sides of the triangle which
forms the northern face of the pyramid. This is the meaning of the Greek text as it stands; but all editors (from
Casaubon down), translators, and archæologists, so far as the
present translator knows, either emend the text or mis-
interpret it, or both (see critical note). Letronne (French
translation), who is followed by the later translators, insists
upon "moderately" as the meaning of μέσως πως (translated
above by "approximately midway between"), and errone-
ously quotes, as a similar use of μέσως πως, 11. 2. 18, where
there is no MS. authority for πως, and translates: "Elle
a sur ses côtés, et à une élévation médiocre, une pierre qui
peut s'ôter." The subsequent editors insert μιᾶς ("one")
before τῶν πλευρῶν ("the sides"); and, following them, even
Sir W. M. Flinders Petrie in his monumental work (*The
Pyramids and Temples of Gizeh*, p. 168) translates: "The
Greater (Pyramid), a little way up one side, has a stone that
may be taken out." These interpretations accord with what
are known facts; but so does the present interpretation,
which also brings out two additional facts of importance:
(1) It was hardly necessary for Strabo to state the obvious
fact that the stone door was "*moderately* high up one side"
of the pyramid (originally "about 55 feet vertically or 71
feet on the slope," according to a private letter from Petrie,

comes to a kind of mountain-brow; on it are numerous pyramids, the tombs of kings, of which three are noteworthy; and two of these are even numbered among the Seven Wonders of the World, for they are a stadium in height, are quadrangular in shape, and their height is a little greater than the length of each of the sides; and one [1] of them is only a little larger than the other.[2] High up, approximately midway between the sides, it has a movable stone,[3] and when this is raised up there is a sloping

dated Sept. 16, 1930), as compared with the height of the vertex (nearly 500 feet), or that the one door was on *one* side of the pyramid. What he means to say is that the door was *literally* high up as compared with the convenient position of an entrance close to the ground, knowing, as he did, that the Aegyptians chose a high position for it in order to keep secret the passage to the royal tombs ; and, through his not unusual conciseness in such cases, he leaves the fact to be inferred. The wisdom of that secrecy is disclosed by the fact that when the Arabs, ignorant of the doorway, wished to enter the pyramid, they forced their way into it from a point near the ground through 100 feet of solid masonry, and thus by chance met the original sloping passage and discovered the original doorway. Moreover, this "movable stone," which was either a flap-door that worked on a stone pivot (Petrie, *l.c.*) or a flat slab that was easily tilted up (Borchardt, *Aegyptische Zeitschrift*, XXXV. 87), must have fitted so nicely when closed that no one unfamiliar with it could distinguish it. (2) "The sides" here must refer to the north-west and north-east *edges* of the pyramid, not to its *northern face*—much less *all four faces*— just as "sides" in the preceding sentence must mean the four sides of the base, not its plane surface. Hence, Strabo means that the doorway was purposely placed to *one side of* ("actually 24 feet," again according to Petrie's letter), and not *at*, a central point between the two edges above-mentioned, which is the fact in the case—a most important part of the ruse, as was later evidenced by the fact that the Arabs began to force their way into the pyramid at the centre (see the "Horizontal Section of the Great Pyramid"

θήκης. αὗται μὲν οὖν ἐγγὺς ἀλλήλων εἰσὶ [1] τῷ
αὐτῷ ἐπιπέδῳ· ἀπωτέρω δ᾽ ἐστὶν ἐν ὕψει μείζονι [2]
τῆς ὀρεινῆς ἡ τρίτη πολὺ ἐλάττων τῶν δυεῖν,
πολὺ δὲ μείζονος δαπάνης κατεσκευασμένη· ἀπὸ
γὰρ θεμελίων μέχρι μέσου σχεδόν τι μέλανος
λίθου ἐστίν, ἐξ οὗ καὶ τὰς θυΐας κατασκευάζουσι,
κομίζοντες πόρρωθεν· ἀπὸ γὰρ τῶν τῆς Αἰθιοπίας
ὀρῶν, καὶ τῷ σκληρὸς εἶναι καὶ δυσκατέργαστος
πολυτελῆ τὴν πραγματείαν παρέσχε. λέγεται δὲ
τῆς ἑταίρας τάφος γεγονὼς ὑπὸ τῶν ἐραστῶν, ἣν
Σαπφὼ μέν, ἡ τῶν μελῶν ποιήτρια, καλεῖ Δωρίχαν,
ἐρωμένην τοῦ ἀδελφοῦ αὐτῆς Χαράξου γεγονυῖαν,
οἶνον κατάγοντος εἰς Ναύκρατιν Λέσβιον κατ᾽
ἐμπορίαν, ἄλλοι δ᾽ ὀνομάζουσι Ῥοδῶπιν· [3] μυθεύουσι δ᾽, ὅτι, λουομένης αὐτῆς, ἐν τῶν ὑποδη-
μάτων αὐτῆς ἁρπάσας ἀετὸς παρὰ τῆς θερα-
παίνης κομίσειεν εἰς Μέμφιν καί, τοῦ βασιλέως
δικαιοδοτοῦντος ὑπαιθρίου,[4] γενόμενος κατὰ κορυφὴν αὐτοῦ ῥίψειε τὸ ὑπόδημα εἰς τὸν κόλπον·

---

[1] ἐπί, before τῷ, Meineke inserts, following Kramer ; ἐν,
Corais.
[2] μείζονι *moxz*, μείζων other MSS.
[3] Ῥοδῶπιν, Corais, for Ῥόδοπιν EF, Ῥοδόπην other MSS.
[4] ὑπαιθρίου, Kramer ; ἐν ὑπαίθρῳ *x*, ὑπαίθριος other MSS.

---

in Richard A. Proctor's *The Great Pyramid*, opposite p. 138).
In short (1) μέσως πως cannot mean "moderately" in a
matter of measurement (if indeed it ever means the same as
μετρίως) and naturally goes with τῶν πλευρῶν, not ἐν ὕψει ;
and in fact some interpreters utterly ignore the πως. (2)
The insertion of μιᾶς is not only unnecessary but eliminates
two important observations.

[1] This passage " sloped steeply down through masonry and
solid rock for 318 feet," passing through an unfinished vault

passage to the vault.[1] Now these pyramids are near one another and on the same level; but farther on, at a greater height of the hill, is the third, which is much smaller than the two, though constructed at much greater expense; for from the foundations almost to the middle it is made of black stone, the stone from which mortars are made, being brought from a great distance, for it is brought from the mountains of Aethiopia; and because of its being hard and difficult to work into shape it rendered the undertaking very expensive. It is called "Tomb of the Courtesan," having been built by her lovers—the courtesan whom Sappho[2] the Melic poetess calls Doricha, the beloved of Sappho's brother Charaxus, who was engaged in transporting Lesbian wine to Naucratis for sale,[3] but others give her the name Rhodopis.[4] They tell the fabulous story that, when she was bathing, an eagle snatched one of her sandals from her maid and carried it to Memphis; and while the king was administering justice in the open air, the eagle, when it arrived above his head, flung the sandal into

(subterranean chamber) "46 feet long, 27 feet wide, and 10.6 feet high," and "ended in a cul-de-sac," being "intended to mislead possible riflers of the" royal "tomb" above (Knight, *l.c.*). Petrie's translation of μέχρι τῆς θήκης ("to the very foundations," instead of "to the vault") is at least misleading. In the very next sentence Strabo refers to the "foundations" (θεμελίων). Since Strabo fails to mention the vaults of the king and the queen high above, the natural inference might be that he regarded the subterranean vault as the actual royal tomb; and in that case one might assume that the tombs were rifled, not by Augustus, but before his time, perhaps by the Persians.

[2] *Frag.* 138 (Bergk) and *Lyra Graeca*, L.C.L., Vol. I, p. 207 (Edmunds).

[3] So Athenaeus, 13. 68.

[4] See Herodotus 2. 134–135.

ὁ δὲ καὶ τῷ ῥυθμῷ τοῦ ὑποδήματος καὶ τῷ
παραδόξῳ κινηθεὶς περιπέμψειεν εἰς τὴν χώραν
κατὰ ζήτησιν τῆς φορούσης ἀνθρώπου τοῦτο·
εὑρεθεῖσα δ' ἐν τῇ πόλει τῶν Ναυκρατιτῶν
ἀναχθείη καὶ γένοιτο γυνὴ τοῦ βασιλέως, τελευ-
τήσασα δὲ τοῦ λεχθέντος τύχοι τάφου.

34. Ἕν δέ τι τῶν ὁραθέντων ὑφ' ἡμῶν ἐν ταῖς
πυραμίσι παραδόξων οὐκ ἄξιον παραλιπεῖν. ἐκ
γὰρ τῆς λατύπης σωροί τινες πρὸ τῶν πυραμίδων
κεῖνται· ἐν τούτοις δ' εὑρίσκεται ψήγματα καὶ
τύπῳ καὶ μεγέθει φακοειδῆ· ἐνίοις δὲ καὶ ὡς ἂν
πτίσμα οἷον ἡμιλεπίστων ὑποτρέχει·[1] φασὶ δ'
ἀπολιθωθῆναι λείψανα τῆς τῶν ἐργαζομένων
τροφῆς· οὐκ ἀπέοικε[2] δέ· καὶ γὰρ οἴκοι παρ'
ἡμῖν λόφος ἐστὶν ἐν πεδίῳ παραμήκης, οὗτος δ'
ἐστὶ μεστὸς ψήφων φακοειδῶν λίθου πωρείας·[3] καὶ
αἱ θαλάττιαι δὲ καὶ αἱ ποτάμιαι ψῆφοι σχεδόν τι
τὴν αὐτὴν ἀπορίαν ὑπογράφουσιν· ἀλλ' αὗται μὲν
C 809 ἐν τῇ κινήσει τῇ διὰ τοῦ ῥεύματος εὑρεσιλογίαν
τινὰ ἔχουσιν, ἐκεῖ δ' ἀπορωτέρα ἡ σκέψις.
εἴρηται δ' ἐν ἄλλοις καὶ διότι περὶ τὸ μέταλλον
τῶν λίθων, ἐξ ὧν αἱ πυραμίδες γεγόνασιν, ἐν
ὄψει[4] ταῖς πυραμίσιν ὂν πέραν ἐν τῇ Ἀραβίᾳ,
Τρωικόν τι καλεῖται πετρῶδες ἱκανῶς ὄρος καὶ
σπήλαια ὑπ' αὐτῷ καὶ κώμη πλησίον καὶ τούτοις καὶ τῷ ποταμῷ, Τροία καλουμένη, κατοικία

---

[1] ἐπιτρέχει s, Corais following.
[2] For ἀπέοικε Letronne conj. ἐπέοικε.
[3] πωρείας, Meineke, for πορίας DEF, πωρίας other MSS.;
πωρίνου Siebenkees and Groskurd.
[4] ὄψει, Corais, for ὄψει; so the later editors.

his lap; and the king, stirred both by the beautiful
shape of the sandal and by the strangeness of the
occurrence, sent men in all directions into the
country in quest of the woman who wore the sandal;
and when she was found in the city of Naucratis,
she was brought up to Memphis, became the wife of
the king, and when she died was honoured with the
above-mentioned tomb.

34. One of the marvellous things I saw at the
pyramids should not be omitted: there are heaps of
stone-chips lying in front of the pyramids; and among
these are found chips that are like lentils both in
form and size; and under some of the heaps lie win-
nowings, as it were, as of half-peeled grains. They
say that what was left of the food of the workmen
has petrified; and this is not improbable. Indeed, in
my home-country,[1] in a plain, there is a long hill
which is full of lentil-shaped pebbles of porous
stone;[2] and the pebbles both of the seas and of the
rivers present about the same puzzling question; but
while these latter find an explanation in the motion
caused by the current of water, the speculation in
that other case is more puzzling. It has been stated
elsewhere[3] that in the neighbourhood of the quarry
of the stones from which the pyramids are built,
which is in sight of the pyramids, on the far side of
the river in Arabia, there is a very rocky mountain
which is called "Trojan," and that there are caves
at the foot of it, and a village near both these and
the river which is called Troy, being an ancient settle-

[1] Strabo was born at Amaseia in Pontus (*Introduction*,
p. xiv).
[2] *i.e.* "tufa."
[3] Not in Strabo's *Geography*; perhaps in his *History* (see
Vol. I, p. 47, note 1).

παλαιὰ τῶν Μενελάῳ συγκατακολουθησάντων
αἰχμαλώτων Τρώων, καταμεινάντων δ᾽ αὐτόθι.

35. Μετὰ δὲ Μέμφιν Ἄκανθος πόλις ὁμοίως
ἐν τῇ Λιβύῃ καὶ τὸ τοῦ Ὀσίριδος ἱερὸν καὶ τὸ τῆς
ἀκάνθης ἄλσος τῆς Θηβαϊκῆς, ἐξ ἧς τὸ κόμμι.[3]
εἶθ᾽ ὁ Ἀφροδιτοπολίτης νομὸς καὶ ἡ ὁμώνυμος
πόλις ἐν τῇ Ἀραβίᾳ, ἐν ᾗ λευκὴ βοῦς ἱερὰ
τρέφεται. εἶθ᾽ ὁ Ἡρακλεώτης νομὸς ἐν νήσῳ
μεγάλῃ, καθ᾽ ἣν ἡ διῶρύξ ἐστιν ἐν δεξιᾷ εἰς τὴν
Λιβύην ἐπὶ τὸν Ἀρσινοΐτην νομόν, ὥστε καὶ
δίστομον εἶναι τὴν διώρυγα, μεταξὺ μέρους τινὸς
τῆς νήσου παρεμπίπτοντος. ἔστι δ᾽ ὁ νομὸς
οὗτος ἀξιολογώτατος τῶν ἁπάντων κατά τε τὴν
ὄψιν καὶ τὴν ἀρετὴν καὶ τὴν κατασκευήν· ἐλαιό-
φυτός τε γὰρ μόνος ἐστὶ μεγάλοις καὶ τελείοις δένδρεσι καὶ καλλικάρποις, εἰ δὲ συγκομίζοι καλῶς
τις, καὶ εὐέλαιος· ὀλιγωροῦντες δὲ τούτου πολὺ
μὲν ποιοῦσιν ἔλαιον, μοχθηρὸν δὲ κατὰ τὴν ὀδμήν
(ἡ δ᾽ ἄλλη Αἴγυπτος ἀνέλαιός ἐστι πλὴν τῶν
κατ᾽ Ἀλεξάνδρειαν κήπων, οἳ μέχρι τοῦ ἐλαίαν
χορηγεῖν ἱκανοί εἰσιν, ἔλαιον δ᾽ οὐχ ὑπουργοῦσιν)·
οἶνόν τε οὐκ ὀλίγον ἐκφέρει σῖτόν τε καὶ ὄσπρια
καὶ τὰ ἄλλα σπέρματα πάμπολλα. θαυμαστὴν
δὲ καὶ τὴν λίμνην ἔχει τὴν Μοίριδος[1] καλουμένην,
πελαγίαν τῷ μεγέθει καὶ τῇ χρόᾳ θαλαττοειδῆ·
καὶ τοὺς αἰγιαλοὺς δέ ἐστιν ὁρᾶν ἐοικότας τοῖς
θαλαττίοις· ὡς ὑπονοεῖν τὰ αὐτὰ περὶ τῶν κατὰ

---

[1] Μοίριδος Ew, Μούριδος other MSS.

---

[1] So Diodorus Siculus 1. 56. 4.   [2] i.e. *Mimosa Nilotica*.
[3] i.e. gum arabic.   [4] See § 37 below.

ment of the captive Trojans who accompanied
Meneläus but stayed there.[1]

35. After Memphis one comes to a city Acanthus,
likewise situated in Libya, and to the temple of Osiris
and the grove of the Thebaïc acantha,[2] from which the
gum [3] is obtained. Then to the Aphroditopolite Nome,
and to the city of like name in Arabia, where is
kept a white cow which is sacred. Then to the
Heracleote Nome, on a large island, where, on the
right, is the canal which leads into Libya to the Arsinoïte Nome, so that the canal has two mouths, a part
of the island intervening between the two.[4] This
Nome is the most noteworthy of all in respect to its
appearance, its fertility, and its material development,
for it alone is planted with olive trees that are large
and full-grown and bear fine fruit, and it would also
produce good olive oil if the olives were carefully
gathered.[5] But since they neglect this matter,
although they make much oil, it has a bad smell (the
rest of Aegypt has no olive trees, except the gardens
near Alexandria, which are sufficient for supplying
olives, but furnish no oil). And it produces wine in no
small quantity, as well as grain, pulse, and the other
seed-plants in very great varieties. It also contains
the wonderful lake called the Lake of Moeris, which
is an open sea in size and like a sea in colour; and its
shores, also, resemble those of a sea, so that one may
make the same supposition about this region as about

[5] In some countries, and generally in Asia, "the olives are
beaten down by poles or by shaking the boughs, or even
allowed to drop naturally, often lying on the ground until the
convenience of the owner admits of their removal; much of
the inferior oil owes its bad quality to the carelessness of the
proprietor of the trees" (*Encyc. Brit.* s.v. "Olive").

Ἄμμωνα τόπων καὶ τούτων (καὶ γὰρ οὐδὲ πάμπολυ ἀφεστᾶσιν ἀλλήλων καὶ τοῦ Παραιτονίου),
μὴ ὥσπερ τὸ ἱερὸν ἐκεῖνο εἰκάζειν ἔστι πρότερον
ἐπὶ τῇ θαλάττῃ ἱδρῦσθαι διὰ τὸ πλῆθος τῶν
τεκμηρίων, καὶ ταῦθ᾽ ὁμοίως τὰ χωρία πρότερον
ἐπὶ τῇ θαλάττῃ ὑπῆργεν. ἡ δὲ κάτω Αἴγυπτος
καὶ τὰ μέχρι τῆς λίμνης τῆς Σιρβωνίτιδος πέλαγος
ἦν, σύρρουν τυχὸν ἴσως τῇ Ἐρυθρᾷ τῇ κατὰ
Ἡρώων πόλιν καὶ τὸν Αἰλανίτην[1] μυχόν.

36. Εὕρηται δὲ περὶ τούτων διὰ πλειόνων ἐν
τῷ πρώτῳ ὑπομνήματι τῆς γεωγραφίας, καὶ νῦν
δ᾽ ἐπὶ τοσοῦτον ὑπομνηστέον τὸ[2] τῆς φύσεως ἅμα
καὶ τὸ τῆς προνοίας ἔργον εἰς ἓν συμφέροντας·
τὸ μὲν τῆς φύσεως, ὅτι τῶν πάντων ὑφ᾽ ἓν[3]
συννευόντων τὸ τοῦ ὅλου μέσον καὶ σφαιρουμένων[4] περὶ τοῦτο, τὸ μὲν πυκνότατον καὶ μεσαί-
C 810 τατόν ἐστιν ἡ γῆ, τὸ δ᾽ ἧττον τοιοῦτον καὶ
ἐφεξῆς τὸ ὕδωρ, ἑκάτερον δὲ σφαῖρα, ἡ μὲν
στερεά, ἡ δὲ κοίλη, ἐντὸς ἔχουσα τὴν γῆν· τὸ δὲ
τῆς προνοίας, ὅτι βεβούληται, καὶ αὐτὴ ποι-
κίλτριά τις οὖσα καὶ μυρίων ἔργων δημιουργός,
ἐν τοῖς πρώτοις ζῷα γεννᾶν, ὡς πολὺ διαφέροντα
τῶν ἄλλων, καὶ τούτων τὰ κράτιστα θεούς τε καὶ
ἀνθρώπους, ὧν ἕνεκεν καὶ τὰ ἄλλα συνέστηκε.
τοῖς μὲν οὖν θεοῖς ἀπέδειξε τὸν οὐρανόν, τοῖς δ᾽
ἀνθρώποις τὴν γῆν, τὰ ἄκρα τῶν τοῦ κόσμου
μερῶν· ἄκρα δὲ τῆς σφαίρας τὸ μέσον καὶ τὸ

---

[1] Ἐλανίτην D. [2] τό, Corais inserts.
[3] εἰς ἕν Dhi.
[4] σφαιρουμένων, Corais, for σφαιρούμενον.

---

[1] See 16. 2. 30, 4. 4, 4, 18. [2] 1. 3. 4, 13.

that of Ammon (in fact, Ammon and the Heracleote
Nome are not very far distant from one another or
from Paraetonium), that, just as from the numerous
evidences one may surmise that that temple was in
earlier times situated on the sea, so likewise these
districts were in earlier times on the sea. And
Lower Aegypt and the parts extending as far as
Lake Sirbonis were sea—this sea being confluent,
perhaps, with the Red Sea in the neighbourhood of
Heröonpolis and the Aelanites [1] Gulf.

36. I have already discussed this subject at greater
length in the First Commentary of my *Geography*,[2]
but now also I must comment briefly on the work of
Nature and at the same time upon that of Providence,
since they contribute to one result.[3] The work of
Nature is this, that all things converge to one thing,
the centre of the whole, and form a sphere around
this; and the densest and most central thing is the
earth, and the thing that is less so and next in order
after it is the water; and that each of the two is a
sphere, the former solid, the latter hollow, having the
earth inside of it. And the work of Providence is
this, that being likewise a broiderer, as it were, and
artificer of countless works, it has willed, among its
first works, to beget living beings, as being much
superior to everything else, and among these the
most excellent beings, both gods and men, on
whose account everything else has been formed.
Now to the gods Providence assigned the heavens and
to men the earth, which are the extremities of the
two parts of the universe; and the two extremities of
the sphere are the central part and the outermost

[3] The reader will remember that Strabo was a Stoic
philosopher (1. 2. 3, 34).

ἐξωτάτω. ἀλλ' ἐπειδὴ τῇ γῇ περίκειται τὸ ὕδωρ,
οὐκ ἔστι δ' ἔνυδρον ζῷον ὁ ἄνθρωπος, ἀλλὰ χερ-
σαῖον καὶ ἐναέριον καὶ πολλοῦ κοινωνικὸν φωτός,
ἐποίησεν ἐξοχὰς ἐν τῇ γῇ πολλὰς[1] καὶ εἰσοχάς,
ὥστ' ἐν αἷς μὲν ἀπολαμβάνεσθαι τὸ σύμπαν ἢ καὶ
τὸ πλέον ὕδωρ ἀποκρύπτον τὴν ὑπ' αὐτῷ γῆν, ἐν
αἷς δ' ἐξέχειν τὴν γῆν ἀποκρύπτουσαν ὑφ' ἑαυτῇ
τὸ ὕδωρ, πλὴν ὅσον χρήσιμον τῷ ἀνθρωπείῳ
γένει καὶ τοῖς περὶ αὐτὸ ζῴοις καὶ φυτοῖς. ἐπεὶ
δ' ἐν κινήσει συνεχεῖ τὰ σύμπαντα καὶ μετα-
βολαῖς μεγάλαις (οὐ γὰρ οἷόν τε ἄλλως τὰ
τοιαῦτα καὶ τοσαῦτα καὶ τηλικαῦτα ἐν τῷ κόσμῳ
διοκεῖσθαι), ὑποληπτέον, μήτε τὴν γῆν ἀεὶ συμ-
μένειν οὕτως, ὥστ' ἀεὶ τηλικαύτην εἶναι μηδὲν
προστιθεῖσαν ἑαυτῇ μηδ' ἀφαιροῦσαν, μήτε τὸ
ὕδωρ, μήτε τὴν ἕδραν ἔχειν τὴν αὐτὴν ἑκάτερον,
καὶ ταῦτα εἰς ἄλληλα φυσικωτάτης οὔσης καὶ
ἐγγυτάτω τῆς μεταπτώσεως· ἀλλὰ καὶ τῆς γῆς
πολλὴν εἰς ὕδωρ μεταβάλλειν, καὶ τῶν ὑδάτων
πολλὰ χερσοῦσθαι τὸν αὐτὸν τρόπον, ὅνπερ καὶ ἐν
τῇ γῇ, καθ' ἣν αὐτὴν[2] τοσαῦται διαφοραί· ἡ
μὲν γὰρ εὔθρυπτος, ἡ δὲ στερεὰ καὶ πετρώδης καὶ
σιδηρῖτις καὶ οὕτως ἐπὶ τῶν ἄλλων. ὁμοίως
δὲ καὶ ἐπὶ τῆς ὑγρᾶς οὐσίας· ἡ μὲν ἁλμυρίς, ἡ
δὲ γλυκεῖα καὶ πότιμος, ἡ δὲ φαρμακώδης καὶ
σωτήριος καὶ ὀλέθριος καὶ ψυχρὰ καὶ θερμή. τί
οὖν θαυμαστόν, εἴ τινα μέρη τῆς γῆς, ἃ νῦν
οἰκεῖται, θαλάττῃ πρότερον κατείχετο, τὰ δὲ νῦν

---

[1] πολλάς, Tzschucke, for πολλοῖς.
[2] καθ' ἣν αὐτήν, Groskurd, for καθ' ἑαυτήν.

part.[1] But since water surrounds the earth, and man
is not an aquatic animal, but a land animal that needs
air and requires much light, Providence has made
numerous elevations and hollows on the earth, so that
the whole, or the most, of the water is received in
the hollows, hiding the earth beneath it, and the
earth projects in the elevations, hiding the water
beneath itself, except so much of the latter as is useful
for the human race, as also for the animals and plants
round it. But since all things are continually in
motion and undergo great changes (for it is not possible
otherwise for things of this kind and number and
size in the universe to be regulated), we must take
it for granted, first, that the earth is not always so
constant that it is always of this or that size, adding
nothing to itself nor subtracting anything, and,
secondly, that the water is not, and, thirdly, that
neither of the two keeps the same fixed place, especially since the reciprocal change of one into the
other is most natural and very near at hand; and
also that much of the earth changes into water, and
many of the waters become dry land in the same
manner as on the earth, where also so many variations
take place; for one kind of earth crumbles easily and
others are solid, or rocky, or contain iron ore, and so
with the rest. And the case is the same with the
properties of liquids: one water is salty, another
sweet and potable, and others contain drugs, salutary
or deadly, or are hot or cold. Why, then, is it marvellous if some parts of the earth which are at present
inhabited were covered with sea in earlier times, and

---

[1] Heaven is the outermost periphery, in which is situated
everything that is divine (Poseidonius, quoted by Diogenes
Laërtius, 7. 138).

πελάγη πρότερον ᾠκεῖτο; καθάπερ καὶ πηγὰς
τὰς[1] πρότερον ἐκλιπεῖν συνέβη, τὰς δ᾽ ἀνεῖσθαι,
καὶ ποταμοὺς καὶ λίμνας, οὕτω δὲ καὶ ὄρη καὶ
πεδία εἰς ἄλληλα μεταπίπτειν· περὶ ὧν καὶ
πρότερον εἰρήκαμεν πολλά, καὶ νῦν εἰρήσθω.

37. Ἡ δ᾽ οὖν Μοίριδος[2] λίμνη διὰ τὸ μέγεθος
καὶ τὸ βάθος ἱκανή ἐστι κατὰ[3] τὰς ἀναβάσεις
τὴν πλημμυρίδα φέρειν καὶ μὴ ὑπερπολάζειν εἰς
τὰ οἰκούμενα καὶ πεφυτευμένα, εἶτα ἐν τῇ ἀπο-
C 811 βάσει τὸ πλεονάζον ἀποδοῦσα τῇ αὐτῇ διώρυγι
κατὰ θάτερον τῶν στομάτων ἔχειν ὑπολειπόμενον
τὸ χρήσιμον πρὸς τὰς ἐποχετείας καὶ αὐτὴ καὶ
ἡ διῶρυξ. ταῦτα μὲν φυσικά, ἐπίκειται δὲ τοῖς
στόμασιν ἀμφοτέροις τῆς διώρυγος κλεῖθρα, οἷς
ταμιεύουσιν οἱ ἀρχιτέκτονες τό τε εἰσρέον ὕδωρ
καὶ τὸ ἐκρέον. πρὸς δὲ τούτοις ἡ τοῦ λαβυρίνθου
κατασκευὴ πάρισον ταῖς πυραμίσιν ἐστὶν ἔργον
καὶ ὁ παρακείμενος τάφος τοῦ κατασκευάσαντος
βασιλέως τὸν λαβύρινθον. ἔστι δὲ κατὰ[4] τὸν
πρῶτον εἴσπλουν τὸν εἰς τὴν διώρυγα προελθόντι
ὅσον τριάκοντα ἢ τετταράκοντα σταδίους ἐπί-
πεδόν τι τραπεζῶδες χωρίον, ἔχον κώμην τε καὶ
βασίλειον μέγα ἐκ πολλῶν βασιλείων,[5] ὅσοι πρότερον ἦσαν νομοί· τοσαῦται γάρ εἰσιν αὐλαὶ
περίστυλοι, συνεχεῖς ἀλλήλαις, εφ᾽ ἕνα στίχον
πᾶσαι καὶ ἐφ᾽ ἑνὸς τοίχου, ὡς ἂν τείχους μακροῦ[6]
προκειμένας ἔχοντος[7] τὰς αὐλάς· αἱ δ᾽ εἰς αὐτὰς

---

[1] καὶ τὰς πηγάς Dh.   [2] Μούριδος Dhimowuz.
[3] All MSS. except E read τε after κατά.
[4] δὲ κατὰ E, δὲ τὸ κατὰ DFh, δὲ τῷ κατά other MSS.
[5] βασιλείων, Corais, for βασιλέων.
[6] μακροῦ, Corais, for μικροῦ.
[7] ἔχοντος, Corais, for ἔχοντες.

if what are now seas were inhabited in earlier times?
Just as fountains of earlier times have given out and
others have sprung forth, and rivers and lakes, so also
mountains and plains have changed one into another.
But I have discussed this subject at length before,[1]
and now let this suffice.

37. Be this as it may, the Lake of Moeris,[2] on
account of its size and its depth, is sufficient to bear
the flood-tides at the risings of the Nile and not overflow into the inhabited and planted parts, and then,
in the retirement of the river, to return the excess
water to the river by the same canal at each of its
two mouths [3] and, both itself and the canal, to keep
back an amount remaining that will be useful for
irrigation. While these conditions are the work of
nature, yet locks have been placed at both mouths
of the canal, by which the engineers [4] regulate both
the inflow and the outflow of the water. In addition to
the things mentioned, this Nome has the Labyrinth,
which is a work comparable to the pyramids, and,
near it, the tomb of the king who built the Labyrinth.[5]
Near the first entrance to the canal, and on proceeding
thence about thirty or forty stadia, one comes to a flat,
trapezium-shaped place, which has a village, and also
a great palace composed of many palaces—as many
in number as there were Nomes in earlier times; [6]
for this is the number of courts, surrounded by colon-
nades, continuous with one another, all in a single
row and along one wall, the structure being as it
were a long wall with the courts in front of it; and the

---

[1] 1. 3. 4, 12–15.   [2] On this lake, cp. Herodotus 2. 149.
[3] Cp. § 35 above.   [4] Literally, "architects."
[5] On this Labyrinth, cp. Herodotus 2. 148, Diodorus Siculus
1. 66. 3, and Pliny 36. 19.
[6] See 17. 1. 3.

STRABO

ὁδοὶ καταντικρὺ τοῦ τείχους εἰσί. πρόκεινται δὲ
τῶν εἰσόδων κρυπταί τινες μακραὶ καὶ πολλαί,
δι᾽ ἀλλήλων ἔχουσαι σκολιὰς τὰς ὁδούς, ὥστε
χωρὶς ἡγεμόνος μηδενὶ τῶν ξένων εἶναι δυνατὴν
τὴν εἰς ἑκάστην αὐλὴν πάροδόν τε καὶ ἔξοδον.
τὸ δὲ θαυμαστόν, ὅτι αἱ στέγαι τῶν οἴκων ἑκάστου
μονόλιθοι,[1] καὶ τῶν κρυπτῶν τὰ πλάτη μονολίθοις
ὡσαύτως ἐστέγασται πλαξίν, ὑπερβαλλούσαις τὸ
μέγεθος, ξύλων οὐδαμοῦ καταμεμιγμένων οὐδ᾽
ἄλλης ὕλης οὐδεμιᾶς. ἀναβάντα τε[2] ἐπὶ τὸ στέγος,
οὐ μεγάλῳ[3] ὕψει, ἅτε μονοστέγῳ, ἔστιν ἰδεῖν
πεδίον λίθινον ἐκ τηλικούτων λίθων, ἐντεῦθεν δὲ
πάλιν εἰς τὰς αὐλὰς ἐκπίπτοντα[4] ἑξῆς ὁρᾶν
κειμένας ὑπὸ μονολίθων κιόνων ὑπηρεισμένας
ἑπτὰ καὶ εἴκοσι· καὶ οἱ τοῖχοι· δὲ οὐκ ἐξ ἐλαττόνων τῷ μεγέθει λίθων σύγκεινται. ἐπὶ τέλει
δὲ τῆς οἰκοδομίας ταύτης πλέον ἢ στάδιον ἐπεχούσης[5] ὁ τάφος ἐστί, πυραμὶς τετράγωνος,
ἑκάστην τετράπλεθρόν πως ἔχουσα τὴν πλευρὰν
καὶ τὸ ἴσον ὕψος· Ἰμάνδης[6] δ᾽ ὄνομα ὁ ταφείς.
πεποιῆσθαι δέ φασι τὰς αὐλὰς τοσαύτας, ὅτι
τοὺς νομοὺς ἔθος ἦν ἐκεῖσε συνέρχεσθαι πάντας
ἀριστίνδην[7] μετὰ τῶν οἰκείων ἱερέων καὶ ἱερειῶν,
θυσίας τε καὶ θεοδοσίας καὶ δικαιοδοσίας[8] περὶ

[1] μονόλιθοι D, μονολίθου F, μονολίθῳ other MSS.
[2] All MSS. except E read ἐστι after τε.
[3] Müller-Dübner, following conj. of Meineke, emend μέγα
τῷ to μεγάλῳ. One would expect ἐν before the οὐ.
[4] For ἐκπίπτοντα, Letronne conj. ἐκκύπτοντα, Kramer
εἰσβλέποντα.
[5] ἐπεχούσης, Corais, for ἀπεχούσης.
[6] Ἰμάνδης, Meineke and Müller-Dübner, for Ἰσμάνδης MSS.,
Μαίνδης Epit. (cp. Ἰσμάνδης § 42 below).

roads leading into them are exactly opposite the wall.
In front of the entrances are crypts, as it were, which
are long and numerous and have winding passages
communicating with one another, so that no stranger
can find his way either into any court or out of it
without a guide. But the marvellous thing is that
the roof of each of the chambers consists of a single
stone, and that the breadths of the crypts are likewise
roofed with single slabs of surpassing size, with no
intermixture anywhere of timber or of any other
material. And, on ascending to the roof, which is at
no great height, inasmuch as the Labyrinth has only
one story, one can see a plain of stone, consisting of
stones of that great size; and thence, descending out
into the courts again, one can see that they lie in a
row and are each supported by twenty-seven monolithic pillars; and their walls, also, are composed of
stones that are no smaller in size. At the end of
this building, which occupies more than a stadium, is
the tomb, a quadrangular pyramid, which has sides
about four plethra in width and a height equal thereto.
Imandes [1] is the name of the man buried there. It
is said that this number of courts was built because it
was the custom for all the Nomes to assemble there
in accordance with their rank, together with their
own priests and priestesses, for the sake of sacrifice
and of offering gifts to the gods and of administering

---

[1] Perhaps an error for "Mandes." The name is spelled
Ismandes in §42 below. Diodorus says "Mendes, whom
some give the name Marrus." The real builder was Maindes,
or Amon-em-hat III, of the twelfth dynasty (Sayce, *The Egypt
of the Hebrews*, p. 281).

---

[7] ἀριστίνδην, Tyrwhitt, for ἄριστον δ' ἦν.
[8] καὶ δικαιοδοσίας, suspected by Corais and Müller-Dübner.

τῶν μεγίστων χάριν. κατήγετο δὲ τῶν νομῶν
ἕκαστος εἰς τὴν ἀποδειχθεῖσαν αὐλὴν αὐτῷ.

38. Παραπλεύσαντι δὲ ταῦτα ἐφ' ἑκατὸν σταδίους πόλις ἐστὶν Ἀρσινόη, Κροκοδείλων δὲ πόλις
ἐκαλεῖτο πρότερον· σφόδρα γὰρ ἐν τῷ νομῷ τούτῳ
τιμῶσι τὸν κροκόδειλον, καί ἐστιν ἱερὸς παρ'
αὐτοῖς ἐν λίμνῃ καθ' αὑτὸν τρεφόμενος, χειροήθης
τοῖς ἱερεῦσι. καλεῖται δὲ Σοῦχος· τρέφεται δὲ
σιτίοις καὶ κρέασι καὶ οἴνῳ, προσφερόντων ἀεὶ τῶν
C 812 ξένων τῶν ἐπὶ τὴν θέαν ἀφικνουμένων. ὁ γοῦν ἡμέ-
τερος ξένος, ἀνὴρ τῶν ἐντίμων, αὐτόθι μυσταγωγῶν
ἡμᾶς, συνῆλθεν ἐπὶ τὴν λίμνην, κομίζων ἀπὸ τοῦ
δείπνου πλακουντάριόν[1] τι καὶ κρέας ὀπτὸν καὶ
προχοΐδιόν τι μελικράτου. εὕρομεν δὲ ἐπὶ τῷ
χείλει κείμενον τὸ θηρίον· προσιόντες δὲ οἱ ἱερεῖς,
οἱ μὲν διέστησαν αὐτοῦ τὸ στόμα, ὁ δὲ ἐνέθηκε
τὸ πέμμα, καὶ πάλιν τὸ κρέας, εἶτα τὸ μελίκρατον
κατήρασε. καθαλόμενος δὲ εἰς τὴν λίμνην διῆξεν
εἰς τὸ πέραν· ἐπελθόντος δὲ καὶ ἄλλου τῶν ξένων,
κομίζοντος ὁμοίως ἀπαρχήν,[2] λαβόντες περιῆλθον
δρόμῳ καὶ καταλαβόντες προσήνεγκαν ὁμοίως τὰ
προσενεχθέντα.

39. Μετὰ δὲ τὸν Ἀρσινοΐτην καὶ[3] τὸν Ἡρακ-
λεωτικὸν νομὸν Ἡρακλέους πόλις, ἐν ᾗ ὁ ἰχνεύμων
τιμᾶται ὑπεναντίως τοῖς Ἀρσινοΐταις· οἱ μὲν γὰρ
τοὺς κροκοδείλους τιμῶσι, καὶ διὰ τοῦτο ἥ τε

---

[1] πλακούντιον E.   [2] ἀπαρχάς E.
[3] καί, Letronne emends to κατά, Groskurd to καὶ κατά.

---

[1] For proposed restorations of the Labyrinth, see the
Latronne Edition, and Petrie (*The Labyrinth, Gerzeh, and*

justice in matters of the greatest importance. And each of the Nomes was conducted to the court appointed to it.[1]

38. Sailing along shore for a distance of one hundred stadia, one comes to the city Arsinoê, which in earlier times was called Crocodeilonpolis; for the people in this Nome hold in very great honour the crocodile, and there is a sacred one there which is kept and fed by itself in a lake, and is tame to the priests. It is called Suchus; and it is fed on grain and pieces of meat and on wine, which are always being fed to it by the foreigners who go to see it. At any rate, our host, one of the officials, who was introducing us into the mysteries there, went with us to the lake, carrying from the dinner a kind of cooky and some roasted meat and a pitcher of wine mixed with honey. We found the animal lying on the edge of the lake; and when the priests went up to it, some of them opened its mouth and another put in the cake, and again the meat, and then poured down the honey mixture. The animal then leaped into the lake and rushed across to the far side; but when another foreigner arrived, likewise carrying an offering of first-fruits, the priests took it, went around the lake in a run, took hold of the animal, and in the same manner fed it what had been brought.

39. After the Arsinoïte and Heracleotic Nomes, one comes to a City of Heracles, where the people hold in honour the ichneumon, the very opposite of the practice of the Arsinoïtae; for whereas the latter hold the crocodile in honour—and on this account

Mazghuneh, p. 28), and Myres (*Annals of Archaeology and Anthropology*, III, 134).

διῶρυξ αὐτῶν ἐστι μεστὴ τῶν κροκοδείλων καὶ
ἡ τοῦ Μοίριδος¹ λίμνη· σέβονται γὰρ καὶ ἀπέ-
χονται αὐτῶν· οἱ δὲ τοὺς ἰχνεύμονας τοὺς ὀλεθριω-
τάτους τοῖς κροκοδείλοις, καθάπερ καὶ ταῖς
ἀσπίσι· καὶ γὰρ τὰ ᾠὰ διαφθείρουσιν αὐτῶν καὶ
αὐτὰ τὰ θηρία, τῷ πηλῷ θωρακισθέντες· κυλισ-
θέντες γὰρ ἐν αὐτῷ ξηραίνονται πρὸς τὸν ἥλιον,
εἶτα τὰς ἀσπίδας μὲν ἢ τῆς κεφαλῆς ἢ τῆς οὐρᾶς
λαβόμενοι κατασπῶσιν εἰς τὸν ποταμὸν καὶ δια-
φθείρουσι· τοὺς δὲ κροκοδείλους ἐνεδρεύσαντες,
ἡνίκ' ἂν ἡλιάζωνται κεχηνότες, ἐμπίπτουσιν εἰς τὰ
χάσματα καὶ διαφαγόντες τὰ σπλάγχνα καὶ τὰς
γαστέρας ἐκδύνουσιν ἐκ νεκρῶν τῶν σωμάτων.

40. Ἑξῆς δ' ἐστὶν ὁ Κυνοπολίτης νομὸς καὶ
Κυνῶν πόλις, ἐν ᾗ ὁ Ἄνουβις τιμᾶται καὶ τοῖς
κυσὶ τιμὴ καὶ σίτισις τέτακταί τις ἱερά. ἐν δὲ
τῇ περαίᾳ Ὀξύρυγχος πόλις καὶ νομὸς ὁμώνυμος.
τιμῶσι δὲ τὸν ὀξύρυγχον καὶ ἔστιν αὐτοῖς ἱερὸν
Ὀξυρύγχου, καίτοι καὶ τῶν ἄλλων Αἰγυπτίων
κοινῇ τιμώντων τὸν ὀξύρυγχον. τινὰ μὲν γὰρ
τῶν ζῴων ἅπαντες κοινῇ τιμῶσιν Αἰγύπτιοι,
καθάπερ τῶν μὲν πεζῶν τρία, βοῦν, κύνα,
αἴλουρον, τῶν δὲ πτηνῶν δύο, ἱέρακα καὶ ἶβιν,
τῶν δ' ἐνύδρων δύο, λεπιδωτὸν ἰχθὺν καὶ
ὀξύρυγχον· ἄλλα δ' ἔστιν, ἃ τιμῶσι καθ' ἑαυτοὺς
ἕκαστοι, καθάπερ Σαῖται πρόβατον καὶ Θηβαῖται,
λάτον δὲ τῶν ἐν τῷ Νείλῳ τινὰ ἰχθὺν Λατοπο-

---

¹ Μοίριδος, Xylander, for Μούριδος.

---

¹ So in § 44 below.
² "City of Dogs."

both their canal and the Lake of Moeris are full of crocodiles, for the people revere them and abstain from harming them [1]—the former hold in honour the ichneumons, which are the deadliest enemies of the crocodile, as also of the asp; for they destroy, not only the eggs of the asps, but also the asps themselves, having armed themselves with a breastplate of mud; for they first roll themselves in mud, make it dry in the sun, and then, seizing the asps by either the head or the tail, drag them down into the river and kill them; and as for the crocodiles, the ichneumons lie in wait for them, and when the crocodiles are basking in the sun with their mouths open the ichneumons throw themselves into their open jaws, eat through their entrails and bellies, and emerge from their dead bodies.

40. One comes next to the Cynopolite Nome, and to Cynonpolis,[2] where Anubis is held in honour and where a form of worship and sacred feeding has been organised for all dogs. On the far side of the river lie the city Oxyrynchus and a Nome bearing the same name. They hold in honour the oxyrynchus[3] and have a temple sacred to Oxyrynchus, though the other Aegyptians in common also hold in honour the oxyrynchus. In fact, certain animals are worshipped by all Aegyptians in common, as, for example, three land animals, bull and dog and cat, and two birds, hawk and ibis, and two aquatics, scale-fish and oxyrynchus, but there are other animals which are honoured by separate groups independently of the rest, as, for example, a sheep by the Saïtae and also by the Thebans; a *latus*, a fish of the Nile, by

[3] *i.e.* "sharp-snouted" (fish). A species of fish like our pike.

λῖται, λύκον τε Λυκοπολῖται, κυνοκέφαλον δὲ
Ἑρμοπολῖται, κῆβον δὲ Βαβυλώνιοι οἱ κατὰ
Μέμφιν· ἔστι δ' ὁ κῆβος τὸ μὲν πρόσωπον
ἐοικὼς σατύρῳ, τἆλλα δὲ κυνὸς καὶ ἄρκτου
μεταξύ, γεννᾶται δ' ἐν Αἰθιοπίᾳ· ἀετὸν δὲ
C 813 Θηβαῖοι, λέοντα δὲ Λεοντοπολῖται, αἶγα δὲ καὶ
τράγον Μενδήσιοι, μυγαλῆν δὲ Ἀθριβῖται, ἄλλοι
δ' ἄλλο τι· τὰς δ' αἰτίας οὐχ ὁμολογουμένας
λέγουσιν.

41. Ἑξῆς δ' ἐστὶν Ἑρμοπολιτικὴ φυλακή,
τελώνιόν τι τῶν ἐκ τῆς Θηβαΐδος καταφερο-
μένων· ἐντεῦθεν ἀρχὴ τῶν ἑξήκοντα σταδίων
σχοίνων, ἕως Συήνης καὶ Ἐλεφαντίνης· εἶτα ἡ
Θηβαϊκὴ φυλακὴ καὶ διῶρυξ φέρουσα ἐπὶ Τάνιν·
εἶτα Λύκων πόλις καὶ Ἀφροδίτης καὶ Πανῶν
πόλις, λινουργῶν καὶ λιθουργῶν κατοικία
παλαιά.

42. Ἔπειτα Πτολεμαϊκὴ πόλις, μεγίστη τῶν
ἐν τῇ Θηβαΐδι καὶ οὐκ ἐλάττων Μέμφεως, ἔχουσα
καὶ σύστημα πολιτικὸν ἐν τῷ Ἑλληνικῷ τρόπῳ.
ὑπὲρ δὲ ταύτης ἡ Ἄβυδος, ἐν ᾗ τὸ Μεμνόνιον,
βασίλειον θαυμαστῶς κατεσκευασμένον ὁλόλιθον [1]
τῇ αὐτῇ κατασκευῇ, ἧπερ τὸν λαβύρινθον ἔφαμεν,
οὐ πολλαπλοῦν δέ· καὶ κρήνη ἐν βάθει κειμένη,
ὥστε καταβαίνειν εἰς αὐτὴν διὰ κατακαμφθεισῶν [2]
ψαλίδων μονολίθων ὑπερβαλλουσῶν τῷ μεγέθει

---

[1] ὁλόλιθον, omitted by E.
[2] κατακαμφθεισῶν (see Diodorus Siculus 2. 9), Corais, for
κατακαμφθέντων. For conjectures, see Kramer.

---

[1] *i.e.* the Aegyptian jackal (*Canis lupaster*).
[2] *i.e.* the dog-faced baboon (*Simia hamadryas*).
[3] See 16. 4. 16 and footnote.

the Latopolitae; a *lycus*[1] by the Lycopolitae; a *cynocephalus*[2] by the Hermopolitae; a *cebus*[3] by the Babylonians who live near Memphis (the *cebus* has a face like a satyr, is between a dog and a bear in other respects, and is bred in Aethiopia); an eagle by the Thebans; a lion by the Leontopolitae; a female and male goat by the Mendesians; a shrew-mouse[4] by the Athribitae, and other animals by other peoples; but the reasons which they give for such worship are not in agreement.

41. One comes next to the Hermopolitic garrison, a kind of toll-station for goods brought down from the Thebaïs; here begins the reckoning of schoeni at sixty stadia,[5] extending as far as Syenê and Elephantinê; and then to the Thebaïc garrison and the canal that leads to Tanis; and then to Lycopolis and to Aphroditopolis and to Panopolis, an old settlement of linen-workers and stone-workers.

42. Then one comes to the city of Ptolemaïs, which is the largest of the cities in the Thebaïs, is no smaller than Memphis, and has also a form of government modelled on that of the Greeks. Above this city lies Abydus, where is the Memnonium, a royal building, which is a remarkable structure built of solid stone, and of the same workmanship as that which I ascribed to the Labyrinth, though not multiplex; and also a fountain[6] which lies at a great depth, so that one descends to it down vaulted galleries made of monoliths of surpassing size and

---

[4] *Mus araneus.*

[5] See § 24 above, and 11. 11. 5.

[6] Known as "Strabo's Well." See Petrie, *The Osireion at Abydos*, p. 2; and Naville, *The Tomb of Osiris, London Times*, March 6 and 17, 1914.

καὶ τῇ κατασκευῇ. ἔστι δὲ διῶρυξ ἄγουσα ἐπὶ
τὸν τόπον ἀπὸ τοῦ μεγάλου ποταμοῦ. περὶ δὲ
τὴν διώρυγα ἀκανθῶν Αἰγυπτίων ἄλσος ἐστὶν
ἱερὸν τοῦ Ἀπόλλωνος. ἔοικε δὲ ὑπάρξαι ποτὲ ἡ
Ἄβυδος πόλις μεγάλη, δευτερεύουσα μετὰ τὰς
Θήβας, νυνὶ δ' ἐστὶ κατοικία μικρά· εἰ δ', ὥς
φασιν, ὁ Μέμνων ὑπὸ τῶν Αἰγυπτίων Ἰσμάνδης [1]
λέγεται, καὶ ὁ λαβύρινθος Μεμνόνιον ἂν εἴη καὶ
τοῦ αὐτοῦ ἔργον, οὗπερ καὶ τὰ ἐν Ἀβύδῳ καὶ τὰ
ἐν Θήβαις· καὶ γὰρ ἐκεῖ λέγεταί τινα Μεμνόνια.
κατὰ δὲ τὴν Ἄβυδόν ἐστιν ἡ πρώτη αὔασις ἐκ
τῶν λεχθεισῶν τριῶν ἐν τῇ Λιβύῃ, διέχουσα
ὁδὸν ἡμερῶν ἑπτὰ ἐνθένδε δι' ἐρημίας, εὔυδρός τε
κατοικία καὶ εὔοινος καὶ τοῖς ἄλλοις ἱκανή·
δευτέρα δ' ἡ κατὰ τὴν Μοίριδος [2] λίμνην· τρίτη
δὲ ἡ κατὰ τὸ μαντεῖον τὸ ἐν Ἄμμωνι· καὶ αὗται
δὲ κατοικίαι εἰσὶν ἀξιόλογοι.

43. Πολλὰ δ' εἰρηκότες περὶ τοῦ Ἄμμωνος
τοσοῦτον εἰπεῖν βουλόμεθα, ὅτι τοῖς ἀρχαίοις
μᾶλλον ἦν ἐν τιμῇ καὶ ἡ μαντικὴ καθόλου καὶ
τὰ χρηστήρια, νυνὶ δ' ὀλιγωρία κατέχει πολλή,
τῶν Ῥωμαίων ἀρκουμένων τοῖς Σιβύλλης χρησμοῖς
καὶ τοῖς Τυρρηνικοῖς θεοπροπίοις διά τε σπλάγ-
χνων καὶ ὀρνιθείας καὶ διοσημιῶν.[3] διόπερ καὶ
τὸ ἐν Ἄμμωνι σχεδόν τι ἐκλέλειπται χρηστήριον, πρότερον δὲ ἐτετίμητο. δηλοῦσι δὲ μάλιστα
τοῦτο οἱ τὰς Ἀλεξάνδρου πράξεις ἀναγράψαντες,

---

[1] Σμάνδης F, Ἰμάνδης xz, Μάνδης w (cp. Ἰμάνδης 17. 1. 37).
[2] Μοίριδος E, Μούριδος other MSS.
[3] διοσημιῶν, Corais, for διασημειῶν.

---

[1] Spelled "Imandes" in § 37 above (see footnote there).

workmanship. There is a canal leading to the place from the great river; and in the neighbourhood of the canal is a grove of Aegyptian *acantha*, sacred to Apollo. Abydus appears once to have been a great city, second only to Thebes, but it is now only a small settlement. But if, as they say, Memnon is called Ismandes[1] by the Aegyptians, the Labyrinth might also be a Memnonium and a work of the same man who built both the Memnonia in Abydus and those in Thebes; for it is said that there are also some Memnonia in Thebes. Opposite Abydus is the first of the above-mentioned three oases in Libya; it is a seven days' journey distant from Abydus through a desert; and it is a settlement which abounds in water and in wine, and is sufficiently supplied with other things. The second oasis is that in the neighbourhood of the Lake of Moeris; and the third is that in the neighbourhood of the oracle in Ammon; and these, also, are noteworthy settlements.

43. Now that I have already said much about Ammon,[2] I wish to add only this: Among the ancients both divination in general and oracles were held in greater honour, but now great neglect of them prevails, since the Romans are satisfied with the oracles of Sibylla, and with the Tyrrhenian prophecies obtained by means of the entrails of animals, flight of birds, and omens from the sky; and on this account, also, the oracle at Ammon has been almost abandoned, though it was held in honour in earlier times; and this fact is most clearly shown by those who have recorded the deeds of Alexander, since,

[2] See references in *Index*.

προστιθέντες μὲν πολὺ καὶ τὸ τῆς κολακείας
εἶδος, ἐμφαίνοντες δέ τι[1] καὶ πίστεως ἄξιον. ὁ
C 814 γοῦν Καλλισθένης φησὶ τὸν Ἀλέξανδρον φιλο-
δοξῆσαι μάλιστα ἀνελθεῖν ἐπὶ τὸ χρηστήριον,
ἐπειδὴ καὶ Περσέα ἤκουσε[2] πρότερον ἀναβῆναι
καὶ Ἡρακλέα· ὁρμήσαντα δ' ἐκ Παραιτονίου,
καίπερ νότων ἐπιπεσόντων, βιάσασθαι· πλανώ-
μενον δ' ὑπὸ τοῦ κονιορτοῦ σωθῆναι, γενομένων
ὄμβρων καὶ δυεῖν κοράκων ἡγησαμένων τὴν ὁδόν,
ἤδη τούτων κολακευτικῶς λεγομένων· τοιαῦτα δὲ
καὶ τὰ ἑξῆς· μόνῳ γὰρ δὴ τῷ βασιλεῖ τὸν ἱερέα
ἐπιτρέψαι παρελθεῖν εἰς τὸν νεὼ μετὰ τῆς συνή-
θους στολῆς, τοὺς δ' ἄλλους μετενδῦναι τὴν
ἐσθῆτα, ἔξωθέν τε τῆς θεμιστείας ἀκροάσασθαι
πάντας πλὴν Ἀλεξάνδρου, τοῦτον δ' ἔνδοθεν·
εἶναι δὲ[3] οὐχ ὥσπερ ἐν Δελφοῖς καὶ Βραγχίδαις
τὰς ἀποθεσπίσεις διὰ λόγων, ἀλλὰ νεύμασι καὶ
συμβόλοις τὸ πλέον, ὡς καὶ παρ' Ὁμήρῳ,

ἦ καὶ κυανέῃσιν ἐπ' ὀφρύσι νεῦσε Κρονίων,

τοῦ προφήτου τὸν Δία ὑποκριναμένου· τοῦτο
μέντοι ῥητῶς εἰπεῖν τὸν ἄνθρωπον πρὸς τὸν
βασιλέα, ὅτι εἴη Διὸς υἱός. προστραγῳδεῖ δὲ
τούτοις ὁ Καλλισθένης, ὅτι τοῦ Ἀπόλλωνος τὸ
ἐν Βραγχίδαις μαντεῖον ἐκλελοιπότος, ἐξ ὅτου
τὸ ἱερὸν ὑπὸ τῶν Βραγχιδῶν σεσύληto ἐπὶ Ξέρξου
περσισάντων, ἐκλελοιπυίας δὲ καὶ τῆς κρήνης,
τότε ἥ τε κρήνη ἀνάσχοι καὶ μαντεῖα πολλὰ οἱ

---

[1] δέ τι, the editors, for δ' ἔτι x, δ' ὅτι other MSS.
[2] ἤκουε DF.　　　　[3] δέ, Meineke inserts.

---

[1] Cp. 2. 1. 5, 11. 6. 4, 15. 1. 21, 28.

although they add numerous forms of mere flattery,[1]
yet they do indicate some things that are worthy of
belief.   At any rate, Callisthenes says that Alexander
conceived a very great ambition to go inland to the
oracle, since he had heard that Perseus, as also
Heracles, had done so in earlier times; and that he
started from Paraetonium, although the south
winds had set in, and forced his way; and that when
he lost his way because of the thick dust, he was
saved by rainfalls and by the guidance of two crows.
But this last assertion is flattery and so are the
next : that the priest permitted the king alone to pass
into the temple in his usual dress, but the rest
changed their clothes; that all heard the oracles
from outside except Alexander, but he inside; that
the oracular responses were not, as at Delphi and
among the Branchidae,[2] given in words, but mostly
by nods and tokens, as in Homer,[3] " Cronion spoke
and nodded assent with his dark brows "—the prophet
having assumed the rôle of Zeus; that, however, the
fellow expressly told the king that he, Alexander, was
son of Zeus.   And to this statement Callisthenes
dramatically adds that,[4] although the oracle of Apollo
among the Branchidae had ceased to speak from the
time the temple had been robbed by the Branchidae,
who sided with the Persians in the time of Xerxes,[5]
and although the spring also had ceased to flow, yet
at Alexander's arrival the spring began to flow again
and that many oracles were carried by the Milesian

[2] *i.e.* at Didyma, near Miletus (14. 1. 5).
[3] *Iliad* 1. 528.
[4] Literally, " although Apollo had deserted the oracle
among the Branchidae."
[5] 11. 11. 4.

Μιλησίων πρέσβεις κομίσαιεν[1] εἰς Μέμφιν περὶ
τῆς ἐκ Διὸς γενέσεως τοῦ Ἀλεξάνδρου καὶ τῆς
ἐσομένης περὶ Ἄρβηλα νίκης καὶ τοῦ Δαρείου
θανάτου καὶ τῶν ἐν Λακεδαίμονι νεωτερισμῶν.
περὶ δὲ τῆς εὐγενείας[2] καὶ τὴν Ἐρυθραίαν Ἀθη-
ναΐδα φησὶν ἀνειπεῖν· καὶ γὰρ ταύτην ὁμοίαν
γενέσθαι τῇ παλαιᾷ Σιβύλλῃ τῇ Ἐρυθραίᾳ. τὰ
μὲν δὴ τῶν συγγραφέων τοιαῦτα.

44. Ἐν δὲ τῇ Ἀβύδῳ τιμῶσι τὸν Ὄσιριν· ἐν
δὲ τῷ ἱερῷ τοῦ Ὀσίριδος οὐκ ἔξεστιν οὔτε ᾠδὸν
οὔτε αὐλητὴν οὔτε ψάλτην ἀπάρχεσθαι τῷ θεῷ,
καθάπερ τοῖς ἄλλοις θεοῖς ἔθος. μετὰ δὲ τὴν
Ἄβυδον Διὸς πόλις ἡ μικρά, εἶτα Τέντυρα πόλις·
ἐνταῦθα δὲ διαφερόντως παρὰ τοὺς ἄλλους
Αἰγυπτίους ὁ κροκόδειλος ἠτίμωται καὶ ἔχθιστος
τῶν ἀπάντων θηρίων νενόμισται. οἱ μὲν γὰρ
ἄλλοι, καίπερ εἰδότες τὴν κακίαν τοῦ ζῴου, καὶ
ὡς ὀλέθριον τῷ ἀνθρωπίνῳ γένει, σέβονται ὅμως
καὶ ἀπέχονται· οὗτοι δὲ πάντα τρόπον ἀν-
ιχνεύουσι καὶ ἐκφθείρουσιν[3] αὐτούς. ἔνιοι δ'
ὥσπερ τοὺς Ψύλλους φασὶ τοὺς πρὸς τῇ Κυρηναίᾳ
φυσικήν τινα ἀντιπάθειαν ἔχειν πρὸς τὰ ἑρπετά,
οὕτω καὶ τοὺς Τεντυρίτας πρὸς τοὺς κροκοδείλους,
ὥστε μηδὲν ὑπ' αὐτῶν πάσχειν, ἀλλὰ καὶ κο-
λυμβᾶν ἀδεῶς καὶ διαπερᾶν, μηδενὸς ἄλλου θαρ-
ροῦντος. εἴς τε τὴν Ῥώμην κομισθεῖσι τοῖς
C 815 κροκοδείλοις ἐπιδείξεως χάριν συνηκολούθουν οἱ
Τεντυρῖται· γενομένης τε δεξαμενῆς καὶ πήγματός
τινος ὑπὲρ μιᾶς τῶν πλευρῶν, ὥστε τοῖς θηρίοις

---

[1] κομίσαιεν, Casaubon, for κομισθέντες.
[2] Meineke conj. διογενείας or θεογενείας.
[3] ἐκφθείρουσιν DF, διαφθείρουσιν other MSS.

ambassadors to Memphis concerning Alexander's
descent from Zeus, his future victory in the neighbourhood of Arbela, the death of Dareius, and the revolu-
tionary attempts in Lacedaemon. And he says that
the Erythraean Athenaïs [1] also gave out an utterance
concerning Alexander's high descent; for, he adds,
this woman was like the ancient Erythraean Sibylla.
Such, then, are the accounts of the historians.

44. At Abydus they hold in honour Osiris; and in
the temple of Osiris [2] neither singer nor flute-player
nor harp-player is permitted to begin the rites in
honour of the god, as is the custom in the case of
the other gods. After Abydus one comes to the
Little Diospolis, and to the city Tentyra, where the
people, as compared with the other Aegyptians, hold
in particular dishonour the crocodile and deem it
the most hateful of all animals. For although the
others know the malice of the animal and how destructive it is to the human race, still they revere it
and abstain from harming it,[3] whereas the Tentyritae
track them and destroy them in every way. Some
say that, just as there is a kind of natural antipathy
between the Psylli [4] near Cyrenaea and reptiles, so
there is between the Tentyritae and crocodiles, so
that they suffer no injury from them, but even dive
in the river without fear and cross over, though no
others are bold enough to do so. When the crocodiles
were brought to Rome for exhibition, they were
attended by the Tentyritae; and when a reservoir
and a kind of stage above one of the sides had been
made for them, so that they could go out of the

[1] 14. 1. 34.
[2] On this temple, see Petrie, *The Osireion at Abydos.*
[3] So in § 39 above.   [4] Cp. 13. 1. 14.

ἐκβᾶσι τοῦ ὕδατος ἡλιαστήριον εἶναι, ἐκεῖνοι
ἦσαν οἱ τοτὲ μὲν ἐξέλκοντες δικτύῳ πρὸς τὸ
ἡλιαστήριον, ὡς καὶ ὑπὸ τῶν θεατῶν ὁραθῆναι,
ἐμβαίνοντες ἅμα εἰς τὸ ὕδωρ, τοτὲ δὲ πάλιν εἰς
τὴν δεξαμενὴν κατασπῶντες. τιμῶσι δὲ Ἀφρο-
δίτην· ὄπισθεν δὲ τοῦ νεὼ τῆς Ἀφροδίτης Ἴσιδός
ἐστιν ἱερόν· εἶτα τὰ Τυφώνια καλούμενα καὶ ἡ
εἰς Κοπτὸν διῶρυξ, πόλιν κοινὴν Αἰγυπτίων τε
καὶ Ἀράβων.

45. Ἐντεῦθέν ἐστιν ἰσθμὸς εἰς τὴν Ἐρυθρὰν
κατὰ πόλιν Βερενίκην, ἀλίμενον μέν, τῇ δ' εὐκαιρίᾳ
τοῦ ἰσθμοῦ καταγωγὰς ἐπιτηδείους ἔχουσαν.
λέγεται δ' ὁ Φιλάδελφος πρῶτος στρατοπέδῳ
τεμεῖν τὴν ὁδὸν ταύτην, ἄνυδρον οὖσαν, καὶ
κατασκευάσαι σταθμούς, ὥσπερ τοῖς ἐμπορίοις [1]
ὁδεύμασι καὶ διὰ τῶν καμήλων, τοῦτο δὲ πρᾶξαι
διὰ τὸ τὴν Ἐρυθρὰν δύσπλουν εἶναι, καὶ μάλιστα
τοῖς ἐκ τοῦ μυχοῦ πλοϊζομένοις. ἐφάνη δὴ τῇ
πείρᾳ πολὺ τὸ χρήσιμον, καὶ νῦν ὁ Ἰνδικὸς φόρτος [2] ἅπας καὶ ὁ Ἀράβιος καὶ τοῦ Αἰθιοπικοῦ
ὁ τῷ Ἀραβίῳ κόλπῳ κατακομιζόμενος εἰς Κοπτὸν
φέρεται, καὶ τοῦτ' ἔστιν ἐμπόριον τῶν τοιούτων
φορτίων. οὐκ ἄπωθεν δὲ τῆς Βερενίκης ἐστὶ
Μυὸς ὅρμος, πόλις ἔχουσα τὸ ναύσταθμον τῶν
πλοϊζομένων, καὶ τῆς Κοπτοῦ οὐ πολὺ ἀφέστηκεν
ἡ καλουμένη Ἀπόλλωνος πόλις, ὥστε καὶ αἱ
διορίζουσαι τὸν ἰσθμὸν δύο πόλεις ἑκατέρωθεν

---

[1] Arrian (*Indica* 41) likewise uses ἐμπορίοις as an adjective,
instead of ἐμπορικοῖς. It is so used nowhere else in Strabo
apparently; but the clause appears to be a direct quotation
from one of Arrian's sources. Kramer and Meineke reject
it as a gloss; Groskurd and C. Müller emend it drastically
(see Kramer). [2] φόρτος *z*, φόρος other MSS.

water and have a basking-place in the sun, these men at one time, stepping into the water all together, would drag them in a net to the basking-place, so that they could be seen by the spectators, and at another would pull them down again into the reservoir. They worship Aphrodite; and back of her shrine is a temple of Isis. And then one comes to the Typhonia, as they are called, and to the canal that leads to Coptus, a city common to the Aegyptians and the Arabians.

45. Thence one crosses an isthmus, which extends to the Red Sea, near a city Berenicê. The city has no harbour, but on account of the favourable lay of the isthmus has convenient landing-places. It is said that Philadelphus was the first person, by means of an army, to cut this road, which is without water, and to build stations, as though for the travels of merchants on camels, and that he did this because the Red Sea was hard to navigate, particularly for those who set sail from its innermost recess. So the utility of his plan was shown by experience to be great, and now all the Indian merchandise, as well as the Arabian and such of the Aethiopian as is brought down by the Arabian Gulf, is carried to Coptus, which is the emporium for such cargoes. Not far from Berenicê lies Myus Hormus,[1] a city containing the naval station for sailors; and not far distant from Coptus lies Apollonospolis,[2] as it is called, so that on either side there are two cities which form the boundaries of

---

[1] But the well-known Berenicê (now Suakim) was about as far from Myus Hormus (now Kosseir) as from Coptus (now Kench); see footnote 2, next page.

[2] "City of Apollo."

εἰσιν. ἀλλὰ νῦν ἡ Κοπτὸς καὶ ὁ Μυὸς ὅρμος
εὐδοκιμεῖ, καὶ χρῶνται τοῖς τόποις τούτοις. πρότερον μὲν οὖν ἐννυκτοπόρουν πρὸς τὰ ἄστρα βλέ-
ποντες οἱ καμηλέμποροι καὶ καθάπερ¹ οἱ πλέοντες
ὥδευον κομίζοντες καὶ ὕδωρ, νυνὶ δὲ καὶ ὑδρεῖα
κατεσκευάκασιν, ὀρύξαντες πολὺ βάθος, καὶ ἐκ
τῶν οὐρανίων, καίπερ ὄντων σπανίων, ὅμως δεξα-
μενὰς πεποίηνται. ἡ δ᾽ ὁδός ἐστιν ἐξ ἢ ἑπτὰ
ἡμερῶν. ἐπὶ δὲ τῷ ἰσθμῷ τούτῳ καὶ τὰ τῆς
σμαράγδου μέταλλά ἐστι, τῶν Ἀράβων ὀρυτ-
τόντων βαθεῖς τινας ὑπονόμους, καὶ ἄλλων λίθων
πολυτελῶν.

46. Μετὰ δὲ τὴν Ἀπόλλωνος πόλιν οἱ Θῆβαι
(καλεῖται δὲ νῦν Διὸς πόλις),

αἵθ᾽ ἑκατόμπυλοί εἰσι, διηκόσιοι δ᾽ ἀν᾽ ἑκάστην
ἀνέρες ἐξοιχνεῦσι σὺν ἵπποισιν καὶ ὄχεσφιν.

Ὅμηρος μὲν οὕτω· λέγει δὲ καὶ τὸν πλοῦτον·

οὐδ᾽ ὅσα Θήβας

C 816 Αἰγυπτίας, ὅθι πλεῖστα δόμοις ἐνὶ κτήματα
κεῖται.

καὶ ἄλλοι δὲ τοιαῦτα λέγουσι, μητρόπολιν τιθέντες
τῆς Αἰγύπτου ταύτην· καὶ νῦν δ᾽ ἴχνη δείκνυται

---

¹ καὶ καθάπερ, omitted by F, καί by Dh.

---

¹ Cp. 2. 5. 12.
² Pliny (6. 26), who speaks only of the route from Coptus
to Berenicê, says that the distance was 257 Roman miles
and required twelve days, and that one of the watering-
places, Old Hydreuma ("Watering-place"), near Berenicê,
could accommodate 2000 persons. Strabo seems to be confused on the subject, since (1) there were two distinct routes ;

the isthmus. But now it is Coptus and Myus Hormus [1] that have high repute; and people frequent these places. Now in earlier times the camel-merchants travelled only by night, looking to the stars for guidance, and, like the mariners, also carried water with them when they travelled; but now they have constructed watering-places, having dug down to a great depth, and, although rain-water is scarce, still they have made cisterns for it. The journey takes six or seven days.[2] On this isthmus are also the mines of smaragdus,[3] where the Arabians dig deep tunnels, I might call them, and of other precious stones.

46. After Apollonospolis one comes to Thebes [4] (now called Diospolis [5]), "Thebes of the hundred gates, whence sally forth two hundred men through each with horses and chariots."[6] So Homer; and he speaks also of its wealth, "even all the revenue of Aegyptian Thebes, where lies in treasure-houses the greatest wealth." And others also say things of this kind, making this city the metropolis of Aegypt. Even now traces of its magnitude are

---

(2) Myus Hormus and the well-known Berenicê were far apart (see footnote above); (3) the journey from Coptus to the latter required about twice as much time as that to the former (cp. Mahaffy, *The Empire of the Ptolemies*, pp. 135, 184, 395, 482), and (4) if Strabo was not thinking of a Berenicê *near* Myus Hormus, his "isthmus" has a very odd shape (see *Map* at end of volume).

[3] Pliny (37. 17) says that there are no fewer than twelve different kinds of smaragdus, and ranks the Aegyptian as third. The Aegyptian appears to have been a genuine emerald. For an account of the mines, see *Encyc. Brit.* s.v. "Emerald."

[4] Luxor.   [5] "City of Zeus."
[6] *Iliad* 9. 383.

τοῦ μεγέθους αὐτῆς ἐπὶ ὀγδοήκοντα σταδίους τὸ
μῆκος. ἔστι δ᾽ ἱερὰ[1] πλείω, καὶ τούτων δὲ τὰ
πολλὰ ἠκρωτηρίασε Καμβύσης. νυνὶ δὲ κωμηδὸν
συνοικεῖται, μέρος μέν[2] τι ἐν τῇ Ἀραβίᾳ, ἐν
ᾗπερ ἡ πόλις, μέρος δέ τι[3] καὶ ἐν τῇ περαίᾳ,
ὅπου τὸ Μεμνόνιον. ἐνταῦθα δὲ δυεῖν κολοσσῶν
ὄντων μονολίθων ἀλλήλων πλησίον, ὁ μὲν σώζεται,
τοῦ δ᾽ ἑτέρου τὰ ἄνω μέρη τὰ ἀπὸ τῆς καθέδρας
πέπτωκε σεισμοῦ γενηθέντος, ὥς φασι. πεπί-
στευται δ᾽, ὅτι ἅπαξ καθ᾽ ἡμέραν ἑκάστην ψόφος,
ὡς ἂν πληγῆς οὐ μεγάλης, ἀποτελεῖται ἀπὸ τοῦ
μένοντος ἐν τῷ θρόνῳ καὶ τῇ βάσει μέρους· κἀγὼ
δὲ παρὼν ἐπὶ τῶν τόπων μετὰ Γάλλου Αἰλίου
καὶ τοῦ πλήθους τῶν συνόντων αὐτῷ φίλων τε
καὶ στρατιωτῶν περὶ ὥραν πρώτην ἤκουσα τοῦ
ψόφου, εἴτε δὲ ἀπὸ τῆς βάσεως εἴτε ἀπὸ τοῦ
κολοσσοῦ εἴτ᾽ ἐπίτηδες τῶν κύκλῳ καὶ περὶ τὴν
βάσιν ἱδρυμένων τινὸς ποιήσαντος τὸν ψόφον, οὐκ
ἔχω διισχυρίσασθαι. διὰ γὰρ τὸ ἄδηλον τῆς
αἰτίας πᾶν μᾶλλον ἐπέρχεται πιστεύειν ἢ τὸ
ἐκ τῶν λίθων οὕτω τεταγμένων ἐκπέμπεσθαι τὸν
ἦχον. ὑπὲρ δὲ τοῦ Μεμνονίου θῆκαι βασιλέων
ἐν σπηλαίοις λατομηταὶ περὶ τετταράκοντα, θαυμαστῶς κατεσκευασμέναι καὶ[4] θέας ἄξιαι. ἐν δὲ
ταῖς θήκαις[5] ἐπί τινων ὀβελίσκων ἀναγραφαὶ

---

[1] Kramer inserts τά after ἱερά; and so the later editors.
[2] μέν, Corais, for δέ.
[3] μέρος δέ τι, Corais, for μέρος δὲ καί E, μέρος δ᾽ ἐστί other
MSS.; and so the later editors.
[4] Omitted by MSS. except EF.
[5] Meineke, following conjecture of Zoega (De Usu Obelisc.
p. 169), which is approved by Kramer and Forbiger, emends
θήκαις to Θήβαις.

pointed out, extending as they do for a distance
of eighty stadia in length;[1] and there are several
temples, but most of these, too, were mutilated by
Cambyses;[2] and now it is only a collection of
villages, a part of it being in Arabia, where was
the city, and a part on the far side of the river,
where was the Memnonium. Here are two colossi,
which are near one another and are each made of a
single stone; one of them is preserved, but the
upper parts of the other, from the seat up, fell
when an earthquake took place, so it is said. It
is believed that once each day a noise, as of a slight
blow, emanates from the part of the latter that
remains on the throne and its base; and I too,
when I was present at the places with Aelius Gallus
and his crowd of associates, both friends and soldiers,
heard the noise at about the first hour,[3] but whether
it came from the base or from the colossus, or
whether the noise was made on purpose by one
of the men who were standing all round and near
to the base, I am unable positively to assert; for on
account of the uncertainty of the cause I am induced
to believe anything rather than that the sound issued
from stones thus fixed. Above the Memnonium, in
caves, are tombs of kings, which are stone-hewn,
are about forty in number, are marvellously constructed, and are a spectacle worth seeing. And
among the tombs,[4] on some obelisks,[5] are inscriptions

[1] Diodorus (1. 45) puts the circuit of the city at 140 stadia.
[2] See § 27 above and 10. 3. 21.
[3] *i.e.* as reckoned from sunrise.
[4] Perhaps an error for "And at Thebes" (see critical note).
[5] One of these obelisks, which were erected by Rameses II,
now stands in the "Place de la Concorde" at Paris, a gift to
Louis XIV from Mehemet Ali.

δηλοῦσαι τὸν πλοῦτον τῶν τότε βασιλέων καὶ
τὴν ἐπικράτειαν, ὡς μέχρι Σκυθῶν καὶ Βακτρίων
καὶ Ἰνδῶν καὶ τῆς νῦν Ἰωνίας διατείνασαν, καὶ
φόρων πλῆθος καὶ στρατιᾶς περὶ ἑκατὸν μυριάδας.
λέγονται δὲ καὶ ἀστρονόμοι καὶ φιλόσοφοι μάλιστα οἱ ἐνταῦθα ἱερεῖς· τούτων δ᾽ ἐστὶ καὶ τὸ
τὰς ἡμέρας μὴ κατὰ σελήνην ἄγειν, ἀλλὰ κατὰ
ἥλιον, τοῖς τριακονθημέροις δώδεκα μησὶν ἐπα-
γόντων πέντε ἡμέρας κατ᾽ ἐνιαυτὸν ἕκαστον· εἰς
δὲ τὴν ἐκπλήρωσιν τοῦ ὅλου ἐνιαυτοῦ, ἐπιτρέχοντος
μορίου τινὸς τῆς ἡμέρας, περίοδόν τινα συντιθέασιν
ἐξ ὅλων ἡμερῶν καὶ ὅλων ἐνιαυτῶν τοσούτων, ὅσα
μόρια τὰ ἐπιτρέχοντα συνελθόντα ποιεῖ ἡμέραν.
ἀνατιθέασι δὲ τῷ Ἑρμῇ πᾶσαν τὴν τοιαύτην[1]
μάλιστα[2] σοφίαν· τῷ δὲ Διί, ὃν μάλιστα τιμῶσιν,
εὐειδεστάτη καὶ γένους λαμπροτάτου παρθένος
ἱερᾶται, ἃς καλοῦσιν οἱ Ἕλληνες παλλάδας·[3]
αὕτη δὲ καὶ παλλακεύει καὶ σύνεστιν οἷς βούλεται,
μέχρις ἂν ἡ φυσικὴ γένηται κάθαρσις τοῦ σώματος·
μετὰ δὲ τὴν κάθαρσιν δίδοται πρὸς ἄνδρα·[4] πρὶν
δὲ δοθῆναι, πένθος αὐτῆς ἄγεται μετὰ τὸν τῆς
παλλακείας καιρόν.

C 817   47. Μετὰ δὲ Θήβας Ἑρμωνθὶς πόλις, ἐν ᾗ ὅ

---

[1] τοσαύτην Cmoxz.

[2] μάλιστα, after τοιαύτην, is omitted by the editors before Kramer.

[3] For παλλάδας Xylander conj. παλλακίδας (see Thesaurus, s.v. παλλακή).

[4] ἄνδρα oz and the editors, ἄνδρας other MSS.

---

[1] i.e. each true "whole day" is $1\frac{1}{1400}$ days, and each true "whole year" is $365\frac{365}{1400}$, or $365\frac{1}{4}$ days. Hence they formed

which show the wealth of the kings at that time, and also their dominion, as having extended as far as the Scythians and the Bactrians and the Indians and the present Ionia, and the amount of tributes they received, and the size of army they had, about one million men. The priests there are said to have been, for the most part, astronomers and philosophers; and it is due to these priests also that people reckon the days, not by the moon, but by the sun, adding to the twelve months of thirty days each five days each year; and, for the filling out of the whole year, since a fraction of the day runs over and above, they form a period of time from enough whole days, or whole years, to make the fractions that run over and above, when added together, amount to a day.[1] They attribute to Hermes all wisdom of this particular kind; but to Zeus, whom they hold highest in honour, they dedicate a maiden of greatest beauty and most illustrious family (such maidens are called "pallades"[2] by the Greeks); and she prostitutes herself, and cohabits with whatever men she wishes until the natural cleansing of her body takes place;[3] and after her cleansing she is given in marriage to a man; but before she is married, after the time of her prostitution, a rite of mourning is celebrated for her.

47. After Thebes, one comes to a city Hermonthis,

---

[1] a period out of enough of these supernumerary fractions, when added together, to make one day; *i.e.* they intercalated a day every fourth year; a practice which later passed into the Julian Calendar. Cp. § 29 (above) and footnote.

[2] *i.e.* "virgin-priestesses," if the text is correct (see critical note). Diodorus Siculus (1. 47. 1) calls these maidens "pallacides (*i.e.* concubines) of Zeus."

[3] *i.e.* until "menstruation."

τε Ἀπόλλων τιμᾶται καὶ ὁ Ζεύς· τρέφεται δὲ
καὶ ἐνταῦθα βοῦς· ἔπειτα Κροκοδείλων πόλις,
τιμῶσα τὸ θηρίον· εἶτα Ἀφροδίτης πόλις καὶ
μετὰ ταῦτα Λατόπολις, τιμῶσα Ἀθηνᾶν καὶ τὸν
λάτον· εἶτα Εἰλειθυίας πόλις καὶ ἱερόν· ἐν δὲ
τῇ περαίᾳ Ἱεράκων πόλις, τὸν ἱέρακα τιμῶσα·
εἶτ᾽ Ἀπόλλωνος πόλις, καὶ αὕτη πολεμοῦσα τοῖς
κροκοδείλοις.

48. Ἡ δὲ Συήνη καὶ ἡ Ἐλεφαντίνη, ἡ μὲν ἐπὶ
τῶν ὅρων τῆς Αἰθιοπίας καὶ τῆς Αἰγύπτου πόλις,
ἡ δ᾽ ἐν τῷ Νείλῳ προκειμένη τῆς Συήνης νῆσος
ἐν ἡμισταδίῳ καὶ ἐν ταύτῃ πόλις ἔχουσα ἱερὸν
Κνούφιδος καὶ νειλομέτριον, καθάπερ Μέμφις.
ἔστι δὲ τὸ νειλομέτριον συννόμῳ λίθῳ[1] κατεσκευασμένον ἐπὶ τῇ ὄχθῃ τοῦ Νείλου φρέαρ, ἐν ᾧ τὰς
ἀναβάσεις τοῦ Νείλου[2] σημειοῦνται τὰς μεγίστας
τε καὶ ἐλαχίστας καὶ τὰς μέσας· συναναβαίνει
γὰρ καὶ συνταπεινοῦται τῷ ποταμῷ τὸ ἐν τῷ
φρέατι ὕδωρ. εἰσὶν οὖν ἐν τῷ τοίχῳ τοῦ φρέατος
παραγραφαί, μέτρα τῶν τελείων καὶ τῶν ἄλλων
ἀναβάσεων. ἐπισκοποῦντες οὖν ταύτας διαση-
μαίνουσι τοῖς ἄλλοις, ὅπως εἰδεῖεν· πρὸ πολλοῦ
γὰρ ἴσασιν ἐκ τῶν τοιούτων σημείων καὶ τῶν
ἡμερῶν[3] τὴν ἐσομένην ἀνάβασιν καὶ προδηλοῦσι.
τοῦτο δὲ καὶ τοῖς γεωργοῖς χρήσιμον τῆς τῶν

---

[1] συννόμῳ λίθῳ, Casaubon, for σὺν μονολίθῳ; so the later
editors.
[2] E reads μονολίθου instead of Νείλου.
[3] For καὶ τῶν ἡμερῶν Casaubon conj. καὶ τεκμηρίων ("evidences"); Corais writes καὶ μέτρων ("measures"), Kramer
approving.

---

[1] See § 40 above.

where both Apollo and Zeus are worshipped; and there, too, a bull is kept. And then to a City of Crocodiles, which holds in honour that animal. And then to a City of Aphroditê, and, after this, to Latopolis, which holds in honour Athena and the *latus*;[1] and then to a City of Eileithuia[2] and a temple; and on the far side of the river lies a City of Hawks, which holds the hawk in honour;[3] and then to Apollonospolis, which also carries on war against the crocodiles.

48. As for Syenê[4] and Elephantinê, the former is on the borders of Aethiopia and Aegypt, and the latter is an island in the Nile, being situated in front of Syenê at a distance of half a stadium, and a city which has a temple of Cnuphis and, like Memphis, a nilometer. The nilometer is a well on the bank of the Nile constructed with close-fitting stones,[5] in which are marks showing the greatest, least, and mean rises of the Nile; for the water in the well rises and lowers with the river. Accordingly, there are marks on the wall of the well, measures of the complete rises and of the others. So when watchers inspect these, they give out word to the rest of the people, so that they may know; for long beforehand they know from such signs and the days[6] what the future rise will be, and reveal it beforehand. This is useful, not only to the farmers with regard to the

---

[2] The goddess of childbirth.
[3] The hawk ("hierax"; see § 49 below) was sacred to Apollo, as was the eagle to Zeus (Aristophanes, *Birds*, 516).
[4] Assuan.
[5] Cp. the structure of the sewers at Rome (5. 3. 8).
[6] *i.e.* apparently, from the times of the observations as compared with the readings of the meter (but see critical note).

ὑδάτων ταμιείας χάριν καὶ παραχωμάτων καὶ
διωρύγων καὶ ἄλλων τοιούτων, καὶ τοῖς ἡγεμόσι
τῶν προσόδων χάριν· αἱ γὰρ μείζους ἀναβάσεις
μείζους καὶ τὰς προσόδους ὑπαγορεύουσιν. ἐν δὲ
τῇ Συήνῃ καὶ τὸ φρέαρ ἐστὶ τὸ διασημαῖνον τὰς
θερινὰς τροπάς,[1] διότι τῷ τροπικῷ κύκλῳ ὑπό-
κεινται οἱ τόποι οὗτοι καὶ ποιοῦσιν ἀσκίους τοὺς
γνώμονας κατὰ μεσημβρίαν.[2] ἀπὸ γὰρ τῶν
ἡμετέρων τόπων, λέγω δὲ τῶν Ἑλλαδικῶν, προϊοῦ-
σιν ἐπὶ τὴν μεσημβρίαν ἐνταῦθα πρῶτον ὁ ἥλιος
κατὰ κορυφὴν ἡμῖν γίνεται καὶ ποιεῖ τοὺς γνώμονας ἀσκίους κατὰ μεσημβρίαν· ἀνάγκη δέ,
κατὰ κορυφὴν ἡμῖν γινομένου, καὶ εἰς τὰ φρέατα
βάλλειν μέχρι τοῦ ὕδατος τὰς αὐγάς, κἂν βαθύ-
τατα ᾖ· κατὰ κάθετον γὰρ ἡμεῖς τε ἔσταμεν καὶ
τὰ ὀρύγματα τῶν φρεάτων κατεσκεύασται. εἰσὶ
δ' ἐνταῦθα τρεῖς σπεῖραι Ῥωμαίων ἱδρυμέναι
φρουρᾶς χάριν.

49. Μικρὸν δ' ὑπὲρ τῆς Ἐλεφαντίνης ἐστὶν ὁ
μικρὸς καταράκτης,[3] ἐφ' ᾧ καὶ θέαν τινὰ οἱ
σκαφῖται τοῖς ἡγεμόσιν ἐπιδείκνυνται· ὁ μὲν γὰρ
καταράκτης ἐστὶ κατὰ μέσον τὸν ποταμόν, πετρώδης τις ὀφρύς, ἐπίπεδος μὲν ἄνωθεν, ὥστε
δέχεσθαι τὸν ποταμόν, τελευτῶσα δ' εἰς κρημνόν,
καθ' οὗ καταρρήγνυται τὸ ὕδωρ, ἑκατέρωθεν δὲ
πρὸς τῇ γῇ ῥεῖθρον, ὃ μάλιστα καὶ ἀνάπλουν
C 818 ἔχει· ἀναπλεύσαντες οὖν ταύτῃ καταρρέουσιν ἐπὶ
τὸν καταράκτην καὶ ὠθοῦνται μετὰ τῆς σκάφης

---

[1] καί, before διότι, the editors omit.
[2] The words καὶ ποιοῦσιν . . . μεσημβρίαν are rejected by
Kramer and Meineke.
[3] καταράκτης DE, καταρράκτης other MSS.; and so in the
succeeding uses of the word.

water-distribution, embankments, canals, and other things of this kind, but also to the praefects, with regard to the revenues; for the greater rises indicate that the revenues also will be greater. But in Syenê[1] is also the well that marks the summer tropic, for the reason that this region lies under the tropic circle and causes the gnomons to cast no shadow at midday; for if from our region, I mean that of Greece, we proceed towards the south, it is at Syenê that the sun first gets over our heads and causes the gnomons to cast no shadow at midday; and necessarily, when the sun gets over our heads, it also casts its rays into wells as far as the water, even if they are very deep; for we ourselves stand perpendicular to the earth and wells are dug perpendicular to the surface. And here are stationed three cohorts as a guard.

49. A little above Elephantinê is the little cataract, on which the boatmen exhibit a kind of spectacle for the praefects;[2] for the cataract is at the middle of the river, and is a brow of rock, as it were, which is flat on top, so that it receives the river, but ends in a precipice, down which the water dashes; whereas on either side towards the land there is a stream which generally can even be navigated up-stream. Accordingly, the boatmen, having first sailed up-stream here, drift down to the cataract, are thrust along with the boat over the precipice, and escape

---

[1] So Pliny (2. 75) and Arrian (*Indica*, 25. 7); but in reality Syenê was slightly to the north of the tropic, its latitude being 24° 1′. The obliquity of the ecliptic in Eratosthenes' time was about 23° 44′, in Strabo's time about 23° 42′, and to-day is about 23° 27′.

[2] *e.g.* Aelius Gallus, whom Strabo accompanied.

ἐπὶ τὸν κρημνὸν καὶ σώζονται σὺν αὐτῇ [1] ἀπαθεῖς.
τοῦ δὲ καταράκτου μικρὸν ἐπάνω τὰς Φιλὰς εἶναι
συμβαίνει, κοινὴν κατοικίαν Αἰθιόπων τε καὶ
Αἰγυπτίων, κατεσκευασμένην ὥσπερ καὶ τὴν
Ἐλεφαντίνην καὶ τὸ μέγεθος ἴσην, ἱερὰ ἔχουσαν
Αἰγύπτια· ὅπου καὶ ὄρνεον τιμᾶται, ὃ καλοῦσι
μὲν ἱέρακα, οὐδὲν δὲ ὅμοιον ἔμοιγε ἐφαίνετο ἔχειν
τοῖς παρ᾽ ἡμῖν καὶ ἐν Αἰγύπτῳ ἱέραξιν, ἀλλὰ καὶ
τῷ μεγέθει μεῖζον ἦν καὶ τῇ ποικιλίᾳ πολὺ ἐξηλ-
λαγμένον. Αἰθιοπικὸν δ᾽ ἔφασαν εἶναι, κἀκεῖθεν
κομίζεσθαι, ὅταν ἐκλίπῃ, καὶ πρότερον.[2] καὶ δὴ
καὶ τότε ἐδείχθη ἡμῖν πρὸς ἐκλείψει ὂν διὰ νόσον.
50. Ἤλθομεν δ᾽ εἰς Φιλὰς ἐκ Συήνης ἀπήνῃ
δι᾽ ὁμαλοῦ σφόδρα πεδίου σταδίους ὁμοῦ τι
ἑκατόν.[3] παρ᾽ ὅλην δὲ τὴν ὁδὸν ἦν ἰδεῖν ἑκατέρωθεν πολλαχοῦ, ὥσπερ ἑρμαῖα, πέτρον ἠλίβατον
στρογγύλον, λεῖον ἱκανῶς, ἐγγὺς σφαιροειδοῦς,
τοῦ μέλανος καὶ σκληροῦ λίθου, ἐξ οὗ αἱ θυῖαι
γίνονται, ἐπὶ πέτρῳ κείμενον μείζονι καὶ ἐπ᾽
ἐκείνῳ πάλιν ἄλλον· ἔστι δ᾽ ὅτε αὐτοὶ καθ᾽ αὑτοὺς
ἔκειντο οἱ πέτροι· ἦν δ᾽ ὁ μὲν μέγιστος τὴν διάμετρον ποδῶν οὐκ ἐλαττόνων ἢ δώδεκα, ἅπαντες
δὲ μείζους ἢ ἡμίσεις τούτων. διέβημεν δὲ εἰς
τὴν νῆσον ἐπὶ πάκτωνος· ὁ δὲ πάκτων διὰ σκυ-
ταλίδων πεπηγός ἐστι σκάφιον, ὥστ᾽ ἐοικέναι

---

[1] αὐτῇ E, αὐταῖς other MSS.
[2] καὶ πρότερον is omitted by F.
[3] For ἑκατόν (ρ΄) Groskurd reads πεντήκοντα (ν΄).

---

[1] Probably an error for "fifty," as Groskurd suggests (see
critical note).

unharmed, boat and all. A little above the cataract
lies Philae, a common settlement of Aethiopians and
Aegyptians, which is built like Elephantinê and is
equal to it in size; and it has Aegyptian temples.
Here, also, a bird is held in honour, which they call
a hawk, though to me it appeared to be in no respect
like the hawks in our country and in Aegypt, but
was both greater in size and far different in the
varied colouring of its plumage. They said that it
was an Aethiopian bird, and that another was brought
from Aethiopia whenever the one at hand died, or
before. And in fact the bird shown to us at the
time mentioned was nearly dead because of disease.

50. We went to Philae from Syenê by wagon
through an exceedingly level plain—a distance all
told of about one hundred[1] stadia. Along the whole
road on either side one could see in many places a
stone like our Hermae;[2] it was huge, round, quite
smooth, nearly sphere-shaped, and consisted of the
black, hard stone from which mortars are made—a
smaller stone lying on a larger, and on that stone
again another.[3] Sometimes, however, it was only
a single stone; and the largest was in diameter no
less than twelve feet, though one and all were
larger than half this measure. We crossed to the
island on a *pacton*. The *pacton* is a small boat constructed of withes, so that it resembles woven-work;

---

[2] *i.e.* quadrangular pillars surmounted by a head or bust
of Hermes, which were used as sign-posts or boundary-marks.

[3] Pocock (*Travels in Egypt*, in *Pinkerton's Voyages and
Travels*, Vol. XV, p. 265), who saw some of these stones,
says that they were rocks of red granite which had turned
blackish on the outside: "a rock standing up like a pillar,
and a large rock on it, hieroglyphics being cut on some of
them."

διαπλοκίνῳ· ἑστῶτες δ' ἐν ὕδατι ἢ καὶ σανιδίοις
τισὶ προσκαθήμενοι ῥᾳδίως ἐπεραιώθημεν, δεδιότες[1] μάτην.[2] ἀκίνδυνα γάρ ἐστιν, ἂν μή τις
ὑπέργομον ποιήσῃ τὸ πορθμεῖον.

51. Καθ' ὅλην δὲ τὴν Αἴγυπτον τοῦ φοίνικος
ἀγεννοῦς ὄντος καὶ ἐκφέροντος καρπὸν οὐκ
εὔβρωτον ἐν τοῖς περὶ τὸ Δέλτα τόποις καὶ περὶ
τὴν Ἀλεξάνδρειαν, ὁ ἐν τῇ Θηβαΐδι φοῖνιξ
ἄριστος τῶν ἄλλων φύεται. θαυμάζειν οὖν
ἄξιον, πῶς ταὐτὸ κλίμα οἰκοῦντες τῇ Ἰουδαίᾳ
καὶ ὅμοροι οἱ περὶ τὸ Δέλτα καὶ τὴν Ἀλεξάνδρειαν, τοσοῦτον διαλλάττουσιν, ἐκείνης πρὸς
ἄλλῳ φοίνικι καὶ τὸν καρυωτὸν γεννώσης, οὐ
πολὺ κρείττονα τοῦ Βαβυλωνίου. διττὸς δ'
ἐστὶν ὅ τε ἐν τῇ Θηβαΐδι καὶ ὁ ἐν τῇ Ἰουδαίᾳ,
ὅ τε ἄλλος καὶ ὁ καρυωτός, σκληρότερος δ' ὁ
Θηβαϊκός, ἀλλὰ τῇ γεύσει εὐστομώτερος. ἔστι
δὲ καὶ νῆσος ἡ μάλιστα ἐκφέρουσα τὸν ἄριστον,
μεγίστην τελοῦσα πρόσοδον τοῖς ἡγεμόσι·
βασιλικὴ γὰρ ἦν, ἰδιώτῃ δ' οὐ μετῆν, καὶ νῦν
τῶν ἡγεμόνων ἐστί.

52. Πολλὰ δ' Ἡρόδοτός τε καὶ ἄλλοι φλυαροῦ-
σιν, ὥσπερ μέλος ἢ ῥυθμὸν ἢ ἥδυσμά τι τῷ
C 819 λόγῳ τὴν τερατείαν προσφέροντες· οἷον καὶ τὸ
φάσκειν περὶ τὰς νήσους τὰς πρὸς τῇ Συήνῃ
καὶ τῇ Ἐλεφαντίνῃ, πλείους δ' εἰσί, τὰς πηγὰς
τοῦ Νείλου εἶναι, καὶ βάθος ἄβυσσον ἔχειν τὸν
πόρον κατὰ τοῦτον τὸν τόπον. νήσους δ' ὁ Νεῖλος
κατεσπαρμένας ἔχει παμπόλλας, τὰς μὲν καλυπ-
τομένας ὅλας ἐν ταῖς ἀναβάσεσι, τὰς δ' ἐκ

---

[1] *moz* read οὐ before δεδιότες.
[2] μάτην EF, omitted by other MSS.

and though standing in water or seated on small boards, we crossed easily, being afraid without cause, for there is no danger unless the ferry-boat is over-laden.

51. Throughout the whole of Aegypt the palm tree is not of a good species; and in the region of the Delta and Alexandria it produces fruit that is not good to eat; but the palm tree in the Thebaïs is better than any of the rest. Now it is a thing worth marvelling at, that a country which is in the same latitude as Judaea and borders on it, I mean the country round the Delta and Alexandria, differs so much, since Judaea, in addition to another palm, produces also the caryotic, which is somewhat better than the Babylonian. There are two kinds in the Thebaïs as well as in Judaea, both the caryotic and the other; and the Thebaïc date is harder, but more agreeable to the taste. There is also an island which is particularly productive of the best date, yielding a very large revenue for the praefects; for it used to be a royal possession, and no private individual shared in it, but it now belongs to the praefects.

52. Both Herodotus[1] and others talk much non-sense, adding to their account marvellous tales, to give it, as it were, a kind of tune or rhythm or relish; as, for example, the assertion that the sources of the Nile are in the neighbourhood of the islands near Syenê and Elephantinê (of which there are several), and that at this place its channel has a bottomless depth. The Nile has very many islands scattered along its course, of which some are wholly covered at its risings and others only partly; but

[1] 2. 28.

μέρους, ἐποχετεύεται δὲ τοῖς κοχλίαις τὰ λίαν
ἔξαλα.

53. Ἦν μὲν οὖν ἡ Αἴγυπτος εἰρηνικὴ τὸ πλέον
ἐξ ἀρχῆς διὰ τὸ αὔταρκες τῆς χώρας καὶ τὸ
δυσείσβολον τοῖς ἔξωθεν, ἀπὸ μὲν τῶν ἄρκτων
ἀλιμένῳ παραλίᾳ καὶ πελάγει τῷ Αἰγυπτίῳ
φρουρουμένη, ἀπὸ δὲ τῆς ἕω καὶ τῆς ἑσπέρας ἐρήμοις
ὄρεσι, τοῖς τε Λιβυκοῖς καὶ τοῖς Ἀραβίοις, ὥσπερ
ἔφαμεν·¹ λοιπὰ δὲ τὰ πρὸς νότον Τρωγλοδύται καὶ
Βλέμμυες καὶ Νοῦβαι καὶ Μεγάβαροι οἱ ὑπὲρ
Συήνης Αἰθίοπες· εἰσὶ δ᾽ οὗτοι νομάδες καὶ οὐ
πολλοὶ οὐδὲ μάχιμοι, δοκοῦντες δὲ τοῖς πάλαι
διὰ τὸ ληστρικῶς ἀφυλάκτοις ἐπιτίθεσθαι πολ-
λάκις· οἱ δὲ πρὸς μεσημβρίαν καὶ Μερόην ἀνή-
κοντες Αἰθίοπες, οὐδ᾽ οὗτοι πολλοὶ οὔτε ἐν
συστροφῇ, ἅτε ποταμίαν μακρὰν στενὴν καὶ
σκολιὰν οἰκοῦντες, οἵαν προείπομεν·² οὐδὲ παρεσ-
κευασμένοι καλῶς οὔτε πρὸς πόλεμον οὔτε πρὸς
τὸν ἄλλον βίον. καὶ νῦν δὲ διάκειται παραπλησίως ἡ χώρα πᾶσα· σημεῖον δέ· τρισὶ γοῦν
σπείραις, οὐδὲ ταύταις ἐντελέσιν, ἱκανῶς ὑπὸ
τῶν Ῥωμαίων ἡ χώρα φρουρεῖται· τολμήσασι δὲ
τοῖς Αἰθίοψιν ἐπιθέσθαι κινδυνεῦσαι τῇ χώρᾳ
συνέπεσε τῇ σφετέρᾳ. καὶ αἱ λοιπαὶ δὲ δυνάμεις
αἱ ἐν Αἰγύπτῳ οὔτε τοσαῦταί τινές εἰσιν οὔτε
ἀθρόαις ἐχρήσαντο οὐδ᾽ ἅπαξ Ῥωμαῖοι· οὐ γάρ
εἰσιν οὔτ᾽ αὐτοὶ Αἰγύπτιοι πολεμισταί, καίπερ
ὄντες παμπληθεῖς, οὔτε τὰ πέριξ ἔθνη. Γάλλος
μέν γε Κορνήλιος, ὁ πρῶτος κατασταθεὶς ἔπαρχος

---

¹ Cp. § 30 above.   ² Cp. § 4 above.
³ See §§ 3 and 4 above.

the exceedingly high parts of the latter are irrigated by means of screws.[1]

53. Now Aegypt was generally inclined to peace from the outset, because of the self-sufficiency of the country and of the difficulty of invasion by outsiders, being protected on the north by a harbourless coast and by the Aegyptian Sea, and on the east and west by the desert mountains of Libya and Arabia, as I have said;[2] and the remaining parts, those towards the south, are inhabited by Troglodytes, Blemmyes, Nubae, and Megabari, those Aethiopians who live above Syenê. These are nomads, and not numerous, or warlike either, though they were thought to be so by the ancients, because often, like brigands, they would attack defenceless persons. As for those Aethiopians who extend towards the south and Meroê, they are not numerous either, nor do they collect in one mass, inasmuch as they inhabit a long, narrow, and winding stretch of river-land, such as I have described before;[3] neither are they well equipped either for warfare or for any other kind of life. And now, too, the whole of the country is similarly disposed to peace. And the following is a sign of the fact: the country is sufficiently guarded by the Romans with only three cohorts, and even these are not complete; and when the Aethiopians dared to make an attack upon them, they imperilled their own country. The remaining Roman forces in Aegypt are hardly as large as these, nor have the Romans used them collectively even once; for neither are the Aegyptians themselves warriors, although they are very numerous, nor are the surrounding tribes. Cornelius Gallus, the first man appointed praefect of the country by Caesar, attacked

τῆς χώρας ὑπὸ Καίσαρος, τήν τε Ἡρώων πόλιν
ἀποστᾶσαν ἐπελθὼν δι᾽ ὀλίγων εἷλε, στάσιν τε
γενηθεῖσαν ἐν τῇ Θηβαΐδι διὰ τοὺς φόρους ἐν
βραχεῖ κατέλυσε. Πετρώνιός τε ὕστερον τοῦ
Ἀλεξανδρέων πλήθους τοσούτων μυριάδων
ὁρμήσαντος ἐπ᾽ αὐτὸν μετὰ λίθων βολῆς, αὐτοῖς
τοῖς περὶ ἑαυτὸν στρατιώταις ἀντέσχε, καὶ
διαφθείρας τινὰς αὐτῶν τοὺς λοιποὺς ἔπαυσε.
Γάλλος τε Αἴλιος μέρει τῆς ἐν Αἰγύπτῳ φρουρᾶς
εἰς τὴν Ἀραβίαν ἐμβαλὼν εἴρηται, τίνα τρόπον
ἐξήλεγξε τοὺς ἀνθρώπους ἀπολέμους ὄντας· εἰ δὴ
μὴ ὁ Συλλαῖος αὐτὸν προυδίδου, κἂν κατεστρέ-
ψατο τὴν Εὐδαίμονα πᾶσαν.

C 820　54. Ἐπειδὴ δὲ οἱ Αἰθίοπες, καταφρονήσαντες
τῷ μέρος τι τῆς ἐν Αἰγύπτῳ δυνάμεως ἀπεσπάσθαι
μετὰ Γάλλου Αἰλίου πολεμοῦντος πρὸς τοὺς
Ἄραβας, ἐπῆλθον [1] τῇ Θηβαΐδι καὶ τῇ φρουρᾷ
τῶν τριῶν σπειρῶν τῶν κατὰ Συήνην καὶ ἑλόντες
ἔφθασαν τήν τε Συήνην καὶ τὴν Ἐλεφαντίνην
καὶ Φιλὰς ἐξ ἐφόδου διὰ τὸ αἰφνίδιον καὶ
ἐξηνδραποδίσαντο, ἀνέσπασαν δὲ καὶ τοὺς
Καίσαρος ἀνδριάντας· ἐπελθὼν δὲ ἐλάττοσιν ἢ
μυρίοις πεζοῖς Πετρώνιος, ἱππεῦσι δὲ ὀκτακο-
σίοις πρὸς ἄνδρας τρισμυρίους, πρῶτον μὲν
ἠνάγκασεν ἀναφυγεῖν αὐτοὺς εἰς Ψέλχιν, πόλιν
Αἰθιοπικήν, καὶ πρεσβεύεται τά τε ληφθέντα
ἀπαιτῶν καὶ τὰς αἰτίας, δι᾽ ἃς ἦρξαν πολέμου·
λεγόντων δ᾽, ὡς ἀδικοῖντο ὑπὸ τῶν νομάρχων, [2]
ἀλλ᾽ οὐκ ἔφη τούτους ἡγεμόνας εἶναι τῆς χώρας,
ἀλλὰ Καίσαρα· αἰτησαμένων δ᾽ ἡμέρας τρεῖς εἰς

----

[1] ἐπῆλθον, Corais, for ἐπελθόντες.

Heroönpolis, which had revolted, and took it with only a few soldiers, and in only a short time broke up a sedition which had taken place in the Thebaïs on account of the tributes. And at a later time Petronius, when all that countless multitude of Alexandrians rushed to attack him with a throwing of stones, held out against them with merely his own body-guard, and after killing some of them put a stop to the rest. And I have already stated [1] how Aelius Gallus, when he invaded Arabia with a part of the guard stationed in Aegypt, discovered that the people were unwarlike; indeed, if Syllaeus had not betrayed him, he would even have subdued the whole of Arabia Felix.

54. But the Aethiopians, emboldened by the fact that a part of the Roman force in Aegypt had been drawn away with Aelius Gallus when he was carrying on war against the Arabians, attacked the Thebaïs and the garrison of the three cohorts at Syenê, and by an unexpected onset took Syenê and Elephantinê and Philae, and enslaved the inhabitants, and also pulled down the statues of Caesar. But Petronius, setting out with less than ten thousand infantry and eight hundred cavalry against thirty thousand men, first forced them to flee back to Pselchis, an Aethiopian city, and sent ambassadors to demand what they had taken, as also to ask the reasons why they had begun war; and when they said that they had been wronged by the Nomarchs,[2] he replied that these were not rulers of the country, but Caesar; and when they had requested three days for delibera-

---

[1] 16. 4. 23.   [2] "Nome-rulers."

---

[2] νομάρχων *s*, μονάρχων other MSS.

βουλὴν καὶ μηδέν, ὧν ἐχρῆν, ποιούντων, προσβαλὼν ἠνάγκασε προελθεῖν εἰς μάχην, ταχὺ δὲ
τροπὴν ἐποίησε, συντεταγμένων τε κακῶς καὶ
ὡπλισμένων· μεγάλους γὰρ εἶχον θυρεούς, καὶ
τούτους ὠμοβοΐνους, ἀμυντήρια δὲ πελέκεις, οἱ δὲ
κοντούς, οἱ δὲ καὶ ξίφη. τινὲς μὲν οὖν εἰς τὴν πόλιν
συνηλάθησαν, οἱ δ᾽ εἰς τὴν ἐρημίαν ἔφυγον, τινὰς
δὲ νῆσος πλησίον ὑπεδέξατο ἐμβάντας¹ εἰς τὸν
πόρον, οὐ γὰρ πολλοὶ ἦσαν ἐνταῦθα οἱ κροκό-
δειλοι διὰ τὸν ῥοῦν. τούτων δ᾽ ἦσαν καὶ οἱ τῆς
βασιλίσσης στρατηγοὶ τῆς Κανδάκης, ἣ καθ᾽
ἡμᾶς ἦρξε τῶν Αἰθιόπων, ἀνδρική τις γυνὴ
πεπηρωμένη τὸν ἕτερον τῶν ὀφθαλμῶν· τούτους
τε δὴ ζωγρίᾳ λαμβάνει ἅπαντας, ἐπιπλεύσας
σχεδίαις τε καὶ ναυσί, καὶ καταπέμπει παρα-
χρῆμα εἰς Ἀλεξάνδρειαν, ἐπελθών τε τὴν Ψέλχιν
αἱρεῖ· προσαριθμουμένου δὲ τοῖς ἑαλωκόσι τοῦ
πλήθους τῶν πεσόντων ἐν τῇ μάχῃ, τοὺς σωθέν-
τας ὀλίγους παντάπασι γενέσθαι συνέβη. ἐκ δὲ
Ψέλχιος ἧκεν εἰς Πρῆμνιν, ἐρυμνὴν πόλιν, διελθὼν
τοὺς θῖνας, ἐν οἷς ὁ Καμβύσου κατεχώσθη
στρατὸς ἐμπεσόντος ἀνέμου. προσβαλὼν δὲ ἐξ
ἐφόδου τὸ φρούριον αἱρεῖ, καὶ μετὰ ταῦτα
ὥρμησεν ἐπὶ Νάπατων· τοῦτο δ᾽ ἦν τὸ βασίλειον
τῆς Κανδάκης, καὶ ἦν ἐνταῦθα υἱὸς αὐτῆς. καὶ
αὐτὴ δ᾽ ἔν τινι πλησίον ἵδρυτο χωρίῳ. πρεσ-
βευσαμένης δὲ περὶ φιλίας καὶ ἀποδούσης τοὺς
ἐκ Συήνης αἰχμαλώτους καὶ τοὺς ἀνδριάντας,
ἐπελθὼν λαμβάνει καὶ τὰ Νάπατα, φυγόντος
τοῦ παιδός, καὶ κατασκάπτει· ἐξανδραποδισά-

---

¹ For ἐμβάντας, Jones conj. ἐμβαλόντας.

tion, but did nothing they should have done, he
made an attack and forced them to come forth to
battle; and he quickly turned them to flight, since
they were badly marshalled and badly armed; for
they had large oblong shields, and those too made of
raw ox-hide, and as weapons some had only axes,
others pikes, and others swords. Now some were
driven together into the city, others fled into the
desert, and others found refuge on a neighbouring
island, having waded [1] into the channel, for on
account of the current the crocodiles were not
numerous there. Among these fugitives were the
generals of Queen Candacê, who was ruler of the
Aethiopians in my time—a masculine sort of woman,
and blind in one eye. These, one and all, he captured
alive, having sailed after them in both rafts and ships,
and he sent them forthwith down to Alexandria; and
he also attacked Pselchis and captured it; and if the
multitude of those who fell in the battle be added
to the number of the captives, those who escaped
must have been altogether few in number. From
Pselchis he went to Premnis, a fortified city, after
passing through the sand-dunes, where the army
of Cambyses was overwhelmed when a wind-storm
struck them; and having made an attack, he took
the fortress at the first onset. After this he set
out for Napata. This was the royal residence of
Candacê; and her son was there, and she herself
was residing at a place near by. But though she
sent ambassadors to treat for friendship and offered
to give back the captives and the statues brought
from Syenê, Petronius attacked and captured Napata
too, from which her son had fled, and rased it to the

[1] See critical note.

μενος δ' ἀναστρέφει πάλιν εἰς τοὐπίσω μετὰ τῶν
λαφύρων, δύσοδα κρίνας τὰ προσωτέρω. τὴν δὲ
Πρήμνιν τειχίσας βέλτιον, φρουρὰν ἐμβαλὼν καὶ
τροφὴν δυεῖν ἐνιαυτῶν τετρακοσίοις ἀνδράσιν,
ἀπῆρεν εἰς Ἀλεξάνδρειαν. καὶ τῶν αἰχμαλώτων
C 821 τοὺς μὲν ἐλαφυροπώλησε, χιλίους δὲ Καίσαρι
ἔπεμψε νεωστὶ ἐκ Καντάβρων ἥκοντι, τοὺς δὲ
νόσοι διεχρήσαντο. ἐν τούτῳ μυριάσι Κανδάκη
πολλαῖς ἐπὶ τὴν φρουρὰν ἐπῆλθε· Πετρώνιος δ'
ἐξεβοήθησε καὶ φθάνει προσελθὼν [1] εἰς τὸ φρούριον, καὶ πλείοσι παρασκευαῖς ἐξασφαλισάμενος
τὸν τόπον, πρεσβευσαμένων, ἐκέλευσεν ὡς Καίσαρα πρεσβεύεσθαι· οὐκ εἰδέναι δὲ φασκόντων,
ὅστις εἴη Καῖσαρ καὶ ὅπη βαδιστέον εἴη παρ'
αὐτόν, ἔδωκε τοὺς παραπέμψοντας· καὶ ἧκον εἰς
Σάμον, ἐνταῦθα τοῦ Καίσαρος ὄντος καὶ μέλλοντος
εἰς Συρίαν ἐντεῦθεν προϊέναι, Τιβέριον εἰς Ἀρ-
μενίαν στέλλοντος. πάντων δὲ τυχόντων, ὧν
ἐδέοντο, ἀφῆκεν αὐτοῖς καὶ τοὺς φόρους, οὓς
ἐπέστησε.

II

1. Πολλὰ δ' εἴρηται περὶ τῶν Αἰθιοπικῶν ἐν
τοῖς πρότερον, ὥστε συμπεριωδευμένα ἂν εἴη τῇ
Αἰγύπτῳ καὶ τὰ τούτων. ὡς δ' εἰπεῖν, τὰ ἄκρα
τῆς οἰκουμένης τὰ παρακείμενα τῇ δυσκράτῳ καὶ
ἀοικήτῳ διὰ καῦμα ἢ ψῦχος ἀνάγκη ἀποτεύγματα
εἶναι τῆς εὐκράτου καὶ ἐλαττώματα· ταῦτα δ'

---

[1] προσελθών F and first hand in D, προσεισελθών C, προεισ-
ελθών other MSS.

ground; and having enslaved its inhabitants, he turned back again with the booty, having decided that the regions farther on would be hard to traverse. But he fortified Premnis better, threw in a garrison and food for four hundred men for two years, and set out for Alexandria. As for the captives, he sold some of them as booty, and sent one thousand to Caesar, who had recently returned from Cantabria; and the others died of diseases. Meantime Candacê marched against the garrison with many thousands of men, but Petronius set out to its assistance and arrived at the fortress first; and when he had made the place thoroughly secure by sundry devices, ambassadors came, but he bade them go to Caesar; and when they asserted that they did not know who Caesar was or where they should have to go to find him, he gave them escorts; and they went to Samos, since Caesar was there and intended to proceed to Syria from there, after despatching Tiberius to Armenia. And when the ambassadors had obtained everything they pled for, he even remitted the tributes which he had imposed.

II

1. In the earlier parts of my work I have already said many things about the Aethiopian[1] tribes, so that the description of their country may be said to be included with that of Aegypt. In general, the extremities of the inhabited world, which lie along-side the part of the earth that is not temperate and habitable, because of heat or cold, must needs be defective and inferior to the temperate part;

---

[1] See *Index*, s.v. "Aethiopians."

ἐκ τῶν βίων δῆλα καὶ τῆς πρὸς τὰς χρείας τὰς
ἀνθρωπικὰς ἀπορίας. κακόβιοί τε δὴ καὶ γυμνῆτές εἰσι τὰ πολλὰ καὶ νομάδες· τά τε βοσκήματα
αὐτοῖς ἐστι μικρά, πρόβατα καὶ αἶγες καὶ βόες·
καὶ κύνες μικροί, τραχεῖς[1] δὲ καὶ μάχιμοι.
τάχα δὲ καὶ τοὺς Πυγμαίους ἀπὸ τῆς τούτων
μικροφυΐας ὑπενόησαν καὶ ἀνέπλασαν· ἑωρακὼς
μὲν γὰρ οὐδεὶς ἐξηγεῖται τῶν πίστεως ἀξίων
ἀνδρῶν.

2. Ζῶσί τ᾿ ἀπὸ κέγχρου καὶ κριθῆς, ἀφ᾿ ὧν καὶ
ποτὸν αὐτοῖς ἐστιν ἀντ᾿ ἐλαίου δὲ[2] βούτυρον καὶ
στέαρ· οὐδ᾿ ἀκρόδρυα ἔχουσι πλὴν φοινίκων
ὀλίγων ἐν κήποις βασιλικοῖς· ἔνιοι δὲ καὶ πόαν
σιτοῦνται καὶ κλῶνας ἁπαλοὺς καὶ λωτὸν καὶ
καλάμου ῥίζαν· κρέασι δὲ χρῶνται καὶ αἵματι
καὶ γάλακτι καὶ τυρῷ. σέβονται δ᾿ ὡς θεοὺς
τοὺς βασιλέας, κατακλείστους ὄντας καὶ οἰκουροὺς
τὸ πλέον. ἔστι δὲ τὸ μέγιστον αὐτοῖς βασίλειον ἡ Μερόη, πόλις ὁμώνυμος τῇ νήσῳ. τὴν
δὲ νῆσον θυρεοειδῆ φασι τὸ σχῆμα, τό τε μέγεθος
τάχα πρὸς ὑπερβολὴν εἴρηται μῆκος μὲν ὅσον
τρισχιλίων σταδίων, εὖρος δὲ χιλίων. ἔχει δ᾿ ἡ
νῆσος[3] συχνὰ καὶ ὄρη καὶ δάση μεγάλα· οἰκοῦσι
δ᾿ οἱ μὲν νομάδες, οἱ δὲ θηρευτικοί, οἱ δὲ γεωργοί·
ἔστι δὲ καὶ χαλκωρυχεῖα καὶ σιδηρουργεῖα καὶ
χρυσεῖα καὶ λίθων γένη πολυτελῶν· περιέχεται δ᾿
ἀπὸ μὲν τῆς Λιβύης θισὶ μεγάλοις, ἀπὸ δὲ τῆς
Ἀραβίας κρημνοῖς συνεχέσιν, ἄνωθεν δ᾿ ἐκ νότου

---

[1] ταχεῖς Eo, perhaps rightly.
[2] The MSS. read ποτὸν ποιοῦσιν αὐτοῖς ἐστιν· ἔλαιον δὲ κτλ.,
except that x omits ἐστιν. Corais reads ποτὸν αὐτοῖς ἐστιν·
ἀντὶ δὲ ἐλαίου κτλ.; but Jones reads as above, copying the
phrase ἀντ᾿ ἐλαίου δέ from 3. 3. 7.

and this is clear from the modes of life of the inhabitants and from their lack of human necessities. They indeed live a hard life, go almost naked, and are nomads; and their domestic animals—sheep, goats, and cattle—are small; and their dogs are small though rough [1] and pugnacious. And perhaps it is from the natural smallness of the people that men have conceived of Pygmies and fabricated them; for no man worthy of belief professes to have seen them.

2. The Aethiopians live on millet and barley, from which they also make a drink; but instead of olive-oil they have butter and tallow. Neither do they have fruit trees, except a few date-palms in the royal gardens. But some use grass as food, as also tender twigs, lotus, and reed-roots; and they use meats, blood, milk, and cheese. They reverence as gods their kings, who generally stay shut up at home. Their greatest royal seat is Meroê, a city bearing the same name as the island. The island is said to be like an oblong shield in shape. Its size has perhaps been exaggerated: about three thousand stadia in length and one thousand in breadth. The island has both numerous mountains and large thickets; it is inhabited partly by nomads, partly by hunters, and partly by farmers; and it has mines of copper, iron, gold, and different kinds [2] of precious stones. It is bounded on the Libyan side by large sand-dunes, and on the Arabian side by continuous

---

[1] Possibly an error for "swift" (see critical note).

[2] Diodorus Siculus (1. 33) says "*all kinds* of precious stones."

---

[3] ἡ νῆσος is omitted by all MSS. except F; E reads ἡ Μερόη.

ταῖς συμβολαῖς τῶν ποταμῶν, τοῦ τε Ἀσταβόρα [1]
C 822 καὶ τοῦ Ἀστάποδος καὶ τοῦ Ἀστασόβα· πρὸς
ἄρκτον δ᾽ ἡ ἐφεξῆς ῥύσις τοῦ Νείλου καὶ μέχρι
Αἰγύπτου κατὰ τὴν λεχθεῖσαν πρότερον σκολιό-
τητα τοῦ ποταμοῦ. ἐν δὲ ταῖς πόλεσιν αἱ οἰκήσεις
ἐκ φοινικίνων σχιζῶν διαπλεκομένων [2] ἢ πλίνθων.
ὀρυκτοὶ δὲ ἅλες, καθάπερ ἐν τοῖς Ἄραψι· πλεο-
νάζει δὲ τῶν φυτῶν ὅ τε φοίνιξ καὶ ἡ περσέα
καὶ ὁ ἔβενος καὶ ἡ κερατία· [3] θήρα δὲ καὶ ἐλεφάντων ἐστὶ καὶ λεόντων καὶ παρδάλεων· εἰσὶ δὲ καὶ
δράκοντες οἱ ἐλεφαντομάχοι καὶ ἄλλα θηρία
πλείω· καταφεύγει γὰρ ἀπὸ τῶν ἐμπυρωτέρων
καὶ αὐχμηροτέρων ἐπὶ τὰ ὑδρηλὰ καὶ ἑλώδη.

3. Ὑπέρκειται δὲ τῆς Μερόης ἡ Ψεβώ, λίμνη
μεγάλη νῆσον ἔχουσα οἰκουμένην ἱκανῶς. συμβαίνει δὲ τοῦ Νείλου τὴν μὲν δυσμικὴν παραπο-
ταμίαν ἐχόντων τῶν Λιβύων, τὴν δὲ πέραν
Αἰθιόπων, παρὰ μέρος αὐτῶν τὴν ἐπικράτειαν εἶναι
τῶν νήσων καὶ τῆς ποταμίας, ἐξελαυνομένων τῶν
ἑτέρων καὶ παραχωρούντων τοῖς κρείττοσι γενο-
μένοις. χρῶνται δὲ καὶ τόξοις Αἰθίοπες τετρα-
πήχεσι ξυλίνοις πεπυρακτωμένοις· [4] ὁπλίζουσι
δὲ καὶ τὰς γυναῖκας, ὧν αἱ πλείους κεκρίκωνται
τὸ χεῖλος τοῦ στόματος χαλκῷ κρίκῳ· κωδιοφόροι
δ᾽ εἰσίν, ἐρέαν οὐκ ἔχοντες, τῶν προβάτων
αἰγοτριχούντων· οἱ δὲ γυμνῆτές εἰσιν, οἳ καὶ [5]

[1] Ἀσταβόρα F, Ἀσταβάρα other MSS.
[2] διαπλεκομένων, Groskurd, for διαπλεκόμεναι, after which
moz read καὶ τοίχων ἐκ πλίνθων, other MSS. τοίχων ἢ πλίνθων.
Jones, following Kramer and C. Müller, ejects τοίχων.
[3] καὶ ἡ κερατία *moxz*, καὶ κεράτια other MSS.
[4] On a conjectural omission here, see C. Müller, *Ind. Var.
Lect.* p. 1042.

precipices, and above, on the south, by the confluences
of the three rivers—the Astaboras, and the Astapus
and the Astasobas [1]—and on the north by the next
course of the Nile, which extends to Aegypt along
the aforesaid windings of the river.   In the cities
the dwellings are made of split pieces of palm-wood
woven together, or of brick.   And they have quarried
salt, as do the Arabians.   And, among the plants,
the palm, the *persea*,[2] the ebony, and the *ceratia*[3]
are found in abundance.   And they have, not only
elephants to hunt, but also lions and leopards.   They
also have serpents, the elephant-fighters, as also
many other wild animals; for the animals flee for
refuge from the hotter and more arid regions to
those that are watery and marshy.

3. Above Meroê lies Psebo, a large lake containing
an island that is rather well settled.   And since the
Libyans hold the land on the western side of the
Nile and the Aethiopians that on the opposite side,
it comes to pass that they take turns in dominating
the islands and the river-land, one of the two being
driven out and yielding place to those who have
proved stronger.   The Aethiopians also use bows,
which are four cubits long, are made of wood, and
are hardened by fire; and they arm the women also,
most of whom have a copper ring through the lip; and
they wear sheep-skins, since they have no wool,
their sheep having hair like that of goats; and some
go naked, or wear round their loins small sheep-

---

[1] Cp. 17. 1. 2.
[2] This tree is carefully described by Pliny (*N. H.*, **13**. 17).
[3] The *carob* or *locust-tree*.

---

[5] οἳ καί EF*h*, ἢ καί other MSS., perhaps rightly.

περιέζωνται μικρὰ κώδια ἢ τρίχινα πλέγματα
εὐυφῆ. θεὸν δὲ νομίζουσι τὸν μὲν ἀθάνατον, τοῦτον δ' εἶναι τὸν αἴτιον τῶν πάντων, τὸν δὲ
θνητόν, ἀνώνυμόν τινα καὶ οὐ σαφῆ. ὡς δ' ἐπὶ
τὸ πολὺ τοὺς εὐεργέτας καὶ βασιλικοὺς θεοὺς
νομίζουσι, καὶ τούτων τοὺς μὲν βασιλέας κοινοὺς
ἁπάντων σωτῆρας καὶ φύλακας, τοὺς δ' ἰδιώτας
ἰδίως τοῖς εὖ παθοῦσιν ὑπ' αὐτῶν. τῶν δὲ πρὸς
τῇ διακεκαυμένῃ τινὲς καὶ ἄθεοι νομίζονται, οὕς
γε καὶ τὸν ἥλιόν φασιν ἐχθαίρειν καὶ κακῶς
λέγειν, ἐπειδὰν προσίδωσιν ἀνίσχοντα, ὡς καίοντα
καὶ πολεμοῦντα αὐτοῖς, καταφεύγειν τε εἰς τὰ
ἕλη. οἱ δ' ἐν Μερόῃ καὶ Ἡρακλέα καὶ Πᾶνα καὶ
Ἶσιν σέβονται πρὸς ἄλλῳ τινὶ βαρβαρικῷ θεῷ.
τοὺς δὲ νεκροὺς οἱ μὲν εἰς τὸν ποταμὸν ἐκρίπτου-
σιν, οἱ δ' οἴκοι κατέχουσι περιχέαντες ὕαλον·
τινὲς δὲ ἐν κεραμίαις σοροῖς κατορύττουσι κύκλῳ
τῶν ἱερῶν, ὅρκον τε τὸν ὑπὲρ αὐτῶν ἀπαιτοῦσι
καὶ πάντων ἁγιστεύουσι μάλιστα. βασιλέας τε
καθιστᾶσι τοὺς κάλλει διαφέροντας ἢ ἀρετῇ
κτηνοτροφίας ἢ ἀνδρείᾳ ἢ πλούτῳ. ἐν δὲ τῇ
Μερόῃ κυριωτάτην τάξιν ἐπεῖχον οἱ ἱερεῖς τὸ
παλαιόν, οἵ γε καὶ τῷ βασιλεῖ προσέταττον ἔσθ'
ὅτε ἀποθνήσκειν πέμψαντες ἄγγελον καὶ κα-
C 823 θίστασαν ἀντ' αὐτοῦ ἕτερον· ὕστερον δὲ κατέλυσέ
τις τῶν βασιλέων τὸ ἔθος, ἐπιὼν μεθ' ὅπλων ἐπὶ
τὸ ἱερόν, ὅπου ὁ χρυσοῦς νεώς ἐστι, καὶ τοὺς
ἱερέας ἀποσφάξας πάντας. ἔστι δὲ καὶ τοῦτο

---

[1] Diodorus Siculus (3. 39) names Zeus in connection with
the three others.

[2] See 17. 1. 8 and footnote on "glass."

skins or girdles of well-woven hair. They regard as
god the immortal being, whom they consider the
cause of all things, and also the mortal being, who
is without name and not to be identified. But in
general they regard their benefactors and royal per-
sonages as gods: of these the kings as the common
saviours and guardians of all, and special individuals
as in a special sense gods to those who have
received benefactions from them. Among those
who live near the torrid zone, some are considered
atheists, since it is said that they hate even the sun,
and revile it when they behold it rising, on the
ground that it burns them and carries on war with
them, and flee for refuge from it into the marshes.
The inhabitants of Meroê worship Heracles, Pan,
and Isis, in addition to some other, barbaric, god.[1]
As for the dead, some cast them into the river,
others enclose them in glass [2] and keep them at
home; but some bury them around the temples in
coffins made of clay; and they exact fulfilment of
oaths sworn over the dead,[3] and consider them the
most sacred of all things. They appoint as kings
those who excel in beauty, or in superiority in cattle-
breeding, or in courage, or in wealth. In Meroê
the highest rank was in ancient times held by the
priests, who indeed would give orders even to
the king, sometimes ordering him through a mes-
senger to die, and would appoint another in his
stead; but later one of the kings broke up the
custom by marching with armed men against the
temple where the golden shrine is and slaughtering
all the priests. The following is also an Aethiopian

---

[3] *i.e.* they make the oath binding by invoking the dead as
witnesses.

ἔθος Αἰθιοπικόν· ὃς γὰρ ἂν τῶν βασιλέων
πηρωθῇ μέρος τι τοῦ σώματος ὁπωσοῦν τὸ αὐτὸ
πάσχουσιν οἱ συνόντες αὐτῷ μάλιστα, οἱ δ' αὐτοὶ
καὶ συναποθνήσκουσιν· ἐκ δὲ τούτου φυλακὴ τοῦ
βασιλέως ἐστὶ πλείστη παρ' αὐτῶν. περὶ μὲν
Αἰθιόπων ἀρκέσει ταῦτα.

4. Τοῖς δ' Αἰγυπτιακοῖς καὶ ταῦτα προσθετέον
ὅσα ἰδιάζοντα, οἷον ὁ Αἰγύπτιος λεγόμενος κύαμος
ἐξ οὗ τὸ κιβώριον, καὶ ἡ βύβλος· ἐνταῦθα γὰρ
καὶ παρ' Ἰνδοῖς μόνον· ἡ δὲ περσέα ἐνταῦθα μόνον
καὶ παρ' Αἰθίοψι, δένδρον μέγα, καρπὸν ἔχον
γλυκὺν καὶ μέγαν, καὶ ἡ συκάμινος ἡ ἐκφέρουσα
τὸν λεγόμενον καρπὸν συκόμορον· σύκῳ γὰρ
ἔοικεν, ἄτιμον δ' ἐστὶ κατὰ τὴν γεῦσιν· γίνεται
δὲ καὶ τὸ κόρσιον καὶ ὅμοιόν τι¹ πεπέρει² τρά-
γημα, μικρῷ αὐτοῦ μεῖζον. ἰχθύες δ' ἐν τῷ
Νείλῳ πολλοὶ μὲν καὶ ἄλλοι χαρακτῆρα ἔχοντες
ἴδιον καὶ ἐπιχώριον, γνωριμώτατοι δὲ ὅ τε
ὀξύρυγχος καὶ ὁ λεπιδωτὸς καὶ λάτος καὶ ἀλάβης
καὶ κορακῖνος καὶ χοῖρος καὶ φαγρώριος, ὃν καὶ
φάγρον καλοῦσιν, ἔτι σίλουρος, κιθαρός, θρίσσα,
κεστρεύς, λύχνος, φῦσα, βοῦς· ὀστρακίων δὲ
κοχλίαι³ μεγάλοι, φωνὴν ὀλολυγόσιν ὁμοίαν
φθεγγόμενοι· ζῷα δ'⁴ ἐπιχώρια καὶ ὁ ἰχνεύμων
καὶ ἡ ἀσπὶς ἡ Αἰγυπτία, ἴδιόν τι⁵ ἔχουσα παρὰ
τὰς ἐν ἄλλοις· διττὴ δ' ἐστίν, ἡ μὲν σπιθαμιαία,
ἥπερ καὶ ὀξυθανατωτέρα, ἡ δ' ἐγγὺς ὀργυιᾶς, ὡς

¹ τό F, τῇ CDhi, τῷ other MSS.
² πεπέρει CE, πέπερι other MSS.
³ The text follows Corais. E reads ὀστράκων δὲ λύχνος,
φῦσα, βοῦς, κοχλίαι; other MSS. ὀστρακίων δίλυχνος. φύσα (F
φύσσα), βοῦς, κοχλίαι.
⁴ δ', Corais inserts.

custom: whenever any one of the kings is maimed
in any part of his body in any way whatever, his
closest associates suffer the same thing, and they
even die with him; and hence these men guard the
king most carefully. This will suffice on the subject
of the Aethiopians.

4. But to my account of things Aegyptian I must
add an enumeration of the things that are peculiar
to that country, as, for example, the Aegyptian
cyamus,[1] as it is called, from which *ciborium* is
derived, and the *byblus*, for the *byblus* is found only
here and among the Indians; and the *persea*[2] is
found only here and among the Aethiopians—a large
tree with large, sweet fruit; and the *sycaminus* that
produces the fruit called *sycomorus*, for it resembles
a *sycum*,[3] though it is not prized for its taste; and
the *corsium* is also found here—a relish somewhat
like pepper, but slightly larger. As for fish in the
Nile, they are indeed many in number and different in
kind, with a special indigenous character, but the best
known are the *oxyrynchus* and the *lepidotus, latus,
alabes, coracinus, choerus*, and *phagrorius*, also called
phagrus, and, besides, the *silurus, citharus, thrissa,
cestreus, lychnus, physa*, and *bos*; and, among shell-
creatures, there are large *conchliae* which emit a
sound like a croak. As for indigenous animals,
Aegypt has also the ichneumon and the Aegyptian
asp, which latter has a peculiarity as compared with
the asp of other countries; but it is of two kinds,
one only a span long, which causes a quicker death,
and the other nearly a fathom, as is stated by

[1] See 17. 1. 15.   [2] See § 2 above.
[3] *i.e.* "fig."

[5] ἴδιόν τι E, ἴδιον δέ τι other MSS.

καὶ Νίκανδρος ὁ τὰ Θηριακὰ γράψας εἴρηκε.
καὶ τῶν ὀρνέων ἶβις καὶ ἱέραξ ὁ Αἰγύπτιος,
ἥμερος παρὰ[1] τοὺς ἄλλοθι, ὡς καὶ ἡ αἴλουρος·
καὶ ὁ[2] νυκτικόραξ ἰδιότροπος ἐνθάδε· παρ' ἡμῖν
μὲν γὰρ ἀετοῦ μέγεθος ἴσχει καὶ φθέγγεται βαρύ,
ἐν Αἰγύπτῳ δὲ κολοιοῦ μέγεθος καὶ φθογγὴ
διάφορος. ἡμερώτατον δ' ἡ ἶβις, πελαργώδης
μὲν κατὰ σχῆμα καὶ μέγεθος, διττὴ δὲ τὴν χρόαν,
ἡ μὲν πελαργώδης, ἡ δὲ ὅλη μέλαινα. μεστὴ δ'
αὐτῶν ἅπασα τρίοδος ἐν Ἀλεξανδρείᾳ, πῇ μὲν
χρησίμως, πῇ δ' οὐ χρησίμως· χρησίμως μέν,
ὅτι πᾶν[3] θηρίον ἐκλέγει καὶ τὰ ἐν τοῖς κρεω-
πωλίοις καὶ τοῖς ὀψοπωλίοις[4] ἀποκαθάρματα·
δυσχρήστως δέ, ὅτι παμφάγον καὶ ἀκάθαρτον καὶ
δυσκόλως ἀπειργόμενον ἀπὸ τῶν καθαρίων καὶ
τῶν ἀλλοτρίων μολυσμοῦ παντός.

5. Ἀληθὲς δὲ καὶ τὸ[5] Ἡροδότου καί ἐστιν
Αἰγυπτιακὸν τὸ τὸν μὲν πηλὸν ταῖς χερσὶ φυρᾶν,
τὸ δὲ στέαρ[6] τὸ εἰς τὴν ἀρτοποιίαν τοῖς ποσί.
C 824 καὶ οἱ κάκεις[7] δὲ ἴδιόν τι ἄρτου γένος, στατικὸν
κοιλίας, καὶ τὸ κίκι καρπός τις σπειρόμενος ἐν
ἀρούραις, ἐξ οὗ ἔλαιον ἀποθλίβεται εἰς μὲν
λύχνον τοῖς ἀπὸ τῆς χώρας σχεδόν τι πᾶσιν, εἰς
ἄλειμμα δὲ τοῖς πενεστέροις καὶ ἐργατικωτέροις

---

[1] ἥμερος παρά E, ἥμερος γὰρ παρά other MSS.
[2] ὁ Cz, ἡ other MSS.
[3] After πᾶν, Jones conj. that πήμονα has fallen out of the text.
[4] ὀψοπωλίοις Casaubon, ὀψοπόλαις E, ὀψοπώλεσιν other MSS.
[5] τοῦ CEFh.
[6] στέας DF, σταῖς second hand Dh, as in Herodotus 2. 36.
[7] οἱ κάκης E, κυλλάστεις conj. Dindorf in *Thesaurus*, s.v.

---

[1] *Theriaca* 168.
[2] A poem on poisonous animals, as the name implies.

Nicander,[1] who wrote the *Theriaca*.[2] Among the
birds are found the ibis and the Aegyptian *hierax*,
which latter is tame, like the cat, as compared with
those elsewhere; and also the *nycticorax*[3] is here of
a peculiar species, for in our country it has the size
of an eagle and a harsh caw, but in Aegypt the size
of a jackdaw and a different caw. The ibis, however,
is the tamest bird; it is like a stork in shape and
size, but it is of two kinds in colour, one kind like
the stork and the other black all over.[4] Every
cross-road in Alexandria is full of them; and though
they are useful in one way, they are not useful in
another. The bird is useful because it singles out
every [5] animal [6] and the refuse in the meat-shops and
bakeries, but not useful because it eats everything,
is unclean, and can only with difficulty be kept away
from things that are clean and do not admit of any
defilement.

5. The statement of Herodotus [7] is also true, that
it is an Aegyptian custom to knead mud with their
hands, but suet for bread-making with their feet.
Further, *kakeis* is a peculiar kind of bread which
checks the bowels; and *kiki* is a kind of fruit sown
in the fields, from which oil is pressed, which is used
not only in lamps by almost all the people in the
country, but also for anointing the body by the
poorer classes and those who do the heavier labour,

[3] *i.e.* "night-crow."
[4] The former is the White or Sacred Ibis; it regularly
visits Aegypt at the time of the inundation, coming from
Nubia.
[5] The translator conjectures that "baneful" has fallen out
of the text after "every" (see critical note).
[6] *e.g.* serpents (Josephus 2. 10), scorpions (Aelian 10. 29),
locusts and caterpillars (Diodorus Siculus 1. 87).
[7] 2. 36.

καὶ ἀνδράσι καὶ γυναιξί. καὶ τὰ κοΐκινα [1] δὲ
πλέγματα Αἰγυπτιακά ἐστι, φυτοῦ τινος, ὅμοια
τοῖς σχοινίνοις ἢ φοινικίνοις. τὸ δὲ ζύθος [2] ἰδίως
μὲν σκευάζεται παρ' ἐκείνοις, κοινὸν δ' ἐστὶ
πολλοῖς, καὶ παρ' ἑκάστοις δὲ αἱ σκευασίαι
διάφοροι. καὶ τοῦτο δὲ τῶν μάλιστα ζηλουμένων
παρ' αὐτοῖς τὸ πάντα τρέφειν τὰ γεννώμενα
παιδία καὶ τὸ περιτέμνειν καὶ τὰ θήλεα ἐκτέμνειν,
ὅπερ καὶ τοῖς Ἰουδαίοις νόμιμον· καὶ οὗτοι δ' εἰσὶν
Αἰγύπτιοι τὸ ἀνέκαθεν, καθάπερ εἰρήκαμεν ἐν τῷ
περὶ ἐκείνων λόγῳ. φησὶ δ' Ἀριστόβουλος, ἐκ
τῆς θαλάττης μηδὲν ἀνατρέχειν ὄψον εἰς τὸν
Νεῖλον πλὴν κεστρέως καὶ θρίσσης καὶ δελφῖνος
διὰ τοὺς κροκοδείλους· τοὺς μὲν δελφῖνας διὰ τὸ
κρείττους εἶναι, τοὺς δὲ κεστρέας τῷ παρα-
πέμπεσθαι ὑπὸ τῶν χοίρων παρὰ γῆν κατά τινα
οἰκείωσιν φυσικήν· τῶν δὲ χοίρων ἀπέχεσθαι
τοὺς κροκοδείλους, στρογγύλων ὄντων καὶ ἐχόντων
ἀκάνθας ἐπὶ τῇ κεφαλῇ φερούσας κίνδυνον τοῖς
θηρίοις· ἀναθεῖν μὲν οὖν ἔαρος τοὺς κεστρέας
γόνον ἔχοντας, μικρὸν δὲ πρὸ δύσεως Πλειάδος
καταβαίνειν τεξομένους ἀθρόους, ὅτε καὶ ἡ ἅλωσις
αὐτῶν γίνεται περιπιπτόντων τοῖς φράγμασιν
ἀθρόων.[3] τοιαύτην δέ τινα εἰκάζειν ἔστι καὶ
περὶ τῆς θρίσσης αἰτίαν. ταῦτα καὶ περὶ
Αἰγύπτου.

---

[1] κοΐκινα (textures "made of the coïx-palm"), Casaubon
and Meineke, for κόκκινα; but Kramer prefers κούκινα ("made
from the coco-palm").
[2] ζύθος Ew, ζύγος other MSS.
[3] ἀθρόων Dh, ἀθρόον other MSS.

both men and women; and further, the *koïkina*[1] are Aegyptian textures made of some plant, and are like those made of rush or the date-palm. And beer is prepared in a peculiar way among the Aegyptians; it is a drink common to many peoples, but the ways of preparing it in the different countries are different. One of the customs most zealously observed among the Aegyptians is this, that they rear every child that is born, and circumcise the males, and excise the females,[2] as is also customary among the Jews, who are also Aegyptians in origin, as I have already stated in my account of them.[3] Aristobulus says that on account of the crocodiles no fish swim up into the Nile from the sea except the *cestreus* and the *thrissa* and the dolphin—the dolphin, because it is stronger than the crocodile, and the *cestreus*, because it is escorted by the *choeri*[4] along the bank, in accordance with some natural affinity; and that the crocodiles keep away from the *choeri*, since the latter are round and have spines on the head which offer danger to the beasts. Now the *cestreus*, he says, runs up the river in spring when it is carrying its spawn, but for the purpose of spawning comes down in schools before the setting of the Pleiad, at which time they are captured, being caught in schools by the fenced enclosures. And some such cause might be conjectured also in the case of the *thrissa*. So much for Aegypt.

[1] See critical note.

[2] *i.e.* remove portions of the *nymphae*, and sometimes of the *clitoris*, of the females. The operation is harmless, and analogous to that of circumcision.

[3] 16. 2. 34.

[4] *i.e.* "pig" fish (see Athenaeus 6).

III

Περὶ δὲ Λιβύης ἐφεξῆς λέγωμεν, ὅπερ λείπεται μέρος τῆς συμπάσης γεωγραφίας.¹ εἴρηται μὲν οὖν καὶ πρότερον πολλὰ καὶ περὶ αὐτῆς, ἀλλὰ καὶ νῦν ὅσα καίρια προσυπομνηστέον, προστιθέντας² καὶ τὰ μὴ λεχθέντα πρότερον. οἱ μὲν οὖν πρὸς τὰς ἠπείρους τὴν οἰκουμένην διελόντες ἀνίσως διεῖλον, ἐμφαίνει γὰρ τὸ τριχῆ τὸ εἰς τρία ἴσα, τοσοῦτο δ᾽ ἀπολείπεται τοῦ τρίτον εἶναι μέρος τῆς οἰκουμένης ἡ Λιβύη, ὥστε καὶ συντεθεῖσα μετὰ τῆς Εὐρώπης οὐκ ἂν ἐξισάζειν δόξειε τῇ Ἀσίᾳ. τάχα δὲ καὶ τῆς Εὐρώπης ἐλάττων ἐστί, κατὰ δὲ τὴν δύναμιν καὶ πολλῷ τινι, ἔρημος γάρ ἐστιν ἡ πολλὴ τῆς μεσογαίας καὶ τῆς παρωκεανίτιδος, κατοικίαις δὲ κατάστικτός ἐστι μικραῖς, καὶ σποράσι καὶ νομαδικαῖς ταῖς πλείσταις· πρὸς δὲ τῇ ἐρημίᾳ καὶ τὸ θηριοτρόφον ἐξελαύνει καὶ ἐκ τῆς δυναμένης C 825 οἰκεῖσθαι· πολὺ δὲ καὶ τῆς διακεκαυμένης ἐπιλαμβάνει ζώνης. ἡ μέντοι καθ᾽ ἡμᾶς εὐδαιμόνως οἰκεῖται πᾶσα παραλία ἡ μεταξὺ Νείλου καὶ Στηλῶν, καὶ μάλιστα ἡ ὑπὸ Καρχηδονίοις γενομένη· ἀνυδρίαι δέ τινες κἀνταῦθα παρεμπίπτουσιν, οἷαι περί τε τὰς Σύρτεις καὶ τοὺς Μαρμαρίδας καὶ τὸν Καταβαθμόν.

Ἔστι δὲ ὀρθογωνίου τριγώνου τὸ σχῆμα, ὡς ἄν τις ἐν ἐπιπέδῳ νοήσειε, βάσιν μεν ἔχον τὴν καθ᾽ ἡμᾶς παραλίαν τὴν ἀπὸ τῆς Αἰγύπτου καὶ

---

¹ γεωμετρίας CDEF.
² προστιθέντας F, προσθέντας other MSS.

¹ 2. 3. 4, and 2. 4. 3.

III

1. Next let me describe Libya, which is the only part left for the completion of my Geography as a whole. Now I have said much about this country before,[1] but I must now comment also on other matters in so far as they may be timely, adding what has not been said before. Now the writers who have divided the inhabited world according to continents have divided it unequally, for the threefold division indicates a division into three equal parts; but Libya lacks so much of being a third part of the inhabited world that even if it were combined with Europe it would seem not to be equal to Asia. Perhaps it is even smaller than Europe; and in power it is much inferior, for the greater part of the interior and of its ocean-coast is desert, and it is dotted with settlements that are small, scattered, and mostly nomadic; and in addition to its deserts, its being a nursery of wild beasts drives out people even from land that could be inhabited; and it overlaps a considerable part of the torrid zone. However, the whole of the coast opposite to us, I mean that between the Nile and the Pillars, and particularly the part which was subject to the Carthaginians, is settled and prosperous; but here too some parts here and there are destitute of water, as, for example, in the regions about the Syrtes, the Marmaridae,[2] and Catabathmus.

Libya has the shape of a right-angled triangle, conceived of as drawn on a plane surface, having as base the coast opposite us, from Aegypt and the

[2] See § 23 following.

Νείλου μέχρι Μαυρουσίας καὶ Στηλῶν, πρὸς
ὀρθὰς δὲ ταύτῃ πλευράν, ἣν ὁ Νεῖλος ποιεῖ μέχρι
Αἰθιοπίας, προσεκβαλλόντων ἡμῶν ἕως Ὠκεανοῦ,
τὴν δ᾽ ὑποτείνουσαν τῇ ὀρθῇ τὴν παρωκεανῖτιν
ἅπασαν τὴν μεταξὺ Αἰθιόπων καὶ Μαυρουσίων.
τὸ μὲν οὖν κατ᾽ αὐτὴν τὴν κορυφὴν τοῦ λεχθέντος
σχήματος, ἤδη πως ὑποπῖπτον τῇ διακεκαυμένῃ,
λέγομεν ἐξ εἰκασμοῦ διὰ τὸ ἀπρόσιτον, ὥστ᾽ οὐδὲ
τὸ μέγιστον πλάτος τῆς χώρας ἔχοιμεν ἂν λέγειν·
τὸ μέντοι τοσοῦτον ἐν τοῖς πρόσθεν λόγοις
ἔφαμεν, ὅτι ἐξ Ἀλεξανδρείας εἰς Μερόην τὸ
βασίλειον τῶν Αἰθιόπων πρὸς νότον ἰόντι στάδιοί
εἰσι περὶ μυρίους, ἐκεῖθεν δ᾽ ἐπ᾽ εὐθείας ἐπὶ τοὺς
ὅρους τῆς διακεκαυμένης καὶ τῆς οἰκουμένης ἄλλοι
τρισχίλιοι.   τὸ γοῦν αὐτὸ θετέον τὸ μέγιστον
πλάτος τῆς Λιβύης, μυρίους καὶ τρισχιλίους ἢ
τετρακισχιλίους στάδιους, μῆκος δὲ μικρῷ ἔλαττον
ἢ διπλάσιον. τὰ καθ᾽ ὅλου μὲν ταῦτα περὶ
Λιβύης· τὰ καθ᾽ ἕκαστα δὲ λεκτέον, ἀρξαμένοις
ἀπὸ τῶν ἑσπερίων μερῶν καὶ τῶν ἐπιφανεστέρων.

2. Οἰκοῦσι δ᾽ ἐνταῦθα Μαυρούσιοι μὲν ὑπὸ
τῶν Ἑλλήνων λεγόμενοι, Μαῦροι δ᾽ ὑπὸ τῶν
Ῥωμαίων καὶ τῶν ἐπιχωρίων,[1] Λιβυκὸν ἔθνος
μέγα καὶ εὔδαιμον, ἀντίπορθμον τῇ Ἰβηρίᾳ.
κατὰ τοῦτο δὲ καὶ ὁ κατὰ τὰς Στήλας τὰς
Ἡρακλείους πορθμός ἐστι, περὶ οὗ πολλὰ εἴρηται.
ἔξω δὲ προελθόντι τοῦ κατὰ τὰς Στήλας πορθμοῦ,
τὴν Λιβύην ἐν ἀριστερᾷ ἔχοντι ὄρος ἐστίν, ὅπερ
οἱ μὲν Ἕλληνες Ἄτλαντα καλοῦσιν, οἱ βάρβαροι
δὲ Δύριν. ἐντεῦθεν δὲ πρόπους ἔκκειταί τις

---

[1] Μαῦροι . . . ἐπιχωρίων, Kramer transfers from a position
after εὔδαιμον.

Nile to Maurusia and the Pillars, and as the side
perpendicular to this that which is formed by the
Nile as far as Aethiopia and by me produced to the
ocean, and as the side subtending the right angle
the whole of the coast between the Aethiopians and
the Maurusians. Now as for the part at the very
vertex of the above-mentioned figure, which begins
approximately with the torrid zone, I speak only
from conjecture, because it is inaccessible, so that I
cannot tell even its maximum breadth, although in
a previous part of my work [1] I have said thus much,
that, as one goes southward from Alexandria to
Meroê, the royal seat of the Aethiopians, the distance
is about ten thousand stadia, and from there in a
straight line to the boundaries between the torrid
zone and the inhabited world three thousand more.
At any rate, the same should be put down as the
maximum breadth of Libya, I mean thirteen or fourteen thousand stadia, and a little less than double
that sum as the length. This, then, is my account
of Libya as a whole, but I must describe it in
detail, beginning with its western, or more famous,
parts.

2. Here dwell a people whom the Greeks call
Maurusians, and the Romans Mauri—a large and
prosperous Libyan tribe, who live on the side of
the strait opposite Iberia. Here also is the strait
which is at the Pillars of Heracles, concerning
which I have often spoken. On proceeding outside
the strait at the Pillars, with Libya on the left, one
comes to a mountain which the Greeks call Atlas
and the barbarians Dyris. From this mountain pro-

[1] 1. 4. 2.

ὕστατος πρὸς δύσιν τῆς Μαυρουσίας αἱ Κώτεις
λεγόμεναι· πλησίον δὲ καὶ πολίχνιον μικρὸν
ὑπὲρ τῆς θαλάττης, ὅπερ Τίγγα[1] καλοῦσιν οἱ
βάρβαροι, Λύγγα[2] δ᾽ ὁ Ἀρτεμίδωρος προση-
γόρευκε, Ἐρατοσθένης δὲ Λίξον· κεῖται δ᾽ ἀντίπορθμον τοῖς Γαδείροις ἐν διάρματι σταδίων
ὀκτακοσίων, ὅσον ἑκάτερα διέχει τοῦ κατὰ τὰς
Στήλας πορθμοῦ· πρὸς νότον δὲ τῇ Λίξῳ καὶ
ταῖς Κώτεσι παράκειται κόλπος Ἐμπορικὸς
C 826 καλούμενος, ἔχων Φοινικικὰς ἐμπορικὰς κατοικίας.
ἔστι μὲν οὖν πᾶσα ἡ συνεχὴς τῷ κόλπῳ τούτῳ
παραλία κολπώδης, ὑπεξαιρουμένῳ δὲ τοὺς κόλπους καὶ τὰς ἐξοχὰς κατὰ τὸ σχῆμα τὸ τριγω-
νοειδές, ὃ ὑπέγραψα, νοείσθω μᾶλλον ἐπὶ τὴν
μεσημβρίαν ἅμα καὶ τὴν ἕω λαμβάνουσα τὴν
αὔξησιν ἡ ἤπειρος. τὸ δ᾽ ὄρος διὰ μέσης ἐκτεινό-
μενον τῆς Μαυρουσίας τὸ ἀπὸ τῶν Κώτεων μέχρι
καὶ Σύρτεων οἰκεῖται καὶ αὐτὸ καὶ ἄλλα παράλ-
ληλα αὐτῇ κατ᾽ ἀρχὰς μὲν ὑπὸ τῶν Μαυρουσίων,
ἐν βάθει δὲ τῆς χώρας ὑπὸ τοῦ μεγίστου τῶν
Λιβυκῶν ἐθνῶν, οἳ Γαίτουλοι λέγονται.

3. Πλεῖστα δὲ πλάσματα τῇ Λιβυκῇ παραλίᾳ
τῇ ἐκτὸς προσεψεύσαντο οἱ συγγραφεῖς, ἀρξάμενοι
ἀπὸ τοῦ Ὀφέλα[3] περίπλου· περὶ ὧν ἐμνήσθημέν
που καὶ πρότερον, καὶ νῦν δὲ λέγομεν, συγγνώμην
αἰτούμενοι τῆς τερατολογίας, ἐάν που βιασθῶμεν

---

[1] Τρίγκα E.   [2] Λύγκα E.
[3] Ὀφρύα Ald.; Tyrwhitt conj. Ἀπέλλα.

---

[1] The same as Tingis (3. 1. 8).
[2] Strabo is confusing Tingis (now Tangiers) with Lynx or
Lixus (now El Araisch or Larasch) ; see § 7 following.
[3] Cadiz.   [4] *i.e.* "Mercantile."

jects a farthermost spur, as it were, towards the west
of Maurusia—the Coteis, as it is called; and near
by is a small town above the sea which the barbarians
call Tinx,[1] though Artemidorus has given it the
name Lynx and Eratosthenes Lixus.[2] It is situated
across the strait opposite Gadeira[3] at a distance of
eight hundred stadia, which is about the distance of
each of the two places from the strait at the Pillars.
To the south of Lixus and the Coteis lies a gulf
called the Emporicus[4] Gulf, which contains settlements of Phoenician merchants. Now the whole of
the coast continuous with this gulf is indented by
gulfs, but one should exclude from consideration the
gulfs and the projections of land, in accordance with
the triangular figure which I have suggested, and
conceive rather of the continent as increasing in
extent in the direction of the south and east.[5] The
mountain,[6] which extends through the middle of
Maurusia from the Coteis to the Syrtes, is inhabited,
both itself and other mountains that run parallel
with Maurusia, at first by the Maurusians but deep
in the interior by the largest of the Libyan tribes,
who are called Gaetulians.

3. The historians, beginning with *The Circumnavigation of Ophelas*,[7] have added numerous other
fabrications in regard to the outside coast of Libya;
and these I have already mentioned somewhere
before,[8] but I am again speaking of them, asking
pardon for introducing marvellous stories, if per-

---

[5] *i.e.* this side forms the hypotenuse and runs in a south-
easterly direction.
[6] Atlas.
[7] Ophelas of Cyrenê (Diodorus Siculus 18. 21, 20. 40–42,
and Plutarch, *Demetrius* 14); see critical note.
[8] 1. 1. 5, and 3. 2. 13.

ἐκπεσεῖν εἴς τι τοιοῦτο, φεύγοντες τὸ πάντα σιγῇ
παραπέμπειν καὶ τρόπον τινὰ πηροῦν[1] τὴν
ἱστορίαν. φασὶ δ' οὖν τὸν Ἐμπορικὸν κόλπον
ἄντρον ἔχειν εἴσω δεχόμενον τὴν θάλατταν ἐν
ταῖς πλημμυρίσι μέχρι καὶ ἑπτὰ σταδίων, προκείμενον δὲ τούτου ταπεινὸν καὶ ὁμαλὸν χωρίον,
ἔχον Ἡρακλέους βωμόν, ὃν οὐκ ἐπικλύζεσθαί
φασιν ὑπὸ τῆς πλημμυρίδος· ἐν δὲ δή τι τῶν
πλασμάτων νομίζω τοῦτο. ἐγγὺς δὲ τούτῳ τὸ ἐν
τοῖς ἑξῆς κόλποις κατοικίας λέγεσθαι παλαιὰς
Τυρίων, ἃς ἐρήμους εἶναι νῦν, οὐκ ἐλαττόνων ἢ
τριακοσίων πόλεων, ἃς οἱ Φαρούσιοι καὶ οἱ
Νιγρῖται[2] ἐξεπόρθησαν· διέχειν δὲ τούτους τῆς
Λυγγὸς φασιν ἡμερῶν τριάκοντα ὁδόν.

4. Τὸ μέντοι τὴν Μαυρουσίαν εὐδαίμονα εἶναι[3]
χώραν πλὴν ὀλίγης ἐρήμου καὶ ποταμοῖς τε καὶ
λίμναις κεχορηγῆσθαι παρὰ πάντων ὁμολογεῖται.
μεγαλόδενδρός τε καὶ πολύδενδρος ὑπερβαλλόντως
ἐστὶ καὶ πάμφορος· τὰς γοῦν μονοξύλους τρα-
πέζας ποικιλωτάτας καὶ μεγίστας ἐκείνη τοῖς
Ῥωμαίοις χορηγεῖ. τοὺς δὲ ποταμοὺς ἔχειν φασὶ
καὶ κροκοδείλους καὶ ἄλλα γένη ζῴων ἐμφερῆ
τοῖς ἐν τῷ Νείλῳ· τινὲς δὲ καὶ τὰς τοῦ Νείλου
πηγὰς πλησιάζειν οἴονται τοῖς ἄκροις τῆς Μαυρουσίας. ἐν ποταμῷ δέ τινι γεννᾶσθαι βδέλλας
ἑπταπήχεις, κατατετρημένα ἐχούσας τὰ βραγχία,
δι' ὧν ἀναπνέουσι. καὶ ταῦτα δὲ λέγουσι περὶ
τῆς χώρας, ὅτι ἄμπελος φύεται δυσὶν ἀνδράσι τὸ
πάχος δυσπερίληπτος, βότρυν πηχυαῖόν πως

---

[1] πηροῦν E, πληροῦν other MSS.
[2] Νιγρῖται Eh, Νηγρῖται D, Νιγρῆται other MSS.
[3] ἔχειν E.

chance I shall be forced to digress into a thing of that sort, since I am unwilling wholly to pass them over in silence and in a way to cripple my history. Now they say that the Emporicus Gulf has a cave which at the full tides admits the sea inside it for a distance of even seven stadia, and that in front of this gulf there is a low, level place containing an altar of Heracles, which, they say, is never inundated by the tide—and it is this that I regard as one of their fabrications. And nearly as bad as this is the statement that on the gulfs which come next after the Emporicus Gulf there were ancient settlements of Tyrians, now deserted—no fewer than three hundred cities, which were destroyed by the Pharusians and the Nigritae; and these people, they say, are at a distance of a thirty days' journey from Lynx.

4. However, it is agreed by all that Maurusia is a fertile country, except a small desert part, and is supplied with both lakes and rivers. It is surpassing in the size and in the number of its trees, and is also productive of everything; at any rate, this is the country which supplies the Romans with the tables that are made of one single piece of wood, very large and most variegated. The rivers are said to contain crocodiles, as also other kinds of animals similar to those in the Nile. Some think that even the sources of the Nile are near the extremities of Maurusia. And they say that in a certain river are found leeches [1] seven cubits long, with gills pierced through with holes, through which they breathe. They also say of this country that it produces a vine so thick that it can hardly be encircled by the arms of two men, and that it yields clusters of

---

[1] They meant leech-*fish*, *i.e.* lampreys.

ἀποδιδοῦσα· βοτάνη τε ὑψηλὴ πᾶσα καὶ λάχα-
νον, οἷον¹ ἄρον² καὶ δρακόντιον, οἱ δὲ τῶν
σταφυλίνων καυλοὶ καὶ ἱππομαράθου καὶ σκο-
λύμων δωδεκαπήχεις, τὸ δὲ πάχος παλαιστῶν
C 827 τεττάρων· καὶ δρακόντων δὲ καὶ ἐλεφάντων καὶ
δορκάδων καὶ βουβάλων καὶ τῶν παραπλησίων
ζῴων, λεόντων τε καὶ παρδάλεων, παντοδαπὴ
τροφὸς ἡ χώρα ἐστί. φέρει δὲ καὶ γαλᾶς αἰλού-
ροις ἴσας καὶ ὁμοίας, πλὴν ὅτι τὰ ῥύγχη προ-
πέπτωκε μᾶλλον, πιθήκων τε πάμπολυ πλῆθος,
περὶ ὧν καὶ Ποσειδώνιος εἴρηκεν, ὅτι πλέων ἐκ
Γαδείρων εἰς τὴν Ἰταλίαν προσενεχθείη τῇ
Λιβυκῇ παραλίᾳ καὶ ἴδοι τῶν θηρίων μεστόν
τινα τούτων ἁλιτενῆ δρυμόν, τῶν μὲν ἐπὶ τοῖς
δένδρεσι, τῶν δ᾽ ἐπὶ γῆς, ἐχόντων ἐνίων καὶ
σκύμνους καὶ ἐπεχόντων μαστόν· γελᾶν οὖν
ὁρῶν βαρυμάστους, ἐνίους δὲ φαλακρούς, τοὺς δὲ
κηλήτας καὶ ἄλλα τοιαῦτα ἐπιφαίνοντας σίνη.

5. Ὑπὲρ ταύτης δ᾽ ἐστὶν ἐπὶ τῇ ἔξω θαλάττῃ ἡ
τῶν ἑσπερίων καλουμένων Αἰθιόπων χώρα, κακῶς
οἰκουμένη τὸ πλέον. ἐνταῦθα δὲ καὶ καμηλο-
παρδάλεις φησὶν Ἰφικράτης³ γεννᾶσθαι καὶ
ἐλέφαντας καὶ τοὺς καλουμένους ῥίζεις, οἳ ταυ-
ροειδεῖς μέν εἰσι τὴν μορφήν, κατὰ δὲ τὴν δίαιταν
καὶ τὸ μέγεθος καὶ τὴν ἀλκὴν τὴν πρὸς μάχην

---

¹ οἷον, Jones inserts (Groskurd οἷον τό).
² ἄρον, Corais, for νεαρόν.   ³ Ὑψικράτης, Corais.

---

¹ They meant in *length*, apparently, and not in *circumference* (cp. 2. 1. 14 and 11. 10. 1).
² Apparently *Arum maculatum* (cuckoo-pint) and *Dracun-
culus* (cp. Pliny 24. 91–92 and Theophrastus 1. 6. 6, 7. 12. 2).
³ A kind of carrot or parsnip.

about one cubit;[1] and that every herb grows high, and every vegetable, as, for example, *arum* and *dracontium*;[2] and the stalks of the *staphylini*[3] and the *hippomarathi*[4] and the *scolymi*[5] grow twelve cubits high and four palms thick. And for serpents, also, and elephants and gazelles and *bubali*[6] and similar animals, as also for lions and leopards, the country is a nurse in every way. It also produces ferrets[7] equal in size to cats, and like them, except that their noses project further; and also a very great number of apes, concerning which Poseidonius states that, when he was sailing from Gadeira to Italy, he was carried close to the Libyan coast and saw on a low-lying shore a forest full of these animals, some in the trees and others on the ground, and some having young and suckling them; that he fell to laughing, however, when he saw some with heavy udders, some with bald heads, and others ruptured or displaying other disabilities of that kind.

5. Above Maurusia, on the outside sea, lies the country of the western Aethiopians, as they are called, a country for the most part poorly settled. Here too, according to Iphicrates,[8] are found camelopards, elephants, and the *rhizeis*,[9] as they are called, which are like bulls in their form, but like elephants in their manner of living and their

---

[4] *i.e.* horse-fennel.   [5] An edible kind of thistle.

[6] Apparently the antelope *bubalis*.

[7] Cp. 3. 2. 6.

[8] Possibly a copyist's error for "Hypicrates" (see Vol. III, p. 245, note 2).

[9] *i.e.* animals with noses "like roots"; perhaps the writer quoted meant the rhinoceros, but elsewhere (16. 4. 15) Strabo himself uses the word "rhinoceros."

ἐλέφασιν ἐοίκασι· δράκοντάς τε λέγει μεγάλους,
ὥστε[1] καὶ πόαν ἐπιπεφυκέναι· τοὺς δὲ λέοντας
τοῖς πώλοις τῶν ἐλεφάντων ἐπιτίθεσθαι, αἱμά-
ξαντας δὲ φεύγειν, ἐπιουσῶν τῶν μητέρων· τὰς
δ᾽, ἐπειδὰν ἴδωσιν ᾑμαγμένους, κτείνειν· ἐπανιόντας
δὲ τοὺς λέοντας ἐπὶ τὰ πτώματα νεκροφαγεῖν.
Βόγον δέ, τὸν βασιλέα τῶν Μαυρουσίων, ἀναβάντα ἐπὶ τοὺς ἑσπερίους Αἰθίοπας, καταπέμψαι
τῇ γυναικὶ δῶρα καλάμους τοῖς Ἰνδικοῖς ὁμοίους,
ὧν ἕκαστον γόνυ χοίνικας χωροῦν[2] ὀκτώ· καὶ
ἀσπαράγων δ᾽ ἐμφερῆ μεγέθη·

6. Εἰς δὲ τὴν ἐντὸς θάλατταν πλέουσιν ἀπὸ
Λυγγὸς πόλις ἐστὶ Ζῆλις καὶ Τίγξ,[3] εἶτα τῶν
Ἑπτὰ ἀδελφῶν μνήματα καὶ τὸ ὑπερκείμενον
ὄρος ὄνομα Ἀβίλη,[4] πολύθηρον καὶ μεγαλόδενδρον.
τοῦ δὲ κατὰ τὰς Στήλας πορθμοῦ τὸ μὲν μῆκος
λέγεται σταδίων ἑκατὸν εἴκοσι, τὸ δ᾽ ἐλάχιστον
πλάτος κατὰ τὸν Ἐλέφαντα ἑξήκοντα. εἰσπλεύσαντι δ᾽ ἑξῆς πόλεις τε καὶ ποταμοὶ πλείους
μέχρι Μολοχὰθ ποταμοῦ, ὃς ὁρίζει τὴν Μαυρουσίων καὶ τὴν Μασαισυλίων[5] γῆν. κεῖται[6]
δὲ καὶ ἄκρα μεγάλη πλησίον τοῦ ποταμοῦ καὶ
Μεταγώνιον, τόπος ἄνυδρος καὶ λυπρός, σχεδὸν
δέ τι καὶ τὸ ὄρος τὸ ἀπὸ τῶν Κώτεων[7] μέχρι
δεῦρο παρατείνει· μῆκος δὲ τὸ ἀπὸ τῶν Κώτεων
ἐπὶ τοὺς ὅρους τοὺς τῶν Μασαισυλίων[8] στάδιοι

---

[1] οἷς γε, Corais.   [2] χωροῦν Eoxz.
[3] Τίγξ, the editors, for Τίγα.
[4] Ἀβήλη oz, Ἀβύλη Dhi.
[5] Μασαισυλίων Eh, Μασαισύλων F, Μασσαισυλίων other MSS.
[6] κεῖται, Kramer, for καλεῖται.
[7] Κώτεων E, Κωταίων other MSS.

size and their courage in fighting. And he speaks
of serpents so large that even grass grows upon
their backs; and says that the lions attack the young
of the elephants, but, after they have drawn blood,
flee when the mothers approach, and that the
mothers, when they see their young stained with
blood, kill them, and that the lions return to the
victims and eat them. And he says that Bogus,
the king of the Maurusians, when he went up
against the western Aethiopians, sent down to his
wife as gifts reeds like those of India, of which each
joint held eight choenices,[1] and also asparagus of
similar size.

6. As one sails into the inner sea from Lynx, one
comes to the city Zelis and to Tinx; and then to
the Monuments of the Seven Brothers [2] and to the
mountain that lies above them, Abilê by name,
which abounds in wild animals and large trees.
The length of the strait at the Pillars is said to
be one hundred and twenty stadia, and the minimum
breadth, measured at Elephas, sixty. On sailing into
the sea, one comes next to several cities and rivers—
to the Molochath [3] River, which forms the boundary
between the lands of the Maurusians and the Masaesylians. Near the river lies a large promontory, and
also Metagonium, a waterless and barren place; and
I might almost say that the mountain which begins
at the Coteis extends as far as this; and its length
from the Coteis to the boundaries of the Masaesylians

---

[1] About a gallon and a half.
[2] The seven "Monuments" or mountain-peaks.
[3] Now the Mulujah.

---

[8] Μασαισυλίων, Kramer, for Μασαισύλων F, Μασσαισυλίων
other MSS.

πεντακισχίλιοι. ἔστι δὲ τὸ Μεταγώνιον κατὰ
νέαν που Καρχηδόνα ἐν τῇ περαίᾳ· Τιμοσθένης
δ᾽ οὐκ εὖ κατὰ Μασσαλίαν φησίν. ἔστι δ᾽ ἐκ
C 828 Καρχηδόνος νέας δίαρμα εἰς Μεταγώνιον στάδιοι
τρισχίλιοι, παράπλους δὲ εἰς Μασσαλίαν ὑπὲρ
ἑξακισχιλίων.

7. Οὕτω δ᾽ εὐδαίμονα χώραν οἰκοῦντες τὴν
πλείστην οἱ Μαυρούσιοι διατελοῦσιν, ὅμως καὶ
μέχρι δεῦρο τοῦ χρόνου νομαδικῶς ζῶντες οἱ
πολλοί. καλλωπίζονται δ᾽ ὅμως κόμης ἐμπλοκῇ
καὶ πώγωνι καὶ χρυσοφορίᾳ σμήξει τε ὀδόντων
καὶ ὀνυχισμῷ· σπάνιον τε ἂν ἴδοις ἁπτομένους
ἀλλήλων ἐν τοῖς περιπάτοις τοῦ παραμένειν
αὐτοῖς ἄθικτον τὸν κόσμον τῶν τριχῶν. μάχονται
δ᾽ ἱππόται τὸ πλέον ἀπὸ ἄκοντος, σχοινοχαλίνοις
χρώμενοι τοῖς ἵπποις καὶ γυμνοῖς, ἔχουσι δὲ καὶ
μαχαίρας· οἱ δὲ πεζοὶ τὰς τῶν ἐλεφάντων δορὰς
ὡς ἀσπίδας προβάλλονται· τὰς δὲ τῶν λεόντων
καὶ παρδάλεων καὶ ἄρκτων ἀμπέχονται καὶ
ἐγκοιμῶνται. σχεδὸν δέ τι καὶ οὗτοι καὶ οἱ
ἐφεξῆς Μασαισύλιοι[1] καὶ κοινῶς Λίβυες κατὰ
τὸ πλέον ὁμοιόσκευοί εἰσι καὶ τὰ ἄλλα ἐμφερεῖς,
μικροῖς ἵπποις χρώμενοι, ὀξέσι δὲ καὶ εὐπειθέσιν,
ὥστ᾽ ἀπὸ ῥαβδίου οἰακίζεσθαι. περιτραχήλια δὲ
ξύλινα ἢ τρίχινα, ἀφ᾽ ὧν ὁ ῥυτὴρ ἀπήρτηται·
ἔνιοι δὲ καὶ χωρὶς ὁλκῆς ἕπονται ὡς κύνες.
πέλτη μικρὰ βυρσίνη, πλατύλογχα μικρά, ἄζω-
στοι πλατύσημοι χιτῶνες, ἐπιπόρπημα, ὡς ἔφην,
δορὰ καὶ προθωράκιον. Φαρούσιοι[2] δὲ καὶ

---

[1] Μασαισύλιοι E, Μασαίσυλοι F, Μασσάσυλοι D, Μασσοίσυλοι
other MSS.

[2] Φαυρούσιοι E, Φαροοούσιοι C

is five thousand stadia. Metagonium is about opposite New Carthage,[1] on the other side of the sea, but Timosthenes wrongly says that it is opposite Massalia.[2] The passage across from New Carthage to Metagonium is three thousand stadia, and the coasting-voyage to Massalia is over six thousand.

7. Although the most of the country inhabited by the Maurusians is so fertile, yet even to this time most of the people persist in living a nomadic life. But nevertheless they beautify their appearance by braiding their hair, growing beards, wearing golden ornaments, and also by cleaning their teeth and paring their nails. And only rarely can you see them touch one another in walking, for fear that the adornment of their hair may not remain intact. Their horsemen fight mostly with a javelin, using bridles made of rush, and riding bareback; but they also carry daggers. The foot-soldiers hold before them as shields the skins of elephants, and clothe themselves with the skins of lions, leopards, and bears, and sleep in them. I might almost say that these people, and the Masaesylians, who live next after them, and the Libyans in general, dress alike and are similar in all other respects, using horses that are small but swift, and so ready to obey that they are governed with a small rod. The horses wear collars made of wood[3] or of hair, to which the rein is fastened, though some follow even without being led, like dogs. These people have small shields made of raw-hide, small spears with broad heads, wear ungirded tunics with wide borders, and, as I have said, use skins as mantles and shields.

---

[1] Now Cartagena.   [2] Now Marseilles.
[3] *i.e.* of tree-wool.

Νίγρητες [1] οἱ ὑπὲρ τούτων οἰκοῦντες πρὸς τοῖς
ἑσπερίοις Αἰθίοψι καὶ τοξεύουσι, καθάπερ καὶ
οἱ Αἰθίοπες· χρῶνται δὲ καὶ δρεπανηφόροις
ἅρμασι. μίσγονται δὲ καὶ τοῖς Μαυρουσίοις οἱ
Φαρούσιοι διὰ τῆς ἐρήμου σπανίως, ὑπὸ ταῖς
κοιλίαις τῶν ἵππων ὑπαρτῶντες τοὺς ἀσκοὺς τοῦ
ὕδατος· ἔστι δ' ὅτε καὶ εἰς Κίρταν ἀφικνοῦνται
διά τινων τόπων ἑλωδῶν καὶ λιμνῶν. τινὰς δ'
αὐτῶν καὶ Τρωγλοδυτικῶς οἰκεῖν φασιν ὀρύτ-
τοντας τὴν γῆν. λέγεται δὲ κἀνταῦθα τοὺς
θερινοὺς ὄμβρους ἐπιπολάζειν, χειμῶνος δὲ εἶναι
ἀνυδρίαν· ἐνίους δὲ τῶν ταύτῃ βαρβάρων καὶ
ὄφεων καὶ ἰχθύων δοραῖς ἀμπεχόναις τε καὶ
στρώμασι χρῆσθαι. τοὺς δὲ Μαυρουσίους [2] ἔνιοί
φασιν Ἰνδοὺς εἶναι τοὺς συγκατελθόντας Ἡρακλεῖ
δεῦρο. μικρὸν μὲν οὖν πρὸ ἡμῶν οἱ περὶ Βόγον [3]
βασιλεῖς καὶ Βόκχον κατεῖχον αὐτήν, φίλοι
Ῥωμαίων ὄντες· ἐκλιπόντων δὲ τούτων, Ἰούβας
παρέλαβε τὴν ἀρχήν, δόντος τοῦ Σεβαστοῦ Καίσαρος καὶ ταύτην αὐτῷ τὴν ἀρχὴν πρὸς τῇ
πατρῴᾳ· υἱὸς δ' ἦν Ἰούβα τοῦ πρὸς Καίσαρα
τὸν θεὸν πολεμήσαντος μετὰ Σκιπίωνος. Ἰούβας
μὲν οὖν νεωστὶ ἐτελεύτα τὸν βίον, διαδέδεκται δὲ
τὴν ἀρχὴν υἱὸς Πτολεμαῖος, γεγονὼς ἐξ Ἀντωνίου
θυγατρὸς καὶ Κλεοπάτρας.

C 829　　8. Ἀρτεμίδωρος δ' Ἐρατοσθένει μὲν ἀντιλέγει,
διότι Λίξον [4] τινά φησι πόλιν περὶ τὰ ἄκρα τῆς

---

[1] Νιγρῆτες DF*h*.
[2] For Μαυρουσίους, Meineke writes Φαρουσίους.
[3] Βόγοι, Casaubon, for Βόκχο. *h*, Βόγκον *i*, Βόγχοι other
MSS.
[4] Λίξον F*s*, Λίξον other MSS.

The Pharusians and Nigretes [1] who live above these
people near the western Aethiopians also use bows,
like the Aethiopians; and they also use scythe-
bearing chariots. The Pharusians mingle only rarely
even with the Maurusians when passing through the
desert, since they carry skins of water fastened
beneath the bellies of their horses. Sometimes,
however, they come even to Cirta, passing through
certain marshy regions and over lakes. Some of
them are said to live like Troglodytes, digging
homes in the earth. And it is said that here too
the summer rains are prevalent, but that in winter
there is a drought, and that some of the barbarians
in this part of the world use also the skins of snakes
and fish both as wraps and as bed-covers. And the
Maurusians [2] are said by some to be the Indians who
came thither with Heracles. Now a little before
my time the kings of the house of Bogus and of
Bocchus, who were friends of the Romans, possessed
the country, but when these died Juba succeeded
to the throne, Augustus Caesar having given him
this in addition to his father's empire. He was the
son of the Juba who with Scipio waged war against
the deified Caesar. Now Juba died lately,[3] but his
son Ptolemy, whose mother was the daughter of
Antony and Cleopatra, has succeeded to the throne.

8. Artemidorus disputes the view of Eratosthenes
because the latter calls a certain city in the neigh-

---

[1] Apparently a copyist's error for "Nigritae" (the spelling
in 2. 5. 33, 16. 4. 37 and 17. 3. 3).

[2] Apparently an error for "Pharusians" (see Sallust,
Jugurtha, 18, Pomponius Mela, 3. 10, Pliny, 5. 8, and
critical note).

[3] About A.D. 19.

Μαυρουσίας τὰ ἑσπέρια ἀντὶ Λυγγός· Φοινικικὰς
δὲ πόλεις κατεσκαμμένας [1] παμπόλλας τινάς, ὧν
οὐδὲν ἰδεῖν ἐστιν ἴχνος· ἐν δὲ τοῖς ἑσπερίοις
Αἰθίοψι, τοὺς ἀέρας πλατεῖς φήσας,[2] ταῖς τε
ὀρθριναῖς ὥραις καὶ ταῖς δειλιναῖς παχεῖς καὶ
ἀχλυώδεις εἶναι τοὺς ἀέρας· πῶς γὰρ ἐν αὐχμώ-
δεσι καὶ καυματηροῖς τόποις ταῦτ' εἶναι ; αὐτὸς
δὲ τούτων πολὺ χείρω λέγει περὶ τοὺς αὐτοὺς
τόπους· μετανάστας γάρ τινας ἱστορεῖ Λωτο-
φάγους, οἳ τὴν ἄνυδρον νέμοιντο, σιτοῖντο δὲ
λωτόν, πόαν τινὰ καὶ ῥίζαν, ἀφ' ἧς οὐδὲν δέοιντο
ποτοῦ· παρήκειν δ' αὐτοὺς μέχρι τῶν ὑπὲρ
Κυρήνης τόπων· τοὺς δ' ἐκεῖ καὶ γαλακτοποτεῖν
καὶ κρεωφαγεῖν, καίπερ ταὐτοκλινεῖς ὄντας. καὶ
Γαβίνιος [3] δὲ ὁ τῶν Ῥωμαίων συγγραφεὺς [4] οὐκ
ἀπέχεται τῆς τερατολογίας τῆς περὶ τὴν Μαυ-
ρουσίαν· πρὸς γὰρ τῇ Λυγγὶ [5] Ἀνταίου μνῆμα
ἱστορεῖ καὶ σκελετὸν πηχῶν ἑξήκοντα, ὃν Σερ-
τώριον γυμνῶσαι καὶ πάλιν ἐπιβαλεῖν γῆν. καὶ
τὰ περὶ τῶν ἐλεφάντων μυθώδη· φησὶ γὰρ τἆλλα
μὲν θηρία φεύγειν τὸ πῦρ, τοὺς δ' ἐλέφαντας
πολεμεῖν καὶ ἀμύνεσθαι, διότι τὴν ὕλην φθείρει·
πρὸς δὲ τοὺς ἀνθρώπους διαμάχεσθαι, κατα-
σκόπους προπέμποντας, καί, ὅταν ἴδωσιν ἐκείνους
φεύγοντας,[6] φεύγειν καὶ αὐτούς, ἐπειδὰν δὲ [7]

[1] κατεσπασμένας F, κατεσκευασμένας mox.
[2] τοὺς ἀέρας πλατεῖς φήσας, Corais and others bracket,
Meineke ejects.
[3] Τανύσιος F, Τανίσιος w.
[4] συγγραφέων MSS.
[5] Λυγγί Dmoxz.
[6] φεύγοντας, Corais inserts.

bourhood of western extremities of Maurusia " Lixus "
instead of Lynx ; and because he calls " Phoenician "
a very great number of rased cities of which no trace
is to be seen ;[1] and because, after calling the air among
the western Aethiopians " salty," [2] he says that the
air is thick and misty in the hours both of early morning
and of evening.   For, argues Artemidorus, how can
these things be in a region that is arid and torrid ?
But he himself gives a much worse account of the
same region, for he tells a story of certain migrants,
Lotophagi,[3] who roam the waterless country and feed
on lotus, a kind of plant and root, from eating which
they have no need of drink ; and that they extend as
far as the region above Cyrenê ; but that those in
that region also drink milk and eat meat, although
they are in the same latitude.   And Gabinius also,
the Roman historian, does not abstain from telling
marvellous stories of Maurusia ; for example, he tells
a story of a tomb of Antaeus near Lynx, and a skeleton
sixty feet in length, which, he says, Sertorius exposed
to view, and then covered again with earth.[4]   And he
tells fabulous stories about the elephants ; for example,
he says that whereas the other animals flee from fire,
the elephants carry on war with it and defend themselves against it, because it destroys the timber, and
that they engage in battle with human beings, sending out scouts before them, and that when they
see them fleeing, they flee too, and that when they

[1] See § 3 (above).
[2] The usual meaning of the Greek adjective is "broad"
or "flat"; but Eratosthenes must have used it in the sense of
"salty."
[3] Lotus-eaters.   [4] So Plutarch (*Sertorius* 9).

---

[7] δέ, omitted by MSS. except E*i*.

τραύματα λάβωσιν, ἱκετηρίαν [1] προτείνειν κλάδους
ἢ βοτάνην ἢ κόνιν.

9. Μετὰ δὲ τὴν τῶν Μαυρουσίων γῆν ἡ τῶν
Μασαισυλίων [2] ἐστίν, ἀπὸ τοῦ Μολοχὰθ ποταμοῦ
τὴν ἀρχὴν λαμβάνουσα, τελευτῶσα δὲ ἐπὶ τὴν
ἄκραν, ἣ καλεῖται Τρητόν, [3] ὅριον τῆς τε Μασαισυλίων [4] καὶ τῆς Μασυλιέων [5] γῆς. στάδιοι δ'
εἰσὶν ἀπὸ τοῦ Μεταγωνίου μέχρι τοῦ Τρητοῦ ἑξα-
κισχίλιοι· οἱ δ' ἐλάττους φασίν. ἔχει δ' ἡ παραλία
πόλεις τε πλείους καὶ ποταμοὺς καὶ χώραν εὐφυῆ,
τῶν δ' ἐν ὀνόματι ἀρκεῖ μνησθῆναι. ἔστι δὲ
πόλις Σίγα ἐν χιλίοις σταδίοις ἀπὸ τῶν λεχθέν-
των ὅρων, καὶ βασίλειον Σόφακος· [6] κατέσπασται
δὲ νῦν· τὴν δὲ χώραν μετὰ Σόφακα [7] κατέσχε
Μασανάσσης, [8] εἶτα Μικίψας, εἶτα καὶ οἱ ἐκεῖνον
διαδεξάμενοι, καθ' ἡμᾶς δὲ Ἰούβας ὁ πατὴρ τοῦ
νεωστὶ τελευτήσαντος Ἰούβα· κατέσπασται δὲ
καὶ Ζάμα τὸ τούτου βασίλειον ὑπὸ Ῥωμαίων·
μετὰ δὲ τὴν Σίγαν [9] Θεῶν λιμὴν ἐν ἑξακοσίοις
σταδίοις· εἶτ' ἄλλοι ἄσημοι τόποι. τὰ μὲν οὖν
ἐν βάθει τῆς χώρας ὀρεινὰ καὶ ἔρημα [10] (ἔσθ' ὅτε
παρέσπαρται, ἃ κατέχουσιν οἱ Γαίτουλοι [11]) μέχρι
καὶ Σύρτεων, τὰ δ' ἐκεῖ πρὸς θαλάττῃ καὶ πεδία

[1] ἱκετηρίαν, Corais, for ἱκητήριον.
[2] Μασαισυλίων EF, Μασσαισυλίων other MSS.
[3] Τρητόν, inserted by the later editors from conj. of
Casaubon.
[4] Μασαισυλίων F, Μασσαισυλίων z, Μασαισύλων other MSS.
[5] Μασυλιέων, Kramer, for Μασυλίβων; Μασσυλιαίων, Corais.
[6] Συόφακος C, Συοφάκας DFhrxz, Σύφακος editors before
Kramer.
[7] Σόφακα (but o above ω) C, Σοφάκα Dh, Συοφάκαν xz.
[8] Μασανάσσης Ci, Μασανίσσης editors before Kramer.
[9] Σίγαν, Corais, for Σίγα.

receive wounds, as suppliants they hold out branches of a tree or an herb or dust.

9. After the land of the Maurusians, one comes to that of the Masaesylians, which takes its beginning at the Molochath River and ends at the promontory which is called Tretum, the boundary between the lands of the Masaesylians and the Masylians. The distance from Metagonium to Tretum is six thousand stadia, though some say less. The coast has several cities and rivers and a goodly territory, but it is sufficient to mention only those of renown. At a distance of one thousand stadia from the above-mentioned boundaries is Siga, which was the royal residence of Sophax, though it is now in ruins. After Sophax the country was possessed by Masanasses, and then by Micipsas, and then by his successors, and in my time by Juba, the father of the Juba who recently died. Zama, his royal residence, has also been laid in ruins by the Romans. After Siga, and at a distance of six hundred stadia, one comes to Theon Limen;[1] and then to the other, insignificant, places. Now the parts deep in the interior[2] are indeed mountainous and desert (sometimes they are interspersed with habitations and these parts are held by the Gaetulians[3]), even as far as the Syrtes, but the

---

[1] "Gods' Harbour."
[2] See 17. 3. 2 (end).
[3] The text of the passage in parentheses is doubtful (see critical note).

---

[10] After ἔρημα Groskurd inserts τινὰ δὲ καὶ οἰκήσιμα; Meineke indicates a lacuna there; Corais conj. ὅπη for πότε.
[11] Γετοῦλοι E, Γέτουλοι other MSS.

εὐδαίμονά ἐστι καὶ πόλεις πολλαὶ καὶ ποταμοὶ καὶ λίμναι.

C 830 10. Ποσειδώνιος δ' οὐκ οἶδ' εἰ ἀληθεύει,[1] φήσας ὀλίγοις καὶ μικροῖς διαρρεῖσθαι ποταμοῖς τὴν Λιβύην· αὐτοὺς γάρ, οὓς Ἀρτεμίδωρος εἴρηκε, τοὺς μεταξὺ τῆς Λυγγὸς καὶ Καρχηδόνος καὶ πολλοὺς εἴρηκε[2] καὶ μεγάλους. ἐν δὲ τῇ μεσογαίᾳ ταῦτ' ἀληθέστερον εἰπεῖν· εἴρηκε δὲ τούτου τὴν αἰτίαν αὐτός, μὴ γὰρ κατομβρεῖσθαι τοῖς ἀρκτικοῖς μέρεσι, καθάπερ οὐδὲ τὴν Αἰθιοπίαν φασί· διὸ πολλάκις λοιμικὰ ἐμπίπτειν ὑπὸ αὐχμῶν καὶ τὰς λίμνας τελμάτων πίμπλασθαι καὶ τὴν ἀκρίδα ἐπιπολάζειν. ἔτι φησὶ τὰ μὲν ἀνατολικὰ ὑγρὰ εἶναι, τὸν γὰρ ἥλιον ἀνίσχοντα ταχὺ παραλλάττειν, τὰ δ' ἑσπέρια ξηρά, ἐκεῖ γὰρ καταστρέφειν. ὑγρὰ γὰρ καὶ ξηρά, τὰ μὲν παρ' ὑδάτων ἀφθονίαν ἢ σπάνιν λέγεται, τὰ δὲ παρὰ τὴν τῶν ἡλίων· βούλεται δὲ λέγειν τὰ παρὰ τοὺς ἡλίους· ταῦτα δὲ πάντες ἀρκτικοῖς καὶ μεσημβρινοῖς κλίμασιν ἀφορίζουσι· καὶ μὴν ἀνατολικά τε καὶ δυσμικά, τὰ μὲν πρὸς τὰς οἰκήσεις λεγόμενα, καθ' ἑκάστην τὴν οἴκησιν καὶ τὴν μετάπτωσιν τῶν ὁριζόντων ἄλλα ἐστίν, ὥστ' οὐδ' ἔνεστι[3] καθολικῶς εἰπεῖν ἐπὶ τῶν ἀπεριλήπτων τὸ πλῆθος, ὅτι τὰ μὲν ἀνατολικὰ ὑγρά, τὰ δὲ δυσμικὰ ξηρά. ὡς δὲ λέγεται πρὸς τὴν οἰκουμένην ὅλην καὶ τὰς

---

[1] ἀληθεύει E, ἀληθής uz, ἀληθῆ other MSS.
[2] τοὺς μεταξὺ ... εἴρηκε, omitted by MSS. except EF.
[3] οὐδ' ἔνεστι, Corais, for οὐδέν ἐστι.

---

[1] The text is corrupt. Strabo probably wrote merely this: "for Artemidorus calls them many and large" (see critical note).

parts there near the sea consist of fertile plains, many cities, rivers, and lakes.

10. I do not know whether Poseidonius tells the truth when he says that Libya is intersected by rivers "only few and small"; for merely the rivers mentioned by Artemidorus, those between Lynx and Carthage, are by him called "both many and large."[1] This statement can be made more truthfully in regard to the interior of the country; and he himself[2] states the cause of this, saying that "no rain falls in the northern parts," as is also said to be the case in Aethiopia, and therefore pestilences often ensue because of droughts, and the lakes are filled with mud, and the locust is prevalent. And he further says that "the eastern regions are moist, for the sun passes quickly when it is rising, whereas the western regions are arid, for there it turns back."[3] For regions are called moist and arid in relation to abundance or scarcity sometimes of waters and partly sometimes of the sun's rays; but Poseidonius means to speak only of the effects of the sun's rays; and these effects are by all writers defined by latitude, north or south; and indeed both the eastern and western regions, when spoken of with reference to the habitations of man, vary according to each several habitation and the change in their horizons, so that it is also impossible to make a general assertion in regard to places whose number passes all comprehension that the eastern are moist and the western arid; but since such statements are made with reference to the in-

[2] Poseidonius.
[3] Thus slowing down in making the turn back, as Strabo interprets it.

ἐσχατιὰς τὰς τοιαύτας, οἷα καὶ ἡ Ἰνδικὴ καὶ ἡ
Ἰβηρία, λέγοι ἄν, εἰ ἄρα,[1] τὴν τοιαύτην ἀπόφα-
σιν. τίς οὖν ἡ πιθανότης τῆς αἰτιολογίας; ἐν
γὰρ περιφορᾷ συνεχεῖ τε καὶ ἀδιαλείπτῳ τοῦ
ἡλίου τίς ἂν εἴη καταστροφή; τό τε τάχος τῆς
παραλλαγῆς[2] πανταχοῦ ἴσον. ἄλλως τε παρὰ
τὴν ἐνάργειαν[3] ἐστι, τὰ ἔσχατα τῆς Ἰβηρίας ἢ
τῆς Μαυρουσίας τὰ πρὸς δύσιν ξηρὰ λέγειν
ἁπάντων μάλιστα· καὶ γὰρ τὸ περιέχον εὔκρατον
ἔχει[4] καὶ πλείστων ὑδάτων εὐπορεῖ. εἰ δὲ τὸ
καταστρέφειν τοιοῦτον εἴληπται, ὅτι ἐνταῦθα τὰ
ὕστατα τῆς οἰκουμένης ὑπὲρ γῆς γίνεται, τί
τοῦτο συντείνει πρὸς ξηρασίαν; καὶ γὰρ ἐνταῦθα
καὶ ἐν τοῖς ἄλλοις τόποις τῆς οἰκουμένης τοῖς
ταὐτοκλινέσι, τὸν ἴσον διαλιπὼν χρόνον τὸν τῆς
νυκτός, ἐπάνεισι πάλιν καὶ θερμαίνει[5] τὴν
γῆν.

11. Ἔστι δέ που αὐτόθι καὶ ἀσφάλτου πηγὴ
καὶ χαλκωρυχεῖα· καὶ σκορπίων δὲ καὶ πτηνῶν[6]
καὶ ἀπτέρων λέγεται πλῆθος, μεγέθει δὲ[7] ἑπτασ-
πονδύλων, ὁμοίως δὲ καὶ φαλάγγια καὶ μεγέθει
καὶ πλήθει διαφέροντα· σαύρας δὲ διπήχεις
φασίν. ἐν μὲν οὖν τῇ παρορείῳ λίθους εὑρίσκεσ-
θαί φασι τοὺς λυχνίτας καὶ καρχηδονίους λεγο-

---

[1] εἰ, moz omit; ἄρα, x omits; the editors before Kramer
read κατά γε instead of εἰ ἄρα.
[2] καταστροφῆς F.   [3] ἐνέργειαν F.
[4] ἔχει, Letronne, for ἔχειν.
[5] διαθερμαίνει E.
[6] E inserts τε after πτηνῶν.
[7] After δέ, Letronne, citing 15. 1. 37 (σκορπίους . . .
ὑπερβάλλοντας μεγέθεσι) and Lucian De Dipsad. 3, inserts
ὑπερβαλλόντων καί.

habited world as a whole and to such extremities of
it as India and Iberia, perhaps he could make such a
statement. What plausibility, however, can there be
in his explanation of the cause? For in the revolution
of the sun, which is continuous and unintermitting,
what "turning back" could there be? And further,
the speed of the sun's transit is everywhere equal.
Besides, it is contrary to the evidence [1] to call the extremities of Iberia or Maurusia, I mean the extremities on the west, the most arid places in the world,
for they not only have a temperate atmosphere but
also are well supplied with numerous waters. But if
the "turning back" of the sun is interpreted in this
way, that there it is last above the inhabited world,
wherein does this contribute to aridity? For there,
as well as in the other places of the inhabited world
that are in the same latitude, the sun leaves an equal
interval of night, and comes back again and warms
the earth.

11. Somewhere here [2] there are also copper mines
and a spring of asphalt; and writers speak also of
a multitude of scorpions, both winged and wingless,
which in size are heptaspondylic,[3] and likewise of
tarantulas [4] which are exceptional both in size and
in number; and lizards which are said to be two
cubits long. Now on the mountain-side [5] are said
to be found the "Lychnite" [6] and Carthaginian

---

[1] One MS. reads "actuality" instead of "evidence" (see
critical note).

[2] *i.e.* in Masaesylia.

[3] *i.e.* they have "seven vertebrae" (the *Pandinus heros*);
see critical note, and cp. 15. 1. 37.

[4] Cp. 16. 4. 12.

[5] Cp. § 19 following.

[6] *i.e.* "Luminous" stones; apparently a tourmaline.

μένους· ἐν δὲ τοῖς πεδίοις ὀστρακίων καὶ χηρα-
μύδων [1] πλῆθος, οἷον ἐν τοῖς περὶ τοῦ Ἄμμωνος
C 831 λόγοις εἰρήκαμεν· καὶ δένδρον δέ ἐστι μελίλωτοι
καλούμενον, ἐξ οὗ σκευάζουσιν οἶνον. τινὲς δ᾽
αὐτῶν καὶ δίκαρπον ἔχουσι τὴν γῆν, καὶ δύο
θεριστικὰ καρποῦνται, τὰ μὲν θερινά, τὰ δ᾽
ἐαρινά· ἔστι δὲ ἡ καλάμη πεντάπηχυς τὸ ὕψος,
πάχος δὲ τοῦ μικροῦ δακτύλου, τὸν δὲ καρπὸν
διακοσιοκαιτετταρακοντάχουν ἀποδίδωσι. τοῦ δὲ
ἔαρος οὐδὲ σπείρουσιν, ἀλλὰ παλιούροις συνδεδε-
μέναις ἐπικαταψήσαντες τὴν χώραν τῷ ἐκπεσόντι
στάχυϊ κατὰ τὸν θερισμὸν ἀρκοῦνται· τελεσι-
καρπεῖ γὰρ τὸν θερινὸν καρπόν. Διὰ δὲ τὸ
πλῆθος τῶν θηρίων κνημῖδας ἔχοντες ἐργάζονται
καὶ τἆλλα δὲ μέρη διφθεροῦνται· καθεύδοντες δὲ
περιχρίουσι τοὺς κλινόποδας σκορόδοις τῶν
σκορπίων χάριν καὶ παλιούροις περιδοῦσιν.

12. Ἦν δ᾽ ἐν [2] τῇ παραλίᾳ ταύτῃ πόλις Ἰωλ
ὄνομα, ἣν ἐπικτίσας Ἰούβας ὁ τοῦ Πτολεμαίου
πατὴρ μετωνόμασε Καισάρειαν, ἔχουσαν καὶ
λιμένα καὶ πρὸ τοῦ λιμένος νησίον. μεταξὺ δὲ
τῆς Καισαρείας καὶ τοῦ Τρητοῦ μέγας ἐστὶ λιμήν,
ὃν Σάλδαν καλοῦσι· τοῦτο δ᾽ ἐστὶν ὅριον τῆς
ὑπὸ τῷ Ἰούβᾳ [3] καὶ τῆς ὑπὸ τοῖς Ῥωμαίοις·
πολυτρόπως γὰρ οἱ μερισμοὶ γεγένηνται τῆς
χώρας, ἅτε τῶν νεμομένων αὐτὴν πλειόνων

---

[1] χημίδων E, χηραμίδων Dx.
[2] δ᾽ ἐν, Casaubon, for δέ.   [3] Ἰόβα E.

---

[1] A carbunculus (see Pliny, 37. 25 and 30).
[2] 1. 3. 4.
[3] i.e. "honey-lotus."   Strabo calls the melilotus a "tree,"

stones,[1] as they are called, and, in the plains, oyster-shells and mussel-shells in great quantities, like those mentioned by me in my description of Ammon.[2] And there is also a tree called melilotus,[3] from which they prepare a wine. And some of the people have land that produces two crops of grain, reaping two harvests, one in spring and the other in summer; and the stalk is five cubits in height, has the thickness of the little finger, and yields a crop 240-fold. In the spring they do not even sow seed, but harrow the ground lightly with bundles of paliuri,[4] and are satisfied with the seed-grain that has fallen out of the ear at the time of the harvest; for this produces a perfect summer crop. On account of the number of wild animals [5] they work with leggings on and also clothe the rest of their bodies with skins. And when they lie down to sleep, they smear the feet of their beds with garlic and tie a bunch of paliuri around them, on account of the scorpions.

12. On this coast was a city named Iol, which Juba, the father of Ptolemy, rebuilt, changing its name to Caesareia; it has a harbour, and also, in front of the harbour, a small island. Between Caesareia and Tretum is a large harbour called Salda, which is now a boundary between the territories subject to Juba and the Romans; for the divisions of the country have been made in various ways, inasmuch as its occupants have been several

both here and in § 17 following, but other writers (*e.g.* Theophrastus, 9. 40, 49) apply the name to a kind of clover.

[4] A kind of thorny shrub (*Rhamnus paliurus*).

[5] *i.e.* reptiles in particular, apparently.

γενομένων καὶ τῶν Ῥωμαίων ἄλλοτ' ἄλλως
τούτων τοῖς μὲν φίλοις χρωμένων, τοῖς δὲ καὶ
πολεμίοις· ὥστε καὶ ἀφαιρεῖσθαι καὶ χαρίζεσθαι
συνέβαινεν ἄλλοις ἄλλα καὶ οὐ τὸν αὐτὸν τρόπον.
ἦν δὲ ἡ μὲν πρὸς τῇ Μαυρουσίᾳ προσοδικωτέρα τε
καὶ δυναμικωτέρα, ἡ δὲ πρὸς τῇ Καρχηδονίᾳ καὶ
τῇ Μασυλιέων [1] ἀνθηροτέρα τε καὶ κατεσκευασμένη βέλτιον, καίπερ κεκακωμένη διὰ τὰ Καρχη-
δόνια τὸ πρῶτον, ἔπειτα διὰ τὸν πρὸς Ἰουγούρθαν
πόλεμον· ἐκεῖνος γὰρ Ἀδάρβαλα ἐκπολιορκήσας
ἐν Ἰτύκῃ καὶ ἀνελών, φίλον ὄντα Ῥωμαίων,
ἐνέπλησε τὴν χώραν πολέμου· εἶτ' ἄλλοι ἐπ'
ἄλλοις συνέστησαν πόλεμοι, τελευταῖος δὲ ὁ πρὸς
Σκιπίωνα Καίσαρι τῷ θεῷ συστάς, ἐν ᾧ καὶ
Ἰούβας ἀπέθανε· συνηφανίσθησαν δὲ τοῖς ἡγεμόσι
καὶ αἱ πόλεις, Τισιαοῦς τε καὶ Οὐάγα [2] καὶ Θάλα,
ἔτι δὲ καὶ Κάψα, τὸ γαζοφυλάκιον τοῦ Ἰου-
γούρθα, καὶ Ζάμα καὶ Ζίγχα [3] καὶ πρὸς αἷς
κατεπολέμησε Καῖσαρ Σκιπίωνα ὁ θεός, πρὸς
Ῥουσπίνῳ [4] μὲν πρῶτον νικῶν, εἶτα πρὸς Οὐζίτοις,
εἶτα πρὸς Θάψῳ καὶ τῇ πλησίον λίμνῃ, καὶ ταῖς
ἄλλαις· πλησίον δὲ καὶ Ζέλλα καὶ Ἀχόλλα,
ἐλεύθεραι πόλεις. εἷλε δ' ἐξ ἐφόδου Καῖσαρ τὴν
Κέρκινναν [5] νῆσον καὶ Θέναν, πολίχνην ἐπιθαλατ-
τιδίαν. τούτων πασῶν αἱ μὲν τελέως ἠφανίσ-
θησαν, αἱ δ' ἡμίσπαστοι κατελείφθησαν· Φαρὰν
δ' οἱ Σκιπίωνος ἱππεῖς ἐνέπρησαν.

---

[1] Μασσαιλίων *moz*, Μασσαισυλίων *x*, Μασσυλιαίων other MSS.
[2] Οὐάγα, Letronne, Kramer, and Meineke, for Οὔατα ; C.
Müller conj. Οὔβατα.
[3] Ζίγχα, Xylander, for Ζάκμα.
[4] Ῥουσπίνῳ, Corais, for Ῥουσπῖνον.

in number and the Romans have dealt with them in different ways at different times, treating some as friends and others as enemies, the result being that different parts were taken away from, or presented to, different peoples, but not in the same way. The country towards Maurusia not only produced more revenue but was also more powerful, whereas that towards Carthage and the Masylians was both more flourishing and better built up, although it had been put in a bad plight, first, on account of the Carthaginian Wars, and then on account of the war against Jugurtha; for he took by siege Adarbal, a friend of the Romans, at Itycê [1] and slew him, and thus filled all Libya with war; and then wars on wars broke out, and, last of all, the war that broke out between the deified Caesar and Scipio, in which even Juba was killed; and with the leaders the cities were wiped out too, I mean Tisiäus, Vaga, and Thala, as also Capsa, the treasure-hold of Jugurtha, and Zama, and Zincha, and those cities near which the deified Caesar defeated Scipio, first winning a victory over him near Ruspinum, and then near Uzita, and then near Thapsus and the lake near by, and the other cities. And near by also are Zella and Acholla, free cities. And Caesar captured at the first onset the island Cercinna, and Thena, a town on the coast. Of all these, some were utterly wiped out and the others left half-destroyed; but Phara was burned by Scipio's cavalry.

[1] *i.e.* "Utica." But Sallust (*Jug.* 25–26) says "Cirta."

---

[5] Κέρκινναν, Casaubon inserts.

C 832   13. Μετὰ δ' οὖν Τρητὸν ἡ Μασυλιέων [1] ἐστὶ
καὶ ἡ Καρχηδονίων παραπλησία χώρα. Κίρτα
τέ ἐστιν ἐν μεσογαίᾳ, τὸ Μασανάσσου [2] καὶ τῶν
ἑξῆς διαδόχων βασίλειον, πόλις εὐερκεστάτη καὶ
κατεσκευασμένη καλῶς τοῖς πᾶσι, καὶ μάλιστα
ὑπὸ Μικίψα, ὅστις καὶ Ἕλληνας συνῴκισεν ἐν
αὐτῇ καὶ τοσαύτην ἐποίησεν, ὥστ' ἐκπέμπειν
μυρίους ἱππέας, διπλασίους δὲ πεζούς. ἥ τε δὴ
Κίρτα ἐνταῦθα καὶ οἱ δύο Ἱππῶνες, ὁ μὲν
πλησίον Ἰτύκης, ὁ δὲ ἀπωτέρω πρὸς τῷ [3] Τρητῷ
μᾶλλον, ἄμφω βασίλεια. ἡ δὲ Ἰτύκη δευτέρα
μετὰ Καρχηδόνα τῷ μεγέθει καὶ τῷ ἀξιώματι·
καταλυθείσης δὲ Καρχηδόνος, ἐκείνη ἦν ὡς ἂν
μητρόπολις τοῖς Ῥωμαίοις καὶ ὁρμητήριον πρὸς
τὰς ἐν Λιβύῃ πράξεις. ἵδρυται δ' ἐν τῷ αὐτῷ
κόλπῳ τῷ Καρχηδονιακῷ, πρὸς θατέρῳ τῶν
ἀκρωτηρίων τῶν ποιούντων τὸν κόλπον, ὧν τὸ
μὲν πρὸς τῇ Ἰτύκῃ καλοῦσιν Ἀπολλώνιον, θάτερον δ' Ἑρμαίαν· καί εἰσιν ἐν ἐπόψει [4] ἀλλήλαις
αἱ πόλεις. ῥεῖ δὲ τῆς Ἰτύκης πλησίον ὁ Βαγρά-
δας [5] ποταμός. εἰσὶ δ' ἀπὸ Τρητοῦ μέχρι
Καρχηδόνος στάδιοι δισχίλιοι πεντακόσιοι. οὔτε [6]
τοῦθ' ὁμολογεῖται δὲ τὸ διάστημα οὔτε τὸ μέχρι
Σύρτεων.

14. Καὶ Καρχηδὼν δὲ ἐπὶ χερρονήσου τινὸς
ἵδρυται, περιγραφούσης κύκλον τριακοσίων ἑξήκοντα σταδίων ἔχοντα τεῖχος, οὗ τὸ ἑξηκοντα-
στάδιον μῆκος [7] αὐτὸς ὁ αὐχὴν ἐπέχει, καθῆκον [8]

---

[1] Μασσυλιέων E, Μασσαισυλίων x, Μασυλιαίων z, Μασυλιαίων
other MSS.

[2] Μασανάσσου, Kramer, for Μασσανάσσου iwx, Μασανάσου
morz, Σανάσσου C, Μασανίσσου other MSS.

182

13. Now after Tretum one comes to the land
of the Masylians, and to the land of the Carthaginians, which is similar thereto. Cirta, the royal
residence of Masanasses and his successors, is in the
interior; it is very strongly fortified and has been
beautifully built up in every way, particularly by
Micipsas, who not only settled a colony of Greeks in
it, but also made it so great that it could send forth
ten thousand cavalry and twice as many infantry.
Cirta, then, is here, and so are the two Hippos,
one near Itycê and the other farther away, rather
towards Tretum; and both are royal residences.
Itycê was second only to Carthage in size and
importance, and when Carthage was destroyed, that
city served the Romans as a metropolis, and as a
base of operations for their activities in Libya. It
is situated in the same gulf as Carthage, near one of
the two promontories which form the gulf, of which
the one near Itycê is called Apollonium and the
other Hermaea; and the two cities are in sight of
one another. Near Itycê flows the Bagradas River.
The distance from Tretum to Carthage is two
thousand five hundred stadia. But neither this distance nor that to the Syrtes is generally agreed upon.

14. Carthage, also, is situated on a kind of
peninsula, which comprises a circuit of three hundred and sixty stadia; and this circuit has a wall;
and sixty stadia of the length of this circuit are
occupied by the neck itself, which extend from sea to

---

³ τῷ, Corais, for τῇ. ⁴ ἐν ὕψει E.
⁵ Βαγράδας E, Μαγάδρας hi, Βαγάδρας other MSS.
⁶ οὔτε, Corais, for οὐδέ.
⁷ τεῖχος Dhi.
⁸ καθῆκον, Groskurd, for καθίκων.

ἀπὸ θαλάττης ἐπὶ θάλατταν, ὅπου τοῖς Καρχηδονίοις ἦσαν αἱ τῶν ἐλεφάντων στάσεις, καὶ τόπος
εὐρυχωρής. κατὰ μέσην δὲ τὴν πόλιν ἡ ἀκρό-
πολις, ἣν ἐκάλουν Βύρσαν, ὀφρὺς ἱκανῶς ὀρθία,
κύκλῳ περιοικουμένη, κατὰ δὲ τὴν κορυφὴν
ἔχουσα Ἀσκληπιεῖον, ὅπερ κατὰ τὴν ἅλωσιν ἡ
γυνὴ τοῦ Ἀσδρούβα συνέπρησεν αὐτῇ.¹ ὑπό-
κεινται δὲ τῇ ἀκροπόλει οἵ τε λιμένες καὶ ὁ Κώθων,
νησίον περιφερὲς εὐρίπῳ περιεχόμενον, ἔχοντι²
νεωσοίκους ἑκατέρωθεν κύκλῳ.

15. Κτίσμα δ' ἐστὶ Διδοῦς ἀγαγούσης ἐκ Τύρου
λαόν· οὕτω δ' εὐτυχὴς ἡ ἀποικία τοῖς Φοίνιξιν
ὑπῆρξε καὶ αὕτη καὶ ἡ μέχρι τῆς Ἰβηρίας τῆς
τε ἄλλης καὶ τῆς ἔξω Στηλῶν, ὥστε τῆς Εὐρώπης
ἔτι νῦν τὴν ἀρίστην νέμονται Φοίνικες κατὰ τὴν
ἤπειρον καὶ τὰς προσεχεῖς νήσους, τήν τε Λιβύην
κατεκτήσαντο πᾶσαν, ὅσην³ μὴ νομαδικῶς οἷόν
τ' ἦν οἰκεῖν. ἀφ' ἧς δυνάμεως πόλιν τε ἀντί-
παλον τῇ Ῥώμῃ κατεσκευάσαντο καὶ τρεῖς ἐπολέ-
μησαν μεγάλους πρὸς αὐτοὺς πολέμους. γένοιτο
δ' ἂν εὔδηλος ἡ δύναμις αὐτῶν ἐκ τοῦ ὑστάτου
πολέμου, ἐν ᾧ κατελύθησαν ὑπὸ Σκιπίωνος τοῦ
Αἰμιλιανοῦ, καὶ ἡ πόλις ἄρδην ἠφανίσθη. ὅτε
C 833 γὰρ ἤρξαντο πολεμεῖν τοῦτον τὸν πόλεμον,⁴
πόλεις μὲν εἶχον τριακοσίας ἐν τῇ Λιβύῃ, ἀνθρώ-
πων δ' ἐν τῇ πόλει μυριάδας ἑβδομήκοντα·
πολιορκούμενοι δὲ καὶ ἀναγκασθέντες τραπέσθαι
πρὸς ἔνδοσιν, πανοπλιῶν μὲν ἔδοσαν μυριάδας

---

¹ αὐτῇ, Corais, for αὑτῇ.
² ἔχοντι, Corais, for ἔχον τε.
³ ὅσην E, ὅσον other MSS.
⁴ πόλεμον EF, τρόπον other MSS.

sea; and this, a spacious place, is where the Carthaginians had their elephant-stalls. Near the middle of the city was the acropolis, which they called Byrsa;[1] it was a fairly steep height and inhabited on all sides, and at the top it had a temple of Asclepius, which, at the time of the capture of the city, the wife of Asdrubal burnt along with herself. Below the acropolis lie the harbours, as also Cothon, a circular isle surrounded by a strait, which latter has ship-houses all round on either side.[2]

15. Carthage was founded by Dido, who brought a host of people from Tyre. The colonisation proved to be so fortunate an enterprise for the Phoenicians, both this at Carthage and that which extended as far as Iberia—I mean the part of Iberia outside the Pillars as well as the rest of it—that even to this day the best part of continental Europe and also the adjacent islands are occupied by Phoenicians; and they also gained possession of all that part of Libya which men can live in without living a nomadic life. From this dominion they not only raised their city to be a rival of Rome, but also waged three great wars against the Romans. Their power might become clearly evident from the last war, in which they were defeated by Scipio Aemilianus and their city was utterly wiped out. For when they began to wage this war they had three hundred cities in Libya and seven hundred thousand people in their city; and when they were being besieged and were forced to resort to surrender, they gave up two hundred thousand full

[1] "Hide."
[2] *i.e.* both on the island and on the mainland.

εἴκοσι, καταπελτικὰ δὲ ὄργανα τρισχίλια,¹ ὡς
οὐ πολεμηθησόμενοι· κριθέντος δὲ πάλιν τοῦ
ἀναπολεμεῖν, ἐξαίφνης ὁπλοποιίαν συνεστήσαντο,
καὶ ἑκάστης ἡμέρας ἀνεφέροντο θυρεοὶ μὲν ἑκατὸν
καὶ τετταράκοντα πεπηγότες, μάχαιραι δὲ τρια-
κόσιαι καὶ λόγχαι πεντακόσιαι, χίλια δὲ βέλη
καταπελτικά, τρίχα δὲ τοῖς καταπέλταις αἱ θερά-
παιναι παρεῖχον. ἔτι τοίνυν ναῦς ἔχοντες δώδεκα
ἐξ ἐτῶν πεντήκοντα κατὰ τὰς ἐν τῷ δευτέρῳ
πολέμῳ συνθήκας, τότε, καίπερ ἤδη συμπεφευ-
γότες εἰς τὴν Βύρσαν, ἐν διμήνῳ κατεσκευάσαντο
ναῦς ἑκατὸν εἴκοσι καταφράκτους, καὶ τοῦ στόματος τοῦ Κώθωνος φρουρουμένου, διώρυξαν ἄλλο
στόμα, καὶ προῆλθεν αἰφνιδίως ὁ στόλος· ὕλη
γὰρ ἦν ἀποκειμένη παλαιὰ καὶ τεχνιτῶν πλῆθος
προσεδρεῦον καὶ σιταρχούμενον² δημοσίᾳ. τοιαύτη
δ᾽ οὖσα Καρχηδὼν ὅμως ἑάλω καὶ κατεσκάφη.
τὴν δὲ χώραν, τὴν μὲν ἐπαρχίαν ἀπέδειξαν
Ῥωμαῖοι, τὴν ὑπὸ τοῖς Καρχηδονίοις, τῆς δὲ
Μασανάσσην ἀπέδειξαν κύριον καὶ τοὺς ἀπογό-
νους τοὺς περὶ Μικίψαν. μάλιστα γὰρ ἐσπου-
δάσθη παρὰ τοῖς Ῥωμαίοις ὁ Μασανάσσης δι᾽
ἀρετὴν καὶ φιλίαν· καὶ γὰρ δὴ καὶ οὗτός ἐστιν ὁ
τοὺς Νομάδας πολιτικοὺς κατασκευάσας καὶ
γεωργούς, ἔτι δ᾽ ἀντὶ τοῦ ληστεύειν διδάξας
στρατεύειν. ἴδιον γάρ τι τοῖς ἀνθρώποις συνέβη

¹ For τρισχίλια Letronne (citing Polybius 36. 4 and Appian
80) conj. δισχίλια.
² σιταρκούμενον xz.

---

suits of armour and three thousand[1] catapults, on
the assumption that they would not be engaged in
war again; but when they resolved to renew the war,
they suddenly organised the manufacture of arms,
and each day produced one hundred and forty
finished shields, three hundred swords, five hundred
spears, and one thousand missiles for the catapults;
and the women-servants furnished hair for the
catapults. Furthermore, although from fifty years
back they had possessed only twelve ships, in
accordance with the treaty made at the second war,
they then, although they had already fled together
for refuge into the Byrsa, built one hundred and
twenty decked ships in two months; and since the
mouth of Cothon was being guarded, they dug
another mouth through and their fleet sallied forth
unexpectedly; for old timber had been stored away
in readiness, and a large number of skilled workmen,
maintained at public expense, had been lying in
wait for this occasion. But though Carthage was so
resourceful, still it was captured and rased to the
ground. As for the country, the Romans proclaimed
one part of it a Province, I mean the part which
had been subject to the Carthaginians, and appointed as sovereign of the other part Masanasses, as
also his descendants, the house of Micipsas;[2] for
Masanasses was held in very high respect among the
Romans because of his valour and friendship; and
indeed it was he who transformed the Nomads into
citizens and farmers, and taught them to be soldiers
instead of brigands. For a peculiar thing had hap-

---

[2] *i.e.* the three sons: Micipsas king, Golossa head of the
department of war, and Mastanaba head of the department of
justice (Appian, § 106).

τούτοις· χώραν γὰρ οἰκοῦντες εὐδαίμονα, πλὴν
τοῦ θηρίοις πλεονάζειν, ἐάσαντες ἐκφθείρειν[1]
ταῦτα καὶ τὴν γῆν ἐργάζεσθαι μετὰ ἀδείας ἐπ'
ἀλλήλοις ἐτρέποντο, τὴν δὲ γῆν τοῖς θηρίοις
ἀφεῖσαν. οὕτω δ' αὐτοῖς συνέβαινε πλάνητα καὶ
μετανάστην βίον ζῆν, μηδὲν ἧττον τῶν ὑπὸ
ἀπορίας καὶ λυπρότητος τόπων ἢ ἀέρων εἰς
τοῦτο περιισταμένων τῶν βίων, ὥστε καὶ ἴδιον
τοῦθ' εὑρίσκεσθαι τοὔνομα τοὺς Μασαισυλίους,
καλοῦνται γὰρ Νομάδες, ἀνάγκη δὲ τοὺς τοιούτους
εὐτελεῖς εἶναι τοῖς βίοις καὶ τὸ πλέον ῥιζοφάγους
ἢ κρεωφάγους, γάλακτι δὲ καὶ τυρῷ τρεφομένους.
ἠρημωμένης δ' οὖν ἐπὶ πολὺν χρόνον τῆς Καρχηδόνος, καὶ σχεδόν τι τὸν αὐτὸν χρόνον, ὅνπερ καὶ
Κόρινθος, ἀνελήφθη πάλιν περὶ τοὺς αὐτούς πως
χρόνους ὑπὸ Καίσαρος τοῦ θεοῦ, πέμψαντος
ἐποίκους Ῥωμαίων τοὺς προαιρουμένους καὶ τῶν
στρατιωτῶν τινας· καὶ νῦν εἴ τις ἄλλη καλῶς
οἰκεῖται τῶν ἐν Λιβύῃ πόλεων.

C 834   16. [2] Κατὰ μέσον δὲ τὸ στόμα τοῦ Καρχηδονίου
κόλπου νῆσός ἐστι Κόρσουρα. ἀντίπορθμος δ'
ἐστὶν ἡ Σικελία τοῖς τόποις τούτοις ἡ κατὰ
Λιλύβαιον, ὅσον ἐν διαστήματι χιλίων καὶ
πεντακοσίων σταδίων· τοσοῦτον γάρ φασι[3]
τὸ ἐκ Λιλυβαίου μέχρι Καρχηδόνος. οὐ πολὺ
δὲ τῆς Κορσούρας διέχουσιν οὐδὲ τῆς Σικελίας

---

[1] ἐκφθείρειν (as in 17. 1. 44), Jones, for ἐκφέρειν.
[2] Meineke ejects Κατὰ μέσον . . . Αἰγίμουρος from the text,
following conj. of Kramer.   [3] φασι F, φησι other MSS.

---

[1] "Nomades" ("Nomads") is the Greek name corres-
ponding to the Latin "Numidae" ("Numidians").

pened in the case of these people, that is, although
they lived in a country blest by nature, except for
the fact that it abounded in wild animals, they
would forbear to destroy these and thus work the
land in security, and would turn against one another,
abandoning the land to the wild animals. In this
way it came to pass that they kept leading a
wandering and migratory life, no less so than
peoples who are driven by poverty and by wretched
soil or climate to resort to this kind of life ; so that
the Masaesylians have obtained this as their special
designation, for they are called Nomades.[1] Such
people of necessity must lead a frugal life, being for
the most part root-eaters and meat-eaters, and using
milk and cheese for food. Be that as it may,
Carthage for a long time remained desolate, about
the same length of time as Corinth,[2] but it was
restored again at about the same time as Corinth by
the deified Caesar, who sent thither as colonists such
Romans as preferred to go there and some soldiers ;
and now it is as prosperous a city as any other
in Libya.

16. Opposite[3] the middle of the mouth of the
Carthaginian Gulf is Corsura,[4] an island. Across
the arm of the sea, opposite this region, is that
part of Sicily wherein lies Lilybaeum, at a distance
of about one thousand five hundred stadia ; for
the distance from Lilybaeum to Carthage is said to
be as great as this. Not far distant from Corsura,

[2] Corinth was destroyed by L. Mummius in 146 B.C., but
was restored by Julius Caesar and Augustus.

[3] This passage, "Opposite . . . other islands," is ejected
from the text by Meineke (see critical note).

[4] "Corsura," unless it is here confused in some way with
Cossura (Pantellaria), is otherwise unknown.

ἄλλαι τε νῆσοι καὶ Αἰγίμουρος.¹ διάπλους
δ᾽ ἐστὶν ἐκ Καρχηδόνος ἑξήκοντα σταδίων
εἰς τὴν προσεχῆ περαίαν, ὅθεν εἰς Νέφεριν ἀνάβασις σταδίων ἑκατὸν εἴκοσι, πόλιν² ἐρυμνὴν
ἐπὶ πέτρας ᾠκισμένην. ἐν αὐτῷ δὲ τῷ κόλπῳ,
ἐν ᾧπερ καὶ ἡ Καρχηδών, Τύνις ἐστὶ πόλις καὶ
θερμὰ καὶ λατομίαι τινές· εἶθ᾽ ἡ Ἑρμαία ἄκρα
τραχεῖα, καὶ ἐπ᾽ αὐτῇ³ πόλις ὁμώνυμος· εἶτα
Νεάπολις· εἶτ᾽ ἄκρα Ταφῖτις, καὶ ἐπ᾽ αὐτῇ λόφος
Ἀσπὶς καλούμενος ἀπὸ τῆς ὁμοιότητος, ὅνπερ
συνῴκισεν ὁ τῆς Σικελίας τύραννος Ἀγαθοκλῆς,
καθ᾽ ὃν καιρὸν ἐπέπλευσε τοῖς Καρχηδονίοις.
συγκατεσπάσθησαν δὲ τῇ Καρχηδονίᾳ ὑπὸ
Ῥωμαίων αἱ πόλεις αὗται. ἀπὸ δὲ τῆς Ταφί-
τιδος ἐν τετρακοσίοις σταδίοις νῆσός ἐστι Κόσ-
σουρος⁴ κατὰ Σελινοῦντα τῆς Σικελίας ποταμόν,
καὶ πόλιν ἔχουσα ὁμώνυμον, ἑκατὸν καὶ πεντήκοντα σταδίων οὖσα⁵ τὴν περίμετρον, διέχουσα
τῆς Σικελίας περὶ ἑξακοσίους σταδίους· ἔστι δὲ
καὶ Μελίτη νῆσος ἐν πεντακοσίοις σταδίοις ἀπὸ
τῆς Κοσσούρου.⁶ εἶτα Ἀδρύμης⁷ πόλις, ἐν ᾗ καὶ
νεώρια ἦν· εἶθ᾽ αἱ Ταριχεῖαι λεγόμεναι, νησία
πολλὰ καὶ πυκνά· εἶτα Θάψος πόλις, καὶ μετὰ
ταύτην νῆσος πελαγία Λοπαδοῦσσα· εἶτα ἄκρα

---

¹ Αἰγίμορος F.   ² δ᾽, after πόλιν, Corais omits.
³ αὐτῆς E, αὐτήν other MSS.   ⁴ Κόρσουρα moz.
⁵ οὖσαν MSS.   ⁶ Κοσσούρας moz.
⁷ Ἀδρυμής F, Ἀδρύμις hix, Ἄδρυμις E, Ἀδρύμη moz.

---

¹ Al Djamur.
² i.e. apparently the eastern side of the Carthaginian
Gulf.
³ Tunis, or Tunes, was situated to the south of Carthage
and at the head of a vast marshy lagoon.

nor yet from Sicily, are Aegimuros [1] and other
islands. The voyage from Carthage across to the
nearest point of the opposite mainland [2] is sixty
stadia, from which the journey inland to Nepheris is
one hundred and twenty stadia—a city fortified by
nature and built upon a rock. But on the same
gulf as that on which Carthage is situated lies a city
Tynis, [3] as also hot springs and stone-quarries; and
then one comes to the rugged promontory Hermaea,
and to a city on it bearing the same name; and
then to Neapolis; and then to a promontory Taphitis,
and to a hill on it, which, from the resemblance, is
called Aspis; [4] this is the hill that Agathocles, the
tyrant of Sicily, colonised at the time when he
sailed against the Carthaginians. But these cities
were demolished by the Romans at the same time
as Carthage. At a distance of four hundred stadia
from Taphitis lies an island Cossurus, [5] opposite the
Selinus River in Sicily, and a city bearing the same
name, which is one hundred and fifty stadia in
circuit and is about six hundred stadia distant from
Sicily; and there is also an island Melitê [6] at a
distance of five hundred stadia from the island
Cossurus. [7] Then one comes to a city Adrymes, [8] at
which there was also a naval arsenal; and then to
the Taricheiae, as they are called, which are
numerous small islands lying close together; and
then to a city Thapsus; and after this to Lopadussa,
an island in the open sea; and then to a promontory

---

[4] *i.e.* "Shield."
[5] The same, apparently, as Cossura (cp. 2. 5. 19 and
6. 2. 11).
[6] Malta.   [7] See preceding footnote.
[8] Also called Adrumetum.

Ἄμμωνος Βαλίθωνος, πρὸς ᾗ θυννοσκοπεῖον·[1]
εἶτα Θένα[2] πόλις παρὰ τὴν ἀρχὴν κειμένη τῆς
μικρᾶς Σύρτεως. πολλαὶ δ᾽ εἰσὶ καὶ ἄλλαι
μεταξὺ πολίχναι οὐκ ἄξιαι μνήμης. παράκειται
δὲ τῇ ἀρχῇ τῆς Σύρτεως νῆσος παραμήκης, ἡ
Κέρκιννα,[3] εὐμεγέθης, ἔχουσα ὁμώνυμον πόλιν,
καὶ ἄλλη ἐλάττων Κερκιννῖτις.[4]

17. Συνεχὴς δ᾽ ἐστὶν ἡ μικρὰ Σύρτις, ἣν καὶ
Λωτοφαγῖτιν Σύρτιν λέγουσιν. ἔστι δ᾽ ὁ μὲν
κύκλος τοῦ κόλπου τούτου σταδίων χιλίων
ἑξακοσίων, τὸ δὲ πλάτος τοῦ στόματος ἑξακοσίων·
καθ᾽ ἑκατέραν δὲ[5] τὴν ἄκραν τὴν ποιοῦσαν τὸ
στόμα προσεχεῖς εἰσι τῇ ἠπείρῳ νῆσοι, ἥ τε
λεχθεῖσα Κέρκιννα καὶ ἡ Μῆνιγξ, πάρισοι τοῖς
μεγέθεσι. τὴν δὲ Μῆνιγγα νομίζουσιν εἶναι τὴν
τῶν Λωτοφάγων γῆν τὴν ὑφ᾽ Ὁμήρου λεγομένην,
καὶ δείκνυταί τινα σύμβολα, καὶ βωμὸς Ὀδυσ-
σέως καὶ αὐτὸς ὁ καρπός· πολὺ γάρ ἐστι τὸ
δένδρον ἐν αὐτῇ τὸ καλούμενον λωτόν, ἔχον
ἥδιστον καρπόν. πλείους δ᾽ εἰσὶν ἐν αὐτῇ πολίχναι,
C 835 μία δ᾽ ὁμώνυμος τῇ νήσῳ. καὶ ἐν αὐτῇ δὲ τῇ Σύρτει
πολίχναι τινές εἰσι. κατὰ δὲ τὸν μυχόν ἐστι
παμμέγεθες ἐμπόριον, ποταμὸν ἔχον ἐμβάλλοντα
εἰς τὸν κόλπον· διατείνει δὲ μέχρι δεῦρο τὰ τῶν
ἀμπώτεων πάθη καὶ τῶν πλημμυρίδων, καθ᾽ ὃν
καιρὸν ἐπὶ τὴν θήραν τῶν ἰχθύων ἐπιπηδῶσιν οἱ
πρόσχωροι κατὰ σπουδὴν θέοντες.

18. Μετὰ δὲ τὴν Σύρτιν Ζοῦχίς ἐστι λίμνη

---

[1] ᾗ θυννοσκοπεῖον, conj. Kramer, for θυννοσκοπίαν; E reads
ἐν ᾗ θυννοσκοπίᾳ.
[2] Θένα, Corais, for Θαῖνα.   [3] Κέρκινα F.
[4] Κερκινῖτις F, Κερκινῆτις i.

of Ammon Balithon, near which is a place for watching for the tunny-fish;[1] and then to a city Thena, which lies near the beginning of the Little Syrtis. In the interval lie numerous small towns not worth mentioning. Near the beginning of the Syrtis lies a long island, Cercinna, which is rather large and contains a city of the same name; and there is another smaller island, Cercinnitis.

17. Continuous with these is the Little Syrtis, which is also called the Syrtis of the Lotus-eaters. The circuit of this gulf is one thousand six hundred stadia, and the breadth of the mouth six hundred; and at each of the two promontories which form its mouth are islands close to the mainland—the Cercinna above-mentioned and Meninx, which are about equal in size. Meninx is regarded as the land of the Lotus-eaters mentioned by Homer; and certain tokens of this are pointed out—both an altar of Odysseus and the fruit itself; for the tree which is called the lotus abounds in the island, and its fruit is delightful. There are several cities on Meninx, and one of them bears the same name as the island. On the coast of the Syrtis itself are several small towns. In the recess of the gulf is a very large emporium, which has a river that empties into the gulf; and the effects of the flow and ebb of the tides extend thus far, at which times the neighbouring inhabitants rush forth on the run to catch the fish.

18. After the Syrtis, one comes to Zuchis, a lake

---

[1] Cp. 5. 2. 6, 8.

---

[5] δέ, omitted by MSS. except *i*.

σταδίων τετρακοσίων στενὸν ἔχουσα εἴσπλουν
καὶ παρ' αὐτὴν πόλις ὁμώνυμος πορφυροβαφεῖα
ἔχουσα καὶ ταριχείας παντοδαπάς· εἶτ' ἄλλη
λίμνη πολὺ ἐλάττων· καὶ μετὰ ταύτην Ἀβρό-
τονον πόλις καὶ ἄλλαι τινές, συνεχῶς δὲ Νεάπολις,
ἣν καὶ Λέπτιν καλοῦσιν· ἐντεῦθεν δ' ἐστὶ δίαρμα
τὸ ἐπὶ Λοκρῶν τῶν Ἐπιζεφυρίων τρισχίλιοι
ἑξακόσιοι στάδιοι. ἑξῆς δ' ἐστὶ ποταμός· καὶ
μετὰ ταῦτα διατείχισμά τι, ὃ ἐποίησαν Καρχηδόνιοι, γεφυροῦντες βάραθρά¹ τινα εἰς τὴν χώραν
ἀνέχοντα· εἰσὶ δὲ καὶ ἀλίμενοί τινες ἐνταῦθα
τόποι, τῆς ἄλλης παραλίας ἐχούσης λιμένας.
εἶτ' ἄκρα ὑψηλὴ καὶ ὑλώδης, ἀρχὴ τῆς μεγάλης
Σύρτεως, καλοῦσι δὲ Κεφαλάς· εἰς ταύτην δὲ τὴν
ἄκραν ἐκ Καρχηδόνος στάδιοί εἰσι μικρῷ πλείους
τῶν πεντακισχιλίων.

19. Ὑπέρκειται δὲ τῆς ἀπὸ Καρχηδόνος παραλίας μέχρι Κεφαλῶν καὶ μέχρι τῆς Μασαισυλίων²
ἡ τῶν Λιβοφοινίκων γῆ μέχρι τῆς τῶν Γαιτούλων³
ὀρεινῆς, ἤδη Λιβυκῆς οὔσης. ἡ δ' ὑπὲρ τῶν
Γαιτούλων ἐστὶν ἡ τῶν Γαραμάντων γῆ παράλληλος ἐκείνῃ, ὅθεν οἱ Καρχηδόνιοι κομίζονται
λίθοι. τοὺς δὲ Γαράμαντας ἀπὸ τῶν Αἰθιόπων
τῶν⁴ παρωκεανιτῶν ἀφεστάναι φασὶν ἡμερῶν
ἐννέα ἢ καὶ δέκα ὁδόν, τοῦ δὲ Ἄμμωνος καὶ
πεντεκαίδεκα. μεταξὺ δὲ τῆς Γαιτούλων καὶ

---

¹ βάθρα Dhi.
² Μασαισυλίων, Kramer, for Μασσαισυλείων F, Μασσαισυλίων
other MSS.
³ Γαιτούλων, Xylander, for Γετούλων.
⁴ καί, before τῶν, Meineke omits.

---

¹ The Cinifo.

with a circuit of four hundred stadia; it has a narrow
entrance, and near it is a city bearing the same
name which contains dye-factories and all kinds of
fish-salting establishments; and then to another
lake, which is much smaller; and after this to a city
Abrotonum and to several others; and contiguous
to these is Neapolis, which is also called Leptis; and
from here the passage across to the Epizephyrian
Locrians is three thousand six hundred stadia.
Next in order one comes to a river;[1] and afterwards to a kind of cross-wall which the Carthaginians built, wishing to bridge over some gorges
which extend up into the interior. There are also
some harbourless regions here, although the rest of
the coast has harbours. Then one comes to a lofty,
wooded promontory, which forms the beginning of
the Great Syrtis and is called Cephalae;[2] and the
distance to this promontory from Carthage is a little
more than five thousand stadia.

19. Above the coast-line which extends from Carthage to Cephalae and to the land of Masaesylians
lies the land of the Libo-Phoenicians, which extends
to the mountainous country of the Gaetulians, where
Libya[3] begins. The land above the Gaetulians is
that of the Garamantes, which lies parallel to the
former and is the land whence the Carthaginian
stones are brought.[4] The Garamantes are said to be
distant from the Aethiopians who live on the ocean
a nine or ten days' journey, and from Ammon fifteen.
Between the Gaetulians and our seaboard[5] there

[2] "Heads."
[3] *i.e.* the true Libya, as distinguished from Libo-Phoenicia.
[4] See 17. 3. 11.
[5] *i.e.* the Mediterranean seaboard.

τῆς ἡμετέρας παραλίας πολλὰ μὲν πεδία, πολλὰ
δὲ ὄρη καὶ λίμναι μεγάλαι καὶ ποταμοί, ὧν τινες
καὶ καταδύντες ὑπὸ γῆς ἀφανεῖς γίνονται. λιτοὶ
δὲ σφόδρα τοῖς βίοις εἰσὶ καὶ τῷ κόσμῳ, πολυ-
γύναικες δὲ καὶ πολύπαιδες, τἆλλα δὲ ἐμφερεῖς
τοῖς νομάσι τῶν Ἀράβων· καὶ ἵπποι δὲ καὶ βόες
μακροτραχηλότεροι[1] τῶν παρ' ἄλλοις. ἱππο-
φόρβια δ' ἐστὶν ἐσπουδασμένα διαφερόντως τοῖς
βασιλεῦσιν, ὥστε καὶ ἀριθμὸν ἐξετάζεσθαι
πώλων κατ' ἔτος εἰς μυριάδας δέκα. τὰ δὲ πρόβατα γάλακτι καὶ κρέασιν ἐκτρέφεται, καὶ
μάλιστα πρὸς τοῖς Αἰθίοψι. τοιαῦτα μὲν τὰ
ἐν τῇ μεσογαίᾳ.

20. Ἡ δὲ μεγάλη Σύρτις τὸν μὲν κύκλον ἔχει
σταδίων τρισχιλίων[2] ἐννακοσίων τριάκοντά που,
τὴν δ' ἐπὶ τὸν μυχὸν διάμετρον χιλίων πεντακοσίων,
τοσοῦτον δέ που καὶ τὸ τοῦ στόματος πλάτος. ἡ
χαλεπότης δὲ καὶ ταύτης τῆς Σύρτεως καὶ τῆς
C 836   μικρᾶς, ὅτι πολλαχοῦ τεναγώδης ἐστὶν ὁ βυθὸς καὶ
κατὰ τὰς ἀμπώτεις καὶ τὰς πλημμυρίδας συμβαίνει
τισὶν ἐμπίπτειν εἰς τὰ βράχη καὶ καθίζειν, σπάνιον
δ' εἶναι τὸ σωζόμενον σκάφος. διόπερ πόρρωθεν
τὸν παράπλουν ποιοῦνται, φυλαττόμενοι, μὴ
ἐμπέσοιεν εἰς τοὺς κόλπους ὑπ' ἀνέμων ἀφύλακτοι
ληφθέντες· τὸ μέντοι παρακίνδυνον τῶν ἀνθρώ-
πων ἁπάντων διαπειρᾶσθαι ποιεῖ, καὶ μάλιστα
τῶν παρὰ γῆν περίπλων· εἰσπλέοντι δὴ τὴν
μεγάλην Σύρτιν ἐν δεξιᾷ μετὰ τὰς Κεφαλάς ἐστι
λίμνη τριακοσίων που σταδίων τὸ μῆκος, ἑβδομήκοντα δὲ τὸ πλάτος, ἐκδιδοῦσα εἰς τὸν κόλπον,

---

[1] μακροτράχηλοι E, μακροχηλότεροι CDhz.
[2] τρισχιλίων (,γ), Kramer inserts.

are not only many plains, but also many mountains, large lakes, and rivers, some of which sink beneath the earth and become invisible. The inhabitants are very simple in their modes of life and in their dress; but the men have many wives and many children, and in other respects are like the nomadic Arabians; and both horses and cattle have longer necks than those of other countries. Horse-breeding is followed with such exceptional interest by the kings that the number of colts every year amounts to one hundred thousand. The sheep are brought up on milk and meats, particularly in the regions near Aethiopia. Such is my account of the interior.

20. The Great Syrtis has a circuit of about three thousand and nine hundred and thirty stadia, and a diameter, to the inmost recess, of one thousand five hundred stadia, and also a breadth at the mouth of about one thousand five hundred. The difficulty with both this Syrtis and the Little Syrtis is that in many places their deep waters contain shallows, and the result is, at the ebb and the flow of the tides, that sailors sometimes fall into the shallows and stick there, and that the safe escape of a boat is rare. On this account sailors keep at a distance when voyaging along the coast, taking precautions not to be caught off their guard and driven by winds into these gulfs. However, the disposition of man to take risks causes him to try anything in the world, and particularly voyages along coasts. Now as one sails into the Great Syrtis, on the right, after Cephalae is passed, one comes to a lake about three hundred stadia in length and seventy in breadth, which empties into the gulf and contains both small islands

ἔχουσα καὶ νησία καὶ ὕφορμον πρὸ τοῦ στόματος.
μετὰ δὲ τὴν λίμνην τόπος ἐστὶν Ἀσπὶς καὶ λιμὴν
κάλλιστος τῶν ἐν τῇ Σύρτει. συνεχὴς δὲ ὁ
Εὐφράντας πύργος ἐστίν, ὅριον τῆς πρότερον
Καρχηδονίας γῆς καὶ τῆς Κυρηναίας τῆς ὑπὸ
Πτολεμαίῳ· εἶτ᾽ ἄλλος τόπος, Χάραξ καλούμενος, ᾧ ἐμπορίῳ ἐχρῶντο Καρχηδόνιοι κομίζοντες
οἶνον, ἀντιφορτιζόμενοι δὲ ὀπὸν καὶ σίλφιον παρὰ
τῶν ἐκ Κυρήνης λάθρα παρακομιζόντων· εἶθ᾽ οἱ
Φιλαίνων βωμοί· καὶ μετὰ τούτους Αὐτόμαλα,
φρούριον φυλακὴν ἔχον, ἱδρυμένον κατὰ τὸν
μυχὸν τοῦ κόλπου παντός. ἔστι δ᾽ ὁ διὰ τοῦ
μυχοῦ τούτου παράλληλος, τοῦ μὲν δι᾽ Ἀλεξανδρείας μικρῷ νοτιώτερος, χιλίοις σταδίοις, τοῦ δὲ
διὰ Καρχηδόνος ἐλάττοσιν ἢ δισχιλίοις· συμ-
πίπτοι¹ δ᾽ ἂν τῇ μὲν καθ᾽ Ἡρώων πόλιν τὴν ἐν τῷ
μυχῷ τοῦ Ἀραβίου κόλπου, τῇ δὲ κατὰ τὴν
μεσόγαιαν τῶν Μασαισυλίων² καὶ τῶν Μαυρου-
σίων.³ τὸ λειπόμενον ἤδη τῆς παραλίας ἐστὶν
εἰς πόλιν Βερενίκην στάδιοι χίλιοι⁴ πεντακόσιοι.
ὑπέρκεινται δὲ τοῦ μήκους τοῦδε⁵ παρήκοντες καὶ
μέχρι τῶν Φιλαίνου βωμῶν οἱ προσαγορευόμενοι
Νασαμῶνες, Λιβυκὸν ἔθνος· ἔχει δὲ τὸ μεταξὺ
διάστημα καὶ λιμένας οὐ πολλοὺς ὑδρεῖά τε
σπάνια. ἔστι δὲ ἄκρα λεγομένη Ψευδοπενιάς,⁶
ἐφ᾽ ἧς ἡ Βερενίκη τὴν θέσιν ἔχει παρὰ λίμνην
τινὰ Τριτωνιάδα, ἐν ᾗ μάλιστα νησίον ἐστὶ καὶ

---

¹ συμπίπτοι, Jones, for πίπτοι.   ² Μασαισύλων MSS.
³ ὅπου, before τὸ λειπόμενον, Kramer ejects.
⁴ χίλιοι, Letronne, for ἐννακισχίλιοι.
⁵ πλάτους, after τοῦδε, the editors omit.
⁶ Ψευδοπελίας E.

and a mooring place in front of its mouth. After
the harbour one comes to a place called Aspis,[1] and
to the finest harbour in the Syrtis. Continuous with
this is the Euphrantas Tower, the boundary between
the former country of the Carthaginians and the
Cyrenaean country as it was under Ptolemy;[2]
and then one comes to another place, called Charax,
which the Carthaginians used as an emporium, taking
wine thither and in exchange receiving loads of
silphium-juice and silphium from merchants who
brought them clandestinely from Cyrenê; and then
to the Altars of the Philaeni; and after these to
Automala, a stronghold which has a garrison and is
situated at the inmost recess of the whole gulf.
The parallel of latitude through this gulf is a little
more to the south than that through Alexandria,
one thousand stadia, and than that through Carthage,
less than two thousand stadia; but it would coincide
with the parallel which passes through the Heroönpolis situated on the recess of the Arabian Gulf
and through the interior of the countries of the
Masaesylians and the Maurusians. The remainder
of the coast from here on to the city Berenicê is one
thousand five hundred stadia in length. Lying
inland above this stretch of coast, and extending
even as far as the Altars of the Philaeni, is the
country of the Nasamones, as they are called, a
Libyan tribe. In the intervening distance there
are only a few harbours; and the watering-places
are scarce. There is, however, a promontory called
Pseudo-penias, on which Berenicê is situated, near a
certain lake, Tritonias, in which the principal things

[1] *i.e.* "Shield."   [2] See 17. 1. 5.

ἱερὸν τῆς Ἀφροδίτης ἐν αὐτῷ. ἔστι δὲ καὶ
λιμὴν[1] Ἑσπερίδων, καὶ ποταμὸς ἐμβάλλει
Λάθων. ἐνδοτέρω δὲ τῆς Βερενίκης ἐστὶ τὸ
μικρὸν ἀκρωτήριον λεγόμενον Βόρειον, ὃ ποιεῖ
τὸ στόμα τῆς Σύρτεως πρὸς τὰς Κεφαλάς.
κεῖται δὲ ἡ Βερενίκη κατὰ τὰ ἄκρα τῆς Πελοπον-
νήσου, κατὰ τὸν καλούμενον Ἰχθύν· καὶ ἔτι κατὰ
τὴν Ζάκυνθον, ἐν διάρματι σταδίων τρισχιλίων
ἑξακοσίων. ἐκ ταύτης τῆς πόλεως τριακοσταῖος
πεζῇ περιώδευσε τὴν Σύρτιν Μάρκος Κάτων, κατά-
γων στρατιὰν πλειόνων ἢ μυρίων ἀνδρῶν, εἰς μέρη
διελὼν τῶν ὑδρείων χάριν· ὥδευσε δὲ πεζὸς ἐν
ἄμμῳ βαθείᾳ καὶ καύμασι. μετὰ δὲ Βερενίκην
πόλις ἐστὶ Ταύχειρα,[2] ἣν καὶ Ἀρσινόην καλοῦσιν·
C 837 εἶθ᾽ ἡ Βάρκη πρότερον, νῦν δὲ Πτολεμαΐς· εἶτα
Φυκοῦς ἄκρα, ταπεινὴ μέν, πλεῖστον δ᾽ ἐκκειμένη[3]
πρὸς ἄρκτον παρὰ τὴν ἄλλην Λιβυκὴν παραλίαν·
κεῖται δὲ κατὰ Ταίναρον τῆς Λακωνικῆς ἐν διάρματι δισχιλίων ὀκτακοσίων σταδίων· ἔστι δὲ
καὶ πολίχνιον ὁμώνυμον τῇ ἄκρᾳ. οὐ πολὺ δὲ
τοῦ Φυκοῦντος ἀπέχει τὸ τῶν Κυρηναίων ἐπίνειον
ἡ Ἀπολλωνία,[4] ὅσον ἑκατὸν καὶ ἑβδομήκοντα
σταδίοις, τῆς δὲ Βερενίκης χιλίοις, τῆς δὲ Κυρήνης
ὀγδοήκοντα, πόλεως μεγάλης ἐν τραπεζοειδεῖ
πεδίῳ κειμένης, ὡς ἐκ τοῦ πελάγους ἑωρῶμεν
αὐτήν.

---

[1] For λίμην, Dodwell conj. λίμνη, and Kramer and Meineke
so write (but see Kramer's note).

[2] Ταύχειρα E, Τάρχειρα CDF*hisw*, Τεύχειρα other MSS.

[3] δ᾽ ἐκκειμένη, Casaubon, for δὲ κειμένη.

[4] Ἀπολλωνία (as in § 21 following), Meineke, for Ἀπολ-
λωνίας.

are an isle and on it a temple of Aphroditê. In this region are also the Harbour [1] of the Hesperides and the river Lathon which empties into it. Farther inside [2] than Berenicê lies the small promontory called Boreium, which with Cephalae forms the mouth of the Syrtis. Berenicê lies opposite the promontories of the Peloponnesus, opposite Ichthys, as it is called, and also opposite Zacynthos, the distance across being three thousand six hundred [3] stadia. Setting out from this city Marcus Cato travelled round the Syrtis by land in thirty days, [4] leading an army of more than ten thousand men, having separated them into divisions on account of the scarcity of watering-places; and he travelled on foot in deep sand and scorching heat. After Berenicê one comes to a city Taucheira, which is also called Arsinoê; and then to a city formerly called Barcê, but now Ptolemaïs; and then to a promontory Phycus, which is low-lying and projects farthest towards the north as compared with the rest of the Libyan coast; it lies opposite Taenarum in Laconia, the distance across being two thousand and eight hundred stadia; and there is also a small town which bears the same name as the promontory. Not far distant from Phycus is the naval station of the Cyrenaeans, Apollonia, about one hundred and seventy stadia from Phycus, one thousand from Berenicê, and eighty from Cyrenê, a large city situated in a trapezium-shaped plain, as it looked to me from the sea.

[1] Some would emend "Harbour" to "Lake" (see critical note).

[2] *i.e.* inside the Syrtis, towards the south (see Map XV, end of vol.).

[3] Cp. 10. 2. 18.

[4] In 47 B.C., on his march to join Metellus Scipio.

21. Ἔστι δὲ Θηραίων κτίσμα, Λακωνικῆς νήσου, ἣν καὶ Καλλίστην ὠνόμαζον τὸ παλαίον, ὥς φησι καὶ Καλλίμαχος·

Καλλίστη τὸ πάροιθε, τὸ δ᾽ ὕστερον οὔνομα
Θήρη,
μήτηρ εὐίππου πατρίδος ἡμετέρης.

κεῖται δὲ τὸ τῶν Κυρηναίων ἐπίνειον κατὰ τὸ ἑσπέριον τῆς Κρήτης ἄκρον, τὸ τοῦ Κριοῦ μέτωπον, ἐν διάρματι δισχιλίων [1] σταδίων· ὁ πλοῦς Λευκονότῳ. λέγεται δὲ ἡ Κυρήνη κτίσμα Βάττου· πρόγονον δὲ τοῦτον ἑαυτοῦ φάσκει Καλλίμαχος· ηὐξήθη δὲ διὰ τὴν ἀρετὴν τῆς χώρας· καὶ γὰρ ἱπποτρόφος ἐστὶν ἀρίστη καὶ καλλίκαρπος, καὶ πολλοὺς ἄνδρας ἀξιολόγους ἔσχε καὶ δυναμένους ἐλευθερίας ἀξιολόγως προΐστασθαι καὶ πρὸς τοὺς ὑπερκειμένους βαρβάρους ἰσχυρῶς ἀντέχειν. τὸ μὲν οὖν παλαιὸν αὐτόνομος ἦν ἡ πόλις· εἶτα οἱ τὴν Αἴγυπτον κατασχόντες Μακεδόνες αὐξηθέντες ἐπέθεντο αὐτοῖς, ἀρξάντων τῶν περὶ Θίβρωνα τῶν ἀνελόντων τὸν Ἅρπαλον· βασιλευθέντες δὲ χρόνους τινὰς εἰς τὴν Ῥωμαίων ἐξουσίαν ἦλθον, καὶ νῦν ἐστιν ἐπαρχία τῇ Κρήτῃ συνεζευγμένη. τῆς δὲ Κυρήνης ἐστὶ περιπόλια ἥ τε Ἀπολλωνία καὶ ἡ Βάρκη καὶ ἡ Ταύχειρα [2] καὶ Βερενίκη καὶ τὰ ἄλλα πολίχνια τὰ πλησίον.

22. Ὁμορεῖ δὲ τῇ Κυρηναίᾳ ἡ τὸ σίλφιον φέρουσα καὶ τὸν ὀπὸν τὸν Κυρηναῖον, ὃν ἐκφέρει τὸ σίλφιον ὀπισθέν. ἐγγὺς δ᾽ ἦλθε τοῦ ἐκλιπεῖν, ἐπελθόντων τῶν βαρβάρων κατὰ ἔχθραν τινὰ καὶ

---

[1] δισχιλίων (͵β) Casaubon, for χιλίων (͵α).
[2] Ταύχειρα (ευ above αυ) E, Τεύχειρα moz.

21. Cyrenê was founded by colonists from Thera, a Laconian island, which in ancient times was called Callistê, as Callimachus says: "Callistê was its first name, but its later name was Thera, mother of my fatherland, famed for its good horses." The naval station of the Cyrenaeans lies opposite the western promontory of Crete, Criumetopon, the distance across being two thousand stadia. The voyage is made with Leuconotus.[1] Cyrenê is said to have been founded by Battus;[2] and Callimachus asserts that Battus was his ancestor. Cyrenê grew strong because of the fertility of its territory, for it is excellent for the breeding of horses and produces beautiful fruit, and it had many men who were noteworthy and who were able to defend its liberty in a noteworthy manner and to resist strongly the barbarians who lived above them. Now in ancient times the city was independent; and then the Macedonians, who had taken possession of Aegypt, grew in power and attacked the Cyrenaeans, under the leadership of Thibron and his associates, who had slain Harpalus; and having been ruled by kings for some time the city came under the power of the Romans and is now joined with Crete into one Province. But Apollonia, Barcê, Taucheira, Berenicê, and the other towns near by, are dependencies of Cyrenê.

22. Bordering on Cyrenaea is the country which produces silphium and the Cyrenaean juice, which latter is produced by the silphium through the extraction of its juice. But it came near giving out when the barbarians invaded the country be-

[1] A south wind (see 1. 2. 21).
[2] About 631 B.C.

φθειράντων[1] τὰς ῥίζας τοῦ φυτοῦ. εἰσὶ δὲ
νομάδες. ἄνδρες δ' ἐγένοντο γνώριμοι Κυρηναῖοι
Ἀρίστιππός τε ὁ Σωκρατικός, ὅστις καὶ τὴν
Κυρηναϊκὴν κατεβάλετο φιλοσοφίαν, καὶ θυγάτηρ,
Ἀρήτη τοὔνομα, ἥπερ διεδέξατο τὴν σχολήν, καὶ
ὁ ταύτην πάλιν διαδεξάμενος υἱὸς Ἀρίστιππος,
ὁ κληθεὶς Μητροδίδακτος, καὶ Ἀννίκερις, ὁ δοκῶν
ἐπανορθῶσαι τὴν Κυρηναϊκὴν αἵρεσιν καὶ παρα-
γαγεῖν ἀντ' αὐτῆς τὴν Ἀννικερίαν. Κυρηναῖος δ'
C 838 ἐστὶ καὶ Καλλίμαχος καὶ Ἐρατοσθένης, ἀμφότεροι
τετιμημένοι παρὰ τοῖς Αἰγυπτίων βασιλεῦσιν,
ὁ μὲν ποιητὴς ἅμα καὶ περὶ γραμματικὴν ἐσπου-
δακώς, ὁ δὲ καὶ ταῦτα καὶ περὶ φιλοσοφίαν καὶ τὰ
μαθήματα, εἴ τις ἄλλος, διαφέρων. ἀλλὰ μὴν
καὶ Καρνεάδης (οὗτος δὲ τῶν ἐξ Ἀκαδημίας
ἄριστος φιλοσόφων ὁμολογεῖται) καὶ ὁ Κρόνος
δὲ Ἀπολλώνιος ἐκεῖθέν ἐστιν, ὁ τοῦ διαλεκτικοῦ
Διοδώρου διδάσκαλος, τοῦ καὶ αὐτοῦ Κρόνου
προσαγορευθέντος, μετενεγκάντων τινῶν τὸ τοῦ
διδασκάλου ἐπίθετον ἐπὶ τὸν μαθητήν. μετὰ δὲ
τὴν Ἀπολλωνίαν ἐστὶν ἡ λοιπὴ τῶν Κυρηναίων
παραλία μέχρι Καταβαθμοῦ σταδίων δισχιλίων
διακοσίων, οὐ πάνυ εὐπαράπλους· καὶ γὰρ
λιμένες ὀλίγοι καὶ ὕφορμοι καὶ κατοικίαι καὶ
ὑδρεῖα. τῶν δὲ μάλιστα ὀνομαζομένων κατὰ τὸν
παράπλουν τόπων τό τε Ναύσταθμόν ἐστι καὶ
τὸ Ζεφύριον πρόσορμον ἔχον καὶ ἄλλο Ζεφύριον
καὶ ἄκρα Χερρόνησος λιμένα ἔχουσα· κεῖται δὲ

---

[1] φθειρόντων E.

cause of some grudge and destroyed the roots of the plant. The inhabitants are nomads. The Cyrenaeans who became famous were Aristippus the Socratic philosopher, who also laid the foundations of the Cyrenaïc philosophy; and his daughter, Aretê by name, who succeeded him as head of the school; and again her son Aristippus, Aretê's successor, who was called Mêtrodidactus;[1] and Anniceris, who is reputed to have revised the doctrines of the Cyrenaïc sect and to have introduced in place of it those of the Annicerian sect. Callimachus, also, was a Cyrenaean, and Eratosthenes, both of whom were held in honour by the Aegyptian kings, the former being a poet and at the same time a zealous student of letters, and the latter being superior, not only in these respects, but also in philosophy, and in mathematics, if ever a man was. Furthermore, Carneades, who by common agreement was the best of the Academic philosophers, and also Apollonius Cronus, were from Cyrenê, the latter being the teacher of Diodorus the Dialectician, who also was given the appellation "Cronus," certain persons having transferred the epithet of the teacher to the pupil. After Apollonia one comes to the remainder of the coast of the Cyrenaeans, which extends as far as Catabathmus, a distance of two thousand two hundred stadia; the coasting-voyage is not at all easy, for there are but few harbours, mooring-places, settlements, and watering-places. Among the places along the coast that are best known are Naustathmus and Zephyrium, which has anchorage, and a second Zephyrium, and a promontory Cherronesus, which has a harbour. This

---

[1] *i.e.* "Mother-taught."

κατὰ Κύκλον[1] τῆς Κρήτης ἐν διάρματι χιλίων
καὶ πεντακοσίων σταδίων νότῳ· εἶτα Ἡράκλειόν τι
ἱερὸν καὶ ὑπὲρ αὐτοῦ κώμη Παλίουρος· εἶτα λιμὴν
Μενέλαος καὶ Ἀρδανίς,[2] ἄκρα ταπεινὴ ὕφορμον
ἔχουσα· εἶτα μέγας λιμήν, καθ᾽ ὃν ἡ ἐν τῇ Κρήτῃ
Χερρόνησος ἵδρυται, δισχιλίων[3] που σταδίων
διάρμα ἀπολείπουσα μεταξύ· ὅλη γὰρ σχεδόν τι
τῇ παραλίᾳ ταύτῃ ἀντίκειται παράλληλος ἡ
Κρήτη στενὴ καὶ μακρά. μετὰ δὲ τὸν μέγαν λιμένα
ἄλλος λιμὴν Πλῦνος, καὶ ὑπὲρ αὐτὸν Τετρα-
πυργία·[4] καλεῖται δὲ ὁ τόπος Κατάβαθμος·
μέχρι δεῦρο ἡ Κυρηναία. τὸ δὲ λοιπὸν ἤδη
μέχρι Παραιτονίου, κἀκεῖθεν εἰς Ἀλεξάνδρειαν,
εἴρηται ἡμῖν ἐν τοῖς Αἰγυπτιακοῖς.

23. Τὴν δ᾽ ὑπερκειμένην ἐν βάθει χώραν τῆς
Σύρτεως καὶ τῆς Κυρηναίας κατέχουσιν οἱ Λίβυες,
παράλυπρον καὶ αὐχμηράν· πρῶτοι μὲν οἱ Νασαμῶνες, ἔπειτα Ψύλλοι καί τινες Γαίτουλοι,[5]
ἔπειτα Γαράμαντες· πρὸς ἕω δ᾽ ἔτι μᾶλλον οἱ
Μαρμαρίδαι,[6] προσχωροῦντες ἐπὶ πλέον τῇ Κυρηναίᾳ καὶ παρατείνοντες μέχρι Ἄμμωνος. τεταρ-
ταίους μὲν οὖν φασιν ἀπὸ τοῦ μυχοῦ τῆς μεγάλης
Σύρτεως τοῦ κατ᾽ Αὐτόμαλά πως[7] βαδίζοντας ὡς

---

[1] For Κύκλον, Corais (citing 8. 5. 1) writes Κόρυκον; but
Kramer rightly objects, proposing Μάταλον instead.

[2] Ἀρδανίς, Meineke, following Kramer, for Ἀρδανίξις.

[3] δισχιλίων, Letronne and most later editors, for τρισχιλίων.

[4] The words καλεῖται . . . Κυρηναία are rightly transposed
from a position after Ἀλεξανδρείαν by Kramer, who also
omits ἢ καί before εἴρηται.

[5] Γέτουλοι MSS.

[6] Μαρμαρίδαι E, Μαρμαρῖται other MSS.

promontory lies opposite Cyclus[1] in Crete; and the
distance across is one thousand five hundred stadia
if one has a south-west wind; and then one comes
to a kind of temple of Heracles, and, above it, to
a village called Paliurus; and then one comes to a
harbour, Menelaüs, and to Ardanis, which is a low-
lying promontory with a mooring-place; and then to
a large harbour, opposite which lies the Cherronesus
in Crete, the interval between the two places being
about two[2] thousand stadia; indeed, I might almost
say that Crete as a whole, being narrow and long,
lies opposite, and parallel, to this coast. After the
large harbour one comes to another harbour, which
is called Plynus, and above it lies Tetrapyrgia;[3] but
the place is called Catabathmus; and Cyrenaea extends thus far. The remaining part of the coast,
extending to Paraetonium and thence to Alexandria,
I have already mentioned in my account of Egypt.

23. The country lying deep in the interior above
the Syrtis and Cyrenaea, a barren and arid region,
is occupied by the Libyans: first by the Nasamones,
and then by the Psyllians and certain Gaetulians,
and then by the Garamantes, and, still more towards
the east, by the Marmaridae, who border to a
greater extent on Cyrenaea and extend as far as
Ammon. Now it is said that persons going on foot
from the recess of the Great Syrtis, from about the
neighbourhood of Automala, approximately in the

---

[1] "Cyclus" is doubtful (see critical note).
[2] The MSS. read "three" (see critical note).
[3] *i.e.* "Four Towers."

---

[7] τοῦ κατ' Αὐτόμαλά πως, Kramer, for τοὺς κατ' αὐτὸ
μαλακῶς.

ἐπὶ χειμερινὰς ἀνατολὰς εἰς Αὔγιλα ¹ ἀφικνεῖσθαι.
ἔστι δὲ ὁ τόπος οὗτος ἐμφερὴς τῷ Ἄμμωνι,
φοινικοτρόφος τε καὶ εὔυδρος· ὑπέρκειται δὲ τῆς
Κυρηναίας ² πρὸς μεσημβρίαν· μέχρι μὲν σταδίων
ἑκατὸν καὶ δενδροφόρος ἐστὶν ἡ γῆ· μέχρι δ'
ἄλλων ἑκατὸν σπείρεται μόνον, οὐκ ὀρυζοτροφεῖ ³
δ' ἡ γῆ διὰ τὸν αὐχμόν. ὑπὲρ δὲ τούτων ἡ τὸ
σίλφιον φέρουσά ⁴ ἐστιν· εἶθ' ἡ ἀοίκητος καὶ ἡ
C 839 τῶν Γαραμάντων. ἔστι δ' ἡ τὸ σίλφιον φέρουσα
στενὴ καὶ παραμήκης καὶ παράξηρος, μῆκος μὲν
ὡς ἐπὶ τὰς ἀνατολὰς ἰόντι ὅσον σταδίων χιλίων,
πλάτος δὲ τριακοσίων ἢ μικρῷ πλειόνων τό γε
γνώριμον· εἰκάζειν μὲν γὰρ ἅπασαν πάρεστι
διηνεκῶς τὴν ἐπὶ τοῦ αὐτοῦ παραλλήλου κειμένην
τοιαύτην εἶναι κατά τε τοὺς ἀέρας καὶ τὴν τοῦ
φυτοῦ φοράν, ἐπεὶ δ' ἐμπίπτουσιν ἐρημίαι πλείους,
οὐ ⁵ τοὺς πάντας τόπους ἴσμεν. παραπλησίως δ'
ἀγνοεῖται καὶ τὰ ὑπὲρ τοῦ Ἄμμωνος καὶ τῶν
αὐάσεων μέχρι τῆς Αἰθιοπίας. οὐδ' ἂν ἔχοιμεν
λέγειν τοὺς ὅρους οὔτε τῆς Αἰθιοπίας οὔτε τῆς
Λιβύης, ἀλλ' οὐδὲ τῆς πρὸς Αἰγύπτῳ τρανῶς,
μή τι γε τῆς πρὸς τῷ ὠκεανῷ.

24. Τὰ μὲν οὖν μέρη τῆς καθ' ἡμᾶς οἰκουμένης ⁶
οὕτω διάκειται· ἐπεὶ δ' οἱ Ῥωμαῖοι τὴν ἀρίστην

---

¹ εἰς Αὔγιλα, Kramer inserts.
² τῆς, after Κυρηναίας, Groskurd ejects.
³ E reads οὐ ῥιζοτροφεῖ, other MSS. ὀρυζοτροφεῖ, before
which Corais and the later editors insert οὐκ.
⁴ φέρουσα, omitted by all MSS. except i.
⁵ οὐ, Hopper inserts.

direction of winter sunrise,[1] arrive at Augila on the
fourth day. This region resembles Ammon, being
productive of palm-trees and also well supplied with
water. It lies above Cyrenaea to the south, and for
a distance of one hundred stadia produces trees,
but for another hundred the land is only sown,
although, on account of its aridity, the land does not
grow rice.[2] Above this region is the country which
produces silphium; and then one comes to the
uninhabited country and to that of the Garamantes.
The country which produces silphium is narrow,
long, and somewhat arid, extending in length, as
one goes approximately towards the east, about one
thousand stadia, and in breadth three hundred or a
little more, at least that part which is known; for
we may conjecture that all lands lying in unbroken
succession on the same parallel of latitude are
similar as regards both climate and plants, but since
several deserts intervene, we do not know all these
regions. Similarly, the regions above Ammon and
the oases as far as Aethiopia are likewise unknown.
Neither can we tell the boundaries either of
Aethiopia or of Libya, nor yet accurately even
those of the country next to Aegypt, much less of
that which borders on the Ocean.

24. This, then, is the lay of the different parts of
our inhabited world; but since the Romans occupy

---

[1] See Vol. I, p. 105.
[2] One major MS. reads "roots" instead of "rice" (see
critical note).

---

[6] Τὰ μὲν οὖν μέρη τῆς καθ᾽ ἡμᾶς οἰκουμένης (as in 2. 5. 34),
Kramer, for τὰ μὲν οὖν μέρη τῆς οἰκουμένης (Dhz adding τά
before μέρη).

αὐτῆς καὶ γνωριμωτάτην κατέχουσιν, ἅπαντας
ὑπερβεβλημένοι τοὺς πρότερον ἡγεμόνας, ὧν
μνήμην ἴσμεν, ἄξιον καὶ διὰ βραχέων καὶ τὰ
τούτων εἰπεῖν. ὅτι μὲν οὖν ἐκ μιᾶς ὁρμηθέντες
πόλεως τῆς Ῥώμης ἅπασαν τὴν Ἰταλίαν ἔσχον
διὰ τὸ πολεμεῖν καὶ πολιτικῶς ἄρχειν, εἴρηται,
καὶ διότι μετὰ τὴν Ἰταλίαν τὰ κύκλῳ προσεκτή-
σαντο, τῇ αὐτῇ ἀρετῇ χρώμενοι. τριῶν δὲ
ἠπείρων οὐσῶν, τὴν μὲν Εὐρώπην σχεδόν τι
πᾶσαν ἔχουσι, πλὴν τῆς¹ ἔξω τοῦ Ἴστρου καὶ
τῶν μεταξὺ τοῦ Ῥήνου καὶ τοῦ Τανάϊδος παρω-
κεανιτῶν· τῆς δὲ Λιβύης ἡ καθ' ἡμᾶς παραλία
πᾶσα ὑπ' αὐτοῖς ἐστιν, ἡ δὲ ἄλλη ἀοίκητός ἐστιν
ἢ λυπρῶς καὶ νομαδικῶς οἰκεῖται· ὁμοίως δὲ καὶ
τῆς Ἀσίας ἡ καθ' ἡμᾶς παραλία πᾶσα ὑποχείριός
ἐστιν, εἰ μή τις τὰ τῶν Ἀχαιῶν καὶ Ζυγῶν καὶ
Ἡνιόχων ἐν λόγῳ τίθεται, ληστρικῶς καὶ νομαδικῶς ζώντων ἐν στενοῖς καὶ λυπροῖς χωρίοις·
τῆς δὲ μεσογαίας καὶ τῆς ἐν βάθει τὴν μὲν
ἔχουσιν αὐτοί, τὴν δὲ Παρθυαῖοι καὶ οἱ² ὑπὲρ
τούτων βάρβαροι, πρός τε ταῖς ἀνατολαῖς καὶ
ταῖς ἄρκτοις Ἰνδοὶ καὶ Βάκτριοι καὶ Σκύθαι,
εἶτ' Ἄραβες καὶ Αἰθίοπες· προστίθεται δὲ ἀεί
τι παρ' ἐκείνων αὐτοῖς. ταύτης δὲ τῆς συμπάσης
χώρας τῆς ὑπὸ Ῥωμαίοις ἡ μὲν βασιλεύεται, ἣν³
δ' ἔχουσιν αὐτοὶ καλέσαντες ἐπαρχίαν, καὶ πέμ-
πουσιν ἡγεμόνας καὶ φορολόγους. εἰσὶ δέ τινες

---

¹ τῶν E.   ² οἵ, omitted by all MSS. except E.
³ ἥν, Corais, for ἥ.

---

¹ 6. 4. 2.   ² Danube.   ³ Rhine.
⁴ Don.   ⁵ See 11. 2. 12.   ⁶ i.e. on the south.

the best and the best known portions of it, having surpassed all former rulers of whom we have record, it is worth while, even though briefly, to add the following account of them. Now I have already stated [1] that, setting out with only one city, Rome, the Romans acquired the whole of Italy through warfare and statesmanlike rulership, and that, after Italy, by exercising the same superior qualities, they also acquired the regions round about Italy. And of the continents, being three in number, they hold almost the whole of Europe, except that part of it which lies outside the Ister [2] River and the parts along the ocean which lie between the Rhenus [3] and the Tanaïs [4] Rivers. Of Libya, the whole of the coast on Our Sea is subject to them; and the rest of the country is uninhabited or else inhabited only in a wretched or nomadic fashion. In like manner, of Asia also, the whole of the coast on Our Sea is subject to them, unless one takes into account the regions of the Achaei and the Zugi and the Heniochi,[5] who live a piratical and nomadic life in narrow and sterile districts; and of the interior and the country deep inland, one part is held by the Romans themselves and another by the Parthians and the barbarians beyond them; and on the east and north live Indians and Bactrians and Scythians, and then [6] Arabians and Aethiopians; but some further portion is constantly being taken from these peoples and added to the possessions of the Romans. Of this whole country that is subject to the Romans, some parts are indeed ruled by kings, but the Romans retain others themselves, calling them Provinces, and send to them praefects and collectors of tribute. But there are also some free cities,

211

καὶ ἐλεύθεραι πόλεις, αἱ μὲν ἐξ ἀρχῆς κατὰ φιλίαν
προσελθοῦσαι, τὰς δ᾽ ἠλευθέρωσαν αὐτοὶ κατὰ
τιμήν. εἰσὶ δὲ καὶ δυνάσται τινὲς καὶ φύλαρχοι
καὶ ἱερεῖς ὑπ᾽ αὐτοῖς. οὗτοι μὲν δὴ ζῶσι κατά
τινας πατρίους νόμους.

C 840   25. Αἱ δ᾽ ἐπαρχίαι διῄρηνται ἄλλοτε μὲν ἄλλως,
ἐν δὲ τῷ παρόντι, ὡς Καῖσαρ ὁ Σεβαστὸς διέ-
ταξεν· ἐπειδὴ γὰρ ἡ πατρὶς ἐπέτρεψεν αὐτῷ τὴν
προστασίαν τῆς ἡγεμονίας καὶ πολέμου καὶ
εἰρήνης κατέστη κύριος διὰ βίου, δίχα διεῖλε
πᾶσαν τὴν χώραν καὶ τὴν μὲν ἀπέδειξεν ἑαυτῷ,
τὴν δὲ τῷ δήμῳ· ἑαυτῷ μέν, ὅση στρατιωτικῆς
φρουρᾶς ἔχει χρείαν (αὕτη δ᾽ ἐστὶν ἡ βάρβαρος
καὶ πλησιόχωρος τοῖς μήπω κεχειρωμένοις ἔθνεσιν
ἢ λυπρὰ καὶ δυσγεώργητος, ὥσθ᾽ ὑπὸ ἀπορίας
τῶν ἄλλων, ἐρυμάτων δ᾽ εὐπορίας ἀφηνιάζειν καὶ
ἀπειθεῖν), τῷ δήμῳ δὲ τὴν ἄλλην, ὅση[1] εἰρηνικὴ
καὶ χωρὶς ὅπλων ἄρχεσθαι ῥᾳδία· ἑκατέραν δὲ
τὴν μερίδα εἰς ἐπαρχίας διένειμε πλείους, ὧν αἱ
μὲν καλοῦνται Καίσαρος, αἱ δὲ τοῦ δήμου. καὶ
εἰς μὲν τὰς Καίσαρος ἡγεμόνας[2] καὶ διοικητὰς
Καῖσαρ πέμπει, διαιρῶν ἄλλοτε ἄλλως τὰς χώρας
καὶ πρὸς τοὺς καιροὺς πολιτευόμενος, εἰς δὲ τὰς
δημοσίας ὁ δῆμος στρατηγοὺς ἢ ὑπάτους. καὶ
αὗται δ᾽ εἰς μερισμοὺς ἄγονται διαφόρους, ἐπειδὰν

---

[1] ὅση F, ὅσην ἦν other MSS.
[2] ἡγεμόνας, Casaubon, for ἡγεμονείας F, ἡγεμονίας other
MSS.

---

[1] i.e. "tribal chiefs."   [2] In Latin principatus.
[3] During office called "propraetors."

of which some came over to the Romans at the
outset as friends, whereas others were set free by
the Romans themselves as a mark of honour.
There are also some potentates and phylarchs [1] and
priests subject to them. Now these live in accordance with certain ancestral laws.

25. But the Provinces have been divided in
different ways at different times, though at the
present time they are as Augustus Caesar arranged
them ; for when his native land committed to him
the foremost place [2] of authority and he became
established as lord for life of war and peace, he
divided the whole of his empire into two parts,
and assigned one portion to himself and the other
to the Roman people ; to himself, all parts that had
need of a military guard (that is, the part that was
barbarian and in the neighbourhood of tribes not
yet subdued, or lands that were sterile and difficult
to bring under cultivation, so that, being unprovided
with everything else, but well provided with
strongholds, they would try to throw off the bridle
and refuse obedience), and to the Roman people
all the rest, in so far as it was peaceable and easy to
rule without arms ; and he divided each of the two
portions into several Provinces, of which some are
called " Provinces of Caesar " and the others
" Provinces of the People." And to the " Provinces
of Caesar " Caesar sends legati [3] and procurators,
dividing the countries in different ways at different
times and administering them as the occasion
requires, whereas to the " Provinces of the People "
the people send praetors or proconsuls, and these
Provinces also are brought under different divisions
whenever expediency requires. But at the outset

κελεύῃ τὸ συμφέρον. ἀλλ' ἐν ἀρχαῖς γε [1] διέθηκε
ποιήσας ὑπατικὰς μὲν δύο, Λιβύην τε, ὅση ὑπὸ
Ῥωμαίοις ἔξω τῆς ὑπὸ Ἰούβα μὲν πρότερον, νῦν
δὲ Πτολεμαίῳ τῷ ἐκείνου παιδί, καὶ Ἀσίαν τὴν
ἐντὸς Ἅλυος καὶ τοῦ Ταύρου πλὴν Γαλατῶν καὶ
τῶν ὑπὸ Ἀμύντα γενομένων ἐθνῶν, ἔτι δὲ Βιθυνίας
καὶ τῆς Προποντίδος· δέκα δὲ στρατηγικάς,[2] κατὰ
μὲν τὴν Εὐρώπην καὶ τὰς πρὸς αὐτῇ νήσους τήν
τε ἐκτὸς Ἰβηρίαν λεγομένην, ὅση περὶ τὸν Βαῖτιν
ποταμὸν καὶ τὸν Ἄναν [3] καὶ τῆς Κελτικῆς τὴν
Ναρβωνῖτιν, τρίτην δὲ Σαρδὼ μετὰ Κύρνου, καὶ
Σικελίαν τετάρτην, πέμπτην δὲ καὶ ἕκτην τῆς
Ἰλλυρίδος τὴν πρὸς τῇ Ἠπείρῳ καὶ Μακεδονίαν,
ἑβδόμην δ' Ἀχαΐαν μέχρι Θετταλίας καὶ Αἰτωλῶν
καὶ Ἀκαρνάνων καί τινων Ἠπειρωτικῶν ἐθνῶν,
ὅσα τῇ Μακεδονίᾳ προσώρισto, ὀγδόην δὲ Κρήτην
μετὰ τῆς Κυρηναίας, ἐννάτην δὲ Κύπρον, δεκάτην
δὲ Βιθυνίαν μετὰ τῆς Προποντίδος καὶ τοῦ Πόντου
τινῶν μερῶν. τὰς δὲ ἄλλας ἐπαρχίας ἔχει Καῖσαρ,
ὧν εἰς ἃς μὲν πέμπει τοὺς ἐπιμελησομένους ὑπα-
τικοὺς ἄνδρας, εἰς ἃς δὲ στρατηγικούς, εἰς ἃς δὲ
καὶ ἱππικούς. καὶ βασιλεῖς δὲ καὶ δυνάσται καὶ
δεκαρχίαι τῆς ἐκείνου μερίδος καὶ εἰσὶ καὶ ὑπῆρξαν
ἀεί.

---

[1] γε, Corais, for τε.

[2] στρατηγικάς, Corais, for στρατηγίας.

[3] καὶ τὸν Ἄναν, editors before Kramer, for καὶ τὸν Ἄτακα
(Ἄτακα MSS.), which is suspected by later editors and
ejected by Meineke.

Caesar organised the Provinces of the People by creating, first, two consular provinces; I mean (1) Libya, in so far as it was subject to the Romans, except the part which was formerly subject to Juba and is now subject to Ptolemy his son, and (2) the part of Asia that lies this side the Halys River and the Taurus, except the countries of the Galatians and of the tribes which had been subject to Amyntas, and also of Bithynia and the Propontis; and, secondly, ten praetorial provinces, first, in Europe and the islands near it, I mean (1) Iberia Ulterior, as it is called, in the neighbourhood of the Baetis and Anas[1] Rivers, (2) Narbonitis in Celtica, (3) Sardo[2] together with Cyrnus,[3] (4) Sicily, (5 and 6) Macedonia and, in Illyria, the country next to Epeirus, (7) Achaea as far as Thessaly and Aetolia and Acarnania and certain Epeirotic tribes which border on Macedonia, (8) Crete along with Cyrenaea, (9) Cypros, and (10) Bithynia along with the Propontis and certain parts of the Pontus. But the rest of the Provinces are held by Caesar; and to some of these he sends as curators men of consular rank, to others men of praetorian rank, and to others men of the rank of knights. Kings, also, and potentates and decarchies are now, and always have been, in Caesar's portion.

[1] "Anas" is a correction for "Atax," the Atax being the present Aude in France.
[2] Sardinia.   [3] Corsica.

INDEX OF NAMES, PLACES, AND SUBJECTS

[The translator has tried to make this *Index* virtually complete. The references are to volume and page.]

A

AARASSUS, a city in Pisidia, **5.** 481

Aba in Phocis, whence Thracian colonists set out for Euboea, **5.** 5

Aba, daughter of Xenophanes and queen of Cilicia, **6.** 343

Abae, the oracle of, in Phocis, **4.** 369

"Abantes," Homer's name for the Euboeans, **5.** 5

"Abantis," a former name of Euboea, **5.** 5

Abaris, "Hyperborian" priest and prophet of Apollo, healer, traveller, and deliverer from plagues; held in high esteem by the Greeks, **3.** 201

Abas the hero, brought a colony to the plain of the Thessalians and named the plain "Pelasgian Argos," **4.** 403; early king of Abantis (Euboea), **5.** 5

Abdera in Iberia, founded by the Phoenicians, **2.** 81

Abdera (Balastra) in Thrace, scene of the myths about Abderus, and ruled over by Diomedes, **3.** 365; named after Abderus, **3.** 367; temple of Jason at, built by Parmenion, **5.** 333; "beautiful colony of the Teïans," **6.** 239

Abderus of Abdera in Thrace; the myths about, **3.** 365; devoured by the horses of Diomedes, **3.** 367

Abeacus, king of the Siraces in the time of King Pharnaces, once sent forth 20,000 cavalry, **5.** 243

Abella (Avella Vecchia), in Campania, **2.** 461

Abii ("Resourceless men"), the Homeric, "men most just," are wagon-dwelling Scythians and Sarmatians, **3.** 179, 181, 189, 195, 205, 209, 245 ("just and resourceless"), **5.** 419

Abilê (or Abilyx, *q.v.*), Mt., in Maurusia, at the Strait of Gibraltar, abounds in wild animals and trees, **8.** 165

Abilyx (Ape) Mountain, in Libya, by some regarded as one of the Pillars of Heracles, **2.** 135

Abisarus, a king in India, **7.** 49

Abonuteichus in Paphlagonia, **5.** 387

Aboracê, in the Syndic territory, near the Cimmerian Bosporus, **5.** 199

Aborras River, the, in Mesopotamia, **7.** 233

Abrettenê, in Mysia in Asia, **5.** 499

Abrotonum, a city on coast of Libya, **8.** 195

Abus, Mt., in Asia, whence flow the Euphrates and the Araxes, **5.** 321; a part of the Taurus, **5.** 335

Abydon (the Homeric Amydon), on the Axius River in Macedonia, **3.** 341, 343, 345, 347

Abydus, **6.** 5; 30 stadia from Sestus, **3.** 379; by Scylax called a boundary of Troy, **6.** 9, 19, 21; the voyage to, from Byzantium, **6.** 13; the parts round, colonised by the Thracians after the Trojan War, **6.** 23; mentioned by Homer, **6.** 37; history and geographical position of, **6.** 41; length of pontoon-bridge at, **6.** 43; after the Trojan War the

INDEX OF NAMES, PLACES, AND SUBJECTS

home of Thracians, and then of Milesians, and later burned by Dareius, **6.** 43; distance from, to the Aesepus River, **6.** 45; 70 stadia from Dardanus, **6.** 59; colonised by Milesians, **6.** 207

Abydus near the Nile, where the Memnonium, of the same workmanship as the Labyrinth, and a marvellous fountain (" Strabo's Well "), **8.** 111; now only a small settlement, **8.** 113; Osiris worshipped at, **8.** 117

Acacesium, in Arcadia, falsified by some writers, according to Callimachus, **3.** 193

Academia, the, at Athens, **4.** 265

Academic philosophers, the; Carneades the best of, **8.** 205

Acalandrus (Salandra) River, the, in southern Italy, **3.** 117

Acamas the Athenian, founded Soli in Cypros, **6.** 381

Acamas, Cape, in Cypros, **6.** 375, 381, 383

Acantha, the Thebaïc (*Mimosa Nilotica*), from which gum arabic is obtained, **8.** 97; the Aegyptian, a grove of, near Abydus, sacred to Apollo, **8.** 113

Acanthus (Hierisos), on the isthmus of Athos, founded by the Andrians, **3.** 353; on the Singitic Gulf near the canal of Xerxes, **3.** 355

Acanthus, in Libya, above Memphis, **8.** 97

Acarnan, son of Alcmaeon; Acarnania named after, **5.** 73

Acarnania, borders on the Ambracian Gulf, **3.** 301; acquired by Diomedes, **3.** 305; bounded by the Acheloüs River, **4.** 17; deserted lands of, well adapted to horse-raising, **4.** 229; borders on Thessaly, **4.** 395; description of, **5.** 23–31; Leucas once a peninsula of, **5.** 31; once ruled by Icarius, father of Penelopê, and his sons, **5.** 35, 69; various places in, **5.** 61, 63; acquired by Laertes and the Cephallenians, **5.** 67; took part in the Trojan war, but was not so-named at that time, **5.** 69, though Ephorus says it did not take part in it, **5.** 71; obtained autonomy from the Romans, **5.** 73;

the Curetes withdrew to, from Aetolia, **5.** 77; now included within a Roman Province, **8.** 215

Acarnanians, the, a Greek people, **4.** 5; joined the Aetolians in war, **4.** 389; disputed the possession of Paracheloïtis with the Aetolians, **5.** 57; now reduced to impotence, **5.** 65; so named, according to Archamachus, because they kept their heads " unshorn," **5.** 185.

Acarnanians, The Polity of the, by Aristotle, **3.** 289

Acathartus Gulf, the, in the Arabian Gulf, **7.** 317

Acê in Phoenicia (see Ptolemaïs), **7.** 271

Acerrae (see Acherrae)

Acesines River, the, in India, **7.** 27, 35, 47, 49, 51

Achaea in Asia, settled by the Achaeans in Jason's crew, **5.** 203; welcomed Mithridates Eupator, **5.** 205; coast of, **5.** 207; life and country of, **8.** 2

Achaea in the Peloponnesus (also referred to as " Ionia ") occupied by the Achaeans from Laconia, **4.** 133; subject to Agamemnon, **4.** 167; colonised by Tisamenus after the return of the Heracleidae, **4.** 235

Achaea in Thessaly, by some called the same as Phthia, **4.** 403

Achaeae, the; abrupt cliffs in Triphylia, **4.** 63

" Achaean Argos," Laconia called, by Homer, **4.** 137, and the whole Peloponnesus called, **4.** 155

Achaean League, the, joined by the Argives, **4.** 185; voluntarily gave Aratus of Sicyon the supreme authority; and places belonging to, **4.** 207; famous for its constitution, arbitrator for the Thebans, and dissolved by the Macedonians, **4.** 211; organisation, administration, and members of, and the time of its reaching the height of its power, and the time of its dissolution, **4.** 217; dissolution of, compared with that of the Amphictyonic, **4.** 357

Achaeans, the; Homeric use of term, **1.** 129, **4.** 401, **5.** 495; migrations of, **1.** 227; in Asia, **1.** 495; cities of, in southern Italy, **3.** 41; sent Leucippus to colonise Metapontium, **3.** 55;

INDEX OF NAMES, PLACES, AND SUBJECTS

an Aeolic tribe, drove the Ionians out of the Peloponnesus, **4.** 7; country of, extends from Cape Araxus to Sicyonia, **4.** 15; once had charge of temple at Olympia, **4.** 103; in Laconia, emigrated to Peloponnesian Ionia (Achaea), **4.** 133, 137; in Thessaly, came with Pelops into the Peloponnesus and settled in Laconia, **4.** 135; came under the dominion of Rome, **4.** 185; drove the Athenian Ionians out of the Aegialus, **4.** 209, 219; long remained a powerful and independent people, both under kings and later under democracy, **4.** 211; after the submersion of Helicê divided its territory among the neighbours, **4.** 215; once surpassed even the Lacedaemonians, **4.** 217; the twelve places settled by, **4.** 219; in Pontus, are a colony of the Orchomenians, **4.** 341; all the Phthiotae in Thessaly, subjects of Achilles, so called, **4.** 401, 413; Naval Station of, at Troy, **6.** 61, 71, about 20 stadia from the present Ilium, if not to be identified with the Harbour of the Achaeans, only about 12 stadia from it, **6.** 73, where are the altars of the twelve gods, **6.** 159; the beach of, in Cypros, **6.** 377

Achaecarus, great diviner among the Bosporeni, **7.** 289

Achaeïum, the, where begins the part of the mainland that belongs to Tenedos, **6.** 63, 89, 91, 93

Achaemenidae, the, a tribe in Persis, **7.** 157

Achaeus, grandfather of Attalus I., **6.** 167

Achaeus, the son of Xuthus, after whom the Achaeans were named, **4.** 209

Achaïa, a city in Aria, **5.** 279

Acharaca in Asia, between Tralleis and Nysa, where is the Plutonium, and also the Charonium, at which remarkable cures occur, **6.** 259

Achardeüs River, the; rises in the Caucasus and empties into Lake Maeotis, **5.** 243

Acheloüs the river-god, defeated by Heracles, **5.** 57, 59

Acheloüs River (Aspropotamos), once

called "Thoas," the; by silting up sea joined isles to mainland, **1.** 221; joined by the Inachus, **3.** 79; empties into the sea, **3.** 309, 311; separates Aetolia from Acarnania, **4.** 17, 5. 23, 25, 55; myths concerning god of, **5.** 57, 59

Acheloüs River (also called Peirus), in Elis, **4.** 43

Acheloüs River, the, in Phthiotis, flows near Lamia, **4.** 413

Acheron (Arconti?) River, the, in Italy, which flows past Pandosia in Bruttium, **3.** 17

Acheron (Phanariotikos) River, the, in Thesprotia, **3.** 17; flows past Pandosia and empties into Glycys Limen ("Sweet Harbour"), **3.** 299; flows from the Acherusian Lake, **3.** 301

Acheron River, the, in Triphylia, empties into the Alpheius; why so named, **4.** 53

Acherrae (Gela), in Campania, **2.** 461

Acherusian Lake (Lago di Fusaro), the, in Campania, **1.** 95, 2. 439, 443; by some identified with Gulf Lucrinus and by Apollodorus with Gulf Avernus, **2.** 447

Acherusian Lake, the (a marsh near Kastri), whence flows the Acheron River in Thesprotia, **3.** 301 (in footnote 2, page 209, "Fusaro" is an error)

Achilleïum in Asia, a village on the Cimmerian Bosporus where the strait is narrowest, **3.** 241; has a temple of Achilles, **5.** 197

Achilleïum, the, in the Troad, fortified by the Mitylenaeans against Sigeium, **6.** 77; where is the monument of Achilles, **6.** 79, 91

Achilles, the shield of, bordered by Oceanus, **1.** 13; sacked Lesbos but spared Lemnos, **1.** 165; the island Leucê, off the mouth of the Borysthenes in the Euxine, sacred to, **3.** 221, 227; the Race Course of (Cape Tendra), **3.** 227, 229; grandfather of the Pyrrhus who ruled over the Molossians, **3.** 309; the subjects of, called Phthians, **3.** 385; promised seven cities on the Messenian and Asinaean Gulfs by Agamemnon, **4.** 109, one of these being Pedasus

INDEX OF NAMES, PLACES, AND SUBJECTS

(Methonê, now Modon), **4.** 111, 115;
promised to bring Patroclus back to
his native city Opus in Locris, **4.**
379; the domain of, in Thessaly, **4.**
399–419; son-in-law of Lycomedes
and father of Neoptolemus, **4.** 427;
"alone knew how to hurl the Pelian
ashen spear," **5.** 21; temple of, at
Achilleium on the Cimmerian Bosporus, **5.** 197; numerous cities in
the Troad outside Ilium sacked by,
and Briseïs taken captive by, at
Lyrnessus, **6.** 15; slew King
Cycnus of Colonae, **6.** 35; monument of, near Sigeium in the Troad,
6. 61; on the cowardice of Hector,
6. 71; pursued Aeneias to Lyrnessus, **6.** 105, 107; laid waste Thebê
and Lyrnessus, taking captive
Chryseïs and Briseïs, **6.** 121;
Palisade of, at Astyra, **6.** 129; slew
Eëtion, **6.** 149, and his seven sons, **6.**
151

Acholla in Libya, a free city, **8.** 181

Acidon River, the, in Triphylia, flows
past Chaa and the tomb of Iardanus, **4.** 65

Acila, Cape, in Arabia, opposite Cape
Deirê, **7.** 315

Acilisenê in Asia; followers of Armenus settled in, **5.** 231, 333; the
Euphrates borders on, **5.** 297, 425;
geographical position of, **5.** 321; annexed to Armenia, **5.** 325; has
many temples of Anaïtis, **5.** 341

Aciris (Agri) River, the, in Italy, **3.** 49

Acisenê (Acilisenê?) in Armenia;
Artaxias the king of, **5.** 325

Acmon, one of the Idaean Dactyli, **5.**
117

Aconite, the plant, grows in the territory of Heracleia Pontica, **5.** 381

Aconites, the, a tribe in Sardinia, **2.**
361

Acontius, Mt., in Phocis, extending
60 stadia to Parapotamii, and
whither the Orchomenians emigrated, **4.** 341

Acorns, eaten two-thirds of the year
by Lusitanian mountaineers, **2.** 75;
the, in Persia, **7.** 181

Acqui (see Aquae Statiellae)

Acra, a village on the Cimmerian Bosporus, **5.** 197

Acraea, in Laconia, **4.** 47

Acraephiae (or Acraephium, q.v.), a
city on Lake Copaïs, **4.** 321

Acraephium (or Acraephiae, q.v., now
in ruins near Karditza) in Boeotia,
on a height near Mt. Ptoüs and Lake
Copaïs, **4.** 329, and identified with
the Homeric Arnê, which by some is
said to have been swallowed up by
Lake Copaïs, **4.** 331

Acragantini, the Emporium of the,
20 Roman miles from the Heracleium, **3.** 57

Acragas, still endures, **3.** 81; the salt-
lakes near, on which people float like
wood, **3.** 91

Acrathos, Cape, on the Strymonic
Gulf, **3.** 353

Acridophagi ("Locust-eaters"), the,
in Aethiopia; manner of capture of
locusts by, **7.** 327

Acrisius, reputed to have been the first
head of the Amphictyonic League,
4. 357

Acritas (Cape Gallo), the beginning of
the Messenian Gulf, **4.** 113

Acrocorinthus, the, one of the two
strategic points in the Peloponnesus, according to Demetrius of
Pharos, **4.** 119, 121; taken by
Aratus from Antigonus Gonatas, **4.**
127; whence Strabo says he beheld
Cleonae, **4.** 187; description of, **4.**
191–195; altitude of, 3½ stadia, **4.**
191; has a small temple of Aphroditê and the spring Peirenê, **4.**
193; wide view from summit of,
4. 195

Acrolissus, a fortress near Lissus in
Illyria, **3.** 265

Acrothoï, a city "near the crest of
Athos," **3.** 355, 357

Actê, the eastern coast of Argolis,
colonised by Agaeus and Deïphontes after the return of the
Heracleidae, **4.** 235

Actê (or Acticê, i.e. Attica), takes a
crescent-shaped bend towards Oropus, **2.** 243

Actian Apollo (see Apollo, the Actian),
the; temple of, near the Ambracian
Gulf, **5.** 25, 31

Actian Games, the, sacred to Actian
Apollo, designated as "Olympian,"
celebrated in the suburbs of Nicopolis Actia, **3.** 305

INDEX OF NAMES, PLACES, AND SUBJECTS

221

INDEX OF NAMES, PLACES, AND SUBJECTS

223

INDEX OF NAMES, PLACES, AND SUBJECTS

Aegyptian Screw, the (see Screw)

Aegyptian Sea, the; the part of the Mediterranean off Aegypt, **1.** 129, 473, 481, **6.** 375, **8.** 31

Aegyptian *Sycaminus* (mulberry-tree), the, found in Aethiopia, **7.** 331

Aegyptian tribes, the, in Judaea, **7.** 281

Aegyptian women, sometimes bear from four to seven children, **7.** 37

Aegyptians, the; migrations of, to Aethiopia and Colchis, **1.** 227; the Island of the, **1.** 235; philosophers, not by nature, but by training and habit, **1.** 395; the fugitive, **1.** 457; custom of, in exposing the sick upon the streets, followed by the Lusitanians in Iberia, **2.** 77; said by some writers to be akin to the Colchians, **5.** 211; often mentioned by Homer, **5.** 423; compared with the Indians, **7.** 21; invented geometry, **7.** 271; regarded as ancestors of the Judaeans, **7.** 281; according to Moses, wrong in representing divine beings by the images of beasts, **7.** 283; use asphalt for embalming corpses, **7.** 297; treacherously murdered Pompey the Great near Mt. Casius, **7.** 299; lead a civilised life, **8.** 9; early kings of, especially prejudiced against the Greeks, **8.** 27–29; native stock of, at Alexandria, **8.** 51; not warriors, **8.** 135; circumcise males and excise females, **8.** 151

"Aegyptians, the Village of the," in Aegypt, **8.** 51

Aegyptus River, the (see Nile)

Aegys, in north-western Laconia, used as a base of operations by Eurysthenes and Procles, **4.** 133; on the borders of Laconia and Arcadia, **5.** 11

Aela, a city near the head of the Arabian Gulf, **7.** 277

Aelana, on the Arabian Gulf, **7.** 313

Aelanites, a gulf in the recess of the Arabian Gulf near Arabia and Gaza, **7.** 277, 313, 341, 343

Aelius Catus (consul with C. Sentius, A.D. 4), transplanted 50,000 persons from among the Getans to Thrace, now called Moesians, **3.** 209

Aelius Gallus, praefect of Aegypt, commander of expedition to Arabia

Felix, **1.** 453; sent by Augustus to explore Arabia, Aethiopia, and other places, **7.** 353; utterly deceived by Syllaeus the Nabataean, and met with great difficulties in his expedition, **7.** 355–363; voyage of, up the Nile, **8.** 83; Strabo at Thebes with, **8.** 123; would have subdued the whole of Arabia Felix, had not Syllaeus betrayed him, **8.** 137

Aemilian Way, the, **2.** 327; built by M. Aemilius Scaurus through Pisa and to Derton, **2.** 329–331; another Aemilian Way, succeeding the Flaminian, **2.** 331

Aemilianus, Quintus Fabius Maximus Allobrogicus, cut down 200,000 Celti at the confluence of the Rhodanus and Isar Rivers, **2.** 197, 219

Aemilius Paulus (see Paulus)

Aenaria, the isle (see Pithecussa)

Aenea, one of the cities destroyed by Cassander, **3.** 343, 349

Aenea (Come?), see Nea Comê, **6.** 91

Aeneias, explorer and founder of cities, **1.** 177; wanderings of, a traditional fact, **2.** 55; activities, and death, of, in Italy, **2.** 379; sojourned at Laurentum and Ardea, **2.** 393; Caïeta, the nurse of, **2.** 397; Dardania in the Troad subject to, **5.** 461; leader of the Dardanians in the Trojan War, **6.** 19, 45; the parts subject to, **6.** 45; by the Romans regarded as their first founder, **6.** 57; Dardania subject to, **6.** 65; with Ascanius the son of, with Scamandrius, founded Scepsis, **6.** 105; variant accounts of, **6.** 107; by some said to have landed at Aegesta in Sicily with Elymus, to have seized Eryx and Lilybaeum, and then to have settled in Italy, **6.** 107, 109; territory subject to, **6.** 119

Aenesippeia, an isle off Aegypt, **8.** 55

Aenesisphyra, a promontory in Aegypt, **8.** 55

Aeniana, a city in Asia, **5.** 249

Aenianians, the; once lived about Dotium and Mt. Ossa, **1.** 227; inhabitants of Mt. Oeta, bordering on the Epicnemidian Locrians, **4.** 387; destroyed by the Aetolians and the Athamanians, **4.** 389; the

INDEX OF NAMES, PLACES, AND SUBJECTS

225

INDEX OF NAMES, PLACES, AND SUBJECTS

mentions the worship of Cotys among the Edonians, **5.** 105, and describes the worship of Dionysus, **5.** 107; in his *Niobê*, confounds things that are different, Mt. Sipylus with Mt. Ida, and places Adrasteia in Phrygia, **5.** 519; in his *Myrmidons*, on the Caïcus and Mysius Rivers, **6.** 139; in his *Persae* refers to Cissia, the mother of Memnon, **7.** 159

Aesepus River, the, in Asia, **5.** 413, 459, 461; borders on the Doliones, **5.** 499, 503; borders on the Troad, **6.** 3, 5, 9, 19, 23, 25, 27, 91; rises in a hill of Mt. Ida, **6.** 85; the Caresus empties into, **6.** 89; Palaescepsis 30 stadia from, **6.** 91

Aesernia (Isernia) in Samnium, destroyed in the Marsic War, **2.** 415, 463

Aesis (Esino) River, the, once a boundary between Cisalpine Celtica and Italy, **2.** 331, 371; distance to, from Garganum, **3.** 133

Aesium, in Italy; geographical position of, **2.** 373

Aesyetes, tomb of, mentioned by Homer, **6.** 67, 75

Aethalia (Elba), isle between Italy and Corsica, **1.** 473; visible from Volaterrae, and contains iron-mines, **2.** 355; Portus Argoüs in, **2.** 357

Aethalŏeis, the, a torrent in the territory of Scepsis, **5.** 115

Aethices, the, an Epeirote tribe; geographical position of Aethicia, the country of, **3.** 311; annexed to Thessaly, once lived on Mt. Pindus, but are now extinct, **4.** 417

Aethicia (see Aethices, the)

Aethiopia, mentioned by Homer, **1.** 5; subject to inundations, **1.** 119; meaning of the term, **1.** 123; Ephorus on, **1.** 125; a desert country, **1.** 501; waters the land of Aegypt, **2.** 189; in many respects like India, **7.** 41; under guard of three Roman cohorts, **8.** 49; extremities of, now reached by large fleets, **8.** 53; boundaries of, unknown, **8.** 209

Aethiopian merchandise, brought to Coptus, **8.** 119

Aethiopian women, some, arm for battle, and wear copper ring through lip, **8.** 145

Aethiopians, the; position of, **1.** 9; "sundered in twain" by the Arabian Gulf, **1.** 111, 119, 129; by the Nile, **1.** 117; more parched than the Indians and divided into two groups, **1.** 395; the western, position of, **1.** 461; Homer quoted on, **3.** 191, 5. 423; mentioned by Hesiod, **3.** 197; compared with the Indians, **7.** 21; explanation of black complexion and woolly hair of, **7.** 39; first subdued by Sesostris the Aegyptian, **7.** 313; weapons used by, **7.** 339; Homer on, **7.** 369; held as subjects the Megabari and the Blemmyes, **8.** 7; modes of life of, **8.** 9; do not use the Red Sea, **8.** 21; now disposed to peace, **8.** 135; once captured Syenê, Elephantinê, and Philae, and pulled down the statues of Caesar, but were repulsed and subdued by Petronius, **8.** 137; their weapons of war, **8.** 139; pardoned by Augustus for their attacks, **8.** 141; life, food, and worship of, **8.** 143; weapons and dress of, **8.** 145; religion, atheism, and customs among, **8.** 147

"Aethiopic" Zone, the, of Poseidonius, **1.** 371

Aetna, Mt., the region of, inhabited by Cyclopes, **1.** 73; the eruptions of, make the land suited to the vine, **2.** 453; Typhon lies beneath, **2.** 457; eruptions of, **3.** 25; the rivers flowing from, have good harbours at mouths, **3.** 63; ash-dust from, has a quality suited to the vine, **3.** 71; regions round, overrun by Eunus, **3.** 85; description of eruptions of, **3.** 87–91; holds in fetters the giant Typhon, **6.** 177

Aetna, the new name given to Catana (*q.v.*) by Hiero, **3.** 67; but later given to city at foot of Mt. Aetna (now Santa Maria di Licodia), **3.** 69, 87

Aetolia, promontories of, formerly islands, **1.** 221; acquired by Diomedes, **3.** 305; Mt. Corax (Vardusia) in, **3.** 327; bounded by the Acheloüs River, **4.** 17; named after Aetolus, **4.** 103; deserted lands of,

INDEX OF NAMES, PLACES, AND SUBJECTS

INDEX OF NAMES, PLACES, AND SUBJECTS

INDEX OF NAMES, PLACES, AND SUBJECTS

5. 151; on "the Cerbesian, a Phrygian melody," 5. 519

Alcyonian Gulf, the, a part of the Crisaean Gulf, 4. 19

Alëian Plain, the, in Cilicia, mentioned by Homer, 5. 423; 6. 355

Aleisium in Elis, 4. 35; by Homer called "Hill of Aleisium," and now Alesiaeum, a territory about Amphidolis, 4. 41

Aleisius River, the, in Elis, 4. 43

Alesia (situated on the Plateau du Mont-Auxois between Alise and Sainte Reine, now in ruins), where Vercingetorix was taken captive, 2. 219

Alessio (see Lissus)

Aletes, the coloniser of Corinth after the return of the Heracleidae, 4. 235

Aletia in Iapygia, 3. 121

Aletrium (Alatri), in Italy, 2. 413

Aleus, father of Augê and grandfather of Telephus; myth of, 6. 135

Alexander the orator, surnamed Lychnus ("Lamp"), contemporary of Cicero, a native of Ephesus, statesman, historian, and author of two poems, one astronomical and the other geographical, 6. 231

Alexander, the Aetolian poet (b. about 315 B.C.), on the Ascanian Lake in Asia Minor, 5. 465, 6. 373; the second man to write the talk of the cinaedi, 6. 253

Alexander, the son of Antiochus, defeated by Demetrius, the son of Seleucus, 6. 169

Alexander Balas (king of Syria 150–146 B.C.), defeated by Demetrius Nicator, 6. 169 and Ptolemy Philometor, 7. 247

Alexander the Great (356–323 B.C.); added to knowledge of geography, 1. 49; advised to treat Greeks as friends and barbarians as enemies, 1. 249; made accurate geographical investigations, 1. 259; crossed the Euphrates, 1. 301; set up altars as limits of his Indian expedition, 2. 139; complained to the Romans about the pirates of Antium (Anzio), 2. 391; expedition of, against the Thracians and Getans, but from scarcity of boats he could

not capture King Syrmus on Peucê Island in the Ister, 3. 201; frankly rebuked by the Celti about the Adriatic, 3. 203; fixed the boundary between Macedonia and Thrace at the Nestus River, 3. 355; received letter from Crates the mining engineer in regard to drainage in the basin of Lake Copaïs, 4. 305; Leonnatus, a comrade of, fell in the Lamian War, 4. 413; said to have had intercourse with Thalestria the queen of the Amazons, 5. 237; exploits of, greatly exaggerated by historians, 5. 239, 247, 255; failed to capture Spitamenes and Bessus, the Persian generals, 5. 269; went to the Iaxartes River, 5. 271; conquered fewer tribes in Asia than the Greeks, 5. 279; broke up a horrible custom in Bactria, and founded and destroyed cities there and in Sogdiana, 5. 283; said to have married Rhoxana, and to have destroyed the city of the Branchidae, 5. 285; attempted an expedition against certain tribes beyond Hyrcania, but later desisted, 5. 287, 289; put an end to the audacity of the Cossaei, 5. 309; sent Menon to gold mines in Armenia, 5. 329; captured Sagalassus in Pisidia, 5. 479; the Selgians in Pisidia voluntarily subject to, 5. 485; utterly defeated the satraps of Dareius near the Granicus River in the Troad, 6. 27; claimed kin with the Ilians, adorned their temple, and otherwise assisted them, 6. 51; Alexandreia (formerly Antigonia) in the Troad named after, by Lysimachus, 6. 53; helped to annotate and preserved the "Recension of the Casket" of Homer, in his zeal for the poet, 6. 55; descended from the Aeacidae, and much admired by Julius Caesar, 6. 57; Agathocles the father of Lysimachus, one of the successors of, 6. 163; captured Miletus, and Halicarnassus, 6. 209; offered to restore the temple of Artemis at Ephesus, but his offer was refused, 6. 227; extended limits of precinct of Ephesian Artemis as place of

INDEX OF NAMES, PLACES, AND SUBJECTS

refuge, **6.** 229; sacred precinct above Chalcideis in Asia dedicated to, **6.** 239; seized Halicarnassus and appointed Ada queen of the Carians, **6.** 285; destroyed Milyas in Pisidia, **6.** 321; led his phalanx along the coast of Cilicia against Issus and the forces of Dareius, **6.** 355; Stasanor of Soli in Cypros appointed general by, **6.** 381; expedition of, to India, **7.** 3; subdued a large part of India and gave it to Porus, **7.** 5; ambition of, when in India, **7.** 7; captured Aornus in India at one assault, **7.** 11; unduly exalted by flatterers, **7.** 13; thought the sources of the Nile were in India, **7.** 41; explored India, **7.** 43; the route thereto taken by, **7.** 45; welcomed by King Taxiles in India, **7.** 47; received 150 dogs from Sopeithes in India, **7.** 55; set sail on the Hydaspes in India, **7.** 55, 57; seriously wounded in India, **7.** 57; conquests of, in India, **7.** 59; said to have advanced as far as the Ganges River, **7.** 61; taught a lesson in endurance by sophists in India, **7.** 107, 109; accompanied by Calanus the Indian sophist, **7.** 119; commended Mandanis the Indian sophist, **7.** 121; campaign of, in Asia, **7.** 133–139; took away certain places from the Arians and founded settlements of his own, **7.** 143; passed through the country of the Paropamisadae, and pursued Bessus into Bactriana, **7.** 145; spent the winter on Mt. Paropamisus, **7.** 147; joined by Craterus in Carmania, **7.** 149; forced his way through various defiles and across various rivers in Persis, **7.** 163; crossed the Araxes River near Persepolis, and burnt up the royal palace there, **7.** 165; carried off Persian treasures to Susa, **7.** 169; deposed King Dareius, **7.** 189; conquered Dareius at Gaugamela near Arbela, **7.** 197; died at Babylon, **7.** 199; destroyed most of the artificial cataracts in the Euphrates and Tigris rivers, **7.** 205; intended to acquire Arabia,

7. 209, 211; found that naphtha in Babylonia was inflammable, **7.** 217; built a mole between Tyre and the mainland, **7.** 267; took Tyre by siege, **7.** 269; rased Gaza in Phoenicia to the ground, **7.** 277; intended to seize Arabia Felix and make it his royal abode, **7.** 373; admired the advantages of the site of Alexandria, fortified it, and made it a great city, **8.** 29 ff.; Rhoxana, his wife, and his children departed from Aegypt to Macedonia, **8.** 37; dramatic story of visit of, to the temple of Ammon and the oracle among the Branchidae, **8.** 113; called the son of Zeus, **8.** 115, 117

Alexander the Judaean, first to proclaim himself king, instead of priest, of Judaea, **7.** 289

Alexander, son of Priam (see Paris)

Alexander the Molossian (appointed king of Epeirus by Philip about 342 B.C.), killed at Pandosia in Bruttium (about 330 B.C.), **7.** 37, 115, 117

Alexander Philalethes, of Laodiceia, head of school of medicine at Carura in Strabo's time, **5.** 519

Alexandreia in the Troad; longest equinoctial day at has 15 equinoctial hours, **1.** 513, **5.** 113; founded by Antigonus and called Antigonia, but changed its name to Alexandreia, **6.** 5, 53, 65; ancient site of, **6.** 93; where the "Judgment of Paris" is said to have taken place, **6.** 103

Alexandreian Games, the, celebrated in honour of Alexander the Great at a precinct above Chalcideis in Asia, **6.** 239

Alexandria in Aegypt (see Map of, at the end of this volume); 4000 stadia from Lycia or Rhodes, **1.** 93, **3.** 23, 483; library of, accessible to Eratosthenes and Hipparchus, **1.** 259; distance from, to equator, **1.** 509; relation of index of sun-dial at, on day of equinox, is as five to three, **1.** 511; healthfulness of, **2.** 315; receives aromatics from Leucê Comê in Arabia, **7.** 359; detailed description and history of, **8.** 23 ff.; the harbours and Heptastadium

INDEX OF NAMES, PLACES, AND SUBJECTS

6. 271; son of Cissus the founder of Argos, 5. 149

Altinum (Altino), near Ravenna, 2. 315

Alura (see Aluris)

Aluris (or Alura, or Dorium) in Messenia, identified by some with the Homeric Dorium, 4. 75

Alus (or Halus, q.v.), the Homeric, in Phthiotis, subject to Achilles, 4. 401; historians in doubt about, 4. 409

Alvena, Mt. (see Minthê)

Alyattes, king of Lydia and father of Croesus, sent gifts to Delphi and consulted oracle, 4. 357; great mound and tomb of, at Sardeis, "a monument of prostitution," 6. 177, 179; source of wealth of, 6. 371; once ruler over a few Greeks in Asia, 7. 187

Alybê (Chalybê?), the Homeric, in Cappadocia Pontica, "the birth-place of silver," 5. 403, 413; term emended by certain critics to "Alopê" or "Alobê," 5. 405, 407, 413, 6. 91

Alyconian Sea, the, in the Corinthian Gulf, extends from Pagae to the boundaries of Boeotia near Creusa, 4. 279

Alyzeus, son of Icarius and brother of Penelopê, 5. 35

Alyzia in Acarnania, 5. 25; geographical position of, 5. 27; thought by Ephorus to have been named after Alyzeus the brother of Penelopê, 5. 35; 15 stadia from the sea, 5. 61

Amadocus II, king of the Odrysae, 3. 371

Amaltheia, the horn of, by some identified with Pacheloïtis, 5. 57, 59

Amanides Gates, the, in Cilicia, where Mt. Amanus ends, 6. 355

Amanus, Mt., the, splits off the Cilician Taurus, 5. 295, 351; extends to the Euphrates River, 5. 297, 6. 355; borders on Syria, 7. 195, 239, 247

Amardi (see Mardi), the, in Asia; geographical position of, 5. 249; live in the Taurus, 5. 259; mountaineers in Atropatian Media, 5. 305

Amarium, sacred precinct of Zeus

Amarius near Aegium, where the common council of the Achaean League convened, 4. 215; belongs to Aegium, 4. 223

Amarynces, lord, buried by the Epeians at Buprasium in Elis, 4. 35

Amarynthium, the; temple of Artemis Amarynthia, 5. 19

Amarynthus, a village seven stadia from Eretria, 5. 15

Amaseia in Cappadocia Pontica, native city of Strabo, a very strongly fortified city, 5. 397, 429; "largest and best of all," 5. 443; detailed description of, 5. 445–447

Amaseno River, the (see Amasenus)

Amasenus (Amaseno) River, the, in Italy, 2. 395, footnote 4

Amasias (Ems) River, the, on which Drusus defeated the Bructeri, 3. 155, 159

Amasra (see Amastris)

Amastris (Amasra), in eastern Paphlagonia, once held by Mithridates Eupator, 5. 371; ten schoeni distant from Enetê (or Eneti), 5. 381; formed out of four settlements by Amastris (niece of Dareius), after whom it was named, 5. 385; not mentioned by Homer, 5. 417

Amathus in Cypros, 6. 379

Amathus River, the (see Pamisus)

Amathusians, the, a Cyprian tribe mentioned by Hipponax, 4. 37

Amaxiki (see Leucas in Acarnania)

"Amazones," an emendation to, in the Homeric text, 5. 405

Amazons, the, home and habits of, 5. 233–239; incredible stories about, 5. 235; said to have founded Ephesus, Smyrna, and other cities, 5. 237; Thalestria, the queen of, said to have had intercourse with Alexander, 5. 239; "swayed a 'Syrian' army," and lived in Themiscyra, 5. 383; placed by certain historians between Mysia, Caria, and Lydia, near Cymê, 5. 405; named Ephesus, Smyrna, Cymê, and Myrina, 5. 407; once lived in Alopê, but now in Zeleia, according to Palaephatus, 5. 409, 413; once fought the Trojans, 5. 413; would not fight on Priam's

233

INDEX OF NAMES, PLACES, AND SUBJECTS

INDEX OF NAMES, PLACES, AND SUBJECTS

237

INDEX OF NAMES, PLACES, AND SUBJECTS

238

INDEX OF NAMES, PLACES, AND SUBJECTS

INDEX OF NAMES, PLACES, AND SUBJECTS

241

INDEX OF NAMES, PLACES, AND SUBJECTS

243

recesses, **7.** 277, 309; separates the Arabians from the Troglodytes, **7.** 355; borders on Arabia, **8.** 3; now navigated by large fleets, **8.** 53

Arabian merchandise, brought to the emporium Coptus, **8.** 119

Arabian "Scenitae" ("Tent-dwellers"), the, now called "Malians" by some writers; country of, borders on Mesopotamia, **7.** 203; occupy certain parts of Mesopotamia, **7.** 233; moderate in exaction of tribute, **7.** 235; border on Syria, **7.** 239; keep herds of all kinds, especially camels, **7.** 301

Arabian tribes, the, in Judaea, **7.** 281

Arabians, the; well-to-do and even rich, **7.** 145; much like the Armenians and Syrians, **1.** 153; unknown to Homer, **3.** 191; some of, who crossed over with Cadmus, settled in Euboea, **5.** 13; the Mesenian, country of, borders on Babylonia, **7.** 203; would not send ambassadors to Alexander, **7.** 211; in part give ear to the Romans and in part to the Parthians, **7.** 235, 237; less civilised than the Syrians, **7.** 255; those in Syria, **7.** 263, 265; desert of, **7.** 307; discussed at length by Artemidorus, **7.** 341; separated from the Troglodytes by the Arabian Gulf, **7.** 355; not very good warriors on land or sea, **7.** 355; by some identified with the Homeric Eremibians, **7.** 371

Arachosia, a part of Ariana, **5.** 277, 279

Arachoti, the, in Asia; geographical position of, **5.** 269, 271, **7.** 141; road through country of, **7.** 143, 145

Arachthus River (see Aratthus)

Aracynthus (Zygos), Mt., in Aetolia, **5.** 27

Aradians, the; seaboard of, in Phoenicia, **7.** 255; history of, **7.** 257; navigate the Jordan and Lycus Rivers, **7.** 261

Aradus, an island in the Persian Gulf, said to have been colonised by the Phoenician Aradus, **7.** 303

Aradus (Ruad), the island, off Phoenicia, **7.** 255; description and history of, **7.** 257, 259

Araethyraea (the Homeric Araethyreê,

q.v.), the country now called Phliasia, **4.** 205

Araethyreê (see Araethyraea), the Homeric, **4.** 185

Aragus River, the, empties into the Cyrus, **5.** 217

"Arambians" (see Eremibians), name of one of the three Arabian tribes, **7.** 371

"Aramaeans," name of one of the three Arabian tribes, **7.** 371; applies to Syrians, **7.** 373

Arammaeans, the; racial likeness of to other peoples, **1.** 153

Arar (Saône) River, the, rises in the Alps and joins the Rhodanus at Lugdunum, **2.** 199, 223; navigable, **2.** 211; claimed as private property by both the Sequani and the Aedui, **2.** 225

Ararenê in Arabia, a desert country and ruled by King Sabos, **7.** 361

Aratthus (or Arachthus, now Arta) River, the, rises in Mt. Tymphê and flows past Ambracia, **3.** 303; empties into the Ambracian Gulf, **3.** 309, 311

Aratus, most illustrious tyrant of Sicyon and general of the Achaean League, **4.** 207; set free the Peloponnesus from tyrants and brought the League to the height of its power, **4.** 217

Aratus of Soli in Cilicia (b. about 315 B.C.), the astronomical poet, author of the *Phaenomena*, **6.** 341, of whose works there remain only two short poems and some recently discovered fragments; on the constellations, **1.** 11; on where "the extremities of east and west join each other," **1.** 397; apocopê in, **4.** 131; on the goat that nursed Zeus, **4.** 223; wrongly says that Mt. Dictê is near Mt. Ida in Crete, **5.** 139; calls Pholegandros "Iron" Island, because of its ruggedness, **5.** 161; in his *Catalepton* mentions the poverty of the isle Gyaros, **5.** 167

Arauris (Hérault) River, the, rises in the Cemmenus Mountain, **2.** 183

Arausio (Orange), **2.** 197

Araxenê in Armenia; bees and honey in, **1.** 273; has an abundance of honey, **5.** 251

INDEX OF NAMES, PLACES, AND SUBJECTS

Araxene Plain, the, in Armenia, very fertile, **5**. 321

Araxes River, the, the mouth of, near that of the Cyrus, **5**. 225, 265; course of, **5**. 187, 305, 321, 327; origin of name of, and description of, **5**. 335

Araxes River, the, in Persis, **7**. 165

Araxus (Kalogria), Cape, opposite Acarnania, **4**. 15, 17; distant 1030 stadia from the isthmus of Corinth, **4**. 19; the beginning of the seaboard of Elis, **4**. 25; 1030 stadia from the isthmus of Corinth, **4**. 227

Arbaces, the empire of, **7**. 195

Arbela, the Babylonian city, **7**. 195; the battle near, **7**. 197; the victory of Alexander at, foretold by oracle, **8**. 117

Arbelus, the son of Athmoneus and founder of Arbela in Assyria, **7**. 197

Arbies, the, a tribe in Ariana, **7**. 129

Arbis River, the, in Ariana, **7**. 129

Arbo, one of the Liburnides, **3**. 259

Arcadia, the home of Pelasgus, father of the Pelasgi, **2**. 345; lies in the interior of the Peloponnesus, **4**. 15; well-known cities in, **4**. 21; description and history of, **4**. 227–233

Arcadian breed of horses, the, are most excellent, **4**. 229

Arcadian colony, Rome an, **2**. 385

Arcadian tribes, the, **4**. 227

Arcadians, the, thought to have been admitted as colonists in the land of the Peucetii, **3**. 127; wholly mountaineers, **4**. 7; by some thought to be one of the three tribes in Triphylia, **4**. 23; fought the Pylians, **4**. 67; held* the priesthood of the Heleian Artemis at Helus in Laconia, **4**. 75; sided with the Messenians in the Messenian War, **4**. 95, 121; called Berethra ("Pits") "Zerethra," **4**. 231

Arcesilaüs of Pitanê in Aeolis (b. about 316 B.C.), founder of the Middle Academy of Philosophy; eminent at Athens, **1**. 53; fellow-student of Zeno under Polemon, **6**. 131

Arceuthus River, the, in Syria, **7**. 247

Archedemus the Stoic philosopher, native of Tarsus, **6**. 347

Archelaüs, grandson of Orestes, first

to lead the Aeolians across to Asia, **6**. 7

Archelaüs I, father of the Archelaüs who was priest at Comana; honoured by Sulla and the Roman Senate, **5**. 437; father of the Archelaüs who married Berenicê, carried on war with Sulla (86 B.C.) and was later honoured by the Romans, **8**. 45

Archelaüs II, son of the Archelaüs who was honoured by the Roman Senate, appointed priest at Comana, **5**. 435; reigned over Aegypt six months but was slain in battle, **5**. 437; pretended son of Mithridates and priest of Comana in Pontus, married Queen Berenicê, **8**. 45; slain by Ptolemy Auletes, **8**. 47

Archelaüs, last king of Greater Cappadocia, given kingdom and other territory by Antony (36 B.C.), **5**. 345, 349, 371; spent most of his time in Cilicia Tracheia, **5**. 361; the miners of, near Galatia, **5**. 369; married Queen Pythodoris, and appointed king of Lesser Armenia, **5**. 427; resided on the isle Elaeussa, **6**. 337; received Cilicia Tracheia from the Romans, **6**. 339

Archelaüs the natural philosopher, disciple of Anaxagoras, **6**. 245

Archelaüs, the, of Euripides, quoted on the Pelasgians, **2**. 345

Archemachus, the Euboean (fl. not later than the third century B.C.), wrote works (now lost) on the *History of Euboea* and *Metonymies* (*Changes in Names*); says the Curetes settled at Chalcis, but later migrated to Aetolia, **5**. 85

Archianax of Mitylenê, built a wall round Sigeium with stones taken from ancient Ilium, **6**. 75

Archias of Corinth, helped Myscellus to found Croton, **3**. 43; founded Syracuse, **3**. 71, **4**. 199; landed at Zephyrium on way to Syracuse, **3**. 73

Archias of Thurii, the commander sent by the Macedonian Antipater to arrest Demosthenes on the island Calauria, **4**. 175

Archidamus III, king of Sparta, born about 400 B.C., lost his life in 338

247

INDEX OF NAMES, PLACES, AND ·SUBJECTS

B.C. when acting as commander for Tarentum, **3**. 115

Archilochus the poet (fl. about 685 B.C.), refers to the Greeks as a whole as "Hellenes" and "Panhellenes," **4**. 157; born in Paros, **5**. 169; robbed of his shield by one of the Saii, **5**. 55, 403, 405; on the misfortunes of the Thasians and Magnesians, **6**. 253

Archimedes of Syracuse (287–212 B.C.), the great mathematician and inventor, nine of whose treatises are extant; his work *On Floating Bodies*, **1**. 201; all water has spherical surface, **1**. 201, 205

Architect, the; qualifications of, **1**. 419

Architects, the, who planned the city Alexandria, **8**. 29

Archons, the ten, in Crete, **5**. 159

Archytas (about 427–347 B.C.), seven times chosen chief magistrate of Taras (Tarentum), famous general, mathematician, and author, on whose life and writings works were written by Aristotle and Aristoxenus; embraced the Pythagorean philosophy, **3**. 115

Arconnesus, the isle, off Halicarnassus, **6**. 283

Arconnesos, the isle (see Aspis), between Teos and Lebedus, **6**. 237

Arconti River, the, in Italy (see Acheron, the, in Italy)

Arctic circle, the; Homer's conception of, **1**. 9; variability of, **1**. 45, 365, **5**. 45; wrongly used by Polybius in defining the zones, **1**. 371, and by others, **1**. 427; Little Bear wholly inside of, and always visible to Cinnamon-producing people, **1**. 507; Great Bear partially visible in, **1**. 509; in the zenith about 1400 stadia north of the Pontus, where the longest day is 15½ equinoctial hours, **1**. 515; relation of, to tropic circle, **1**. 519

Arcton-oros, near Cyzicus, **5**. 501

Arcturus, stands in the zenith, 400 stadia south of Alexandria, **1**. 511; rains cease in India at time of rising of, **7**. 25

Ardanis, Cape, in Cyrenaea, **1**. 147, **8**. 207

Ardea, the ancient, in Italy, **2**. 379; devastated by the Samnitae, **2**. 393

Ardeatae, the territory of the, in Latium; marshy and unhealthy, **2**. 389

Ardennes, the (see Arduenna)

Ardia, the southern part of Dalmatia, near the Adriatic, **3**. 251

Ardiaei (later called Vardiaei), the; geographical position of, **3**. 257, 261, 263, 325; because of piracy pushed back into the interior by the Romans and forced to till the soil, and now virtually obliterated, **3**. 263; in earlier times continually at war with the Autariatae over the salt-works on the common frontiers, **3**. 271

Ardian Mountain (Dinara), the, in Dalmatia, **3**. 251

Arduenna (Ardennes), the forest, **2**. 233

Arecomisci, the (see Volcae)

Aregon, the Corinthian; famous painting of, entitled "Artemis Borne Aloft on a Griffin," in the temple of Artemis near the mouth of the Alpheius River, **4**. 49

Areion, the fleet horse on which Adrastus escaped, **4**. 295

Areius, friend of Xenarchus of Seleuceia in Cilicia, and contemporary of Strabo, **6**. 335

Arelatē (Arles), a large emporium near the Rhodanus, **2**. 183

Arenē in Messenia (see Erana)

Arenē in Triphylia, mentioned in the Homeric *Catalogue*, perhaps to be identified with Samicum, **4**. 61; lies in the country now called Hypaesia, **4**. 63; wrongly identified by some with Erana in Messenia, **4**. 117

Ares (Mars), the god of war, worshipped by the Lusitanians, **2**. 73; temple of, built at the confluence of the Rhodanus and Isar Rivers by Aemilianus, **2**. 197; the father of Romulus and Remus by Rhea Silvia, **2**. 381; statue of, dedicated along with that of Athenē at her temple near Coroneia (?), **4**. 325 (see footnote 1); cheered the Trojans, **6**. 69; an offering hung up to, in the temple of Athenē Glaucopis,

INDEX OF NAMES, PLACES, AND SUBJECTS

INDEX OF NAMES, PLACES, AND SUBJECTS

INDEX OF NAMES, PLACES, AND SUBJECTS

INDEX OF NAMES, PLACES, AND SUBJECTS

Poseidonius, **2**. 67; on the origin of the large stones in Stony Plain in Celtica, **2**. 185; on "river-stones, formed of sand, but melted by the rains," **3**. 193; on the Leleges of Ionia and their conquests and settlements in Greece, **3**. 289; born at Stageira in Macedonia, **3**. 355, which belongs to the Chalcidians, **3**. 359; on the Cauconians in Coelê Elis, **4**. 55; says the Arcadian Dryops settled Dryopians in Asinê in Argolis, **4**. 173; says the Carians seized Epidaurus, **4**. 175; says the peoples of the island Tenedos and the Corinthian Tenea are akin, **4**. 199; sojourned and died at Chalcis in Euboea, **5**. 19; recension of the *Iliad* by, called the *Iliad of the Casket*, **6**. 55 (see **6**. 56, footnote 1); history of the library of, **6**. 111, 113; sojourned at Assus, **6**. 115; and consorted there with the niece of the tyrant Hermeias, **6**. 117; changed the name of Tyrtamus to Theophrastus, **6**. 145; reports that one Aegyptian woman bore seven children at one time, and discusses the Nile and rivers in India, **7**. 37; does not believe the statement that nothing floats on the Silus River in India, **7**. 67; on the cause of the risings of the Nile, **8**. 21

Aristoxenus of Tarentum (fl. about 330 B.C.), pupil of Aristotle, philosopher, musician, and author of *Elements of Harmony*, of which three incomplete books are preserved; holds that music tends to discipline character, **1**. 57

Aristus, author of a history of Alexander the Great, born at Salamis in Cypros, **6**. 379; on the tombs of the Persian kings at Pasargadae, **7**. 167

Arithmetic, invented by the Phoenicians, **7**. 269, 271; **8**. 11

Arius River, the, in Aria and Margiana, **5**. 277; is at last absorbed by the sand, **5**. 285

Ariusia, a district in Chios, produces the best of Greek wine, **6**. 243

Arkadia (see Cyparissia)

Arles (see Arelatê)

Armenê in Paphlagonia; the proverb applied to, **5**. 387

Armenia, visited by Jason, **1**. 177; once under water, according to Xanthus, **1**. 181; fertile districts of, **1**. 273; north and south dimension of, still unmeasured, **1**. 303; the pass leading from, into Iberia, **5**. 221; named after Armenus of Thessaly, **5**. 231; best part of, once occupied by the Sacae, **5**. 263; for the most part given to brigandage, and lies inside the Taurus, **5**. 301; an exceptionally good "horse-pasturing" country, **5**. 311; detailed description of, **5**. 317–341; geographical position of, **5**. 317; intersected by the Euphrates, **5**. 319; the fertility of, **5**. 321; in earlier times a small country, **5**. 323; the cities in, **5**. 325; the rivers and lakes in, **5**. 327, 335; the mines in, **5**. 329; the wealth, power, and size of, **5**. 331; visited by Jason, **5**. 333; the more recent history of, **5**. 337, 339; follows the sacred rites of the Persians, **5**. 341; borders on Cappadocia, **5**. 345; borders on Babylonia, **7**. 203

Armenia, the Greater; the Euphrates flows through, **5**. 297, **7**. 215; lies east of Atropatian Media, **5**. 303, 319; Zenon, son of Queen Pythodoris, now king of, **5**. 427

Armenia, the Lesser; the Euphrates borders on, **5**. 297; situated above Trapezus and Pharnacia, **5**. 339; sea-coast as far as, annexed to Cappadocia Pontica by Mithridates, **5**. 371; extent of empire of, **5**. 423; separated from Acilisenê by the Euphrates, **5**. 425; Archelaüs appointed king of, **5**. 427; borders on Culupenê and Camisenê, **5**. 441; the Euphrates flows in, **7**. 215

Armenian Gates, the, **1**. 303

Armenians, the; much like the Syrians and Arabians, **1**. 153; geographical position of, **1**. 497; are excellent subjects, but from neglect by the Romans sometimes attempt revolutions, **3**. 145; hold a part of the Moschian country, **5**. 215; manner of fighting of, **5**.

INDEX OF NAMES, PLACES, AND SUBJECTS

Arsinoê (Sydrê ?, Syedra ?, or Aunesis ?) in Cilicia, between Coracesium and Hamaxia, **6.** 331

Arsinoê in Cilicia, between Nagidus and Melania, **6.** 333

Arsinoê (in earlier times called Crocodeilonpolis) near the Nile; reveres a sacred crocodile, **8.** 107

Arsinoê, the city (also called Cleopatris), on the isthmus near where the canal empties into the Red Sea and the Arabian Gulf, **8.** 77

Arsinoê, harbour and city in Cyprus, between Salamis and Leucolla, **6.** 379

Arsinoê in Cyprus, between Soli and Cape Acamas, **6.** 381

Arsinoê, between Zephyria and Hierocepis in Cyprus, **6.** 381

Arsinoê, the Lycian (see Patara)

Arsinoê, city and harbour near Cape Deirê, **7.** 331

Arsinoê, on the coast between Philotera and Myus Harbour, **7.** 315

Arsinus River (see Erasinus)

Arta, the city (see Ambracia)

Arta, the Gulf of (see Ambracian Gulf)

Arta, the River (see Aratthus)

Artabazus, father-in-law of Seleucus Nicator, **5.** 509

Artabrians (also called Arotrebians, **2.** 71); the, in Iberia, live in neighbourhood of Cape Nerium, **1.** 461, **2.** 69; have thickly-settled cities on the "Harbour of the Artabrians," **2.** 71

Artacaëna, a city in Aria, **5.** 279

Artacê on Cyzicus, colonised by Milesians, **6.** 9, 207

Artacê, an island in the Propontis, **5.** 505

Artacê, Mt., in Cyzicus, **5.** 505

Artacenê, in Assyria, **7.** 197

Artageras, a strong fortress on the Euphrates, **5.** 327

Artaki (see Cyzicus)

Artanes (Arsaces ? or Armenias ?), the Sophenian, an Armenian king, dethroned by Tigranes, **5.** 337

Artavasdes, the son of Tigranes; king of Armenia; betrayed Antony, **5.** 307; the treasury of, near Artaxata, **5.** 327; invaded Media

with Antony, **5.** 331; betrayed Antony to the Parthians and later was slain, **5.** 339, 341

Artaxata (also called Artaxiasata) in Armenia; the country round ruled by Zariadris, **5.** 325

Artaxias, formerly a general of Antiochus the Great and later king of Sophenê and other countries in Asia; enlarged Armenia, **5.** 323, 325; once king of part of Armenia, **5.** 337

Artaxiasarta (see Artaxata)

"Artemeas," epithet of Artemis (see Artemis Artemeas)

Artemidorus of Ephesus (fl. about 100 B.C.), geographer, and author, among other works, of a work in 11 books, of which only fragments preserved in an abridgment by Marcianus now remain; likens the Sacred Cape of Iberia to a ship, and denies existence of temple or altar of Heracles thereon, **2.** 7; his stories about sunsets in Iberia, **2.** 9, 11; contradicts Eratosthenes regarding "Tartessis," "Blest Isle," the tides, and other things, **2.** 49; on Odysseia and Athene's temple in Iberia, and on the Lotus-eaters, **2.** 83; says Tarraco has poor places for anchorage, **2.** 91; on the barbaric customs of women in Iberia, **2.** 109, 111; on the dimensions of the larger Gymnesian (Balearic) Island, **2.** 125; on Hera's isle, **2.** 137; on the spring at Gades, **2.** 145; says the Rhodanus has three mouths, **2.** 189; on Aeria (Orange) in Celtica, **2.** 197; on the harbour called "Two Crows" on the ocean-coast of Celtica, **2.** 249; his fabulous story of Demeter and Corê, **2.** 251; on the distance from Cyrnus (Corsica) and Sardo to the mainland, **2.** 357; identifies Avernus with Lake Acherusia, **2.** 447; on the distance round the Tarantine Gulf, **3.** 39; on the distance from Cape Pachynus to Cape Taenarum and from the Alpheius to the Pamisus, **3.** 61; on certain distances between points in Italy, **3.** 131, 133; says the Hebrus is 3100 stadia from

INDEX OF NAMES, PLACES, AND SUBJECTS

255

INDEX OF NAMES, PLACES, AND SUBJECTS

Thessaly subject to, according to Homer, 4. 433

Asclepiades of Myrlea on the Propontis (fl. in first century B.C.), historian, grammarian, and teacher of grammar in Turditania; on Odysseia and Athene's temple in Iberia, and on memorials of wanderings of Odysseus in Iberia, 2. 83; on the Igletes, in Iberia, 2. 119

Asclepiades, the physician, of Prusa; a native of Bithynia, 5. 467

Asclepieium, the; famous temple in Cos, 6. 287

Asclepieium, the, in the Troad, founded by Lysimachus, 6. 89

Asclepius, the remarkable ivory image of, made by Colotes, at Cyllenê in Elis, 4. 25; temple of, at Gerenia in Messenia, 4. 113; famous temples of, at Epidaurus, Triccê, and on Cos, 4. 177; temple of, 40 stadia from Dymê and 80 from Patras, 4. 219; earliest and most famous temple of, at Triccê in Thessaly, 4. 429; the statue of, at Epidaurus, brought to Italy by oracle of the Sibyl, 5. 471; said to have been born in Triccê in Hestiaeotis in Thessaly, 6. 249; grove of, in Phoenicia, 7. 267; temple of, on acropolis of Carthage, burnt up by wife of Asdrubal, 8. 185

Ascrê, native city of Hesiod, on a high and rugged hill about 40 stadia from Thespiae, and ridiculed by Hesiod, 4. 315, 317, 6. 161; "Árnê" in the *Iliad* ignorantly emended to "Ascrê" by Zenodotus, 4. 331

Asculum Picenum (Ascoli Piceno), in Picenum, well fortified by nature, 2. 429

Asdrubal (Hasdrubal), son-in-law and successor (reigned 229–221 B.C.) of Hamilcar Barcas, founded New Carthage, 2. 87; wife of, burnt up the temple of Asclepius and herself along with it when Carthage was captured (by Scipio, 146 B.C.), 8. 185

Asea (also called Asia), a village in the territory of Megalopolis, whence flows the Eurotas, 3. 93, 4. 47, 199

Ash-dust, the, from Aetna, makes the soil suitable for the vine, 3. 69, 71

Asia in Arcadia (see Asea)

"Asia," perhaps applied to "Meïonia" by Homer, 6. 179

Asia, revealed to geographers by Alexander, 1. 51; shape of, as compared with Europe and Libya, 1. 467; bounded by the Nile, 1. 485; divisions of, 1. 495; subject to rulers appointed by the Romans, 3. 145; "wheat-producing," 3. 207; separated from Europe by the Cimmerian Bosporus, 3. 329; Corinth on the direct route from, to Italy, 4. 189; consecrated to Dionysus, 5. 109; borders on Europe along the Tanaïs River, and is bisected by the Taurus range, 5. 183; description of the northern division of, 5. 185; shape and dimensions of eastern portion of, 5. 289; whole of, once ruled by Greater Media, 5. 307; now largely subject to the Romans, 8. 211; in part a consular Province, 8. 215

Asia (Minor), called "Asia" in the special sense of the term, 1. 483; defined as the part of Asia this side the Taurus, 5. 295, 347; or Asiatic peninsula; discussion of boundaries of, 6. 359–365

"Asiarchs," the, in Tralleis, 6. 255

Asiatic peninsula, the (Asia Minor); discussion of boundaries of, 6. 359–365

Asiatic Stathmi, The, written apparently by a certain Amyntas who accompanied Alexander, 7. 141

Asidigis, now Medina Sidonia (see Baetis)

Asii, the, in Asia, helped to take away Bactriana from the Greeks, 5. 261

Asinaean Gulf (see Messenian Gulf), the, named after the Messenian Asinê, 4. 109, 113

Asinê, the Hermionic, in Argolis, 4. 113, 153, 171, 173, 181

Asinê in Laconia, 4. 127

Asinê (Koron, or Koroni), in Messenia, 4. 109; the Asinaean (Messenian) Gulf named after, 4. 113

Asinius Pollio (76 B.C.–A.D. 4), orator, poet, historian, and consul (40 B.C.); wrongly says the Rhenus is 6000 stadia long, 2. 227

Asioneis (or Esioneis), the, in Asia;

257

INDEX OF NAMES, PLACES, AND SUBJECTS

country of, invaded by the Cimmerians, **6.** 179

Asius the son of Dymas and the uncle of Hector, who dwelt in Phrygia; mentioned by Homer, and not to be confused with Asius the son of Hyrtacus, **6.** 41

Asius, the hero; hero-temple of, near Nysa in Caria, **6.** 261

Asius, son of Hyrtacus, mentioned by Homer and leader in the Trojan War, **6.** 19, 21, 37

Asius of Samos (lived, apparently about 700 B.C.), epic and iambic poet, of whose works only fragments remain; on Dius and Melanippê at Metapontium, **3.** 53

Asopia, a district in Sicyonia, through which the Asopus flows, **4.** 313

Asopus, a city in Laconia (now in ruins near Xyli), **4.** 129

Asopus River, the, on the island Paros, **4.** 205

Asopus (Hagios Giorgios) River, the, rises in Argolis and flows past Sicyonia, **3.** 79, **4.** 205, 313

Asopus (Asopo) River, the; flows past Thebes, Plataea, and Tanagra, **4.** 205; divides the Parasopii into several settlements, and empties near Tanagra, **4.** 315, 325

Asopus River, the, in Thessalian Phthiotis, flows past the village Parasopii in the Trachinian Heracleia, **4.** 205, 313; receives the Phoenix River and empties near Thermopylae, **4.** 391

Asp, the Aegyptian, of two kinds, **8.** 149

Aspaneus, the market for timber from Mt. Ida in the Troad, **6.** 103

Aspendus in Pamphylia, founded by the Argives, **5.** 479, **6.** 325

Asphalt; the mine of, near Apollonia (Pollina) in Illyria, **3.** 267; discharged from Hieron Oros into the Propontis (Sea of Marmora), **3.** 377; used in the wall, temples, and palace at Susa, **7.** 159; liquid (naphtha) and dry, produced respectively in Susis and Babylonia, **7.** 215, 217; the Dead Sea full of, **7.** 293–295; used by the Aegyptians for embalming corpses, **7.** 297; a spring of, in Masaesylia in Libya, **8.** 177

Asphaltic vine-earth, the, at Pierian Seleuceia and in Rhodes, kills vine-infesting insects, **3.** 267

Asphaltites Lake (Dead Sea), by Strabo confused with Lake Sirbonis; description of, **7.** 293–295

Aspionus, a satrapy in Bactria, taken from Eucratides by the Parthians, **5.** 281

Aspis (also called Arconnesos), an island between Teos and Lebedus, **6.** 237

Aspis ("Shield"), a Carthaginian city whose Latin name is Clupea, **3.** 103, **8.** 199

Aspis ("Shield"), a hill on the promontory Taphitis in Carthaginia; colonised by Agathocles at the time when he attacked the Carthaginians, **8.** 191

Aspledon (see Eudeielos), the Homeric, by some called Spledon; name of, changed to Eudeielos, **4.** 339

Aspordene (Asporene?) Mother, the; temple of, on Mt. Aspordenum (Asporenum?) near Pergamum, **6.** 147

Aspordenum (Asporenum?), Mt., near Pergamum, **6.** 147

Asporene Mother, the (see Aspordene Mother)

Asporenum, Mt. (see Aspordenum)

Aspra Spitia (see Anticyra)

Aspromonte (see Sila, Mt.)

Aspropotamos (see Acheloüs River)

Asps, the, in India, **7.** 79

Aspurgiani, the, a tribe of the Maeotae, caught King Polemon alive and killed him, **5.** 201; one of the barbarian tribes round Syndicê, **5.** 427

Ass, the, not bred in the region of Lake Maeotis because this animal is sensitive to cold, **3.** 225

Assacanus, the land of, in India, **7.** 25, 47

Asses; the wild, in the Scythian plains, **3.** 249; in Bagadania in Cappadocia, **5.** 367; used by the Carmanians, even in war, and are sacrificed to Ares, **7.** 153

Assuan (see Syenê)

Assus, territory of, **6.** 5, 99; 120 stadia from Lectum, **6.** 101; description and history of, **6.** 115, 117;

INDEX OF NAMES, PLACES, AND SUBJECTS

259

INDEX OF NAMES, PLACES, AND SUBJECTS

INDEX OF NAMES, PLACES, AND SUBJECTS

upright, but the Homeric was seated (as at various places to-day), **6.** 83; priestess of, at Pedasa in Caria, grows a beard when misfortune is imminent, **6.** 119; saved Augê and her son Telephus, **6.** 135; temple of, near Smyrna, **6.** 203; colossal statue of, at temple of Hera on Samos, **6.** 215; born from the head of Zeus, **6.** 277; famous temple of, at Lindus in Crete, **6.** 279; temple of, at Sidê in Pamphylia, **6.** 325; temple of, among the Elymaeans, robbed by the Parthian king, **7.** 223; Cyrrhestis, temple of, near Heracleia in Syria, **7.** 247; temple of, at Saïs in Aegypt, **8.** 67

Athenians, the; dispute of, with Boeotians about Oropus, **1.** 245; fond of letters, not by nature, but by habit, **1.** 395; colonised Neapolis, **2.** 449; destroyed the rebuilt Sybaris in Italy, and founded Thurii, **3.** 47; re-founded Cardia on the Melas Gulf, **3.** 373; regarded as an indigenous people, **4.** 7; rebuilt the Messenian Pylus as a fortress against the Lacedaemonians, **4.** 109; captured 300 Lacedaemonians on Sphacteria, **4.** 111; rivalled by the inhabitants of Aegina in the sea-fight at Salamis, **4.** 179; divided Aegina by lot among Athenian settlers but lost it to the Lacedaemonians, **4.** 181; joined Eurystheus in expedition against Iolaüs, **4.** 187; ancestors of the Ionians, **4.** 207; turned over their government to Ion the son of Xuthus, and sent a colony of Ionians to occupy the Aegialus in the Peloponnesus, **4.** 209; called the wind Argestes "Sceiron," **4.** 245; voluntarily received Melanthus the king of Messenia as their king, **4.** 249; once in strife with the Megarians for Salamis, but now hold it, **4.** 253; wont to despatch 400 ships on expeditions, **4.** 261; history of the forms of government of, **4.** 269, 271; hold Haliartus, as a gift from the Romans, **4.** 325; conquered by Philip at Chaeroneia, **4.** 333; the road taken by, on the Pythian procession to Delphi, **4.** 367; fought the

Macedonians in the Lamian War, **4.** 413; 2000, from the deme of the Histiaeans, colonised Histiaea (Oreus) in Euboea, **5.** 7; founded Athenae Diades in Euboea, **5.** 9; said to have founded Chalcis and Eretria before the Trojan War, **5.** 13; always hospitable to all things foreign, especially foreign religious rites, **5.** 109; once slew most of the inhabitants of Melos from youth upwards, **5.** 163; now hold Delos, **5.** 167; once besieged Ceos, **5.** 169; under Athenocles colonised Amisus, **5.** 395; with the Megarians founded Astacus on the Propontis, **5.** 455; under Phrynon the Olympian victor seized Sigeium in the Troad, **6.** 75; Adramyttium a colony of, **6.** 103; ordered slaughter of all Mitylenaeans from youth up, but rescinded decree, **6.** 145; with Menestheus founded Elaea in Asia in Trojan times, **6.** 159; fined Phrynichus the tragic poet 1000 drachmas because of his play on *The Capture of Miletus by Dareius*, **6.** 209; sent Pericles and Sophocles the poet to capture Samos, and allotted land to 2000 Athenians there, **6.** 219

Athenocles, and Athenians, colonised Amisus in Cappadocia Pontica, **5.** 395

Athenodorus of Canana near Tarsus (about 74 B.C.–A.D. 7), pupil of Poseidonius, friend of Strabo, learned scientist; on the tides, **1.** 19, 203, 2. 147; teacher of Julius Caesar and for a time ruled over Tarsus, **6.** 349, 351; praises the government of the Petraeans in Arabia, **7.** 353

Athenodorus Cordylion, lived with Marcus Cato; native of Tarsus, **6.** 347

Athens, parallel of latitude through, **1.** 241, 253; distance of parallel of, from Meroê, **1.** 255; parallel of, perceptibly different from that of Rhodes as shown by sun-dial, **1.** 333; rivalled by Massalia as a centre of learning, **2.** 179; once inhabited by Pelasgi, **2.** 347; occupied by Maleos the Pelasgian, **2.** 365; belonged to a kind of Amphictyonic

INDEX OF NAMES, PLACES, AND SUBJECTS

INDEX OF NAMES, PLACES, AND SUBJECTS

Philip, and died in old age, **6.** 165, 167

Attalus II (Philadelphus), son of Attalus I and brother of Eumenes II, embellished Pergamum, appointed guardian of Attalus III (Philometor), and reigned at Pergamum for 21 years (159–138 B.C.), **6.** 167; helped Demetrius the son of Seleucus to defeat Alexander the son of Antiochus, fought with the Romans against the Pseudo-Philip, made an expedition against Thrace, slew Prusias, and left the empire to his nephew Attalus III, **6.** 169; deceived in regard to the mole he had built at Ephesus, **6.** 229; settled the Dionysiac artists between Teos and Lebedus, **6.** 237; founded Attaleia in Pamphylia and sent a colony to the neighbouring Corycus, **6.** 323

Attalus III (Philometor), reigned only five years (138–133 B.C.) and left the Romans his heirs, **6.** 169

Attasii, the, a tribe of the Sacae and Massagetae in Asia, **5.** 269

Attea in Asia, **6.** 103

"Attes hyes" (see "Hyes attes")

"Atthis," and "Attica," derived from Atthis the son of Cranaüs, **4.** 265

Atthis, the son of Cranaüs, gave name to "Atthis" (Attica), **4.** 265

Atthis (Attica), the *Land of*, the histories of, **2.** 347, **4.** 247

Attic dialect, the ancient; the same as the Ionic, **4.** 5

Attic people, the, of ancient times, called Ionians, **4.** 5

Attic Tetrapolis, the, **4.** 175

Attica (see Atthis), once held by the Thracians under Eumolpus, **3.** 287; the Tetrapolis of (or Marathonian Tetrapolis), founded by Xuthus the son of Hellen, **4.** 209; once held by the Ionians, **4.** 245; in early times called Ionia and Ias, and was divided up between the sons of Pandion, **4.** 247; invaded by the Heracleidae, **4.** 249; "the sanctuary of the gods," **4.** 263; once called "Ionia," after Ion, **4.** 207; has 170, or 174, demes, **4.** 263; in earlier times called "Acticê," "Mopsopia" and "Ionia," **4.** 267;

people of, settled by Cecrops in 12 cities, but later by Theseus united into one city, Athens, **4.** 267; demes of, in the interior, too tedious to recount, **4.** 275; the rivers of, **4.** 275, 277; Plataeae on the confines of, **4.** 325; people of, akin to the Trojans, **6.** 95

Aturia, a region in Assyria, **7.** 193, 195; plains of, surround Ninus, **7.** 197

Atys, the Lydian, whose son Tyrrhenus colonised Tyrrhenia in Italy, **2.** 337

"Auases," the Aegyptian word for "oases," **1.** 501

Aude River, the (see Atax)

Aufidus (Ofanto) River, the, **2.** 395 (where "Aufidus" is an error for "Ufens"); distance from, to Barium, **3.** 127

Augaeae in Laconia, the Homeric "Augeiae," **4.** 131

Augê, mother of Telephus; myth of, **6.** 135

Augeiae in Laconia; name now spelled Aegaeae, **4.** 131

Augeiae in Locris, the Homeric, no longer existent, **4.** 131, 383

Augeias (or Augeas), the king of the Epeians, **4.** 29, **5.** 59; slain by Heracles, **4.** 39, 91; a foe of Neleus, **4.** 83; by some called king of Pisatis, **4.** 95

Augila, in the interior of Libya, a four days' journey from Automala, **8.** 209

Augusta in Sicily (see Xiphonia)

Augusta Emerita, in the country of the Turdulians in Iberia, **2.** 61, 121

Augusta Praetoria (Aosta), founded by Augustus, **2.** 281

Augustonemetum (see Nemossus)

Augustus Caesar (see Caesar Augustus)

Aulis, rightly called "rocky" by Homer, **3.** 189; mentioned by Homer in connection with Hyria; the Aeolic fleet despatched to Asia from, by the sons of Orestes, **4.** 283; a rocky place, a village of the Tanagraeans, and its harbour only large enough for 50 ships, and therefore the large harbour was probably the naval station of the Greeks, **4.** 289; Hyria situated near, **4.** 295, 313

263

INDEX OF NAMES, PLACES, AND SUBJECTS

"Aulon," the, of Messenia, **4**. 75

Aulonia (see Caulonia)

Aunesis (see Arsinoë in Cilicia)

Aurochs, the, in India (see Bisons)

Aurunci, the (see Argyrusci)

Ausar (Seschio) River, the, joins the Arnus at Pisa, **2**. 351

Auscii, the, in Aquitania, **2**. 217; given the "Latin right" by the Romans, **2**. 219

Ausonian Sea (see Sicilian Sea), the; forms a boundary of Italy, **1**. 493; named after the Ausonians, **2**. 395

Ausonians, the; country of, **2**. 393, 395; another name of the Opici, **2**. 435; founded Temesa in Bruttium, **3**. 17

Autariatae, the, border on Paeonia, **3**. 251, 275, 325; virtually destroyed by their wars with the Macedonians and the Romans, **3**. 263; once the largest and best Illyrian tribe, holding sway over the rest of the Thracians and Illyrians, but were overthrown by the Scordisci and later by the Romans, **3**. 271, 273

Autesion, descendant of Polyneices and father of Theras the founder of Thera, **4**. 63

Autolycus, a burglar, **4**. 435; regarded as founder of Sinopé and honoured as god; statue of, carried off by Leucullus, **5**. 391

Automala, a stronghold on the Great Syrtis, **8**. 199

Auxumum (Osimo), in Picenum, **2**. 429

Avella Vecchia (see Abella)

Avendo (see Vendo)

Avenio (Avignon), **2**. 197

Aventine, Mt., joined to Rome by Ancus Marcius, **2**. 401

Avernus, Lake (Lake Averno), **1**. 95, **2**. 439, 441, 443

Avigliana (see Ocelum)

Avignon (see Avenio)

Axes; double-edged, used in battle by the Negrani in Arabia, **7**. 361; used as weapons by some of the Aethiopians, **8**. 139

Axine Sea, the (see Euxine)

Axis, the, of the earth and the heavens, **1**. 425

Axius (Vardar) River, the, receives

the waters of the Erigon, **3**. 311, 341; flows through a certain pass in Macedonia, **3**. 325; the Paeonians lived on both sides of, **3**. 331, 333; joined by the Erigon and supplies Lake Ludias, **3**. 341; a muddy river, **3**. 343, 345, 347; flows from Paeonia, **3**. 361

Azamora, a stronghold in Cataonia, **5**. 357

Azanes, the, in the Peloponnesus, **4**. 19; an ancient Arcadian tribe, **4**. 227

Azani, a city in Phrygia Epictetus, **5**. 505

Azanitis in Asia; the Rhyndacus River rises in, **5**. 503

Azara, epithet of the Elymaean Artemis, **7**. 223

Azaritia, a spring in Bithynia which breeds little crocodiles, **5**. 455

Azeneis, the Attic deme, **4**. 271

Azorus, a city in Pelagonia, **3**. 311

Azotians, the, a tribe in Syria, **7**. 239

Azotus in Phoenicia, **7**. 277

B

Babanomus, borders on the territory of Amaseia in Cappadocia Pontica, **5**. 449

Baboons, the, in Aethiopia, **7**. 337

Babylon, geographical position of, **1**. 307; founded by Semiramis, **1**. 319; 3000 stadia from the mouth of the Euphrates, **7**. 163; preferred by Alexander to all other Persian cities, **7**. 169; description of, **7**. 197, 201; wall and hanging garden of, called one of the Seven Wonders of the world, **7**. 199; now almost deserted, **7**. 201; in ancient times the metropolis, **7**. 219; 4800 stadia from Thapsacus, **7**. 231; road from Syria to, **7**. 233

Babylon, a stronghold on the Nile, **8**. 85; now an encampment of three Roman legions, **8**. 87

Babylonia, **1**. 499; produces rice, **7**. 29; description of, **7**. 197–227; has set apart a special settlement for its philosophers, the Chaldaeans, **7**. 201; boundaries of, **7**. 203; rivers and canals in, **7**. 205–209; various products of, **7**. 215–217;

INDEX OF NAMES, PLACES, AND SUBJECTS

INDEX OF NAMES, PLACES, AND SUBJECTS

Barnichius River, the (see Enipeus River)

Barnus (Neretscha Planina) Mountain, the, in western Macedonia, whither runs the Egnatian Way, 3. 295

Barter (and money) in Lusitania, 2. 75; among the Scythians and other nomads, 3. 197; in Albania in Asia, 5. 227

Basgoedariza, a stronghold built by Mithridates, 5. 425

Basileius River, the, between the Euphrates and Tigris, 7. 233

Basoropeda in Media, annexed to Armenia, 5. 325

Bastarnians, the geographical position of, 1. 493; 3. 153; beyond Germany, 3. 173; called "Peucini" when they seized the island Peucê, 3. 217; of Germanic stock, 3. 221

Bastetania, in Iberia, where women dance with men, 2. 75; geographical position of, 2. 79, 103, 105; mountain-chain in, and mines of gold and other metals, 2. 81

Bastetanians (also called Bastulians), the, in Iberia, 2. 15; divisions of, 2. 19

Bastulians, the (see Bastetanians)

Bata, a city and harbour, in Asia, 5. 205, 207

Bathynias River, the, empties into the Propontis, 3. 379

Bathys Limen (Deep Harbour), near Aulis, 4. 289

Batiae, a town in Thesprotia, 3. 301

Batieia, in the Trojan Plain, called by the immortals "the tomb of much-bounding Myrina," 5. 493; mentioned by Homer, 6. 67; Myrina the Amazon buried at, 6. 163

Bato, the Daesitiatian leader, who fought the Romans in A.D. 6, put Bato the Breucian to death in A.D. 8, and shortly afterwards surrendered to the Romans, 3. 257

Bato (fl. second half of third century B.C.), born at Sinopê and author of *The Persica*, 5. 391

Bats, the, at Borsippa in Babylonia, much larger than elsewhere, and prepared for food, 7. 203

Battus, founder of Cyrenê (631 B.C.), 8. 203

Beans, the Aegyptian, found in the Acesines River in India, 7. 41

Bear, the Great, partially visible in arctic circle from certain points, 1. 9, 509

Bear, the Little, wholly inside arctic circle to people in Cinnamon-producing Country, 1. 507

Bears, the; the setting of, according to Deïmachus and others, 1. 287, 291

Beavers, found in Iberia, and yield medicinal castor inferior to that from beavers of the Pontus, 2. 107

Bebrycians, the, are in origin a Thracian tribe, 3. 177; in Asia, were Thracians, 5. 375; conquered by Mariandynus, 5. 377; colonised the parts about Abydus after the Trojan War, 6. 23; not mentioned by Homer, 6. 363

Beer, used by Lusitanian mountaineers, 2. 75; a kind of, made of grain and honey by inhabitants of Thulê, 2. 261; by the Ligures, 2. 265; used at Alexandria, 8. 57; made in a peculiar way by the Aegyptians, 8. 153

Bees, the, in Hyrcania, have hives in trees, as also in Matiana (in Media), and in Sacasenê and Araxenê (districts of Armenia), 1. 273, 5. 251; none in India, 7. 33

Beetle (*cantharos*), the, dies when it touches Cantharolethron near Olynthus, 3. 351

Beirut in Syria (see Berytus)

Belbina (Hagios Giorgios), the island, off Aegina in the high sea, 4. 179, 251; off Attica, 4. 271

Belgae, the, one of the three divisions of Transalpine Celtica, 2. 163; geographical position of, 2. 165; description of, 2. 235; bravest of the Celti, 2. 239; alone held out against the Cimbri and Teutones, 2. 241

Belion (or Limaeas) River, the, in Iberia, 2. 69

Bellerophon, caught the winged horse Pegasus at the spring Peirenê, 4. 195; the Palisade of, in Phrygia, 6. 191; fought against the Solymi, 6. 321

Bellerophontes (Bellerophon), set out from Lycia and "fought with the

INDEX OF NAMES, PLACES, AND SUBJECTS

269

INDEX OF NAMES, PLACES, AND SUBJECTS

with the Lacedaemonians under Epameinondas, almost gained the supremacy of Greece, fought with the Phocians and with the Macedonians, and is now in bad plight, **4.** 287; the dire results of earthquakes in, **4.** 301, 303; once ruled by Cecrops, being then called Cecropia, **4.** 307

Boeotian cities, the, are now, except Thespiae and Tanagra, only ruins or names, **4.** 319

Boeotians, the; dispute of, with Athenians, about Oropus, **1.** 245; naturally not fond of letters, **1.** 395; once called "Syes" ("swine"), according to Pindar, **3.** 287; once called Aonians, devastated Attica, **4.** 267; mostly under the command of the Phoenicians and the house of Cadmus, **4.** 283; war of, with the Thracians, **4.** 283–287; advised by the oracle at Dodona to commit an act of sacrilege, burnt up the priestess herself, **4.** 285; took possession of Orchomenus and Coroneia after the Trojan War, **4.** 323; conquered by Philip at Chaeroneia, **4.** 333; in the Trojan War, **4.** 407; call locusts "pornopion," **6.** 127

Boeotus, son of Melanippê the prisoner by Poseidon, at Metapontium, **3.** 53

Boerebistas, king of the Getans (see Byrebistas)

Boethus the Sidonian, Aristotelian philosopher and friend of Strabo, **7.** 271

Boethus, of Tarsus, bad poet and bad citizen, in power by favour of Antony for a time at Tarsus, **6.** 349

Boetylus (see Oetylus)

Boeüm, city of the Dorian Tetrapolis, **4.** 387

Boeüm, Mt., in Orestis, from which, according to some, one can see both the Aegaean Sea and the Ambracian Gulf, **3.** 329

Bogiodiatarus, by Pompey presented with Mithridatium in Pontus, **5.** 469

Bogus, king of Maurusia in Libya about 110 B.C.; neighbour to Aethiopians and visited by Eudoxus of Cyzicus, **1.** 383; urged by Eudox-

us to make expedition to India, **1.** 383, 389; ally of Antony, put to death at Methonê by Agrippa, **4.** 111; went up against the western Aethiopians, **8.** 165; kings of house of, held possession of Maurusia, being friendly to the Romans, **8.** 169

Bohemia (see Boihaemum)

Bohemians, the; Forest of (see Gabreta Forest)

Böhmer Wald, or Forest of the Bohemians (see Gabreta)

Boihaemum (cp. Bohemia), the domain of Marabodus, **3.** 155, 157

Boii, the, migrated across the Alps from Transalpine Celtica, **2.** 235; geographical position of, **2.** 281; one of the largest Celtic tribes, and driven out of Italy by the Romans, **2.** 311; opposed by the Cenomani in Roman battles, **2.** 323; the desert of, borders on the Lake of Constance, **3.** 165; in earlier times dwelt in the Hercynian Forest, **3.** 169; a Celtic tribe, **3.** 179, 253; destroyed by the Getans, **3.** 211; subdued by the Dacians, **3.** 253; virtually destroyed in wars with the Macedonians and the Romans, **3.** 263

Bolbê (Beschikgoel), Lake, **3.** 361

Bolbitine mouth of the Nile, the, **8.** 65, 67

Bologna in Italy (see Bononia)

Bolsena (see Volsinii)

Bolsena, Lake, near Volsinii, **2.** 367

Bombyces, the, a kind of reed-flute, **5.** 107

Bomians, the, in Aetolia, **5.** 29

Bonones, son of Phraates IV, sent by his father as hostage to Rome, **7.** 237, 239

Bononia (Bologna), not far from Ravenna, **2.** 327

Böos Aulê ("Cow's Stall"), a cave in Euboea, where Io is said to have given birth to Epaphus, **5.** 5

Boosura in Cypros, **6.** 381

Bordeaux (see Burdigala)

Boreas the North Wind, snatched up Oreithyia, the daughter of Erechtheus, **1.** 105, **3.** 175

Boreium, Cape, with Cephalae forms the mouth of the Great Syrtis, **8.** 201

Borkum the island (see Burchanis)

Bornfornello in Sicily (see Himera)

INDEX OF NAMES, PLACES, AND SUBJECTS

271

INDEX OF NAMES, PLACES, AND SUBJECTS

INDEX OF NAMES, PLACES, AND SUBJECTS

2. 227; expedition of Julius Caesar to, 2. 229; distance from, to mouths of rivers in Celtica, 320 stadia, 2. 231; an island near, on which sacrifices are made similar to those in Samothrace to Demeter and Corê, 2. 251; detailed description of, 2. 253–259; shape and dimensions of, 2. 253; products, exports, and physique of inhabitants of, 2. 255; conquered by Julius Caesar, 2. 257; islands near, 2. 259

Britannic (British) Islands, the; outside the Pillars, 1. 493

Britomartis, fled from violence of Minos, 5. 139; the temple of, at Cherronesus in Crete, 5. 143

Britons, the, taller than the Celti, make no cheese, and have no experience in agriculture, 2. 255; chieftains of, won friendship of Augustus and dedicated offerings in the Capitolium, 2. 257; readily submit to heavy duties on imports and exports, 2. 259

Briula in Asia, near Nysa, 6. 261

Brixia (Brescia), in Italy, 2. 311

Bromius, another name of Dionysus, 5. 101

Bronze vessels, found at Corinth, sold at high price at Rome, 4. 203

Brothers, Monuments of the Seven (mountain-peaks in Libya), 8. 165

Bructeri, the, defeated by Drusus in a naval battle on the Ems River, 3. 155; live near the ocean, 3. 159; captives from, led in triumphal procession at Rome, 3. 163

Brundusium (see Brentesium)

Brutii, the (see Bretii)

Bruttium (see Brettii, the), description of, 3. 11–49

Brutus, Decimus (b. about 84 B.C.); his flight from Mutina (43 B.C.), 2. 279

Brutus, D. Junius (consul 138 B.C.), surnamed Callaïcus (from victory over Callaïcans); subjected Lusitanians in Iberia, 2. 63; campaign of, in Iberia, ended at Baenis (Minho) River, 2. 69, 77

Brutus, M. (and Cassius), defeat of, at Philippi (42 B.C.), 3. 363

Bruzzano, Capo (see Zephyrium, Cape)

Bryanium, a populous city on the Erigon River, 3. 311

Brygi (or Brigi, q.v.), the, an Illyrian tribe, 3. 307; are the same people as the Bryges and Phrygians, 5. 403, 405

Bubali (apparently the antelope bubalis), in Maurusia in Libya, 8. 163

Bubastus, near the Delta of Aegypt, 8. 79

Bubon in Phrygia, 6. 193

Buca (Termoli), on the coast of the Frentani, 3. 135

Bucephalia, a city founded by Alexander in India, 7. 49

Bucephalus, favourite horse of Alexander, killed in India, 7. 49

Buchetium, a small town of the Cossopaeans in Thesprotia, 3. 301

Bucolopolis in Phoenicia, 7. 275

Budorus, Mt., in Salamis, 5. 9

Budorus River, the, in Euboea, 5. 9

Bull, a, led the way for Sabine colonists, 2. 465

Bull-fights, the, at Memphis in Aegypt, 8. 89

Bulls, the wild, in Aethiopia, 7. 337

Buprasis, the territory of Buprasium, occupied by Cauconians, 4. 55

Buprasium in Elis, mentioned by Homer, 4. 35, 37, 39; separated from Dymê by the Larisus River, 4. 225

Bura, engulfed because of earthquake, 1. 99, 219; one of the twelve cities in which the Achaeans settled, 4. 219; about 40 stadia above the sea, swallowed up by an earthquake, 4. 221

Burchanis (called by the Romans Fabaria; now Borkum), the island, subjugated by Drusus, 3. 159

Burdigala (Bordeaux), emporium of the Bituriges, 2. 215

Busiris, a city in Aegypt, maligned as inhospitable, 8. 69

Busiris, the tyrant or king in Aegypt who never existed, 8. 69

Bustards, numerous in Iberia, 2. 107

Buthrotum (Butrinto), on Pelodes Harbour in Epeirus, has Roman settlers, 3. 299

Buticê, Lake, in Aegypt, 8. 67

INDEX OF NAMES, PLACES, AND SUBJECTS

INDEX OF NAMES, PLACES, AND SUBJECTS

remaining inhabitants of other Epeirote cities to Nicopolis, **3.** 303; has put the Actian Games in great honour, **3.** 305; at Corinth, on his way to celebrate the Triumph after the victory at Actium, **5.** 165; friendship of, attained by Atropatian Media, **5.** 305; generals of, destroyed the fortress Artageras on the Euphrates, **5.** 327; set Amisus free after the Battle of Actium, **5.** 395; put Adiatorix and his second son to death, but appointed his eldest son priest of Comana in Cappadocia Pontica, **5.** 439; restored cities damaged by earthquakes in Asia Minor, **5.** 517; gave back the statue of Aias to the Rhoeteians in the Troad, **6.** 59, as also other statues to their owners, **6.** 61; appointed Marcus Pompey of Mitylenê Procurator of Asia, **6.** 145; pupil of Apollodorus of Gadara, **6.** 171; restored the colossal statues of Athenê and Heracles to the temple of Hera on Samos, but transferred that of Zeus to the Capitolium at Rome, **6.** 215; nullified extension of limits of precinct of temple of Artemis at Ephesus as place of refuge, **6.** 229; dedicated the *Aphroditê Anadyomenê* of Apelles to Julius Caesar, **6.** 289; friendship of, with Xenarchus of Seleuceia in Cilicia, **6.** 335; received gifts from King Pandion of India, **7.** 5; the Indian embassy to, **7.** 125, 127; on friendly terms with Phraates IV the king of the Parthians, **7.** 237; appointed Herod king of Judaea, **7.** 299; sent Aelius Gallus to explore Aethiopia, Arabia, and other places, **7.** 353; wished to win over, or subjugate, the Arabians, because of their wealth, **7.** 355; now appoints the priest in charge of the Museum at Alexandria, **8.** 35; exploits of, at Nicopolis near Alexandria, **8.** 43; pursued Antony and Cleopatra to Aegypt and put an end to her reign, **8.** 47; property of, in Aegypt, **8.** 49; appointed Cornelius Gallus first praefect of Aegypt, **8.** 135; statues of, pulled down by the

Aethiopians, **8.** 137; pardoned the Aethiopians and remitted the tributes, **8.** 141; gave Maurusia to Juba, **8.** 169; his division and administration of the Provinces, **8.** 213–215

Caesar, Germanicus (see Germanicus)

Caesar, Julius; made journey from Rome to Obulco in Iberia in 27 days, **2.** 97; defeated Afranius and Petreius, Pompey's generals, at Ilerda in Iberia, **2.** 99; generals of, fought by Sextus (Pompey) in Iaccetania, **2.** 101; his division of Transalpine Celtica (Gaul) into three parts, **2.** 165; Pompey's sedition against, **2.** 179; acted with moderation towards Massalia, **2.** 181; war of, against Vercingetorix, **2.** 219; navy-yard of, in Celtica, when he sailed to Britain, **2.** 227; destroyed 400,000 Elvetii, **2.** 229; defeated the Veneti, a tribe of the Belgae, in a naval battle, **2.** 235; his expedition to Britain, **2.** 253; won victories over the Britons, **2.** 257; added 5000 colonists to Comum, among them 500 notable Greeks, **2.** 311; builder of beautiful structures at Rome, **2.** 407; subdued Transalpine and Cisalpine Celtica, and Liguria, **3.** 143; planned an expedition against Byrebistas king of the Getans, **3.** 187 (cp. **3.** 211); restored Corinth, colonising it mostly with freedmen, **4.** 203; set free Amisus in Cappadocia Pontica, **5.** 395; greatly honoured Cleon the pirate, even appointing him priest of Comana in Pontus, **5.** 499; emulated Alexander in bestowing great honour upon Ilium, **6.** 55, 57; a friend to Mithridates the Pergamenian, **6.** 169; Trebonius, one of the murderers of, slain by Dolabella at Smyrna, **6.** 247; the *Aphroditê Anadyomenê* dedicated to, at Rome, by Augustus, **6.** 289; pupil of Athenodorus of Tarsus, **6.** 349; established Cleopatra as queen of Aegypt, having slain her young brother, **8.** 47; fought by Scipio and the elder Juba, **8.** 169; victories of, over Scipio, in Libya, **8.** 181

276

INDEX OF NAMES, PLACES, AND SUBJECTS

Caesar, Tiberius (Roman emperor A.D. 14–37); placed three legions over certain tribes in Iberia, **2.** 79; subjugated the Carni and Norici, **2.** 283; makes Augustus the model for his own administration and is assisted by his sons Germanicus and Drusus, **3.** 147; used an island in the Lake of Constance as a base of operations in his naval battle with the Vindelici, **3.** 163; saw the sources of the Ister at a day's journey from the Lake of Constance, **3.** 165; made Greater Cappadocia a Roman province, **5.** 349; restored places damaged by earthquakes, **5.** 517; Marcus Pompey of Mitylenē one of best friends of, **6.** 145; recently restored Sardeis, after the earthquakes, **6.** 179; sent by Augustus from Samos to Armenia, **8.** 141

Caesareia in Libya (see Iol)

Caesarium, the, at Alexandria. **8.** 39

Caesena, on the Aemilian Way, **2.** 327

Caïcus River, the, in Asia, **5.** 487; the Mysians settled above sources of, **5.** 489; geographical position and extent of, **6.** 5; outlets of, **6.** 103, 133; Teuthrania lies this side of **6.** 135; does not flow from Mt. Ida **6.** 137; borders on domain of Eurypylus, **6.** 153; flows past Pergamum, **6.** 169; Plain of, about the best land in Mysia, **6.** 169; Plain of, created by silt, **7.** 23

Caïetanus Sinus (Caïetan Kolpos; see Caïetas, Gulf of)

Caïta (Gaëta), in Italy, **2.** 397

Caïtas, the Gulf of, in Italy, **2.** 397; borders on the Caecuban Plain, **2.** 399

Calabrians (see Galabrii), the; country of, comprises one of the two parts of Iapygia, **3.** 103

Calachenē, in Assyria, **7.** 193

Calaguris, a city of the Vasconians, in Iberia, where Sertorius fought, **2.** 99

Calamine, obtained from Cyprian copper, **2.** 107

Calamis (fl. at Athens about 450 B.C.), made the colossal statue of Apollo in the temple of Apollo on the Apollonian isle in the Euxine, which was carried off to Rome by Lucullus, **3.** 277

Calanus, the Indian sophist, accompanied Alexander to Persis and perished on funeral pyre, **7.** 7, 109, 111; different accounts of, **7.** 119, 121

Calasarna in Leucania, **3.** 11

Calatia (Galazze), on the Appian Way, **2.** 461, **3.** 125

Calauria (Poros), the isle, in the Myrtoan Sea, **1.** 477; four stadia from the mainland and has a circuit of 130 stadia, **4.** 153; had an asylum sacred to Poseidon, and was given in exchange by Leto to Poseidon for Delos, **4.** 173

Calbis River, the, in the Peraea of the Rhodians, **6.** 265

Calchas, the seer; the temple of, in Daunia; description of worship at, **2.** 131; founded Selgē in Pisidia, **5.** 481; story of contest, grief, and death of, **6.** 233, 235; led from Troy the ancestors of the Pamphylians, but, according to Callinus, died at Clarus, **6.** 325; contest of, with Mopsus, **6.** 353

Caledonian boar, the, **4.** 197

Calendar, the, of the astronomers at Heliupolis, **8.** 85; and at Aegyptian Thebes, **8.** 125

Calenian wine, **2.** 437

Cales (Calvi), the city of the Caleni, in Campania, **2.** 413, 461

Caleti, the, in Celtica; geographical position of, **2.** 211, 233

Callaïcans, the, in Iberia; geographical position, and military prowess of, **2.** 65; by some formerly called Lusitanians, **2.** 67; modes of life of, **2.** 77; some of, live on west of the Celtiberians, **2.** 103; have no god, **2.** 109; formerly called Lusitanians, **2.** 121

Callaïcia, settled by companions of Teucer, **2.** 83

Callas (Xeropotamos) River, the, in Euboea, **5.** 7

Callatis (Mangalia), on the Euxine, **3.** 273, 277; colonised by Heracleia Pontica, **5.** 379

Calliarus in Locris, now a beautifully tilled plain, **4.** 383

Callias, the interpreter of Sappho and

INDEX OF NAMES, PLACES, AND SUBJECTS

INDEX OF NAMES, PLACES, AND SUBJECTS

279

INDEX OF NAMES, PLACES, AND SUBJECTS

INDEX OF NAMES, PLACES, AND SUBJECTS

2. 383; walled by the first founders of Rome, 2. 399; the works of art on the, 2. 409; received the most precious treasures of Mithridates, 5. 431; received the colossal statue of Zeus which had been in the temple of Hera on Samos, 6. 215

Capitulum (Piglio), above Praeneste, 2. 415

Capo dell' Armi (see Leucopetra, Cape)

Capo d'Orlando (see Agathyrnum)

Capo di Schiso (see Naxus)

Capo Spartivento (see Heracleium, Cape)

Cappadocia, position of, 1. 497; produces herbs out of which thorn-stuffs are woven, 2. 157; separated from Armenia by the Euphrates River, 5. 297; the annual tribute paid by, to Persia, 5. 313; description of, 5. 345–349; the tribes of, 5. 345; constitutes an isthmus, 5. 347; political divisions of, 5. 347; further description of, 5. 367–371; dimensions and fertility of, 5. 367; Sinopean earth and different kinds of stones found in, 5. 369; allowed by the Romans to choose their own kings, 5. 371

Cappadocia Pontica (or the Pontus), 5. 295, 349, 361; Mithridates Eupator established himself as king of, 5. 371

Cappadocia Proper, or the Greater, 5. 349, 369, 371, 449

Cappadocian kings, the line of the, failed, 3. 145

Cappadocians, the, distinguished from the Cataonians by the ancients, 5. 345; have the same language and usages as the Cataonians, 5. 347; greatly revere the Cataonian Apollo, 5. 357; empire of, attacked by Sisines in Strabo's Time, 5. 359; by Callisthenes called the " White Syrians," 5. 377; not mentioned by Homer, 5. 423, 6. 363, 367; called " White Syrians," 7. 193

Capreae (Capri), the isle, a fragment broken off from Promontory of Athenê in Italy, 1. 223; 3. 25; an isle off Campania, 1. 473; private property of Augustus, 2. 459

Capri (see Capreae)

Capria, Lake, in Pamphylia, 6. 325

Caprus, the harbour of Stageira, and the isle (Kapronisi) there, 3. 355, 359

Caprus River, the, in Assyria, 7. 197

Caprus River, the, in Phrygia, joins the Maeander at Laodiceia, 5. 511, 7. 197

Capua (Santa Maria di Capua, now in ruins, not the Capua of to-day), capital of the Tyrrhenians, 2. 435, 459; on the Appian Way, 3. 125

Capua, the modern (see Casilinum)

Capyae, near Mantaneia in Arcadia, by some said to have been founded by Aeneias, 6. 107

Capys, after whom Capyae in Arcadia was named, 6. 107

Caracoma, a little town opposite Samothrace, 3. 369

Caralis, a city in Sardinia, 2. 361

Carambis (Kerembe), Cape, in Paphlagonia, 1. 479; lies opposite Cape Criumetopon, 3. 235, 5. 205, and with it divides the Euxine into two seas, 5. 387; 700 stadia from Sinopê, 5. 391

Carana in Cappadocia Pontica, 5. 443

Carbo, Gnaeus (consul 113 B.C.); his battle with the Cimbri, 2. 319

Carcathiocerta, the royal city of Sophenê in Asia, 5. 321

Carcinites Gulf (also called Tamyracê, now Karkinit Bay), the, in the Euxine, 3. 229, 241

Cardaces, the, in Persia, 7. 181

Cardamum, a kind of cress in Persia, 7. 181

Cardamylê(Skardamula), the Homeric in Laconia, 4. 109; situated on a rock, 4. 113; one of the seven cities promised by Agamemnon to Achilles, 4. 115

Cardia on the Melas Gulf, founded by Milesians and Clazomenians, later refounded by the Athenians, 3. 373, 375

Carduchians, the, in Asia (see Gordyaeans)

Carenitis, annexed to Armenia, 5. 325; the country in Cappadocia Pontica formerly held by Ateporix, 5. 443

Caresenê, extends alongside Dardania, 6. 87, 89

Caresus in the Troad, now deserted, 6. 89

Caresus River, the, mentioned by

INDEX OF NAMES, PLACES, AND SUBJECTS

INDEX OF NAMES, PLACES, AND SUBJECTS

INDEX OF NAMES, PLACES, AND SUBJECTS

Cenchrius River, the, near Ephesus, **6.** 223

Cenomani, the, live in Transpadana, and used to help the Romans in their battles, **2.** 323

Census, the Roman, in Iberia, **2.** 131; of Patavium in Italy, **2.** 313

Centaurs, certain of the, washed off poison in the Anigrus River and gave it an offensive odour, **4.** 61; tomb of, on Taphiassus, a hill in Aetolia, **4.** 385; driven to the land of the Aethices on Mt. Pindus, **4.** 417; forced from Mt. Pelion by Peirithoüs, **4.** 439

Centoripa (or Centuripae, now Centorbi), in Sicily, restored by Augustus, **3.** 79; lies above Catana, **3.** 81, near the town Aetna, **3.** 87

Ceos, the city, on Ceos, lies 25 stadia from the sea, **5.** 169

Ceos, the island, one of the Cyclades, once ruled by the Eretrians, **5.** 17; Simonides and other famous men natives of, **5.** 169

Cephalae, Cape, forms the western boundary of the Great Syrtis, being 5000 stadia from Carthage, **8.** 195

Cephallenia, the island, off the Corinthian Gulf, **1.** 477; not more than eighty stadia from Cape Chelonatas, **4.** 27 ("eight" there is an error for "eighty")

Cephallenians, the; with Odysseus at Troy, **4.** 255; Laertes lord over, **5.** 31, 33; all subjects of Odysseus so called, **5.** 35; by some called "Taphians" and Teleboans, but were subject to Odysseus, **5.** 47

Cephaloedis (Cephaloedium) in Sicily, **3.** 81

Cephaloedium (or Cephaloedis, now Cephalu), in Sicily, 30 Roman miles from Alaesa, **3.** 57, 81

Cephalon, native of Gergithes in the territory of Cymê, **6.** 37

Cephalus, the son of Deïoneus, said to have leaped off Cape Leucatas into the sea, **5.** 33; expedition of, to Cephallenia, **5.** 47; an exile from Athens, reigned over Taphos and Cephallenia, **5.** 61; said to have gained the mastery over Acarnania, and to have been the first to leap off Cape Leucatas, **5.** 67

Cephisia, one of the twelve cities in Attica settled by Cecrops, **4.** 267

Cephissis (or Hylicê), Lake, near Lake Copaïs, and between Thebes and Anthedon, is filled from Lake Copaïs through subterranean channels, **4.** 309

"Cephissis Lake"; the name applied by Pindar to Lake Copaïs, **4.** 323

Cephissus, the fountain, at Apollonia near Epidamnus, **4.** 375

"Cephissus," the name of six different rivers, **4.** 375

Cephissus River, the, in Attica; description of course of, **4.** 275, 277, 375

Cephissus River, the, in Boeotia, empties near Larymna, **4.** 297; supplies Lake Copaïs, goes underground, and issues forth again near Upper Larymna, **4.** 305; the sources (at Lilaea in Phocis) and course of, **4.** 307, 309, 373; receives the waters of the Pindus River near Lilaea, **4.** 387

Cephissus River, the, n Salamis, **4.** 375

Cephissus River, the, in Scyros, **4.** 375

Cephissus River, the, in Sicyon, **4.** 375

Cephissus River, the; Parapotamii in Phocis situated on, **4.** 373; winding course of, described by Hesiod, **4.** 375

Cepi, near the Cimmerian Bosporus, **5.** 199

Ceprano (see Fregellae)

Ceramus, a town near Cnidus, **6.** 283

Cerasus in Cappadocia Pontica, **5.** 399

Cerata ("Horns") Mountains, the, between Megaris and Attica, **4.** 257

Ceratia (carob or locust tree), the, found in abundance in Aethiopia, **8.** 145

Ceraunia (apparently an error for "Cerynia"), situated on a high rock near Aegium in Achaea, **4.** 223

Ceraunian Mountains, the; distance from to Corcyra, Leucas, and the Peloponnesus, **1.** 405; with Cape Iapygia bar the mouth of the Ionian Gulf, **3.** 117; voyage from, to Brundisium, **3.** 125; where the Ionian Gulf and the Adriatic begin, **3.** 267, 277, 299, 307; in Asia, a part of the Caucasian Mountains so called, **5.** 223, 233

INDEX OF NAMES, PLACES, AND SUBJECTS

INDEX OF NAMES, PLACES, AND SUBJECTS

Charmides, the father of Pheidias the great sculptor, **4**. 89

Charmoleon of Massalia, host of Poseidonius in Liguria, **2**. 113

Charmothas Harbour, the, in the Arabian Gulf; description of, **7**. 345

Charon of Lampsacus (lived about 460 B.C.), on the boundaries of the Troad, **6**. 9; the historian (author of a *Persian History* and *Annals of the Lampsaceni*, **6**. 37

Charondas, ancient lawgiver of Catana; laws of, used by the Mazaceni in Cappadocia, **5**. 367

Charonia (or Plutonia, *q.v.*), the, at Acharaca in Nysaïs, near Magnesia and Myus, and at Hierapolis in Phrygia, **5**. 513

Charonium (cp. Plutonia), the, near Thymbria in Caria, a sacred cave which emits deadly vapours, **6**. 211; at Acharaca near Nysa in Caria, **6**. 259

Charybdis, a monstrous and destructive deep, **3**. 67, 77, 159; infested by brigands, **1**. 73; substantially correct account of, given by Homer, **1**. 91

Charybdis, a chasm in Syria into which the Orestes flows, **3**. 93

Chatramotitae, the, in Arabia, **7**. 311

Chatramotitis in Arabia, produces myrrh, **7**. 311

Chatti, the, an indigent German tribe, **3**. 159; captives from, led in triumphal procession at Rome, **3**. 161, 163

Chattuarii, the, an indigent German tribe, **3**. 159; captives from, led in triumphal procession at Rome, **3**. 163

Chaubi, the, a German tribe near the ocean, **3**. 159

Chaulotaeans, the, in Arabia, **7**. 309

Chazenê, in Assyria, **7**. 193

Cheese, on island near Gades, made of milk mixed with water, **2**. 133; not made in Britain, **2**. 255; made in the Alps, **2**. 283; made in Attica, not touched by priestess of Athenê Polias, **4**. 257; the Salonian, from Salon in Bithynia, **5**. 463; used by the Aethiopians, **8**. 143; and by the Masaesylians, **8**. 189

Cheimerium, Cape, in Epeirus, **3**. 299

Cheirocrates (Deinocrates?), completed the restoration of the temple of Artemis at Ephesus, and proposed to Alexander to fashion Mt. Athos in his likeness, **6**. 227

Chelidonia in Phrygia; the road through, **6**. 309

Chelidonian Isles (Khelidonia), the, at the beginning of the coast of Pamphylia, **5**. 295; off Lycia, form the beginning of the Taurus, **6**. 263, 319; 1900 stadia from Cypros, **6**. 377

Chelonatas, Cape, the most westerly point of the Peloponnesus, **4**. 25; lies 180 stadia from Cephallenia, **5**. 51

Chelonophagi (" Turtle-eaters "), the, in Aethiopia, **7**. 329

Chersicrates, left by Archias to colonise Corcyra, **3**. 71, after driving out the Liburnians, **3**. 73

Chersiphron, first architect of the temple of Artemis at Ephesus, **6**. 225

Cherso Island (see Apsyrtides)

Chersonesus, a stronghold slightly to the west of Alexandria, **8**. 57

Chersonesus in Crete, the seaport of Lyctus, has the temple of Britomartis, **5**. 143

Chersonesus, the Great (the Tauric Chersonese, now the Crimea), **3**. 225, 229, 231, 233; similar to the Peloponnesus in size and shape, and ruled by the potentates of the Bosporus, **3**. 241; mostly level, exceedingly fertile, yielding thirty-fold, paid enormous tribute to Mithridates, and supplied the Greeks with grain and fish, **3**. 243; the isthmus of, fortified by Asander against the Scythians, **3**. 245

Chersonesus Heracleotica (or Heracleia) in the Crimea, **3**. 231

Chersonesus, the Little, a part of the Great Chersonesus (the Crimea), **3**. 233

Chersonesus, the New, a city on the Little Chersonesus in the Crimea, **3**. 233; subject to the present day to the potentates of the Bosporus, **3**. 233; the wall of, and the salt-works near, **3**. 247

Chersonesus, the Old, in the Crimea now in ruins, **3**. 233

INDEX OF NAMES, PLACES, AND SUBJECTS

INDEX OF NAMES, PLACES, AND SUBJECTS

INDEX OF NAMES, PLACES, AND SUBJECTS

and could be traversed only with difficulty by Hannibal, **2.** 329;

Cisses (the Homeric), apparently the ruler of Cissus in Macedonia, **3.** 343, 349

Cissus, one of the cities destroyed by Cassander, **3.** 343, 349

Cissus, father of Althaemenes and coloniser of Argos after the return of the Heracleidae, **4.** 235, **5.** 149

Cis-Tauran regions of Asia, the, **1.** 495, **5.** 189, 295

Cisterns, the, at Rome, **2.** 405

Cisthenê, a deserted city with a harbour outside the Gulf of Adramyttium, **6.** 103

Cisthenê, an island off Lycia, **6.** 319

Citaris, the Median, **5.** 313

Cithaeron, Mt., joins the mountains of Megara and Attica, bends into the plains and ends near Thebes, **4.** 301, 313; Plataeae lies at foot of, **4.** 325

Cithara (see Lyre), the; the Asiatic, **5.** 109; played by Arion and Terpander, **6.** 145

Citharists, and flute-players, played the accompaniment to the Pythian Nome at Delphi, **4.** 363

Citharoedes, the, sang paeans at Delphi in honour of Apollo, **4.** 361, 363

Citharus, the, a fish indigenous to the Nile, **8.** 149

Citium in Cypros, home of Zeno the Stoic and Apollonius the physician, **6.** 379

Citrum, the Roman name of Pydna (*q.v.*) in Macedonia, **3.** 341

Cius, a companion of Heracles, founded the city of Cius in Asia, **5.** 457

Cius (see Prusias, the city), **5.** 453, 455

Civilisation, the development of, according to Plato, **6.** 47, 49

Civita Tommasa (see Foruli)

Clanis (Chiana) River, the (see Liris River), sources of the, **2.** 287; runs through Tyrrhenia, **2.** 403

Clarus near Colophon in Asia, **6.** 233, where the seer Calchas is said to have died, **6.** 325

Clastidium (Casteggio), near the Aemilian Way, **2.** 327

Claterna, on the Aemilian Way, **2.** 327

Claudius, Publius Pulcher, Roman tribune, sent Marcus Cato to take Cypros away from King Ptolemy, **6.** 385

Clautenatii, the; one of the boldest tribes of the Vindelici, **2.** 281

Clazomenae, once an island, **1.** 217

Clazomenae in Asia, founded by Paralus, **6.** 201; the Old and New, **6.** 245

Clazomenians, the, on Lake Maeotis; with Milesians founded Cardia, **3.** 373; engage in fishing, **5.** 195; live on an isthmus, **6.** 239

Cleandria in the Troad, **6.** 89

Cleandridas, an exile from Lacedaemon, served as general for the Thurii, **3.** 51

Cleantacidae, the; tyrants of Mitylenê, **6.** 143

Cleanthes, the Corinthian; famous paintings of, entitled the "Capture of Troy" and the "Birth of Athenê," in the temple of Artemis near the mouth of the Alpheius River, **4.** 49

Cleanthes, the Stoic philosopher and successor of Zeno, a native of Assus, **6.** 115

Cleides, the, two isles off Cypros, **6.** 375, 377, 379, 383

Cleitarchus the historian, who accompanied Alexander the Great on his Asiatic expedition; on the saltrock in India, **2.** 357; on the danger of the tides on the coast of Celtica, **3.** 167; on the isthmus of Asia Minor, **5.** 187; on the birds used in processions in India, **7.** 123

Cleitor (Palaeopoli near Kliteras) in Arcadia, no longer exists, **4.** 229

Cleobulus, one of the Seven Wise Men, a native of Lindus in Rhodes, **6.** 279

Cleochares, the rhetorician, a native of Myrleïa in Bithynia, **5.** 467

Cleomachus the pugilist, imitated the dialect and mannerisms of the *cinaedi*, **6.** 253

Cleombrotus, supposed founder of Heraea in Arcadia, **4.** 21

Cleon, chieftain of bands of robbers on the Mysian Olympus in Strabo's time; useful to Antony, later joined Caesar's side, and even received the priesthood of Comana, **5.** 497, 499

INDEX OF NAMES, PLACES, AND SUBJECTS

INDEX OF NAMES, PLACES, AND SUBJECTS

Romans got a remission of 100 talents of the appointed tribute in return for the *Aphroditê Anadyomenê* of Apelles, **6.** 289

" Cobialus," " Aegialus " (the Paphlagonian) emended to, by some, **5.** 387

Cobus the Treran Chief; expeditions of, **1.** 227

Cocalus, the Sicilian king who harboured Daedalus when in flight from Minos, **3.** 85; at whose home Minos died, **3.** 109

Cocceius, constructed the tunnels from Avernus to Cumae and from Dicaearchia to Neapolis, **2.** 445

" Cocces " (" Scarlet "), nickname of the Ptolemy from Syria, **8.** 37

Coccus (the kermes-berry), used for dyeing, **6.** 189

Codridae, the, led an Ionian colony from Athens to Caria and Lydia, **4.** 209, 211

Codrus, the son of Melanthus, and king of Attica when the Heracleidae invaded it, **4.** 249; father of Androclus the leader of the Ionian colonisation, and of several bastards who founded cities in Asia, **6.** 199, 201; Megara founded after death of, **6.** 271

" Codrus," a barbarian name, **3.** 287

" Coela " (" Hollows "), the, of Euboea, **5.** 5

Coelê (" Hollow ") Elis (see Elis), **4.** 21

Coelius, Lucius Antipater (b. about 175 B.C.), the Roman historian; says that Rome was founded by Greeks, **2.** 385

Coeüs, the father of Leto, **5.** 163

Coffins, of clay, in Aethiopia, **8.** 147

Cogaeonum, Mt. (now Mt. Gogany? or Mt. Kaszon), a sacred mountain among the Getans, **3.** 187

Cohortes vigilum, the; a city-militia at Rome, composed of freedmen, **2.** 403

Cohorts, nine Roman, stationed in Aegypt, **8.** 49; three at Syenê, **8.** 129

Colapis (Kulpa) River, the, joins the Saüs near Segestica, **2.** 289; meets the Danuvius near the country of the Scordisci, **3.** 255

Colchians, the; Homer's knowledge of, **1.** 75; founded Pola (Polae), an Italian city, **1.** 169, **2.** 323; in the Mithridatic War, **5.** 207; by some writers said to be akin to the Aegyptians, **5.** 211; hold a part of the Moschian country, **5.** 215

Colchis, made known to geographers by Mithridates, **1.** 51; wealth and geographical position of, **1.** 167; lies at the foot of the Caucasian Mountains, **5.** 191; produces bitter honey, but is noted for its linen, hemp, wax, and pitch, **5.** 211; fame and history of, **5.** 213; borders on Armenia, **5.** 323; and on Cappadocia, **5.** 345; the sea-coast as far as, annexed to Cappadocia Pontica by Mithridates, **5.** 371, 425

Coldui (Coaduï?), the, a tribe of the Suevi, **3.** 155

Collatia (Castellaccio), **2.** 383

Colline Gate, the, at Rome, **2.** 401

Colobi, Grove of, near the Arabian Gulf, **7.** 323, 327

Coloê, Lake, near Sardeis (the Homeric Gygae, *q.v.*), where is the temple of Coloënian Artemis, **6.** 173; where are the monuments of the kings, **6.** 177; said to be an artificial lake, **6.** 199

Colonae, a place in the Erythraean territory in Ionia, **6.** 35

Colonae on the outer Hellespontine sea, birthplace of the Cycnus who was slain by Achilles, **6.** 35, 95

Colonae near Lampsacus, a colony of the Milesians, **6.** 35

Colonae, in Phocis, **6.** 35

Colonae, in Thessaly, **6.** 35

Colonies, numerous, sent out from Chalcis and Eretria, **5.** 13

Colony, the Roman, at Eporedia (Ivrea), **2.** 279; at Comum, **2.** 311

Colophon, city in Asiatic Ionia, founded by Andraemon of Pylus, **6.** 199; whither the Smyrnaeans fled for refuge, **6.** 203; position and history of, **6.** 233–237; famous men of, **6.** 235; Homer a native of, according to some, **6.** 237

Colophonians, the, in Asia had notable naval and cavalry forces, **6.** 235

Colos, the, an animal in Scythia

INDEX OF NAMES, PLACES, AND SUBJECTS

INDEX OF NAMES, PLACES, AND SUBJECTS

"Convenae," the, in Aquitania, **2.** 217; given the "Latin right" by the Romans, **2.** 219

Copae, mentioned by Homer, **4.** 305; the region of, forms the deepest recess of Lake Copaïs, and hence the name of the latter, **4.** 321, 323

Copaïs, Lake, cities on, swallowed up, **1.** 219; filled by the Cephissus River, and partly drained by Crates the mining engineer from Chalcis, **4.** 305; receives the waters of the Cephissus, Permessus and Olmeius Rivers, **4.** 307; has a circuit of 360 stadia, **4.** 309; names of various cities around, **4.** 321–341; in early times had no common name, but several restricted names, but later the restricted name Copaïs (from "Copae") prevailed, **4.** 321; dry ground and tilled when owned by the Orchomenians, **4.** 339; the Cephissus River empties into, **4.** 373

Cophes River, the, in India, **7.** 45, 47

Cophus Harbour, the, near Cape Derrhis in Macedonia, **3.** 353

Copiae (Torre Brodognato), the later name of Thurii, **3.** 47

Copper (and gold) mined at Cotinae in Iberia, **2.** 25; greatest quantity and best quality of, in Turdetania, **2.** 39; of Cypros alone yields calamine, chalcanthite, and spodium, **2.** 107; once mined in the Lelantine Plain in Euboea, **5.** 13; abundant in the land of the Massagetae in Asia, **5.** 267; abundant in mines at Tamassus in Cypros, **6.** 383; used in India, **7.** 123

Copper, found on the island Meroê in the Nile, **8.** 143

Copper mine, the, at Temesa in Italy, **3.** 17; the fame of, **5.** 411; above Cisthenê in Asia Minor, **6.** 103; in Carmania, **7.** 153; in Masaesylia in Libya, **8.** 177

Copper, mountain-, prepared at Andeira in Asia Minor, **6.** 115

Copper vessel and scourge, the, at Dodona in Thesprotia, **3.** 325

Copratas River, the, in Persis, **7.** 163

Copria ("Dung-hill") in Sicily (see Tauromenian shore)

Coptus, a city common to the Aegyptians and the Arabians, and great emporium, from which a road runs to Berenicê, **8.** 119–121

Cora (Cori), in Italy, **2.** 413

Coracesium, a fortress in Cilicia Tracheia, **6.** 325, 331; used as base of operations by Diodotus Tryphon, **6.** 327

Coracinus, the, a fish indigenous to the Nile, **8.** 149

Coracius, Mt., near Colophon in Asia, sacred to Artemis, **6.** 237

Coralis, Lake, in Lycaonia, 5. 475

"Coralius" River, the, the name wrongly applied to the Cuarius by Alcaeus, **4.** 323, 329

Coralli, the, a brigandish tribe in the neighbourhood of the Haemus Mountain, **3.** 275

Corassiae, the islands, among the Sporades, **5.** 173

Coraüs, Fortress and Hunting-ground of, near the Arabian Gulf, **7.** 323

Corax (Vardusia), Mt., in Aetolia, **3.** 327, **4.** 345, **5.** 27

Corbianê, a province of Elamaïs in Asia, **7.** 223

Corbilo, on the Liger River in Celtica, **2.** 215

Corcoras (Gurk) River, the, flows past Nauportus, **2.** 289, **3.** 255

Corcyra (Corfu); distance from, to Leucas and the Ceraunian Mountains, **1.** 405, and to Ithaca, **1.** 409; off the coast of Epeirus, **1.** 475; colonised by Chersicrates, companion of Archias, **3.** 73; identified by Callimachus with Scheria, the Isle of the Phaeacians, **3.** 193; the western extremity and eastern headland of, **3.** 299; according to some, was a part of Macedonia, **3.** 309; ruined by wars and became a proverbial joke, **3.** 327

Corcyra, Black (Curzola), founded by the Cnidians, lies near the Pleraei, **3.** 261, 263

Corcyraeans, the, founded Epidamnus (Dyrrachium, now Durazzo), and, with the Corinthians, Apollonia (Pollina), **3.** 265; the copper scourge of, at Dodona, **3.** 325

Corduba, founded by Marcellus, **2.** 21; distance to, from the sea, 1200

299

stadia, 2. 23; through which runs the main road, 2. 97

Cordylê, the, a kind of fish in the Euxine off Pharnacia, 5. 403

Corê (Persephonê), Proserpina, sacrifices to, in Samothrace and in island near Britain, 2. 251; used to visit neighbourhood of, to gather flowers, 3. 19; trampled underfoot Minthê the concubine of Hades in Triphylia, 4. 51; worshipped there, 4. 53

Corebus, the Eleian, victor at Olympia in the first Olympiad, 4. 93

Coressia in Ceos, 5. 169

Coressus, Mt., near Ephesus, 6. 203, 225

Corfinium (Pentima), whither the Valerian Way runs, 2. 415; the metropolis of the Peligni, 2. 431

Corfu (see Corcyra)

Corinth; a tyrant of, was betrothed to, and murdered, Rhadinê of Samus in Triphylia, 4. 65; Cypselus, the tyrant of, dedicated the Zeus of beaten gold at Olympia, 4. 89; destroyed, but rebuilt by the Romans, 4. 121; once subject to Agamemnon, 4. 167; "wealthy," 4. 185; description and history of, 4. 189–203; the "key" of the Peloponnesus, 4. 189; the temple of Aphroditê at, with 1000 courtesans, 4. 191; including Acrocorinthus, about 85 stadia in circuit, 4. 193; the two harbours of, 4. 197; rased to the ground by Mummius, 4. 199; pitied by Polybius, 4. 201; restored by Julius Caesar, 4. 203; in proverb called "beetle-browed," 4. 205; added by Aratus to the Achaean League, 4. 217; colonised by Aletes after return of Heracleidae, 4. 235; persuaded the Heracleidae to make an expedition against Attica, 4. 249; and Calchis, by Philip called "the fetters of Greece," 4. 391; Comana in Cappadocia Pontica likened to, because of its multitude of courtesans, 5. 439; remained desolate about as long as Carthage, 8. 189

Corinth, Gulf of, water-level of, thought to be higher than that of the Aegaean Sea, 1. 201, 3. 297;

description of, and of cities on, 4. 15–19; 2100 stadia in perimeter from the Evenus to Cape Araxus, 4. 17; begins at mouth of the Achelöus River, 4. 25; Mychus Harbour considered by some the inmost recess of, but the inmost is at Pagae and Oenoê, 4. 317

Corinth, Isthmus of; canal through attempted by Demetrius, 1. 201; inscribed pillar erected on, as boundary between Ionia and the Peloponnesus, 2. 139; distant 1030 stadia from Cape Araxus (Kalogria), 4. 19; narrowest at the "Diolcus," 4. 155

Corinthia, extends from Sicyonia to the isthmus, 4. 15; lies on the Crisaean Gulf, 4. 195; the Nemea River a boundary of, 4. 207

Corinthians, the, with the Corcyraeans founded Apollonia (Pollina) in Illyria, 3. 265; founded Potidaea, 3. 349; Tenea revolted from, 4. 199; sided with Philip and insulted the Romans, but suffered the destruction of Corinth by Mummius, 4. 199; conquered at Chaeroneia by Philip, 4. 333; dug canal through isthmus of Leucas, 5. 33

Coriscus, the Socratic philosopher, native of Scepsis, 6. 111

Cornel-wood, the, of which javelins are made, 5. 483

Cornelius Gallus (d. 26 B.C.), the first man to be appointed praefect of Aegypt, by Augustus, and took Heröonpolis with only a few soldiers, 8. 135

Corneto (see Tarquinia)

Corocondamê, a village on the Cimmerian Bosporus, 5. 197. 205

Corocondamitis, Lake, near the Cimmerian Bosporus, 5. 199

Coronaeis, the; inhabitants of Coronê in Messenê called, 4. 325

Coronê (Petalidi) in Messenia, by some writers identified with the Homeric Pedasus, 4. 117; inhabitants of, called Coronaeis, 4. 325

Coroneia (Camari) the Homeric, in Boeotia; the Cephissus River flows near, 4. 307; lies near Lake Copaïs, 4. 321; description and history of, 4. 323; inhabitants of,

INDEX OF NAMES, PLACES, AND SUBJECTS

INDEX OF NAMES, PLACES, AND SUBJECTS

INDEX OF NAMES, PLACES, AND SUBJECTS

INDEX OF NAMES, PLACES, AND SUBJECTS

INDEX OF NAMES, PLACES, AND SUBJECTS

INDEX OF NAMES, PLACES, AND SUBJECTS

Datis the Persian general; army of, utterly destroyed by Miltiades at Marathon, 4. 273

Datum (see Philippi) in Macedonia, has dockyards and gold mines, 3. 355, 359 (see footnote 4)

Daulia (see Daulis)

Daulians, the; boundary of territory of, 4. 373

Daulis (or Daulia) in Phocis, once held by Tereus the Thracian, 3. 287; belongs to Phocis, 4. 343; scene of the mythical story of Philomela and Procnê, 4. 369

Daunia in Italy, has hero-temples of Calchas and Podaleirius, 3. 131

Daunians, the, in Apulia; historical and mythical accounts of, 2. 319; a tribe of the Apuli, 2. 433, 3. 103; co-operated with the Tarantini against the Messapians, 3. 117; the mule-road through country of, 3. 123; geographical position of, 3. 127, 129; language of, 3. 135

"Daüs," the name given a Dacian slave in Attica, 3. 213

Dead Sea, the (see Asphaltites Lake)

Debae, a tribe in Arabia, consisting partly of nomads and partly of farmers, 7. 345

Decaeneus, priest and god of the Getans in the time of Julius Caesar, 3. 187; wizard and prognosticator, 3. 211; diviner of Byrebistas and contemporary of Strabo; regarded as god by the Getans, 7. 289

Deceleia (Taτόϊ), deme of Attica, the base of operations of the Peloponnesians in the Deceleian War, 4. 263; one of the twelve cities in Attica settled by Cecrops, 4. 267

Deceleian War, the, 4. 263

Decietae, the, a tribe of the Ligures, 2. 265

Deer; numerous in Iberia, 2. 107; a peculiar animal like a, in the Alps, 2. 289; those among the Eneti herd with wolves, 2. 321; in the Scythian marshes (see Colos), 3. 249; found in Arabia, 7. 343

Degmenus the Epeian champion, defeated by Pyraechmes the Aetolian champion, 4. 103

Deïaneira, wife of Heracles; the painting of Heracles in torture in the robe of, at Corinth, 4. 201; attempted violation of, by Nessus in Aetolia, 5. 29; the daughter of Oeneus, 5. 57

Deïmachus, ambassador of Antiochus Soter (reigned 281–262 B.C.) to Allitrochades, king of Palimbothra in India, and author of a work on India, which was thoroughly discredited by Strabo but quoted approvingly by Hipparchus, 1. 257, 263, 265; estimates distance to pass that leads over to Bactriana and Sogdiana, 1. 273; on certain distances, 1. 279; on the geographical position of the Bactrians, 1. 285; on the tropics, 1. 289; says the Bears do not set in India, 1. 291; on the size of India, 7. 19

Deinocrates (see Cheirocrates)

Deïoneus, father of the Cephalus who leaped off Cape Leucatas into the sea, 5. 33, 47, 61

Deïotarus, the son of Castor and surnamed Philadelphus, the last king of Paphlagonia, 5. 453

Deïotarus, one of the twelve tetrarchs of the Galatians and appointed king of Galatia by Pompey, and presented by Pompey with a part of Gazelonitis, and with Pharnacia and Trapezusia, 5. 393, 469; Blucium the royal residence of, 5. 471; slayer of his son-in-law Castor and of his own daughter, 5. 473

Deïphontes, colonised the region about Actê in Argolis after the return of the Heracleidae, 4. 235

Deirê, Cape, at mouth of Arabian Gulf, 7. 313, 327

Delians, the, invoke an Apollo "Ulius" (god of "healing"), 6. 207

Delium (Dilisi) in Boeotia, 4. 149; the sanctuary of Apollo near Tanagra, 30 stadia from Aulis, 4. 289

Delium in Laconia, sacred to Apollo, 4. 149

Dellius, companion of Antony, wrote an account of his expedition against the Parthians, 5. 305

Delos, given in exchange by Poseidon to Leto for Calauria, 4. 173; reproduction of temple of Apollo in, at Delium in Boeotia, 4. 289; where are the temple of Apollo and the

311

INDEX OF NAMES, PLACES, AND SUBJECTS

Letoüm, and where Apollo and Artemis were born, **5.** 163; famous for its festivals, **5.** 165; famous as a commercial centre, **5.** 167; the great slave-market in, **6.** 329

Delphi (Pytho), invaded by Brennus the Prausan, **2.** 205; treasures from, at Tolosa, **2.** 207; treasury of the Spinitae at, **2.** 315; the treasury of the Agyllaei at, **2.** 341; Chalcidians emigrated from, and founded Rhegium, **3.** 21; dedications of Metapontium at, **3.** 51; temple of Apollo at, adorned by Lipara, the Liparaean Isle, **3.** 95; the myths about, **3.** 315; given in exchange by Poseidon to Apollo for Cape Taenarum, **4.** 173; temple at, robbed by the Phocians, **4.** 287; the offering taken to, by the Pythaïstae from Athens, **4.** 295; description of, **4.** 347-369; most famous city in Phocis, **4.** 347; temple at, has priority of age, is a rocky, theatrelike place, **4.** 349; has a circuit of 16 stadia, **4.** 351; description of the seat of the oracle at, **4.** 353; temple at, had the most truthful of all oracles, is the centre of Greece as a whole, was believed to be at the centre of the inhabited world, and was easy of access for the Greeks as a whole, **4.** 355; the temple of, in earlier times rich in treasures but now plundered and poor, **4.** 359; the contests at, **4.** 361; founding of the oracle at, by Apollo, **4.** 365, and slaying of the Dragon by, **4.** 367; the oracle of Apollo at, often consulted by the ancients, **7.** 287

Delphians, the, were indigenous inhabitants of Parnassus in olden times, **4.** 365; induced by the Lacedaemonians to revolt from the common organisation of the Phocians (about 457 B.C.), **4.** 371

Delphinium, the Sacred Harbour, at Oropus, **4.** 289

Delta, the Aegyptian, "gift of the Nile," **1.** 111 (see other references *s.v.* "Herodotus"); description of, **8.** 13-15; boundaries of, **8.** 65

Demaratus (father of Tarquinius Priscus), once in power at Corinth, fled

to Tarquinii in Italy and became its ruler, **2.** 339, **4.** 191

Demes, the, in Attica, are 170, or 174, in number, **4.** 263; several named, **4.** 271

Demeter, sacrifices to, in Samothrace, and sacrifices similar thereto in island near Britain, **2.** 251; the temple of, at Enna in Sicily, **3.** 81; the sacred grove of, in Triphylia, **4.** 51; temple of there, **4.** 53; the Eleusinian, welcomed the serpent Cychreides to Eleusis, **4.** 253, 257, and descendants of King Codrus and his son Androclus superintend sacrifices in honour of, **6.** 199; worshipped by the assemblymen of the Amphictyonic League, **4.** 357, 393; the leader-in-chief, or genius, of, called Iacchus, **5.** 95; the ministers of, **5.** 97

Demetrias (Goritza) in Magnesia in Thessaly, called one of the three "shackles of Greece," **4.** 391, since it commanded Tempê, **4.** 393; founded by Demetrius Poliorcetes, **4.** 423, 433, 445; lies on the sea between Nelia and Pagasae, **4.** 423, 433, 445; long a naval station and residence of the Macedonian kings, held the mastery over Tempê and Mts. Pelion and Ossa, is now reduced in power, but surpasses all other cities in Magnesia, **4.** 425; 27 stadia from Ormenium and seven from the site of Iolcus, **4.** 435; more than 1000 stadia from the mouth of the Peneius, **4.** 451

Demetrias, a city in Assyria, **7.** 197

Demetrium in Thessaly, mentioned by Homer as "sacred precinct of Demeter" and by him called "Pyrasus"; subject to Protesilaüs, and 20 stadia from Phthiotic Thebes, **4.** 421; now rased to the ground, **4.** 423

Demetrius Aetolicus (son of Antigonus Gonatas, reigned over Macedonia, 239-229 B.C.), devastated Aetolia, **5.** 27

Demetrius of Callatis (fl. about 200 B.C.), historian, and author of a work on the geography and ethnography of the Euxine regions; his

313

INDEX OF NAMES, PLACES, AND SUBJECTS

Dictynnaean temple, the, on Mt. Tityrus in Crete, **5.** 139

Dictys, drew to land in Seriphos the chest in which Perseus and his mother Danaë were enclosed, **5.** 171

Didyma near Miletus; temple of Apollo near, presided over by Branchus, descendant of Machaereus the Delphian, **4.** 361; robbed by Xerxes, **5.** 285

Didyman Hills, the, at the Dotian Plain in Thessaly, **4.** 449; mentioned by Hesiod, **6.** 251

Didymê, the "Twin" city of Gades, **2.** 131

Didymê (Salina), one of the Liparaean Isles, **3.** 99

Diegylis, king of the Caeni in Thrace, defeated by Attalus II, **6.** 169

Dilisé (see Delium in Boeotia)

Dinara, Mt. (see Ardian Mountain)

Dindymenê (Mother Rhea); named after Mt. Dindymus in Galatia, **5.** 471; temple of, on Mt. Dindymus in territory of Cyzicus, founded by the Argonauts, **5.** 501; temple of, at Magnesia on the Maeander, no longer in existence, **6.** 251

Dindymus, Mt., in territory of Cyzicus, has a temple of Mother Dindymenê, which was founded by the Argonauts, **5.** 501

Dindymus, Mt., in Galatia, **5.** 471

Dio of Syracuse (b. about 410 B.C.), made an expedition against Dionysius the Younger, **3.** 15

Diochares, the Gates of, near the Lyceium at Athens, **4.** 267

Diocles in Pherae, visited by Telemachus, **4.** 145

Diocopenê in Cappadocia Pontica, **5.** 447

Diodorus the Elder, of Sardeis, called Zonas; a great orator, who many times pleaded the cause of Asia, and acquitted himself of the charge of trying to cause cities to revolt from King Mithridates, **6.** 179

Diodorus the Younger, of Sardeis, friend of Strabo, author of historical treatises, and various poems, **6.** 181

Diodorus, general in the Mithridatic War, slew the members of the city council of Adramyttium, and died in disgrace at Amaseia in Pontus, **6.** 129

Diodorus, nicknamed "Cronus," a native of Iasus in Caria, **6.** 291

Diodorus the Dialectician, of Iasus in Caria, pupil of Apollonius Cronus of Cyrenê, **8.** 205

Diodorus the grammarian, a native of Tarsus, **6.** 351

Diodotus, the sculptor, by some said to have made the remarkable statue of Nemesis at Rhamnus, **4.** 263

Diodotus the Sidonian philosopher, friend of Strabo, **7.** 271

Diodotus Tryphon, gained the upper hand over Arsaces I, king of Parthia, **5.** 275; caused Syria to revolt from the kings, responsible for the organisation of the Cilician gangs of pirates, forced by Antiochus the son of Demetrius to kill himself, **6.** 327

Diogenes the Cynic, a native of Sinopê, **5.** 391

Diogenes the philosopher and poet, a native of Tarsus, **6.** 351

Diogenes the Stoic philosopher, a native of Seleuceia on the Tigris, but called "the Babylonian," **7.** 219

Diolcus, the; the narrowest part of the Corinthian isthmus, **4.** 13, 155, 197

Diomedeae (Tremiti), the; isles off the Italian coast in the Adriatic, **1.** 475, **2.** 319; mythical story about, **3.** 129; off Cape Garganum, **3.** 131

Diomedes, the Greek hero; his opinion of Odysseus, **1.** 61; wanderings of, a traditional fact, **2.** 55; temple of, in the recess of the Adriatic, **2.** 317; the Islands and worship of, **2.** 319, 321; founded Canusium and Argyrippa in Apulia; and story of early dominion of, in the regions of Apulia, the land of the Frentani, and the land of the Heneti, **3.** 129; further stories about, **3.** 131; with Alcmaeon acquired Acarnania and Aetolia, **3.** 305; ruled over the Bistonian Thracians, **3.** 365; the horses of, devoured Abderus, **3.** 369; expeditions of, with Alcmaeon, and participant in the Trojan expedition, **4.** 369, **5.** 71

315

INDEX OF NAMES, PLACES, AND SUBJECTS

Dionê, the temple-associate of Zeus at Dodona, 3. 317

Dionysiac artists, the, in Ionia live, and have festivals, at Lebedus in Asia; migrated from Teos, 6. 237

Dionysiac arts, the, 5. 121

Dionysiac rites, the, in India, 7. 97

Dionysides, great tragic poet, a native of Tarsus, 6. 353

Dionysium, the, in Rhodes, contains many votive offerings, 6. 269

Dionysius Atticus, the Pergamenian; sophist, historian, and speech-writer, pupil of Apollodorus the Pergamenian, 6. 171

Dionysius of Chalcis in Euboea (fl., apparently, in the fourth century B.C.), author of a work on the *The Foundings* of cities; says the *Thracian* Bosporus was in earlier times called the *Mysian* Bosporus, 5. 465

Dionysius the Dialectician, a native of Bithynia, 5. 465

Dionysius the Elder (430–367 B.C.), the tyrant of Sicily; his stud of wild horses in the land of the Heneti in Italy, 2. 309; robbed the temple of Eilethyia at Pyrgi, 2. 365; the tyranny of, 2. 427; destroyed Rhegium, 3. 27

Dionysius the Younger (succeeded his father Dionysius the Elder as tyrant of Syracuse in 367 B.C.); expedition against, by Dio, 3. 15; restored a part of Rhegium, 3. 27; banishment of, from Syracuse (357 B.C.), and immorality of, 3. 31; tried to build a wall across the Italian isthmus, 3. 37

Dionysius the historian, contemporary of Strabo, a native of Halicarnassus, 6. 285

Dionysius the tyrant; son of Heracleon, once ruled three towns in Syria, 7. 247

Dionysius, the tyrant of Heracleia Pontica, and husband of Amastris, 5. 385

Dionysius Thrax, though an Alexandrian, was called a Rhodian, 6. 281

Dionysocles, famous orator, native of Magnesia on the Maeander, 6. 257

Dionysodorus of Melos, the mathematician, native of Amisus, 5. 399

Dionysus; long journeys of, 1. 177; erected pillars at limits of his Indian expeditions, 2. 139, which are no longer to be seen, 2. 141; the women of the Samnitae in Celtica possessed by, 2. 249; the temple of, at Limnae in the suburbs of Sparta, 4. 125; the celebrated painting of, by Aristeides, at Corinth, carried to Rome and seen by Strabo on the walls of the temple of Ceres, 4. 201; also called Iacchus, 5. 95; the rites of, in Greece, akin to those of Rhea in Phrygia, 5. 99, 101; takes delight in the Triennial Festivals, 5. 103; the rites of, identified with those of the Edonian Lycurgus, 5. 107; Asia consecrated to, 5. 109; reputed expedition of, to India, 5. 239; Priapus, worshipped at Ornea and at Priapus, called the son of, 6. 27; called "Pyrigenes," and with good reason, 6. 183; honoured with games and festival at Lebedus in Asia, 6. 237; expedition of, to India, 7. 7–13; praises of, hymned in India, 7. 97; worshipped by the Arabians, 7. 211

Dionysus, a City of, in Libya, which "the same man can never find twice," 3. 193

Diophanes the rhetorician, born at Mitylenê, 6. 143

Diophantus, general of Mithridates, vanquished the Roxolani and Bosporians, 3. 223; founded Fort Eupatorium, 3. 247

Diophorti, Mt. (see Lycaeus)

Dioscuri (Castor and Pollux), the; why called "guardians of the sea" and "saviours of sailors," 1. 177; temple of, in the Forum at Rome, 2. 393; the altars of, on the Sagra River in Bruttium, 3. 35; once captured Las, 4. 131; and hence called "the Lapersae," 4. 133; sacked Aphidna and recovered Helen, 4. 263; charioteers of, 5. 203

Dioscurias (Iskuria), in Colchis, in inmost recess of Euxine Sea, 3000 stadia farther east than Gulf of Issus, 1. 175, 479; most easterly point of the Mediterranean, 1. 485;

INDEX OF NAMES, PLACES, AND SUBJECTS

the coast of, **5.** 207; occupies the most easterly point of the Euxine, and is the common emporium of seventy tribes called Caucasians, **5.** 209, 211, 241

Diospolis in Cappadocia Pontica (see Cabeira)

Diospolis, or "City of Zeus" (see Thebes, the Aegyptian)

Diospolis, Little, on the Nile, **8.** 117

Diospolis, a, near Mendes in Aegypt, **8.** 69

Diotimus, son of Strombichus, the Athenian ambassador; contemporary of Damastes, and said to have sailed from Cilicia on Cydnus and Choaspes Rivers to Susa in 40 days, **1.** 175

Diotrephes, native of Laodiceia on the Maeander, teacher of Hybreas the greatest orator in Strabo's time, **6.** 191

Diphilus, the comic poet, contemporary of Menander, a native of Sinopê, **5.** 391

Dircê, the spring near Phara in Achaea, bearing the same name as that at Thebes, **4.** 227; the spring near Thebes, **4.** 313

Dirk, the, used by the Iberians, **2.** 107

Diseases, of animals, a cure-all for, at the temple of Podaleirius in Daunia in Italy, **3.** 131; cured by waters of Cytherius River in Elis, **4.** 99

Dithyramb, a, of Pindar, quoted, **5.** 99

Ditiones, the, a Pannonian tribe, **3.** 257

Dium, a city of Athos, **3.** 355, 357

Dium (Lithada), near Cape Cenaeum in Euboea, colonised Canae in Aeolis, **5.** 9

Dium (Malathria), in southern Macedonia, in the foot-hills of Olympus, **3.** 339

Diurnal period, the, **2.** 149

Dius, father of Hesiod, native of Cymê Phryconis in Asia, but moved to "wretched" Ascrê in Boeotia, **6.** 161

Dius, legendary hero of Metapontium, **3.** 53

Divination; juggling and magic closely related to, **5.** 121

Division, the Northern, of the in-

habited world, **1.** 293, 351; the Southern, divided into Sections (Sphragides), **1.** 293

Dnieper River, the (see Borysthenes)

Dniester River, the (see Tyras)

Doberus, near the Strymon River, **3.** 361

Docimaea, a village in Phrygia, where is the quarry of "Docimaean" marble, **5.** 507

Docimaean Marble, the, **4.** 429

"Dodo," an apocopated form of "Dodona," **4.** 131

Dodona, seat of the oracle of Dodonaean Zeus in Epeirus (near what is now Dramisi), **3.** 17, 297; the oracle at, now virtually extinct, **3.** 313; once under the rule of the Thesprotians and later of the Molossians, **3.** 315; temple of, according to Suidas, was transferred from Dodona in Thessaly, **3.** 317; oracle of, transferred in accordance with an oracle of Apollo, **3.** 321, 323; the copper vessel and copper scourge ("scourge of the Corcyraeans") at, **3.** 325; the oracle at, advised the Boeotians to commit an act of sacrilege, **4.** 285; a tripod secretly dedicated at, every year, by the Boeotians, **4.** 287; oracle of Zeus at, consulted by Greek statesmen, **7.** 287

Dodona, "wintry," in Thessaly, held by the Perrhaebians, **4.** 443; the oracle at, transferred to Dodona in Epeirus, **3.** 317, 321, 323

Doedalsus, a founder of Astacus on the Propontis, **5.** 455

Dog-fish (see Galeotae)

Dogs, hunting, produced by Britain, **2.** 255; in Bactria and Sogdiana, called "undertakers," **5.** 283; the brave, in India, **7.** 65, 67; the large hunting, among the Cynamolgi in Aethiopia, **7.** 323; worshipped at Cynonpolis on the Nile, **8.** 109; of the Aethiopians, are small, **8.** 143

Dolabella, captured and slew Trebonius, one of the murderers of Caesar, at Smyrna, **6.** 247; almost caused the ruin of Laodiceia in Syria and was killed there (43 B.C.), **7.** 249

Dolicha (see Dulichium)

Dolion, son of Silenus and Melia, lived

INDEX OF NAMES, PLACES, AND SUBJECTS

INDEX OF NAMES, PLACES, AND SUBJECTS

319

INDEX OF NAMES, PLACES, AND SUBJECTS

the Homeric Cephallenia, **5.** 47;
Meges the king of, **5.** 59

Dunax, Mt., in Thrace, compared
with the Alps, **2.** 293

Duras River, the, rises in the Apennine Mountains, **2.** 287

Durazzo (see Epidamnus in Illyria)

Durias River, the, rises in the Alps,
2. 271; an aid in mining, **2.** 277;
lies along road to Ocelum, **2.** 327

Duricortora (Rheims), metropolis of
the Remi, **2.** 233

Durio (Malaucène?), **2.** 197

Duris of Samos (fl. about 350 B.C.),
author of a *History of Greece and
Macedon* and other historical works,
of which only fragments are extant;
on Rhagae in Media, **1.** 223

Durius (Douro) River, the, in Iberia;
courses the country of the Vaccaeans, **2.** 65; navigable for 800
stadia, **2.** 69; rises in Celtiberia, **2.**
101

Dye-works, the numerous, in Tyre,
7. 269; at Zuchis in Libya, **8.**
195

Dyeing, roots useful for, in Iberia, **2.**
107

Dyestae, the, **3.** 307

Dymas, father of Hecabê, a Phrygian,
6. 41

Dymê (near Kato-Akhaia), made up
of eight communities, **4.** 23; 60
stadia from Cape Araxus, **4.** 25; an
Epeian city, not mentioned by
Homer, **4.** 39; called "Cauconian,"
4. 43, 45; where the Homeric
Cauconians lived, **4.** 55–59; joined
the Achaean League, **4.** 207; member of a new league after the dissolution of the Achaean League, **4.**
211; one of the twelve cities in
which the Achaeans settled, **4.** 219;
in earlier times called Stratos, has
no harbour, is farthest towards the
west, as its name indicates, and
received from Pompey a mixed
group of captured pirates, **4.** 225;
borders on Phara, **4.** 227; colonised
with pirates by Pompey, **6.** 315

Dyras River, the, tried to quench the
funeral pyre of Heracles, **4.** 391

Dyris (see Atlas) Mountain, the,
occupied by Aethiopians, **1.** 119

Dyrrachium (see Epidamnus in Illyria)

Dyspontium, between Olympia and
the city Elis, **4.** 101

Dyteutus the son of Adiatorix,
appointed priest of Comana by
Augustus, **5.** 437; the domain of,
5. 443

E

Eagle, the, not found in the region of
Lake Maeotis, **3.** 249; worshipped
at Thebes in Aegypt, **8.** 111

Eagles (or Crows?), the, set free by
Zeus, met at Delphi, **4.** 355

Earth, the; spheroidal in shape, **1.**
179, 233, 361, 425; 180,000 stadia
in circumference, according to
Poseidonius, and by him divided
into five zones, **1.** 365; divided into
seven zones by Polybius, **1.** 367;
sometimes rises and undergoes
settling processes, **1.** 391; surface
of, spherical, **1.** 421, 431; spherically
concentric with the heavens, and
otherwise described in relation
thereto, **1.** 425; circumference of,
1. 429, 437, 505; largest circle of,
divided into 360 sections (*i.e.*
degrees); discussion of sphericity
of, and its relation to the heavens,
8. 99; of the changes it undergoes,
8. 101–103

Earth, the Circuit of the, by Hesiod,
cited in regard to the Galactophagi,
i.e. Scythians, **3.** 205

Earth, Mother, shrouded the Giants
at Leuca, **3.** 119; worshipped by
the Derbices in Asia, **5.** 293

Earthenware, the, found at Corinth,
sold at high price at Rome, **4.** 203

Earthquake, an, broke up wall of
Elateia, **1.** 225; almost destroyed
Tyre, **7.** 269

Earthquakes, caused destruction of
Bura and Bizonê, **1.** 199; and of
Helicê; wreaked havoc in various
places, **1.** 217; cause of name of
Rhagae ("Rent") in Media, and
formed the Euripus, **1.** 223; account
of results of in numerous places in
Greece, **1.** 223–227; changes resulting from, **1.** 391; called "Brastae"
by Aristotle, **2.** 185; earthquakes
common in region of Italy and
Sicily, **2.** 457, 459; not now frequent

INDEX OF NAMES, PLACES, AND SUBJECTS

in region of Sicilian Strait, **3.** 5; effects of, on rivers and lakes in Boeotia, **4.** 301, and the dire results, **4.** 303; split Mt. Ossa off from Mt. Olympus, **4.** 397; frequent in territory of Laodiceia, Carura, and the Maeander River, **5.** 513; also in other places in Asia Minor, **5.** 515, 517; recently damaged Magnesia in Asia, **6.** 159; recently damaged Sardeis greatly, **6.** 179; occur frequently at Philadelphia in Mysia, **6.** 181, and at Laodiceia on the Maeander, **6.** 189; frequent in a certain region in India, **7.** 29; and eruptions, in the region of the Dead Sea, destroyed several cities, **7.** 297

Ebony-tree, the, in India, **7.** 65; abundant in Aethiopia, **8.** 145

Ebura, the city, in Iberia, **2.** 19

Eburones, the, in Celtica; geographical position of, **2.** 233

Ebusus (Ibiza), the island, lies off Tarraco, **2.** 91; one of the Pityussae, **2.** 125, 473

Ecbatana (Hamadan), royal seat of the Median empire, and later the summer-residence of the Parthian kings, **5.** 303, and also of the Persian and Macedonian kings, **5.** 307; Persian treasures worth 180,000 talents assembled at, **7.** 169; summer residence of the Parthian kings, **7.** 219

Echedorus (Gallikos) River, the, in Macedonia, **3.** 343

Echeiae in Laconia, colonised by Teleclus, **4.** 115

Echelas (see Archelaüs the son of Penthilus)

Echinades (Kurtzolares), the islands; off the Gulf of Corinth, **1.** 477, **4.** 77; "the sacred," mentioned by Homer, **5.** 35; subject to Meges, **5.** 49, 59; geographical position of, **5.** 55, 57

Echinus, damaged by an earthquake, **1.** 225; above the Maliac Gulf, subject to Achilles, **4.** 419

Eclipses, the, **1.** 23; worked out by astronomers, **1.** 425

Ecregma, the; outlet of Lake Sirbonis into Mediterranean, **1.** 243

Edessa (Vodena), through which the Egnatian Way passes, **3.** 295

Edessa in Mesopotamia (see Bambycê)

Edetania, geographical position of, **2.** 103

Edetanians, the, in Iberia; geographical position of, **2.** 81; extend to New Carthage, **2.** 105

Edones, the, in Thrace, a tribe of the Edoni, **3.** 331

Edoni, the, in Macedonia; geographical position of, **3.** 331; over whom Rhesus reigned, **3.** 359; worship Cotys, **5.** 105

Education, and intercourse with mankind, neglected by the Boeotians, and hence their failure to gain the supremacy in Greece, **4.** 281

Eels, cause of large size of, in ocean, **2.** 37; feed on mud, **2.** 183

Eëtion, father of Andromachê, **6.** 17; one of the two Cilician dynasties subject to, **6.** 121; king of Thebê and Chrysa, **6.** 17, 121; slain before the *Catalogue*, **6.** 149

Egelasta in Iberia, through which the road formerly ran, **2.** 95

Egeria, a spring which feeds Lacus Nemorensis, **2.** 423

Egertius, founded Chios, **6.** 201

Egesta (see Aegesta)

Egnatia (also spelled Gnathia, Gnatia, Ignatia; now Torre d'Agnazzo), on the mule-road from Brundisium to Beneventum, **3.** 125; on the coast of the Adriatic, **3.** 127

Egnatian Way, the, from Apollonia (Pollina) to Cypsela (Ipsala), on the Hebrus (Maritza) River, **3.** 293, 309; the southern boundary of Macedonia, **3.** 329; ends at Thessaloniceia, **3.** 333

Egra, a village in Arabia, **7.** 363

Egypt (see Aegypt)

Egyptians (see Aegyptians)

Eidomenê, a city in Macedonia, **3.** 361

Eilethyia, goddess of childbirth; a temple of, at Pyrgi in Italy, **2.** 365, and at Amnisus in Crete, **5.** 129; City of, on the Nile south of Thebes, **8.** 127

Eiones, a village in Argolis, once a naval station of the Mycenaeans but no longer existent, **4.** 173

Eiresionê (Olive-branch), the Attic, **1.** 59

321

INDEX OF NAMES, PLACES, AND SUBJECTS

from 300 to 500 years, **7.** 75; used in processions at festivals in India, **7.** 121; 500 kept by Seleucus at Apameia in Syria, **7.** 251; captured near Ptolemaïs, **7.** 313, 319; hunting-ground of, near Saba harbour in the Arabian Gulf, **7.** 319; hunting-grounds of, near Melinus Harbour in the Arabian Gulf, **7.** 323; description of capture of, near Daraba in Aethiopia, by the Elephantophagi, **7.** 325; several hunting-grounds of, in region of Cape Deirê, **7.** 327, 331, 331; numerous to the south of Cape Deirê, **7.** 335; in Aethiopia, hunted by men sent out by the Ptolemies, **8.** 17, 145; found in Maurusia in Libya, and in western Aethiopia, **8.** 163, 165; fabulous stories about, **8.** 171–173

Elephas, Mt., in Aethiopia, **7.** 333

Eleus (or Elaeus), a city at the southern end of the Thracian Chersonesus and opposite Cape Sigeium in the Troad; has the temple of Protesilaüs, and its name is masculine, **3.** 375; distant 170 stadia from the place of the pontoon-bridge, **3.** 377

Eleus, in the Peraea of the Rhodians, **6.** 281

Eleusinian Demeter, the (see Demeter)

Eleusinian Gulf, the, in a way the same as the Saronic, **4.** 197

Eleusis; the serpent called Cychreides welcomed at, by Demeter, **4.** 253; the temple at, **4.** 257; the inspiration of, according to Hegesias, **4.** 261; one of the twelve cities in Attica settled by Cecrops, **4.** 267; the processions from Athens to, **4.** 277

Eleusis in Aegypt, a notorious resort, **8.** 61

Eleusis in Boeotia, on the Triton River, **4.** 305; founded by Cecrops, and submerged by Lake Copaïs, **4.** 307

Eleussa, the island, opposite Pitanê, **6.** 131

Eleussa (Eleus?), in the Thracian Chersonesus, where is a temple of Protesilaüs, **6.** 61

Eleussa, the island, off Cape Astypalaea in Greece, **4.** 271

Eleutherae (Gyftocastro); lies near the deme Oenoê, **4.** 181; according to some belongs to Attica, to others, to Boeotia, **4.** 325

Eleutherian Games, the, at Plataea, where the victor received a crown, **4.** 327

Eleutherokhori in Macedonia (see Methonê)

Eleutherus River, the, in Phoenicia, **7.** 255, 259

Elimeia, a mountainous region on the confines of Epeirus and Thessaly, **3.** 307; used to be called a part of Upper Macedonia, **3.** 309

Elimiotae, the, annexed to Macedonia, **4.** 417

Elis (Kaliscopi), the city, made up several communities in the surrounding country, **4.** 23; left without walls because it was regarded by all as sacred, **4.** 105; once sent settlers to Eretria in Euboea, **5.** 17; statue of Oxylus at, **5.** 77

Elis (Eleia), the country; geographical position of, **4.** 15; detailed description of, **4.** 19–107; the Pylus in Coelê Elis not the Homeric Pylus, **4.** 23; "goodly," according to Homer, **4.** 35, 37; said once to have been called Cauconia, **4.** 55; "where the Epeians hold sway," **4.** 77; now comprises all the country as far as Messenê, **4.** 95; by oath made sacred to Zeus, **4.** 103, 105; length of present coast of, 1200 stadia, **4.** 106; colonised by Cresphontes after the return of the Heracleidae, **4.** 235

Elisa River, the (see Elison)

Elison River (or Elisa), the, in Elis, **4.** 27

Elixus River, the, in Ceos, **5.** 169

Elk, the European (see footnote 5, Vol. II, p 289)

Ellopia, a place in Euboea founded by Ellops, **5.** 7

"Ellopia," a former name of Euboea, **5.** 7

Ellopians, the, forced to migrate to Euboea after the battle at Leuctra, **5.** 7; made war on the Oreitae, **5.** 9

Ellops the king, son of Ion; Euboea formerly named Ellopia after, and

INDEX OF NAMES, PLACES, AND SUBJECTS

by some called the brother of
Aïclus and Cothus, **5**. 7

Elonê, the Homeric, subject to
Polypoetes, **4**. 437; a Perrhaebian
city, changed its name to Leimonê,
now in ruins, **4**. 443

Elpiae, among the Daunians in Italy,
founded by the Rhodians, **6**. 277

Elui, the, a tribe in Aquitania, **2**.
217

Elvetii (or Helvetii, *q.v.*), the; the first
of all the peoples who live on the
Rhenus, **2**. 225; 400,000 of, destroyed by Julius Caesar, **2**. 225;
number of the, **2**. 229, 241; geographical position of, **2**. 281

Elymaeans, the, in Assyria, mountainous country of, **5**. 301, 309;
once assisted by the Cossaei
against the Susians and Babylonians, **5**. 307, 309; a predatory
people, **7**. 173, 193; country of,
borders on Babylonia, **7**. 203;
country and military power of, **7**.
221; would not submit to the
Parthians or to the Macedonians,
and slew Antiochus the Great, **7**.
221, 223

Elymaïs, borders on Susis and Media,
7. 221; provinces of, **7**. 223

Elymus the Trojan, companion of
Aeneias, **6**. 109

Elysian Plain, the, placed by Homer
in the far west, **2**. 55

Emathia, the name of Macedonia in
earlier times and also of a city near
the sea, **3**. 329

"Emathoëis," Homer's epithet of
Pylus, **4**. 21, 51; "Sandy" (?), **4**.
33

Embalming, at Necropolis, a suburb
of Alexandria, **8**. 41

Emerald (see Smaragdus), the, in
India, **7**. 123; found in gold mines
in Arabia, **7**. 351

Emeseni, the, a tribe in Syria, **7**. 253

Emoda, Mt., a part of the Caucasus, **5**.
259

Emodus, Mt., where Alexander got
timber for shipbuilding, **7**. 15, 49,
125

Empedocles the philosopher, of
Acragas (Agrigentum) in Sicily
(fl. about 490 B.C.); according to
certain stories leaped into the crater

of Aetna, **3**. 89, 97; *apocopê* in,
4. 131

Emporicus Gulf, the, on the western
coast of Libya, where are settlements
of Phoenician merchants, **8**. 159;
the fabulous cave on, **8**. 161

Emporitans, the, in Iberia, once lived
on an island (now Medas) off the
coast of Emporium, **2**. 93; port of,
2. 93; skilful in flax-working, **2**. 95

Emporium, the, at Alexandria, **8**. 39

Emporium, a naval station near
Medma in Bruttium, **3**. 19

Emporium of the Canusitae (Cannae,
now Canne, apparently), on the
Aufidus River, **3**. 127

Emporium, near north-eastern corner
of Iberia, founded by people of
Massalia (Marseilles), and description of, **2**. 93

Ems River, the (see Amasias)

Enchelii (or Sesarethii), the, **3**. 307

Endera, deep in the interior of
Aethiopia, a settlement of naked
people; habits of people at, **7**.
321–323

Endymion, father of King Aetolus,
5. 77; sepulchre of, in Caria, **6**. 209

Enetê (or Eneti), on the coast, ten
schoeni from Amastris in Paphlagonia, **5**. 381; identified with
Amisus by Hecataeus, **5**. 417

Enetian (Venetian) country, the, in
Italy, settled by the Enetians
(or Henetians) from Paphlagonia,
5. 381

Enetians (see Henetians), the; migrations of, from Paphlagonia to the
Adriatic, **1**. 227; accorded civic
rights by the Romans, **2**. 299; the
seaboard of, **2**. 303; origin of, **2**.
307; noted for their horses and
mules, **2**. 309; territory of, does not
include Aquileia, **2**. 317; decreed
honours to Diomedes, and worship
Hera and the Aetolian Artemis, **2**.
321; used to assist the Romans in
battle, **2**. 323; in Paphlagonia,
mentioned by Homer, and the most
notable tribe of the Paphlagonians,
5. 381; crossed over to Thrace after
capture of Troy, and finally landed
in the Enetian (Venetian) country
(in Italy), **5**. 383, 415

Engineer, the; qualifications of, **1**. 419

INDEX OF NAMES, PLACES, AND SUBJECTS

Engineering, a branch of mathematics, **1**. 201

England (see Britain)

Enianians, the Homeric (see Aenianians), **4**. 443

Eniconiae, a town in Corsica, **2**. 359

Enipeus, god of the Enipeus River in Elis, loved by Tyro, **4**. 99

Enipeus (Lestenitza) River, the, in Elis, now called the Barnichius, empties into the Alpheius, **4**. 99

Enipeus (Tsanarlis) River, the, in Thessaly (by some spelled "Eniseus"), flows from Mt. Othrys, **4**. 99; the course of, **4**. 405

"Eniseus" River, the (see Enipeus River), the, in Thessaly, **4**. 99

Enispê, windy, the Homeric, now deserted, **3**. 385, **4**. 229

Enna in Sicily, where is the temple of Demeter, **3**. 81; taken by Eunus, **3**. 85; lies midway between Syracuse and Eryx, **3**. 87

Ennea Hodoi (see Amphipolis)

Ennius (b. 239 B.C.), the Roman poet, born at Rodiae, **3**. 119

Enopê, the Homeric, **4**. 109; by some identified with Pellana (now Zugra), and by others with Gerenia, **4**. 115

Enos (see Aenus)

Enotocoetae, the, in India, sleep in their ears, **7**. 95

Enydra in Phoenicia, **7**. 255

Enyo (Goddess of War), also called "Ma"; the temple of, at Comana in Greater Cappadocia—and the priest of, ranks next to the king, **5**. 351, 353, 357; temple of, also at Comana in Cappadocia Pontica, **5**. 433

Eordi, the, in Macedonia, through whose country the Egnatian Way passes, **3**. 295, 307

Eoubes (see Olbia)

Epacria, one of the twelve cities in Attica settled by Cecrops, **4**. 267

Epameinondas, conquered the Lacedaemonians in the Battle at Mantineia, but lost his life therein, **4**. 229; all but gained the supremacy of Greece for Thebes, **4**. 281, 287; defeated the Lacedaemonians at Leuctra, **4**. 335

Epeians, the, lived in Elis, **4**. 19; one of the three tribes in Triphylia,

4. 23; Otus, a chief of the, **4**. 25; discussion of Homer's statement in regard to, **4**. 35–43; a different people from the Eleians, **4**. 39; extent of territory of, **4**. 55; "held sway in Elis," according to Homer, **4**. 77; conceived a contempt for Neleus, **4**. 81; many of, embarked for Troy, **4**. 83; joined by the Aetolians under Oxylus, **4**. 91; Salmoneus the king of, drove Aetolus out of Eleia, but the Epeians were later driven out by Oxylus, **4**. 103; with Aetolus took up their abode in Aetolia, but were destroyed by the Aeolians, **4**. 369; occupied the Echinades Islands, **5**. 49; and Oxeiae Islands, **5**. 59; with the Aetolians founded the earliest cities in Aetolia, **5**. 77, 81

Epeirotes, the, live on the flank of the Greeks, **3**. 287; 70 cities of, destroyed by Paulus Aemilius, **3**. 293; consist of 14 tribes, **3**. 297, 333

Epeirotic tribes, names of certain, **3**. 289; certain, now included within a Roman Province, **3**. 215

Epeirus, geographical position of, **3**. 249, 299; rugged, but in earlier times populous, **3**. 311; once held a part of Macedonia, **3**. 329

Epeius, born at Panopeus in Phocis, **4**. 371

Ephebeia, the, at Neapolis, **2**. 449

Ephebi, the, at Athens; Epicurus and Menander enrolled among, at the same time, **6**. 219

Ephesians, the; certain of, called Sisyrbitae, **6**. 201; exchanged Neapolis for Marathesium, **6**. 223; defeated by the Magnesians, according to Callinus, **6**. 251

Ephesium, the; the temple of the Ephesian Artemis at Massalia, **2**. 173

Ephesus, the Selinus River flows through, **4**. 233; said to have been founded by the Amazons, **5**. 237, and given its name by them, **5**. 407; the greatest emporium in Asia Minor, **5**. 509; the Caÿster Plain in territory of, **6**. 155; 320 stadia from Smyrna, **6**. 197; parts round, in earlier times occupied by Carians, **6**. 199; founded by Androclus the

325

INDEX OF NAMES, PLACES, AND SUBJECTS

INDEX OF NAMES, PLACES, AND SUBJECTS

to Crete, **5.** 151; says Cytorum was named after Cytorus the son of Phrixus, **5.** 387; on the abode of the Amazons, **5.** 405; on the boundaries of Aeolis in Asia, **6.** 9, 79; on "many-fountained Ida," **6.** 11; author of the *History* and a work on *Inventions*, a native of Cymê Phryconis in Asia, **6.** 161; ridiculed for his references to his countrymen, **6.** 163; tells the history of Miletus, **6.** 205; says that the Asiatic peninsula (Asia Minor) was inhabited by 16 tribes, **6.** 361, 367; misjudged by Apollodorus, **6.** 363; placed the Homeric Halizones in the interior, **6.** 365

"Ephyra," the earlier name of Cichyrus in Thesprotia, **3.** 301; nine cities so named, **3.** 339

Ephyra, an Aetolian village, **4.** 29

Ephyra, the, "in the inmost part of Argos," **4.** 165

Ephyra, the Corinthian (Korakou?), **4.** 27

Ephyra (Palaea Larissa), another name of Crannon in Thessaly, **3.** 335, 337

Ephyra (apparently the Homeric), on the Selleëis River in Elis, 120 stadia from the city Elis, **3.** 315; **4.** 27

Ephyra, a Sicyonian village, **4.** 29

Ephyra, the Thesprotian, **4.** 27, 29; whence the sons of Thessalus invaded Thessaly, **4.** 455

Ephyra, the Thessalian, **4.** 27

Ephyri, the Aetolian, Perrhaebian and Thesprotian, **4.** 29; the Homeric, "from Thrace," **4.** 447

"Ephyri," in earlier times the name of the Crannonians in Thessaly, **4.** 447

Epicarus (see Epidaurus)

Epicharmus of Cos (about 540–483 B.C.), the comic poet; *apocopê* in, **4.** 131

Epicnemidian Locrians (see Locrians), the, named after Mt. Cnemis, **4.** 343; **4.** 377; the territory of, **4.** 381; progenitors of the Ozolian Locrians, **4.** 387

Epicteti (Privy-councillors), the, at Ephesus, **6.** 225

Epicteti, the Phrygian, live about the Mysian Olympus, **5.** 499

Epicurus, "in a sense a Lampsacenian"; Metrodorus of Lampsacus a comrade of, **6.** 37; grew up in Samos and Teos, and became an *ephebus* at Athens, **6.** 219

Epidamnus (Durazzo) in Illyria; the distance from, to Thessaloniceia, **1.** 409; voyage from, to Brundisium, **3.** 125; founded by the Corcyraeans and now called Dyrrachium, **3.** 265; 535 Roman miles, by the Egnatian Way, to Cypsela (Ipsala) on the Hebrus (Maritza) River, **3.** 293; whither went many of the inhabitants of Dyspontium in Elis, **4.** 101

Epidaurian breed of horses, the, is most excellent, **4.** 229

Epidaurians, the, once colonised Aegina, **4.** 181

Epidaurus (once called Epicarus, now Epidavra), on the Saronic Gulf, **4.** 153; settled by emigrants from Tiryns, **4.** 171; belonged to a kind of Amphictyonic League, **4.** 173, 175; seized by Carians, **4.** 175; famed for its temple of Asclepius, and has a circular coast of 15 stadia, **4.** 177

Epidaurus Limera in Laconia, **4.** 151

Epidavra (see Epidaurus)

Epigoni, the; expedition of, against Thebes, **3.** 305, **4.** 283, **5.** 71; captured Thebes, **4.** 333

Epigram, an, of Callimachus, in regard to a poem of Creophilus the Samian, **6.** 219

Epimenides the Cretan wizard, said to have been from Phaestus, **5.** 141

Epistrategi, the, in Aegypt, **8.** 53

Epistrophus, the Homeric, leader of the Halizones, **5.** 403, 407, 409; slain by Achilles at Lyrnessus, **6.** 15, 121, 151

Epitalium in Macistia, the present name of the Homeric Thryum, **4.** 49, 71, 73

Epithets in Homer, **1.** 57, 91, 133

Epizephyrian Locrians (see Locrians), the, were colonists from the Ozolian Locrians, **4.** 387

Epopeus (Epomeo), Mt., on Pithecussae; shaken by earthquake, cast forth fire, **2.** 459

Epopis, a hill in Italy, on the brow of

INDEX OF NAMES, PLACES, AND SUBJECTS

which Locri Epizephyrii is situated, **3.** 29

Eporedia (Ivrea), a Roman colony in Italy, **2.** 279

Equator, the; the limit of the southerly peoples, **1.** 231; geographical position of, **1.** 279; divides earth into two hemispheres, **1.** 371; region of, temperate, according to Eratosthenes and Polybius, **1.** 373; distance from, to pole, one-fourth of earth's largest circle, **1.** 429; measures 250,000 stadia, according to Eratosthenes, **1.** 437; distance from, to Cinnamon-bearing country and Syenê, **1.** 507; between which and tropic circle shadows fall in both directions, **1.** 509; distance from, to the tropic, $\frac{4}{60}$ of the greatest circle, **1.** 521

Equestrian rank, the, a praefect of, governs certain of the Ligures, **2.** 271; from men of, in Luca, the Roman Senate recruits its ranks, **2.** 329

Equinoctial hours, the; meaning of, **1.** 283 (footnote 4); at Meroê and other places, **1.** 507, 509, 511, 513, 515, 517

" Equinoctial rising " of the sun, the; a variable term, **1.** 415

Equinoctial signs, the, **2.** 153

Equinoctial west, the; the Tagus River flows towards, **2.** 65

Equinoxes, the, **1.** 287, 291, **2.** 151

Erae in Asia, near Erythrae, **6.** 239

Erana (Kuriaki) in Messenia, by some said to have been called Arenê in earlier times, by the same name as the Pylian Arenê, **4.** 69; wrongly identified by some with the Homeric Arenê, **4.** 117

Erasinus River, the, which flows from Arcadia to the coast near Bura, **3.** 93, **4.** 161

Erasinus River, the, near Brauron in Attica, **4.** 163

Erasinus (or Arsinus) River, the, in Argolis, flows underground from the Stymphalian Lake, **4.** 161, 231

Erasinus River, the, near Eretria, **4.** 163

Erasistrateian school of medicine, the, at Smyrna, **5.** 519

Erasistratus the physician (fl. in the

first half of the third century B.C.), from Iulis in Ceos, **5.** 169; the Erasistratean school of medicine at Smyrna, **5.** 519

Erastus, the Socratic philosopher, native of Scepsis, **6.** 111

Erato, the clear-voiced muse, **4.** 65

Eratosthenes of Cyrenê (about 276–194 B.C.), learned Alexandrian scholar; geographer and philosopher, **1.** 3; on the aim of a poet, **1.** 23, 55, 57; on additions to geographical knowledge, **1.** 49; his wide knowledge of geography, **1.** 51; never saw Athens, according to Polemon, but in fact studied under Zeno there, **1.** 53; his treatises *On the Good* and his *Studies in Declamation* show superficiality, **1.** 55; says " Homer never lets fall an inappropriate epithet," **1.** 57; on limitations of Homer's knowledge, **1.** 59; misrepresents Homer, **1.** 67, 81, 97; on Hesiod's geography, **1.** 85; on Aeolus, king of the winds, **1.** 87; on the original level of the Mediterranean, **1.** 141; relies too much on poor authorities, *e.g.* Damastes, **1.** 173; believed Gulf of Issus most easterly point of Mediterranean, and believes fabulous stories told about northern parts of the Adriatic, and even mentions an island Cerne, **1.** 175; on the shape of the earth and its changes, **1.** 179; explains finding of oyster-shells and salt-marshes 2000 or 3000 stadia from sea, **1.** 181; does not confirm doctrine of Archimedes on the sphericity of liquid bodies, **1.** 201; on changes about Mt. Casius and Gerrha, **1.** 207; does not believe in uniform level of the seas, **1.** 209; on the Hyperboreians, **1.** 229; reviser of geography, **1.** 231, 253, 267; on Iernê, **1.** 237; says parallel through Athens is less than 200,000 stadia in circuit, **1.** 241; on the division of the continents, **1.** 243; diets upon disputation, **1.** 245; opposes dividing mankind into two groups, Greeks and barbarians, **1.** 249; divides inhabited world into two parts by line parallel to equator, **1.** 253; discredited by Hipparchus, **1.** 257; had access to library at

INDEX OF NAMES, PLACES, AND SUBJECTS

329

INDEX OF NAMES, PLACES, AND SUBJECTS

"Eremni" ("Black"), not applicable to the Arabians, **7.** 373

Eressus in Lesbos, the home of Theophrastus and Phanias, the Peripatetic philosophers, **6.** 145

Eretria, now a market-place at Athens, said to have colonised Eretria in Euboea, **5.** 15

Eretria in Euboea; across the strait 40 stadia from Oropus, **4.** 289; second largest city in Euboea, **5.** 11, 17; said to have been founded by the Athenians before the Trojan War, and many colonies sent out by, **5.** 13; by some said to have been colonised from Triphylian Macistus by Eretrieus, and in earlier times called Melaneïs and Arotria, **5.** 15; destroyed by the Persians but rebuilt, **5.** 17; the school of Eretrian philosophers at, **5.** 19

Eretria in Phthiotis, subject to Achilles, **4.** 413; near the Pharsalus in Thessaly, **5.** 15

Eretrian sect, the, of philosophers, **4.** 251

Eretrians, the, in Euboea, were colonists from the Attic deme of the Eretrians, **5.** 7; now hold the territory of Carystus, **5.** 11; once powerful, ruling over several islands, and rhotacised the letter *s*, **5.** 17; were carried off by the Persians, and said to have settled in Gordyenê in Asia, **7.** 233

Eretum (near Grotta Marozza), a village, **2.** 375; at the junction of the Salarian and Nomentane Ways, **2.** 377, 417

Erginus, tyrant of Orchomenus in Boeotia, received tribute from the Thebans, **4.** 335

Ericaceae, the botanical term, **3.** 99, footnote 6

Erichthonius, an original founder in both the Trojan and Attic tribes, **6.** 95

Ericodes (or Ericussa), distance from, to Phoenicodes, **3.** 103

Ericussa (Alicudi), one of the Liparaean Isles, named from its plant "heather," **3.** 99

Eridanus River, the, at Athens, **4.** 267

Eridanus, the, in Italy, a mythical river, **2.** 319

Erigon River, the, receives many streams from the Illyrian Mountains and empties into the Axius River, **3.** 311, 339, 341, 345; "the river in Thrace that is now called Rheginia," **3.** 371

Eriko (see Oricum)

Erimokastron (see Thespeia)

Erineus, the home of the poet Tyrtaeus, **4.** 123; a city of the Dorian Tetrapolis, **4.** 387; subject to Achilles, **4.** 413

Erineus, in the Troad, mentioned by Homer, **6.** 67; lies below the ancient Ilium, **6.** 71

Erymanthus River, the, empties into the Alpheius, **4.** 47; forms a boundary of Arcadia, **4.** 101

Erymnae in Thessaly, **4.** 451

Erysichaeans, the, a people in the interior of Acarnania, **5.** 65

Erytheia, the ancient, identified with Gadeira and called "Blest Isle," **2.** 49; scene of the adventures of Geryon, **2.** 133; necessity of bleeding animals at, **3.** 69

Erythini, "the lofty," in Paphlagonia (now called Erythrini), mentioned by Homer, **5.** 377, 387

"Erythra" ("Red"), name given by some to Erythraean Sea—and explanation of, **7.** 349

Erythrae, the Homeric, in Boeotia, by some writers regarded as subject to the Plataeans, **4.** 315, 321

Erythrae (Ritri) in Ionia, a colony of the Erythrae below Mt. Cithaeron, **4.** 297; founded by Cnopus, bastard son of King Codrus, **6.** 201, 239

Erythraean (Red) Sea, the, unknown to Homer, according to Apollodorus, **3.** 191; origin of name of, **7.** 349–351

Erythraeans, the, at Mimas, worship Heracles Ipoctonus, **6.** 127

Erythras, a harbour near Erythrae in Asia, **6.** 241

Erythras the king, a certain Persian, or son of Perseus, after whom, according to certain writers, the Erythraean ("Red") Sea was named, **7.** 305, 351

Eryx, a city in Sicily, seized by Aeneias, **6.** 109

INDEX OF NAMES, PLACES, AND SUBJECTS

INDEX OF NAMES, PLACES, AND SUBJECTS

INDEX OF NAMES, PLACES, AND SUBJECTS

333

INDEX OF NAMES, PLACES, AND SUBJECTS

334

INDEX OF NAMES, PLACES, AND SUBJECTS

335

INDEX OF NAMES, PLACES, AND SUBJECTS

of the Celti; once seized Roman territory, **2.** 311, in Cispadana, **2.** 323; destroyed by the Romans, **2.** 325

Gaius Julius, son of Eurycles the Lacedaemonian ruler, **4.** 139

Galabrii, the, a Dardanian tribe in Illyria, thought to be the ancestors of the Italian Calabrians; have an ancient city, **3.** 265

Galactophagi (" Curd-eaters "), the Homeric, are wagon-dwelling Scythians and Sarmatians, **3.** 179, 181, 189, 195, 197, 205, 209, 243, **5.** 419; by Apollodorus called a fabrication of Homer, **5.** 423

Galata, the Harbour of (see " Fig-tree, Under the ")

Galatia; in Greater Phrygia, a territory seized by Tectosages from Celtica, who were " Galatians " (Gauls), **2.** 205; description and history of, **5.** 467–473; has three tribes, **5.** 467, 471; has a Council and twelve Tetrarchs, **5.** 469

Galatians (Gauls), the; emigrations of, **1.** 227; inhabit country as far west as Gades, according to Eratosthenes, **1.** 411; rank their mines with those of Turditanians, **2.** 41; trained by the Massaliotes to write Greek, **2.** 179; as a whole, by the Greeks called " Celti", **2.** 211; the fourteen tribes of, between the Garumna and Liger, **2.** 213; in common dedicated temple to Augustus at Lugdunum, **2.** 223; the Cisalpine, accorded civic rights by the Romans, **2.** 299; defeated Rome (390 B.C.), **2.** 339, 341; captured Rome, **3.** 141; the " Genuine " (*i.e.* Germans), **3.** 153; the Scordiscan, **3.** 169; in Asia, extent of territory of, **5.** 345; in Asia, given over to the hereditary Tetrarchs by Pompey, **5.** 373; some of, settled in Paphlagonia, **5.** 383; overran the country subject to the Attalic and Bithynian kings in Asia Minor, and finally, by voluntary cession, received the present Galatia, **5.** 469; occupied a part of Greater Phrygia, **5.** 485; onsets of, in Asia Minor, **5.** 495; who crossed over to Asia, found Ilium lacking in walls,

6. 53; conquered by Attalus I, **6.** 167; tribe of, said by Apollodorus to be more recent than the time of Ephorus, **6.** 361, 367

Galatic Gulf (Gulf of Lyons), the, on the southern side of Celtica, **1.** 491, **2.** 5, 181, 215

Galatic Gulfs, the two, **2.** 119

Galatic (Gallic, or Celtic) race (the Gauls, the); the traits and habits of, **2.** 237–249; are war-mad, **2.** 237; are akin to the Germans, **2.** 239; the armour of, **2.** 241; structure of the homes of, **2.** 243; have three sets of men who are held in particular honour, **2.** 245; barbaric customs of, **2.** 247

Galatic tribes, the, beyond the Rhenus and Celtica, **3.** 151, 153

Galaxidi (see Oeantheia)

Galazze (see Calatia)

Galeotae, the; a kind of fish caught in the Strait of Messina, also called sword-fish and dog-fish, **1.** 87

Galepsus, between the mouths of the Strymon and Nestus Rivers, **3.** 355; rased to the ground by Philip, **3.** 359

Galilee, **7.** 281

Gallesius, Mt., between Ephesus and Colophon, **6.** 213

Galli, the (priests of Cybelè), eunuchs at the Plutonium at Hierapolis in Phrygia, **6.** 187

Gallia Aquitanica (see Aquitania)

Gallia Belgica, **2.** 167 (footnote 2), 223

Gallia Lugdunensis, **2.** 167 (footnote 1), 223 (footnote 3)

Gallia Narbonensis (see Narbonitis)

Gallikos River (see Echedorus River)

Gallipoli (see Callipolis)

Gallo, Cape (see Acritas)

Gallo-Graecia, a part of Phrygia in Asia Minor, ceded to the Galatae, **1.** 497, **5.** 469

Gallus, Aelius (see Aelius Gallus)

Gallus, Cornelius (see Cornelius Gallus)

Gallus River, the, which rises at Modra in Phrygia Hellespontica, joins the Sangarius, **5.** 379

Gamabrivii, the, an indigent German tribe, **3.** 159

Gambarus, competent ruler in Syria, **7.** 255

Games, the Actian, at Nicopolis in

337

INDEX OF NAMES, PLACES, AND SUBJECTS

Greece, **3.** 305; the Eleutherian, at Plataea, where the victor received a crown, **4.** 327; the Nemean, **4.** 187; the Olympian, **4.** 87, 91–95; the Pythian, **4.** 361; the quinquennial, at Neapolis near Alexandria in Aegypt, **8.** 41

Gandaris in India, subject to Porus, **7.** 53

Gandaritis, a district in India, **7.** 45

Gangamê, an instrument with which fish are caught in the ice at the Strait of Kertch, **3.** 225

Ganges, the city, in India, **7.** 125

Ganges River, the, in India, **7.** 17; has many tributaries, and is the largest river in India, **7.** 19; largest of all rivers, **7.** 61, 63; course of, **7.** 125

Gangitis, a stone found in Gordyaea which is avoided by reptiles, **7.** 233

Gangra, a small town and fortress in Paphlagonia, residence of Morzeus, **5.** 453

Ganymede, snatched away either at Harpagia or at the Dardanian Promontory in the Troad, **6.** 27, 59

Garabuza, Cape (see Cimarus)

Garamantes, the, in Libya; geographical position of land of, **8.** 195, 207, 209

Gardiki (see Larisa Kremastê)

Gardinitza (see Opus in Locris)

Garescus in Macedonia, one of the cities destroyed by Cassander, **3.** 343, 361

Gargano (see Garganum)

Garganum (Gargano), the promontory, in Apulia, **3.** 131; distance from, to Brundisium, **3.** 133; the deep gulf at, **3.** 135

Gargara in Aeolis in Asia; territory of, **6.** 13, 99; on the Gulf of Adramyttium, **6.** 103, 115; founded by the people of Assus, **6.** 117

Gargarians, the, live on the borders of the Amazons, **5.** 233; cohabit with the Amazons, and live in Themiscyra, **5.** 235

Gargarum, a place high up on Mt. Ida, **6.** 13

Gargarus, Mt., the Homeric, a summit of Mt. Ida, **6.** 11

Gargettus (near Garito in Attica),

where the headless body of Eurystheus was buried, **4.** 187

Garindaeans, the, in Arabia, coast of, **7.** 343

Garmanes (Sramans), the, in India, **7.** 99; life and tenets of, **7.** 103

Garonne River, the (see Garumna)

Garsaüra, a town on the borders of Lycaonia, said once to have been a metropolis, **5.** 359

Garsaüra in Cappadocia, near Soatra, **5.** 475; the road through, **6.** 309

Garsauritis, one of the ten prefectures of Cappadocia, **5.** 349

Garumna (Garonne) River, the, navigable and empties into the ocean, **2.** 211; approximately parallel to the Pyrenees, **2.** 213; whence is one of the four passages to Britain, **2.** 253

Gascogne, Gulf of, **1.** 491 (footnote 2)

Gastuniotikos River, the (see Peneius River, the, in Elis)

"Gasys," a Paphlagonian name used in Cappadocia, **5.** 417

Gaudos, **3.** 103; called the Isle of Calypso by Callimachus, **3.** 193

Gaugamela ("Camel's House"), a village in Aturia, where Dareius was conquered and lost his empire, **7.** 197

Gauls, the (see Galatic race, Celti, and Galatians)

Gaza, in Phoenicia, harbour and city, **7.** 277; sandy country of, **7.** 279

Gazaca (near Leilan), royal summer residence of kings of Atropatian Media, **5.** 305

Gazacenê in Cappadocia; Paphlagonian names prevalent in, **5.** 417

Gazaeans, the, a tribe in Syria, **7.** 239

Gazelles (see Deer), the, in the Scythian plains, **3.** 249; many, in Gazelonitis in Cappadocia Pontica, **5.** 393; in India, **7.** 125; horns of, used as weapons by the Simi in Aethiopia, **7.** 325; in Arabia, **7.** 343; abound in Maurusia in Libya, **8.** 163

Gazelon, a city in Gazelonitis in Cappadocia Pontica, **5.** 395

Gazelonitis in Cappadocia Pontica, fertile, level, and has gazelles and fine sheep, **5.** 393; Paphlagonian names prevalent in, **5.** 417; boundaries of, **5.** 443

INDEX OF NAMES, PLACES, AND SUBJECTS

INDEX OF NAMES, PLACES, AND SUBJECTS

Gergithium, in the territory of Lampsacus, rich in vines, **6**. 35

Gergithium, in the territory of Cymê near Phryconian Larissa, **6**. 37

Gergovia (Gergovie), near which Julius Caesar fought Vercingetorix, **2**. 219

Gergovie (see Gergovia)

Germanic tribes, the, beyond the Rhenus and the Ister, **3**. 151, 153

Germanic War, the, **2**. 231

Germanicus, the Younger, son of Nero Claudius Drusus and Antonia; his triumph over the Cherusci, **3**. 161

Germanicus, son of Tiberius Caesar, assists his father, **3**. 147

Germans, the, joined by the Sequani in their war upon Italy, **2**. 225; kinsmen of the Gauls, **2**. 239; country of, overrun by Italians, **2**. 281; now being fought by the Romans, **3**. 143; called Germani ("Genuine" Galatae) by the Romans, **3**. 153; the country and tribes of, **3**. 153–173; enemies to the Romans, **3**. 217

Germany, divided into two parts by Albis River, **1**. 51; bounded by the Rhine and Danube, **1**. 491, 493

Geron, a river in Coelê Elis, **4**. 33

"Gerontes" ("old men"), the word for "senators" among the Laconians and the Massaliotes, **3**. 323; in Crete and Sparta, **5**. 151, 159

Gerrha in Arabia, on the road from Phoenicia to Aegypt, **7**. 279; inhabited by Chaldaeans exiled from Babylon, **7**. 303

Gerrha in Phoenicia, formerly covered with shoal water, **1**. 185, 207

Gerrhaeans, the, convey aromatics from Arabia to Palestine, **7**. 343; riches of, **7**. 349

Gerrhaeïdae, a harbour, 30 stadia from Teos, **6**. 239

Geryon, the neat-herd of, **2**. 49; kine of, sought by Heracles, **2**. 57, 385, 445; adventures of, in Erytheia, **2**. 133

"Geta," the name given a Getan slave in Attica, **3**. 213

Getans, the; border on the Ister River, **1**. 493; geographical position of, **3**. 173; precise boundaries

of, uncertain, **3**. 175; religion among, and abstention of, from meat, **3**. 185; have regarded their priest, or the counsellor of the king, as god, **3**. 187; held the region on the far side of the Ister, **3**. 201; straightforwardness of, **3**. 203; expedition of Lysimachus against, **3**. 203, 217; history of, **3**. 211–217; the language of, the same as that of the Dacians, **3**. 215; the Desert of, flat and waterless, **3**. 217, 221; border on the Ister, **3**. 251; regarded the prophets Zamolxis and Decaeneus as gods, **7**. 289

Gezatorix, the country of, in western Paphlagonia, **5**. 451

Ghuiloje More (see Sapra, Lake)

Giants, the, in the Phlegraean Plain, **2**. 439, 447; the Leuternian, shrouded by Mother Earth at Leuca, **3**. 119; in earlier times lived on Pallenê (the Macedonian peninsula now called Kassandra), **3**. 349, 351; attacked Aphroditê at Phanagoreia near the Cimmerian Bosporus, but were slain by Heracles, **5**. 201

Gibraltar (see Calpê), the strait at, formerly non-existent and how formed, **1**. 183, 191, 207

Gigartus, a stronghold of robbers at foot of Mt. Libanus, **7**. 263

Gindarus in Syria, **7**. 247

"Ginni" (stunted horses or mules), the, among the Ligures, **2**. 267

Giraffe (see Camelopard)

Girdles, the, of the Amazons, made of skins of wild animals, **5**. 233; made of hair in Aethiopia, **8**. 147

Gladiators, the Roman, trained at healthful Ravenna, **2**. 315; extravagantly entertained by the Campani, **2**. 467

Glass-sand, the, in Phoenicia, **7**. 271

Glass vessels, imported to Britain from Celtica, **2**. 259

Glass-ware, the, at Rome, **7**. 273

Glass-workers, the, at Alexandria, **7**. 273

Glaucê (not named), the spring at Corinth, connected with Peirenê, **4**. 193

Glaucias the tyrant, fled for refuge to Sidenê in time of Croesus, **6**. 83

Glaucopium, falsified by some writers,

INDEX OF NAMES, PLACES, AND SUBJECTS

INDEX OF NAMES, PLACES, AND SUBJECTS

Greece, education in, by poetry, **1**. 55; a country of mountains and rocks, **1**. 487; bounded by the Ister, **1**. 493; the more direct route from, to Italy, is to Brundisium, **3**. 123; well known by Homer, **3**. 195; geographical position of, **3**. 249; the whole of, originally, and most of now, inhabited by barbarians, **3**. 287; northern districts belonging to, **3**. 295; washed on two sides by the Aegaean, **3**. 297; in earliest times held by the Pelasgians, **3**. 313; includes Macedonia, **3**. 327; detailed description of, **4**. 3–395; has the same number (four) of tribes as dialects, **4**. 5; consists of five peninsulas, **4**. 9–13; as a whole called "Argos" by Homer, **4**. 155, 163; the three peninsulas of, **4**. 239; the hegemony of, lost by the Lacedaemonians in the battles at Leuctra and Mantineia, **4**. 335; the "omphalos" ("navel") at Delphi the centre of, **4**. 355; Chalcis and Corinth called "the fetters" of, by Philip, **4**. 391; with Thessaly and other lands now a praetorial Province, **8**. 215

Greek, onomatopoetic words abound in, **6**. 305

Greek culture, preserved at Neapolis, **2**. 449

Greek decorum and usages in Cumae in Italy, **2**. 439

Greeks, the, wrongly named the three continents, **1**. 245; as against barbarians, **1**. 247; interested in government, arts, and in science of living, **1**. 487; upbuilders of Europe, **1**. 489; custom of, in offering hecatombs, followed by the Lusitanians in Iberia, **2**. 75, and also in marrying, **2**. 77; most talkative of men, **2**. 117; most of, represent Pillars of Heracles as near Strait of Gibraltar, **2**. 137; beloved by the Massaliotes, **2**. 179; 500 notable, at Comum in Italy, **2**. 313; founded Rome, according to Coelius, the Roman historian, **2**. 385; kinship of, with the Romans, **2**. 391; had the repute of wisdom in choosing sites of cities, **2**. 405; founded Praeneste and Tibur, **2**. 417;

sometimes make vows, **2**. 465; occupied Magna Graecia in Italy, **3**. 7; held the seaboard of Sicily, **3**. 73; call Iapygia "Messapia," **3**. 103; took sides with the Carthaginians, and hence were later subdued by the Romans, **3**. 141, 143; named the Cimbri "Cimmerians," **3**. 169; supposed the Getans were Thracians, **3**. 175; regard the Scythians as the most straightforward of men, **3**. 199, and held in high esteem Anacharsis and Abaris, **3**. 201; once received 2,100,000 medimni of grain from Leuco, king of the Cimmerian Bosporians, **3**. 243; certain of, inhabit the seaboard of the Propontis, the Hellespont, the Gulf of Melas, and the Aegaean Sea, **3**. 295; call the Thracian paeonismos "titanismos," **3**. 363; as a whole were called "Argives" because of the fame of Argos, **4**. 163; wiped out Mardonius and 300,000 Persians at Plataea, **4**. 325; the Thessalians the most ancient composite part of, **4**. 393; discussion of religion of, **5**. 93; call the ministers of Rhea "Curetes," **5**. 99; founded Panticapaeum and other cities in the Cimmerian Bosporus, **5**. 197; call the boats of certain Asiatic pirates "camarae," **5**. 203; knew the circuit of the Caspian Sea, **5**. 245; caused Bactria to revolt, and became masters of Ariana and India, **5**. 279; took possession of Eucratidia in Bactria, and also held Sogdiana, **5**. 281; joined by the Sinopeans in many struggles, **5**. 387; migrations and invasions of, in ancient times, **5**. 489; inhabited Rhodes and Cos before the Trojan War, **5**. 495; colonised Asia, **6**. 3, 5; witlessness of, at Troy, **6**. 71; rased Ilium to the ground, **6**. 83; Theophanes of Mityléné the most illustrious of, **6**. 145; the Rhodians friendly to, **6**. 269; caused Bactriana to revolt from the Syrian kings, **7**. 5; many beliefs of, like those of the Indians, **7**. 103; avenged by Alexander in Persis, **7**. 165; learned geometry from the Aegyptians and astronomy and

343

arithmetic from the Phoenicians, **7.** 271; according to Moses, wrong in modelling gods in human form, **7.** 283; in their governments follow the mandates of both gods and men, **7.** 287; hated by the earlier Aegyptian kings, **8.** 29; progenitors of one class of the people at Alexandria, **8.** 165; learn astronomy and astrology from the Aegyptians and Chaldaeans, **8.** 85; a colony of, settled by King Macipsas at Cirta in Masylia in Libya, **8.** 183

Grium, Mt., by some identified with the Homeric "mountain of the Phtheires," **6.** 209

Groats, made from Campanian wheat, superior to rice or any other grain-food, **2.** 435

Grosphus, the, a kind of spear used by the Gauls, **2.** 243

Grumentum (Saponara) in Italy, **3.** 11

Grynium in Asia Minor, where is a temple of the Grynian Apollo, **6.** 159

Guadalquivir River, the (see Baetis)

Guadiana River, the (see Anas)

Gubbio in Italy (see Iguvium)

Guinea-fowls, the, on the fabulous Electrides Islands, **2.** 319; numerous, on an island of Myus Harbour in the Arabian Gulf, **7.** 317

Gum, arabic (see Acantha)

Gum, a substance like, in Pisidia, used as frankincense, **5.** 483

Guneus, the domain of, in Thessaly, **4.** 443

Guranii, the, in Asia, **5.** 335

Gurk River, the (see Corcoras)

Gyaros, one of the Cyclades Islands, **5.** 165; the poverty of, **5.** 167

Gygaea, the Homeric, mother of Mnesthles and Antiphus, **6.** 175

Gygaea (later called Coloë), Lake, the Homeric, where is the temple of Coloënian Artemis, **6.** 173

Gygas, Cape, near Dardanus in the Troad, **6.** 41

Gyges, king of Lydia, deposited gifts in treasure-house at Delphi with name inscribed thereon, **4.** 359; permitted the Milesians to found Abydus, **6.** 41; source of wealth of, **6.** 371

Gymnasia, the, at Neapolis, **2.** 449

Gymnasium, the, near Nicopolis in Epeirus, **3.** 305; in the city Elis, **4.** 23; at Sinopê in Paphlagonia, **5.** 389; at Nysa in Asia Minor, **6.** 257; at Alexandria, **8.** 41

Gymnesian (Balearic) Islands, the, **1.** 473; once plagued by hares, **2.** 35; lie off Tarraco, **2.** 91; geographical position of, **2.** 125–129; description of, **2.** 125–129; by some said to have been founded by the Rhodians after their departure from Troy; also called "Balearides"—and explanation of two names of, **6.** 277

Gymnesians, the, inhabitants of the Balearic Islands, spoken of as best of slingers, **2.** 125; forced to appeal to the Romans because of pest of rabbits, **2.** 129

Gymnosophists, the, revered by the Indians, **7.** 289

Gynaeconopolis in Aegypt, **8.** 73

Gyrton (or Gyrtonê), in Thessaly, a Magnetan and Perrhaebian city, in which Peirithoüs and Ixion ruled, **3.** 335, 337, 339, **4.** 437; near Mt. Pelion and the Peneius, **4.** 447, 453

Gyrtonê (see Gyrton), the Homeric, subject to Polypoetes, **4.** 437, 453

Gyrtonians, the, in Thessaly, in earlier times called "Phlegyae," **4.** 447

Gythium (Palaeopoli), near Marathonisi), naval station of Sparta, **4.** 47; 240 stadia from Sparta, **4.** 127

H

Hades, a myth, **1.** 79; associated with night and Tartarus, **2.** 51; placed by Homer at "the ends of the earth," in the far west, **2.** 57; the entrance to, at Avernus, **2.** 441–445; much revered in Triphylia, **3.** 387; sacred precinct of, in Triphylia, **4.** 51, 53; a statue of, dedicated with that of Athenê at her temple near Coroneia, **4.** 325

Hadylius, Mt., in Phocis, extends over a distance of 60 stadia, **4.** 373

Haemon; Thessaly, or a part of it, named "Haemonia" after, by his son Thessalus, **4.** 453; the father of the Oxylus who, from Aetolia, settled Elis, **5.** 77

INDEX OF NAMES, PLACES, AND SUBJECTS

Haemonia, a former name of Thessaly, or of a part of it, **1.** 169, **4.** 453

Haemus Mountain (the Balkans), the, near the Euxine, compared with Alps, **2.** 293; is the largest and highest mountain in that part of the world, and cleaves Thrace almost in the centre, **3.** 251; occupied by tribes of brigands, **3.** 275; reaches the sea at Naulochus, **3.** 279; a boundary of Macedonia, **3.** 329, 361

Hagii Apostoli in Macedonia (see Pella)

Hagion Oros, Gulf of (see Singitic Gulf)

Hagios Dimitrios, Cape (see Sepias, Cape)

Hagios Elios, Mt. (see Ochê)

Hagios Georgios, the island (see Belbina)

Hagios Georgios River, the (see Asopus in Argolis and Sicyonia)

Hagios Nikolaos, Cape (see Astypalaea, Cape)

Halae Araphaenides (Rafina), on the eastern coast of Attica, where is the temple of Artemis Tauropolus, **4.** 273; passage to, from Marmarium in Euboea, **5.** 11

Halae in Boeotia, a village, "where that part of the Boeotian coast which faces Euboea terminates," **4.** 297, 377

Halesian Plain, the, near Cape Lectum, **6.** 97

Halex River, the, marks the boundary between the territories of Rhegium and Locri Epizephyrii, **3.** 33

Haliacmon (Vistritza) River, the, flows into the Thermaean Gulf, **3.** 325, 331, 333, 339, 343, 345

Haliartus (Mazi), rightly called "grassy" by Homer, **1.** 57, **3.** 189, **4.** 307, 323; the Permessus and Olmeius Rivers meet, and empty into Lake Copaïs, near, **4.** 307, 309; near Lake Copaïs and 30 stadia from Ocaleê and 60 from Alalcomenium, **4.** 321; the spring Tilphossa flows near, **4.** 323; no longer in existence, was destroyed by Perseus, and now belongs to the Athenians as gift from the Romans, **4.** 325; Amphictyonic Council used to convene in territory of, at Onchestus, **4.** 329

Halicarnassus (formerly called Zephyra) in Caria, founded by Anthes from Troezen in Argolis, **4.** 175; six cities united into, by Mausolus, **6.** 119; captured by Alexander, **6.** 209, 285; people of, are Dorians, **6.** 271; not in existence in Homer's time, **6.** 273; description and history of, **6.** 283–287; famous natives of, **6.** 283–285

Halicyrna in Aetolia, **5.** 63

Halieis, on the Argolic Gulf, near Hermionê, **4.** 171

Halimusii, the Attic deme, **4.** 271

Halisarna, a, in Cos, **6.** 287

Halius in Locris; some substitute for "Alopê" in Homeric text, **4.** 409

Halizones (see Halizoni), the; hypothesis of Demetrius about, **6.** 89; mentioned by Homer, **6.** 361; placed in the interior by Ephorus, **6.** 365; fabricated by Apollodorus, **6.** 369

Halizoni (or Halizones), the Homeric, came from Cappadocia Pontica, **5.** 403; near Pallenê, by some identified with the Homeric Halizones, **5.** 407; the home of, round Pharnacia, **6.** 359

Halonnesos, an Ionian isle near Mt. Corycus in Asia, **6.** 241

Halonnesos, the isle off Magnesia, **4.** 427

"Halonnesos," the second n redundant in, **6.** 147

Halus in Locris, **4.** 409

Halus in Phthiotis (see Alus), about 60 stadia from Itonus, founded by Athamas, destroyed, and then colonised by the Pharsalians, **4.** 409; placed by Artemidorus on the seaboard, **4.** 411; subject to Protesilaüs, **4.** 421, 423

Halys River, the, not mentioned by Homer, **3.** 189; empties into the Euxine on the borders of Cappadocia, **5.** 345; "the country this side" ruled by Croesus, **5.** 347; confused with the Euphrates, **5.** 363; separates the Paphlagonians from the Pontic Cappadocians, **5.** 373; course of, according to Herodotus, **5.** 383; named after the "halae" ("salt-works") past which it flows,

345

INDEX OF NAMES, PLACES, AND SUBJECTS

INDEX OF NAMES, PLACES, AND SUBJECTS

wins the approval of Demetrius of Scepsis, **5.** 407, 409, 413; author of the *History*, **6.** 207; says Mt. Latmus is the Homeric "mountain of the Phtheires," **6.** 209; a native of Teos, **6.** 239

Hecatê, the goddess, **5.** 95; chapel of, at the temple of Artemis at Ephesus, **6.** 229; temple of, at Lagina in Caria, **6.** 297

Hecaterus, grandfather of nymphs, satyrs and the Curetes, **5.** 111

Hecatomnos, king of the Carians and father of Mausolus, **6.** 285

Hecatompylus (Damegam), in Asia, 1960 stadia from the Caspian Gates, and royal seat of the Parthians, **5.** 271

Hecatonnesi, the; islands between Asia and Lesbos, named after Hecatus (Apollo), **6.** 147

Hector, the Trojans led by, **6.** 19; nephew of the Phrygian Asius, **6.** 41; praised by the present Ilians, **6.** 55; Andromachê the wife of, once queen of the Molossians, **6.** 57; sacred precinct of, at Ophrynium, **6.** 59; territory of Ilium subject to, **6.** 65; reproached by Achilles, **6.** 71; father of Scamandrius, **6.** 105; had the few remaining Cilicians under his command, **6.** 149

Hedylus of Samos or Athens, contemporary of Callimachus, and supposed author of a certain elegy, **6.** 379

"Hedyosmos" ("Sweet-smelling"), a kind of garden-mint found near the Triphylian Pylus, **4.** 51

Hegesianax (fl. 196 B.C.) of Alexandreia in the Troad, on the lack of walls at Ilium, **6.** 53

Hegesias of Magnesia on the Maeander (fl. about 250 B.C.), on the Acropolis at Athens, on Eleusis, and Attica in general, **4.** 261, 263; initiated the Asiatic style of oratory, **6.** 253

Heilesium in Boeotia, so named from the "helê" ("marshes") near it, **4.** 303, 321

Heleians (see Helots)

Heleii ("Marsh-men"), the, in Aethiopia, **7.** 321

Helen, The Reclaiming of, title of a tragedy by Sophocles, **6.** 235

Helen, entertained in Sidon, **1.** 149; carried off by Paris, **2.** 189; by Homer called the "Argive," **4.** 165; the rape of, by Theseus, at Aphidna, **4.** 263; with Paris landed on the island Cranaê, **4.** 273; later wife of Paris, **6.** 65; with Menelaüs, said to have been entertained in Aegypt by King Thon, **8.** 63

Helenê (Makronisi), the island, lies off Attica between Thoricus and Cape Sunium, and was referred to by Homer as "Cranaê," **4.** 273; where Helen and Paris stopped, **4.** 275; 60 stadia in length, **5.** 165

Heleon in Boeotia, a village belonging to Tanagra, named from the "helê" ("marshes") there, **4.** 297; one of the "Four United Villages," **4.** 301, 303

Heliadae, the, according to the mythical story, once took possession of Rhodes, **6.** 275

Heliades, the, story of, **2.** 319

Helicê in Achaea, wiped out by a wave from the sea (372 B.C.), **1.** 219; description of its temple and sacrifices, and of its destruction, **4.** 185, 213, 215; one of the twelve cities in which the Achaeans settled, **4.** 219

Helicê, a, in Thessaly, mentioned by Hesiod, **4.** 215

Helicê, Is from, founded Sybaris in Italy, **3.** 47

Helicon, Mt., on which is the spring called Hippucrenê; is visible from the Acrocorinthus, **4.** 195; the Permessus and Holmius Rivers rise in, **4.** 307; geographical position of, **4.** 317; rivals Parnassus both in height and in circuit, and was dedicated to the Muses by the Thracians, **4.** 319; Mychus Harbour lies below, **4.** 369; consecrated to the Muses by Thracians in Boeotia, **5.** 107

"Heliopolitae," the, in Asia, led by Aristonicus, **6.** 247

Heliupolis, where the sacred ox Mneuïs is kept, **8.** 73; once a remarkable city, but now deserted, **8.** 79; once a centre of study of philosophy and astronomy, where Plato and Eudoxus spent 13 years, **8.** 83; is in Arabia, **8.** 85

347

INDEX OF NAMES, PLACES, AND SUBJECTS

tory, in Iberia, **2.** 89; where Sertorius fought, **2.** 99

Hemispheres, the northern and southern, divided by equator, **1.** 371, 427

Hemp, made in quantities in Colchis, **5.** 211

Henetians (Enetians, *q. v.*, Venetians), the; explorers, and founders of cities, **1.** 177, 227; the wanderings of, a traditional fact, **2.** 55; came from Paphlagonia and settled colony in Italy, **2.** 235, 307; observed rites in honour of Diomedes, **3.** 129, and tell of his apotheosis in their country, **3.** 131; held Cytorum, near the Parthenius River in Asia, **5.** 377

Heniochi, the, in Asia, **1.** 495, **5.** 191, 207; coast of, **5.** 203; at one time had four kings, **5.** 205; country and life of, **8.** 211

Heorta, a city of the Scordisci, **3.** 273

Hephaesteium, the, at Memphis; bull-fights in the *dromus* of, **8.** 89

Hephaestus, the Forum of (Forum Vulcani, La Solfatara), **2.** 449; grandfather of three Cabeiri, **5.** 115

Hepta Phreata (" Seven Wells "), in Arabia, **7.** 363

Heptacomitae, the, by the ancients called Mosynoeci, occupy Mt. Scydises above Colchis, live in trees, and cut down three maniples of Pompey's army, **5.** 401

Heptaporus (or Polyporus) River, the, mentioned by Homer, **5.** 421, **6.** 25, 59, 87; flows from Mt. Ida in the Troad, **6.** 11; crossed seven times by the same road, **6.** 89

Heptastadium, the, bridged by Xerxes, **6.** 41

Heptastadium, the, at Alexandria, **8.** 27, 39

Hera, the Argive, worshipped by the Eneti, **2.** 321; " Cupra," temple of, in Picenum, **2.** 429; the Argoan, temple of, built by Jason, in Leucania, **3.** 3; the power of, as described by Homer, **4.** 91; temple of, at Prosymna near Tiryns, **4.** 169; oracle of, between Lechaeum and Pagae, **4.** 197; born at Argos, **4.** 331; temples of, at Pharygae in Locris and at Pharygae in Argolis, **4.** 383, 385; with Hypnos came to Mt. Ida, **6.** 11; ancient temple and

shrine of, in Samos, had three colossal statues, all upon one base, **6.** 213; frightened by the Curetes when spying on Leto, **6.** 223

Hera's Island, close to Pillars of Heracles, **2.** 129; by some regarded as one of the Pillars, **2.** 137

" Heracleia," ancient name of Carteia, **2.** 15

Heracleia, The (Adventures of Heracles), supposedly written by Peisander, **6.** 281, **7.** 13

Heracleia in Caria, **6.** 291

Heracleia in the Crimea, **3.** 231

Heracleia in Elis, near Olympia, **4.** 99

Heracleia below Latmus, near Miletus, **6.** 209

Heracleia (Polycoro) in Leucania, in the territory of Tarentum, between the Aciris and Siris Rivers, **3.** 49, 51; the seat of the general festal assembly of the Greeks in southern Italy, **3.** 115

Heracleia Lyncestis (Monastir); the Egnatian Way runs through, **3.** 295

Heracleia in Media, lies near Rhagae, **5.** 273; founded by the Macedonians, **5.** 309

Heracleia, a village of the Mytylenaeans in Asia, **6.** 103

Heracleia Pontica (Erekli), founded Chersonesus Heracleotica in the Crimea, **3.** 231; once held by Mithridates Eupator, **5.** 371, 373; by the Romans added to Cappadocia Pontica, and said to have been founded by the Milesians, **5.** 375; history of, **5.** 379; 1500 stadia from the Chalcedonian temple and 500 from the Sangarius River, **5.** 381; 2000 stadia from Sinopê, **5.** 391; not mentioned by Homer, **5.** 417

Heracleia Sintica (Zeroökori), **3.** 361

Heracleia in Syria, lies to the east of Antiocheia, **7.** 245, 247, 249

Heracleia (see Trachin), the Trachinian, in Thessaly near Thermopylae, damaged by an earthquake, **1.** 225; where flows an Asopus River, **4.** 205, 313; six stadia from the old Trachin, **4.** 391, and forty from Thermopylae, **4.** 393, 415, 449

Heracleian Cape, the, in Cappadocia Pontica, **5.** 399

INDEX OF NAMES, PLACES, AND SUBJECTS

Heracleides, the Herophileian physician, native of Erythrae in Asia, **6**. 243

Heracleides of Pontus (b. about 380 B.C.); pupil of Plato and Aristotle, and author of numerous works on a variety of subjects, including certain *Dialogues* mentioned by Strabo; makes a certain Magus say that he had circumnavigated Libya, **1**. 377, 385; on the submersion of Helicê, **4**. 215; Platonic philosopher, **5**. 371; on the sacred mice round the temple of Sminthian Apollo at Chrysa, **6**. 95

Heracleiotic (or Canobic) mouth, the, of the Nile, **8**. 13, 63

Heracleitus the poet, comrade of Callimachus, native of Halicarnassus, **6**. 285

Heracleitus of Ephesus (about 535–475 B.C.), founder of metaphysics and called "dark philosopher" because of the obscurity of his writings; on "the Bear" in Homer, **1**. 11, **6**. 231

Heracleium, the, near Canobus, in Aegypt, **8**. 65

Heracleium in Crete, the seaport of Cnossus, **5**. 129

Heracleium (Temple of Heracles), the, at Gades; behaviour of spring in, **2**. 143, and wells in, **2**. 145

Heracleium, near Lake Maeotis, **5**. 197

Heracleium, the, in Sicily, 75 Roman miles from Lilybaeum, **3**. 57

Heracleium in Syria, **7**. 247, 255

Heracleium, Cape (Capo Spartivento), last cape of Italy, **3**. 27

Heracleotae, the; city of (Chersonesus Heracleotica or Heracleia), in the Crimea, **3**. 231

Heracleotis, a district in the territory of the Ephesians, revolted from the Ephesians, **6**. 233

Heracles, son of Zeus and Alcmenê; invaded Iberia, **1**. 7; wise from travel, **1**. 31; mythical labours of, **1**. 69; Pillars of, 22,500 stadia distant from Cape Malea, **1**. 93; long journeys of, **1**. 177; Pillars of, at end of inhabited world on west, **1**. 253, and distance from, to Peloponnesus, **1**. 403, to Strait of Sicily and

to Sacred Cape, **1**. 407, to Massalia and the Pyrenees, **1**. 409, and lie in the equinoctial west, **1**. 411, and width and length of strait at, **1**. 469, and at most westerly point of Mediterranean, **1**. 485; temple and altar of, on the Sacred Cape of Iberia, **2**. 7; said to have founded Calpê in Iberia, **2**. 15; expedition of, in quest of kine of Geryon and apples of the Hesperides, **2**. 57; certain companions of, colonised Iberia, **2**. 83; temple of, on the isle of Gades, and twelve labours of, **2**. 133; different theories as to site of Pillars of, **2**. 135–143; wont to erect pillars at limits of his expeditions, **2**. 139; pillars of, in India, no longer to be seen, **2**. 141; informed by Prometheus of route from Caucasus to the Hesperides, **2**. 187; temple of, built by Aemilianus at confluence of the Rhodanus and Isar Rivers, **2**. 197; "Monoecus," temple of, on Port of Monoecus (Monaco), **2**. 267; Atys the Lydian, a descendant of, by Omphalê, **2**. 337; some children of, settled in Sardinia, **2**. 361; Harbour of, at Cosa in Italy, **2**. 363; entertained by Evander, mythical founder of Rome, and destined to become a god, **2**. 385; temple of, at Tibur, **2**. 417; Fortress of (Herculaneum), **2**. 451; completed mound at Gulf Lucrinus, **2**. 445; the Harbour of (Tropea), in Bruttium, **3**. 19; the colossal bronze statue of, taken by Fabius Maximus from Tarentum to the Capitolium at Rome, **3**. 107; drove out the Leuternian Giants, **3**. 119; defeated the giants in Pallenê (Kassandra) the Macedonian peninsula, **3**. 351; connected a hollow place in Thrace with the sea and thus created Lake Bistonis, **3**. 365; the voyage of, from Troy, **3**. 381; father of Tlepolemus of Ephyra, **4**. 27; joined by the Epeians against Augeias, **4**. 39; temple of, in Triphylia, **4**. 65; ravaged the Pylian country, slaying all the twelve sons of Neleus except Nestor, **4**. 81, 85; humbled the Eleians, **4**. 91; by some said to have

INDEX OF NAMES, PLACES, AND SUBJECTS

been the first to contend in the Olympian Games and win the victory, **4.** 93; captured cities in Elis, **4.** 105; brought up Cerberus from Hades near Cape Taenarum, **4.** 127; drove the birds away from the Stymphalian Lake, **4.** 161; said to have driven out the Dryopians, **4.** 173; the sons of, **4.** 187; the painting of, in torture in the robe of Deïaneira, **4.** 201; slew Erginus the tyrant of the Orchomenians, **4.** 335; the hot waters of, at Aedepsus in Euboea, **4.** 379; death of, on Mt. Oeta, **4.** 387; hot waters near Thermopylae sacred to, **4.** 389; funeral pyre of, **4.** 391; captured Oechalia, **4.** 433; ancestor of Thessalian kings, **4.** 455; killed the ferryman Nessus at the Lycormas (Evenus) River in Aetolia, **5.** 29; defeated the river-god Acheloüs and thus won the hand of Deïaneira, **5.** 57; drained Paracheloïtis, **5.** 59; harbour and precinct of, in Acarnania, from which latter the "Labours of Heracles," by Lysippus, was carried to Rome, **5.** 61; the last of the giants destroyed by, lie beneath the isle Myconos, **5.** 171; slew the giants who attacked Aphroditê at Phanagoreia near the Cimmerian Bosporus, **5.** 201; reputed expedition of, to India, **5.** 239; Pillars of, 30,000 stadia from Issus, **5.** 289; Hylas, a companion of, carried off by the nymphs from Mt. Arganthonium in Asia, and Cius, a companion of, founded Cius, **5.** 457; not honoured by the Ilians, because he sacked their city, **6.** 61, 63; ruined Augê the mother of Telephus, **6.** 135; colossal statue of, in Samos, **6.** 215; father of Thessalus, **6.** 273; expedition of, to India, **7.** 7–13; worshipped by Indian philosophers, **7.** 97; temple of, on the Heracleium in Aegypt, **8.** 65; the City of, near the Nile, holds in honour the ichneumon, **8.** 107; said to have visited the temple of Ammon, **8.** 115; worshipped at Meroê, **8.** 147; altar of, on the Emporicus Gulf in Libya, **8.** 161; took Indian natives with him to

Libya, **8.** 169; a kind of temple of, in Cyrenaea, **8.** 207

Heracles, one of the Idaean Dactyli, not the son of Zeus and Alcmenê, said by some to have been the first to contend in the Olympian Games and win the victory, **4.** 93

Heracles, Island of (see Scombraria)

Heracles Cornopion ("Locust-killer"), worshipped by the Oetaeans, **6.** 127

Heracles Ipoctonus ("Ips-slayer"), worshipped by the Erythraeans in Mimas, **6.** 127

Heracleïdae, the, brought back the Dorians, **4.** 7; the return of, after the Trojan War, **4.** 9, 91, 107, 175; guided back to the Peloponnesus by Oxylus, **4.** 103; under Eurysthenes and Procles seized Laconia, **4.** 133; succeeded the Pelopidae at Mycenae and Argos, **4.** 187; held all the Peloponnesus except Achaea, **4.** 211; invaded Attica, but were defeated, and founded Megara, **4.** 251; as some think, built their fleet at Naupactus, **4.** 385; returned to the Peloponnesus from the Dorian Tetrapolis, **4.** 387; once inhabited Rhodes, **6.** 273

Heraea (near Aïanni) in Arcadia, settled either by Cleombrotus or Cleonymus from nine communities, **4.** 21; no longer exists, **4.** 229

Heraeum, the Argive, 40 stadia from Argos, **4.** 151, and common to Argos and Mycenae, and contains remarkable statues made by Polycleitus, **4.** 165, 167 (see footnote 1)

Heraeum, the, on the isle Samos, **6.** 213

Hérault River, the (see Arauris)

Herculaneum (see Heracles, Fortress of), **2.** 451

Hercynian (Black) Forest, the; near the sources of the Ister, **2.** 287; geographical position of, **3.** 155; description of, **3.** 163, 165

Herdonia (Ordona), on the mule-road between Brundisium and Beneventum, **3.** 123

Hermae, the, between Syenê and Philae; description of, **8.** 131

Hermaea, the promontory and city on the coast of Carthaginia, **8.** 183, 191

351

INDEX OF NAMES, PLACES, AND SUBJECTS

INDEX OF NAMES, PLACES, AND SUBJECTS

INDEX OF NAMES, PLACES, AND SUBJECTS

"Tamassus," **3.** 17; Islands of Aeolus of, **3.** 19; scourged by Zoïlus (surnamed Homeromastix, "Scourge of Homer"), **3.** 79; hinted at the truth when he called Aeolus "steward of the winds," **3.** 97, 99; on "the Mysians, hand-to-hand fighters," **3.** 177, 181, 187, 189, 209; on the Hippemolgi, Galactophagi, and Abii, **3.** 179, 181, 195, 197, 205, 209; accused of ignorance of distant places by Apollodorus and Eratosthenes, but conceded accurate knowledge of places near by, never using an inappropriate epithet, **3.** 189–199; placed the wanderings of Odysseus in Oceanus, **3.** 193; wrongly reproached by Eratosthenes and Apollodorus for ignorance of geography, though he knew Greece and also regions remote, **3.** 195; correctly describes the Scythians and other similar tribes, **3.** 199, 205; knew of the potter's wheel (*Iliad* xviii. 600), **3.** 207; did not invent the "Galactophagi" and the "Abii," **3.** 209, 243, 245; invokes "Zeus, Dodonaean, Pelasgian," and describes the people (the Selli) of Dodona, **3.** 313; the *Odyssey* of, quoted on the "tomouroi of great Zeus" at Dodona; the proper interpretation of his words "themistes" and "boulai," **3.** 317; calls the Europus River "Titaresius," **3.** 335; by "Phlegyae" means the Gyrtonians, **3.** 335, 337; calls Abydon on the Axius River "Amydon," **3.** 341, 343, 345; calls the Axius River "water most fair," **3.** 343, 345; on Iphidamas, "whom Cisses reared," **3.** 343, 349; on the "Sinties" (*i.e.* "Sinti") in Lemnos, **3.** 367; invoked as witness by some writers in regard to the extent of the Hellespont, **3.** 381, 383; on "Rhipê, Stratiê, and windy Enispê," all now deserted, **3.** 385, **4.** 229; the first author to discuss Greece, **4.** 3; calls the land of the Epeians Elis, **4.** 19; knew of Pylus, both land and city, **4.** 21; his words not to be contradicted, **4.** 25; mentions Cyllenê in Elis, **4.** 25; apparently means by "Ephyra"

the city in Elis (five citations), **4.** 27, 29; distinguishes between places bearing the same name by appropriate epithets, **4.** 29; means by "Pylus" the Triphylian Pylus, **4.** 31, 33, 57; divides the Eleian country into four parts, **4.** 35; often by a poetic figure names a part with the whole, **4.** 37; a case of *hyperbaton* in, **4.** 41; on Athene's visit to the Cauconians, **4.** 45, 57; mentions Helus near Sparta, **4.** 47; means by "Pylus" (Nestor's home) the "Lepreatic (or Triphylian) Pylus" and calls it "emathóeis," **4.** 51; means that Telemachus found the Pylians offering sacrifice at the temple of the Samian Poseidon, and says the Cauconians came as allies of the Trojans, **4.** 55; refers to the Eleian, not the Triphylian Cauconians, **4.** 57; on Arenê and Pylus, **4.** 61; prolongs the Pylian Sea to the seven cities promised by Agamemnon to Achilles, **4.** 67; his fame and knowledge, **4.** 69; on the country that was subject to Nestor, **4.** 71, 73; according to his statements the Pylus of Nestor could not lie on the sea, **4.** 75; on the return voyage of Telemachus from Sparta, **4.** 77; only the Triphylian Pylus could be the Pylus of Nestor, according to his account, **4.** 77–87; his characterisation of Zeus followed by Pheidias in making the great image at Olympia, **4.** 89; "alone has seen, or alone has shown the likenesses of the gods" (*e.g.* in his descriptions of Zeus and Hera), **4.** 91; does not mention the Olympian Games, but certain funeral games in Elis, **4.** 93; calls Lesbos the "city of Macar," **4.** 97; most of the Pylian districts mentioned in his *Catalogue* thought to be Arcadian, **4.** 101; on the seven cities promised by Agamemnon to Achilles, **4.** 109; on the city Helus in Laconia, **4.** 129; *Catalogue* of, quoted on Messê, **4.** 129; calls Laconia "Achaean Argos," **4.** 137; on the journey of Telemachus to Sparta via Pherae (Pharis), **4.** 145; his

357

INDEX OF NAMES, PLACES, AND SUBJECTS

359

INDEX OF NAMES, PLACES, AND SUBJECTS

6. 245; especially claimed by Smyrna, **6.** 247; on the "Asian meadow" (Leimon), **6.** 261; Rhodes and Cos in existence in time of, but not Halicarnassus and Cnidus, **6.** 273; on the Carians "of barbarian speech," **6.** 301; the "Solymi" of, not Lycians but Milyae, **6.** 321, 323; on the Cilicians in the Troad, **6.** 357; in his *Catalogue* names the various Trojan allies, **6.** 361; does not mention the Pamphylians and various other tribes, **6.** 363, 367, 369; misunderstood by Apollodorus, **6.** 371, 373; on the worship of Dionysus on Mt. Nysa, **7,** 9, 11; on the war between the pygmies and the cranes, **7.** 95; knows nothing about the empires of the Medes and Syrians, **7.** 187; does not mention Tyre, **7.** 267; on the skill of the Sidonians in beautiful arts, **7.** 269; on the oracle of Zeus at Dodona and his conversations with Minos in Crete, **7.** 287; says Persephonê granted reason to Teiresias after his death, **7.** 289; on the Aethiopians, Sidonians, and Erembians, **7.** 369, 371; on the Nile, "heaven-fed river," **8.** 21; cited in regard to Alexandria, **8.** 35; on where Helen got her "goodly drugs," **8.** 63; on the nods of Zeus, **8.** 115; on the Aegyptian Thebes, **8.** 121; Meninx (Jerba), in the Little Syrtis, regarded as "the land of the Lotus-eaters" of, **8.** 193

Homereium, the, at Smyrna, a quadrangular portico with shrine and statue of Homer, **6.** 245

Homeric Catalogue of Ships, The; the work of Apollodorus of Athens on, **3.** 187; most Pylian districts mentioned in, thought to be Arcadian, **4.** 101; writers on, have supplied Strabo with materials, **4.** 341

Homeridae, the, in Chios; mentioned by Pindar, **6.** 243, 245

Homolê (see Homolium in Magnesia)

Homolium, a city in Macedonia and Magnesia close to Mt. Ossa, **3.** 337, **4.** 449, 453

Homonadeis, the, in Pisidia; the country of, invaded by Amyntas, **5.** 477, 479, 481

Honey; in Hyrcania, drips from leaves of trees, as also in Matianê (in Media) and in Sacasenê and Araxenê (districts of Armenia), **1.** 273; exported from Turdetania, **2.** 33; produced in the Alps, **2.** 283; the "Hyblaean," at Megara Hyblaea in Sicily, **3.** 365; superior in Sicily, **3.** 85; excellent, at Brundisium, **3.** 121; the best, produced on Mt. Hymettus, **4.** 275; in the Sporades Islands, rivals that of Attica, **5.** 179; in Colchis, generally bitter, **5.** 211; abundant in Hyrcania, in Matianê in Media, and in Sacasenê and Araxenê in Armenia, **5.** 251; a crazing kind of mixture of, made by the Heptacomitae in Asia Minor, **5.** 401; yielded by the palm-tree, **7.** 215; abundant in Arabia, **7.** 311

Hoop-trundling, at Rome, **2.** 407

Horizon, change of, **1.** 45

Hormina (or Hyrmina), a mountain promontory near Cyllenê in Elis, **4.** 41

Horn, the, of the Byzantines, a gulf resembling a stag's horn, **3.** 281, 283

Horse, a white, sacrificed to Diomedes by the Eneti, **2.** 321

Horse-meat, eaten by the Scythian Nomads, **3.** 243

Horse-race, a, instituted by Romulus in honour of Poseidon (Neptune), **2.** 385

Horse-raising, in Aetolia, Acarnania, and Thessaly, **4.** 229

Horses, good qualities of, determined by training as well as by locality, **1.** 395; in Iberia, trained to climb mountains and to obey promptly, and swift, like those of Parthia, **2.** 107; superior, bred by the Eneti, **2.** 309, but practice now discontinued, **2.** 321; which drink from the Sybaris River in Italy are made timid, **3.** 47; excellent, in neighbourhood of Mt. Garganum in Apulia, **3.** 131; small, in region of Lake Maeotis, **3.** 225; castrated in Scythia and Sarmatia, **3.** 249; the breed of, in Arcadia, Argolis, and Epidauria, is most excellent, **4.** 229; the, of the Amazons, **5.** 233; the Nesaean, originated either in Greater Media or in Armenia, **5.** 311,

INDEX OF NAMES, PLACES, AND SUBJECTS

20,000 being sent annually from Armenia to the Persian king, 5. 331; those in Parthia, 5. 311; in India, possession of, a royal privilege, 7. 69, 87; certain in India, have one horn and the head of a deer, 7. 93; scarce in Carmania, 7. 153; more than 30,000 kept at royal stud at Apameia in Syria, 7. 251; not found at Nabataea in Arabia, 7. 369; the, in Masaesylia, are small, but quick, and obedient, 8. 167; raised in great numbers between the seaboard and Getulia, 8. 197

Horses, stunted (see Ginni)

Hortensius, married Marcia the wife of Marcus Cato, 5. 273

Hot springs, the, in Pithecussae, a cure for gall-stones, 2. 459

Hungarians, the (see Urgi)

Hya (see Hyampolis)

Hyacynthian Festival, the, in the temple of Amyclaean Apollo in Laconia, 3. 109

Hyameitis, one of the five capitals of Messenia, 4. 119

Hyampeia on Parnassus, not the same as Hyampolis, 4. 373

Hyampolis (near Vogdhani) in Phocis, lies above the territory of Hyampolis, 4. 341; later called Hya by some, whither the Hyantes of Boeotia were banished, is far inland and not to be confused with Hyampeia on Parnassus, 4. 373

Hyantes, the, lived in Boeotia in earlier times, 3. 287, 4. 281; founded a city Hya in Phocis, 4. 283; banished from Boeotia to Hyampolis in Phocis, 4. 373; left Boeotia and settled in Aetolia, 5. 81

Hyarotis River, the, in India, 7. 35, 47, 51

Hybla in Sicily (see Megara Hyblaea)

Hyblaean honey, the, at Megara Hyblaea in Sicily, 3. 65

Hybreas of Mylasa in Caria, greatest orator in Strabo's time, 6. 191; remarkable career of, 6. 295-297; provoked Labienus, withdrew to Rhodes, but returned and resumed power, 6. 297

Hybrianes (Agrianes?), the, 3. 275

Hydara, a stronghold built by Mithridates, 5. 425

Hydarnes, one of the "Seven Persians," 5. 337

Hydaspes River, the, in India, 7. 5, 25, 47, 49, 55, 57

Hydatos-Potamoi (see Seleuceia in Pieria, in Syria)

Hydê, the Homeric, at foot of Mt. Tmolus in Lydia, 4. 309; reputed home of the Homeric "Tychius, the best of workers in hide," and by some identified with Sardeis, 6. 175

"Hydê," an incorrect reading, for "Hylê" in Boeotia, in Homer, 4. 309, 311

Hydra (see Lysimachia), Lake, in Aetolia, 5. 65

Hydra, the monster, poisoned certain of the Centaurs, 4. 61; killed by Heracles at the lake called Lernê, in Argolis, 4. 151, 163

Hydra, the promontory, with Harmatus forms the Elaïtic Gulf, 6. 159

Hydraces, the, a tribe in India, summoned as mercenary troops by Cyrus, 7. 9

Hydrelus, the Lacedaemonian, founded a city in Asia Minor, 6. 261

Hydruntum (see Hydrus)

Hydrus (or Hydruntum, now Otranto), in Iapygia, 3. 119

Hydrussa the island, off Attica, 4. 271

Hyelê (see Elea)

"Hyes attes," a cry uttered in the ritual of Sabazius and the Mother, 5. 109

Hylas; Mt. Arganthonium in Asia the scene of myth of, 5. 457

Hylê, the Homeric (Hydê not being the correct reading), in Boeotia on Lake Cephissis (Hylicê), 4. 309, 311, 321

Hylicê (the Homeric Cephissis), Lake, 4. 309

Hyllus the eldest son of Heracles, adopted by Aegimius the king of the Dorian Tetrapolis, 4. 387

Hyllus (now called Phrygius) River, the, mentioned by Homer, 5. 421; empties into the Hermus, 6. 173

Hylobii, the, in India, a sect of the Garmanes in India, 7. 103

Hymettus, Mt., one of the most famous mountains in Attica, has marble quarries and produces the

INDEX OF NAMES, PLACES, AND SUBJECTS

INDEX OF NAMES, PLACES, AND SUBJECTS

Hyria, and is a colony of Hyria, having been founded by Nycteus the father of Antiopê, **4.** 297

Hysiatae, the; inhabitants of Hysiae in Argolis, **4.** 297

Hyssus (the Roman javelin), can be used both in close combat and as a missile for hurling, **5.** 19

Hystaspis, father of Dareius, **6.** 217

I

Iaccetania in Iberia, where Sertorius waged war against Pompey, and Sextus (Pompey) against Caesar's generals, **2.** 101

Iaccetanians, the; geographical position of, **2.** 99

Iacchus (Dionysus), the "horned," **7.** 9

Ialmenus, led a colony of Orchomenians to the Pontus, after the capture of Troy, **4.** 341

Ialysus, tutelary hero of Rhodes and grandson of Helius, **6.** 273; son of Cercaphus, **6.** 275

Ialysus, a city in Rhodes, mentioned by Homer, **6.** 273; origin of name of, **6.** 275

Iamblichus, chieftain of a tribe in Syria, **7.** 253

Iambus, the, suited to reproaches (in the Pythian Nome), **4.** 363

Iamneia, a village near Iapê in Phoenicia, **7.** 275, 277

Iaonians, the Homeric, "with trailing tunics," **4.** 407

Iapodes, the, a mixed tribe of Illyrians and Celts, **3.** 253, 259, 287

Iapyges, the; the name of the inhabitants of the country of the Tarantini, **3.** 13; the three capes of, **3.** 39; once lived at Croton, **3.** 43; named after Iapyx, son of Daedalus and a Cretan woman, **3.** 111

Iapygia; the promontory of, **1.** 417; the early boundary of, **3.** 53; called Messapia by the Greeks, **3.** 103; forms a sort of peninsula, **3.** 105; happy lot of part of, **3.** 117; called Messapia by Messapus, **4.** 299

Iapygian Cape (Capo di Leuca), the, **1.** 147, **2.** 301, **3.** 29, 103, 117

Iapyx, the son of Daedalus, after

whom the Iapyges were named, **3.** 111; colonised Brundisium, **3.** 121

Iardanus; the meadow and tomb of, in Triphylia, **4.** 63, 67

Iardanus, the streams of, as mentioned by Homer, **4.** 45

"Iasian Argos," the Homeric, **4.** 155, means the Peloponnesus, **4.** 157

Iasidae, the, and "Iasian Argos," referred to by more recent writers, **4.** 165

Iasion, who lived in Samothrace, was struck by thunderbolt for sinning against Demeter, **3.** 371

Iasus, on an island close to Caria; amusing story concerning, **6.** 291

Iaxartes River, the, empties into the Caspian Sea, **5.** 245; the boundary between the Sacae and the Sogdiani, **5.** 269; about 5000 stadia from Bactra, **5.** 271; borders on Sogdiana, and forms the boundary between it and the nomads, **5.** 281; empties into the Caspian Sea but should not be confused with the Oxus, **5.** 287

Iazyges, the, beyond Germany, **3.** 173

Iberia in Asia, invaded by Pompey, **5.** 187; bounded by the Caucasus, **5.** 207; bounded on the north by the Caucasus, **5.** 207; detailed description of, **5.** 217-221; four passes lead into, **5.** 219; has four castes of people, **5.** 221, 323

Iberia in Europe; wealth of, **1.** 7; like an ox-hide in shape, **1.** 317; length of, **1.** 409; promontory of, **1.** 417; shape and dimensions of, **1.** 489; description of, in detail, **2.** 3-123; cold and rugged in northern parts, fertile in southern, **2.** 3; shape (like an ox-hide) and dimensions of, **2.** 5; western and southern sides of, **2.** 11; betrays signs of Odysseus' wanderings, **2.** 53; wealth of, **2.** 57; description of seaboard of, from the Pillars to the Pyrenees, **2.** 79-101; colonised by companions of Heracles and emigrants from Messenê, **2.** 83; coast of, from Pillars to Tarraco, has poor harbours, but, from Tarraco to Emporium, fine ones, **2.** 93; the number of its cities, the poverty of much of its soil, and the traits of

363

INDEX OF NAMES, PLACES, AND SUBJECTS

its people, 2. 105; animals, birds, medicinal castor, copper, roots for dyeing, olives, grapes, and figs in, 2. 107; variations in use of the term by historians, 2. 117, 119; except Baetica, belongs wholly to Augustus, being governed by two legati, 2. 221; islands off coast of, 2. 123–159; the passes leading to, from Italy, long barred by the Ligures, 2. 269; profitable mines in, 2. 333; much of, acquired by the Romans in the Third Carthaginian War, 3. 141; colonised by Rhodians in early times, 6. 275

Iberia, Ulterior, now a praetorial Province, 8. 215

Iberian earth, the, rivals the Sinopean, 5. 369

Iberian Sea, the; definition of, 1. 471

Iberians, the Asiatic, are excellent subjects, but from neglect by the Romans sometimes attempt revolutions, 3. 145; hold a part of the Moschian country, 5. 215; perhaps so named from the gold mines in their country, 5. 215; assemble for war in great numbers, 5. 219

Iberians, the (in Europe; use of the term, 1. 123; migrations of western Iberians to regions beyond the Pontus and Colchis, 1. 227; traits and modes of life of, and why they could be subdued by various foreign nations, 2. 87; armour, infantry, and cavalry of, 2. 107; some of, sleep on the ground, 2. 109, and have other barbaric customs, 2. 111; ride double on horseback, though in battle one of two fights on foot, 2. 113; commit suicide upon occasion, and die for those to whom they have "devoted" themselves, 2. 115; say that the Pillars of Heracles are in Gades, 2. 137; taught the sacred rites of Artemis by the Massaliotes, 2. 175; more difficult to conquer than the Gauls, 2. 239; the first barbarian settlers of Sicily, 3. 73; began the war with the Romans, 3. 143

Iberus (Ebro) River, the; distant about 2200 stadia from New Carthage, 2. 81; the course of, 2. 91; geographi-

cal position of, 2. 97; a stone bridge over, at Celsa, 2. 99; crossing of, at Varia, 2. 101; formerly a boundary of Iberia, 2. 119; novel and peculiar in respect to its overflows, 2. 155

Ibex, the Alpine (see footnote 5, Vol. II., p. 289)

Ibis, the, found in the neighbourhood of Cape Deirê in Aethiopia, 7. 331; worshipped by the Aegyptians, 8. 109; description and habits of, 8. 151

Ibiza, the isle (see Ebusus)

Ibycus the Greek lyric poet, of Rhegium (fl. about 540 B.C.); on the mole connecting Syracuse with the island, 1. 219; says the Asopus in Sicyonia rises in Phrygia, 3. 79

Icaria, or Icaros (Nikaria), one of the Sporades Islands, a famous isle, 5. 173; the isle near Samos, where Icarus fell; description of, 6. 221

Icarian Sea, the; extent of, 1. 477, 5. 173; named after the isle Icaria, 6. 221

Icarius, father of Penelopê by Polycastê, had two sons who reigned over Acarnania with him, 5. 35; banished from Lacedaemon, settled in Acarnania, 5. 69

Icaros (or Icaria), colonised by Milesians, 6. 207

Icaros, an island in the Persian Gulf, has a temple of Apollo and an oracle of Artemis Tauropolus, 7. 303

Icarus, son of Daedalus; story of flight of, and of fall of, on the isle Icaria, 6. 221

Ichnae in Thessaly, where the Ichnaean Artemis is worshipped, 4. 421

Ichneumon, the, held in great honour by the people of the City of Heracles on the Nile, 8. 107; kills crocodiles and asps, 8. 109; indigenous to Aegypt, 8. 149

Ichthyophagi (" Fish-eaters "), the, live in narrow zones beneath the tropics, 1. 367, 7. 131, 153, 313, 327; life and habits of, 7. 329

Ichthys, Cape (Catakolo) in Elis, 120 stadia from Cephallenia, 4. 47; lies opposite Berenicê in Libya, 8. 201

Icizari, a strong fortress, now deserted, on Lake Stephanê in Cappadocia Pontica, 5. 445

INDEX OF NAMES, PLACES, AND SUBJECTS

INDEX OF NAMES, PLACES, AND SUBJECTS

366

INDEX OF NAMES, PLACES, AND SUBJECTS

INDEX OF NAMES, PLACES, AND SUBJECTS

Ipni in Magnesia, where some of Xerxes' ships were destroyed, **4.** 451

Ips, the vine-eating; Heracles the destroyer of, **6.** 127

Ipsela (see Cypsela)

Ireland (see Iernê)

Iri River, the (see Eurotas River, the, in the Peloponnesus), **4.** 231

Iris, the Selgic (orris-root), and the ointment made from it in Pisidia, **5.** 485

Iris River, the; silting up at mouth of, **1.** 193; rises in Cappadocia Pontica and flows through Themiscyra, **5.** 395; flows through Comana and Dazimonitis, and past Gaziura and Amaseia, and then into Phanaraea, **5.** 397, 429, 445

Iron, greatest quantity and best quality of, in Turditania, **2.** 39; mines of, near Hemeroscopeium in Iberia, **2.** 89; collars of, worn by women in Iberia, **2.** 109; produced in Britain, **2.** 255; mined in island Aethalia (Elba), **2.** 355, 357; once mined in the Lelantine Plain in Euboea, **5.** 13; first worked on Mt. Ida in the Troad, **5.** 117; with zinc, yields "mock-silver," at Andeira in Asia Minor, **6.** 115; skilful embossing of, at Cityra in Phrygia, **6.** 193; first worked by the Telchines in Rhodes, according to some writers, **6.** 275; found on the island Meroê in the Nile, **8.** 143

Iron mines, the, in Pharnacia in Cappadocia Pontica, **5.** 401, 403

Iron-works, the, among the Petrocorii and Bituriges Cubi in Aquitania, **2.** 217; in the territory of Aquileia and the Eneti, **2.** 319

Is, of Helicê, founder of Sybaris in Italy, **3.** 47

Isander, the Homeric (see Peisander)

Isar (Isère) River, the, confluence of, with the Rhodanus, **2.** 195, 197

Isaras River, the, **2.** 285 (see footnote)

Isaura, Old and New, in Lycaonia, **5.** 475, **6.** 327

Isauricê, in Lycaonia, **5.** 475

Ischia, the Italian isle (see Pithecussa)

Ischopolis in Cappadocia Pontica, now in ruins, **5.** 399

Isère River, the (see Isar River)

Isernia (see Aesernia)

Isinda in Asia, **6.** 193

Isinglass, the, in Cappadocia; see **5.** 369, footnote 2

Isis; temple of, at Soli in Cypros, **6.** 381; temple of, on a mountain near the Arabian Gulf, built by Sesostris, **7.** 319; river-land of, in Aethiopia, **7.** 333; mythical story of her hiding of body of Osiris from Typhon, **8.** 75; temple of, at Tentyra on the Nile, **8.** 119; worshipped at Meroê, **8.** 147

Iskuria (see Dioscurias)

Ismahan (see Ismarus in Thrace)

Ismara (see Ismarus in Thrace)

Ismaris, Lake, in Thrace, sends forth the stream called Odysseium, **3.** 365, 367

Ismarus (or Ismara, now Ismahan) in Thrace, **3.** 365, 367

Ismenus River, the, flows through the plain in front of Thebes, **4.** 313

Isodromian Mother, the (Cybelê); temple of, near Tralleis and Larisa in Asia, **4.** 441

Isola Longa, one of the Liburnides, **3.** 259

Issa (or Lesbos, *q.v.*)

Issa (Lissa), isle in the Adriatic, **1.** 475, **3.** 259

Issican Sea, the, **1.** 481

Issus, the road from, to Amisus and Sinopê, **6.** 311; small town in Cilicia, **6.** 345, 355

Issus, the Gulf of; distance from, to the Euxine, **1.** 255, and to the Sacred Cape of Iberia, **1.** 407; about 40,000 stadia from the Indian Sea, and 30,000 from the western extremity of Europe, **5.** 289

Ister (Karanasib), a city on the Euxine, **3.** 275; founded by the Milesians, **3.** 277

Ister (Danube) River, the; revealed to geographers by Alexander, and regions beyond by the Romans, **1.** 51; rises in region above the Adriatic, **1.** 211; bisects eastern Europe and forms a boundary of Germany and other countries, **1.** 493; the Atesinus empties into, **2.** 285; rises near the Suevi and the Black Forest, **2.** 287; bisects eastern Europe, and is the largest European river, **3.** 151; sources of,

369

INDEX OF NAMES, PLACES, AND SUBJECTS

INDEX OF NAMES, PLACES, AND SUBJECTS

Maurusia, with Scipio waged war against Julius Caesar, **8**. 169; king of Masaesylia, **8**. 173; killed in war against Caesar, **8**. 181

Juba II, invested by the Romans with the rule, not only of Maurusia, but also of other parts of Libya, **3**. 143; by gift of Augustus, succeeded to the throne of Maurusia, but recently (A.D. 19) died, **8**. 169, 215; father of Ptolemy, his successor, **8**. 179

Jucar River, the (see Sucro)

Judaea, a part of Syria, **7**. 239; geographical position of, **7**. 267; description and history of, **7**. 281–299; first kings of, **7**. 289; later kings of, **7**. 299; Aegypt difficult to enter from, **8**. 71; produces good palm-trees, **8**. 133

Judaeans, the, a tribe in Syria, **7**. 239; seized Gadaris in Phoenicia, **7**. 277; ancestors of, regarded as Aegyptians, **7**. 281; the shrewd practice of, in increasing revenues, adopted by certain Aegyptians, **8**. 61; are Aegyptian in origin, and practise circumcision and excision, **8**. 153

Judicum praefectus, the, a local official in Alexandria, **8**. 49

Juggling, closely related to religion and divination, **5**. 121

Jugurtha, the war against, caused much damage in Libya, **8**. 181

Julia Ioza, name of city (Zelis in Libya) transplanted to Iberia, **2**. 17

Juliopolis in Galatia, the home of Cleon (see Gordium)

Julius Caesar (see Caesar, Julius)

Juncarian Plain, the, in Iberia, **2**. 95

Jura, Mt., lies in the territory of the Sequani, **2**. 229; the pass over, **2**. 291

Juri dicendi praefectus, the, a Roman official in Aegypt, **4**. 49

Jurisconsults, the, expound the law to the Romans, **5**. 367

Jury, a trial by a, of men who murdered the priestess at Dodona, **4**. 285

Justice, Plato's definition of, **1**. 39; a cardinal principle of the Scythians, **3**. 201; wherein the Scythians excel all men, **3**. 205

K

Kainon Chorion, an impregnable rock in Cappadocia Pontica, **5**. 429

Kalamaki (see Schoenus)

Kalogria, Cape (see Araxus)

Kalpaki (see Orchomenus, the Arcadian)

Kandia (see Asinê, the Hermionic)

Kaprena (see Chaeroneia)

Kapronisi, the isle (see Caprus)

Karadje, Cape (see Criumetopon)

Karanasib (see Ister)

Karvura, Cape (see Zoster)

Karystos (see Carystus)

Kassandra (see Pallenê and Potidaea)

Kastri in Argolis (see Hermionê)

Kastri (see Pandosia, in Epeirus)

Kastro, Mt. (see Cynthus)

Kaszon, Mt., on the borders of Transylvania and Moldavia (see Cogaeonum)

Kato-Akhaia (see Dymê)

Kavarna (see Bizonê)

Kavo Grosso (see Thyrides)

Kempten (see Cambodunum)

Kerembe, Cape (see Carambis)

Kerka River, the (see Titius River)

Kermes, the dye-stuff, exported from Turdetania, **2**. 33

Kettle, the most sacred among the Cimbri, presented to Augustus, **3**. 165

Khaiaffa (see Macistus)

Kharkia (see Chalcia, the island)

Khelidonia Islands (see Chelidoniae)

Khryso (see Crisa)

Kiki, a fruit in Aegypt from which oil is pressed, **8**. 151

Kiladia (see Mases)

Kilissa-Hissar (see Tyana)

Kilissa-Kieui (see Ancyra in Phrygia)

Kimolos (see Cimolos)

Kisamo Kasteli (see Cisamus)

Kitros in Macedonia (see Pydna)

Klituras (see Cleitor)

Knights (see Hippeis), the, at Patavium, **2**. 313

Koïkina, Aegyptian textures made of some plant, **8**. 153

Kokhla (see Plataeae)

Konia (see Iconium)

Korakou (see Ephyra, the Corinthian)

Koron, or Koroni (see Asinê)

INDEX OF NAMES, PLACES, AND SUBJECTS

373

INDEX OF NAMES, PLACES, AND SUBJECTS

INDEX OF NAMES, PLACES, AND SUBJECTS

history of, **5.** 511; subject to earthquakes, **5.** 513; once seriously damaged, but restored by Caesar, **5.** 517; rivers in territory of, change water into stone, **6.** 189; the road through, **6.** 309

Laodiceia (Ladikieh) in Syria, on the sea, **7.** 241; description of, **7.** 249

Laodiceians, the (near the Lycus), derive splendid revenue from their sheep, **5.** 511

Laomedon; Heracles said to have sacked Ilium on account of horses of, **6.** 63

Lapathus in Cypros, founded by Laconians under Praxander, **6.** 377

Lapê (see Napê)

"Lapersae, the," the Dioscuri so called by Sophocles, **5.** 133

Lapis Specularis; see **5.** 369, footnote 2

Lapiths, the; the Peneius flows through the cities of, **3.** 333; under Ixion and Peirithoüs humbled and ejected the Perrhaebians, **4.** 437, 439; according to Homer and Simonides, lived intermingled with the Perrhaebians, **4.** 443, 445; Hieronymus on, **4.** 453

Lapsaki (see Lampsacus)

Laralon River, the, in Italy, **2.** 371

Laranda in Lycaonia, held by Antipater Derbetes, **5.** 477

Larimnum, a most fragrant incense, produced in the country of the Sabaeans in Arabia, **7.** 349

Larisa in Syria, **7.** 253

Larisa, daughter of Piasus and violated by him, killed him, **6.** 157

Larisa, the acropolis of Argos, has a temple of Zeus, **4.** 159, 441

Larisa Cremastê (Gardiki), also called Pelasgia, in the Pelasgian Plain in Thessaly, shocked by earthquake, **1.** 225; subject to Protesilaüs, **4.** 403, 419, 421, 433, 441, 453

Larisa, a city in Crete, **4.** 441

Larisa, a city between Elis and Dymê, **4.** 441

Larisa, the Ephesian, **4.** 441

Larisa, a village in the territory of Ephesus in the Caÿster Plain, once a city and had a temple of Larisaean Apollo, **6.** 155, 157

Larisa on the Euxine, near the end of Mt. Haemus, **4.** 441

Larisa, a place on Mt. Ossa, **4.** 441

Larisa Pelasgia (see Larisa Cremastê)

Larisa (Larisa Phriconis), inhabited by the Pelasgi, **2.** 345; near Cymê in Asia, **4.** 441; "fertile" abode of the Pelasgi, **6.** 153, 157

Larisa in Syria, **4.** 441

Larisa (Yenicheher) in Thessaly, suffered from earthquake, **1.** 225; 340 stadia from Thaumaci, 240 from outlets of the Peneius, **4.** 233; lies on the Peneius River, **3.** 337, **4.** 333, **5.** 231, 333; had land that was deposited, and sometimes washed away, by the Peneius, **4.** 439, **6.** 157

Larisa, a village near Tralleis in Asia, **4.** 441

Larisa near Hamaxitis in the Troad, **4.** 441; used to belong to the Tenedians, **6.** 93; in plain sight of Ilium, **6.** 153

Larisaean Rocks, the, 50 stadia from Mitylenê on the road to Methymnê, **4.** 441

Larisaeans, the, on the Peneius River, seized Perrhaebia and exacted tribute until Philip overcame them, **4.** 439

Larisian Plain, the, in Crete, **4.** 441

Larisus River, the; the boundary between Dymê and Buprasium, **4.** 225; between Dymê and Elis, **4.** 441

Larius (Como), the Lake, filled by the Addua River, **2.** 227; geographical position of, **2.** 271, 273, 313; dimensions of, **2.** 295

Larma (see Larymna, Upper)

Lartolaeëtans, the, in Iberia; fertile country of, **2.** 93

Larymna (see Larymna, Upper) in Boeotia, a village near the mouth of the Cephissus River, **4.** 297

Larymna, Upper (Larma), in Locris, annexed to the Boeotian (Lower) Larymna, **4.** 305

Las (Passova), the Homeric, once captured by Castor and Pollux, **4.** 131, and hence the inhabitants were called Lapersae, **4.** 133

Lasion in Elis, **4.** 27

Lathon River, the, empties into the

375

INDEX OF NAMES, PLACES, AND SUBJECTS

Harbour of the Hesperides in Libya, **6.** 249, **8.** 201

Latin country, the (see Latium)

"Latin right," the, given to Nemausus, **2.** 201; to certain Aquitani, to the Auscii, and to the Convenae, **2.** 219

Latin Way, the, **2.** 411, 413, 415

Latini, which the Turdetani have become, **2.** 59; country of the, **2.** 335; name applied by Aeneas to all his subjects; offered sacrifice to Zeus at Alba, **2.** 379; hold religious festivals at Ardea, **2.** 393; now hold Campania as far as Sinuessa, **2.** 395; treated by the Romans as partners after the expulsion of Tarquinius Superbus, **3.** 139; later made subject, **3.** 141

Latinus, king of the aborigines, who lived where Rome now is, was killed in the battle against the Rutuli and succeeded by Aeneias, **2.** 379

Latitudes (see Climata), the, determined by Hipparchus, **1.** 22 (footnote 2); the observation of differences in, **1.** 331; of peoples, do not determine success of human institutions, **1.** 393; the graphic representation of, **1.** 463; parallels of, between Rome and Naples, and through Apollonia in Epeirus and other places, and distance from, to equator and other parallels, **1.** 513

Latium (the Latin country); bounded by the Tiber, **2.** 335; description of, **2.** 377-425; where is Rome, **2.** 377; has fertile soil and produces everything, **2.** 389; the other cities and roads in, **2.** 409-425; present extent of seaboard of, **2.** 389; the cities on seaboard of, **2.** 391-399; Rome, **2.** 399-409; other cities in, **2.** 409-425

Latmian Gulf (at first called "Latmus"), the, near Miletus, **6.** 209

Latmus, the gulf (see Latmian Gulf)

Latmus, Mt., the Homeric "mountain of the Phtheires," near Miletus, **6.** 209

Latomiae ("Quarries"), the; six isles in the Arabian Gulf, **7.** 319, 327

Latopolis, on the Nile, south of Thebes, worships Athenê and the *Latus*, **8.** 127

Latus, the (a fish), worshipped at Latopolis on the Nile, **8.** 109, 127; indigenous to Aegypt, **8.** 149

Laurel, the, in India, **7.** 97; in the Red Sea, **7.** 305

Laurel groves; numerous in the region of Cape Deirê in Aethiopia, **7.** 331

Laurentum (Torre di Paterno) in Italy; where Aeneias put in, **2.** 379; geographical position of, **2.** 393

Laurium, silver-mines of ("Attic silver-mines"), **2.** 43; riddle applied to, **2.** 45; have now failed, **4.** 275, **5.** 15

Laüs (near Laino), in Leucania, a colony of the Sybaritae, **3.** 5; a boundary of the Brutii, **3.** 13

Lava, the, from Aetna, solidifies, **3.** 69, 87

Laviansenê, one of the ten prefectures of Cappadocia, **5.** 349, 369; borders on Culupenê and Camisenê, **5.** 441

Lavican Way, the, **2.** 411

Lavinium (near Laino), named by King Latinus after his daughter Lavinia, **2.** 379; Titus Tatius murdered at, **2.** 385; geographical position of, **2.** 393; Aeneias landed at, **6.** 109

Lead, mines of, at Castalo in Iberia, **2.** 47; in the Cassiterides Islands, **2.** 157

League, the Achaean (see Achaean League)

League, a new, formed by Patrae, Dymê, Tritaea, and Pharae after the dissolution of the Achaean League, **4.** 211

League, the Chrysaorian in Caria, **6.** 299

League, the Lycian, **6.** 313, 315

Lebadeia (Livadia) near Lake Copaïs, **4.** 331; has the oracle of the Trophonian Zeus, in an underground chasm, **4.** 333; Panopeus and Trachin in Phocis border on region of, **4.** 371

Lebedus in Asia, founded by Andropompus, **6.** 199; great centre of worship of Dionysus, **6.** 237

Leben (Leda) in Crete, emporium of Gortynia, **5.** 137, 139

Lebinthos (Levintha), one of the Sporades Islands, **5.** 173

INDEX OF NAMES, PLACES, AND SUBJECTS

Lecce (see Lupiae)

Lechaeum, level of waters at, higher than at Cenchreae, as was thought, **1**. 209; the western harbour of Corinth and connected therewith by long walls, **4**. 197

Lectum, Cape; Mt. Ida in the Troad extends to, **6**. 5; between Tenedos and Lesbos, **6**. 11, 13; Hamaxitus adjacent to, **6**. 93; has an altar of the twelve gods, founded by Agamemnon, **6**. 97

Leda in Crete (see Leben)

Leda, daughter of Thestius the Aetolian and wife of Tyndareus, **5**. 69

Leeches (lampreys) seven cubits long found in a river in Maurusia in Libya, **8**. 161

Leëtanians, the, in Iberia; fertile country of, **2**. 93

Legae, the, a Scythian people, live between the Amazons and the Albanians, **5**. 233

Legati (propraetors), sent by Augustus to his Provinces, **8**. 213

Legati, two (praetorian and consular), govern Caesar's territory in Iberia, **2**. 121

Legatus, a, serves as assistant to a praetor in governing Baetica in Iberia, **2**. 121

Legions, three Roman, stationed in Aegypt, **8**. 49

Leibethra, near Dium in southern Macedonia, **3**. 339

Leibethrides, the, cave sacred to nymphs on Mt. Helicon, **4**. 319, **5**. 109

Leibethrum, in Pieria in Macedonia, consecrated by Thracians to the Muses, **4**. 319, **5**. 107

Leimon ("Meadow") in Asia Minor, where the Nysaeans celebrate festivals, **6**. 269

Leimonê (see Elonê)

Lelantine Plain, the, in Euboea, suffered a volcanic eruption, **1**. 215; contains disease-curing fountains, and once had a mine of copper and iron, **5**. 13; an object of dispute between the Eretrians and the Chalcidians, **5**. 19; an object of contention, **5**. 85

Leleges, the, obtained a portion of the Peloponnesus, **3**. 287; Lelex the

founder of, **3**. 289; Locrus, a chieftain of, **3**. 291; lived in Boeotia in earlier times, **4**. 281; certain of, settled in Pisidia, **5**. 481, by aid of the Cretans, **5**. 491; dynasty of, **6**. 17; majority of, placed by Homer on the Gulf of Adramyttium, **6**. 97; Pedasus a city of, **6**. 15, 99, as also Assus, **6**. 115, 117; different from the Carians, **6**. 117; founded many cities in Caria, seized part of Pisidia, invaded Greece, became distributed throughout it, and disappeared, **6**. 119; traces of, in Caria and Miletus, **6**. 121; closely related to the Trojans, but not included with them in the *Catalogue*, **6**. 149; present at the Trojan battles, **6**. 151; occupied parts of the Asiatic coast in early times, but were driven out by the Ionians, **6**. 199, 205; once inhabited Ephesus, **6**. 225; subject to Minos and occupied Aegaean isles, **6**. 301; mentioned by Homer, **6**. 363

" Lelegian forts," the, in Caria, **3**. 289

Lelex, founder of the tribe of the Leleges, **3**. 289

Lemenna Lake (Lake of Geneva), traversed by the Rhodanus River, **2**. 199, 273, 291

Lemnos, spared by Achilles, **1**. 165; the Aegaean isle, **1**. 477; settled by Pelasgians, **2**. 347; lies east of Athos, **3**. 353, 365; first settled by the Thracian Sinti, **3**. 367; the Minyans driven out of, **4**. 63; the sacred rites in, **5**. 89; the Cabeiri worshipped in, **5**. 115

Lemovices, the, a tribe in Aquitania, **2**. 217

Lenae, the; ministers of Dionysus, **5**. 97

"Length" and "breadth"; geographical definition of, **1**. 321

Lentil-shaped pebbles, the, at the pyramids of Gizeh and at Amaseia in Pontus; explanation of, **8**. 95

Leocorium, the, at Athens, **4**. 263; has a myth connected with it, **4**. 265

Leon, the Lookout of, in Aethiopia, **7**. 333; Pillars and Altars of, **7**. 335

Leondari (see Leuctrum)

Leones (Lions), City of, in Phoenicia, **7**. 267

377

INDEX OF NAMES, PLACES, AND SUBJECTS

INDEX OF NAMES, PLACES, AND SUBJECTS

INDEX OF NAMES, PLACES, AND SUBJECTS

INDEX OF NAMES, PLACES, AND SUBJECTS

"Lychnite" (Tourmaline?) stones, the, said to be found in Masaesylia in Libya, **8**. 177

Lychnus, the, a fish indigenous to the Nile, **8**. 149

Lycia, 4000 stadia from Alexandria, **1**. 93; a part of the Cis-Halys country, **1**. 497; colonised by the Cauconians, **3**. 385; home of the Cyclopes who helped to build the walls of Tiryns, **4**. 169; the Homeric, in which Zeleia was situated, was subject to Pandarus, **5**. 461; discussion of, **5**. 491–495; origin of name of, **5**. 491; the present, separated from the country of the Cibyrans by a ridge of the Taurus, **6**. 265; description of, **6**. 311–323

Lycians, the, were Trojans, according to Homer, **5**. 37, 423; two groups of, the Trojan and that near Caria, **5**. 491; the same as the Homeric "Solymi"(?), **5**. 493; by some confused with the Carians, **5**. 495, 6. 315; in the Troad, were led by Pandarus, **6**. 19, held Zeleia, **6**. 23, and "fight in close combat," **6**. 45; in southern Asia Minor, captured Sardeis, **6**. 179; continued to live in a decent and civilised way, **6**. 313; by Homer made a different people from the Solymi, but by others said once to have been called "Solymi," and later "Termilae," and still later named after Lycus the son of Pandion, **6**. 323, 361

Lycomedes the King, with Polemon captured Arsaces at Sagylium, **5**. 445

Lycomedes, king of the isle Scyros, and father-in-law of Achilles, **4**. 427

Lycomedes, priest of Comana in Cappadocia Pontica, **5**. 437

Lycoreia, above the temple at Delphi, where the Delphians lived in earlier times, **4**. 351

Lycormas River (see Evenus River)

Lyctians, the, in Crete, possess Minoa, **5**. 123

Lyctus (or Lyttus, *q.v.*) in Crete, at one time, with Gortyna, took precedence over Cnossus, **5**. 129; Cherronesus the seaport of, **5**. 143; institutions at, **5**. 149

Lycupolis, a, in the Sebennytic Nome in Aegypt, **8**. 69

Lycurgus, the Edonian, identified with Dionysus, **5**. 107; mentioned by Homer, **7**. 11

Lycurgus, the lawgiver, responsible for the Laconian supremacy, **4**. 137; wrongly ignored by Hellanicus, who ascribes the Spartan Constitution to Eurysthenes and Procles, **4**. 139; a member of the house of the Eurypontidae, **4**. 141; sixth in descent from Procles, **4**. 141; for a time reigned as king at Sparta, sojourned in Crete and Aegypt, and then returned home as law-giver, **5**. 153; often consulted the Pythian priestess at Delphi, **7**. 287

Lycurgus, a work on, by Pausanias, one of the Eurypontidae, **4**. 141

Lycurgus the orator (b. about 396 B.C.), agrees that the Homeric Ilium was wiped out, **6**. 83

Lycus, son of King Pandion, received Euboea from his father, **4**. 247, 249; named the Lycians after himself, **5**. 493; banished from home and settled in Lycia, **6**. 323

Lycus, the (*Canis lupaster*, jackal), worshipped at Lycopolis, **8**. 111

Lycus (wrongly called the "Thermodon" by Eratosthenes) River, the, empties into the Euxine, **5**. 327; rises in Armenia and joins the Iris River in Cappadocia Pontica, **5**. 397, 429

Lycus River, the, between Ninus and Arbela, **7**. 195, 197

Lycus River (Tchorouk Sou), the, in Phrygia, joins the Maeander, **5**. 511

Lycus River, the, in Syria, navigable, **7**. 261, 263

Lydia, The History of, by Xanthus, **5**. 517

Lydia, a part of the Cis-Halys country, **1**. 497; whence Tyrrhenus colonised Tyrrhenia in Italy, **2**. 337; colonised by Ionians from Athens, **4**. 209

Lydian Gate, the, at Adramyttium, **6**. 127

Lydian language, the; no trace of, now left in Lydia, **6**. 193

Lydians, the, caused flight of certain Ionians to Italy, **3**. 49; once held the mastery after the Trojan War, **5**. 463; confused with other peoples in Asia, **5**. 487, 495; Gyges the king of, **6**. 41; once held Adramyttium,

INDEX OF NAMES, PLACES, AND SUBJECTS

385

INDEX OF NAMES, PLACES, AND SUBJECTS

"Macar, the city of," in Homer, means the island Lesbos, **4.** 97

Macaria, a spring near Tricorynthus in Attica, **4.** 187

Macaria Plain, the, on the Pamisus River, **4.** 117

Maccaresa (see Fregena)

Macedon, name of an ancient chieftain of Macedonia, **3.** 329

Macedonia (in earlier times called Emathia), **3.** 329; geographical position of, **3.** 249; now held by Thracians, **3.** 287; according to some writers, extends from the Strymon (Struma) to the Nestus (Mesta), **3.** 297; fortified against Greece by the Peneius River, where it flows through Tempê, **3.** 325; a part of Greece, **3.** 327, **4.** 3; like a parallelogram in shape, **3.** 327; boundaries of, **3.** 329, 369, **4.** 395, 399; coast of, extends from Cape Sunium to the Thracian Chersonese, **3.** 333; the Epeirotic tribes annexed to, **3.** 369; Thrace now called, **3.** 349; much of, as now, occupied by the Paeonians, **3.** 363; divided into four parts by Paulus, **3.** 369; countries annexed to, **4.** 415, 417; with the country next to Epeirus, now a praetorial Province, **8.** 215

Macedonia, Lower, **3.** 341, **4.** 399

Macedonia, Upper (or Free), consisted of the regions about Lyncus, Pelagonia, Orestias, and Elimeia, **3.** 309, 331, **4.** 399

Macedonian Kings, the, molested Athens, but let its government remain democratic, **4.** 269

Macedonians, the, upbuilders of Europe, **1.** 489; under Alexander, believed that Heracles and Dionysus preceded them in expedition to India, **2.** 141; sided with the Carthaginians, and hence the later conquest of them by the Romans, **3.** 141; greatly reduced certain tribes of the Galatae, Illyrians, and Thracians, **3.** 263; subdued by Paulus Aemilius, **3.** 293; inhabit the districts between the Paeonian Mountains and the Strymon (Struma) River, **3.** 295; subjugated the Epeirote cities, **3.** 303; the empire of, broken up by

the Romans, **3.** 309, 345; called their senators "peligones," **3.** 323; gained the hegemony of Greece, **4.** 137; revered the temple of Poseidon on Calauria, **4.** 175; dissolved the Achaean League, **4.** 211; reduced the Dorian Tetrapolis, **4.** 389; war of, with the Athenians, near Lamia, **4.** 413; for a time strongly resisted by the Aetolians and Acarnanians, **5.** 67; once ruled over Hyrcania, **5.** 253; gave the name "Caucasus" to all the mountains which follow in order after the country of the Arians, **5.** 259; received tribute from the Parthians and Hyrcanians, **5.** 271; imposed their own names on conquered places, **5.** 285; overthrew the Persians and occupied Syria, **5.** 307; once ruled over Armenia, **5.** 337; allowed the two satrapies of Cappadocia to change to kingdoms, **5.** 349; succeeded the Persians as masters in Asia, **5.** 463; onsets of, in Asia, **5.** 495; certain, live about Mt. Tmolus in Lydia, **6.** 173; Stratoniceia in Caria a settlement of, **6.** 297; once used Cyinda in Cilicia as a treasury, **6.** 341; gave Ariana to the Indians, **7.** 15; subdued the Persians, **7.** 159, 187; planted the vine in Susis and Babylonia, **7.** 173; conquered Dareius at Gaugamela near Arbela, **7.** 197; seized Phoenicia, **7.** 257; took possession of Aegypt, and attacked the Cyrenaeans, **8.** 203

Macestus River, the, in Asia, flows from Ancyra and empties into the Rhyndacus, **5.** 503

Machaereus, a Delphian, slew Neoptolemus the son of Achilles, **4.** 361

Machaerus, a stronghold in Syria, destroyed by Pompey, **7.** 291

Macistia, in Triphylia, separated by a mountain from Pisatis, **4.** 49; where is the temple of Leto, **4.** 73

Macistians, the, used to have charge of the temple of Poseidon at Samicum, **4.** 49; revere Hades, **4.** 51

Macistus, the Triphylian, said to have colonised Eretria in Euboea, **5.** 15

Macistus (or Platanistus, now Khaiaffa) in Triphylia, seized by the Cauconians, **3.** 23, **4.** 55

INDEX OF NAMES, PLACES, AND SUBJECTS

of, according to present historians,
4. 407; description and history of,
4. 423, 425; most of, annexed to
Macedonia, **4.** 427; indistinctly
mentioned by Homer, **4.** 445, 447;
Hieronymus on, **4.** 453

Magnesians, the, in Caria, near the
Maeander River, settled in the
Antiocheia near Pisidia, **5.** 507;
descendants of the Magnesians in
Thessaly, utterly destroyed by the
Trerans, **6.** 251

Magnesians (or Magnetans), the, in
Thessaly; geographical position of,
4. 395, 427, 447, 449; Homolium
belongs to, **4.** 449, 451; colonised
Magnesia on the Maeander River,
6. 211, 251

Magnetans, the (see Magnesians)

Magnetis in Macedonia, **3.** 349

Magnopolis in Phanaroea in Cappadocia Pontica (see Eupatoria)

Magoedi, the, corrupters of Melic
poetry, **6.** 253

Magus, a circumnavigator of Libya,
according to Heracleides, and a
visitor at court of Gelo, **1.** 377

Maïtos (see Madytus)

Makri, Cape (see Serrhium, Cape, in
Thrace)

Makriplagi, Mt. (see Gerania)

Makronisi the island (see Helenê)

Malaca (now Malaga) in Iberia, bears
the stamp of a Phoenician city, **2.** 81

Malaga (see Malaca)

Malaria (?), the disease, **2.** 315

Malathria in southern Macedonia (see
Dium)

Malatia (see Melitina)

Malaucênê (see Durio)

Malaüs, descendant of Agamemnon,
founded Phriconian Cymê in Asia,
6. 7

Malea (or Maleae, *q.v.*) Cape, distant
22,500 stadia from Pillars of Heracles,
1. 93; promontory ending in, **1.** 417

Maleae, Cape, 670 stadia from Cape
Taenarum, **4.** 127, 129, 149, 151,
155; the sea beyond, hard to navigate, **4.** 189; the distance from, to
the Ister River, **4.** 233, 235

Maleos, the Pelasgian king, **2.** 365

Malia, Mt. (see Aegaleum)

Malia, southernmost promontory of
Lesbos, **6.** 139

Maliac Gulf, the, next to the Opuntian Gulf, **3.** 353, **4.** 381; has about
the same length as the territory of
Achilles, **4.** 407; enumeration of
cities near, that were subject to
Achilles, **4.** 413, 417, and cities on
coast of, that were subject to
Achilles, **4.** 417, 419

Malian War, the; Styra in Euboea
destroyed during, **5.** 11

Malians, the Arabian, **7.** 233

Malians, the, in Thessaly; geographical
position of, **4.** 395; subject to
Achilles, **4.** 413, 449

Malli, the, a tribe in India, **7.** 57

Mallus in Cilicia, founded by Amphilochus and Mopsus, **6.** 353; birthplace of Crates the grammarian, **6.**
355

Malotha, a village in Arabia, **7.** 363

Malta (see Melitê)

Malus, in the Troad, **6.** 89

Malvasia (see Minoa the island)

Mamaüs River, the, flows past the
Lepreatic Pylus, **4.** 51

Mamertine wine, the, made at
Messenê in Sicily, rivals the best
of the Italian wines, **3.** 67

Mamertini, the, a tribe of the Campani, settled at Messenê in Sicily, **3.**
65; got control of the city, **3.** 67

Mamertium, in Bruttium, **3.** 35

Mandanis, the Indian sophist, commended Alexander, **7.** 111; refused
to visit Alexander, **7.** 121

Mandilo, Cape (see Geraestus)

"Manes," a name given Phrygian
slaves in Attica, **3.** 213; a name
used in Cappadocia, **5.** 415

Manes River, the (see Boagrius River,
the, in Locris), **4.** 381

Mangalia (see Callatis)

Manius Aquillius (consul 129 B.C.),
organised a province in Asia, **6.** 249

Mantianê, a large lake in Armenia;
next to Lake Maeotis in size, **5.** 327

Mantineia (Palaeopoli) in Arcadia,
settled by Argive colonists, **4.** 21;
made famous by the Battle of
Mantineia, but no longer exists,
4. 229, 335

Manto, daughter of Teiresias the
prophet and mother of Mopsus by
Apollo, **4.** 253, **6.** 233, 353

Mantua, in Italy, **2.** 311

INDEX OF NAMES, PLACES, AND SUBJECTS

Mantudi (see Cerinthus)

Map, the, of the inhabited world; revised by Eratosthenes, **1.** 231, 253, 267; "our geographical" (Map of Agrippa?), **1.** 465; how to make, **1.** 449, **2.** 358 (footnote 3)

Maps, the early, **1.** 257, 267

Marabodus, the royal residence of, at Boihaemum; enjoyed favour of Augustus and ruled many German tribes, **3.** 157

Maracanda in Sogdiana, destroyed by Alexander, **5.** 283

Maranitae, the coast of, now called coast of the Garindaeans, **7.** 343

Marathesium in Asia, once belonged to the Samians, but now to the Ephesians, **6.** 223

Marathon, expedition of Eurystheus to, **4.** 187; belonged to the Tetrapolis of Attica, **4.** 209; deme of Attica where Miltiades utterly destroyed the Persian army, **4.** 263, 273

Marathon Plain, the, in Iberia (see Fennel Plain)

Marathonian Tetrapolis, the, also called Tetrapolis of Attica, founded by Xuthus the son of Hellen, **4.** 181, 209; colonised certain cities in Euboea, **5.** 11

Marathus, an ancient city in Phoenicia, now in ruins, **7.** 255

Marble, the Carystian, in Euboea, **4.** 427, **5.** 9

Marble, the Docimaean, or Synnadic, **4.** 429

Marble, the Hierapolitic, **4.** 429

Marble, the, at Mylasa in Caria, excellent, **6.** 293

Marble, the Proconnesian white, at New Proconnesus in the Troad, **6.** 33

Marble, the Parian, the best for sculpture, **2.** 357, **5.** 171

Marble, the Pentelic, and the Hymettian, **4.** 275

Marble, the Scyrian variegated, is famous, **4.** 427; has taken precedence at Rome, **4.** 429

Marble, the Synnadic (see Marble, the Docimaean)

Marble quarries of Carrara, the, near Luna, **2.** 349; near Pisa, **2.** 353

Marble quarry, the, in Chios, is famous, **6.** 243

Marcellus, Marcus, founder of Corduba (in his third consulship, 152 B.C.), **2.** 21; exacted tribute of 600 talents from Celtiberia, **2.** 105

Marcellus, son of Octavia, was a pupil of Nestor the Academician, **6.** 351

Marcomanni, the, migrated with Marabodus to Boihaemum, **3.** 157

Mardi (or Amardi), the; extent of coast of, on the Caspian Sea, **5.** 245; in Persis and Armenia, **5.** 305; a predatory tribe situated next to the Persians, **5.** 309, **7.** 157

Mardonius, with 300,000 Persians, wiped out by the Greeks at Plataea, **4.** 325

Mareia (also called Mareotis, *q.v.*), Lake, borders on Alexandria, and of vast importance commercially, **8.** 31; description of, **8.** 57–59, 73

Mare-milkers (see Hippemolgi)

"Mareotic" wine, the, in Aegypt, is excellent, **8.** 59

Mareotis (also called Mareia, *q.v.*), Lake, in Aegypt, loses its baneful qualities because of overflow of the Nile, **2.** 315; connected by canals with the Nile, **8.** 15, 39, 73; borders on Alexandria, **8.** 31

Mare Piccolo, the harbour of Tarentum (see Taras)

Mare's milk, used by the Scythian Nomads, **3.** 157

Margalae, the, in Amphidolia, **4.** 71

Margiana, mild climate, and fertility, of, and huge grape-vines in, **1.** 273; a powerful district in Asia, **5.** 277; well suited to the vine, **5.** 279

Margus River, the, in Aria and Margiana, **5.** 277

Margus (or Bargus, now Morava) River, the, empties into the Ister, **3.** 273

Mariaba, metropolis of the Sabaeans in Arabia, **7.** 311; description of, **7.** 349

Mariandyni, the, in Asia, appear to be in origin a Thracian tribe, **3.** 177; in Asia Minor, by some called Caucones, **5.** 373; variant accounts of, **5.** 375; border on Paphlagonia, **5.** 383; not mentioned by Homer, **5.** 423, **6.** 363

Mariandynus, king of part of Paphla-

INDEX OF NAMES, PLACES, AND SUBJECTS

INDEX OF NAMES, PLACES, AND SUBJECTS

which the Boeotian Medeon was named, **4**. 321, 369

Medes, the; geographical position of, **1**. 497, 499; ancient history of, untrustworthy, **5**. 247; once ruled over Hyrcania, **5**. 253; border on the Cadasians, **5**. 269; customs of, adopted by the Armenians and Persians, **5**. 313–317; pride themselves upon their cavalry, **5**. 331; once ruled over Armenia and are in a way descendants of Jason and Medeia, **5**. 337; follow the sacred rites of the Persians, **5**. 341; language and customs of, used by Carmanians, **7**. 155; overthrown by the Persians under Cyrus, **7**. 157, 195; country of, borders on Babylonia, **7**. 203; wont to attack the Armenians and the Babylonians, **7**. 225

Medi, the, a Thracian tribe bordering on the Illyrian Thunatae, **3**. 265; some of, live in the neighbourhood of the Haemus Mountain, **3**. 275

Media, visited by Jason, **1**. 177, **5**. 213, 231; former domain of, **5**. 273; separated from Babylonia by Mt. Zagrus, **5**. 295, 301; description of, **5**. 303–317; divided into Greater and Atropatian Media, **5**. 299, 303; annual tribute paid by, to Persia, **5**. 313; lost Caspianê, Phaunitis, and Basoropeda to Armenia, **5**. 325; borders on Elamaïs, **7**. 221; now subject to the Parthians, **7**. 233

Media, the Atropatian; a peculiar custom of people in, **5**. 241

Media, the Greater, in ancient times ruled over all Asia—and boundaries of, **5**. 307, 309; description and customs of, **5**. 311–317

Medic juice, the, from the silphium in Media, **5**. 311

Medimnus of grain, a, sold for 200 drachmae at Casilinum, **2**. 461

Mediolanium (Milan), once the metropolis of the Insubri, **2**. 311

Mediolanium (Saintes), city of the Santoni, **2**. 215

Mediomatrici, the, live along the Rhenus, **2**. 229

Mediterranean (Our Sea), the; boundaries of, **1**. 19; formerly not connected with the Atlantic Ocean, **1**. 183; its bed higher, **1**. 189; level lowered by outflow at Strait of Gibraltar, **1**. 207; maximum breadth of, 5000 stadia, **1**. 443; one of the four large gulfs, **1**. 467; boundaries and dimensions of, **1**. 471; its most southerly, northerly, westerly, and easterly points, **1**. 483; routes over, for ships, pass through zone of fair weather, **2**. 31; probably once confluent with the Red Sea, **8**. 99

Medius, the Larisaean, accompanied Alexander on his Asiatic expedition, **5**. 333

Medma (Mesima), in Bruttium, founded by the Locrians, **3**. 19

Medoaci, the, live in Transpadana, **2**. 323

Medoacus (Brenta) River, the, in Italy, navigable from the sea to Patavium, **2**. 313

Medobithynians, the, are in origin a Thracian tribe, **3**. 177

Medon, marshal of the forces of Philoctetes at Troy, **4**. 407

Medulli, the, hold the loftiest peaks of the Alps, **2**. 195, 271; live above the confluence of the Isar and the Rhodanus, **2**. 273

Medus, the son of Medeia, is said to have succeeded to the empire of Media, **5**. 315

Medus River, the, in Media, **7**. 165

Medusa, the Gorgon, from whose neck Pegasus the horse sprang, **4**. 195

Megabari, the; weapons of, **7**. 339; subject to the Aethiopians, **8**. 7; situated to the south of Aegypt, **8**. 135

Megabates, the Persian admiral, slew Salganeus, the Boeotian guide, near the Euripus, **4**. 291

Megabyzi, the; eunuchs who served as priests at the temple of Artemis at Ephesus, **6**. 229

Megalokhorion (see Methana)

Megalopolis, "the Great City," in Arcadia; the Homeric Hirê near, **4**. 115; added to the Achaean League by Aratus of Sicyon, **4**. 217; "the Great City now a great desert," **4**. 229; like Babylon, now in ruins, **7**. 201

INDEX OF NAMES, PLACES, AND SUBJECTS

Megalopolitis in Cappadocia Pontica, subject to Queen Pythodoris, **5.** 431, 441

Meganisi (see Taphos)

Megara in Greece, founded by the Dorians, **4.** 7; added to the Achaean League by Aratus of Sicyon, **4.** 217; joined to Nisaea, its naval station, by walls; not mentioned by Homer because not yet founded, **4.** 245; founded by the Heracleidae, and still endures, **4.** 251; in early times a part of Attica, **4.** 257; scene of myth of Philomela and Procnê, **4.** 369; founded by Dorians after the death of Codrus, **6.** 271

Megara Hyblaea (formerly called Hybla, near Agosta) in Sicily, no longer existent, **3.** 63; founded by Theocles the Athenian and some Megarians, **3.** 65; abandoned about the same time as Syracuse, **3.** 71

Megara in Syria, **7.** 253

Megarian sect, the, of philosophers, **4.** 251

Megarians, the, in Greece, founded Megara in Sicily, **3.** 65; founded Selinus in Sicily, **3.** 83; founded Chalcedon, opposite Byzantium, **3.** 283; Nisaea the naval station of, **4.** 11; once in strife with the Athenians for Salamis, **4.** 253, 255; founded Chalcedon and Astacus, the latter with the Athenians, **5.** 455

Megarians, the Hyblaean, in Sicily, forced by the Carthaginians to migrate, **4.** 223

Megarians, Polity of the, by Aristotle, **3.** 289

Megaris, lies on the Crisaean Gulf, **4.** 195; includes Crommyon, **4.** 239; in Homer's time a part of Ionia, and obtained by Nisus the son of King Pandion, **4.** 247; has rather poor soil and is mostly occupied by the Oneian Mountains, **4.** 251

Megasthenes of Chalcis (in Euboea), joint founder of Cumae in Italy, **2.** 437

Megasthenes, ambassador of Seleucus Nicator (reigned 312–328 B.C.) to Sandrocottus, king of Palimbothra

in India; author of a historico-geographical work, which was thoroughly discredited by Strabo but quoted approvingly by Hipparchus, **1.** 257, 261, 265; on the setting of the Bears, **1.** 287, 291; discounts all ancient stories about India, **7.** 7; on the expeditions of Heracles and Dionysus to India, **7.** 9; on the size of India, **7.** 17, 19; on the fertility of India, **7.** 31; on the size of the Ganges River, **7.** 63; says the largest tigers are found in the country of the Prasii in India, **7.** 65; on the seven castes in India, **7.** 67–83; describes the gold-mining ant-lions in India, **7.** 75; on the honesty and habits of the Indians, **7.** 87, 89, 93; tells mythical stories about India, **7.** 95, 97; on the two sects of philosophers in India, **7.** 99; on suicide in India, **7.** 119

Meges, the Homeric, son of Phyleus; the corselet of, **4.** 27; king of the Echinades Islands, **5.** 49, 59

Megillus, on the growing of rice, **7.** 29

Megistê, island and city off Lycia, **6.** 319

Meïonia (see Maeonia)

"Meïonia," perhaps applied to "Asia" sometimes, **6.** 179

Meïonians, the Homeric, are the same people as the Mysians and the Maeonians, **5.** 405, 487; the Lydian, colonised Thebê in the Troad after the Trojan War, **6.** 23; are Lydians, **6.** 171, 361, 365; led by Mnesthles and Antiphus, according to Homer, **6.** 175; an unknown tribe, according to Apollodorus, **6.** 369

Melaena, Cape, in Chios, **6.** 243

Melaenae (or Melaniae) in Cilicia, 1900 stadia to the borders of Syria, **7.** 281

Melaenae in the Troad, **6.** 89

Melamphylus, one of the earlier names of the Ionian Samos, **5.** 53, **6.** 215

Melampus, first physician, and founder of the worship of Dionysus in Greece, used the water of the Anigrus River in Triphylia to purify the Proetides, **4.** 61

393

INDEX OF NAMES, PLACES, AND SUBJECTS

Melanchrus, tyrant of Mitylenê, railed at by Alcaeus, **6.** 143

Melaneïs, an earlier name of Eretria, **5.** 15

Melania (also called Melaenae and Melaniae) in Cilicia, **6.** 333

Melaniae (see Melaenae)

Melanippê the prisoner, at Metapontium, **3.** 53

Melanippus, the Homeric, pastured kine in Percotê, **6.** 19

Melanthus, king of the Messenians, **4.** 109; also reigned over the Athenians, **4.** 249; father of Codrus, accompanied by many Pylians to Athens, **4.** 199

Melanus, a promontory between Cyzicus and Priapus, **5.** 505

Melas, the Homeric, son of Porthaon, **5.** 75

Melas Gulf (Gulf of Saros), the, formed by the Thracian Chersonesus, **1.** 477, **3.** 373, 375

Melas River, the, in Boeotia, flowed through the territory of Haliartus and emptied into a fissure in the earth near Orchomenus, but has now disappeared, **4.** 307; flows between Eudeielos and Orchomenus, **4.** 341

Melas River, the, in Cappadocia, spreads out into marshes and lakes and renders the stone-quarry hard to work, **5.** 363

Melas River, the, in Pamphylia, **6.** 325

Melas River, the, in Thessaly, flows five stadia from Trachin, **4.** 391

Melas River, the, in Thrace, which flows into the Melas Gulf, not sufficient to supply the army of Xerxes, **3.** 373

Meldi, the, live on the Sequana River, **2.** 233

Meleager, of Gadaris in Phoenicia, **7.** 277

Meleager, with Oeneus, fought with the sons of Thestius, **5.** 87

Meleager, the palisade of, in Syria, **7.** 247

Meles River, the, flows past Smyrna, **5.** 421, **6.** 247

Melia, wife of Silenus and mother of the Dolion who dwelt on the Ascanian Lake, **5.** 465, **6.** 373

Melia, the mother of Tenerus the Boeotian prophet by Apollo, **4.** 329

Meliboea (near Aghia), in Thessaly, whence Philoctetes fled, **3.** 9; subject to Philoctetes, **4.** 427; where some of Xerxes' ships were wrecked, **4.** 451

Melilotus, a tree in Masaesylia in Libya whence wine is made, **8.** 179

Melinus Harbour, the, in the Arabian Gulf, **7.** 323

Melitaea in Thessaly, formerly called Pyrrha, and the tomb of Hellen at, **4.** 405; subject to Achilles, **4.** 413

Melitê (Malta), off Cape Pachynus, whence come the little dogs, **3.** 103, **8.** 191

Melitê (Lezini), a lake in Acarnania, **5.** 61

Melitê, the Attic deme, **1.** 243, 247

Melitê, the name of Samothrace in olden times, **3.** 371

Melitena, one of the ten prefectures of Cappadocia, **5.** 297, 319, 345, 349; description of, **5.** 351; has strongholds, but no cities, **5.** 357

Melo, leader of the Sugambri in their war against the Romans, **3.** 161

Melos (Milo), one of the Cyclades Islands, a notable island, **5.** 161; most of inhabitants of, from youth upwards, once slain by the Athenians, **5.** 163

Melpis (Melfa) River, the, flows past Aquinum, **2.** 413

Melsus River, the, flows through Asturia, **2.** 121

Memnon, son of Tithonus; tomb of, above the outlet of the Aesepus River, **6.** 27; said to have been buried near Paltus in Syria, by the Badas River, **7.** 159; called Ismandes by the Aegyptians, **8.** 113

Memnon of Rhodes, general of the Persians, arrested Hermeias the tyrant of Assus, and sent him up to the king of the Persians to be hanged, **6.** 117

Memnon's Village, in the Troad, **6.** 27

Memnonia, the, in Abydus and Thebes, **8.** 113

Memnonium, the, at Abydus near the Nile, remarkable royal building

INDEX OF NAMES, PLACES, AND SUBJECTS

of the same workmanship as the Labyrinth, 8. 111–113

Memnonium, the; name of the acropolis of Susa, 7. 159

Memoirs, the Aegyptian, Babylonian, and Indian, on the straightforward character of the Scythians, 3. 201

Memphis in Aegypt; temples of the Cabeiri and Hephaestus in, destroyed by Cambyses, 5. 115; "royal residence of the Aegyptians," keeps the sacred bull Apis, 8. 73, 87; distance from, to Thebaïs, 8. 75; a curious kind of hall at, 8. 83; description of, 8. 87–89

Men, mythical, who are "half-dog," or "long-headed," or "pygmies," or "web-footed," or "dog-headed," or "have eyes in their breasts," or "one-eyed," invented by the poets, 3. 191

Mēn (see Mēn Ascaeus), the temple of, in the country of the Antiocheians (at Saghir?), 5. 433

Mēn Arcaeus (Ascaeus?), the priesthood of, at Antiocheia near Pisidia, 5. 507

Mēn Ascaeus; temple of, near the Antiocheia that is near Pisidia, 5. 431

Mēn of Carus; temple of, in place of same name, between Carura and Laodiceia, 5. 431, 519

Mēn of Pharnaces, the temple of, at Cabeira in Cappadocia Pontica, 5. 431

Menander the comic poet, of Athens (b. 342 B.C.); on the polygamy of the Thracians and Getans, 3. 183; on the money and time spent by women on religious observances, 3. 183, 185; says that Sappho the poetess was the first to leap off Cape Leucatas into the sea, 5. 33; on a certain law in the isle Ceos, 5. 169; says that the isle Samos "produces everything but birds' milk," 6. 215, 217; became an *ephebus* at Athens, 6. 219

Menander, king of Bactria; far-reaching conquests of, 5. 279–281

Menapii, the, live on both sides of the Rhenus near its mouths, 2. 231; border on the Marini, 2. 253; fogs among, 2. 257

Mendê, a city on Pallenê, 3. 351

Mendes in Aegypt, where Pan and a he-goat are worshipped, 8. 69

Mendesian mouth of the Nile, the, 8. 65, 71

Menecles, the orator, teacher of Apollonius Malacus and Apollonius Molon, 6. 281, 299

Menecrates of Elaea, a disciple of Xenocrates; opinions of, approved by Demetrius of Scepsis, 5. 407; in his *Circuit of the Hellespont* discusses the Halizones, 5. 409; regards the Mysians as Lydian in origin, 5. 489; in his work on the *Foundings of Cities* discusses the Pelasgians in Asia, 6. 157

Menecrates, pupil of Aristarchus and native of Nysa in Asia, 6. 263

Menedemus, founder of the Eretrian sect of philosophers, 4. 251, 5. 19

Menelaüs, the brother of Ptolemy I; the Menelaïte Nome in Aegypt named after, 8. 65

Menelaïs, a city in Aegypt, 8. 73

Menelaüs, the Greek hero, destined for Elysian Plain, 1. 7; travelled much, and hence a wise man, 1. 29; traveller and braggart, 1. 111; wanderings of, 1. 137, 139; the prophecy uttered to, by Proteus, 1. 141; wealthy palace of, 1. 143; sojourned in Sidon, 1. 149; wanderings of, a traditional fact, 2. 55, 359; domain of, included Messenia, 4. 87; accompanied to Troy by men of Pherae (Pharis), 4. 109; also held Messenia as subject at time of Trojan War, 4. 107, 109; palace of, at Sparta, visited by Telemachus, 4. 147, 149; came into possession of Laconia, 4. 167; in haste to return home from Troy, 5. 105; said to have been entertained in Aegypt by King Thon, 8. 63; took captive Trojans with him, who settled in Arabia, 8. 95–97

Menelaüs Harbour, in Cyrenaea, 8. 207

Menestheus, port and oracle of, in Iberia, 2. 17; Greek charioteer at Troy, 4. 255; with Athenians, founded Elaea in Asia in Trojan times, 6. 159

395

INDEX OF NAMES, PLACES, AND SUBJECTS

INDEX OF NAMES, PLACES, AND SUBJECTS

INDEX OF NAMES, PLACES, AND SUBJECTS

INDEX OF NAMES, PLACES, AND SUBJECTS

INDEX OF NAMES, PLACES, AND SUBJECTS

Minturnae (near Traetto), in Italy, **2.**
395; midway between Formiae and
Sinuessa, **2.** 397, 413

Minyans, the, one of the three tribes in
Triphylia, **4.** 23; settlements of, in
Lemnos, Lacedaemon, Triphylia,
and the isle Thera, **4.** 63; the inhabitants of Orchomenus in Boeotia,
as also the Argonauts so called, and
in early times were a rich and
powerful people, **4.** 335

Minyeius (or Minteius) River (see
Anigrus River), the, empties into
the sea near Arenê, **4.** 61, 63

Misenum (Miseno), named after
Misenus, **2.** 435, 439, 447, 449

Misenus, companion of Odysseus, **1.**
95

Misogynes, the, of Menander (see
Woman-hater)

Mithras (*i.e.* "Helius," the "Sun"),
worshipped by the Persians, **7.** 175

Mithridates "Ctistes" ("Founder"),
reigned 337–302 B.C.; used Cimiata
as base of operations, **5.** 453

Mithridates Euergetes, king of Pontus
and friend to Dorylaüs, the military
expert and distant relative of
Strabo, **5.** 133; slain at Sinopê, and
succeeded by his son Mithridates
(Eupator) who was only eleven
years old, **5.** 135

Mithridates Eupator, king of Pontus
(120–63 B.C.), most formidable
enemy of the Romans in the East;
made known to geographers northern regions as far as Lake Maeotis
(Sea of Azov) and Colchis, **1.** 51;
victor over barbarians at mouth of
Lake Maeotis, **1.** 277; deposed by
the Romans, **3.** 145; waged war
with the Roxolani, **3.** 223; Neoptolemus, a general of, defeated the
barbarians in both a naval and
cavalry engagement in the Strait of
Kertch, **3.** 227; by request became
guardian of Old Chersonesus, **3.**
233; given the sovereignty of
Panticapaeum by Parisades, **3.**
235, 239; received a tribute of
180,000 medimni of grain and 200
talents of silver from the region of
the Cimmerian Bosporus, **3.** 243;
completely defeated by the Romans
at Chaeroneia (86 B.C.), **4.** 333;

son of Mithridates Euergetes and
succeeded to the rule when only
eleven years old, **5.** 135; generals of,
completely ruined Delos, **5.** 167;
attacked by Pompey, **5.** 189; in
flight from his own country made
long journey in Asia, **5.** 203; won
Colchis, but later lost it, **5.** 213;
overthrown by Pompey, **5.** 263,
373; became king of Cappadocia
Pontica and other countries this
side and beyond the Halys River,
5. 371, 373, 385; born and reared at
Sinopê, **5.** 389; adorned Amisus, **5.**
395; once master of Colchis, but
fled from Pompey, **5.** 425; the most
precious treasuries of, stored at
Kainon Chorion in Cappadocia, and
later dedicated in the Capitolium at
Rome by Pompey, **5.** 431; the war
of, against Leucullus and Pompey,
5. 435; arranged terms with Sulla
at Dardanus in the Troad, **6.** 59;
joined by Diodorus the general, **6.**
129; Adobogion the mother of
Mithridates of Pergamum said to
have been a concubine of, **6.** 169;
attacked Sardeis and absolved
Diodorus the Elder from blame, **6.**
181; extended limits of precinct of
temple of Artemis at Ephesus as
place of refuge, **6.** 229; Archelaïs,
pretended son of, married Berenicê
the queen of Aegypt.

Mithridates of Pergamum (contemporary of Strabo), robbed the oracle
of Phrixus, **5.** 213; son of Meno-
dotus and Adobogion (the latter said
to have been a concubine of Eupator), friend of Julius Caesar, and
king of the Bosporus and other
countries, but overthrown by
Asander, **6.** 169

Mithridatic War, the, resulted in
tyrants at Athens, **4.** 269; names of
peoples engaged in, **5.** 207; brought
misfortune to Adramyttium, **6.** 129

Mithridatium in the Pontus, given to
Bogiotarus by Pompey, **5.** 469

Mithropastes, son of Aristes, a satrap
of Phrygia, banished by Dareius,
served as guide to Nearchus in his
voyage over the Persian Gulf, **7.** 305

Mitylenaeans, the (and Cumaeans),
founded Aenus on the Melas Gulf,

401

INDEX OF NAMES, PLACES, AND SUBJECTS

Taurus into Pamphylia, **6.** 325; founded Mallus in Cilicia, died in duel with Amphilochus there, **6.** 353, 355

Mopsus the Lapith who sailed with the Argonauts, after whom Mopsium in Thessaly was named, **4.** 453

Morals, the, of the barbarians, corrupted by " our mode of life," **3.** 199

Morava River (see Margus)

Morenê in Asia; a part of, subject to Cleon, **5.** 499

Morgantium (or Murgantia), in Sicily, took its name from the Morgetes, **3.** 23; settled by the Morgetes, **3.** 73

Morgetes, the, inhabited southern Italy in earlier times, **3.** 23; settled in Morgantium in Sicily, **3.** 73

Morimenê, one of the ten prefectures of Cappadocia, **5.** 349; the temple of Venasian Zeus in, **5.** 359

Morini, the, in Celtica; geographical position of, **2.** 233; from whose coast some sail to Britain, **2.** 253; fogs among, **2.** 257

Moron (Al-Merim), a city on a mountain near the Tagus River in Iberia, about 500 stadia from the sea, used as base of operations by Brutus, **2.** 63

" Mortuaries," the, found at Corinth, sold at high price at Rome, **4.** 203

Morys (the Homeric), son of Hippotion, led forces from Ascania, **5.** 461

Morzeus: Gangra in Paphlagonia the royal residence of, **5.** 453

Moschian country, the, held partly by the Colchians, partly by the Iberians, and partly by the Armenians, **5.** 213, 215

Moschian Mountains, the, in Asia Minor, **5.** 209, 299; joined by Mt. Scydises above Colchis, **5.** 401

Moschians, the, in the Mithridatic War, **5.** 207

Moses, an Aegyptian priest; his tenets, and his kingdom at Jerusalem, **7.** 283–285; revered as ruler and prophet, **7.** 289

Mosynoeci (see Heptacomitae), the, lost territory to the Armenians, **5.** 325

Mouse, the, carved at foot of image of

Apollo at Chrysa in the Troad, **6.** 95; the *mus araneus* worshipped at Athribis, **8.** 111

Mudania on the Propontis (see Myrlea)

Muga River, the (see Clodianus)

Mugilones, the, a German tribe, ruled by Marabodus, **3.** 157

Mulberry-tree (see Sycaminus, the Aegyptian)

Mule, a, tows the boat on the canal alongside the Appian Way, **2.** 397

Mules, superior, bred by the Eneti in Italy, **2.** 309; the famous Reatebreed of, in the Sabine country, **2.** 375; wild, in Eneti (or Enetê?), **5.** 417; in Arabia, **7.** 343

Mules, stunted (see Ginni)

Mulius, the Epeian spearman, slain by Nestor, **4.** 29

Mullets, the " dug," in Celtica, **2.** 183

Mummius, Leucius, the consul (who destroyed Corinth by fire in 146 B.C.), **4.** 121, 199; personally indifferent to works of art, **4.** 201, 203

Munda in Iberia, where the sons of Pompey were defeated, **2.** 21; a capital city; distance from, to Carteia, **2.** 23; the battle at, **2.** 97

Mundas (Mondego) River, the, in Iberia; affords short voyages inland, **2.** 67

Munychia, the hill at Peiraeus; description and history of, **4.** 259, 261

Murgantia in Sicily (see Morgantium)

Murviedro in Spain (see Saguntum)

Musaeus, the musician, called a Thracian, **5.** 109; a prophet often consulted, **7.** 289

Muses, the, met Thamyris the Thracian singer at Dorium, **4.** 71; temple of, on Mt. Helicon, dedicated by Thracians, **4.** 319; are goddesses in a special sense, and preside over the choruses, **5.** 95; worship of, Thracian in origin, **5.** 107, 109

Museum, the, at Alexandria, **8.** 35

Music, in education, **1.** 55; at Neapolis, **2.** 449; brings one in touch with the divine, **5.** 93; our system of education based on; and made synonymous with philosophy by Plato and the Pythagoreians, **5.** 95; all, regarded as Thracian and Asiatic in origin, **5.** 107

INDEX OF NAMES, PLACES, AND SUBJECTS

Musicanus, the country of, in India, **7.** 33, produces a grain like wheat, and a vine from which wine is produced, **7.** 35, and is highly praised by Onesicritus, **7.** 59; slavery a success in country of, **7.** 91

Musmones, the; a kind of sheep in Sardinia, **2.** 363

Mussel-shells, found in great quantities in the plains of Masaesylia, **8.** 179

Mussels, both large and abundant on ocean-coast of Iberia, **2.** 35

Mutina (Modène), one of the famous cities of Italy, **2.** 327; region of, produces the finest wool, **2.** 333

Mycalê, Mt., parts round, in earlier times, occupied by Carians, **6.** 197; with Samos forms a narrow strait, and is well supplied with figs and wild animals, **6.** 211, 213; in Ionia opposite Samos, from which Samians settled in Samothrace, **3.** 371

Mycalessus (or Mycalettus), the Homeric, a village in the territory of Tanagra, on the road from Thebes to Chalcis, **4.** 293; one of the "Four United Villages," **4.** 301

Mycalettus (see Mycalessus)

Mycenae, lies 10 stadia from the Argive Heraeum, **4.** 151; one of the two capitals, **4.** 165; gained the ascendency, but was later destroyed by the Argives, **4.** 167; cities named by Homer as subject to, **4.** 185; history of, **4.** 185–187

Mychus (in the Galitza Gulf), the last harbour (on the east) in Phocis, is considered the deepest recess of the Crisaean Gulf, and lies 90 stadia from Creusa, **4.** 317; lies between Mt. Helicon and Ascrê, **4.** 369

Myconos, one of the Cyclades Islands, **5.** 165; beneath which lie the last of the giants destroyed by Heracles, **5.** 171

Mygdonians, the, in Mesopotamia, live below Mt. Masius, **5.** 319; on the Euphrates, **7.** 231

Mygdonians, the, are a Thracian tribe in origin, **3.** 177; live about Lake Bolbê in Macedonia, **3.** 331, 361

Mygdonians, the, in the Troad, **5.** 499, 503; boundaries of confused, **5.** 459

Mygdonis, mastered by the Paeonians, **3.** 363

Mylae (Milazzo) in Sicily, 25 Roman miles from Cape Pelorias, **3.** 57

Mylasa in Caria, a noteworthy city, **6.** 291; description, history, and notable men of, **6.** 293–297

Mylasians, the, in Caria have two temples of Zeus, **6.** 293

Myndus in Caria, **6.** 119, 289

Mynes, "the divine," ruler of Lyrnessus in the Troad, fell in battle against Achilles, **6.** 15, 17, 121, 151; one of the two Cilician dynasties subject to, **6.** 121

Myonnesus, a town between Teos and Lebedus, **6.** 237

Myonnesus, a small island in the Maliac Gulf, **4.** 419

"Myonnesus," the second *n* redundant in, **6.** 147

Myra in Lycia, member of the Lycian League, **6.** 315, 319

Myrcinus, on the Strymonic Gulf, **3.** 355

Myriandrus in Cilicia, on the Gulf of Issus, **6.** 357

Myrina the Amazon, buried in the Trojan Plain, **5.** 493; the city Myrina named after, **6.** 163

Myrina in Asia Minor, said to have been founded by the Amazons, **5.** 237, 407; named after Myrina the Amazon, **6.** 163

Myrleia (Mudania) on the Propontis; home of Asclepiades the grammarian, **2.** 83; the Halizones live in mountains above, according to Menecrates, **5.** 409; destroyed by Philip the son of Demetrius with the aid of Prusias, but by the latter restored and named "Apameia" after his wife, **5.** 457

Myrmecium, a little city 20 stadia from Panticapaeum in the Crimea, **3.** 239, **5.** 197

Myrmidons, The, of Aeschylus, quoted, **6.** 139

Myrmidons (see Aeginetans), the Homeric, in Thessaly, **4.** 157; subject to Achilles, **4.** 401; all who fled with Peleus from Aegina were so called by Homer, **4.** 413

Myron the sculptor (fl. about 430 B.C.), made the three colossal statues in

INDEX OF NAMES, PLACES, AND SUBJECTS

the temple of Hera on Samos, **6.** 213

Myrrh, produced in Aethiopia near Cape Deirê, **7.** 331, 333, and in the country of the Sabaeans in Arabia, **7.** 347; produced from trees, **7.** 365

Myrrh trees, the, in India, **7.** 133

Myrrhinus (Merenda), a deme on the eastern coast of Attica, **4.** 273

Myrsilus of Lesbos, an historical writer of uncertain date; says that Antissa, now a city of Lesbos, was formerly an island, **1.** 223; says that Assus was founded by Methymnaeans, **6.** 117

Myrsilus, tyrant of Mitylenê, railed at, by Alcaeus, **6.** 143

Myrsinus in Elis, **4.** 35, 39; the present Myrtuntium, **4.** 41

Myrtle, the, in India, **7.** 97

Myrtoan Sea, the; dimensions of, **1.** 477, **3.** 279

Myrtuntium, a salt-lake between Leucas and the Ambracian Gulf, **5.** 61

Myscellus, founder of Croton, in Italy, **3.** 43; oracle given out to, at Delphi, **3.** 71; came from Rhypes in Achaea, **4.** 225

Mysia (or Maeonia or Meïonia) Catacecaumenê ("Burnt"), in Lydia, where some place the Homeric "Hydê," **6.** 177; description of, **6.** 181; scene of the mythical story of Typhon, according to some, **6.** 183; produces fine wine, **6.** 215

Mysia, bordering on the Troad, once occupied by the Thracian Bebryces, **5.** 375; geographical position of, **5.** 455, 459, 463, 505; divided into two parts, **5.** 485, 487; name of the country round Cyzicus, **6.** 373

Mysians, the, in Asia, are the same people as the Maeonians and the Meïonians, **5.** 405; not mentioned by Homer, **5.** 423; boundaries of, confused with those of the Bithynians and Phrygians, **5.** 459; once held the mastery after the Trojan War, **5.** 463; settled round the Ascanian Lake, **5.** 463, 467; apparently Thracian in origin, **5.** 465; the abode of, in Asia, and the origin of name of, **5.** 487, 489, 499; accounts of, go back to earlier times than the Trojan War, **5.** 491; certain survivors of, colonised the Plain of Thebê after the Trojan War, **6.** 23, 127; are next to the Lydians, **6.** 181, 185; as brothers worship the Carian Zeus with the Carians and Lydians, **6.** 293; by the poets confused with other peoples, **6.** 315; tribes of, mentioned by Homer, **6.** 361; Apollodorus on, **6.** 373

Mysians (Moesians), the, in Europe, were Thracians and identical with the present Moesians, **3.** 175; discussion of, **3.** 177–181; the Homeric, **3.** 187, 189, 195, 209, bordered on the little Scordisci, **3.** 273, living on the far side of the Ister, and colonised Mysia in Asia, **5.** 487

Mysians, the, of Sophocles, refers to land of Mysia as "city of the Mysians," **4.** 99

Mysius River, the, in Asia, empties into the Caïcus, **6.** 137

Myth, the aim of, **1.** 91; used by Homer for a useful purpose, **1.** 97

Mythical men and places, invented by the poets, **3.** 191

Mythology, makes Ares (Mars) the father of Romulus and Remus, **2.** 381; borders on theology, **5.** 119

Myths, sanctioned by poets, states, and lawgivers as a useful expedient, **1.** 67, 71; distasteful to Strabo, but must be taken into consideration, **5.** 119; wrongly included by historians, **5.** 247

Myus in Asia, in earlier times occupied by Carians, **6.** 197; founded by Cydrelus the bastard son of King Codrus, **6.** 199; one of the twelve Ionian cities, now incorporated into Miletus, **6.** 211

Myus Hormus (Harbour), also called Aphroditê's Harbour, on the Arabian Gulf, **7.** 315, 317; Aelius Gallus with his army sailed across to, from Arabia, **7.** 363; on the Red Sea near Berenicê, **8.** 119

N

Nabataea, a populous country in Arabia, **7.** 343

Nabataean Arabians, the; Rock of, on the Arabian Gulf, **7.** 341

INDEX OF NAMES, PLACES, AND SUBJECTS

405

INDEX OF NAMES, PLACES, AND SUBJECTS

station of the Argives, 4. 151; near the Cyclopeian caverns, 4. 153, 169; inhabitants of, withdrew to Messenia, 4. 171; belonged to a kind of Amphictyonic League of seven cities, 4. 175

Nauplians, the; dues of, at temple of Poseidon on Calauria, paid by the Argives, 4. 175

Naupleis (see Nauplia)

Nauplius, the founder of Nauplia, 4. 151, whom Strabo confuses with Nauplius the son of Poseidon and Amymonê, 4. 153 (see footnote 1)

Nauportus (Ober-Laibach); imports to, 2. 287; a settlement of the Taurisci, 350 stadia from Aquileia, 3. 255

Naustathmus, in Cyrenaea, 8. 205

Navigators, taught how to steer course in straits by Danaüs, 1. 85

Naxians, the, founded Callipolis in Sicily, 3. 83; always shared in the misfortunes of the Syracusans, but not always in their fortunes, 3. 87

Naxos, one of the Cyclades Islands, 5. 165, 169

Naxos (on Capo di Schiso) in Sicily, no longer existent, 3. 63; founded by Theocles the Athenian and some Chalcidians, 3. 65; founded at about the same time as Syracuse, 3. 71

Nea, a village near Scepsis in Asia, 5. 411; between Polichna and Palaescepsis (Aenea Comê?), 6. 91

Neaethus (Neto) River, the, in Italy; origin of name of, 3. 41

Neandria, incorporated into Alexandreia in the Troad, 5. 113, 6. 93

Neandrians, the, in the Troad; territory of, 6. 101

Neanthes of Cyzicus (fl. in third century B.C.), voluminous writer on historical subjects, though only a few fragments are extant; credits Argonauts with erecting sanctuary of Cybelê near Cyzicus, 1. 165

Neapolis in Asia, once belonged to the Ephesians, but now to the Samians, 6. 221, 223

Neapolis, a fort in the Crimea (site unknown), built by Scilurus and his sons, 3. 247

Neapolis (formerly called Phazemon) in Cappadocia Pontica, so named by Pompey, 5. 443

Neapolis (Kavala) in Macedonia, marks the limit of the Strymonic Gulf, 3. 353, 359

Neapolis (Naples); description of, 2. 449-451, 457; Gulf of, called "Crater," 2. 435; tunnel from, to Dicaearchia, 2. 445; now non-Greek, 3. 7

Neapolis, on the eastern coast of Carthaginia, 8. 191

Neapolis (also called Leptis), a city near the Great Syrtis, 8. 195

Neapolitans, the, once held Capreae, 2. 459

Neapolitis in Cappadocia Pontica, 5. 443

Nearchus, admiral under Alexander the Great; (in 325 B.C.) made expedition from the mouth of the Indus to the Persian Gulf; an abstract of his voyage is contained in Arrian's *Indica*. He was discredited by Strabo, 1. 263; on the Bears, 1. 291; on four predatory tribes in Asia, 5. 309; on the ambition of Alexander when in India, 7. 7; on the size of India, 7. 19; on the alluvial deposits of various rivers, 7. 23; on the rains in India, 7. 27; on the cotton in India, 7. 33; attributes the risings of the Nile and the rivers in India to the summer rains, 7. 41; on the mouths of the Indus River in India, 7. 59; on the capturing of elephants in India, and on the antlions there, 7. 75; on the vicious reptiles in India, 7. 77; on slavery in India, 7. 91; on the sophists in India, 7. 115, and on the skill of the Indians in handiwork, 7. 117; on the Arbies in India, 7. 129; commander of Alexander's fleet, 7. 133, 135; difficult voyage of, in the Persian Gulf, 7. 149; his account thereof, 7. 151; on the language and customs of the Carmanians, 7. 155; on the seaboard of Persis, 7. 161; found no native guides on voyage from India to Babylonia, 7. 173; navigated the Persian Gulf, 7. 303, 305, 307

INDEX OF NAMES, PLACES, AND SUBJECTS

INDEX OF NAMES, PLACES, AND SUBJECTS

(Lisbon), **2.** 67; the end of western and northern sides of Iberia, and inhabited by Celtic people, **2.** 67

Nero, Mt. (see Aenus)

Neroassus (see Nora)

Nervii, the, a Germanic tribe in Celtica, **2.** 231

Nesaea, a district in Hyrcania, **5.** 253

Nesaean horses, the, in Media, **5.** 311; in Armenia, **5.** 331

Nesson, the son of Thessalus; both Thessaly and Lake Nessonis named after, **4.** 455

Nessonis, Lake, in Thessaly, **4.** 397; the Peneius flows into, **4.** 439; not mentioned by Homer, **4.** 445; named after Nesson the son of Thessalus, **4.** 455

Nessus, the Centaur; tomb of, on Taphiassus, a hill in Aetolia, **4.** 385

Nessus the ferryman, killed by Heracles at the Lycormas (Evenus) River in Aetolia, **5.** 29

Nestor, son of Neleus, travelled much, **1.** 29; on the wanderings of Menelaüs, **1.** 139; accompanied by Pisatae to Troy, **2.** 351; companions of, founded Metapontium in Italy, **3.** 51; called by Homer "the Gerenian" after "Gerena" in Messenia, according to some writers, **3.** 193, **4.** 33, 85; ruler of Triphylian Pylus, **4.** 19, 21, not of the Pylus of Coelê Elis, **4.** 23; slew Mulius the Epeian spearman, son-in-law of Augeas, **4.** 29; "the Gerenian," claimed by three different Pyluses, **4.** 33, 113; lived in the Lepreatic, or Triphylian Pylus, according to Homer (Strabo says), **4.** 51, 57; Chloris the mother of, from Minyeian Orchomenus, **4.** 63; the subjects of, **4.** 71, 75, 87; various proofs of his having lived at the *Triphylian* Pylus, **4.** 77–87; his recital to Patroclus of the war between the Pylians and Eleians proves it, **4.** 79, 81; descendants of, sided with the Messenians in the Messenian War, **4.** 95; not mentioned by Homer as going forth to battle at Troy, **4.** 401; knew nothing about affairs in Crete after he set out for Troy, **5.** 145; founded temple of Nedusian Athenê on

Ceos on his return from Troy, **5.** 169; by the more recent poets called a Messenian, **6.** 199

Nestus (Mesta) River, the; the northern boundary of Macedonia, **3.** 297, 355, 357, 363, 365, 367

Netium (Noja), on the mule-road between Brundisium and Beneventum, **3.** 123

Neto River, the (see Neaethus)

New Carthage (Cartagena), famous silver-mines at, **2.** 47; founded by Hasdrubal, **2.** 87; a powerful city, **2.** 89; where the consular governor administers justice in winter, **2.** 123; has a tree from the bark of which woven stuffs are made, **2.** 155

Nibarus, Mt., in Asia, extends as far as Media, **5.** 321; a part of the Taurus, **5.** 335

Nicaea, daughter of Antipater, and wife of Lysimachus; Nicaea, the metropolis of Bithynia, named after, **5.** 463

Nicaea (Antigonia), metropolis of Bithynia, on the Ascanian Lake, first founded by Antigonus the son of Philip, who called it Antigonia, and later by Lysimachus, who changed the name to that of his wife, **5.** 463; description of, **5.** 463–465

Nicaea, a city in India founded by Alexander, **7.** 49

Nicaea in Locris, **4.** 383; a fort near Thermopylae, **4.** 389

Nicaea (Nice), founded by the Massaliotes, **2.** 175, 191; subject to the Massaliotes, belongs to Province of Narbonitis, **2.** 193

Nicander (lived about 185–135 B.C.), poet, grammarian, and physician, and author of the *Theriaca*; on the two kinds of Aegyptian asps, **8.** 151

Nicatorium, Mt., near Arbela, so named by Alexander after his victory over Dareius, **7.** 197

Nice (see Nicaea)

Nicephorium in Assyria, **7.** 231

Nicias, contemporary of Strabo, native of Cos, reigned as tyrant over the Coans, **6.** 289

"Nicias, the Village of," to the west of Alexandria, **8.** 57

Nicolaüs Damascenus, on the embassy

408

INDEX OF NAMES, PLACES, AND SUBJECTS

from India to Augustus Caesar, **7.** 125, and on the gifts sent to Augustus, **7.** 127

Nicomedeia in Bithynia, about 300 stadia from the Sangarius River, **5.** 379; lies on the Astacene Gulf and was named after Nicomedes I, the Bithynian king (264 B.C.), **5.** 455

Nicomedes, the son of Prusias, king of Bithynia; incited against his father by Attalus II, **6.** 169; forces of, utterly destroyed by Mithridates, **5.** 449, 455; fought against Aristonicus, **6.** 247

Niconia (near Ovidiopol), on the Tyras River, **3.** 219

Nicophorium at Pergamum, planted with a grove, **6.** 169

Nicopolis in Acarnania; Anactorium an emporium of, **5.** 25

Nicopolis, near Alexandria, greatly honoured by Augustus because of his victory there, **8.** 43

Nicopolis in Lesser Armenia, founded by Pompey, **5.** 425

Nicopolis in Cilicia, on the Gulf of Issus, **6.** 357

Nicopolis Actia (near Prevesa) in Epeirus, founded by Augustus in honour of his victory over Antony, **3.** 301; a populous and wealthy city, **3.** 303; Actian Games celebrated near, and it has several dependent settlements, **3.** 305

Nicostratê, mother of Evander, mythical founder of Rome; skilled in divination, **2.** 385

Nigritae (or Nigretes?), the, and the Pharusians, said to have destroyed 300 Tyrian cities on the western coast of Libya, **8.** 161; use bows and scythe-bearing chariots, **8.** 169

Nikaria (see Icaria)

Nile (Aegyptus) River, the; mouths of, **1.** 107; boundary between two continents, **1.** 119, 129, 243, 415; "heaven-fed," **1.** 133; cataracts of, impassable for ships, **1.** 139; alluvial deposits of, **1.** 193; fed by rains from mountains of Aethiopia, **1.** 375; navigated by Eudoxus of Cyzicus, **1.** 377; nearly on the same meridian as the Tanaïs, **1.** 415; by its overflows causes Lake Mareotis to lose its baneful qualities, **2.** 315;

flows underground for a distance near its sources, **3.** 93; risings of, unknown to Homer, according to Apollodorus, **3.** 189; the silting up of, like that of the Pyramus River, and Aegypt called by Herodotus the "gift" of, **5.** 357; produces huge creatures, **7.** 37; largest of all rivers except the Ganges, Indus, and Ister, **7.** 61; certain fish found in, **7.** 79; confusion in boundaries of lands caused by, gave rise to science of geometry, **7.** 271; joined by the Astaboras, **3.** 319; joined by the Astasobas near Meroê, **7.** 321; position and description of, **8.** 3–5; effects like results in Aegypt and Aethiopia, **8.** 7; confuses boundaries, rising as high as 14 cubits, **8.** 11; forms the Delta, **8.** 13–15; filled from summer rains in Aethiopia, **8.** 17–21; timely risings of, **8.** 31; mouths of, **8.** 65 ff.; canals of, **8.** 75 ff.; level of, marked by Nilometer, **8.** 11, 127; has numerous islands, **8.** 133; by Herodotus foolishly said to rise near Syenê, **8.** 133; names of fish indigenous to, **8.** 149; the fish and crocodiles in, **8.** 153; sources of, by some thought to be near the extremities of Maurusia, **8.** 161

Nilometer, the, in Aegypt, **8.** 11, 13; construction and utility of, **8.** 127

Nîmes (see Namausus)

Nineveh (see Ninus)

Ninia, a city in Dalmatia, set on fire by Augustus, **3.** 261

Ninus (Nineveh), the city, founded by Ninus, **1.** 319; wiped out after the overthrow of the Syrians (608 B.C.), **7.** 193, 195; surrounded by the plains of Aturia, **7.** 197

Ninus, husband of Queen Semiramis and founder of Nineveh, called a Syrian, **1.** 319

Niobê, the, of Aeschylus, quoted, **5.** 519

Niobê, given in marriage to Amphion by her brother Pelops, **4.** 113; the home of, in Phrygia, **5.** 487

Nios (see Ios)

Niphates, Mt., a part of the Taurus, **5.** 299, 301, 305, 321

Nisa in Boeotia, the Homeric, no-

409

INDEX OF NAMES, PLACES, AND SUBJECTS

where to be seen, unless one identifies it with Isus, **4.** 299

Nisa in Megaris, has now disappeared, **4.** 299

Nisaea, the naval station of the Megarians, 18 stadia from Megara and joined to it by walls, **4.** 11, 245; betrayed to King Minos by Scylla, **4.** 173; alleged by the Megarians to have sent ships to Troy, **4.** 255

Nisibis in Assyria, or Mesopotamia, also called Mygdonian Antiocheia, at the foot of Mt. Masius, **5.** 299, 319, **7.** 231

Nisus, the father of the Scylla who was drowned by Minos, **4.** 173; son of King Pandion, received Megaris from his father and founded Nisaea, **4.** 247, 249

Nisyrians, Isles of the, near Nisyros, **5.** 177, 179

Nisyros, a city on the isle Carpathos, **5.** 177, 179

Nisyros, one of the Sporades Islands, mentioned by Homer, **5.** 175; description of, **5.** 177; in the high sea opposite Cnidus, **6.** 283; 60 stadia from Cape Laceter in Cos, **6.** 287

Nitiobriges, the, a tribe in Aquitania, **2.** 217

Nitre-beds (sodium carbonate, not saltpetre), the two, near Momemphis in Aegypt, **8.** 73

Noarus River, the, flows near Segestica, **3.** 255; empties into the Ister, **3.** 273

Nocera (see Nuceria)

Noega in Iberia, **2.** 121

Noja (see Netium)

Nola, in Campania, **2.** 453, 461

Nomads, the; in north-eastern Europe, of no use to the Romans and only require watching, **3.** 145; known by Homer, **3.** 197; have become morally worse under the influence of "our mode of life," **3.** 199; modes of life of, **3.** 205–209, 223; those beyond the Crimea eat horse-meat, cheese, and curd, **3.** 243; the Scythian, in Asia, **5.** 191; the Asiatic and European, used Tanaïs as a common emporium, **5.** 193; called Nabiani and Panxani, live between Lake Maeotis and the Caspian Sea,

5. 243; Scythian and Sarmatian, **5.** 245, 259; who live north of Sogdiana in Asia, **5.** 281; on the Arabian Gulf, **7.** 317; call the elephant hunters "Acatharti" ("Unclean"), **7.** 325; those in Arabia called "Debae" fight from the backs of camels and subsist upon their milk and flesh, **7.** 345; among the Aethiopians, often attacked like brigands, **8.** 135; in Maurusia and Masaesylia, **8.** 167; in Massaesylia taught by King Masanasses to be citizens, farmers, and soldiers, **8.** 187–189

Nomantini (or Numantini), the, in Iberia, driven out by the Romans, **3.** 143

Nomarchs, the, in Aegypt, **8.** 53; accused of injustice by the Aethiopians, **8.** 137

Nome, the Pythian (see Pythian Nome)

Nomentan Way, the, joins the Salarian Way at Eretum, **2.** 377, 417

Nomentum (Mentana), a small town in Latium, **2.** 375

Nomes, the thirty-six, in Aegypt, **8.** 9; the Heracleïotic and Arsinoïte, **8.** 15; Menelaïte, **8.** 65; Saïtic and Sebennytic, **8.** 67; Busirite, **8.** 69; Athribite, Prosopite, Mendesian, Leontopolite, Pharbetite, and Tanite, **8.** 71; Gynaeconopolite, Momemphite, and Nitriote, **8.** 73; Sethroïte, **8.** 77 (see footnote on page 76); Phagroriopolite, and Bubastite, **8.** 79; Letopolite, **8.** 85; Aphroditopolite, Heracleote, and Arsinoïte, **8.** 97; Cynopolite and Nome of Oxyrynchus, **8.** 109

Nora, now called Neroassus; a lofty stronghold in Cappadocia, where Eumenes held out against a siege for a long time, **5.** 357; served as the treasury of Sisines in Strabo's time, **5.** 359

Noreïa (Neumarkt in Austria), to which there is a voyage of 1200 stadia by river from the Adriatic, **2.** 317; near which Graeus Carbo fought the Cimbri, **2.** 319

Norici, the; geographical position of, **2.** 281, 283; **3.** 165

INDEX OF NAMES, PLACES, AND SUBJECTS

411

INDEX OF NAMES, PLACES, AND SUBJECTS

413

INDEX OF NAMES, PLACES, AND SUBJECTS

INDEX OF NAMES, PLACES, AND SUBJECTS

Ophelas (or Ophellas) of Pella in Macedonia, ruler of Cyrenê (322–308 B.C.) and a historian; wrote a *Circumnavigation of Libya*, but added a number of fabrications, **8.** 159

Ophians, the, in Aetolia, **5.** 29

Ophiodes, an island in the Arabian Gulf; topaz found in, **7.** 317

Ophiogeneis ("Serpent-born"), the, in the Troad; mythical story of, **6.** 31

Ophiussa (Afsia), one of the Pityussae; description of, **2.** 125

Ophiussa, an earlier name of Rhodes, **6.** 273

Ophiussa, on the Tyras River, **3.** 219

Ophlimus, Mt., in Asia, protects Phanaroea on the west, **5.** 429

Ophrynium in the Troad, near which is the sacred precinct of Hector, **6.** 59

Opici, the, once lived in Campania and are also called Ausones, **2.** 435; ejected by the Sabini, **2.** 465

Opis (to be identified, apparently, with Seleuceia); the village, about 200 stadia distant from the Euphrates, **1.** 305; on the Tigris River, **5.** 329; the Tigris River navigable to, **7.** 205

Opisthomarathus in Phocis, near Anticyra, **4.** 369

Opitergium (Oderzo) in Italy, **2.** 317

Opsicella in Iberia, founded by Ocelas, a companion of Antenor, **2.** 83

Opuntian Locrians, the, named after their metropolis Opus, **4.** 343

Opuntians, the, in Elis, claim kinship with the Locrian Opuntians, **4.** 379

Opuntians, Polity of the, by Aristotle, **3.** 289

Opus (near Gardinitza), damaged by earthquake, **1.** 225; the metropolis of the Epicnemidian Locrians, **4.** 341; the pillar dedicated by, at Thermopylae; 15 stadia from the sea and 60 from Cynus its seaport; by Homer called the home of Patroclus, **4.** 379

Oracle, the, of Zeus, at Dodona, deceived Alexander the Molossian, **3.** 17; founded by the Pelasgians, now virtually extinct, **3.** 313; given

out to the Tyrians on the founding of Gades, **2.** 135; regarded by Poseidonius as a Phoenician lie, **2.** 137; of the dead at Avernus, **2.** 441, 443, 445; given out at Delphi to Archias, founder of Syracuse, and to Myscellus, founder of Croton, **3.** 71; to Phalanthus, coloniser of Tarentum, **3.** 109; in regard to the exchange of Delos for Calauria and Delphi for Cape Taenarum, **4.** 173; "Blest is Corinth, but Tenea for me," **4.** 199; ordering Xenophon to buy a plot of land for Artemis in Elis, **4.** 223; at Dodona, advised the Boeotians to commit sacrilege, **4.** 285; in regard to flashes of lightning through Harma, **4.** 293; at Delphi, personally consulted by Agamemnon, **4.** 307; of Apollo, on Mt. Ptoüs, **4.** 329; of Trophonian Zeus at Lebadeia, **4.** 333; at Delphi, described, **4.** 353, the most truthful of all oracles, **4.** 353; consulted by Croesus and other foreigners, **4.** 357; devised by Apollo to help mankind, **4.** 365; of Abae, in Phocis, **4.** 369; given out to people of Aegium, meaning that the Chalcidians are the best of all fighters, **5.** 21; for sleepers, at Aniaricê in Asia, **5.** 251; in regard to the Pyramus River, **5.** 355; of the Sibyl, requiring the Romans to bring to Italy certain statues from Galatia and Epidaurus, **5.** 471; of Apollo Actaeus at Adrasteia, abolished, as also that at Zeleia, **6.** 29; to the Teucrians, to remain "where the earth-born should attack them," **6.** 95; at Ammon, and those of Sibylla, **8.** 113

Oracles, the, at Delphi, given out in words, but, at the temple of Ammon and other places, mostly by nods and signs, **8.** 115

Orange, in France (see Arausio)

Oratory, the Asiatic style of, initiated by Hegesias, **6.** 253

Orbelus, Mt. (Perim-dagh), on the northern boundary of Macedonia, **3.** 329

Orbis River, the, rises in the Cemmenus Mountain, **2.** 183

INDEX OF NAMES, PLACES, AND SUBJECTS

Orcaorci, a town in Galatia; region of, cold and bare of trees, grazed by wild asses, and has extremely deep wells, 5. 473, 475

Orcheni, the, a tribe of the Chaldaean philosophers, 7. 203

Orchistenê, in Armenia, has a large cavalry, 5. 323

Orchomenians, the, called by Homer "Minyae," joined the Thebans and helped the Thebans to drive out the Pelasgians and the Thracians, 4. 283; Homer gives catalogue of, separating them from the Boeotians, 4. 335; Lake Copaïs dry ground and tilled in time of, 4. 339; emigrated when the waters overflowed the plain, 4. 341; Mt. Acontius lies near, and the Cephissus River flows through, 4. 375

Orchomenus (Kalpaki), the Arcadian, "abounding in flocks," 4. 29; no longer exists, 4. 229

Orchomenus (Skripu), the Boeotian, "Minyeian," 4. 29, 175; Chloris the mother of Nestor came from, 4. 63; the site of, 4. 305, 333; a fissure in the earth opened up near, admitting the Melas River, and the Cephissus River flows near, 4. 307; occupied by the Boeotians after the Trojan War, 4. 323; by Homer called "Minyeian," and extremely wealthy, 4. 335, 339

Orchomenus near Carystus in Euboea, 4. 341

Ordona (see Herdonia)

Oreitae, the, a tribe in Asia, 7. 129

Oreitae, the, in Euboea, formerly called Histiaeans; Philistides the tyrant of, 5. 7; fought by the Ellopians, 5. 9

Oreithyia, snatched up by Boreas the North Wind, 3. 175

Ores, found in mountains between the Anas and Tagus Rivers, 2. 25

Orestae, the, an Epeirote tribe, 3. 307, 327, 341; annexed to Macedonia, 4. 417

Orestes, son of Agamemnon, said to have occupied Orestias and left it bearing his name, and to have founded a city which he called Argos Oresticum, 3. 307; Tisamenus the son of, powerful king of Achaea,

4. 211; sons of, despatched the Aeolian fleet from Aulis to Asia, 4. 283; with Iphigeneia, thought to have brought sacred rites in honour of Artemis Tauropolus to Comana in Cappadocia, 5. 353, 359; first leader of the Aeolian colonisations, but died in Arcadia, 6. 7

Orestes, the, of Euripides, where "Argos" and "Mycenae" are used synonymously, 4. 187

Orestias, occupied by Orestes and so named by him, 3. 307; used to be called a part of Upper Macedonia, 3. 309; geographical position of, 3. 325; said to have been the earlier name of Pelagonia, 3. 363

Oretania, borders on Turdetania, 2. 19; cities of, Castalo and Oria, very powerful, 2. 65; mountain-chain in, 2. 81; traversed by the Baetis, 2. 101

Oretanians, the, in Iberia; geographical position of, 2. 13, 65, 81, 103; extend almost to Malaca, 2. 105

Oreus (Histiaea in early times, now Oreï) in Euboea; walls and houses of, collapsed because of earthquake, 1. 223; Philistides the tyrant of, and site and history of, 5. 7, 9

Oria, a district of Histiaeotis in Euboea, 5. 7

Oria (see Uria)

Oria (now, apparently, Nuestra Senora de Oreto), in Iberia; a powerful city, 2. 65

Oricum (Erico), in Illyria, 3. 267

Orion; the; the bird in India that has the sweetest voice, 7. 123

Orion, reared at Oreus in Euboea, 5. 9

Ormenium (or Orminium) in Thessaly; territory of, now regarded as belonging to Magnesia, 4. 407; inhabitants of, transferred to Demetrias, 4. 423; a village at the foot of Mt. Pelion, 27 stadia from Demetrias and 20 from Iolcus, 4. 433, and the home of Phoenix, 4. 435

Ormenus the king, grandfather of Phoenix; the different accounts of, 4. 435

Orminium (see Ormenium)

Ornaments, barbaric, of women in Iberia, 2. 109, 111

Orneae in Argolis; unknown to

417

Homer, and bears the same name as the city between Corinth and Sicyon, **4.** 183

Orneae near Corinth, now deserted, formerly well peopled and had a highly revered temple of Priapus, **4.** 205, **6.** 27

Orneiae, the Homeric (see Orneae), **4.** 185

Ornithes ("Birds"), City of (Ornithopolis), between Tyre and Sidon, **7.** 271

Ornithopolis (see Ornithes)

Oroatis River, the, in Persis, **7.** 155; about 2000 stadia from the Pasitigris, **7.** 163

Orobiae, or Orobia, in Euboea, now Rovias (destroyed by a tidal wave 426 B.C.), near Aegae, **4.** 297; where was an oracle of Apollo Selinuntius, **5.** 7

Orodes, the Parthian king, surnamed "Arsaces," **7.** 63, 237 (footnote 3)

Orontes, descendant of Hydarnes, once held Armenia, **5.** 337

Orontes River (Nahr-el-Asi), the (formerly called Typhon), flows underground for a distance between Apameia and Antiocheia, **3.** 93; 1130 stadia from Orthosia, **6.** 333; course of, **6.** 357; in Syria, **7.** 243; course of, **7.** 245, 247, 249, 251; sources of, **7.** 265

Oropus, on the common boundary of Attica and Boeotia; has often been disputed territory, **1.** 245, **4.** 273; across the strait 40 stadia from Eretria, **4.** 289, 291; temple of Amphiaraüs and monument of Narcissus near, **4.** 293

Oros, Hieron (see Hieron Oros)

Orospeda, the mountain, in Iberia; geographical position of, **2.** 97

Orpheus, lived at Pimpleia in southern Macedonia; wizard, musician, and soothsayer, **3.** 339; Thamyris the Thracian like, **3.** 357; the rites of, originated among the Thracians, **5.** 105; a Thracian himself, **5.** 109; a prophet often consulted, **7.** 289

Orphic arts, the, **5.** 121

Orris-root (see Iris, the Selgic)

Orthagora in Thrace, **3.** 367

Orthagoras, says the isle Ogyris lies 2000 stadia from Carmania, **7.** 305

Orthanês, Attic deity similar to Priapus, **6.** 29

Orthê, the Homeric, subject to Polypoetes, **4.** 437; by some called the acropolis of the Phalannaeans, **4.** 439

Orthopolis, a city in Macedonia, **3.** 361

Orthosia in Caria, **6.** 261

Orthosia in Phoenicia, **7.** 255, 259, 265; 3650 stadia from Pelusium and 1130 from the Orontes River, **7.** 281

Orthosia in Syria, 3900 stadia from Pelusium, **6.** 333

Ortilochus, the home of, in Pherae, visited by Telemachus, **4.** 145

Orton (Ortona), the port-town of the Frentani, **2.** 433

Ortospana in Asia; geographical position of, **5.** 271

"Ortygia," name of nurse at travail of Leto, **6.** 223

Ortygia, a grove above Ephesus, said to be the scene of the travail of Leto, whose nurse was named "Ortygia," **6.** 223

Ortygia, the earlier name of Rheneia, the desert isle near Delos, **5.** 167

Ortygia, the island off Syracuse, **3.** 75, 79

Osca (Huesca), in Iberia; geographical position of, and where Sertorius was killed, **2.** 99

Oscan tribe, the Sidicini an, **2.** 435

Osci, the; country and dialect of, **2.** 395; have disappeared, **2.** 413; the mountains of, **2.** 435; once held Herculaneum and Pompeii, **2.** 453

Osimo (see Auxumum)

Osiris, the asylum of, in Aegypt, **8.** 73; mythical story of, **8.** 75; same as the bull Apis, **8.** 87; rites of, temple of, **8.** 117

Osismii (Ostimii), the, live on a promontory in Celtica, **2.** 237

Ossa, Mt., in Greece, broken off from Olympus, **1.** 223; neighbourhood of, once inhabited by the Aenianians, **1.** 227; compared with the Alps, **2.** 293; belongs to Thessaly, **3.** 335; held by Demetrias, **3.** 393, 425; split off from Mt. Olympus by earthquakes, **4.** 397; the Dotian Plain lies near, **4.** 449; the voyage along coast of, long and rough, **4.** 451

INDEX OF NAMES, PLACES, AND SUBJECTS

distance from, to Criumetopon in
Crete and to Strait of Sicily, **1**. 407;
one of the three capes of Sicily, **3**.
55, 57; 50 Roman miles from
Camarina and 36 from Syracuse, **3**.
59; 4000 stadia from the Alpheius,
3. 61; 4600 stadia from Cape
Taenarum, **4**. 127

Pacorus (eldest son of Orodes the king
of Parthia, with Labienus overran
Syria and part of Asia Minor, but
was defeated in 39 B.C. by Ventidius,
a legate of Antony. Again invaded
Syria but fell in battle there);
reverses of, **7**. 237; killed by Ventidius, **7**. 247

Pactolus River, the, rises in Mt.
Tmolus, **5**. 421; once brought down
quantities of gold-dust, **6**. 173

Pacton, a boat made of withes, used at
Philae, an isle in the Nile, **8**. 131

Pactyê on the Propontis, **3**. 373, 375,
377

Pactyes, Mt., in the territory of
Ephesus, **6**. 249

Padua (see Patavium)

Padus (Po) River, the, **2**. 271; the
largest of all European rivers except
the Ister, **2**. 227, 271, 273, 295, 307,
309, 311, 313, 327, 329, 435

Paean, the, to Apollo, originated at the
slaying of the Python by Apollo at
Delphi, **4**. 367

Paeanismos, the, of the Thracians,
called *titanismos* by the Greeks, **3**.
363

Paeans, the Cretic, invented by
Thales, **5**. 147; adopted at Sparta,
5. 151

Paeonia, boundaries of, **3**. 251, 275,
325, 333; land of, contains gold
nuggets, **3**. 355; the Axius and
Strymon Rivers flow from, **3**. 361;
traditions about, **3**. 363

Paeonians, the, in Asia, mentioned by
Homer, **6**. 117; in Trojan battles, **6**.
151

Paeonians, the, a Thracian tribe, lived
in Amphaxitis, *i.e.* on both sides of
the Axius River, **3**. 331, 333, 341,
345; in early times, as now, occupied much of Macedonia, **3**. 363

Paerisades (see Parisades)

Paeseni, the, in the Troad, changed
their abode to Lampsacus, **6**. 35

Paestan Gulf, the (see Poseidonian
Gulf)

Paesus (or Apaesus), a city and river
between Parium and Lampsacus, **6**.
35; former colonised by Milesians,
6. 207

Pagae (Psatho), a stronghold in
Megaris, nearly 350 stadia from
Peiraeus, **4**. 197, 243; situated in the
inmost recess of the Corinthian Gulf,
4. 317

Pagasae (Angistri) in Thessaly, seaport of Pherae, and 90 stadia from
it, **4**. 423

Pagasitic Gulf, the; position of, on the
Aegaean, **3**. 353, **4**. 425, 433

Pago, one of the Liburnides, **3**. 259

Pagrae, a stronghold near Antiocheia
in Syria, **7**. 247

Palacium, a fort in the Crimea (site
unknown), built by Scilurus and his
sons, **3**. 247

Palacus, son of Scilurus, a prince in the
Tauric Chersonese, assisted by the
Roxolani in his war against Mithri-
dates, **3**. 223, 235

"Palae," apparently a native Iberian
word for "nuggets," **2**. 41

Palaea in Asia, 130 stadia from Andeira, **6**. 131

Palaea, a town in Cypros, **6**. 379

Palaea-Akhaia (see Olenus in Achaea)

Palaebyblus (Old Byblus) in Syria, **7**.
263

Palaeo-Episcopi (see Gomphi)

Palaeo-Episcopi (see Tegea)

Palaeokastro in Euboea (see Eretria)

Palaeokastro (see Lilaea in Phocis)

Palaeokastro near Navarino (see Pylus,
the Messenian)

Palaeokastro (see Thuria)

Palaeopoli near Klituras (see Cleitor)

Palaeopoli (see Mantineia)

Palaepaphos in Cypros, where is a
temple of the Paphian Aphroditê, **6**.
381

Palaephaetus, author of a work *On
Incredible Things*; opinions of,
approved by Demetrius of Scepsis,
5. 407; on the Homeric Halizones,
5. 409

Palaepharsalus in Thessaly; Pompey
fled from, to Aegypt, **8**. 47

Palaerus in Acarnania, **5**. 25, 61

Palaescepsis (Old Scepsis), in the

INDEX OF NAMES, PLACES, AND SUBJECTS

Troad, **6.** 89, 91, 101; lay near the highest part of Mt. Ida, but its inhabitants were removed to the present Scepsis, 60 (260?) stadia lower down, **6.** 105

Palaestine, whither Minaeans and Gerrhaeans convey their aromatics, **7.** 343

Palamedes, The, of Euripides, quoted, **5.** 103

Palamedes, the son of Nauplius, **4.** 151

Palatium, the, walled by the first founders of Rome, **2.** 399; the works of art on, **2.** 409

Paleis, a city in Cephallenia, **5.** 47, 49, 51

Palermo (see Panormus)

Palestrina (see Praeneste)

Palibothra (or Palimbothra) in India, on the Ganges River, **7.** 17, 125; description of, **7.** 63

Palici, the, territory of, in Sicily, has craters that spout up water, **3.** 91

Palinthus (Plinthus?), the name of the tomb of Danaüs at Argos, **4.** 163

Palinuro, Cape (see Palinurus)

Palinurus (Palinuro), Cape of, in Italy, **3.** 5

Palinurus, in Cyrenaea, **8.** 207

Pallades, or *pallacides* ("dedicated maidens"), the, at Aegyptian Thebes, **8.** 125

Pallantia (Palencia), in Iberia, belongs to the Arvacans, **2.** 103

Pallas, "breeder of giants," son of King Pandion, received southern Atthis (Attica) from his father, **4.** 247, 249

Pallenê (in earlier times called Phlegra, but now Kassandra), the Macedonian peninsula, **3.** 349; where the Trojan women set on fire the ships of their Greek captors, **3.** 351; colonised by the Eretrians, **5.** 13

Palm, the; most abundant in Babylonia, at Susa, and on the coast of Persis and Carmania, **7.** 201; 360 uses of, **7.** 215; limited cultivation of, by Judaeans, in order to increase revenues, **8.** 61; in general not of good species in Aegypt, though good in Judaea, **8.** 133; found in abundance in Aethiopia, **8.** 145

Palma, a city on the larger of the Gymnesiae, **2.** 125

Palm-trees, great grove of, in Plain of Jericho, **7.** 291; abundant in region of Cape Deirê in Aethiopia, **7.** 331; excellent grove of, near Cape Poseidium on the Arabian Gulf, **7.** 341

Palms, the sweet-smelling, in Arabia, **7.** 347

Palmys, the Homeric, led forces from Ascania, **5.** 461

Paltus in Syria, where Memnon was buried, **7.** 159, 255

Pamboeotian Festival, the, held at the temple of Athenê near Coroneia, **4.** 325

Pamisus (Mavrozumenos) River, the, flows in Messenia, and is not the boundary between Laconia and Messenia, as Euripides says, **4.** 87, 117, 143

Pamisus River, the, a torrential stream flowing near the Laconian Leuctrum, **4.** 119

Pamisus (or Amathus) River, the, in Triphylia, flows past the Lepreatic Pylus, **4.** 21, 31, 51, 119

Pamphylia in Asia; the Chelidoniae Islands at beginning of coast of, **5.** 295; borders on Lycia, **6.** 311; description of, **6.** 323–325

Pamphylian Sea, the, **1.** 481; boundaries of, **6.** 375

Pamphylians, the, in Asia, not mentioned by Homer, **5.** 423, **6.** 363; do not wholly abstain from piracy, **5.** 481; engaged in piracy, and gained mastery of the sea as far as Italy, **6.** 313; said to be descendants of the peoples led from Troy by Calchas and Amphilochus, **6.** 325

Pan, the god, worshipped at Mendes in Aegypt, **8.** 69; and at Meroê, **8.** 147

Panaenus, the painter, assisted his uncle Pheidias in making the image of Zeus in the temple at Olympia, and also made many paintings therefor, **4.** 89

Panaetius the philosopher; Apollonius of Nysa the best of disciples of, **6.** 263; native of Rhodes, **6.** 279; reputed to have been pupil of Crates of Mallus, **6.** 355

Panaria (see Euonymus)

421

INDEX OF NAMES, PLACES, AND SUBJECTS

INDEX OF NAMES, PLACES, AND SUBJECTS

5. 381; the boundaries of country of—and by Herodotus called the "White Syrians," 5. 383, 385; Homer ignorant of seaboard of, 5. 423; have many temples on Mt. Olgassys, 5. 449; tribes of, mentioned by Homer, 6. 361

Paphus in Cyprus, founded by Agapenor, 6. 381, 383

Papyrus (see Byblus); transported from Tyrrhenia to Rome, 2. 367; found round the edges of a lake near Cape Deirê in Aethiopia, 7. 331

Parachelöitae in Phthiotis, subject to Achilles, 4. 413

Parachelöitis, in Acarnania and Aetolia; formed by silt from the Acheloüs River, 5. 57; rendered dry by Achilles, 5. 59

Parachoathras, Mt., the, in Armenia, 5. 259, 299, 319; the Cadusii live at foot of, 5. 269

Paradeisus, a place in Syria, 7. 265

Paradoxes, the, of the Stoics, 2. 145

Paraetacae (see Paraetaceni), the, in Aturia; the Araxes River flows from country of, 7. 165; country of, borders on Babylonia, 7. 193, 203

Paraetacenê, borders on Carmania, 7. 221

Paraetaceni, the; the mountainous country of, 5. 301; a predatory tribe bordering on Greater Armenia and Persia, 5. 309, 7. 173, but engage mainly in agriculture, 7. 221

Paraetonium (or Ammonia) in Aegypt, a city on the coast west of Alexandria, 8. 55; Alexander set out from, to the temple of Ammon, 8. 115

Paralus, founded Clazomenae in Asia, 6. 201

Paralysis, afflicted the Roman soldiers in Arabia, 7. 359

Parapotamia, the, of the Arabian chieftains, 7. 255

Parapotamia in Phocis (or Parapotamii, q.v.)

Parapotamii in Phocis, through which flows the Cephissus River, 4. 307; near Mt. Acontius, 4. 341; geographical position of, according to Theopompus, 4. 373; the narrow pass near, 4. 375

Parasang, the Persian, equals 60 stadia

according to some, but 30 or 40 according to others, 5. 287

Parasopia, in the Trachinian Heracleia, through which the Asopus flows, 4. 313; in the Oetaean country (see Parasopias), 4. 415

Parasopias (see Parasopia in the Trachinian Heracleia), in the Oetaean country, 4. 415

Parasopii, a village in the Trachinian Heracleia, 4. 205, 313

Parasopii, the, in Boeotia, divided into several settlements by the Asopus River, 4. 315

Parati, the, a tribe in Sardinia, 2. 361

"Pareisactus," nickname of the Ptolemy from Syria, 8. 37

Parhelia, the, in the clouds (" mock-suns "), 3. 227

Parian marble, the; the best for sculpture, 5. 171

Parians, the, in the Troad, founded the island Paros, later called Pharos, in the Adriatic, 3. 261, 263; founded Thasos, as also Parium on the Propontis, 5. 169; curried favour with the Attalic kings, and thus gained more territory, 6. 31

Parians, the, a tribe of Däae above Lake Maeotis, 5. 275

Paris, with Helen, entertained in Sidon, 1. 149; would have saved Greeks and barbarians from ruin if he had been shipwrecked on voyage to Sparta, 2. 189; stopped with Helen on the island " Cranaë " (Helenê, now Makronisi), 4. 273; tomb of, in Cebrenia in the Troad, 6. 65; the Judgment of, said to have taken place on Mt. Alexandreia above Antandrus, 6. 103

Parisades (or Paerisades), king of the Cimmerian Bosporus, presented his country to Mithridates, 3. 235, 237; regarded as god, 3. 239

Parisii, the, live about the Sequana (Seine) River, 2. 233

Parisus (or Tisia, now Theiss) River, the, the boundary between Illyria and Dacia, 3. 253 (see footnote 4)

Parium, city in the Troad, founded by the Parians, 4. 169, 6. 9; noted for its altar, its sides being a stadium in length, 5. 171; temple of Apollo Actaeus and Artemis transferred to,

423

INDEX OF NAMES, PLACES, AND SUBJECTS

summer at Ecbatana and in Hyrcania, **7.** 219

Parthian War, the, **5.** 437

Parthians, the; have added to knowledge of geography, **1.** 49; geographical position of, **1.** 499; have now yielded to the pre-eminence of the Romans, **3.** 145; have sent to Rome the trophies of their former victory, **3.** 147; the supremacy of, disclosed more geographical knowledge, **5.** 247; once ruler over Hyrcania, **5.** 253; Hecatompylus the royal seat of, **5.** 273; the Council of, described, **5.** 277; wrested the satrapies Turiva and Aspionus away from Eucratides, **5.** 281; use Ecbatana as summer-residence for their kings, **5.** 303, 307; wont to plunder Atropatian Media, **5.** 305; joined Labienus against Mylasa in Caria, **6.** 297; got possession of region on far side of the Euphrates, **6.** 329, 331; give the surname "Arsaces" to all their kings, **7.** 63; geographical position of, **7.** 145; now rule over the Persians, **7.** 159; present empire of, **7.** 173, 233; now rule over the Medes and Babylonians, but never once over the Armenians, **7.** 225; friendly towards the Romans, but defended themselves against Crassus, and later sent to Augustus the trophies of their victory, **7.** 237

Parthica, The, of Apollodorus, **7.** 5

Parthini, the, an Illyrian tribe, **3.** 307

Partridge, the, famous painting of, at Rhodes, by Protogenes, **6.** 269, 271; larger than a vulture, sent to Augustus by King Porus in India, **7.** 127

Partridges, the, in India, as large as geese, **7.** 95

Paryadres, Mt., in Asia, **5.** 209, 299; geographical position of, **5.** 319, 401; contained several fortified treasuries of Mithridates, **5.** 425; protects Phanaroea, **5.** 429

Parysatis, by barbarians called Pharziris, **7.** 373

Pasargadae, royal palace, treasures, and tombs at, **7.** 159; description of tomb of Cyrus at, **7.** 165

Pasiani, the, in Asia, helped to take away Bactriana from the Greeks, **5.** 261

Pasitigris River, the; the name of the Tigris River at its outlets, **7.** 161, 163

Passo di Civita (see Teanum Apulum)

Patala, a notable city in India, **7.** 59

Patalenê in India, occupied by Euthydemus the king of Bactria, **5.** 281; similar to the Delta of Aegypt, **7.** 19, 25; is an island, **7.** 57

Patara in Lycia, has a temple of Apollo; by Ptolemy Philadelphus named the Lycian Arsinoë, **6.** 317

Patarus, founder of Patara in Lycia, **6.** 317

Patavium (Padua), like Gadeira, has 500 knights, **2.** 131; an important city, **2.** 313; region of, produces wool of medium quality, **2.** 333

Pateischoreis, the, a tribe in Persis, **7.** 157

Patmos, the isle, **5.** 173

Patrae (Patras), made up of seven communities, **4.** 23; member of a new league after the dissolution of the Achaean League, **4.** 211; one of the 12 Achaean cities, **4.** 219; where the Romans settled a large part of the army after the Battle of Actium; a very populous city, and has a fairly good anchoring-place, **4.** 225

Patraeus, a village on the Cimmerian Bosporus, **5.** 197, 199

Patras (see Patrae)

Patrocles (about 312–261 B.C.); Macedonian general under Seleucus I and Antiochus I, explorer, author of geographical treatises now lost, and regarded as trustworthy by Strabo, **1.** 259, 261, 265; on the distance from the southern capes of India to the Caucasus Mountains, **1.** 255; discredited by Hipparchus, **1.** 257, 261; governor in the Orient, **1.** 281; on the Cadusii and the Caspian Sea, **5.** 251; on the Oxus River, **5.** 253; says the mouths of the Oxus and Iaxartes Rivers are 80 parasangs distant from one another, **5.** 287; on the possible voyages from India to Hyrcania, **5.** 289; on the length of India, **7.** 17

425

INDEX OF NAMES, PLACES, AND SUBJECTS

INDEX OF NAMES, PLACES, AND SUBJECTS

428

INDEX OF NAMES, PLACES, AND SUBJECTS

429

INDEX OF NAMES, PLACES, AND SUBJECTS

intermingled with the Lapiths, according to Simonides, **4.** 445; lived about Mt. Pelion and the Peneius, **4.** 447; little or no trace of, now preserved, **4.** 449; carried off the Histiaeans of Euboea into Thessaly, **5.** 9

Persea, a luscious fruit in Aethiopia, **7.** 331; the tree in Aethiopia, **8.** 145, and in Aegypt, **8.** 149

Persephonê (see Corê), the festival of, **1.** 377; endowed Teiresias with reason after his death, **7.** 289

Persepolis, 4200 stadia from Susa, **7.** 157; royal palace, treasures, and tombs at, **7.** 159; second only to Susa, **7.** 165

Perseus, king of Macedonia, overthrown by Paulus Aemilius, **3.** 143, 293, 345; captured by Paulus, **3.** 369; rased Haliartus to the ground, **4.** 325; son of Philip V the son of Demetrius II, **5.** 457; fought by the Romans and Eumenes II, **6.** 167

Perseus, the ancient, father of Helius, **4.** 129; founded Mycenae, **4.** 185; rescued by Dictys at Seriphos, **5.** 171; father of Erythras, **7.** 351; the Watchtower of, in Aegypt, **8.** 67; said to have visited the temple of Ammon, **8.** 115

Perseus, the constellation; star on the right elbow of, slightly to north of arctic circle, at 1400 stadia north of the Pontus, **1.** 515

Persia, geographical position of, **1.** 499; annual tributes paid to, by Cappadocia and Media, **5.** 313

Persian battle, the, at Marathon, **4.** 263; near Plataeae, **4.** 287

Persian fleet, the, destroyed at Cape Sepias in Magnesia, **4.** 451

Persian Gates, the, passed through, by Alexander, **7.** 163

Persian Gulf (or Persian Sea), the; one of the four large gulfs, **1.** 467; the Euphrates and Tigris Rivers empty into, **5.** 297; spouting whales in, **7.** 149; can be crossed in one day at its mouth, **7.** 155; borders on Babylonia, **7.** 203; description of, **7.** 301–303; borders on Arabia, **8.** 3

Persian Letters, the, on the straightforward character of the Scythians, **3.** 201

Persian Sea (see Persian Gulf)

Persian War, the; meteor fell at Aegospotami during, **3.** 377; the sea-fight at Salamis in time of, **4.** 179

Persians, the; blundered from ignorance of geography, **1.** 35; 300,000 wiped out by the Greeks at Plataeae, **4.** 325; for a time withstood by Leonidas at Thermopylae, **4.** 393; most of customs of, imitated by the Siginni, **5.** 293; overthrown by the Macedonians, **5.** 307; once ruled over Armenia, **5.** 337; sacred rites of, followed by the Medes and Armenians, **5.** 341; divided Cappadocia into two satrapies, **5.** 349; once held mastery in Asia Minor after Trojan War, **5.** 463; onsets of, in Asia, **5.** 495; hanged Hermeias the pupil and friend of Aristotle, **6.** 117; built an arcade of white marble on Mt. Tmolus near Sardeis, **6.** 173; named the "Hyrcanian Plain" and the "Plain of Cyrus," **6.** 185; once captured Miletus, **6.** 209; hanged Polycrates the powerful tyrant of Samos (522 B.C.), **6.** 217; said to have deposited treasures in the temple of Artemis at Ephesus, **6.** 227; once ruled over Ariana, **7.** 15, 129; language and customs of, used by the Carmanians, **7.** 155; country, customs, and history of, **7.** 155–189; established royal seat of their empire at Susa, **7.** 157; now subject to the king of the Parthians, **7.** 159; once collected tributes from all Asia, **7.** 163; conquered by Alexander, **7.** 165, 169; customs and worship of, **7.** 175–187; the hegemony of, over Asia, lasted 250 years, **7.** 189; overthrew the Medes, **7.** 195; ruined Babylon, **7.** 199; constructed cataracts in the Euphrates and Tigris to prevent navigation, **7.** 205; seized Phoenicia, **7.** 257; used Ptolemaïs in Phoenicia as base of operations against Aegypt, **7.** 271; revere the Magi and other diviners, **7.** 289; wont to guide ambassadors treacherously, **8.** 71

Persica, The, of Baton the Sinopean, **5.** 391

INDEX OF NAMES, PLACES, AND SUBJECTS

431

INDEX OF NAMES, PLACES, AND SUBJECTS

433

INDEX OF NAMES, PLACES, AND SUBJECTS

INDEX OF NAMES, PLACES, AND SUBJECTS

INDEX OF NAMES, PLACES, AND SUBJECTS

437

INDEX OF NAMES, PLACES, AND SUBJECTS

INDEX OF NAMES, PLACES, AND SUBJECTS

440

INDEX OF NAMES, PLACES, AND SUBJECTS

INDEX OF NAMES, PLACES, AND SUBJECTS

INDEX OF NAMES, PLACES, AND SUBJECTS

443

INDEX OF NAMES, PLACES, AND SUBJECTS

Euxine); peoples beyond, unknown, **3**. 173; forty rivers empty into, **3**. 189; " left parts " of, extend from the Ister to Byzantium, **3**. 285, 327

Ponza (see Pontia)

Poplar-trees, the Heliades changed into, **2**. 319

Poplonium (or Populonia, near Piombino), distance from, to Cosa, **2**. 347; visited by Strabo, **2**. 355

"Pordalis," an indecent name, **6**. 149

Pordoselenê (Poroselenê?), near Lesbos, **6**. 147

"Pornopion," the name of a certain month among the Aeolians in Asia, **6**. 127

Poros, the isle (see Calauria)

Poroselenê (see Pordoselenê)

Porsinas, the king of Clusium (Chiusi) in Tyrrhenia, tried to restore Tarquinius Superbus to the throne, **2**. 339

Porta Collina, at Rome, **2**. 377

Porthaon, the Homeric, father of "Agrius, Melas, and Oeneus, who lived in Pleuron and steep Calydon," **5**. 75

Porticanus, the country of, in India, **7**. 59

Porto di Fermo (see Castellum Firmanorum)

Portugal (a part of ancient Iberia, *q.v.*)

Porus, the king, captured by Alexander and presented with a large part of India by Alexander, **7**. 5; country of, has about 300 cities, **7**. 49, 51

Porus, the Indian; country of, in India, called Gandaris, **7**. 25; a relative of the Porus whom Alexander captured, **7**. 51

Porus, ruler of 600 kings in India, wished to become a friend of Augustus Caesar, sending ambassadors and gifts to him, **7**. 127

Poseidium, the, at Alexandria, containing a temple of Poseidon, **8**. 39

Poseidium, a small town in Syria near Laodiceia, **7**. 249, 255

Poseidium, Cape, in Arabia, **7**. 341

Poseidium, Cape, in Chios, **6**. 241, 243

Poseidium, Cape (Punta della Licosa), promontory in Leucania, **3**. 3

Poseidium, Cape, of the Milesians;

end of coast of Ionia, **6**. 197, 205, 263, 291; altar on, erected by Neleus, **6**. 199

Poseidium, Cape, on the isle Samos, has a temple of Poseidon, **6**. 213

Poseidium (Cape Scala), the, in Thesprotia, **3**. 299

Poseidium, Cape, north of Euboea in Thessaly; position of, in the Aegaean, **3**. 353

Poseidon; Asphalius, temple of, on new volcanic isle, **1**. 215; according to Homer, halted his horses at the Euboean Aegae, whence, probably, the Aegaean Sea took its name, **2**. 221; a horse-race instituted in honour of, by Romulus, **2**. 385; numerous temples of, in capes in Elis, **4**. 49; temple of the " Samian " at Samicum in Triphylia, **4**. 49, 59, 63, where Telemachus found the Pylians offering sacrifices, **4**. 53; temple of, on Cape Taenarum, **4**. 127; father of the mythical Nauplius, **4**. 153; the Isthmian, temple of, on the Isthmus of Corinth, **4**. 155, 197; Troezen in Argolis sacred to; asylum in Calauria, sacred to; gave Leto Delos for Calauria, and Apollo Delphi for Cape Taenarum, **4**. 173, 175; the Heliconian, temple of, at Helicê, submerged by tidal wave, **4**. 213, 215; sacred precinct of, at Onchestus, **4**. 329; notable temple of, on Cape Geraestus in Euboea, **5**. 11; great temple of, on the island Tenos, **5**. 173, and on the island Nisyros, **5**. 177; worshipped in Phrygia, in the interior—and explanation thereof, **5**. 515; destroyed Aias (Ajax), **6**. 81; temple of, on Cape Poseidium in Samos, **6**. 213; the Heliconian, sacrifices to, at Panionium in Asia, **6**. 221; temple of, at Alexandria, **8**. 39

Poseidonia (Pesto) in Leucania, **2**. 469, **3**. 3; people of, conquered by the people of Elea, **3**. 5

Poseidonia, Gulf of, in Leucania, **2**. 299, 305, 469

Poseidonia, the earlier name of Troezen in Argolis, **4**. 173

Poseidonius of Apameia in Syria (b. about 130 B.C.), author of a history in 52 books, now lost, and

445

INDEX OF NAMES, PLACES, AND SUBJECTS

a geographical and astronomical scholar of peculiar value to Strabo and other later scientific writers; philosopher, **1**. 3; on the tides, **1**. 15, 19, 203; praised by Strabo, **1**. 53; on the winds, **1**. 107; on the Erembians, **1**. 151; on the Syrians and kindred peoples, **1**. 153; on the silting-up process, **1**. 199; on the partial destruction of Sidon by an earthquake, **1**. 215; his treatise on Oceanus and his discussion of the zones, **1**. 361; estimates circumference of earth at 180,000 stadia, **1**. 365; his "Aethiopic" and "Scythico-Celtic" zones, **1**. 371; on the oblique motion and celerity of the sun at equator, **1**. 375; believes the ocean flows in a circle round the inhabited world, **1**. 385; philosopher and master of demonstration, **1**. 391; thinks migration of Cimbrians was caused by inundation of sea, and approves of division of inhabited world into three continents, **1**. 393; would emend Homer's text, **1**. 395; views of, on physics, **1**. 397; imitates Aristotle, **1**. 399; says Cnidus lies on same parallel as Rhodes and Gades, **1**. 461; on the Perisicans, Amphiscians, and Heteroscians, **1**. 517; on sunsets in Iberia, **2**. 9; made observations of the sun on visit to Gades (Cadiz), **2**. 11; on the east winds of the Mediterranean, **2**. 31; praises extravagantly quantity and quality of silver and gold ores in Turdetania, **2**. 41–47; says Aristotle wrongly attributes tides to "high and rugged coasts" of Maurusia and Iberia, **2**. 67; says the Baenis (Minius) River rises in Cantabria, **2**. 69; on Odysseia and Athenē's temple in Iberia, **2**. 83; says Marcus Marcellus exacted tribute of 600 talents from Celtiberia, but denies that the country had 300 cities, **2**. 105; on three by-products of Cyprian copper, on Iberian crows, and on Celtiberian and Parthian horses, **2**. 107; on the fortitude of women in some countries, notably in Liguria at child-birth, **2**. 113; on the Pillars of Heracles, **2**. 137;

on two wells in the Heracleium at Gades, **2**. 145; on the causes of the tides, **2**. 147–151; on a peculiar tree (*Dracaena Draco*?) in Iberia, **2**. 155; on the origin of the large stones in Stony Plain in Celtica, **2**. 185; on the treasures found at Tolosa, **2**. 207; on the width of the isthmus between Narbo and the ocean, **2**. 209; on barbaric customs of the Gauls, **2**. 247; on a certain isle off the mouth of the Liger where no male sets foot, **2**. 249; on quarrying stones in Liguria, **2**. 335; says the circuit of Sicily is 4400 stadia, **3**. 57; on the geographical position of the three capes of Sicily, **3**. 59, 61; on the effects of the eruptions of Aetna, **3**. 69; on Syracuse, Eryx, and Enna, **3**. 87; on a submarine eruption between Hiera and Euonymus, **3**. 101; on the expedition of the Cimbri to the region of Lake Maeotis, **3**. 169; on the Homeric Mysians, **3**. 177, 179, 195; would emend "Mysi" to "Moesi" in Homer, **3**. 181; says Scilurus, the king of the Bosporus, had 50 sons, **3**. 235; says the earth poured into the trenches at the mine of asphalt near Apollonia in Illyria changes to asphalt, and describes the asphaltic vine-earth at the Pierian Seleuceia (Kabousi) and in Rhodes (where he was Prytanis), which kills the insects on infected vines, **3**. 267; known by Strabo (?), **3**. 383 (see footnote 6); wrote treatises on *Physics* and *Mathematics*, **4**. 3; more accurate in matter of distances than Polybius, **5**. 83; on the width of the isthmuses (1) between Colchis and the mouth of the Cyrus River, (2) between Lake Maeotis and the Ocean, and (3) between Pelusium and the Red Sea, **5**. 187; wrote a history of Pompey, **5**. 189; on the earthquakes round Rhagae, **5**. 273; on the Council of the Parthians, **5**. 277; on bricks in Iberia that float on water and are used to clean silver, **6**. 133; sojourned and taught in Rhodes, **6**. 279; on the springs of naphtha in Babylonia, **7**. 217;

INDEX OF NAMES, PLACES, AND SUBJECTS

says that Seleucis in Syria was divided into four satrapies, **7.** 241; most learned of all philosophers in Strabo's time, native of Apameia, **7.** 255; on the huge dragon seen in Syria, **7.** 261; says that the ancient dogma about atoms originated with Mochus the Sidonian, **7.** 271; on the sorcerers about the Dead Sea, **7.** 295; on the fragrant salts in Arabia, **7.** 351; emends the Homeric "Erembians" to "Arambians," and says that the Arabians consist of three tribes, **7.** 371; on the cause of the risings of the Nile, **8.** 19; on the breadth of the isthmus between Pelusium and Heröonpolis, **8.** 71; amused by the apes on the coast in Maurusia, **8.** 163; says that the rivers in Libya are "only few and small," and discusses the effect of the sun on different regions, **8.** 175–177

Potamia in western Paphlagonia, **5.** 453

Potamon of Mitylenê, contemporary of Strabo, **6.** 143

Potamus, the Attic deme, north of Cape Sunium, **4.** 271

Potentates, the, subject to the Romans, **8.** 213

Potidaea (later called Cassandreia, now Kassandra), founded by the Corinthians, **3.** 349

"Potistra" (see "Pistra")

Potniae near Thebes, scene of the myth of the Glaucus who was torn to pieces by the Potnian mares, **4.** 313; by some identified with the Homeric Hypothebes, **4.** 327

Potnian mares, the, which tore Glaucus to pieces, **4.** 313

Practius (see Practius River), a supposed place in the Troad, **6.** 39; mentioned by Homer, **6.** 37

Practius River, the, in the Troad, **6.** 9, 19, 23, 39

Praefect, a, of equestrian rank, sent to govern certain Ligures, **2.** 271

Praefect, the, of Aegypt, has the rank of king, **8.** 49

Praefects, the; in Iberia, reside at Tarraco, **2.** 91; sail up the Nile in cabin-boats, **8.** 63; the Nilometers

useful to, in determining revenues, **8.** 129; hold as personal property a certain island in the Nile, **8.** 133; sent by the Romans to the Provinces, **8.** 211

Praeneste (Palestrina), between the Latin and Valerian Ways, **2.** 415; description of, **2.** 417–419

Praenestine Way, the, **2.** 415

Praenestini, the, 540 in number, who long held out against Hannibal at Casilinum, **2.** 461

Praetor, a, governs Baetica, **2.** 121

Praetor nocturnus, the, a local official in Alexandria, **8.** 49

Praetorian *legatus*, a, administers justice to the Lusitanians, **2.** 121

Praetors, the, insulted by the Lacedaemonians, **4.** 137; sent by Augustus to all "Provinces of the People," **8.** 213

Pramnae, the, a sect of philosophers in India, **7.** 123; life and habits of, **7.** 125

Prasia (or Prasiae), a deme on the eastern coast of Attica, **4.** 271

Prasiae (Prasto, near Leonidi), in Laconia, belongs to the Argives, **4.** 151; belonged to a kind of Amphictyonic League of seven cities, **4.** 175

Prasians, the, in the Argolis; dues of, at temple of Poseidon on Calauria, paid by the Lacedaemonians, **4.** 175

Prasians, the, in Crete, called the Corybantes sons of Athenê and Helius, **5.** 111; country of, **5.** 139

Prasii, the, superior to all other tribes in India, **7.** 63

Prasto (see Prasiae)

Prasus in Crete, where is the temple of the Dictaean Zeus, **5.** 127; lies 60 stadia above the sea and was rased to the ground by the Hierapynians, **5.** 139

Praxander, founded Lapathus in Cypros, **6.** 377

Praxiphanes the philosopher, native of Rhodes, **6.** 279

Praxiteles, the great sculptor (b. about 390 B.C.); the "Eros" of, at Thespiae, brought fame to that city, **4.** 319; works of, filled whole of altar in temple of Artemis at Ephesus, **6.** 229

447

INDEX OF NAMES, PLACES, AND SUBJECTS

INDEX OF NAMES, PLACES, AND SUBJECTS

INDEX OF NAMES, PLACES, AND SUBJECTS

285–247 B.C.); Timosthenes the admiral of, writer on *Harbours* and composer of melody of the Pythian Nome, **4.** 363; Arsinoê, wife and sister of, founded the city Arsinoê in Aetolia, **5.** 65; Philotera named after sister of, **7.** 315; sent Eumedes to the hunting-grounds for elephants, **7.** 319; much interested in the sciences, **8.** 17–19; succeeded Ptolemy Soter, and was succeeded by Euergetes, **8.** 43; built the road from Coptus to Berenicê on the Red Sea, **8.** 119

Ptolemy III, Euergetes, succeeded Ptolemy Philadelphus and was succeeded by Philopator, **8.** 43

Ptolemy IV, Philopator or Tryphon (reigned 222–205 B.C.); partly walled Gortynia, **5.** 137; fought Antiochus the Great at Rhaphia, **7.** 279; son of Agathocleia, succeeded Euergetes and was succeeded by Epiphanes, **8.** 43

Ptolemy V, Epiphanes, succeeded Philopator and was succeeded by Philometor, **8.** 43

Ptolemy VI, Philometor (reigned 181–146 B.C.); conquered Alexander Balas in Syria (146 B.C.), but died from a wound (fell from his horse), **7.** 247; succeeded Epiphanes and was succeeded by Euergetes II (Physcon), **8.** 43

Ptolemy VII, Euergetes II, Physcon (reigned 146–117 B.C.); received favourably Eudoxus of Cyzicus, **1.** 377; succeeded by his wife Cleopatra, **1.** 379; his scarcity of competent pilots, **1.** 387; knew nothing about India, **1.** 397; succeeded Philometor and was succeeded by Ptolemy Lathurus, **8.** 43; sent masses of people against soldiers, thus causing their destruction, **8.** 51

Ptolemy VIII, Lathurus, succeeded Ptolemy Euergetes II (Physcon) and was succeeded by Auletes, **8.** 43

Ptolemy IX, Auletes (reigned 80–58 B.C. and 55–51 B.C.); illegitimate son of Ptolemy VIII, Lathurus; banished by the Aegyptians (58 B.C.), but restored to the throne by Gabinius the proconsul, **5.** 437;

father of Cleopatra and brother of Ptolemy the king of Cypros, **6.** 385; successor of Ptolemy Lathurus and father of Berenicê and Cleopatra, **8.** 43; the reign of, **8.** 45–47; worst king of all, but received large revenues, **8.** 53

Ptolemy, last king of Cypros (reigned 80–57 B.C.), younger brother of Ptolemy IX, Auletes; being deposed, and refusing to surrender to Marcus Cato, committed suicide, **6.** 385

Ptolemy, grandson of Antony and Cleopatra and son of Juba the Younger, succeeded to the throne of Maurusia, **8.** 169, 179, 215

Ptolemy "Cocces" and "Pareisactus," from Syria, plundered the gold sarcophagus of Alexander, **8.** 37

Ptoüs (Skroponeri), Mt., in Boeotia; the oracle of Apollo on, **4.** 329

Publicans, Roman, worked the gold mines in the land of the Salassi, **2.** 277

Pulse, sown in the winter season, **7.** 21

Purple, the marine, used for dyeing, **6.** 189; the Tyrian, most beautiful of all, **7.** 269

Purple-fish of huge size at Carteia, **2.** 37

Puteoli (see Dicaearchia); origin of name of, **2.** 447

Pydna (Citrum, now Kitros), a Pierian city, **3.** 339, 341, 345, 359

Pygela, a town in Asia, founded by Agamemnon, has a temple of Artemis Munychia, **6.** 223

Pygmies, the, slaughtered by cranes, **1.** 127; explanation of reputed size of, **8.** 143

Pylae, boundary between Cilicia and Syria, **6.** 357

Pylae (see Thermopylae), **4.** 11; the Amphictyonic League convened at, twice a year, **4.** 357

Pylaean Assembly, the, of the Amphictyons at Thermopylae, **4.** 393

Pylaemenes, the descendants of, given by Pompey the kingship over certain of the Paphlagonians, **5.** 371; the leader of the Eneti of the Paphlagonians in the Trojan War, **5.** 381

Pylaeus, scion of Ares, ruler of the Pelasgians at Larisa Phryconis, **6.**

451

INDEX OF NAMES, PLACES, AND SUBJECTS

INDEX OF NAMES, PLACES, AND SUBJECTS

and other countries, **5.** 213, 427, 431, 441, 443; daughter of Pythodorus of Tralleis, **6.** 257

Pythodorus of Tralleis, contemporary of Strabo, native of Nisa, friend of Pompey, father of Queen Pythodoris, and very wealthy, **5.** 427, **6.** 257

Pytholaüs, Cape of, in Aethiopia, **7.** 331; Pillars and Altars of, **7.** 335

Python, according to Ephorus, a cruel man known as the Dragon, slain by Apollo, **4.** 367

Pytna, a peak of Mt. Ida in Crete, **5.** 113

Pyxus (Buxentum, now Policastro), in Leucania, colonised from Messenê in Sicily, **3.** 5

Q

Quaestor, a, serves as assistant to a praetor in governing Baetica in Iberia, **2.** 121; the, at Nemausus, a Roman citizen, **2.** 203

Quarries of stone, the, near Tibur, **2.** 417, and near Tunis, **8.** 191

Quarry, the, above Cape Amphialê in Attica, **4.** 257

Quirinal Hill, the, walled by the first founders of Rome, but easy to capture, **2.** 399

" Quirites," the, origin of term, **2.** 375

R

Rabbits (see Hares), the, in the Gymnesiae no longer a pest, **2.** 129

Rafina (see Halae Araphaenides)

Rain, no, in Babylonia, at Susa, and in Sitacenê, **7.** 201

Rains, the cause of, at the equator, **1.** 373

Ram, a, never sacrificed at the oracle of Phrixus, **5.** 213

Rams, in Turdetania, bought at a talent apiece, **2.** 33

Rasa near Olympia (see Scillus)

Ras-al-Razat (see Phycus)

Rat (?), a, sold for 200 drachmae at Casilinum, **2.** 461 (footnote 3)

Ravenna, in Umbria, **2.** 301, 327; largest city in the marshes; description of, **2.** 313, 315, 337; where the Ombrici (Umbri) begin, **2.** 369

Reate (Rieti), a Sabine city, **2.** 375

Red-rust, often ruins crops in Triphylia, **4.** 53

Red Sea (see Arabian Gulf and Erythraean Sea), the, **1.** 119, 123, **8.** 7; once extended to Gerrha, **1.** 185, 207, 209; thought by Dareius I to lie at a higher level than Aegypt, **8.** 77; probably once confluent with the Mediterranean, **8.** 99; the road from Coptus to, **8.** 119–121

Reed, the kind of, used for flutes, produced by a marsh in Boeotia, **4.** 325; the, in India, are tremendous in size, **7.** 93; uses of, on the Euphrates, **7.** 205, 207; in Lake Gennesaritis, **7.** 261; abundant in the country of Coracius in Aethiopia, **7.** 321; in country of the Sabaeans in Arabia, **7.** 347

Reed-roots, used as food by the Aethiopians, **8.** 143

Reeds, in western Aethiopia, whose joints each hold eight *choinices*, being like those in India, **8.** 165

Reggio d'Emilia (see Regium Lepidum)

Regis Villa, between Ossa and Gravisci, where once was a palace of Maleos the Pelasgian, **2.** 365

Regium Lepidum (Reggio nell' Emilia), on the Aemilian Way, **2.** 311, 327

Religion, chiefly supported by women, **3.** 183; the, of the Greeks and barbarians, **5.** 93

Remi, the, a notable tribe in Celtica, **2.** 233

Remus (Romus), the story of, **2.** 381; slain as result of a quarrel, **2.** 383

Rentina (see Arethusa)

Reptiles (see Serpents and Snakes), the deadly, in Albania in Asia, **5.** 229; with wings like bats, in India, **7.** 65; numerous and vicious in India, **7.** 77, 79; in Gordyaea, avoid a certain stone called Gangitis, **7.** 233; on the isthmus between Pelusium and Heröonpolis, **8.** 71

Republic, Plato's, cited on founding cities as far as possible from the sea, **3.** 205

Resin, produced in the Alps, **2.** 283

Revolutions, the, of the heavenly bodies, **1.** 425

INDEX OF NAMES, PLACES, AND SUBJECTS

455

INDEX OF NAMES, PLACES, AND SUBJECTS

Rhetia, mother of the Cyrbantes, by Apollo, **5.** 115

Rhetoric, definition of, **1.** 61; Homer an expert in, **1.** 63

Rhetoric, a work on, by Apollodorus the Pergamenian, **6.** 171

Rhetoric, The Art of, by Hermagoras of Temnus, **6.** 159

Rhine River, the (see Rhenus River)

Rhinoceros, the, in southern Aethiopia; description of, **7.** 335

Rhinoceros, the (see " *Rhizeis,*" **8.** 163)

Rhinocolura in Phoenicia, the lakes and pits near, **7.** 211; origin of name of, **7.** 279; receives aromatics from Leucê Comê in Arabia, **7.** 359

Rhipae (see Rhipê)

Rhipaean Mountains, the mythical, **3.** 175, 191

Rhipê, the Homeric (perhaps also called Rhipae), now deserted, **3.** 385, **4.** 229

Rhium, in Messenia, by Cresphontes made one of the five capitals of Messenia, **4.** 117, 119

Rhium (Rion), Cape, at the entrance of the Corinthian Gulf, **4.** 17, 241

Rhizeis (rhinoceros ?), found in western Aethiopia, **8.** 163

Rhizo (Risano), on the Rhizonic Gulf, **3.** 263

Rhizonic Gulf (Gulf of Cattaro), the, in Illyria, **3.** 257, 263

Rhizophagi (" Root-eaters "), the, in Aethiopia, **7.** 321

Rhizus in Thessaly, now a village belonging to Demetrias, **4.** 425, 451

Rhodanus (Rhone) River, the, formerly called the boundary between Celtica and Iberia, **2.** 117; a navigable river, **2.** 167; empties into the Galatic Gulf, **2.** 181; controversy as to number of mouths of, **2.** 189; the largest river in Celtica, **2.** 195; joins the Cemmenus Mountain and the Isar River, **2.** 197; passes through Lemenna Lake, **2.** 199; navigable, **2.** 211; borders on the land of the Sallyes, **2.** 269; traverses Lake Lemenna, **2.** 273; rises in the Alps, **2.** 291; flows through Lake Lemenna, **3.** 77

Rhodaspes, son of Phraates IV, sent by his father as hostage to Rome, **7.** 237, 239

Rhodes, about 4000 stadia from Alexandria, **1.** 93, 323; parallel of, perceptibly different from that of Athens as shown by sun-dial, **1.** 333; distance from, to various points, **1.** 407, 447, 483; longest day at, at about centre of, has 14½ equinoctial hours, **1.** 513; ledges of rock in, **2.** 357; the colossus of, **3.** 107; has asphaltic earth which cures the infested vine, **3.** 267; the nine Telchines lived in, some accompanying Mother Rhea thence to Crete, **5.** 111; type of adornment of, like that of Cyzicus, **5.** 501; the city, terraced like Munychia at Peiraeus, **4.** 259; description and history of, **6.** 269–281; maritime supremacy of, **6.** 269; government of, not democratic but beneficent, **6.** 271; earlier names of, **6.** 273; the present city, founded in the time of the Peloponnesian War, **6.** 275; colonies of, **6.** 277; notable men of, **6.** 279, 281

Rhodians, the, erected temple on new volcanic isle, **1.** 215; thought by some to have founded Siris and Sybaris in Italy, **3.** 51; city of, terraced like Munychia at Peiraeus, **4.** 259; worship Apollo "Erythibius," **6.** 127; fleet of joined the Romans against Philip, **6.** 167; the Peraea (Mainland) of, **6.** 191, 263, 265, 311; friends to the Romans and Greeks, **6.** 269; take care of their poor people, and are Dorians in origin, **6.** 271; even in early times sailed far and wide, and founded several cities, **6.** 277; famous men among, **6.** 279; unfriendly to the Syrians, **6.** 329

Rhodius River, the, mentioned by Homer, **5.** 421; empties between Abydus and Dardanus, and is mentioned by Homer, **6.** 59, 87; source of, **6.** 89

Rhodopê, Mt. (Despoto-Dagh); compared with the Alps, **2.** 293; a boundary of Paeonis, **3.** 251; borders on the country of the Bessi, **3.** 275; on northern boundary of Macedonia, **3.** 329; position of, with reference to the Strymon River, **3.** 361; the

INDEX OF NAMES, PLACES, AND SUBJECTS

Agrianes live in neighbourhood of, **3**. 363

Rhodopis the Courtesan (see Doricha)

Rhoduntia, a stronghold near Thermopylae, **4**. 391

Rhodus (see Rhoê), near north-eastern corner of Iberia, belonging to city of Emporium, but by some said to have been founded by the Rhodians, **2**. 93; founded by the Rhodians, and later taken by the Massaliotes, **6**. 277

Rhoê (Rhodê?) Agathê (Rosas?), in Iberia, founded by the Massaliotes, **2**. 175

Rhoeïtes River, the (see Rhesus River)

Rhoetaces River, the, empties into the Cyrus River, **5**. 219

Rhoeteïum in the Troad, where is a temple, tomb, and statue of Aias, **6**. 59, 67; received part of the territory of ancient Ilium, **6**. 85

Rhombites River, the, Greater, 800 stadia from Tanaïs and noted for its fish, **5**. 195

Rhombites River, the Lesser, 800 stadia from the Greater Rhombites, noted for its fish, **5**. 195

Rhone River, the (see Rhodanus)

Rhosus on the Gulf of Issus in Cilicia, **6**. 357

Rhoxana, daughter of Oxyartes in Bactriana, reputed to have married Alexander the Great, **5**. 285

Rhyndacus River, the, in Mysia, **5**. 409; borders on the Doliones, **5**. 499; course of, **5**. 503

Rhypes, one of the twelve cities in which the Achaeans settled, **4**. 219; now uninhabited, and its territory, Rhypis, held by Aegium and Pharae, **4**. 225

Rhypis, the territory of Rhypes, in Achaea, **4**. 225

Rhytium in Crete, belongs to the Gortynians, **5**. 141

Rice, sown in rainy seasons in India, **7**. 21; the sowing and harvesting of, **7**. 27, 29

Riddle, a, attributed to Homer and applied to failure of silver-mines at Laurium, **2**. 45

Rieti (see Reate)

Rimini (see Ariminum)

Ritri (see Erythrae in Ionia)

Road, the mule-, from Brundisium to Beneventum, **3**. 123; joins the Appian Way near Beneventum, **3**. 125

Roads, the Roman, in Iberia, **2**. 95

Rocking Stones, on the Sacred Cape of Iberia, **2**. 7

Rodiae (Rudiae, now Rugge), a Greek city in Iapygia and birth-place of Ennius the poet, **3**. 119, 121

Roïnos, Mt. (see Parthenius)

Roman forces, the, in Aegypt, **8**. 135

Roman freedmen, the, with whom Julius Caesar colonised Corinth, ransacked all graves, **4**. 203

Roman generals, tactics used by, in Corsica, **2**. 359, and in Sardinia, **2**. 361

Roman Senate, the; recruits ranks from men of equestrian rank in Luca, **2**. 329; sent deputation to offer sacrifices on new island created by volcanic eruption in Mediterranean, **3**. 101

Romans, the, occupied Iberia, **1**. 7; have added to our knowledge of geography, **1**. 49; victims of plague of mice and famine in Cantabria, **1**. 113; called refined by Eratosthenes, **1**. 249; scorned to hold Britain because of its lack of importance, **1**. 445; recently invaded Arabia Felix, **1**. 453; civilisers of many savage nations, **1**. 487; upbuilders of Europe, **1**. 489; join the Nomads (Numidians) in hunting, **1**. 503; transferred certain Lusitanians to interfluvial region in Iberia, **2**. 13; beloved by inhabitants of Gadeira, **2**. 17; carried on war against Lusitanians, of all Iberians, for longest time, **2**. 65, reducing most of their cities to mere villages, **2**. 71; civilising influences of, in Lusitania, **2**. 77–79; carried on piecemeal war with the Iberians, **2**. 87; some officers of, thought crazy by Vettonians in Iberia when seen walking for mere exercise, **2**. 109; historians among, imitators of the Greeks, **2**. 117; finally learned about the Cassiterides Islands, **2**. 157; friendly to the Massaliotes, **2**. 177; most notable of, went to school at Massalia rather

457

than at Athens, **2.** 179; sold lakes at Tolosa containing hidden gold and silver for public treasury, **2.** 207; gave the "Latin right" to certain of the Aquitani, **2.** 219; in complete control of Celtica, **2.** 225, 233; have enslaved the Gallic race, **2.** 237, 241; conquered these more easily than the Iberians, **2.** 239; put a stop to barbaric customs in Gaul, **2.** 247; virtually acquired Britain, **2.** 257; after 80 years conquered the Ligures, **2.** 269, and the Salassi, **2.** 277; given pretexts for war by the Salassi, **2.** 279; control all gold mines, **2.** 293; shared civic rites with certain peoples, **2.** 299; drove out of Italy, or destroyed, certain tribes, **2.** 311; founded Aquileia as a fortress, **2.** 317; helped by the Eneti in their battles, **2.** 323; have been intermingled with the Ombrici and Tyrrheni, **2.** 325; surpassed all others in men, cities, and wealth, **2.** 331; surrendered to the Galatae (390 B.C.), **2.** 341; call Cyrnus "Corsica," **2.** 359; defeated the Carthaginians, **2.** 361; colonised some towns, humbled others, **2.** 365; at last realised the wealth of the Sabini, **2.** 377; worship Nicostratè (Carmenta) the mother of Evander, **2.** 385–387; destroyed Alba, **2.** 389; accused of sending out pirates from Antium, **2.** 391; put a stop to that practice, **2.** 393; still preserve the dialect of the Oscans, **2.** 395; depend on arms and valour rather than on fortifications, **2.** 401; used foresight in city-improvements, **2.** 405; have filled Rome with beautiful structures, **2.** 407; regard the Campus Martius as holiest place of all, **2.** 409; destroyed Fregellae, **2.** 413; founded certain cities, **2.** 415; used Alba as a prison, **2.** 425; settled a colony at Dicaearchia, **2.** 447; some of, retire permanently at Neapolis, **2.** 431; disciplined the Campani, **2.** 467; took Paestum (Pesto) from the Leucani, **2.** 469; ejected the Picentes, **2.** 471; crushed the Brettii at Temesa, **3.**

15; took Hipponium and changed its name to Vibo Valentia, **3.** 17; colonised Thurii and changed its name to Copiae, **3.** 47; used Messenè in Sicily as a base of operations against the Carthaginians, **3.** 67; drove the Carthaginians out of Sicily and took Syracuse by siege, **3.** 73; besieged Eunus at Enna, **3.** 81, 83; took possession of Sicily, **3.** 85; took Tarentum by storm, **3.** 107; colony of, received at Tarentum, **3.** 117; suffered great losses at Battle of Cannae, **3.** 135; the causes of their preeminence and a description of their conquests and hegemony, **3.** 137–147; transferred some of the Germanic tribes across the Rhine to Celtica, **3.** 155; wars of, against the Germans, **3.** 159; subdued the Cimbri and the Helvetii, **3.** 169; have not yet advanced beyond the Albis (Elbe) River, **3.** 171; found the Getans a formidable enemy and prepared to make an expedition against them, **3.** 211; completely humbled the Getans and Dacians, who once could marshal 200,000 men, but now only 40,000, **3.** 213, 215; campaign against, planned by Mithridates, **3.** 233; have held the Cimmerian Bosporus since the time of Mithridates, **3.** 237; appoint the kings of the Bosporians, **3.** 247; have virtually wiped out certain tribes of the Galatae, Illyrians, and Thracians, **3.** 263; subdued the Autariatae and Scordisci, **3.** 273; derive great revenue from the *Pelamydes* fish at Byzantium, **3.** 283; encamp in houses in depopulated regions, **3.** 291, 293; have colonists at Buthrotum in Epeirus, **3.** 299; reduced the Epeirote cities, and transferred remaining inhabitants to Nicopolis, **3.** 303; broke up the Macedonian empire, **3.** 309; set Corcyra free, **3.** 327; defeated Perseus before Pydna, **3.** 345; destroyed, but rebuilt, Corinth, **4.** 121; overthrew Helot-slavery in Laconia, **4.** 135; gained the supremacy over Greece, **4.** 137; joined by the Perioeci and Helots

INDEX OF NAMES, PLACES, AND SUBJECTS

in Laconia, **4.** 139; extravagance
of, in the importation of marble
from Laconia, **4.** 143; joined by
Tenea against Corinth, **4.** 199; all
Greece became subject to, **4.** 201;
wished to destroy some Greek states
and preserve others, **4.** 217; settled
a large part of the army at Patrae
after the Battle of Actium, **4.** 225;
leave Athens free and hold it in
honour, **4.** 269, 271; became lords
of all by their intercourse with
mankind, and by applying themselves to training and education,
4. 281; annexed Upper Larymna
to Larymna, **4.** 305; gave Haliartus
to the Athenians, **4.** 325; completely defeated the forces of
Mithridates at Chaeroneia, **4.** 333;
found the Dorian Tetrapolis virtually extinct, **4.** 389; under Titus
Quintius Flamininus, conquered
Philip the son of Demetrius at
Cynoscephalae in Thessaly, **4.** 445;
strongly resisted and tricked by
the Acarnanians, **5.** 67, 73; broke
up the piracy of the Cilicians,
5. 133; Lagetas, great-uncle of
Strabo, betrayed kingdom of
Mithridates Eupator to, **5.** 135;
now rule Crete, **5.** 159; made Delos
a great commercial centre, **5.** 167;
the supremacy of, disclosed more
geographical knowledge, **5.** 247;
a marriage-custom among, **5.** 273;
received large tribute from Tigranes
the king of Armenia, **5.** 331; now
rule over Armenia, **5.** 341; assigned
an eleventh prefecture to pre-
decessors of Archelaüs, and to
Archelaüs still further territory, **5.**
349; allowed the Cappadocians
and others to collect large damages
from Ariathres, **5.** 365; jurisconsults of, expound the law, **5.**
367; conquered Antiochus and
began to administer affairs of Asia,
5. 369; granted autonomy to
Cappadocia, **5.** 371; made various
different administrative changes in
Asia Minor through their prefects,
5. 373; occupied Heracleia Pontica,
5. 379; boundaries of the Pontic
Province of, **5.** 385; colonised
Sinopê, **5.** 391; pulled down part of

the walls of Kainon Chorion in
Cappadocia Pontica, **5.** 429; assign-
ments of territory by, in Cappadocia
Pontica, **5.** 443; gave freedom to
the Prusians in Asia, **5.** 457;
succeeded the Macedonians as
masters in Asia, **5.** 463; have united
into one province all the country
subject to Amyntas, **5.** 469; made
famous the temple of Mother
Agdistis at Pessinus in Galatia, **5.**
471; subdued Lycaonia and
Cilicia, **5.** 475; gave Isaura to
Amyntas, **5.** 477; now hold Pisidia,
5. 485; honoured Cyzicus, giving it
further territory, **5.** 503; set free
Antiocheia near Pisidia from its
kings, and gave Eumenes II his
kingdom in Asia, **5.** 507; export
great monolithic pillars of Synnadic
marble from Phrygia, **5.** 507;
found the present Ilium to be only
a village when they expelled Antiochus from Asia, **6.** 53; under Fimbria,
in the time of the Mithridatic War,
ruined Ilium, **6.** 55; regard Aeneias
as their original founder, **6.** 57;
Attalus I and Rhodian fleet fought
on side of, against Philip, and by
Eumenes II against Antiochus the
Great and Perseus, **6.** 167; assisted
by Attalus II against the Pseudo-
Philip, **6.** 169; left as heirs of
Attalus III, and proclaimed his
empire a Roman province, **6.** 169;
confused the boundaries of Lydia,
Phrygia, and Caria by making their
own administrative divisions, **6.** 183;
restored revenues to Artemis at
Ephesus, **6.** 233; restored the
Caunians in Asia to the Rhodians,
6. 267; the Rhodians friendly to,
6. 269; remitted to the Coans 100
talents of the appointed tribute in
return for the *Aphroditê Anadyomenê*
of Apelles, **6.** 289; left the Lycians
in Asia free, **6.** 315; gave Telmessus
in Lycia to Eumenes II, **6.** 317;
became rich after the destruction of
Carthage and Corinth, and used
many slaves, **6.** 329; finally overthrew the Cilicians, **6.** 331; gave
Cilicia Tracheia to Archelaüs, **6.**
339; proclaimed Tarcondimotus in
Cilicia king, **6.** 355; took possession

459

INDEX OF NAMES, PLACES, AND SUBJECTS

Royal Valley, the, in Syria, above the Massyas Plain, **7.** 265

Ruad, the island off Phoenicia (see Aradus)

Rubicon (Rugone) River, the, in Italy, **2.** 327; once the boundary between Italy and Cisalpine Celtica, **2.** 331, 371

Rucantii, the, one of the boldest tribes of the Rhaeti, **2.** 281

Ruddle, exported from Turdetania, **2.** 33; the, in Carmania, **7.** 153

Rudiae (see Rodiae)

Rue, nourished by wood-ashes, **3.** 71

Rugge (see Rodiae)

Ruphia River, the (see Alpheius River)

Ruscino, river (Têt) and city (Castel Roussillon, near Perpignan); the river, rises in the Pyrenees, **2.** 183

Rush, grows in Triphylia, **4.** 53; aromatic, in Lake Gennesaritis, **7.** 261

Rush Plain, the (see Spartarian Plain)

Ruspinum in Libya; Scipio defeated by Julius Caesar near, **8.** 181

Ruteni, the, a tribe in Aquitania, **2.** 217

Rutuli, the, who held the old Ardea, and fought the Romans, **2.** 379; the overthrow of, **2.** 387; settlements of, devastated by the Samnitae, **2.** 393

S

Saba, name of a harbour, and also of a hunting-ground for elephants, on the Arabian Gulf, **7.** 319

Sabae, a good-sized city on the Arabian Gulf, **7.** 323

Sábaeans, the, a large tribe in Arabia Felix, **7.** 311; description of people and country of, **7.** 347, 349; often overran Syria, **7.** 351

Sabaïtic Mouth, the, in the Arabian Gulf, **7.** 319

Sabata (Sawa) in Arabia, a royal city in Arabia, **7.** 311

Sabata (Bracciano), Lake, in Italy, **2.** 369

Sabazius, the Phrygian, transmitted the rites of Dionysus, **5.** 105; the ritual of, **5.** 109

" Sabelli," a nickname of the Samnitae, **2.** 465

Sabine women, the rape of the, **2.** 385; avenged by Titus Tatius, **2.** 401

Sabini, the; geographical position of, **2.** 335, 337; description of country of, **2.** 373, 375; excellent characteristics of, **2.** 377; also called Sabelli and Samnitae, **2.** 465; treated as partners by the Romans after the expulsion of Tarquinius Superbus, **3.** 139

Sabos, king of Ararenê in Arabia, fled when Aelius Gallus approached, **7.** 361

Sabre, a long, used by the Gauls, **2.** 243, 247

Sabus, the country of, in India, **7.** 57

Sacaea, the; a sacred festival at Zela in Cappadocia, **5.** 263; so named by Cyrus the Elder, **5.** 265

Sacarauli, the, in Asia, helped to take away Bactriana from the Greeks, **5.** 261

Sacasenê in Armenia, has an abundance of honey, **1.** 273, **5.** 251; named after the Sacae, who once occupied it, **5.** 263; borders on Albania and the Cyrus River, **5.** 321

Saccopodes ("Sack-feet"), the (see Adiobeni)

Sacians, the, in Asia; a Scythian tribe, **3.** 207, **5.** 261; seized Bactriana and the best part of Armenia, but were wiped out by the Persians, **5.** 263, 267; separated from the Sogdiani by the Iaxertes River, **5.** 269

Sacred Cape (St. Vincent Cape) of Iberia, the, distance from, to Gulf of Issus, **1.** 407; most westerly point of inhabited world, **1.** 459, **2.** 7; distance from, to Gadeira and the Anas River, **2.** 19, 49; points north of, **2.** 61

Sacred Mouth, the, of the Ister River, **3.** 217, 219

Sacred War, the; temple at Delphi robbed in time of, **2.** 207

Sacrifices in Gaul, **2.** 247, 249

Sadacora in Cappadocia, the road through, **6.** 311

Sadracae, royal residence of Dareius the son of Hystaspes, **7.** 197

Saffron, superior, in Sicily, **3.** 85

Sagalasseis, the, occupy a region this side the Taurus, **5.** 481

INDEX OF NAMES, PLACES, AND SUBJECTS

Sagalassus (also called Selgessus) in Pisidia, **5.** 477, **6.** 193; captured by Alexander, **5.** 479

Sagapeni, the, in Asia, **7.** 223

Sagaris, the, a weapon of the Amazons, **5.** 233, and of the Massagetae in Asia, **5.** 267

Sagi (coarse cloaks), the Ligurian, **2.** 267

Sagra River, the, near Locri Epizephyrii, near which the armies of Locri and Croton fought, **3.** 35, 37, 45

Sagrus (Sangro) River, the, separates the Frentani and the Peligni, **2.** 433

Saguntum (Murviedro) in Iberia (founded by the Zacynthians), north of the Sucro, destroyed by Hannibal, **2.** 91; the road through, **2.** 95

Sagus, the, a coarse cloak worn by the Gauls, **2.** 241

Sagylium in Cappadocia Pontica, has a strong fortress on a high mountain, **5.** 445

Saïï, the Thracian, once inhabited Samothrace, and are mentioned by Archilochus, **5.** 55; formerly called Sinties and Sinti, **5.** 403; robbed Archilochus of his shield—and are now called Sapaei, **5.** 405

Saint-Cyr de Provence (see Tauroentium)

Saint-Gothard, Mt. (see Adula)

Saintes (see Mediolanium)

Saïs, metropolis in Aegypt, where is a temple of Athena, wherein lies the tomb of Psammitichus, **8.** 67; near the asylum of Osiris, **8.** 73

Salacia (Alcacer-do-Sal) in Lusitania, where delicate fabrics are woven, **2.** 33; geographical position of, **2.** 63

Salaminiac Gulf, the (see Saronic Gulf)

Salamis in Cypros, founded by Teucer, **6.** 377, 379

Salamis in the Myrtoan Sea, **1.** 477; the sea-fight at, **4.** 179, 187, 271; 70 or 80 stadia in length, **4.** 251; in early times a separate state, **4.** 257; last wreckage of ships after fight at, cast forth in Attica at temple of Aphroditê Colias, **4.** 271

Salamvria River (see Peneius)

Salandra River, the (see Acalandrus)

Salapia (Salpi) in Apulia, the seaport of the Argyrippini, **3.** 127

Salarian Way, the, runs through the Sabine country, **2.** 377

Salas (Thüringian Sasle) River, the, near which Drusus Germanicus met his end, **3.** 159

Salassi, the; country of, traversed by the Durias River, **2.** 271; geographical position of, **2.** 273, 303; has gold mines, **2.** 277; the road through, **2.** 289, 293

Salda, a large harbour between Caesareia and Tretum, the boundary between the territories subject to Juba and the Romans, **8.** 179

Salduba (see Caesar Augusta)

Salentini, the, country of, comprises one of the two parts of Iapygia, **3.** 103; said to be a Cretan colony, **3.** 117

Salerno, Gulf of (see Poseidonian Gulf)

Salernum (Salerno), fortified by the Romans against the Picentes, **2.** 471

Salganeus, a place in Boeotia, on a height, near the Euripus, named after Salganeus the Boeotian, **4.** 291

Salganeus the Boeotian guide, wrongly executed by the Persians, **1.** 35, **4.** 291

Salina (see Didymê)

Salix, a tree of genus of, found in Aegypt, **2.** 155

Sallyes, the; the geographical position of, **2.** 169, 181, 193, 195, 201, 269; precautions taken against, by the Massaliotes, **2.** 169, 175

Salmacis, a fountain at Halicarnassus, said to render effeminate all who drink of it, **6.** 283

Salmonê, a city in Pisatis, **4.** 97; a spring there whence flows the Enipeus River, **4.** 99

Salmoneus, the Homeric, said to have reigned in Pisatis, and in Eleia, **4.** 97, 99; Ephorus' account of, **4.** 103

Salmonium, the eastern cape of Crete; distance from, to Rhodes and Criumetopon, **1.** 407

Salmydessus, covered with shoal waters, **1.** 183, 193; a desert and stony beach in Thrace, 700 stadia long, **3.** 279

Salo (Salona), the seaport-city of the

INDEX OF NAMES, PLACES, AND SUBJECTS

INDEX OF NAMES, PLACES, AND SUBJECTS

465

INDEX OF NAMES, PLACES, AND SUBJECTS

INDEX OF NAMES, PLACES, AND SUBJECTS

questioned people of Massalia and Narbo about Britain, **2.** 215 (see footnote there); the tomb of, at Liternum, **2.** 437

Scipio, Gaius, added 3000 colonists to Comum, **2.** 311

Scipio, Metellus Pius (died 46 B.C.); war of, against Julius Caesar in Libya, in which he was defeated (decisively, at Thapsus 46 B.C.), **8.** 181

" Scira," a place in Attica named after the hero Scirus, **4.** 253

" Sciras," the earlier name of the city Salamis, and an epithet of Athenê, **4.** 253

Scirus the hero, after whom two places and the month Scirophorion were named, **4.** 253

Scoleces, an insect which breeds in the snow on the Caucasian Mountains, **5.** 323

Scollis, Mt., by Homer called the Olenian Rock, **4.** 225

Scollis, Mt. (see Scollium)

Scollium, Mt. (Scollis, now Santameriotiko), in Elis, **4.** 31, 41

Scolus, the Homeric, **4.** 183; a wretched village at the foot of Mt. Cithaeron, whence Pentheus was taken when he was torn to pieces by the Bacchantes, **4.** 313; by some writers regarded as subject to the Plataeans, **4.** 315

Scolus, a city near Olynthus, **4.** 313

Scolymi (an edible kind of thistle), found in Maurusia, **8.** 163

Scombraria (Island of Heracles), near New Carthage, **2.** 91

Scopas of Paros (fl. first half of fourth century B.C.), the great sculptor, made the image of Apollo at Chrysa, **6.** 95; works of, in the grove Ortygia near Ephesus—one showing Leto holding a sceptre, with the nurse Ortygia holding the infants Apollo and Artemis in her arms, **6.** 225

Scordisci (or Scordistae), the, who are called Galatae, lived intermingled with the Illyrian and Thracian tribes, and often served the Dacians as allies, **3.** 253; country of, **3.** 255; border on the Pannonians, **3.** 271; overpowered the Autariatae, and

widely extended their sway, but at last were subdued by the Romans, **3.** 273

Scordistae (see Scordisci), the, virtually destroyed by wars with the Macedonians and the Romans, **3.** 263

Scorpions, the, in Albania in Asia, **5.** 229; the winged, in India, **7.** 65; the large, in India, **7.** 79; the multitude of, rendered a certain region in Aethiopia uninhabitable, **7.** 327; abound in Masaesylia in Libya, **8.** 177

Scotussa, in Thessaly Pelasgiotis, where was the original oak-tree and temple of Dodonaean Zeus, **3.** 317, 319, 321, 323, 361, **4.** 445

Screw, the Aegyptian, used by Turdetanians in mining, **2.** 45

Screws (see Wheels), used for the irrigation of islands in the Nile, **8.** 135

Scriba publicus, the, a local official in Alexandria, **8.** 49

Scripu (see Orchomenus, the Boeotian)

Scultenna (Scoltenna in its upper course, Panaro in its lower) River, the, in Italy, **2.** 333

Scurvy, afflicted the Roman army in Arabia, **7.** 359

Scydises, Mt., in Asia, **5.** 209; geographical position of, **5.** 319; joins the Moschian Mountains above Colchis, **5.** 401

Scylacium (see Scylletium)

Scylax of Caryanda, navigator and geographer (sent by Dareius Hystaspes to explore the Indus River and did not return for two and a half years), says that Bithynia was settled by the Mysians, **5.** 465; on the boundaries of the Troad, **6.** 9; native of Caryanda, **6.** 289

Scylax River, the, in Cappadocia Pontica, **5.** 397

Scylla, the daughter of Nisus; Cape Scyllaeum in Argolis named after, **4.** 173

Scylla (see Scyllaeum), infested by brigands, **1.** 73; Odysseus' passage by, **1.** 77; shape of, **1.** 79; description of, by Homer, corresponds with fact, **1.** 87, 97

Scyllaeum, the (Scilla, see Scylla),

467

INDEX OF NAMES, PLACES, AND SUBJECTS

INDEX OF NAMES, PLACES, AND SUBJECTS

INDEX OF NAMES, PLACES, AND SUBJECTS

to have unearthed a skeleton 60 cubits long near Lynx in Maurusia, **8.** 171

Servilius, Publius Isauricus, an acquaintance of Strabo, subjugated Isaura in Lycaonia and destroyed most of strongholds of pirates on the sea, **5.** 475; demolished Isaura and wiped out piracy, **6.** 315; seized various places in Lycia and Pamphylia, **6.** 339

Servius Tullius, legendary king of Rome, joined Esquiline and Viminal Hills to Rome, **2.** 401

Sesamê, sown in rainy seasons in India, **7.** 21

Sesamê-oil, used in Babylonia, **7.** 215; used instead of olive-oil in Nabataea in Arabia, **7.** 369

Sesamus in Paphlagonia, one of the four cities incorporated into Amastris, **5.** 385

Sesarethii, the (see Enchelii)

Seschio River, the (see Ausar)

Sesithacus, son of Segimerus and chieftain of the Cherusci, led captive in triumph at Rome, **3.** 161

Sesostris (Rameses II, king of Aegypt about 1333 B.C.), abandoned building canal through Aegyptian isthmus, **1.** 141; expeditions of, to remote lands, **1.** 227; advanced as far as Europe, **7.** 7, leading his army from Iberia to Thrace and the Pontus, but did not reach India, **7.** 9; remarkable exploits of, **7.** 313; built a temple of Isis on a mountain near the Arabian Gulf, **7.** 319; travelled over the whole of Aethiopia, **8.** 19; said to have been the first to cut the canal that empties into the Red Sea and the Arabian Gulf, **8.** 77

Sessa (see Suessa Aurunca)

Sestias, Cape, in the Thracian Chersonesus, where Xerxes' pontoon-bridge was built, **3.** 377

Sestus (Boghaly), 80 stadia from Aegospotami, **3.** 377; a colony of the Lesbians 30 stadia from Abydus, **3.** 379; at end of seaboard of the Propontis, **6.** 5; the voyage to, from Byzantium, **6.** 13; mentioned by Homer, **6.** 37; best of the cities in the Chersonesus, and by the Romans assigned to the same governor as Abydus, **6.** 41; length of pontoon-bridge at, **6.** 43; mistress of the strait, **6.** 45

Set, the Aegyptian god, **8.** 75 (see footnote 2)

Setabis in Iberia, the road through, **2.** 95

Setia (Sezze), territory of, marshy and unhealthful, **2.** 389; between the Latin and Appian Ways, and produces an expensive wine, **2.** 413

Setinian wine, the, **2.** 399

Setium, Mt. (Cape de Cette), divides the Galatic Gulf into two gulfs, **2.** 181

Settia in Crete (see Minoa)

Seusamora, a fortified city on the Aragus River, **5.** 221

Seuthes, the, at Rome, **2.** 405

Seuthes, king of the Odrysae, **3.** 369

Sewers, the, at Rome, **2.** 405

"Sex" (see "Hexi"), the name of the city of the Exitanians in Iberia, according to Ptolemaeus, **2.** 81 (footnote 4)

Sextius, Titus, one of Caesar's legates in Gaul and at the time of Caesar's death (44 B.C.) governor of Numidia; defeated the Sallyes and founded Aquae Sextiae (now Aix), **2.** 177

Sezze (see Setia)

Sheep, a, sacrificed at only one place in Aegypt, **8.** 73

Sheep, the, in Celtica have rough and flocky wool, **2.** 241; in Sardinia grow goat-hair instead of wool, **2.** 363; in neighbourhood of Mt. Aetna, choke from fatness, **3.** 69; excellent, about Mt. Garganum in Apulia, **3.** 131; large, in the region of Lake Maeotis, **3.** 225; which drink from a certain river in Euboea turn white and from another black, **5.** 21; the skin-clad, in Gazelonitis in Cappadocia Pontica, yield soft wool, **5.** 393; in Lycaonia, numerous but have coarse wool, **5.** 475; of the Laodiceians, noted for softness and raven-black colour of their wool, **5.** 511; fattened on date-stones in Babylonia, **7.** 215; in Nabataea in Arabia, are white-fleeced, **7.** 369; of the Aethiopians, are small, **8.** 143, and have hair like that of goats, **8.** 145; in certain parts of

INDEX OF NAMES, PLACES, AND SUBJECTS

INDEX OF NAMES, PLACES, AND SUBJECTS

313; colony of the Cymaeans, **6.** 325

Sidenê in Cappadocia Pontica, 3000 stadia from Dioscurias, **1.** 485; a low-lying country, **1.** 193; subject to Themiscyra, **5.** 395; a fertile plain, **5.** 397; borders on Pharnacia, **5.** 427

Sidenê in the Troad, on the Granicus River, now in ruins, **6.** 27; refuge of the tyrant Glaucias and destroyed by Croesus, **6.** 83

Sideros, Cape (see Samonium)

Sidicini, the, an Oscan tribe, once occupied Campania, **2.** 435

Sidon, two-thirds of, engulfed because of an earthquake, **1.** 215; longest day at, has 14¼ equinoctial hours, **1.** 511; belongs to the Phoenician Tripolis, **7.** 259; near Mt. Antilibanus, **7.** 261; description and history of, **7.** 267

Sidoni, the, a Bastarnian tribe, **3.** 221

Sidonians, mentioned by Homer, **1.** 5, **3.** 191, **7.** 369; makers of beautiful works of art, **1.** 151; skilled in many arts, in astronomy, mathematics, and seamanship, **7.** 269; famous men among, **7.** 271; discussion of, **7.** 371

Sifanto (see Siphnos)

Siga in Masaesylia in Libya, royal residence of Sophax, now in ruins, 1000 stadia from Maurusia, **8.** 173

Sigeium, Cape (Yeni-Scheher), in the Troad, **3.** 375, **6.** 61, 91

Sigeium in the Troad, now in ruins, **6.** 61, 67; a wall around built with stones from ancient Ilium, **6.** 75; has been rased to the ground by the Ilians, **6.** 79; received part of the territory of ancient Ilium, **6.** 85

"Sigelus's," the monument of Narcissus near Oropus so called, **4.** 293

Sigerdis, the kingdom of, in Asia, **5.** 281

Sigia, once the name of the site of Alexandreia in the Troad, **6.** 93

Siginni, the, in Asia, imitate the Persians in most of their customs, **5.** 293

Signia (Segni), between the Latin and Appian Ways, produces the Signine Wine, **2.** 413

Sigri, Cape (see Sigrium)

Sigrianê, in Asia, **5.** 313

Sigrium (Sigri), Cape, in Lesbos, **3.** 381, **6.** 139, 141, 145

Sila, Mt. (Aspromonte), in Bruttium, **3.** 35

Silaceni, the, in Asia, **7.** 223

Silanus the historian, on the behaviour of a spring at Gades, **2.** 145

Silaris (Sele) River, the, flows between Campania and Leucania, **2.** 469, **3.** 3; any plant let down into, turns to stone, **2.** 471

Silas River, the, in India, **7.** 67

Sileni, the, ministers of Dionysus, **5.** 87, 97

Silenus, father of the Dolion who dwelt on the Ascanian Lake, **5.** 465, **6.** 373

Silli ("Lampoons"), the, of Xenophanes, **6.** 235

Silo (Pompaedius Silo)

Silphium, produced in zones beneath the tropics, **1.** 367; in Libya, **1.** 501; whence the "Medic juice," **5.** 311; in Asia, helpful in the digestion of raw food, **7.** 147; the Cyrenaean, **8.** 199, 203, 209

Silting-up, the, of the Rhodanus, **2.** 189; of the sea at the mouth of the Nile, unknown to Homer, according to Apollodorus, **3.** 189; at the mouths of the Cyrus River, **5.** 223; at the mouth of the Pyramus River, like that of the Nile, **5.** 355, 357; at the mouth of the Maeander, has made Priene an inland city, **5.** 515

Silurus, the, a fish indigenous to the Nile, **8.** 149

Silva Gallinaria, on the Gulf of Cumae, where pirates assembled, **2.** 439

Silver, plentiful in regions of Ilipa and Sisapo in Iberia, **2.** 25; largest quantity and best quality of, in Turdetania, **2.** 39, 45; a composite part of "electrum," **2.** 41; "effloresces" from the soil in Artabria, **2.** 45; description of mines of, at New Carthage, **2.** 47; found mixed in small quantities with lead at mines at Castalo in Iberia, **2.** 47; produced in Britain, **2.** 255; first coined (in Crete) by Pheidon, **4.** 181; Alybê in Cappadocia "the birthplace of," **5.** 403, 405; cleaned with

473

INDEX OF NAMES, PLACES, AND SUBJECTS

bricks of clay-like earth, in Iberia, **6.** 133; " birthplace " of, **6.** 369; in the country of Musicanus in India, **7.** 61; exchanged for gold in Arabia at ratio of two to one, **7.** 347; great quantities of, among the Sabaeans and Gerrhaeans in Arabia, **7.** 349; plentiful among the Nabataeans in Arabia, **7.** 369

Silver, mock-, prepared at Andeira in Asia Minor, **6.** 115

Silver bullion, found at Tolosa, **2.** 207

Silver mines, the, among the Ruteni and the Gabales in Aquitania, **2.** 219; of Damastium, **3.** 307; in Mt. Pangaeum in Macedonia, **3.** 355; at Laurium in Attica, have now failed, **4.** 275, **5.** 15; in Pharnacia in Cappadocia Pontica, **5.** 401; in Cypros, **6.** 383; in India, **7.** 53; in Carmania, **7.** 153

" Silver " Mountain, in Iberia, wherein the Baetis is said to rise, and so called on account of its silver-mines, **2.** 49

Silvium (Garagone, apparently), on the western borders of the Peucetii, **3.** 127

Simi, the, in Aethiopia, use the horns of gazelles as weapons, **7.** 327

Simmias of Rhodes (fl. about 300 B.C.), poet and grammarian of the Alexandrian school, **6.** 281; *apocopē* in, **4.** 131

Simnus River, the (see Siris)

Simoedia, a melic poem by Simus, **6.** 253

Simöeis River, the, near Aegesta in Sicily, so named by Aeneias, **6.** 109

Simöeis River, the, in the Troad, joins the Scamander, **6.** 61, 67, 69; Polium on, **6.** 83

Simöeisian Plain, the, in the Troad, **6.** 67

Simonides, the melic poet, uncle of Bacchylides, from Iulis in Ceos, **5.** 169; uses the indecent adjective " pordacian," **6.** 149; on the Hyperboreans, **7.** 97; in his dithyramb entitled *Memnon*, one of his Delian poems, says that Memnon was buried near the Badas River in Syria, **7.** 159

Simonides, the iambic poet, born in Amorgos, **5.** 173

Simus, the melic poet, corrupted the style handed down by earlier melic poets and introduced the *Simoedia*, **6.** 253

Simus the physician, a native of Cos, **6.** 289

Simyra in Phoenicia, **7.** 255

Sinda, a city in Pisidia, lies on the border of Phrygia and Caria, **5.** 431, **6.** 189

Sindi, the, across the Cimmerian Bosporus in Asia, **3.** 243, **5.** 201; royal seat of, at Gorgipia, near the Cimmerian Bosporus, **5.** 199; a tribe of the Maeotae, **5.** 201

Sindicê, land of the Sindi across the Cimmerian Bosporus in Asia, paid enormous tribute to Mithridates, **3.** 243, **5.** 201

Sindomana, in India, **7.** 57

Singitic Gulf (Gulf of Hagion Oros), the, between Derrhis and Athos, **3.** 353

Singus (Sykia), on the Singitic Gulf, **3.** 353

Sinna, a fortress on Mt. Libanus, **7.** 263

Sinnaca in Assyria, where Crassus was slain, **7.** 231

Sinno River, the (see Siris River)

Sinopê, traces of expedition of Jason near, **1.** 169; suburbs of, planted with olive-trees, **1.** 275; on the Euxine, where the *Pelamydes* fish are caught and pickled, **3.** 283; a famous city founded by the Milesians; description and history of, **5.** 387–391; Mithridates Eupator born and reared at, **5.** 389; captured first by Pharnaces and then by Leucullus, and has received a Roman colony, **5.** 389–391; not mentioned by Homer, **5.** 417; the road from, to Issus, **6.** 311

Sinopean earth (see Ruddle), the; the Iberian ruddle not inferior to, **2.** 33; the best in the world, found in Cappadocia, **5.** 367, 369

Sinopitis in Paphlagonia, has excellent timber for ships and tables, and abounds in olive-trees, **5.** 393

Sinoria (later called Synoria), a stronghold close to the borders of

474

INDEX OF NAMES, PLACES, AND SUBJECTS

INDEX OF NAMES, PLACES, AND SUBJECTS

INDEX OF NAMES, PLACES, AND SUBJECTS

INDEX OF NAMES, PLACES, AND SUBJECTS

INDEX OF NAMES, PLACES, AND SUBJECTS

hearsay, **1.** 451; ascended Nile with Aelius Gallus the Roman praefect, **1.** 455; quoted by Athenaeus as saying that he (Strabo) says that he knew Poseidonius, **3.** 383; not alien to Cnossus in Crete—and the history of relatives of, **5.** 133–137; distinguished ancestors of, **5.** 433, 435; took entire course of Aristodemus at Nysa in Asia, **6.** 263

Stratarchas, son of Dorylaüs the military expert, **5.** 135

Stratiê, the Homeric, now deserted, **3.** 385, **4.** 229

Stratius the priest, at Panticapaeum, **1.** 277

Strato of Lampsacus in Mysia in Asia Minor; became head of Peripatetic school of philosophy in 287 B.C.; called the "physicist," and praised by Eratosthenes for his explanation of physical changes of lands and seas, **1.** 181; prophesies silting up of whole Euxine Sea, **1.** 183; on the bed-levels of the Mediterranean and the Atlantic, **1.** 187; says that the bed of the Euxine is higher than that of the Propontis, **1.** 189

Strato, an isle in the Arabian Gulf, **7.** 319

Strato, the Tower of, in Phoenicia, **7.** 275

Stratocles, the Athenian archon (425 B.C.), went on the second Sicilian expedition (?), **4.** 111 (see footnote)

Stratocles the philosopher, native of Rhodes, **6.** 279

Straton the tyrant, put Amisus in Cappadocia Pontica in bad plight, **5.** 395

Stratonicê, daughter of King Ariathres, wife of Eumenes II, and mother of Attalus III, **6.** 167

Stratoniceia in Caria, a noteworthy city, **6.** 291; description and history of, **6.** 297–299

Stratonicus the citharist, utters a proverb on the city Assus, **6.** 115; on the paleness of the Caunians in the Peraea of the Rhodians, **6.** 267

Stratos, the earlier name of Dymê in Achaea, **4.** 225

Stratus (near Lepenu) in Acarnania,

on the Acheloüs River, **5.** 25; geographical position of, **5.** 27

Strombichus, father of the Athenian ambassador Diotimus, **1.** 175

Stromboli (see Strongylê)

Strongoli (see Petelia)

Strongylê (Stromboli), one of the Liparaean Isles, the home of Aeolus, "steward of the winds," **3.** 99

Strophades Islands, the, lie about 400 stadia off the Messenian Cyparissia, **4.** 111

Strovitzi (see Lepreum)

Struma River, the (see Strymon River)

Strumitza (see Callipolis in Macedonia)

Struthophagi ("Bird-eaters"), the, in Aethiopia; manner of capture of birds like ostriches by, **7.** 325

Strymon (Struma) River, the, **3.** 295, 297, 325, 331, 335, 355, 359, 363

Strymonic Gulf, the; position of, on the Aegaean, **3.** 353, 357, 363

Stubara, a populous city on the Erigon River, **3.** 311

Stura (see Styra)

Stymphalian Lake, the, in Arcadia, whence Heracles drove out the birds, **4.** 161; source of the Erasinus River, **4.** 231, 233

Stymphalides, the; name of the birds at the Stymphalian Lake, **4.** 161

Stymphalus in Arcadia, no longer exists, **3.** 93, **4.** 161, 229; once on the Stymphalian Lake, but now 50 stadia away, and why, **4.** 231 (see footnote 5); besieged by Iphicrates, **4.** 233

Styptic earth, a kind of, used in refining gold, **2.** 41

Styra (Stura) in Euboea, **5.** 9; destroyed in the Malian War by Phaedrus the Athenian general, **5.** 11

Styrax (or Storax) shrub, or tree, abundant in a certain region of Aethiopia, **7.** 329

Styrax-tree, the, abounds in the region of Mt. Taurus, **5.** 483

Styx River, the, at Avernus in Italy, **2.** 443

Styx River, the, in Rhodes, water

481

INDEX OF NAMES, PLACES, AND SUBJECTS

INDEX OF NAMES, PLACES, AND SUBJECTS

INDEX OF NAMES, PLACES, AND SUBJECTS

Mentes, **5.** 47, 59 ; said once to have lived in Acarnania, **5.** 67

Taphiassus, a hill in Aetolia, where are the tombs of Nessus and other Centaurs, whence flow putrid waters, **4.** 385 ; lies above Molycreia, **5.** 27, 63

Taphitis, the promontory, on the coast of Carthaginia, **8.** 191

Taphos (Meganisi), the island, by some identified with the Homeric Cephallenia, **5.** 47 ; now called Taphius, **5.** 49 ; distinct from the Echinades, **5.** 59

Taposeiris, a place to the east of Alexandria, **8.** 57 ; called the " Little " Taposeiris, **8.** 63

Taposeiris, an inland place to the west of Alexandria, where a great festival is held, **8.** 57

Taprobanê (Ceylon), position of, **1.** 235 ; position and size of, **1.** 271 ; lies off India, and is as large as Britain, **1.** 497 ; description and geographical position of, **7.** 21, 23

Tapyri, the, live between the Hyrcanians and the Arians, **5.** 269 ; formerly subject to Media and live between the Derbices and Hyrcanians, **5.** 273 ; strange customs of, **5.** 293 ; mountaineers in Atropatian Media, **5.** 305

Tarantine Gulf (Gulf of Tarentum), the ; distance around, **3.** 39

Tarantini, the ; fabricated an epithet for the Samnitae, **2.** 465 ; country of, borders on Metapontium, **3.** 13 ; took the Thurii away from the Leucani, **3.** 47 ; colonised Heracleia from Siris, **3.** 49, 51 ; hated by the Achaeans, **3.** 53 ; once exceedingly powerful, **3.** 113 ; through bad policies deteriorated, **3.** 115 ; defeated by the Romans, **3.** 141

Tarantulas (see Phalangia) ; the "tetragnathi" ("four-jawed") rendered a certain region in Aethiopia uninhabitable, **7.** 327 ; abound in Masaesylia in Libya, **8.** 177

Taras (Tarentum) ; towards the end of the Appian Way, **2.** 395 ; still in existence, **3.** 41 ; description and history of, **3.** 105–117 ; the harbour of (Mare Piccolo), **3.** 123 ; the Appian Way runs through, meeting

the mule-road near Beneventum, **3.** 125 ; about 700 stadia distant from Brundisium and Barium, **3.** 127 ; distance from, to Phalacrum in Thesprotia, **3.** 299

Tarbassus, a city in Pisidia, **5.** 481

Tarbelli, the, live on the western coast of Celtica in Aquitania, **2.** 215

Tarco, under direction of Tyrrhenus the Lydian founded twelve cities in Italy, among them Tarquinia (Corneto), **2.** 337

Tarcondimotus, contemporary of Strabo, lord of the strongholds of Mt. Amanus in Cilicia, and proclaimed king by the Romans, **6.** 355

Tarente (see Taras)

Tarentum (see Taras)

Tarentum, the Gulf of, **2.** 305 ; held by the Greeks, **3.** 7

Taricheae in Phoenicia, has an excellent fish-pickling industry, **7.** 297

Taricheiae, the, islands off the coast of Carthaginia, **8.** 191

Tarnê, the Homeric, in Lydia, **4.** 331

Taronitis, annexed to Armenia, **5.** 325

Tarpetes, the, a tribe of the Maeotae, **5.** 201

Tarphê in Locris, 20 stadia from Thronium, is now called Pharygae, and has a temple of Pharygaean Hera, **4.** 383

Tarquinia (Corneto), founded by Tarco, **2.** 337

Tarquinii in Italy (see Tarquinia)

Tarquinius Superbus, son of Tarquinius Priscus and king of Rome, banished (509 B.C.), **2.** 339 ; captured Suessa the metropolis of the Volsci, **2.** 387

Tarquinius Priscus, son of Demaratus of Corinth, at first called Lucumo, **2.** 339 ; king of Rome, destroyed Apiola and sacked several cities of the Aequi, **2.** 387 ; father of Tarquinius Superbus, **4.** 191

Tarracina (Terracina), the territory of, marshy and unhealthful, **2.** 389 ; on the Appian Way, **2.** 395

Tarraco (Tarragone), in Iberia, description of, **2.** 91 ; the road through, **2.** 95 ; where Sertorius fought, **2.** 99 ; where the consular governor administers justice in winter, **2.** 123

485

INDEX OF NAMES, PLACES, AND SUBJECTS

INDEX OF NAMES, PLACES, AND SUBJECTS

INDEX OF NAMES, PLACES, AND SUBJECTS

INDEX OF NAMES, PLACES, AND SUBJECTS

489

INDEX OF NAMES, PLACES, AND SUBJECTS

Theodosia (Feodosia or Kaffa) in the Crimea, **3.** 235; situated in a fertile plain and has a large harbour, **3.** 237

Theodosius, the mathematician, and his sons, natives of Bithynia, **5.** 467

Theology, borders on mythology, **5.** 119

Theomnestus, contemporary of Strabo, renowned harper, political opponent of Nicias, a native of Cos, **6.** 289

Theon Limen (God's Harbour) in Masaesylia in Libya, **8.** 173

Theophanes of Mitylene (fl. about 62 B.C.; intimate friend of Pompey, and wrote a history of his campaigns), on the course of the Tanaïs River, **5.** 193; made the expedition with Pompey and tells where Amazons lived, **5.** 233; on certain insects in Armenia, **5.** 323; on the size of Armenia, **5.** 331; changed the spelling of " Sinoria " to " Synoria," **5.** 425; father of Marcus Pompey, contemporary of Strabo, historian, statesman, friend of Pompey, and most illustrious of all the Greeks, **6.** 143, 145

Theophilus, son of Tibius the cousin of Strabo's grandfather, slain by Mithridates, **5.** 435

Theophrastus the Peripatetic philosopher (d. 278 B.C.), teacher of Demetrius of Phalerum, who reigned at Athens by appointment of Cassander the king of Macedonia, **4.** 269; pupil of Aristotle, author of treatise *On Love*; on Leucocomas and Euxynthetus, **5.** 139; inherited the library of Aristotle, **6.** 111; disciple of Aristotle, native of Eressus in Lesbos, first named Tyrtamus, his name being changed by Aristotle, and most eloquent of Aristotle's disciples, **6.** 145

Theopompus of Chios (b. about 380 B.C., pupil of Isocrates and historian of Greece (411–394 B.C.) and of Philip of Macedon (360–336 B.C.); professedly narrates myths in his histories, **1.** 159; on the "Land of Panchaea," an invention, **3.** 191; on the origin of the names "Ionian Gulf" and "Adriatic (Adrias) Gulf," **3.** 267; wrong on the length

of the Adriatic and Illyria, and makes a number of incredible statements, **3.** 269; says there were 14 tribes of the Epeirotes, **3.** 297; on the conquests and hospitality of the Lacedaemonians, **4.** 171; on Methonê in Macedonia and Methonê (Methana) in Argolis, **4.** 177; on the geographical position of Parapotamii, **4.** 373; on the Larisa between Elis and Dymê, **4.** 441; on Histiaea (Oreus) in Euboea, **5.** 7; says that Mariandynus ruled over part of Paphlagonia, took possession of the country of the Bebryces, and left the country named after himself, **5.** 375; on Amisus, **5.** 395; on the strait at Sestus, **6.** 45; on Mt. Mesogis in Asia, **6.** 185; native of Chios, **6.** 243

Theopompus of Cnidus, contemporary of Strabo, friend of Julius Caesar, **6.** 283

Thera (formerly called Callistê), the island, founded by Theras, a descendant of Polyneices, **4.** 63; metropolis of the Cyrenaeans and a colony of the Lacedaemonians, **5.** 161, **8.** 203

Therapnae, in the territory of Thebes, **4.** 315

Theras, son of Autesion, descendant of Polyneices, founded Thera, the mother-city of Cyrenê, **4.** 63

Therasia (Thirasia), the island, near Thera, **5.** 161

Theriaca, the, a poem on poisonous animals by Nicander, **8.** 151

Therikos (see Thoricus)

Therma (earlier name of Thessaloniceia, *q.v.*)

Therma in Aetolia; statue of Aetolus at, **5.** 77

Thermaean Gulf (Gulf of Saloniki), the, **3.** 297; receives the waters of the Haliacmon, **3.** 325; Alorus in inmost recess of, **3.** 341; cities on, destroyed by Cassander the son-in-law of Philip, **3.** 343, 345, 349; position of, on the Aegaean, **3.** 353, 381

Thermessa (or Hiera, now Vulcanello), one of the Liparaean Islands, **3.** 95

Thermodon (see Lycus) River, the;

491

INDEX OF NAMES, PLACES, AND SUBJECTS

silting-up at mouth of, **1**. 193; not mentioned by Homer, **3**. 189; flows through Themiscyra, **5**. 395

Thermopylae (or Pylae), treason of Ephialtes at pass of, **1**. 35; hot springs at, once ceased to flow because of earthquake, **1**. 223; the Amphictyonic League convened at, **4**. 357; memorial pillar at, dedicated by the Locrians, **4**. 379; Mt. Oeta highest at, **4**. 389; 15 stadia from the Asopus River, **4**. 391; Leonidas fought the Persians at, and is 40 stadia by land from the Trachinian Heracleia, and 70 by sea from Cape Cenaeum and 530 from the Euripus, **4**. 393, 395, 411, 417, 419

Theseium, the, at Athens, **4**. 263; has a myth connected with it, **4**. 265

Theseus, the legendary Attic hero; mythical deeds of, **1**. 69; long journeys of, and reputed to have visited Hades, **1**. 177; said to have colonised Brentesium, with Cretans, from Cnossus, **3**. 121; slew the Crommyonian sow, **4**. 197; killed Sciron and Pityocamptes the robbers, **4**. 245; snatched Helen at Aphidna, **4**. 263; incorporated the 12 cities in Attica into one city, Athens, **4**. 267; slew the Marathonian bull, **4**. 273; adventures of, in Crete, **5**. 131

Thesmophoria, the; celebration of, at Alponus, **1**. 225

Thespeia (or Thespiae, *q.v.*, now Erimokastron), the Homeric, **4**. 183

Thespiae (or Thespeia), has held out fairly well to this day, **4**. 287; Creusa the naval station of, **4**. 299; geographical position of, **4**. 315; well known in earlier times because of the Eros of Praxiteles there, and still endures, **4**. 319

Thespians, the; the Homeric village Eutresis belonged to, **4**. 323

Thesprotians, the, a barbarian tribe, now hold part of the country above Acarnania and Aetolia, **3**. 287, 289, 297

Thessalian horses, the, praised as best in oracle, **5**. 21

Thessalians, the, had serfs called "Penestae," **5**. 377

Thessalians, the, said to have founded Ravenna in Italy, **2**. 315; are the most ancient composite part of the Greeks, **4**. 393

Thessaliotis, one of the four divisions of Thessaly, **4**. 397; geographical position of, **4**. 399, 421, 433

Thessalonicê, daughter of Philip and wife of Cassander, after whom Thessaloniceia was named, **3**. 343, 347

Thessaloniceia (in earlier times called Therma, now Saloniki); distance from, to Epidamnus, **1**. 409; whither runs the Egnatian Way from Apollonia (Pollina) in Illyria, **3**. 295; now the largest city in Macedonia, **3**. 297, 329, 333, 341, 347, 349, 369; named after Thessalonicê the daughter of Philip and wife of Cassander, **3**. 343; 260 stadia from the outlets of the Peneius and 3200 from the Ister, **4**. 233

Thessalus, the son of Haemon, Thessaly named after, **4**. 453

Thessalus, son of Heracles, and father of the two Coan leaders, Pheidippus and Antiphus, **6**. 273

Thessaly, once called "Haemonia," **1**. 169; certain parts of, now held by Thracians, **3**. 287; Pelasgiotis, where (at Scotussa) was the original temple of Dodonaean, or Pelasgian, Zeus, **3**. 319; well adapted to horse-raising, **4**. 229; description and history of, **4**. 395-455; boundaries of, **4**. 395; wholly a plain except Pelion and Ossa, **4**. 397; divided into four parts, **4**. 397; divided into ten parts by Homer, **4**. 399; ruled by Deucalion, **4**. 405; the domain of Achilles in, **4**. 399-419; the domain of Phoenix in (the Dolopians), **4**. 401, 415 (cp. **4**. 435); the domain of Protesilaüs in, **4**. 405, 407, 411, 415, 419, 421; the domain of Philoctetes in, **4**. 405, 407, 425, 427, 451; the domain of Eurypylus in, **4**. 407, 413, 421, 433, 435, 437; the domain of Eumelus in, **4**. 423, 425, 437, 447, 451; the domain of Polypoetes in, **4**. 437;

492

INDEX OF NAMES, PLACES, AND SUBJECTS

INDEX OF NAMES, PLACES, AND SUBJECTS

Thynians, the Pontic, are in origin a Thracian tribe, **3.** 177

Thynians, the Thracian, gave their name to Thynias, the coast between Salmydessus and Apollonia Pontica, **5.** 375

Thynias (Iniada), Cape, on the Euxine, **3.** 279

Thyreae, possession of, disputed by Argives and Lacedaemonians, **1.** 245, 247 ; on the confines of Laconia and Argolis, not mentioned by Homer, **4.** 183

Thyrides (Kavo Grosso), **4.** 15, 113, 125

Thysa, daughter of Dionysus, mentioned by Euripides, **5.** 103

Thyssus, a city of Athos, **3.** 355, 357

Tiara, the Median, **5.** 313

Tibareni, the, in Asia ; geographical position of, **5.** 319, 399, 423 ; subject to Mithridates Eupator, **5.** 371 ; subject to Lesser Armenia and later to Mithridates, **5.** 425 ; now ruled by Queen Pythodoris, **5.** 427

Tiber River, the, borders on Tyrrhenia, **2.** 335 ; navigable, **2.** 349 ; tributaries of, from Tyrrhenia, **2.** 367 ; silting-up of, at mouth of, **2.** 391 ; tributaries of, from Umbria, and elsewhere, **2.** 403

Tiberius (see Caesar, Tiberius)

Tiberius Gracchus (consul 177 B.C.), by Polybius said to have destroyed 300 cities in Celtiberia, **2.** 105

"Tibius," a name given Paphlagonian slaves in Attica, **3.** 213 ; a Paphlagonian name used in Cappadocia, **5.** 415

Tibius, cousin of Strabo's grandfather, slain by Mithridates, **5.** 435

Tibur (Tivoli), visible from Rome, **2.** 415 ; description of, **2.** 417–419

Tiburtine stone, the quarries of, near Tibur, **2.** 417

Ticinum (Pavia), in Italy, **2.** 327

Ticinus (Tessin) River, the, tributary of the Padus, **2.** 295, 327

Tides, the, understood by Homer, **1.** 13 ; thoroughly investigated by Poseidonius and Athenodorus, **1.** 19, 203 ; at the Strait of Messina, **1.** 85 ; caused by the rising and

sinking of the beds of the seas, **1.** 187 ; compared with currents at straits, and correspond to rising and setting of the moon, **1.** 203 ; inundations of, in Iberia, **2.** 27, 29 ; ebb and flow of, responsible for large size of oysters and cetaceans, **2.** 37 ; cast ashore quantities of acorns, **2.** 39 ; said by Eratosthenes to come to an end at the Sacred Cape, **2.** 49 ; form estuaries on west coast of Iberia, **2.** 63 ; wrongly explained by Aristotle, according to Poseidonius, **2.** 67 ; effect of, on a spring at Gades, **2.** 143, 153, and on wells there, **2.** 145 ; increase of, at time of the full moon, **2.** 257 ; behaviour of, at head of the Adriatic, **2.** 309 ; on the coast of the Cimbri, **3.** 165, 167

Tieium, the city of the Cauconians in Bithynia, **5.** 377 ; home of Philotaerus, head of the family of the Attalic kings, **5.** 381 ; further history of, **5.** 385 ; Bithynium lies above, **5.** 463

Tigers, the largest, twice as large as lions, found in the country of the Prasii in India, **7.** 65

Tigranes, king of Armenia 96–56 B.C. ; father of Artavasdes ; treasury of, near Artaxata, **5.** 327 ; paid large tribute to the Romans, **5.** 331 ; descendant of Artaxias, and king of Armenia properly so called, **5.** 337 ; the remarkable career of, **5.** 337 ; seized Syria and Phoenicia, **5.** 339 ; forced the Mazaceni to migrate to Mesopotamia and founded Tigranocerta with them, **5.** 367 ; sent Metrodorus back to Mithridates, **6.** 115 ; opposed all attacks successfully, **7.** 225 ; held the Gordyaeans in subjection, and favoured by Pompey, **7.** 231 ; slew Selenê, surnamed Cleopatra, **7.** 241 ; by Pompey shut off from Antiocheia in Syria, **7.** 249

Tigranocerta, lies below Mt. Masius, **5.** 299, **7.** 231 ; founded by Tigranes the king of Armenia, **5.** 339, 367

Tigris River, the, flows from Armenia southwards, and with the Euphrates encloses Mesopotamia, **1.** 305 ; flows underground for a distance near

INDEX OF NAMES, PLACES, AND SUBJECTS

its sources, **3**. 93; description of course of, **5**. 297; empties into the Red Sea (!), **5**. 327; origin of name of, **5**. 329; at its outlets is called "Pasitigris," **7**. 161; navigable to Opis, or Seleuceia, **7**. 205; Polycleitus on, **7**. 213; distances from, to the Euphrates, **7**. 229

Tigyreni, the, a tribe of the Helvetii, joined the Cimbri, **3**. 169

Tilos (see Telos)

Tilphossa, a spring near Lake Copaïs, **4**. 323; at the foot of Mt. Tilphossius, **4**. 333

Tilphossium (see Tilphusium) in Boeotia, near Lake Copaïs, **4**. 331

Tilphossius, Mt., in Boeotia, where rises the spring Tilphossa, **4**. 323; lies above Alalcomenae, **4**. 333

Tilphusium (Tilphossium ?) in Boeotia, near Lake Copaïs, **4**. 321

Timaeus (also called "Epitimaeus") of Tauromenium (b. about 352 B.C. and lived 96 years), the historian, his greatest work being a history of Sicily from the earliest times to 264 B.C., in 38 books or more, of which only fragments remain; on the number of the mouths of the Rhodanus, **2**. 189; on the results of earthquakes in the Pithecussae Islands, **2**. 459; on the contest between Eunomus and Ariston at the Pythian Games, **3**. 35; connects the fountain of Arethusa with the Alpheius River, **3**. 75; accused of falsifying by Demetrius of Scepsis, **6**. 77; on the means used to restore the temple of Artemis at Ephesus, **6**. 227; on the size of the larger of the Gymnesian Isles, **6**. 277

Timagenes, a rhetorician and historian from Alexandria, contemporary of Augustus and author of a history of his exploits; on the fate of consul Caepio's daughters, **2**. 207; says that brass rained from the skies and was swept down by rivers, **7**. 97

Timavi Fons (Timavo), the, empties into the Adriatic, **2**. 319

Timavum, the name of a temple of Diomedes in the recess of the Adriatic, **2**. 319, 323

Timavus (Timavo) River, the, in

Italy, **2**. 319; runs underground for a distance, **3**. 93

Timon the "Misanthrope," imitated by Antony at Alexandria, **8**. 39

Timonitis in western Paphlagonia, **5**. 451

Timonium, the name given by Antony to his royal lodge at Alexandria, **8**. 39

Timosthenes of Rhodes (fl. about 280 B.C.), admiral under Ptolemy Philadelphus; on the winds, **1**. 107; author of a work on *Harbours*, **1**. 353; mistakes of, in regard to promontories in the Mediterranean, **1**. 353; entirely ignorant of Iberia, Celtica, Germany, Britain, and other countries, **1**. 357, 361; says that Calpê in Iberia was in ancient times called Heracleia, **2**. 15; composed the melody of the Pythian Nome, and wrote a work on *Harbours* in ten books, **4**. 363; wrongly says there are *forty* islands between Asia and Lesbos, **6**. 147; wrongly says that the promontory Metagonium lies opposite Massalia, **8**. 167

Timotheus Patrion, a native of Sinopê, **5**. 391

Timouchos, the title of an Assemblyman at Massalia, **2**. 175

Tin, is dug from the ground in Turdetania, not found on surface as among Artabrians; also found in the Cassiterides and the Britannic Islands, and exported to Massalia, **2**. 45, 157; found in the country of the Drangae in Asia, **7**. 145

Tingis (Tangier, see Tinx) in Maurusia; passage from, to Belon in Iberia, **2**. 15

Tinos (see Tenos)

Tinx (Tingis), by some confused with "Lynx" and "Lixus" (*q.v.*), **8**. 159; geographical position of, **8**. 165

Tirizis (Kaliakra), Cape, in Thrace, once used as a treasury by Lysimachus, **3**. 279

Tiryns "of the great walls"; acropolis of, now deserted, **4**. 169; inhabitants of, migrated to Epidaurus, **4**. 171

Tisamenus, son of Orestes, persuaded by Philonomus to emigrate with Achaeans in Laconia to Ionia (Achaea), **4**. 133, 211, 235

497

INDEX OF NAMES, PLACES, AND SUBJECTS

INDEX OF NAMES, PLACES, AND SUBJECTS

499

INDEX OF NAMES, PLACES, AND SUBJECTS

INDEX OF NAMES, PLACES, AND SUBJECTS

INDEX OF NAMES, PLACES, AND SUBJECTS

Romans, **1.** 51; flows between the Tanaïs (Don) and the Ister (Danube) into the Euxine, **1.** 413; 900 stadia from the Ister—and cities on, **3.** 219

Tyre, once an island, **1.** 217; longest day at, has 14¼ equinoctial hours, **1.** 511; Io first disappeared in, **7.** 243; belongs to the Phoenician Tripolis, **7.** 259; largest and oldest city of the Phoenicians, wholly an island—and description and history of, **7.** 267–271; a host of people from, under Dido, founded Carthage, **8.** 185

Tyre, an island in the Persian Gulf, said to have been colonised by the Phoenician Tyre, **7.** 303

Tyregetans, the, bounded by the Ister, **1.** 493; geographical position of, **3.** 153, 175, 221

Tyriaeum, on the borders of Phrygia and Lycaonia; the road through, **6.** 309

Tyrians, the, overran and subdued most of Iberia, **2.** 87; founded Gades, **2.** 135; adjudged autonomous by the kings and later by the Romans, and pay extravagant honours to Heracles, **7.** 269; ancient settlements of, on western coast of Libya, **8.** 161

Tyro, fell in love with Enipeus, god of the Enipeus River, **4.** 99

Tyrranion the grammarian, at Rome, native of Amisus, teacher of Strabo, **5.** 399; got possession of the libraries of Aristotle and Theophrastus, which Sulla had brought there, **6.** 113

Tyrrhenia (Etruria), borders on Liguria, **2.** 333; general description of, **2.** 347–369; bounded by the Macra River, **2.** 351; has numerous valuable lakes, **2.** 367; and numerous hot springs, **2.** 369

Tyrrhenian nativity-casters, the, revered by the Romans, **7.** 289

Tyrrhenian (Etruscan) images, the; images like, in Aegyptian temples, **8.** 83

Tyrrhenian prophecies, the, used by the Romans, **8.** 113

Tyrrhenian pirates, the, in early times made trafficking impossible in the region of Sicily, **3.** 65

Tyrrhenian Sea, the; definition of, **1.** 471; forms a boundary of Italy, **1.** 493, **2.** 305

Tyrrhenians, the; have been intermingled with the Romans, **2.** 325; geographical position of, **2.** 335, 347; called by the Romans "Etrusci" and "Tusci," **2.** 337; captured Caere, **2.** 341; otherwise mentioned, **2.** 315, 353, 365; pirates, **2.** 391; founded Cuprae Fanum, **2.** 429; founded twelve cities, and ejected the Cumaei from Campania, **2.** 435; once held Herculaneum and Pompeii, **2.** 451–453; stopped from their unrestrained licence by the Romans, **3.** 141; more than any other people ravaged the Mediterranean, **5.** 133; call "pitheci" ("monkeys") "arimi," and hence, according to some, the Homeric "Arimi" lived in the Pithecussae Islands, **6.** 175

Tyrrhenus, the son of Atys, the Lydian, who colonised Tyrrhenia in Italy, **2.** 337; accompanied by Pelasgi, **2.** 347

Tyrtaeus the elegiac poet, on the capture of Messenê in the twentieth year of the war, **3.** 113; on the Messenian Wars, **4.** 121; author of *Eunomia*, and by some said to have been an Athenian, **4.** 123; on the fertility of Laconia, **4.** 143

Tyrtamus the philosopher, name of, changed by Aristotle to Theophrastus, **6.** 145

U

Ubii, the, transferred across the Rhenus by Agrippa, **2.** 231, **3.** 154 (footnote)

Ucromirus, chieftain of the Chatti and father of Rhamis, **3.** 161

Ufens (Ufente) River, the, **2.** 395 (footnote 4)

Ufente River, the (see Ufens)

Ulia in Iberia, where the sons of Pompey were defeated, **2.** 21

"Ulius" (god of "health"), epithet of Apollo (see Apollo Ulius)

Ulysses (see Odysseus)

Umbria (Ombrica) in Italy, colonised by Aeginetans, **4.** 181

INDEX OF NAMES, PLACES, AND SUBJECTS

Undalum (now Sorgnes, apparently), **2**. 197

Universe, the, sphere-shaped, **1**. 233, 361, 521

Uranopolis, on the isthmus of Athos, founded by Alexarchus, **3**. 357

Urgi, the (Hungarians?, or Turks?), a nomadic race, **3**. 221

Uria, a lake in Aetolia, **5**. 63

Uria (Oria) in Iapygia, **3**. 121, 123

Urium, a small town near the headland of Garganum in Apulia, **3**. 131

Urso in Iberia, where the sons of Pompey were defeated, **2**. 21

Utica in Libya (see Itycê)

Utility, urges reference to customs and constitutions no longer existent, **1**. 467

Uxia, on the borders of Persis and Susis, **7**. 219

Uxii, the, a predatory tribe on the borders of Persis and Susis, **5**. 309, **7**. 161; narrow defiles in country of, **7**. 163

Uxisamê (Ushant), the island, **1**. 239

Uzita in Libya; Scipio defeated Julius Caesar near, **8**. 181

V

Vaccaeans, the, in Iberia, geographical position of, **2**. 65, 67; home of some of, on west of Celtiberians, **2**. 103

Vacua River, the, in Iberia; affords short voyages inland, **2**. 69

Vada Sabatorum (Vado), near Genua (Genoa), **2**. 263

Vaga in Libya, destroyed in war between Scipio and Julius Caesar, **8**. 181

Valerian Way, the, **2**. 411, 415; runs from Messenê to Cape Lilybaeum, **3**. 59

Valerius Flaccus, Roman consul, in command against Mithridates (86 B.C.), slain by Fimbria the quaestor, **6**. 551

Vapanes, a town in Corsica, **2**. 359

Var River, the (see Varus)

Varagri, the, live on peaks of the Alps, **2**. 273

Vardusia, Mt., in Aetolia (see Corax, Mt., in Aetolia), **5**. 27

Vari, the Cavaran, in Celtica, **2**. 197

Varia (Varea) in Iberia, at the crossing of the Iberus River, **2**. 101

Varia (Vicovara), on the Valerian Way, **2**. 415

Varna (see Odessus)

Varro, Terentius, overthrew the Salassi, **2**. 279

Varus, Quintilius (consul 13 B.C.), with three Roman legions, destroyed by ambush in Germany, **3**. 161

Varus (Var) River, the, forms the boundary between Narbonitis and Italy, **2**. 169; between Antipolis and Nicaea, **2**. 191; a boundary of the Ligures, **2**. 271; geographical position of, **2**. 299

Vasconians, the; geographical position of, **2**. 77, 99

Vates, the, of the Gauls; diviners and physicists, **2**. 245

Vatika (see Boea)

Vegetables, the, grown in Campania, **2**. 437

Veglia the island (see Cyrictica)

Veii, a city on the Tiber, **2**. 365

Veils, barbaric, used by women in Iberia, **2**. 109

Velika, Mt. (see Albian Mountain)

Velina (see Aquileia)

Velitrae (Velletri), in Italy, **2**. 413

Vellavii, the, a tribe in Aquitania, **2**. 217

Velletri (see Velitrae)

Velukhi, Mt. (see Typhrestus, Mt.)

Venafro (see Venafrum)

Venafrum (Venafro), in Italy, produces the finest olive-oil, **2**. 415; territory of, well supplied with the olive, **2**. 437

Venasa in Cappadocia, the temple of Venasian Zeus in, where the priest serves for life, **5**. 359

Vendo (or Avendo), a city of the Iapodes, **2**. 287, **3**. 259

Veneti (see Eneti and Heneti), tribe of the Belgae who fought the naval battle with Julius Caesar, and perhaps settled the colony on the Adriatic, **2**. 235

Venetian country, the, in Italy, settled by the Eneti (or Heneti) from Paphlagonia, **5**. 381

Venetus Lake (Lake Constance), by Strabo mentioned merely as " a

503

INDEX OF NAMES, PLACES, AND SUBJECTS

INDEX OF NAMES, PLACES, AND SUBJECTS

505

INDEX OF NAMES, PLACES, AND SUBJECTS

Rhaetic, **2**. 281; stored in wooden jars, and bartered by Illyrians at Aquileia, **2**. 317; in Cisalpine Celtica, stored in jars larger than houses, **2**. 333; the Caecuban, **2**. 389; the Fundanian, Caecuban, Setinian, Falernian, Alban, and Statanian, **2**. 399; the Setinian expensive, and the Signian best for checking the bowels, **2**. 413; good, made at Ancona, **2**. 429; the Falernian, Statanian and Calernian best, with the Surrentine as rival, **2**. 437; the Lagaritan, sweet, mild and medicinal and that of Thurii famous, **3**. 49; the Mamertine, made at Messenê in Sicily, rivals the best of the Italian wines, **3**. 67; the Getans persuaded to live without, **3**. 211; the "Carystian," from the Laconian Carystus, **5**. 11; sold by European to Asiatic nomads at Tanaïs, **5**. 195; abundance of, in Aria, **5**. 279; in Media, **5**. 317; the "Monarite" in Melitenê rivals the Greek wines, **5**. 351; abundant in Phanaroea, **5**. 427; the "Ambladian," from Amblada in Pisidia, good for medicinal purposes, **5**. 481; the Catacecaumenite, in Asia; inferior to no other, **6**. 181, 183; that of Samos not good, those of Chios, Lesbos, and Cos excellent, those of Ephesus and Metropolis good, and those of Mt. Mesogis, Mt. Tmolus, the Catacecaumene country, Cnidos, Smyrna, exceptionally good, **6**. 215; the best produced in Ariusia in Chios, **6**. 243, 287; the Aromian, the best Mesogitan, **6**. 261; that in Chios and Lesbos, excellent, **6**. 287; according to some, not made in India, **7**. 35; the Chalymonian in Syria, used by the Persians, **7**. 185; yielded by the palm-tree, **7**. 215, 365; that used at Alexandria comes mainly from Laodiceia in Syria, **7**. 249; the "Libyan," not good, **8**. 57; the "Mareotic" in Aegypt, excellent, **8**. 59; the "Lesbian," exported to Aegypt, **8**. 93; abounds in the oasis opposite Abydus, **8**. 113; in Masaesylia in Libya, made from the tree called *Melilotus*, **8**. 179; exchanged by the Carthagin-

ians for "Cyrenaean" silphium at Charax, **8**. 199

Winter-sunrise, a variable term, **1**. 415, **3**. 41

Winter-sunset, **3**. 57

Wise Men, the, in India, cure diseases, **7**. 79

Wolf, a, suckled Romulus and Remus, **2**. 381; the, in Celtica, no match for a hog, **2**. 243; a, led the way for the Hirpini, **2**. 467

Wolves, the, among the Eneti, herd with deer, **2**. 321; in Arabia (jackals?), **7**. 343

Woman-hater (*Misogynes*), the, of Menander, **3**. 185

Woman-rule, no mark of civilisation, **2**. 115

Women, the chief founders of religion, **3**. 183; spend much time and money thereon, **3**. 185

Wonders, the Seven, of the World; two of the pyramids of Gizeh numbered among, **8**. 91

Wood-ashes, nourish rue, **3**. 71

Woodpecker (*Picus*), a, led the way for colonisers of Picenum, **2**. 427

Wooers, the, of Penelopê, set their ambush against Telemachus "in the Cephallenian Strait between Ithaca and rugged Samos," **4**. 77

Wool, the colour of, in Turdetania, **2**. 33; the, of sheep in Celtica, rough and flocky, **2**. 241; the soft kind, produced in the region of Mutina and the Scultenna (Panaso in its lower course) River in Italy; the coarse kind, in Liguria and Symbria; the medium kind in the region of Patavium, **2**. 333; abundant in Sicily, **3**. 87; excellent in territory of Brundisium, **3**. 121; produced in Gazelonitis in Cappadocia Pontica, is soft, **5**. 393; of the sheep of the Laodiceians, noted for its softness and raven-black colour, even surpassing the Milesian, **5**. 511; not produced in Aethiopia, the sheep there having hair like goats, **8**. 147

Wool-tree, the, in Libya; horse-collars made of, **8**. 167

World, the inhabited, an island and circumnavigable, **1**. 17; extreme limits of, **1**. 25; breadth of,

INDEX OF NAMES, PLACES, AND SUBJECTS

1. 233, 271; dimensions of, 1. 237, 5. 291; a fraction of temperate zone, 1. 243; ends on west at Pillars of Heracles and on east at capes of India, 1. 253; divided into Northern and Southern Divisions and into "Sphragides" ("Seals") by Eratosthenes, 1. 293; length of, about 70,000 stadia, breadth of, slightly less than half of length, 1. 315; divided by Eratosthenes into two parts by the Taurus Range and the Mediterranean, 1. 317, 321; definition of "length" and "breadth" of, 1. 321; 70,000 stadia in length and extends over one-half of whole circle, 1. 393, 407, 437; length of, measured along line parallel to equator, 1. 415; lies like an island in a quadrilateral area, 1. 433; chlamys-shaped, 1. 435, 447, 455, 457, 463; breadth of, less than 30,000 stadia, 1. 437, 447, 455; Sacred Cape most westerly point of, 1. 459; division of, by meridians and "climata," *i.e.* by parallels of longitude and latitude, 1. 463; limits of, on south and north, 1. 505; the "omphalos" ("navel") at Delphi, the centre of, 4. 355; divided into three continents, 8. 155

Wrestling, at Rome, 2. 407

X

Xandii (Xanthii?), the, a tribe of Dáae above Lake Maeotis, 5. 275
Xantheia in Thrace, 3. 365
Xanthians, the Thracian, 6. 41
Xanthii (Xandii?), the, in Asia, a tribe of the Dáae, 5. 261
Xanthus the king of the Boeotians, defeated in single combat by Melanthus the king of Messené, 4. 249
Xanthus in Lycia, member of the Lycian League, 6. 315; largest city in Lycia, 6. 317
Xanthus of Lydia, the historian; on physical changes in Asia Minor, 1. 181; regards the Mysians as Lydian in origin, 5. 489; author of the *History of Lydia*; on the strange changes caused by earthquakes in

Lydia and Phrygia, 5. 517; a Lydian, but his city unknown to Strabo, 6. 181; says that Arimus was king of Mysia Catacecaumené, 6. 183; says that the Phrygians came from Europe after the Trojan War, 6. 371
Xanthus River, the, in Lycia, in earlier times called Sirbis, 6. 317
Xanthus River, the, in the Troad, 6. 41
Xenarchus, Peripatetic philosopher, contemporary of Strabo, teacher of Seleuceia in Cilicia, teacher of Strabo and friend of Augustus, 6. 335
Xenocles, the famous orator, of Adramyttium, made a speech before the Roman Senate, 6. 131; praised by Cicero, 6. 299
Xenocles, Alexander's treasurer, 1. 261
Xenocrates the philosopher, of Bithynia; Menecrates of Elaea a disciple of, 5. 407; native of Bithynia, 5. 465; along with Aristotle a guest of Hermeias the tyrant of Assus, 6. 117
Xenophanes the philosopher, a native of Colophon in Asia, author of the *Silli*, in verse, attacking Homer and Hesiod, 6. 235
Xenophon, bought a plot of land in Elis for Artemis in accordance with an oracle, 4. 223
Xeropotamos River, the (see Callas)
Xerxené, annexed to Armenia, 5. 325
Xerxes, blundered from ignorance of geography, 1. 35; expeditions of, 1. 227; the canal of, across the isthmus of Athos, 3. 355, 357; enumerated his army at Doriscus in Thrace, 3. 369; army of, not sufficiently supplied by the Melas River, 3. 373; built his pontoon-bridge at Madytus and Cape Sestias, 3. 377; defeated near Salamis, 4. 253; attempted to build a mole from Attica to Salamis, 4. 257; fleet of, destroyed by a tempest at Cape Sepias, 4. 451; gave the Branchidae a city because they had betrayed to him the riches of the god at Didymi, 5. 285; gave Lampsacus in the Troad to Themistocles, to supply him with wine, 6. 29; bridged the Hepta-

INDEX OF NAMES, PLACES, AND SUBJECTS

INDEX OF NAMES, PLACES, AND SUBJECTS

Left Map

29 30 31 33 34 35 36

ÆGYPTUS

Iope
Jamnia · Hierapicus · Philadelphia
Azotus
Ascalon · HIEROSOLYMA
Gaza

32
Zephyrion Ostium
Bolbitinum Ostium · Sebennyticum Ostium · Phatniticum · Taniticum
Taposiris · Heracleum · Naucratis · Mendesium Ostium · Pelusiacum Ostium · Casium · Gerrha · Pelusiacum Ostium · Chabriae Charax
Nicopolis · Bubastis · Pelusium
Alexandria · Pharos · Phœnicon
Chersonesus · Saïs · Sebennytus
Plinthine · Gynæcopolis · Xois · Busiris · Tanis · Heroopolis
Leontopolis · Aphroditopolis · Bubastis · Aphroditopolis
Prosopis · Athribis · Sais · Hieracon · Phragonopolis
Momemphis · Delta · Lycus · Lacus Amarus · Serbonis L. Rhinocolura
Menelaïs · Heliopolis · Babylon · Arsinoë · Idumœi
Latopolis · Cercasura · Trojanum Cleopatris (Cleopatra)
Pyramid · Troja Cleopatris · Trojanus M.
MEMPHIS
Acanthus
Aphroditopolis · Petra
Mœris L. · Fontes calidi (Hammam el Farûm) · Aelana
Arsinoë, Crocodeilopolis
Labyrinthus
Heracleopolis
Posidium Pr.
Oxyrynchus
Phœnicon
Cynopolis
Tanis · Hermupolis · Arsinoë · Insulæ Nabatæorum Phocarum I.
Hermopolitana Phylace
Thebana Phylace
Philotera
Lycopolis
Myus Hormus
Aphroditopolis
Panopolis
Ptolemais
Abydus
Diospolis Minor · Tentyra · Coptus · Isthmus
Hermonthis · THERÆ · Diospolis
Crocodeilopolis · Aphroditopolis · Latopolis · Hieracompolis
Apollonospolis
Myus Hormus
Smaragdi Metalla
Syene et Elephantine I.
Philae I. · Cataractes Minor
Berenice
Ophiodes I.

Stadia
0 500 1000

Pselchis

ÆTHIOPIA

ΦΟΙΝΙΚΗ
Idumœi
SINUS ARABICUS sive MARE ERYTHRÆUM
Mons Alius

Right Map

30 32 34 36 38 40 42 44

ÆGYPTUS
ÆTHIOPIA

AEGYPTUS
Nabatæa · Leuce Come
Charmothas port. · Egra
Elephantine I. · Syene
Phylae I. · Berenice · Ophiodes I.
Pselchis
Premnis
Stadia
0 1000 2000
Cataractes Major
Napata · Ladis M.
Sabaiticum Ostium
Ptolemais
MEROË INSULA · Meroë
Saba · Elaea I.
Rhizophagi · Melinus Portus
Spermatophagi · Autiphili Portus
Acridophagi · Endera · Creophagi
Struthophagi · Elephantophagi · Berenice Dargada · Saba
Canimulgi sive Agrii · Arsinoë · Acila
Psebo Lacus · Deire
Elephas M. · Notu Ceras Pr.
Lichae Venatio · Deire Pr. · Elephantum
Lacus aquae amarae · Myrrha Fera Regio · Ptolemai portus promont. in quo populetum sacrum
Lacus aquae dulcis · Pseudocassiae et Thuris Regio · Cinnamom.fera Regio
Thuri Fera Regio

SINUS ARABICUS sive MARE ERYTHRÆUM
ARABIA
BLEMMYES
MEGABARI
NUBÆ
TENESIS SEMBRITARUM REGIO
ROMATEGIFERA

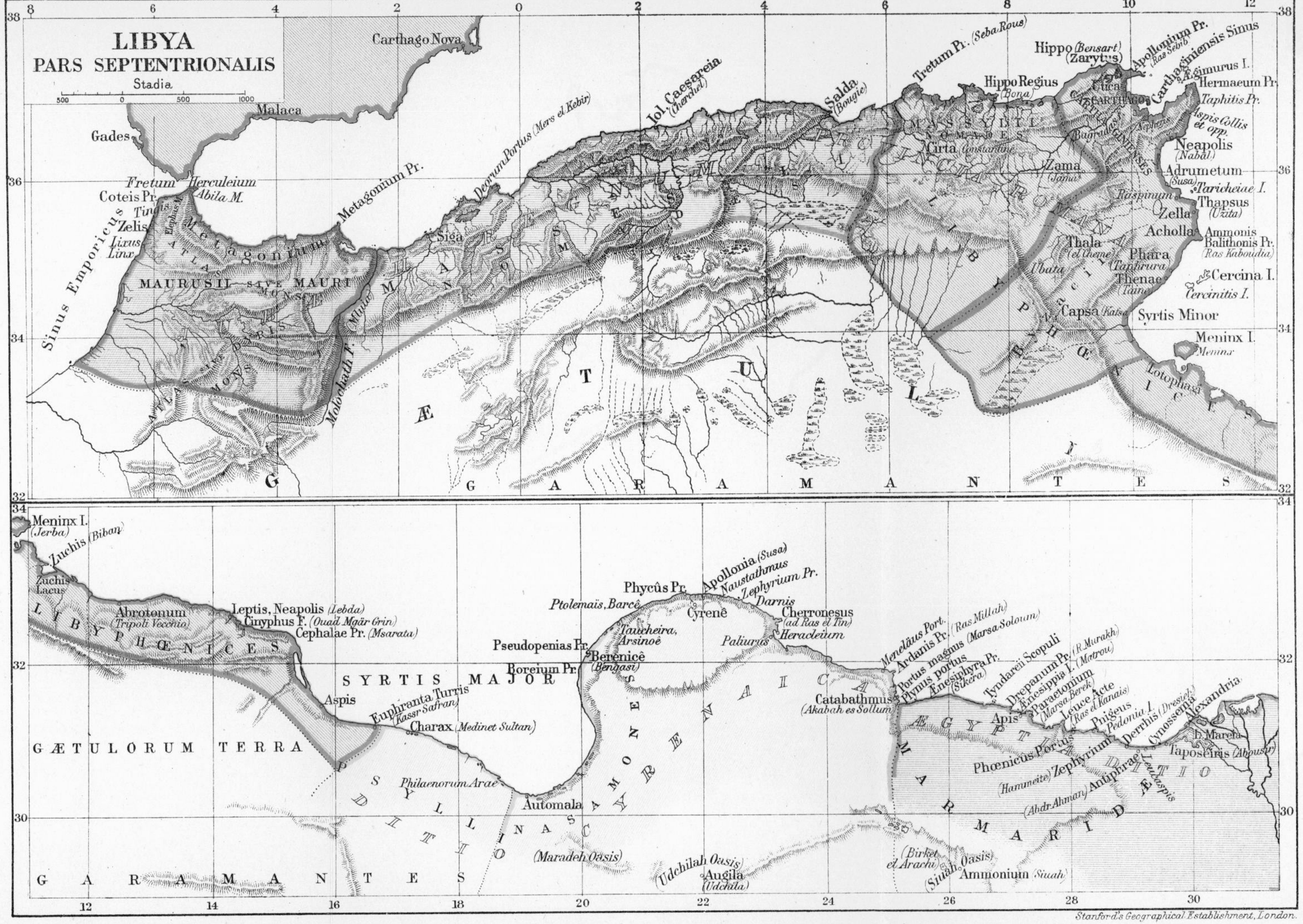

Map XV.

LIBYA
PARS SEPTENTRIONALIS

Stadia.

500   500   1000

Carthago Nova

Malaca

Gades

Fretum Herculeium
Coteis Pr.
Tingis
Zelis
Lixus *(Larasch)*
Linx

Abila M.

MAURUSII SIVE MAURI

ATLAS MAJOR MONS

MALVA F.

Metagonium Pr.

Siga

Magnum Pr.

Deorum Portus *(Mers el Kebir)*

Jol Caesareia *(Cherchel)*

Salda *(Bougie)*

Cirta *(Constantine)*

Hippo Regius *(Bona)*

Tretum Pr. *(Seba Rous)*

Hippo *(Bensart)* *(Zaryt̄vs)*

Apollonium Pr. *(Ras Sedi)*

Carthaginiensis Sinus

Æsurus I.

Utica
CARTHAGO

Hermaeum Pr.
Taphitis Pr.

Apis Collis et opp.

Bagradas F.

Neapolis *(Nabal)*

Zama *(Jama)*

Adrumetum *(Susa)*
Tarichciae I.
Thapsus *(Uzita)*

Raspinum Pr.

Zella

Thala *(el Chame)*

Ammonis
Balithonis Pr.
(Ras Kaboudia)

Acholla

Phara
(Henchura)

Thenae
(Tina)

Cercina I.
Cercinitis I.

Capsa *(Kafsa)*

Syrtis Minor

Meninx I.
(Meninx)

MAURUSIA MONS

AEG

NUM

TULI

GARAMANTES

Lotophagi

LIBYPHOE

GÆTULI

Sinus Emporicus

Meninx I. *(Jerba)*
Zuchis *(Biban)*
Zuchis Lacus

Abrotonum *(Tripoli Vecchio)*

Leptis, Neapolis *(Lebda)*
Cinyphus F. *(Ouad Moâr Grin)*
Cephalae Pr. *(Msarata)*

LIBYPHŒNICES

SYRTIS MAJOR

Aspis

Euphranta Turris *(Kassr Safran)*
Charax *(Medinet Sultan)*

GÆTULORUM TERRA

SYRTIOL PSYLLINA

Philaenorum Arae

Automala

Pseudopenias Pr.

Boreium Pr.
Berenicē *(Benghasi)*

Taucheira,
Arsinoē

Ptolemais, Barcē

Phycûs Pr.

Apollouia *(Susa)*
Naustathmus
Zephyrium Pr.

Cyrenē

Paliurus

Darnis
Cherronesus
(ad Ras el Tin)
Heracleium

CYRENAII

Catabathmus
(Akabah es Sollum)

Maradeh Oasis

Augila *(Udchila)*

Udchilah Oasis

Birket
el Arach

Siuah Oasis

Ammonium *(Siuah)*

GARAMANTES

MARMARID

Menelaus Port.
Ardanis Pr. *(Ras Millah)*
Portus magnus *(Marsa Soloum)*
Plynus portus
Ænesiphyra Pr. *(Tobruk)*

Tyndareii Scopuli

Drepanum Pr. *(R. Marakh)*
Ænesippia I. *(Matrou)*
Paraetonium *(Marsa Berek)*
Luce Acte
Pedonia I. *(Ras el Kanais)*
Derthis I. *(Dresich)*

Apis
Phoenicus Portus
(Hamunete)
Zephyrium Pr.
(Abdr Ahman)

Antiphrae

Phthenus
Cynossema

Plinthine

Taposiris *(Abusir)*

Marea

Alexandria

AEGYP

ÆTHIO

PRINTED IN GREAT BRITAIN BY
RICHARD CLAY & SONS, LIMITED,
BUNGAY, SUFFOLK.

Map XIII

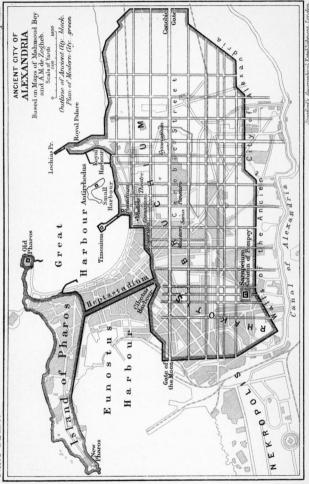

ANCIENT CITY OF
ALEXANDRIA
Based on Maps of Mahmoud Bey
and A.M. de Zogheb.
Scale of Yards

Outline of Ancient City ... black.
Plan of Modern City .. green.

Royal Palace
Lochias Pr.
Royal Harbour
Antirrhodus
Small Harbour
Posidium
Theatre
Chaliate
Imperium (Caesarium)
Timonium
Old Pharos
New Pharos
Island of Pharos
Great Harbour
Heptastadium
Cibotus Harbour
Eunostus Harbour
Gate of the Moon
Gymnasium
Canobic Street
Canobic Gate
Museum Soma
Serapeum
Column of Pompey
Walls of the Ancient City of Alexandria
Canal of Alexandria
NEKROPOLIS

Stanford's Geographical Establishment, London.

THE LOEB CLASSICAL LIBRARY

VOLUMES ALREADY PUBLISHED

Latin Authors

APULEIUS. THE GOLDEN ASS (METAMORPHOSES).
W. Adlington (1566). Revised by S. Gaselee. (*4th Imp.*)

AULUS GELLIUS. J. C. Rolfe. 3 Vols.

AUSONIUS. H. G. Evelyn White. 2 Vols.

BEDE. J. E. King. 2 Vols.

BOETHIUS: TRACTS AND DE CONSOLATIONE
PHILOSOPHIAE. Rev. H. F. Stewart and E. K. Rand.
(*2nd Imp.*)

CAESAR: CIVIL WARS. A. G. Peskett. (*3rd Imp.*)

CAESAR: GALLIC WAR. H. J. Edwards. (*5th Imp.*)

CATULLUS. F. W. Cornish; TIBULLUS. J. B. Postgate;
AND PERVIGILIUM VENERIS. J. W. Mackail. (*9th
Imp.*)

CICERO: DE FINIBUS. H. Rackham. (*3rd Imp. revised.*)

CICERO: DE OFFICIIS. Walter Miller. (*3rd Imp.*)

CICERO: DE SENECTUTE, DE AMICITIA, DE
DIVINATIONE. W. A. Falconer. (*3rd Imp.*)

CICERO: DE REPUBLICA AND DE LEGIBUS. Clinton
W. Keyes.

CICERO: LETTERS TO ATTICUS. E. O. Winstedt.
3 Vols. (Vol. I. *4th Imp.*, Vol. II. *3rd Imp.* and III. *2nd Imp.*)

CICERO: LETTERS TO HIS FRIENDS. W. Glynn
Williams. 3 Vols.

CICERO: PHILIPPICS. W. C. A. Ker.

CICERO: PRO ARCHIA, POST REDITUM, DE DOMO, DE HARUSPICUM RESPONSIS, PRO PLANCIO. N. H. Watts.

CICERO, PRO QUINCTIO, PRO ROSCIO AMERINO, PRO ROSCIO COMOEDO, CONTRA RULLUM. J. H. Freese.

CICERO: TUSCULAN DISPUTATIONS. J. E. King.

CICERO: PRO CAECINA, PRO LEGE MANILIA, PRO CLUENTIO, PRO RABIRIO. H. Grose Hodge.

CICERO: PRO MILONE, IN PISONEM, PRO SCAURO, PRO FONTEIO, PRO RABIRIO POSTUMO, PRO MARCELLO, PRO LIGARIO, PRO REGE DEIOTARO, N. H. Watts.

CICERO: VERRINE ORATIONS. L. H. G. Greenwood. 2 Vols. Vol. I.

CLAUDIAN. M. Platnauer. 2 Vols.

FLORUS: E. S. Forster, and CORNELIUS NEPOS: J. C. Rolfe.

FRONTINUS: STRATAGEMS AND AQUEDUCTS. C. E. Bennett.

FRONTO: CORRESPONDENCE. C. R. Haines. 2 Vols.

HORACE: ODES AND EPODES. C. E. Bennett. (*9th Imp. revised.*)

HORACE: SATIRES, EPISTLES, ARS POETICA. H. R. Fairclough. (*3rd Imp. revised.*)

JUVENAL AND PERSIUS. G. G. Ramsay. (*5th Imp.*)

LIVY. B. O. Foster. 13 Vols. Vols. I.-V. (Vol. I. *2nd Imp. revised.*)

LUCAN. J. D. Duff.

LUCRETIUS. W. H. D. Rouse. (*3rd Imp. revised.*)

MARTIAL. W. C. A. Ker. 2 Vols. (*3rd Imp. revised.*)

OVID: THE ART OF LOVE AND OTHER POEMS. J. H. Mozley.

OVID: FASTI. Sir James G. Frazer.

OVID: HEROIDES AND AMORES. Grant Showerman. (*3rd Imp.*)

OVID: METAMORPHOSES. F. J. Miller. 2 Vols. (Vol. I. *5th Imp.*, Vol. II. *4th Imp.*)

OVID: TRISTIA AND EX PONTO. A. L. Wheeler.

PETRONIUS. M. Heseltine; SENECA: APOCOLO-CYNTOSIS. W. H. D. Rouse. (*5th Imp.*)